Educational Foundations

in Canada

Educational Foundations *in Canada*

Alan Edmunds Jodi Nickel Ken Badley

with Gail Edmunds

OXFORD
UNIVERSITY PRESS

Oxford University Press is a department of the University of Oxford. It furthers the University's objective of excellence in research, scholarship, and education by publishing worldwide. Oxford is a registered trade mark of Oxford University Press in the UK and in certain other countries.

Published in Canada by
Oxford University Press
8 Sampson Mews, Suite 204
Don Mills, Ontario M3C 0H5 Canada

www.oupcanada.com

Library and Archives Canada Cataloguing in Publication

Edmunds, Alan Louis, 1956–, author
Educational foundations in Canada / Alan Edmunds, Jodi Nickel, and Ken Badley.

Includes bibliographical references and index.
ISBN 978-0-19-543380-7 (pbk.)

1. Education—Canada. 2. Teaching—Canada. I. Nickel, Jodi, 1968–, author II. Badley, Ken, author III. Title.

LA412.E27 2014 370.971 C2014-905483-1

Cover image: Image Source/Photodisc/Getty Images

Printed and bound in Canada

7 8 9 — 23 22 21

Contents

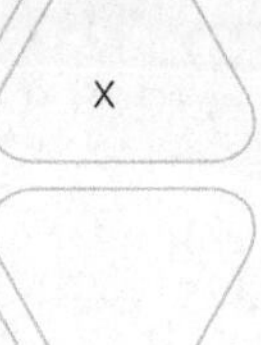

Preface

Teaching and the education it produces are reflections of society and all that occurs therein. Educational foundations, therefore, is the examination of the societal and contextual constructs that influence teaching. However, without teaching as the universal focal point, these constructs are nothing more than loosely related descriptions of a variety of sociocultural perspectives. It is not until their specific influences on education are carefully examined and directed towards teaching that the essence of educational foundations materializes.

We wrote this Canadian text because we all hold several deep beliefs about educational foundations. One of the underpinnings of education is the significant influence that context has on teaching. The Canadian context and the influence it exerts on teaching and teachers in Canadian schools is paramount. While we believe that the fundamental canon of educational foundations includes the specific contextual influences that affect teaching, we do not believe that these influences are the canon. Somehow in the last two decades, these influences seem to have become more important than teaching itself. We think it is important to provide you with both direct and potential teaching outcomes that can result from all such influences. We have explicitly outlined the implications that each influence has for teaching. To unify the book, we have included a recurring feature that describes how each influence can have an impact on today's teachers. We believe we have produced a comprehensive and manageable Canadian text that focuses on teaching.

Many texts portray how the influences we have mentioned affect education, but we believe these influences work in two directions. After all, if educational influences are socially constructed and teaching is a social event, then influence is necessarily a bidirectional occurrence. For this reason, in this text we continually examine the reciprocity between teaching and its influences. We think our examination of how each affects the other will present education, teacher educators, teaching, and teachers from a far richer and more nuanced perspective. Therefore, a central theme explored in this text is how and why teaching and teachers are affected by these influences, and which aspects of each influence must teachers consider in order to use them appropriately in their classrooms.

To this end, the book begins with the topic of teaching as the focus, because we feel that it is only after students understand teaching that they will be in a position to appreciate fully how all the influences described in the subsequent chapters play a role. This sequence of chapters will provide you with a rich understanding of teaching and education so that you can properly contextualize teaching and education within all the spheres of influence. It is our contention that the best way to learn these related aspects of teaching is to learn what teaching is first, and then integrate these other aspects into this established cognitive framework.

Foremost among the many traits, characteristics, and behaviours exhibited by exemplary teachers stands the almost intangible notion of *reflective practice*: a deep and sincere desire to make one's teaching better. Chapter 1 carefully illustrates teaching excellence; it conveys to aspiring teachers the importance of being a reflective practitioner, and it demonstrates how all other laudable teaching qualities result from such reflection. It examines the premises, practices, and instructional elements of teaching, the central theme being that teaching is at once an art, a science, and a craft with an emphasis on requiring from teachers a dedication to the profession through continual reflective and skilful teaching. The discovery of self as teacher requires honest perceptions of what is known, the courage to accept that what we know about teaching is always changing, and the determination to reshape it until it matches our inspirations.

The second chapter describes how teachers can design and implement effective models of behaviour and classroom management. It introduces the reader to the underlying psychological principles of behaviour and the motivating forces that cause students to act as they do. The fundamental premise here is that how teachers achieve classroom order is as important as whether order is achieved. To this end, good classroom order requires a well-planned and comprehensive approach that is explicitly defined, reasonably flexible, and firmly implemented. We also disagree with the notion that teachers are the only individuals responsible for good classroom order. Co-operative and collaborative efforts toward establishing suitable rules, rewards, and consequences result in better teacher–student and student–student interactions. Based on the above, teachers can design and implement a comprehensive approach to behaviour and classroom management that results in more positive student behaviours, enhanced student psychological security, and better teaching and learning.

Curriculum is what emerges from answering the question, what is worth knowing? Chapter 3 considers the various influences upon curriculum, including the provincial guidelines, ideological influences, and the decisions of the individual teacher. We demonstrate the importance of establishing clear outcomes for effective curriculum planning that will ultimately foster deep understanding. We also examine the approaches to teaching and learning that provide students greater control over their own learning and the strategies to be successful in that learning process.

In its simplest form, the primary function of education is that teachers teach, students learn, and then teachers assess whether students have learned. Chapter 4 describes the optimum interplay between teaching, learning, and assessment, with a focus on using assessment as an *a priori* part of the instructional process, as opposed to a secondary byproduct of teaching. This chapter connects curricular issues to assessment decisions and demonstrates how both act as precursors to good teaching. In this regard, this chapter specifically outlines how to determine what students will learn; how best to assess if they have learned; what to teach to achieve that learning; and how best to teach the material. One of the fundamental questions this chapter answers is, what tools should teachers use when assessing student progress, and why?

The terra firma of Chapter 5 is the position advocated by the Spanish-born philosopher and poet George Santayana, that those who cannot learn from history are doomed to repeat it. As reflective practitioners, teachers need to draw on what has passed before in order to improve what lies ahead. Although the education system in ancient Greece, for example, may seem far removed from the contemporary classroom, principles such as the Socratic method are still employed by teachers as a pedagogical instrument. In large measure, modern education is a product of the past and, while many educators may not consciously realize the influence history has on their daily classroom practice, this reality is unquestionable. This chapter establishes the inextricable links between the past and the present. Consequently, specific attention is devoted to the form and practice of education in the period of classical antiquity, through the Middle Ages and the Renaissance, and up to and including the development of an indigenous education system in Canada. This chapter is governed by the overall goal of answering a fundamental question: what impact does history have on my teaching, and how does it influence what I teach my students?

Although most teachers may not consciously concern themselves with issues of philosophy when planning a lesson or marking an exam, philosophy has a significant impact on much of what we do as teachers. In fact, the growth and shape of public education has been largely driven by the extant dominant philosophical forces at work in society. In Chapter 6, we expose the reader to the normative philosophies of idealism, realism, pragmatism, existentialism, and essentialism. We then show how these "isms" have shaped philosophies of education including essentialism, perennialism, progressivism, and social constructivism. This chapter also addresses two interrelated questions: (1) why is it important for me as a teacher to study philosophy, and (2) what impact do these philosophical positions have on me as a classroom teacher? If you are able to begin to grapple with these issues here, you will be much better equipped to begin to formulate your own personal philosophy of education.

The Canadian classroom of today is quite unlike the one-room schoolhouses of years gone by. In fact, the cornerstone of today's classroom is its diversity. As a nation, Canada prides itself for its multiculturalism, and Canadian schools have become microcosms of society. The fundamental question Chapter 7 addresses is, how can schools and those who teach within them educate children from diverse cultural backgrounds? To answer this question, we consider the sociocultural changes that Canada has undergone. Besides addressing the political and demographic trends that have created the Canadian mosaic, we give attention to the manner in which schools and teachers have changed to meet emerging multicultural realities. We then outline the expectations placed on schools and teachers to create respectful and inclusive learning environments. Finally, we offer practical advice on how to teach within diverse classrooms, with the goal of equipping teachers with the knowledge and skills required to create equitable learning environments.

It is neither assumed nor expected that teachers be lawyers, economists, or politicians and policy makers. However, it is incumbent upon teachers to have a healthy respect and appreciation for the manner in which law, economics, and policy shape what teachers can and cannot do in classrooms. The final chapter, Chapter 8, discusses the dynamics of public education in Canada with particular reference to the legal, economic, and political dimensions. After reading this chapter, you will understand how the Canadian education system is structured, and that in spite of many similarities among the provinces, education is essentially a local responsibility with real differences from one province or territory to the next. Furthermore, you will realize that federal government involvement in education, though minimal, is an undeniable fact of life for teachers throughout this country.

We have attempted to deal with these eight perspectives and influences on teachers' classroom work in one book, rather than in eight books. On first glance, that task might seem impossible, or at least intimidating. But we believe these perspectives and influences all connect into a single whole. Students and teachers do the great work of learning and teaching in a space. That space is typically a literal, physical space such as a classroom, gym, lab, hallway, or public place where students and teachers might go on a field trip. But it is also a very social space; a web of stories, relationships, and expectations. During any given school day, students and teachers in Canada's classrooms focus primarily on the tasks of learning, teaching, and assessment. But their work and the spaces in which they do it are heavily shaped by the influences, forces, and factors we describe between the covers of this book. In this way, the eight chapters of this text form a cohesive entity. We trust that as you read this book, you will become better equipped to more fully create the kinds of spaces where students love to engage with you, with each other, and with the curriculum you have planned.

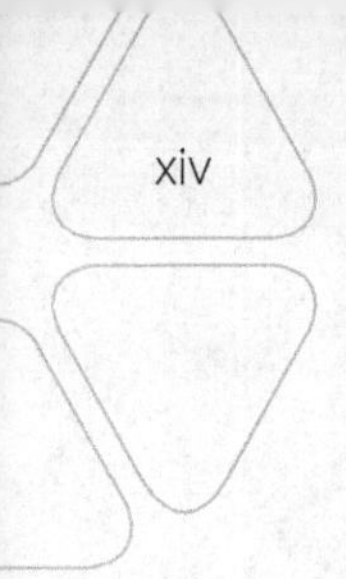

Acknowledgements

It is with sincere indebtedness that I acknowledge the inspiration provided by many students over my career. They made me strive to become a better teacher of teachers. Thanks also to David Young for initial conceptualizations for this book.

—Alan Edmunds

I would like to acknowledge my colleagues who prize teacher education so highly and inspired many of these ideas. Thanks to Ken Nickel and Karim Dharamsi for advice on early drafts.

—Jodi Nickel

I would like to acknowledge the support of George Fox University, which granted me a sabbatical for the fall semester of 2013, during which time I completed much of the work on chapters 5 and 8.

— Ken Badley

1

Teaching as Reflective Practice

Learning Objectives

After reading this chapter, you should understand

1. What reflective practice is and how it is embodied by teachers
2. The importance of reflective practice to teacher professionalism
3. How research and practice influence evidence-based practice
4. The importance of reflective practice
5. The difference between routine expert teachers and adaptive expert teachers
6. The use of a teaching log to engage in reflective practice
7. The importance of values in teaching and education
8. The common practices of highly effective teachers

 Becoming a Really Good Teacher

Teacher education has undergone many changes over the years, especially over the last four or five decades. Despite all these changes, the issues that are of primary importance to the discipline remain as dominant as ever. Coming to grips with these issues and recognizing how they affect teachers specifically and education in general is vital to our growth and advancement as a profession. Otherwise, both teachers and the discipline will stagnate. One of the most prominent and enduring issues is how different aspects of education can impact on teachers' educational practice and how analyses of such aspects can be used to improve practice. By continually engaging in systematic and progressive investigations of all that encompasses the educational enterprise, we establish and distill a solid and defensible foundation for classroom practice and hopefully avoid the risk of developing educational programs or methods of practice based on mottos, aphorisms, and quick fixes.

There are many descriptions of what really good teaching is, and these descriptions are as varied and diverse as the educators who provide them. For example, on the technical side, good teaching ranges from demonstrating curricular expertise, to implementing innovative instructional methods, to constructing classroom environments that are conducive to learning, to designing and using appropriate forms of assessment to measure and signify student progress. Good teaching in this sense is often measured by indicators of student achievement. All of these facets, along with many others, form the vital core of interrelated parts that typically make up good teacher education programs. On the other hand, from the human side, good teachers run the gamut from being well organized, having a sense of humour, being flexible, and accommodating student differences to being involved in extracurricular activities, having an open and inclusive classroom, acting as a vehicle for social change, and serving an integral function within society at large. Good teaching in this sense is often indicated by the inter- and intrapersonal growth of students and by educators' contributions to advancements toward a more literate and informed world. While these humanistic and holistic aspects of teaching are obviously less measureable and tangible than the technical aspects mentioned, they too are vitally important features within teacher education programs. Having said that, the humanistic traits and behaviours that contribute to good teaching are considerably more difficult for university instructors to teach and for aspiring educators to learn.

This raises the following questions: What are the mechanisms by which an aspiring teacher transforms into a really good teacher? Are good teachers born or made? Is it simply experience that separates the novice from the expert, the really good from the also-rans? What can teacher educators do to teach the seemingly unteachable and intangible but highly desirable humanistic traits that everyone agrees always seem to make the real difference?

Ever since the first teacher–learner relationship was realized, either formally or informally, humankind has wondered about how to make teaching better and, by extension, make learning better. There have been numerous attempts by renowned educational researchers, teacher educators, and practising teachers to answer these questions in cogent and meaningful ways. From time to time, historians, sociologists, psychologists, and philosophers have also chimed in, and we have been intermittently deluged with analogous efforts from the worlds of business and industry as well as from sport and the arts. In fact, a raucous and interesting debate still rages over how much of teaching is science and how much of it is art.

Those who support the *teaching-as-science* position will vigorously contend, amongst other things, that the scientific principles that govern the statistical analyses of educational programs or the numerical accuracy of teacher evaluations bring conceptual rigour to the discipline of teaching, especially when these principles are coupled with students' large-scale test results and comprehensive check lists requiring multipedagogical approaches. This perspective also contends that scientifically derived group results (about teachers, students, or both) can be validly projected onto each and every individual classified in either group. From this perspective, insights into effective teaching are derived from a wealth of experiences supported by enriched and strong subject expertise. Finally, in an attempt to remedy a perceived lack of instructional and curricular rigour, some in this camp have even portrayed the science of education as requiring a stricter and more rigid adherence to lesson plan design and execution.

On the other hand, those who support the *teaching-as-art* position contend that educators should use educationally scientific principles to inform their practice, but that their practice must ultimately be an accurate reflection of their own skilful judgment and decision making. Such decision making involves an intricate artistic weaving of on-the-spot actions and reactions with the attitude that teaching is a delicate learning process that requires trial and error rather than the false guarantees of overly prescribed methods. This perspective also contends that each individual is worthy of special attention, even though that individual shares many if not most of the traits and characteristics of their identity group. Advocates of this perspective will certainly build lesson plans using the same templates and frameworks as their teaching-as-science brethren, but with more and larger allowances for creativity, ingenuity, and flexibility in their design and execution. Teachers who successfully capture the art of teaching are frequently portrayed as having insight similar to that of an artist or choreographer, and their teaching more closely embodies the "true spirit" of the craft. In this light, teaching is deemed to be more about creative and intuitive processes about instruction and learning that are personal to the individual rather than the utilization of methods and principles that are allocated for all teachers. William James (1842–1910), widely considered to be the central figure behind the establishment of educational psychology as a separate discipline from psychology in North America, weighed in on the art-versus-science debate with the following:

> I say moreover that you make a great, a very great mistake, if you think that psychology, being the science of the mind's laws, is something from which you can deduce definite programmes and schemes and methods of instruction for immediate schoolroom use. Psychology is a science, and teaching is an art; and sciences never generate arts directly out of themselves. An intermediary inventive mind must make the application, by using its originality. (James, 1899/1983, pp. 7–8)

There is no mistaking that James's intermediary inventive mind is the mind of the teacher. It is the teacher whose work is based on sound educational principles (the science) who will generate and create novel approaches (the art) to educational instruction.

The art–science juxtaposition is but one of a plethora of paired contrasts by which teaching has been analyzed, critiqued, and argued about. Examples of such contrasts are teacher-oriented versus student-oriented instruction, direct instruction versus discovery learning, and lecturing versus the Socratic method. Notwithstanding these intriguing conceptual matchups and our instinctive desire to wade in and tease out solutions, the answer to "What makes for really good teaching?" does not actually lie in settling these debates.

This is because despite protracted and pointed discussions of these issues over many decades, these debates usually result in agreements to disagree, at best. While the honour and validity of coming to a consensus is not in question, such amiability has not really advanced our understandings about good teaching. Moreover, and unfortunately, the vast efforts to resolve these debates have been at the expense of serious inquiry delving into the crucial issues of practice. Answering the "Is teaching art or is it science?" type question must be, at most, a secondary consideration.

As educators, our first consideration for improving teacher practice has to be the careful examination and explanation of the soul of excellent teaching: one's attitude about one's teaching. A great attitude can turn a bad lesson plan into a good teaching and learning experience, while a less-than-great attitude will turn a great lesson plan into a disaster. As you will see in the sections that follow, it is primarily because of professionally positive attitudes that good teaching happens. Yes, all of the variously described and widely touted teaching approaches, methods, and perspectives that you will encounter in this text and in the other courses of your education program are inherently important to this thing we call practice, but it is primarily your attitude about your teaching that will truly make these elements come alive and result in teaching excellence in your classroom.

Before we attempt to provide potential answers to the questions raised above, we would like to explain the purpose of this chapter. A lot of what you will encounter in your preservice education program will be content—the straightforward information that you will need to learn and know to a high degree to be a proficient teacher. Amongst other things, this content will include the information found in the remaining chapters of this text, such as the historical, sociological, and philosophical foundations of education; the fundamental principles behind sound classroom management and effective and appropriate assessment; and the broad and specific policies that educators must be aware of and adhere to. This chapter is a bit different. It provides you with an overarching approach for teaching that contains both content to be learned and understood and a strategy that is to be learned, practised, and refined. This chapter explains the "what to do" and the "how to do it."

The content of this chapter is a detailed description of what reflective practice is, while the chapter's strategy is an outline of how to properly engage in reflective practice. We like to think of both parts of this approach, collectively called **reflective practice**, as a lifelong or career-long learning tool. Moreover, we call reflective practice a *career-long learning tool* because you will be able to apply, adapt, and modify it throughout your career regardless of how the content may change. We draw your attention to this conception because we believe that teachers learn, develop, and prosper if they are provided with content that is directly connected to self-perpetuating strategies (see Cole & Knowles, 2000). These vital connections enable teachers to learn and develop independently and continuously. Therefore, the focus of this chapter is not on content that may be either entirely static or wildly susceptible to change, but on a content–strategy combination than can be universally applied. The design of this chapter is to help you understand and practise what it takes to become a professional teacher who is an **adaptive expert**. Hammerness, Darling-Hammond, and Bransford (2005) describe an adaptive expert as a teacher who has the habit of mind to inquire continually into their practice; a lifelong learner who balances instructional efficiency with instructional innovation. There is a major difference, however, between merely knowing what teaching is and how you put it into practice. There is an even further distinction to be made between how you put teaching into practice and why and how you may need to consider changing it, or not.

reflective practice
The process of purposefully thinking about one's teaching practice and actively considering whether it can be changed.

adaptive expert
A teacher who has the habit of mind to inquire continually into their practice; a lifelong learner who balances instructional efficiency with instructional innovation.

The Teacher's Attitude

From our perspective, the first pedagogical consideration of every teacher should be the recognition and acceptance of the one element that truly transforms teaching into really good and even excellent teaching. It is an attitude that unabashedly states, "*I will do everything necessary to be the very best teacher I can be.*" Now, it is quite likely that you have heard and even stated similar expressions of wholesome intent in the past. For example, your enrolment and participation in your teacher education program (for which you are reading this text) is a clear start toward acquiring and nurturing this contagious spirit. To prevent your attitude from being perceived as facile or naive, it must be accompanied by your unerring and unshakeable sense of obligation to act purposefully to fulfill your declared goal. Do not be fooled by its perceptible simplicity. The mere stating of your purpose or goal is not enough. You literally and figuratively have to be prepared to walk the talk—to actually do what you say, what you believe. To merely say it without doing it would be superficial at best and disingenuous at worst. Worse still, because your statement was made superficially and was not deeply rooted within your beliefs as a teacher, your perspectives on your teaching and your confidence in your approach will be poorly conceived. This sets your teaching up to be phony, fragile, and highly malleable, and in this state educators are extremely susceptible to the myriad educational fads that come along. By adopting this professionally positive attitude, however, we mean that you have to strive to develop and cultivate a deep and genuine desire to make your teaching better. By embracing this attitude you cannot help but actively seek out, work at, modify, put into place, and test and retest all the actions, characteristics, and behaviours that have been exhibited by exemplary teachers over the millennia.

John Dewey (1859–1952) is considered by many to have been one of the greatest teachers. He was a high school teacher at one point, but his main contributions to education resulted from being a teacher of teachers at the University of Chicago. He was the first to directly link children's abilities to make their own meaning from information to the instructional approaches that fostered that meaning making. At a time when teachers were reciting lessons to students to fill them up with knowledge and the societal emphasis was on punctuality and industriousness, Dewey suggested that teachers ask students to respond and react to what they were saying and to consider whether their will or motivations played a role in their learning. Dewey was primarily a pedagogue, more interested in how children learned than how teachers taught. How children learned eventually led to his revelations for instructional practice, but always from the perspective of the learner. While Dewey was not necessarily reflecting on his own teaching, he was determined to be the best teacher of teachers he could be. He analyzed what teachers were doing and what and how children seemed to be learning (and not learning) and, as a result of this reflective process, found there was a better way to teach. He then went against the instructional norm and suggested a radical change that still resonates within education today: Design instructional practice so that it takes advantage of what we know about how children learn best.

By having this inquisitive and reflective attitude, you, like Dewey, will transform and personalize all available facets of teaching into your own style, framed and moulded by your own beliefs and subsequent emerging beliefs about teaching. This will give you the very best chance to be the best teacher *you* can be. Without this attitude, however, any and all of your teacher actions, characteristics, and behaviours will become nothing more than a laundry list—a series of items to be collected and used (or abused) that will morph into a bland recipe for teaching, or worse, a bunch of steps to be blindly followed and duplicated.

While many of the elements that make up good teaching are necessary, in and of themselves they do not constitute good teaching. Here is an example of an absence of this attitude that occurred during one of the authors' observations of student teaching:

> Because of traffic congestion and heavy snow conditions, he quietly slipped into the teacher candidate's Grade 8 room just as the lesson was starting. Usually he arrived early to go over the lesson, to discuss how that lesson was connected to the rest of the course/lessons, and to discuss what the teacher candidate wanted the professor to watch for in terms of teaching methods. Except for significant pauses to allow students to take notes from the transparencies, the 40-minute lesson went fairly well. During his postlesson debriefing with the teacher and the teacher candidate, the teacher described in great detail how the teacher candidate was doing a good job using his carefully assembled set of overhead slides. Holding a hefty and well-organized four-inch, three-ring binder containing several hundred overheads, the teacher proudly stated that it had taken him nearly two years to create and assemble his "course" and that he had been using these diligently for the last four years. In glowing terms, the teacher commented on how well the teacher candidate had paused (as he had instructed) to allow for student note-taking. When demurely asked by the professor if lessons were ever accompanied by classroom activities, the teacher explained that the transparencies were the best way for students to "get" the information. He said activities were too time consuming and difficult to create and often cumbersome and troublesome to use. "Besides" he said, "activities allow for too many chances for bad behaviour. The slides force them to pay attention because the information will be on their test."

In this instance, the use of overhead slides is a good teaching element, as is the use of note-taking to enhance student learning and accountability. It could even generously be argued that the use of both elements resulted in a calm and quiet classroom atmosphere with few disruptive behaviours. Given that disruptive behaviours have a considerable negative effect on student learning and demonstrated achievement, this is a laudable accomplishment. However, there is not much else here that can be considered good teaching. In fact, there is lots that would be considered to be the epitome of poor teaching.

Practical Applications

Based on the above example, list and describe all aspects of teaching that you feel are examples of less-than-good teaching. Include in your description explanations showing how these examples are not indicative of the positive attitude we provided above.

At this point, you are hopefully asking how you can get this professionally positive attitude, or you may be wondering whether you already have it. Whether you have it or not is not what is important; what is important is that you have to want it. If you want it, you will get it. After all, an attitude is nothing more than a disposition, a way of thinking, an outlook. Attitude is one of the few things in life that we have nearly complete control over. Having an attitude about teaching is quite unlike a teaching skill that we can be good or not-so-good at, or a body of knowledge that we can understand, only partially understand, or not understand at all. Just as you did not have to ask someone's permission or pass some sort of test to be inspired to become a teacher, neither do you have to ask or qualify in any way to *desire* to become a great teacher. You simply have to think it. Oberg (1988) encapsulated the essence of such an attitude:

> Required attitudes include a willingness to question what seems firmly established and taken-for-granted with respect to yourself as well as other people and institutions; a commitment to act justly, wisely, and equitably for all; an openness and sensitivity to other points of view and unthought-of possibilities; the temerity to risk exposing your own situation and point of view to careful scrutiny; and faith in yourself as a source of more educative actions. (p. 191)

The process of acquiring this attitude starts with making a simple and heartfelt, yet conscious and determined, decision to be the very best teacher you can be. There is consistent and exceptionally strong evidence from research on teachers and teaching that *as you think about yourself as teacher, you will be* (Sockett, 2008). From a similar but slightly different perspective, research on the dispositional attributes of teachers also supports the powerful positive relationships amongst inspired teacher beliefs and attitudes, teacher self-efficacy, and effective teacher practice (Woolfolk Hoy, Davis, & Pape, 2006). However, it behooves you to be aware that initially adopting this attitude is the easy part; it is as easy as simply saying the definitive statement above. What has to be adopted next, and this is the sticky part, is coming to grips with your own honest perceptions of who you are as a teacher, having the courage to accept that what is known about good teaching is forever changing, and summoning the determination to reshape your teaching until it matches your inspirations. You have to be willing to identify and scrutinize your assumptions and perceptions about teaching and, after having done so, go back to teaching with renewed and revised assumptions and perspectives. And then you have to be willing to do it all over again. This cyclical process is called reflective practice.

What Is Reflective Practice?

Reflective practice is the process by which educators study their own teaching methods. This is a process mostly driven by a desire to reshape the design and delivery of instruction so that it best serves student learning and achievement. It is underpinned by the firm belief that the teaching–learning process is invariably complex and that no one right approach exists. The concept of reflective practice was first written about by Dewey and others in earlier times, but it became a fundamental tenet of education with the landmark book by Donald Schön titled *The Reflective Practitioner: How Professionals Think in Action* (1983). Schön outlined for us the importance of integrating theory and practice via a cyclical procedure of reflecting on one's teaching experiences, mulling them over, evaluating them for possible change, and enacting these changes with the expectation that this process will inherently have to be done again.

Let's put reflective practice into context. Think of the statement "I will do everything necessary to be the very best teacher I can be" as your attitude or mental mindset, and think of your knowledge, assumptions, and perspectives about teaching as those things you will bring your newfound attitude to bear upon. It naturally follows, then, that the systematic process by which you will think about (reflect on) and change your thoughts and actions (in practice) so you can become a great teacher is called *reflective practice.*

While this form of heightened awareness and self-examination is labelled differently by different vocations, the process of self-examination is one of the landmark criteria by which a profession is defined. In Sockett's (2008) description of teaching as a profession and of teachers as professionals, **professionalism** is referred to as the qualitative moniker

professionalism
Teacher professionalism comprises high levels of competence, performance, and conduct in regard to educating students, engaging in professional development, and being an exemplar of the discipline.

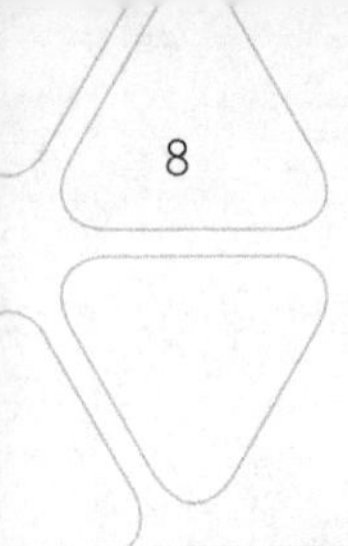

that can only be accurately applied once five very specific criteria are met: (a) judgments based on scholarly knowledge/experience, (b) autonomy of the individual, (c) continual enhancement of service, (d) self-governance by the professional body, and (e) public recognition of merits. Relative to teaching, then, professionalism is embodied in reflective practice, and many say that for education reflective practice is the ***sine qua non*** of professionalism. By engaging in reflective practice (judgment), each teacher works on his or her own (autonomous) professional perspective and practice (service), which enhances the overall effectiveness of the entire discipline (self-government) and for which teachers are well regarded and remunerated by the clientele they serve (public recognition).

sine qua non
A necessary, indispensable, and essential principle, action, or condition of an entity without which there is nothing.

A real-life example of how teacher professionalism and reflective practice has impacted society is found in the recent advances made in teacher education. For a long time, teacher preparation requirements in North America were set or mandated by governments (distant and local) with little consideration paid to the actual practices that teachers engaged in or the manner by which they improved their practice. While the various institutions across the continent charged with teacher education developed programs containing varying practicum components and courses, it would have been quite incorrect to state that these disparate programs represented a coherent system of teacher preparation. Drawing on much of the current research on teacher practice and the reflective process by which it is reshaped and improved, Darling-Hammond and Bransford (2005), in collaboration with the National Academy of Education, edited an exemplary compilation of *what teachers should learn and be able to do* that serves as the gold standard for the knowledge base for professional practice and standards for the work of teachers. It is based on strong professional consensus in conjunction with established research evidence about the learning and actions required of and evident in highly successful teachers. The result was a comprehensive set of recommended learnings, practices, and dispositions drawn from more than two decades worth of work done by teachers and researchers to codify disconnected elements of teaching into a unified front.

The Role of Research in Reflective Practice

By encouraging, if not demanding, that our profession engage in reflective practice, educators are stating that we understand and can clearly articulate the agreed-upon theoretical and practicable elements that make for good teaching. This does not mean, however, that there is only one **epistemology** from which these elements are drawn, nor does it mean that some elements are more or less important than others (epistemology is the branch of philosophy concerned with the nature and scope of knowledge and how it is constructed). In fact, it is a widely and enthusiastically agreed-upon tenet within education that an individual teacher's selected and preferred teaching elements will be different or will be applied differently depending on his or her individual philosophical, theoretical, and experiential perspectives. You will encounter many of these perspectives in the later chapters of this text and in other courses in your program. Furthermore, because of personality differences and personal preferences, no two teachers will teach in exactly the same manner even if they embrace the same beliefs about teaching.

epistemology
The branch of philosophy concerned with the nature and scope of knowledge addressed by questions like, "What is knowledge?" "How is knowledge constructed?" "How do we know what we know?" It is usually accompanied by a healthy skepticism about different knowledge claims.

Nevertheless, when all possible elements of good teaching are subjected to reflective practice, teachers, both individually and collectively, provide the discipline with a consensus about preferred elements. Some elements will be universally accepted, some will be conditionally accepted, while others will be universally rejected. This self-iterative process provides teaching with a significant degree of professional coherence while at the same time allowing for teacher ingenuity, creativity, and variation. Thus, reflective practice is the concrete foundation upon which each individual teacher's praxis can be created and re-created. By praxis we mean the process of using theory to engage in teaching such that practice and theory become intertwined. Sockett (2008) described the teacher as clinician–professional as follows:

praxis
The process of engaging, applying, exercising, or practising a theory, lesson, or skill such that practice and theory become intertwined.

> A person who reflectively uses research-based knowledge to inform practice, either by simply applying scientifically grounded conclusions somewhat like a technician, or more positively in making reflective judgments about research conclusions and their applicability to his or her own practice. (p. 54)

Thus, from the perspective of reflective practice, scholarly evidence and research-based knowledge about teaching must be considered as educational premises to be tested, not as accepted gospels to be followed. If the elements of good teaching are viewed as testable possibilities, teachers will become intimately familiar with both those they adopt and those they discard. By seeking out, analyzing, testing, modifying, and then either adopting or discarding certain elements, each teacher's overall approach becomes better grounded. As a result, you will know what you prefer and why, and you will know what you dislike and why. In this manner, reflective practice consolidates teachers' philosophical perspectives, broadens their epistemological bases, and enhances their day-to-day practice. This evidence-based practice is the preferred professional ideal because of "the professional autonomy it implies for teachers to be able to warrant autonomously their actions rather than simply pointing to the authority of the research" (Sockett, 2008, p. 57). This approach makes teachers masters of their own instructional destiny and responsible and accountable for it for the very best reasons.

evidence-based practice
Teacher practices that are based on established and consistent research findings.

Theory and Practice Connections

The above section primarily explains how research-based knowledge can augment teaching. It is equally important to realize that when this process is engaged at the macrosystem level by vast numbers of teachers, reflective practice reciprocally changes the very research that teachers look to for guidance. In the ongoing process of testing and retesting the elements of good teaching, the profession naturally calls into question "what the research states" and the respective educational conclusions that are drawn. While such questioning and testing does not necessarily resolve these issues into definitive answers, it does an excellent job of raising topical awareness, which can lead to potentially resolving at least the ambiguities surrounding those issues. For example, questioning educational theories regarding their functionality and applicability has proven an invaluable tool for shedding much-needed light on controversial topics such as multiple intelligences, learning styles, and the phonics versus whole-language debate in reading. Here we provide a brief overview of the phonics versus whole-language issue and the outcomes of this decades-old debate.

Reflective Practice in the Phonics versus Whole-Language Debate

The dispute over whether phonics or whole-language learning constitutes the best form of reading instruction has been engaged in since the early part of the 20th century. The heart of the argument has always been the juxtaposition of supposedly idyllic whole-language learning by immersion against the allegedly overly systematic and rigorous methods of phonics. Phonics theory frames learning to read as a process by which children master a set of sound-to-symbol correspondences. By learning the 26 letters of the alphabet and the vast array of letter combinations that communicate the 44 sounds or phonemes in the English language, children become able to read words by decoding them or sounding them out. Decoding is deemed an especially important learning-to-read skill when children need to understand unfamiliar words to make sense of text, otherwise defined as reading comprehension. Whole-language theory, on the other hand, contends that learning to read is comparable to learning to speak in that it is a natural and unconscious process best advanced by being immersed in language and print. By being exposed to text, being read to, and reading aloud themselves children make associative connections between their understandings of alphabet letters and whole words. In the whole-language scheme, unfamiliar words are skipped, guessed at, or deduced from context so as to not interrupt the flow of reading comprehension. There is typically little mention of the sounds made by letters and no mention of the sounds formed by letter combinations.

The instructional emphasis for reading vacillated between phonics and whole-language learning several times from the 1930s to the late 1980s. By the mid-1990s there was consensus that the whole-language movement was largely to blame for the repeated evidence of poor reading skills in students and their poor overall educational performances throughout North America. Nonetheless, this did not mean that phonics as it was originally conceived and practised was the answer. Research on reading instruction today studies the effects of actual teaching practices on student reading abilities and how instructional practice can be scrutinized and changed to produce better educational outcomes.

In the specific case of the opposed educational positions of phonics and whole-language learning, the primary function of reflective practice—to question the functionality and applicability of all theories—proved invaluable. The "naturalness" of whole-language learning has been debunked, as have the rote memory methods of early phonics. In their place is now a consensus description of the combined instructional and curricular elements necessary for successful early reading programs. Teaching practices strongly associated with improvements in children's reading achievement are "the systematic teaching of phonemic awareness, guided repeated oral reading, direct and indirect vocabulary instruction with careful attention to readers' needs, and a combination of reading comprehension techniques that include metacognitive strategies" (Bransford, Darling-Hammond, & LePage, 2005, p. 27).

The main point here is that current approaches to reading instruction are not merely a combination of phonics and whole-language learning; that would be facile and misleading. Current proven approaches to reading instruction are the result of teachers and researchers being willing to question and hold accountable the theories that dictate instructional practice. By reflecting on the educational outcomes that result from teacher practices, educators constantly engage in investigative procedures that examine the functionality and applicability of theory and practice. Reflective practice thus provides a more objective means for examining not only teaching practices, but also research on teaching practices. This necessitates that teachers have an open mind about the potential for proving true or falsifying all elements of teaching and the research each is based on as they are performed within the context of each and every teacher's classroom.

Why Engage in Reflective Practice?

While a lot of the research on teacher practice has centred on pedagogy, curriculum knowledge, and theories of motivation and learning, more attention is now being paid to the significance of teachers' awareness and understandings of their own practice. Teachers need a clear vision of what teaching expertise is or what they want it to be so they can observe their own work with an eye toward growth and progress, and can envision themselves making changes as required: "[W]ithout a clear vision of one's ultimate goals and responsibilities as a professional, the metacognitive reflection needed for assessing progress is difficult if not impossible to achieve" (Bransford, Derry, Berliner, Hammerness, & Beckett, 2005, p. 76). Therefore, it is imperative to develop the inquiry skills needed to look critically at one's own practice and to adapt as one sees fit. Inquiry of this sort breeds a kind and depth of understanding that cannot be gained from keeping a laundry list of good practices in a special folder or by memorizing them. Without reflective practice, 20 years of teaching is not 20 years of experience; it is one year of experience taught 20 times! You may want to reconsider the Grade 8 science teacher in the example given earlier in this chapter. Was his teaching really any better after four years of using his beloved slides?

metacognition
Higher-order thinking skills such as planning, monitoring, and evaluating that oversee and control the cognitive processes used in learning.

The predominant thinking that drives the concept of reflective practice is the fact that teachers will continually acquire and construct new knowledge and skills. This even happens during initial preservice practicum placements, short as they may be. Reflective practice is also predicated on the notion that teachers do not acquire complete and finite sets of skills or knowledge before crossing the threshold of their own classroom in a full-time role. If changes to educational practice are inevitably going to happen, then we believe these should happen by design rather than by accident. When formulated, executed, and examined by design, teaching is less likely to be a series of disconnected facts and methods that are a mile wide but only an inch deep, attempting to be everything to everyone at once yet not really resulting in much of anything for anyone. Good teaching developed by intent stimulates a grounded perspective that is deeply rooted and defensible and upon which well-thought-out judgments and choices can be confidently decided.

CASE STUDY

Teachers' Perspectives on Reflective Practice

Case #1: A Student Teacher's Perspective: Reflecting and Writing Showed Me My Strengths and Weaknesses

From the six weeks here [in classes], I got a lot of great ideas and met colleagues whom I could contact in case of need. From the practicum I learned how to put all of these ideas, and my previous experiences, into practice in the classroom. The only way for me to learn my strengths and my weaknesses is to reflect on my teaching, and this is what I did in my placement. I found my associate's comments useful, but my students' comments were often more practical and comforting in a way. They know I'm still learning, so most of them were great about letting me know what would help them learn better.

Getting up in front of the classroom this time seemed to be very different from my previous teaching rounds. I was anxious to get up and teach, rather than continuing to observe my associate. I wanted to see what *I* could do! One factor which was very helpful was that I taught two Grade 11

continued

chemistry classes as well as two Grade 10 science classes (plus an enriched Grade 11 chemistry class from hell!). This meant that I was teaching every lesson twice. I almost always found that my second lesson went better, as I learned where the trouble spots were and how to anticipate any questions that might come up. I also found that my second lesson always took longer, because I was explaining things more fully.

One major factor I noticed was that I was able to relax much more by the last week. I was much more confident with what I was doing and how my students learned best. Both my associates and my students noticed and commented on this. That's all I can think of right now. I'm all written out. It was really good (for me) to be writing journals and comments every day and I'm to the point now where I don't want to do anymore! Time to relax! (Featherstone, Munby, & Russell, 1997, pp. 51–52).

Case #2: A First-Year Teacher's Perspective: Teaching as Inquiry

As a reflective practitioner I have gained a greater insight into and knowledge of my personal pedagogy and have expanded my visions of effective teaching practices. Through nontraditional methods the students and I have become self-researchers and each has participated in our individual reflexive inquiries. We have used vehicles such as imagery, poetry, mask making, and finger painting to explore our inner selves and to express our deeply held truths.

As this inquiry evolved it became an exploration of inner self and the primacy of emotions. Although the journey was travelled together, each of us followed a personal path. Along the way our separate paths merged as we developed a deep level of trust and found ways to share our self-discoveries.

The timing of the experience was of an essence for me in my first year of teaching both Grade 8 and visual arts. It has reaffirmed my commitment to work with intermediate-level students and to develop, for next year, an integrated language arts and visual arts curriculum. My principal hears the power of our voices and sees the expanse of our work. He supports me as an agent of change and hopes that I will work as a mentor with other intermediate teachers within our school (Cole & Knowles, 2000, p. 81).

Case #3: A Veteran Teacher's Perspective: Ongoing Learning Experiences

Until this point in my teaching journey, my contacts with other teachers had been opportunistic. I would gain information and assurances in the quick exchanges of stories, the casual camaraderie of the staff room, and even through a few enduring friendships. These stories of teaching may have exerted undetected influence upon me. Some stories revealed more than others a colleague's knowledge, intentions, classroom practice, or a view of students. Several close friendships became a collegial relationship accompanied by the ready availability of mutual aid or helping. As I consistently sought and accepted radical changes in my teaching assignments, I made certain requests of those more familiar with the subject area, grade level, student population, and community. Throughout, I routinely shared materials and methods or openly exchanged ideas and opinions with other teachers on staff. I also learned that amongst the "hidden costs of sharing expertise" with new teachers and other colleagues is the potential risk of an added planning and preparation burden and an erosion of the accumulated ideas, methods, and materials that served as the basis for my reputation as a teacher (Skau, 1995, pp. 95–96).

Case #4: Perspective from a Teacher of Teachers: How Can I Help Student Teachers Improve the Quality of Their Learning and Teaching?

This is the story of a personal action project in which I took a leap of faith, as a teacher of physics teachers, and returned to the physics classroom to see if I could still be a successful physics teacher myself. I also wanted to see how the experiences of daily high school teaching would affect my ways of thinking about my regular work with people learning to teach physics. I had not taught high school for more than 20 years. I have always wanted to be seen as a teacher educator who attended to reality as well as theory, as one who could practice what he preached. It seems appropriate to review my personal stance toward the topic of reflective practice. What is my concern about my practice? What am I going to do about it? What evidence will I gather to enable me to judge my own actions? How will I validate the claims I make about my actions?

I committed myself to keeping notes as extensively as possible as a process for analyzing each day's work with a view to that of the next day. I relied extensively on written comments from my students, asking each to participate in a 30-minute interview and to write a final assignment about the year's experience learning to teach. In my excitement and enthusiasm about being a teacher as I was also a teacher educator, I moved too quickly for some of the preservice teachers in my physics method course, just as I moved too quickly through the physics curriculum for some of the Grade 12 students. Next year I will adjust the pace, accepting the student teachers' initial need for fine details. I will also accept their need to be trained in strategies. My two semesters of Grade 12 physics teaching convinced me that teacher educators must always look for parallels between what we advocate as good learning for students in schools, what we advocate as good learning for new and experienced teachers, and what we advocate as good learning for ourselves. How different would preservice teacher education programs be if courses and practice teaching experiences were framed by the question, "How can I help these student teachers to improve the quality of their learning? (Russell, 1995, pp. 95–112).

Expert Teachers

The pervasive mindset of teachers, therefore, should be to embody an explicit plan to reflect on, appraise, and learn from their teaching in a continual and organized fashion. This plan has to include a variety of sources of information about good teaching that ranges from evidence contained in the literature, to the perceived abilities of colleagues and mentors, to one's local knowledge about specific students and classrooms. These intertwined perspectives provide an informed expert base that is indispensable when exercising one's professional judgment. This is not to say that teachers without this specific type of plan are not good teachers; but it does say that teachers with this type of plan will be much better teachers and will continue to get better throughout their careers. Bransford, Derry, Berliner, Hammerness, and Beckett (2005) elaborate on this crucial distinction by describing the difference between a routine expert and an adaptive expert. While both types of expert teachers will continue to learn over their careers, "routine experts develop a core set of competencies that they apply throughout their lives with greater and greater efficiency. In contrast, adaptive experts are much more likely to change their core competencies and continually expand the breadth and depth of their expertise" (pp. 48–49). As Figure 1.1 outlines quite clearly, experts can work across and within the dimensions of innovation (vertical axis) and/or efficiency (horizontal axis).

From the figure we can see that efficiency at the expense of innovation tends to produce routine experts. These teachers are very good at what they do, but they are not well armed to tackle curricular or instructional changes that take them outside their comfort zone. These types of teachers struggle mightily when a Ministry of Education changes a curriculum guide, and they often resist such changes. This is how 20 years of experience becomes one year of experience taught 20 times. On the other hand, innovation at the expense of efficiency tends to produce frustrated and perpetual novices, regardless of their years of experience. These teachers are constantly searching for and experimenting with new curricular and instructional approaches, so much so that they end up poorly grounded

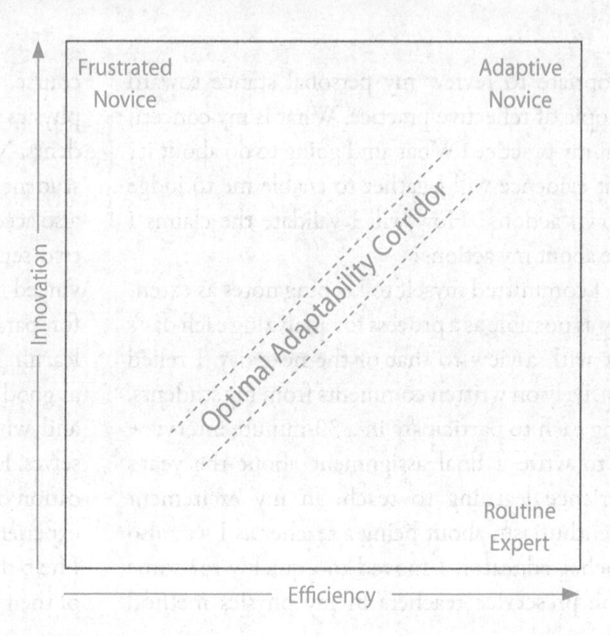

FIGURE 1.1 The Dimensions of Adaptive Expertise

Source: From Bransford, Derry, Berliner, Hammerness, & Beckett, 2005. Figure 2.1, p. 49.

and are susceptible to any and all suggestions about teaching. This is how unproven but enticing educational fads have secured footholds of varying durations within our discipline. For example, the notion that all learners display one of four innately different and preferred learning styles has had great appeal because it speaks to a more individualistic approach to instruction rather than teaching all students in an identical way with no consideration for individual differences. Despite this appeal, adjusting one's teaching to exclusively accommodate those specific learning styles has not been shown to improve student academic achievement (Klein, 1997).

According to Bransford and colleagues (2005), adaptive experts are comfortable with both innovation and efficiency and they tend to function at the high ends of both dimensions. As their years of experience accumulate, these teachers entertain and experiment with innovations and efficient ways of using them as they move along the optimal adaptability corridor. The optimal adaptability corridor balances innovation with efficiency, and this interplay provides an impetus that continually moves our teaching forward. This multidimensional approach to analyzing and improving one's teaching is seen in many quarters as the gold standard for teacher development (e.g., National Research Council, 2000).

You should anticipate that embarking on a path of self-analysis will lead to challenges and perhaps a complete retooling of one's teaching practices, and this is bound to feel risky. You will experience discomfort with new ideas and probably even clumsiness when executing new skills, and nobody likes to appear or feel incompetent. That is why embarking on this path should begin immediately during your preparation to be a teacher, not later in your career when it is harder to change. With reflective practice as an expected and established part of your professional development repertoire, conducting an analysis of your practice with the view toward potentially changing it will feel like a natural part of your life as a teacher. As you engage in reflective practice more and more, you will quickly realize that what started out as a new, somewhat risky, and perhaps tricky process will evolve into a way of life that is routine, fluent, even welcomed. What may initially feel onerous and time consuming to carry out will become an easier part of your normal approach and, thus, it will deliver more effective results. Finally, it must be reiterated that engaging in reflective practice is a choice—a choice to improve one's practice to best serve one's students. It is also a choice that will provide an immeasurable sense of professional fulfillment throughout your career. For these reasons, therefore, we want to emphasize that reflective practice is a choice that cannot be made in an effort to discharge some sort of evaluation criteria or administrative obligation. If reflective practice gets reduced to an item on an annual performance checklist, it may just as well not be on the list at all for all the good it will do.

How to Engage in Reflective Practice

There are many different descriptions of how to engage in reflective practice. You can find a wide variety of them in different texts and research articles and on educational sites on the Internet. The method we describe below is an amalgam of several approaches that we have read about, personally encountered or participated in, or taught over many years. We have attempted to make our method as straightforward and practical as possible while at the same time strictly adhering to the fundamental principles that govern meaningful and effective reflective practice. In our view, if reflective practice is not conducted according to these principles, the process can quickly descend into nothing more than frivolous navel-gazing or annoying busy work and the end product will be worthless. When executed properly, however, reflective practice has been shown to result in a plethora of benefits for the user:

1. Examining our teaching practices will illuminate our ideological and philosophical views of teaching. Your ideological and philosophical perspectives on education come from how you perceive the fundamental nature of educational knowledge and the sets of ideas that make up your expectations, actions, and overall vision of education. At a minimum, if nothing else results, these perspectives will be reaffirmed and consolidated.
2. By starting with the fundamental premise that teaching practice is something that is formulated and constructed we speak to the fact that it can be changed. Knowing something can be changed is the vital first step in seeking ways to change it.
3. Building on the above point, seeing something changed speaks to the fact that it can be changed more than once. This portrays teaching as something that will likely be under continual reformation.
4. A carefully analyzed and recrafted teaching practice creates flexibility and adaptability. By actively considering which elements of teaching to include, discard, or change, we develop the wherewithal to make slight but significant changes without having to completely abandon everything we did before.
5. Self-knowing makes for meaningful teaching. If we definitively know who we are as teachers, our teaching practice will always be genuine and purposeful—and nothing plays a more powerful role in student learning. We may still make mistakes and want to change things, but these functions will not occur because we were untrue to ourselves or the professional process.

Our last comment about reflective practice is to alert you to its greatest potential pitfall: thinking that reflective practice means making changes. This is certainly not the case. There will be many elements of your practice that are well executed and wonderfully effective, and there is no reason to change these. To be most effective, reflective practice should be considered more as an opportunity to determine *whether* certain elements of your teaching need changing. To use a medical analogy, reflective practice should be thought of as a required annual physical, a checkup to make sure things are functioning satisfactorily, not as elective surgery to indiscriminately replace a part.

Perspective Taking

To gain an honest and comprehensive viewpoint of one's teaching so as to tease out meaningful insights requires an examination from all pertinent perspectives. Here we borrow a page from Brookfield's (1995) book *Becoming a Critically Reflective Teacher,* in which he articulates four interrelated lenses through which teachers can look at their practice: (a) the autobiographical lens, (b) the learner lens, (c) the peer/colleague lens, and (d) the research lens. We have adapted Brookfield's lenses to act as an organizing frame upon which we then articulate our collective perspectives on reflective practice. While some of our details are similar to Brookfield's, our tenets and principles do not materialize from his philosophical archetype of primarily hunting for assumptions of power and hegemony. By power and hegemony Brookfield means that governments or school boards exert dominance over teachers by dictating the internal policies and processes of education. That is not the philosophical position of this chapter or text. In this section, we first outline what looking through each of these lenses entails and why we should do it. Secondly, we outline the systematic process by which you can evaluate the information you gather so you can complete your analysis. Finally, we provide examples of what keeps the process on track and how it can result in a more realistic plan for improving your practice.

The *autobiographical lens* allows self-examination from the perspective of understandings one's teaching practices and lived teaching experiences. It includes everything and everyone that has influenced our teaching, such as the role models who have inspired us, all that we have studied and learned about teaching, anecdotes about our teaching from a variety of sources, and reflections on how we were taught as students. It is equally about the good and the not-so-good aspects of our practice, because teachers often use their strengths to facilitate or circumvent real or imagined weaknesses. One of the fundamental battles you will have to settle in your autobiographical analyses is to come to terms with the stark reality of the differences between what you like and want as a teacher versus what works well. To avoid becoming myopic and resting comfortably with what you mostly want or like, you must also focus an eye through the other three lenses. Details on the specific types of questions you can ask to find out what you want to know in this regard are found in the next section entitled "My Teaching Log."

By setting out to purposefully compile evidence from all four perspectives, you are assured of gaining an invaluable triangulation of the issues in your reflections on your practice. Via **triangulation** (examining how multiple perspectives bear on the same issue), these disparate but related views will coalesce, thereby providing you with a hierarchy of issues that details which aspects of your teaching need immediate attention and which of them can be left as is for the time being. For example, because learning is inextricably dependent on at least a basic level of psychological security and comfort, classroom management issues will need to be addressed before you can start to investigate the possibility of changing more subtle nuances of your instructional approach. If student engagement and involvement is critical to how you have designed your instruction and it is a fundamental part of how your lessons need to unfold to be effective, doing so in a classroom that feels chaotic (to your

triangulation
The combined analysis of related pieces of information to establish the validity of a research conclusion.

students) will be impossible. On the other hand, resolving classroom management issues may change the tone of the room so dramatically that you will decide to do other things in addition to creating more student engagement, such as allowing for more independent and autonomous seatwork, something that may never have occurred to you while teaching in your previously troublesome environment.

The *learner lens* allows for an examination of our teaching from our students' perspectives. As much as it would be desirable, we can never literally see ourselves through our students' eyes, but we can work at getting as figuratively close to that perspective as possible. The intent here is to find out whether your teaching intentions match how your students receive and perceive your intentions. Is how you presented the core topics of the curriculum and how these topics interact exactly how your students interpreted and understood them? Did your chosen method of instruction facilitate or hinder these understandings? Did your interpersonal skills and behaviours convey respect and fairness, or are these behaviours motivational for some students while demoralizing for others? The best feedback comes from student perspectives that are provided anonymously.

While we may want it to be otherwise, the power relationship that invariably exists between teachers and students is omnipresent, even if it is positively and respectfully constructed and executed. This reality dictates that students are more likely to provide you with sincere suggestions and critiques if their anonymity is protected. This is especially true in the case of less-than-complimentary comments and feedback, which sometimes are our best indicators of things that need attention.

Perhaps the riskiest of the perspectives we seek about our teaching are those acquired through the *peer/colleague lens*. But they can also be the most insightful and rewarding. By asking fellow educators to observe and comment on your practice, some peers (including department heads and principals) will unfortunately see this as a sign of perceived self-incompetence. As if that were not risky enough, it is also anxiety provoking that when we ask others for their perceptions of our practice, we must share what our own perspectives are—complete with glories and warts. These thoughts and practices are personal; they are the very essence of who we are as teachers and to share them, even as a starting point for what is intended as a constructive reformulation process, exposes us. By engaging in this intimate conversation we are holding our proverbial classroom door wide open, a door behind which we privately teach and reign supreme and, to a large extent, are mostly only accountable to ourselves. This is the very door we often use to avoid the curious eyes of other educators because they, unlike our students, are fully aware of what comprises good teaching and they are our ideological and methodological equals. At the same time, this peer expertise is exactly what makes their potential insights invaluable and worth seeking. The foremost criterion you should use to discern which peers should provide this information, therefore, is a willing confidante who understands that you want them to provide you with an objective and clearer perspective of your teaching and that you will take their feedback *into consideration for potential changes*. It has to be made perfectly clear that their role is not to change your teaching.

Your peers and colleagues can also serve you well in another important way. As our ideological and methodological equals, you can casually and informally observe their practice and listen to their views on teaching and compare and contrast these with your own. Invariably, it will be clear that they face or have faced the same dilemmas about teaching that you encounter. The realization that you are not the only teacher who has experienced shortcomings and doubts about your practice is reassuring and can be a major motivator for change. At the same time, in case the exercise of self-reflection plunges you into blind recriminatory self-flagellation, you will also see that you share with them the splendor and brilliance of really good teaching.

If the peer/colleague lens is the riskiest of the perspectives to take on, the *research lens* is the least risky. Perusing great books and articles on good teaching and participating in exemplary professional development workshops can be an exclusively private matter. Nobody knows whether these knowledge sources change our thinking, nor will anyone know whether we choose to implement any of the demonstrated practices. And if we do decide to do so, who is to know if these changes worked or failed? Naively comfortable as this use of the research may be, gazing through the research lens confronts us with the challenge of staring down one of the most powerful assumptions amongst educated individuals: the false hypothesis that "answers" to teaching dilemmas lie in mystical solutions just waiting to be discovered in some book, article, conference, or workshop. This assumption is often accompanied by the artificial hope that if we look hard enough and long enough, the answers will be revealed, our worries will be over, and our teaching will be the better for it. Looking through the research lens can also serve as a much-needed wake-up call when we ruefully realize that our newfound ideas will remain utterly worthless unless we sculpt and hone them to suit our own teaching preferences and contexts. Unlike a doctor's prescribed medicine, merely using an educational idea without making it our own does not make things better.

My Teaching Log

There are an infinite number of simple and exotic ways of designing and using a teaching log. These can range from simple weekly records of particular aspects of teaching or designated events, to daily notes about all that happens in a teacher's life, both inside and outside the classroom. Teaching logs are designed to be informal places where you write about your reactions to experiences so that you can improve your conversation with yourself about your teaching and whether there are some aspects that need to change. This approach makes better sense of our experiences because it forces us to summarize our thoughts; then we have to purposefully and carefully attempt to understand and come to grips with them. Not only does a teaching log produce a lasting record of our thoughts and feelings, it allows us to go back and "see" what we were thinking and to reflect on it based on newer thoughts or more recent developments.

Practical Applications

OTHER WAYS OF RECORDING REFLECTION

There are other ways to record thoughts and reflections in addition to traditional writing. For example, you may be familiar with *mind mapping*, a technique developed by Tony Buzan (1993). Also called *radiant thinking*, this visual approach can be used to assist problem solving by associating ideas and representing them, often colourfully, in webs of linkages. There are thousands of websites devoted to mind mapping, with software available to help the process; see www.tonybuzan.com/about/mind-mapping/.

There is also a very useful summary document entitled *Journal Writing and Adult Learning* by Sandra Kerka (1996).

Our careful examination of numerous approaches and types of logs revealed that there are three primary tenets that make for effective logs. First, your log has to be a conscious, purposeful, and deliberate part of your overall approach to teaching. If it is not planned, it will not happen. Second, it has to be an autonomous process devoid of the obligatory duties that may be imposed by faculty advisers, associate teachers, principals, or department heads. Doing it because you want to is considerably more professional and effective than doing it because you have to or because someone will evaluate it. And third, the process is simple, so keep it simple. The risk here is to turn being reflective into something that is more convoluted and troublesome than it has to be. To keep it simple and effective, follow these five steps:

Step 1: Identify and analyze the elements of your teaching that you think need attention (e.g., lesson planning, instructing, transitions, dealing with misbehaviour).

Step 2: Gather new information about these elements (or these types of elements).

Step 3: Decide *whether* the new knowledge has implications for your identified elements (it may not).

Step 4: Design and implement your desired changes.

Step 5: Choose a time when you will go through this process again.

The remainder of this section provides details on how to accomplish these five steps.

You may be wondering why we have emphasized writing all this information down in a teaching log. After all, you could simply think about it and just do it. While that is true, there is lots of research evidence that demonstrates that writing about something is a more powerful and longer-lasting learning process than merely thinking about it, even if we think about it a lot. Just thinking about something usually leads to processing the information once and predominantly in our most habitual way. The entire process happens very quickly. On the other hand, writing forces us to slow down and process information more times and in a multitude of ways. This is a much more measured and reflective procedure. When we write, (a) we think about the information (the first time we process), (b) we write it (the second time we process), (c) we read what we write as we write it (the third time we process), and (d) we read over what we have written (the fourth time we process). There is also something intuitively obligatory about thinking about and reflecting on what is written and carrying out one's intentions when they are on paper; it becomes a personal contract; your promise to yourself. Graham (2006), in his seminal chapter in the *Handbook of Educational Psychology*, provided the most cogent description of the intrinsic connections between writing and learning:

> Writing is an indispensable tool for learning. It makes it possible to gather, preserve, and transmit information with great detail and accuracy. The permanence of writing makes ideas readily available for review and evaluation; its explicitness encourages the establishment of connections between ideas; and its active nature may foster the exploration of unexamined assumptions. E. M. Forster's observation, "How can I know what I think until I see what I say" (Brodie, 1997, p. 135), captures the potential of writing as a tool for refining and extending one's knowledge. (p. 457)

For a comprehensive review of the merits and contributions of writing to the learning process, see Graham (2006).

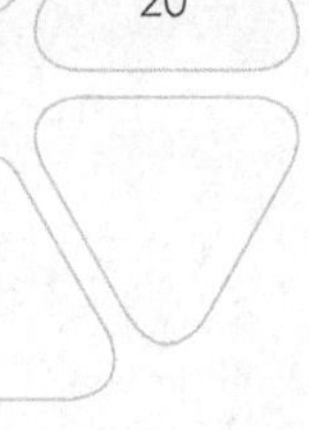

Step 1: Identify and Analyze Elements for Consideration

To keep the process simple, pick a time when you are not in the act of teaching or planning to record your thoughts about a particular lesson or group of lessons. Small sections of teaching are easier to remember and carefully think about than longer sections. The elements of your practice that you want to identify for further consideration are those that you obviously found exasperating, wearisome, or annoying or, by contrast, teaching elements that were very satisfying, effective, and interesting or those that you are excited to try again or perhaps try in a different way. All elements of teaching practice typically fall into one of three broad categories: They are either knowledge, skills, or dispositions. The following are examples of some questions you can ask pertaining to each category:

1. *Knowledge*: Was I fully aware of my students' potential misconceptions associated with this curricular topic? How could I circumvent that the next time or use these likely misunderstandings to my benefit?
2. *Skills*: Did I properly implement the **Socratic method** during my lesson? In the Socratic method, teachers ask students open-ended questions that require generative and rationalized answers that are discussed/debated. Was it inappropriate to use this method to teach this topic? If not, why did this approach still seem to cause problems?
3. *Dispositions*: Did I give my students the benefit of the doubt when I marked their recent essay assignment, or did I adhere too rigidly to my marking rubric?

Socratic method
A dialogue-based instructional approach where teachers ask students open-ended questions that require generative and rationalized answers. These usually prompt further questions, deeper analysis, and better understandings.

To make sure you capture the entire moment, write about (a) how you felt, (b) what you thought, and (c) what you and your students said and did relative to that element. Example #1 below describes how a classroom management problem affected instructional efficiency and how the teacher made use of research he had previously encountered to solve the dilemma:

Example #1

Frequently, after I teach the essence of my planned lesson or demonstrate how to do what a task requires, I provide my students with seatwork to reinforce basic concepts. It's not only a chance for them to practise and become familiar with the task, it's also an opportunity for me to help them with that process. Instead of completing their assigned seatwork, however, lots of students tended to talk, act out, and disrupt those who were working. As time went on, this problem progressed from mildly annoying to downright problematic. I tried nipping this in the bud by assigning their unfinished seatwork as homework, but this did not solve the disruption problem, I received lots of complaints about having to complete seatwork for homework, the homework was not being done, and my students were not learning from my lessons.

I shared my frustrations with my students and together we took 20 minutes to discuss it and try to come to a resolution. They shared with me that they did not mind seatwork but had a great aversion to doing extra homework. They also said they wished they had more free time to just talk and mingle in class. From my perspective, I described how I had a professional duty to make sure they understood the concepts of the lessons and that it was not appropriate that some students were disrupting others who were trying to work. I pointed out this resulted in everyone having extra homework, not just some students.

As a compromise, we agreed that I would reduce the volume of daily seatwork and if they completed the seatwork before the end of class, they would get 10 minutes of free time next class (and for all future seatwork). The next day they did it. This eliminated the disruptive behaviour and they enjoyed the free time. This solution was based on an approach to classroom management that I read about in one of my textbooks.

Next, analyze each element from the following five perspectives in the following order. Each perspective is accompanied by suggestions about the types of critical and analytical reasoning you should engage in. These suggestions will definitely serve the purpose, but they can also be used as starting points for your own thinking and analysis. The order is important because it is more revealing and enlightening to start with an analysis of "why" we decided to do something than it is to delve immediately into why it did or did not work. We also highly recommend that you be frank and honest with yourself and willing to take credit for things that went well, as well as lament about those that did not. A comfortable way of doing this is to think of this analysis as an attempt to find explanations, not to assign blame or glory.

1. *What was my goal in using this element?* Why did I chose it over others? What end did I want to achieve? Maybe the element is fine but its targeted purpose was unclear or improper.
2. *In striving toward this goal, what were my assumptions about the curriculum, my students' abilities to learn, the element itself, and my overall classroom circumstances?* Did I miss/forget a crucial part of the lesson that caused the element to fail? Were my students really ready to participate in that type of activity? Did I try to stretch that element too far in its application? Is that element, effective as it may be, really suitable in this very small (large) classroom?
   - You should be so well versed in your basis for these underlying assumptions that you would be willing to express them publicly to anyone that asked.
3. *If it was an unsuccessful element, how unsuccessful was it (a little or a lot)? Why did this element not achieve its intended purpose?* Is the nonsuccess of this element significant enough to warrant further examination, or is it a minor irritant? What seemed to interfere with the success of this element?
   - The point here is to not only work to rectify this element, but to also rectify similar elements or their applications.
4. *If it was a successful element, how successful was it (a little or a lot)? Why did this element achieve its intended purpose?* Is the success of this element significant enough to warrant further examination, or is it more of a minor celebration? What seemed to cause the success of this element?
   - The point here is to not only revel in the success of this element, but also to determine whether it or its features could be used elsewhere in the application of similar elements.
5. *What mitigating conditions may have affected my use of this element?* Did I have enough time to properly use the element? What would have happened if the fire alarm had not gone off? Did that spate of student misbehaviours for 20 minutes ruin the atmosphere needed for the element? Is it possible that I am trying to use the element to make up for a lack of adequate supports or resources?

Practical Applications

Using the five perspectives outlined above, classify and describe how each perspective was implemented by the teacher in Example #1. You may have to make some assumptions about what the teacher actually did or was thinking about for some perspectives.

Step 2: Gather New Information

This stage of the process is where you seek out new or more information. To accomplish this, you will need to use the four lenses mentioned previously. A brief description of each lens is followed by leading questions and issues that should be considered when searching for information or soliciting feedback.

1. The *autobiographical lens* is self-examination from the perspective of one's understandings of one's teaching practices and lived teaching experiences. A key thought while engaging in this part of the exercise is to focus on teaching events that infuriated, energized, or truly puzzled you. The purpose and function of our teaching reveals much more about ourselves when it is directly connected to deep emotional feelings.

   Questions and Ideas. This list can be expanded but should be used in a written format:

   a) What part of my teaching proved especially stressful or exciting?

   b) What is my overarching philosophy of teaching, and did it play a role in selecting or executing this teaching element? If so, how and why did my philosophy affect my desired outcome?

   c) Is it possible that I saw/heard someone else use this element before?

   d) Did I use this element exactly as it should be used, or did my modification of it affect it in some way?

   e) Are any of my answers to these questions supported by other potential sources of information?

   f) What do I most need to learn about for my teaching?

   g) What do I worry about the most regarding my teaching?

2. The *learner lens* is an examination of our teaching from our students' perspectives. A key thought here is to try to become more aware of how your students are experiencing learning. For example, figuring out why they are apathetic about or enthralled with your teaching is far more informative than getting them to comment on the use of PowerPoint slides. As a cautionary note, you have to be quite precise in what you ask them to comment on or you will get feedback on everything and anything. The topics you want them to comment on are the key elements you identified as part of the exercise above. The fundamental premise behind this line of questioning is to resolve the question "Is it possible that my students just did not get what I intended? If so, why?" There are two things that you have to make perfectly clear: (a) You value their input and you will take their comments seriously, and (b) their feedback "will be considered for possible changes" as opposed to guaranteeing changes.

   Questions and Ideas. These questions are typically presented to students in written format and are completed and submitted anonymously. Limit the list to 10 questions or fewer to avoid being overwhelmed with data. You will have to adjust these to suit the age of your students.

   > *I would like to get your feedback on how my teaching is going. Your comments will help me to see things through your eyes. I will take your comments into consideration for any changes that I might want to make.*

a) Yesterday I did/used ____________ when I taught the lesson. That did not seem to go as well as I wanted. Can you tell me any reasons why it was not effective?
b) A few days ago I did/used ________ when I taught the lesson. That seemed to work very well. Can you tell me why it was so effective?
c) Do you think that using ________ to deal with behaviour problems in our classroom is effective? Why?
d) Having the rule that ________________ seems to work very well in dealing with assignments. Can you tell me why it is so effective?

These questions are of a more general nature:

a) What aspects of classroom behaviour do you think need to be improved? How could they be improved?
b) Does __________ make you want to participate in my class? Why or why not?
c) What was the most important thing that happened to you in my class this week?
d) What do you feel most dissatisfied with regarding our class?

3. The *peer/colleague lens* provides perspectives on our teaching from colleagues and peers. The key thought at this stage is that you want to gain multiple perspectives on your practice from well-informed individuals so you can acquire a clearer picture about your practice, not change the entire picture (see Jones, 1995). Because this process requires you to share personal ideas about teaching it is a risky venture; therefore, you must carefully chose your observers. You can also formally or informally observe others for more ideas about teaching. We provided an example of these types of influences in "Case #3: A Veteran Teacher's Perspective" in the Case Study earlier in this chapter.

Questions and Ideas: It is best to be as precise as you can in soliciting your colleagues' comments.

I would appreciate your feedback on certain aspects of my teaching. When I am teaching my lesson/class, I'd like you to take note of the following two (or three) teaching elements and make specific comments on how well they seem to work. I'd also appreciate it if you would comment on one other thing that you happen to notice during the lesson. I will take your comments into consideration when deciding what changes, if any, I may want to make.

a) The two to three elements of my teaching that I would like you to focus on are . . .
b) What have you heard from students about my use of these two to three elements?

4. The *research lens* provides further or new information about teaching elements found in books, articles, workshops, and so on. There are two key thoughts for this part of the process. The first is that any information you find may or may not prove useful, but you should consider all of it carefully. We say this because it is instinctive to think that "answers" can be found outside the classroom in books, resources, or workshops or that we need help from experts and consultants. At this point in the process you have a fairly good idea of what elements of your teaching need attention

and you have likely come to some fairly reasoned conclusions as to what to do about them. Therefore, consider new information as something *that may prove useful*. Your second key thought is that you should use research evidence to satisfy or disprove your hunches and intuitions. Rather than thinking of putting theory into practice, think of putting yourself into practice whereby you test and retest what you practise against what the research says. Unfortunately, you will often hear researchers and educators contrasting educational theory and research with educational practice. This is an inappropriate and untenable portrayal of the symbiotic relation between epistemology and **pedagogy**. We are all theorists and practitioners, at once using our acquired theoretical perspectives to support our practice and using our teaching processes to prove or disprove these perspectives. It is the failure of practice that leads to demands that theorists ask more and different questions to help us untangle the educational dilemmas we come up against.

pedagogy
The principles, methods, and activities of instruction that compose the profession of a teacher; sometimes referred to as "how one teaches."

Step 3: Does the New Information Have Implications for Your Practice?

Typically, if you seek out information about your identified teaching elements, that information will apply to those elements. This does not mean, however, that it will necessarily have implications for *your* practice. Your best bet is to look for commonalities amongst the various pieces of data you have gathered. By triangulating your own understandings, feedback you gathered from your students and colleagues, and the research evidence you sourced, it will become clear which bits of information will have implications for your practice and which will not. The key questions to ask are as follows:

1. Why and how will this information help my practice?
2. If I implement it, will it make a small change to what I do or will it require a significant departure?
3. Does this potential change feel like a logical step or does it seem to come out of left field?

Step 4: Design and Implement Your Desired Changes

Once you have decided on the changes you'd like to make, there can be no holding back or second guessing (unless, of course, you see that the changes will be just as bad or worse than the original). The point here is to use your changes to engage your teaching with the same conviction and determination you taught with before you even suspected that changes were needed. We do not mean for you to throw caution to the wind, but you have to rely on the sound judgment you used to discern the required changes, your ability to properly meld them into your teaching, and your expert ability to professionally carry out your new teaching. To hold back at this juncture will undermine all the hard work you have put in and it will contradict your positive attitude of "I will do everything necessary to be the very best teacher I can be." Therefore, make thoughtful and meaningful changes, then go teach assertively.

Step 5: When to Repeat the Process?

The cyclical nature of reflective practice is inevitable. There is an inherent human desire to make everything we do better or more efficient, and because we enact and experience our teaching practice daily, we can easily be drawn into a never-ending full-scale review of our work. Therefore, while reflective practice must be a continual and career-long process, you have to be judicious in its use or it can become reflection for reflection's sake. Just as you carefully selected a lesson or series of lessons for your initial attempt at the process, you have to be equally vigilant about when you might next entertain employing it. If nothing about your teaching is of great interest to you or causes you grave concern, there is no need for further reflection with the exception of an annual or end-of-term review; this is the minimum action you should take. However, when you are starting your career, you may want to select one or two minor elements of your teaching for reflection each month or two. Additionally, thinking about and tinkering with your practice is highly encouraged as long as it adheres to the fundamental principles outlined above. Sometimes stop-gap measures can be greatly beneficial, especially on a day-to-day or week-to-week basis, but they should not be thought of as viable substitutes for the real thing.

Suggestions for Engaging in Reflective Practice

This section provides you with things to think about when engaging in reflective practice. Each suggestion is based on recurring evidence from the experiences of numerous individuals who worked through this reflective process. Over two decades, this group of individuals has included many teachers and teacher-candidates, several university professors, and some coaches.

1. Don't only look back at what you did; look forward to what you want to do.
2. It is perfectly acceptable to dream about what you envision for your teaching. As long as you keep it realistic and specific, you will not go wrong.
3. Triangulating various perspectives about your teaching will provide you with accurate views and prevent the accumulation of limited and distorted views.
4. Do not let your path to personal professional growth be deterred by skeptics and naysayers, and that includes you.
5. Providing a critique of your teaching is not criticism of your teaching.
6. Reflective practice is an ongoing pattern of growth, not a collection of bandages.
7. Be proud of your accomplishments and your growth as a teacher, but be humble enough to acknowledge that you will always be a reflective practitioner open to further growth.

Exemplary Teaching

It is quite difficult and it can be overly simplistic to try to describe all of what composes exemplary teaching. Really good teaching involves the understanding and coordination of so many instructional and contextual variables that any attempt to define it can end up being nothing more than an extensive list. And, while this list or table may be comprehensive and contain all the important components of teaching, it could not hope to accurately explain the complexity of teacher–student interactions that form the basis for all good teaching. In this instance, think of this comprehensive list as part of the science of teaching, while the complexities and nuances of teacher–student interactions are part of the art of teaching. In the case of the list, it would probably be a fairly straightforward scientific assemblage of all that is good about teaching in terms of required knowledge and skills.

A few of the components certain to be on that list include subject matter expertise, teaching method proficiency, excellent organizational skills, and the ability to alter your teaching to reach a variety of students. In the case of teacher–student interactions, however, these represent the more subtle and artistic elements of teaching that require a disposition that is conducive to positive interpersonal outcomes. Here we are talking about teachers having a personal characteristic and attitude that makes them consciously choose to have their students' best interests at heart, to embrace the concept of being firm but fair and flexible, to appreciate that school is not the first priority for all students, and to accept that how much students learn is far more important than how much you teach. You should think of these conceptions as logical and necessary extensions of the attitude "I will do everything necessary to be the very best teacher I can be."

To attempt to catalogue, define, or list all the elements of good teaching, therefore, is not the purpose of this final section. The curriculum and methods courses of your teacher education program will provide you with much better and more specific explanations and demonstrations of these fundamental aspects of teaching. Our purpose here is to outline for you the overarching and basic tenets and principles that should govern your use of those aspects of teaching. For example, if you hold to the principle that the primary purpose of teaching is to incite good learning in all students, you will carefully consider whether methods such as lecturing and assessment tools such as essays are the best ways to accomplish that purpose. Therefore, this final part of the chapter will include a description of those elements of education that are widely agreed upon as composing good teaching, a framework to organize them, and an outline of the basic values that enable teachers to thrive as educators.

As we mentioned at the beginning of this chapter, teacher education has undergone some fairly dramatic changes over the last four or five decades. In that time, several attempts have been made to outline the details of what composes good teaching. Over the last 25 years, the teaching profession has been similarly engaged in the process of developing a systematic and standardized collection of descriptions regarding the knowledge, skills, and dispositions of professional teaching. This **codification** of the knowledge and standards of professional practice is based on an ever-growing consensus about exemplary practice and valid, reliable, and replicable research that has been conducted in classrooms with actual students and teachers. The fundamental difference driving this consensus and codification of teaching is that its descriptions of exemplary teaching are primarily based on what is known about high-quality student learning that is derived from exceptional teaching. This perspective places effective and proven student learning outcomes at the forefront of the discussion, rather than as a secondary consideration or afterthought whereby good teaching is primarily or exclusively considered from the teacher's perspective.

codification
The assembly, arrangement into order, and systematization of principles that govern a professional body.

Here we outline the critical components of exemplary teaching practice based on the above consensus. The conceptual structure we use to organize these components is from Bransford, Darling-Hammond, and LePage's (2005) *Preparing Teachers for a Changing World*. As shown in Figure 1.2, the framework outlines the three specific areas of knowledge, skills, and dispositions that are important for teachers to acquire and implement. The three key components of the framework are as follows:

1. Knowledge of learners and how they learn and develop within social contexts
2. Conceptions of curriculum content and goals; an understanding of subject matter and skills to be taught in light of the social purposes of education
3. An understanding of teaching in light of the content and learners to be taught, as informed by assessment and supported by classroom environments (Bransford, Darling-Hammond, & LePage, 2005, p. 10)

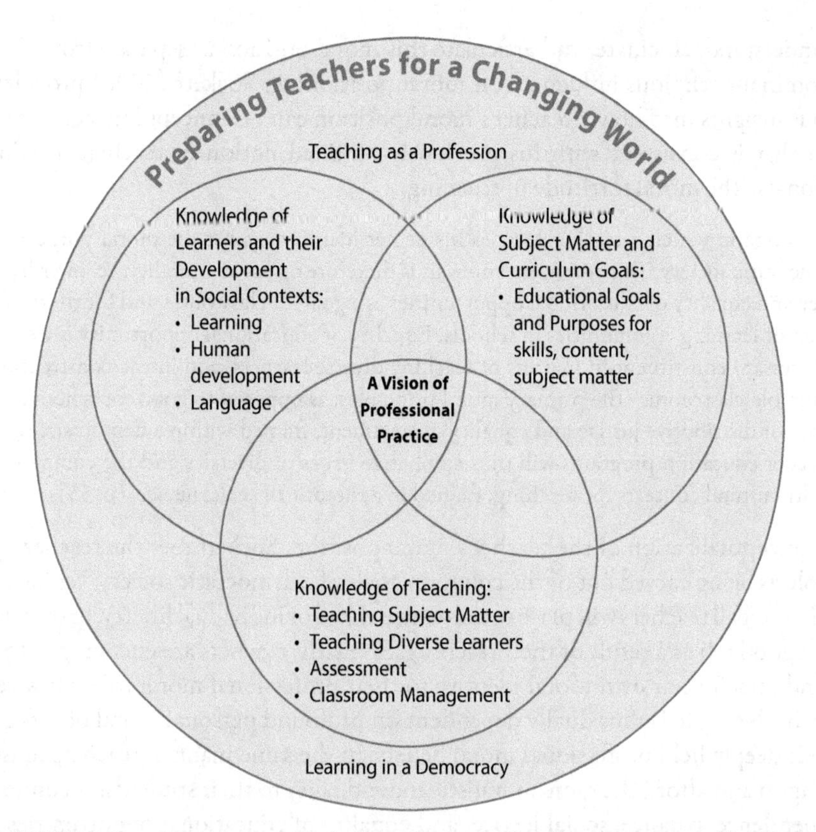

FIGURE 1.2 A Framework for Understanding Teaching and Learning
Source: From Bransford, Darling-Hammond, & LePage, 2005). Figure 1.1, p. 11.

These three areas are overlaid by two important conditions of practice: (a) Teaching is a profession, and (b) education must serve the purposes of a democracy. Thus, in addition to developing excellent knowledge, skills, and dispositions, teachers are charged with two additional obligations. First, they need to have or develop a strong sense of moral purpose so that they can provide students with a meaningful education. This means understanding that education, and schools and teachers in particular, have a larger duty to produce caring, loving, and loveable people as well as competent individuals. Second, teachers have to provide an education that serves fundamental democratic purposes so that students can fully participate in the political, civic, and economic facets of society. This means understanding that schools, in addition to functioning as places of learning, also function as places that fulfill vocational, civic, personal, and social needs. Given that students' academic needs might not necessarily be their first priority, teachers have to try to balance students' other needs and priorities as best they can without compromising student educational progress. What we can deduce from this is that in addition to acquiring and honing traditional sets of knowledge, skills, and dispositions, teachers also need to know, care about, and be able to work in classrooms that are increasingly diverse.

Teaching with a Moral Purpose

The one element of teaching that makes it a profession rather than a job is its sense of moral purpose. This is probably the single greatest change in teacher education and teacher practice over the last 50 years, and it has occurred because educators and researchers sought to better understand, elucidate, and articulate this moral position as separate from the previously dominant religious influences on moral positioning. Sockett (2008) provides some illustrious insights into how a teacher's moral position can be conceptualized. It is a moral position that is consistent with his previously outlined notion of teachers as clinician–professionals. The moral fortitude of teaching

> . . . is one in which a teacher forgoes his or her identity against the moral purposes of a democratic society. This common emphasis is therefore on social morality, i.e. interdependence and equality of educational opportunities as a goal for classrooms and for the development of learning communities in schools. Equality of educational opportunity is viewed as a necessary constituent in matters of teaching diverse learners, and in the construction of equitable classrooms. The primary moral principles, as opposed to goals for schooling, are those of distributive justice and equality of treatment, framed within a democratic society. Teacher education programs will thus emphasize issues of diversity and the complexity of multi-cultural contexts for teaching, framed in a rhetoric of social justice. (p. 55)

In this conceptualization of the teacher's moral position, Sockett sees the teacher's professional role as being carved out of the common goals of a democratic society, yet he acknowledges that not all teachers will place social justice ahead of individual liberty, or that students will get a good job as a result of their teaching. Similarly, teachers are encouraged to create, build, and attach their own moral identity to their professional moral role. How teachers perform in their role is thus dually dependent on profound personal moral beliefs coupled with their deeply held professional moral beliefs. In the same manner, teachers must bring to bear upon and afford the same moralistic individuality to their students. A commitment to independence, balance, social justice, and equality of educational opportunities is seen as an equally admirable objective for teachers as well as their students so that they, too, can develop and nurture the virtues and propensities of a democratic citizen.

Not only do teachers need a moral compass to follow through on their commitment to educating their students, they need a compass that holds dear and reflects the virtues of truth, respect, openness, and impartiality as well as the qualities of tolerance, reason, and compassion. This is necessary because in the responsibility of educating the next generations, teachers are allocated the highest moral authority. Education is a moral end and teachers cannot shrink from this obligation, just as they cannot only partially implement or shy away from a robust and sound instructional strategy. The difficulty for teachers is that morality is seldom visible or on display except perhaps in the enactment of classroom management. Unless it is part of a specific formal curriculum, teachers will have to create their own opportunities to demonstrate the moral actions and reflections that contribute to their students' social, moral, ethical, and emotional development. The potential catch-22 here is that teachers must be careful not to be seen to be imposing their morals and values on the students within whom they are required to strongly encourage moral individuality and identity.

The Values of Teaching and Education

Hansen's (2008) definitive work on the purposes of teacher education outlines the five intrinsic values that influence the scope and structure of teaching. In the broadest sense, this set of values first and foremost embraces the premise that teachers need to be properly educated for their role in society. Once prepared, teachers can carry out and embody the greater values of society wherein education is seen as a necessary preparatory phase for later work and life and as fulfilling the modern need for academic learning, the enhancement of human development, and the call for social justice. We have paraphrased Hansen's five intrinsic values below.

1. From the initiation of formal schooling, the most widely shared value amongst educators and members of the public, particularly parents, is that education should primarily be designed and delivered to prepare the young for a productive economic, social, and adult life.
2. Teacher educator programs should cultivate teachers' disciplinary knowledge in conjunction with instructional knowledge about how to bring subject matter to life. This moves teacher-candidates from mindless memorization to genuine understanding.
3. Every teacher is charged with generating activities that engage students' powers to understand, explain, and come to grips with the significance of new academic knowledge, and it is an injustice not to expose the young to such mind-expanding values.
4. Teacher educators and teachers hold in high esteem the values embedded in a variety of theoretical conceptions of learning. Each group is enthralled by the sheer fact that human beings can learn and grow in remarkable, unfathomable ways.
5. Social justice means a commitment to rectify, through teacher education and schooling, historic injustices in society based on racism, sexism, classism, homophobia, and other forms of systemic prejudice. Also, through a call for and an enactment of civic and democratic education, teachers have an important role to play in societal transformation.

Hansen presents these values in a heuristic manner all the while acknowledging that teachers will and should ask urgently pressing questions about each. We have provided some of our own sample questions here:

1. Relative to life preparation: What is meant by a productive life? Who gets to judge whether someone is living a productive life, and by what measures? Is one person's fulfillment another person's emptiness?
2. Relative to knowledge: Whose knowledge is accepted, how has it been determined, and who decides what is important? How and why should the acquisition of knowledge be filtered?
3. Relative to teaching students: When and how should academic knowledge be introduced to students? What are the compromises that must be made in using certain methods?
4. Relative to learning theory: Which theory should be used and why (or why not)? How do you determine the effectiveness of adhering to a particular theory?
5. Relative to social justice: What is meant by *justice* and how do we know it when we see it? Does justice for one mean justice for all, and vice versa?

To provide specific directions to teachers for developing their own values for teaching, Hansen directly connects them to Dewey's theory of public interest. In his theory, Dewey (1988) suggested that the public—or *a public*—is never static; rather, it is an ever-emerging entity that comes into being when the consequences of human activity in one place affect people elsewhere and when those people seek to respond to those consequences. Therefore, the public has an inherent and pervasive common interest in having these consequences systematically cared for. Given that teachers will internalize and cause intellectual and social consequences and that the public interest constitutes a living and dynamic process, teachers need to think of life preparation, academic learning, diversity, civic education, and social justice as points of departure for investigations into how to create the richest of educational experiences possible for their students. This global outlook will prevent education from becoming too closely associated with only one theoretical perspective. This also suggests that societal values are constantly changing, so teachers should be prepared to be aware of and open to such changes (see Cochran-Smith, Feiman-Nemser, McIntyre, & Demers, 2008).

The values described above will change over time to keep pace with and accurately reflect the changing mores of society. They will also change to accommodate conceptual and methodological transformations within education. In turn, these values will modify teachers' perceptions and attitudes, causing them to need to adapt and change their everyday practice. This does not mean that all teachers will be the same, but it should mean that they will draw on the same omnipresent values and principles to guide their practice. To add scope and depth to these values, we conclude the chapter with examples of the common kinds of practices exhibited by highly effective teachers.

Common Practices among Highly Effective Teachers

Carter (2003) conducted a comprehensive study for the Public Education Foundation examining 92 elementary and middle school teachers who were ranked as highly effective educators based on a variety of indicators. During the study, the teachers were interviewed, surveyed, and observed over the course of one teaching year. This research found that although the 92 teachers differed in age, experience, background, and personality and varied widely in their teaching styles, they displayed and practised a remarkably common set of teaching elements:

1. Expectations for students were clearly stated and exemplars of previous year's assignments were shown as models of what to produce.
2. Student work could be found everywhere: inside classrooms, outside the door, and down the hall.
3. Teachers did not stand still and lecture; they covered every part of the room and monitored every activity that took place within it.
4. Multiple small-group activities were often evident, while the traditional arrangement of desks in rows was practically nonexistent.
5. There were high levels of "instructional discourse": Students were encouraged to ask questions, discuss ideas, and comment on statements made by teachers and other students.
6. The organization of the room and the lessons was clearly evident. Materials were easily accessible when needed, and no class time was wasted from lack of preparation. (Bransford, Darling-Hammond, & LePage, 2005, p. 6)

It is our contention that a central part of being an effective teacher is making a steadfast commitment to doing one's best to help all students succeed—hence our persistence that a good teacher's attitude has to be "I will do everything necessary to be the very best teacher I can be." This means, however, that this desire must be facilitated by expert knowledge and skills, and the values and attitudes that are conducive to teaching excellence as reflected by outstanding student achievement. These core ideas will have an omnipresent and direct influence on the ways in which curricula are interpreted, the perceived benefits and various implementations of particular instructional methods, and the types of assessment strategies selected. The ideas presented in this chapter are the linchpins around which teachers can mould their understandings and practice. By following these principles and values of education, teachers, like their students, will be primed to succeed.

Discussion Questions

1. What is reflective practice and how is it embodied by teachers?
2. How can my professionalism as a teacher be enhanced through reflective practice?
3. How can I use a teaching log to conduct my own reflective practice?
4. How do these fundamental values influence my professionalism?
5. What are the common practices of highly effective teachers?

Further Resources

1. Cochran-Smith, M., Feiman-Nemser, S., McIntyre, D. J., & Demers, K. E. (Eds.). (2008). *Handbook of research on teacher education: Enduring questions in changing contexts* (3rd ed.). New York, NY: Routledge, Taylor & Francis Group and the Association of Teacher Educators.

   This handbook was initiated to ferment change in education based on solid evidence. Beyond simply conceptualizing the broad landscape of teacher education, this volume presents research evidence and commentaries written by researchers, teachers, teacher educators, policy-makers, and foundation directors that reflect a wide spectrum of ideological stances on education. It particularly frames these issues relevant to the development of strong teacher education programs and the proper preparation of teachers.

2. Cole, A. L., & Knowles, J. G. (2000). *Researching teaching: Exploring teacher development through reflexive inquiry*. Toronto, ON: Allyn & Bacon.

   Explorations of practice and the improvement of practice are the primary functions of this book. It places teaching at the centre of all that is done in education and focuses on exploring teaching from grade school through to university instruction and beyond to teacher professional development. It contains both insights about and suggested practices for the process of reflective inquiry.

3. Danielson, C. F. (2007). *Enhancing professional practice: A framework for teaching* (2nd ed.). Alexandria, VA: ASCD.

   This framework for professional practice includes four domains: planning and preparation, the classroom environment, instruction, and professional responsibilities. Using rubrics and illustrative examples, the author provides specific examples to demonstrate characteristics of effective teaching.

4. Jones, D. C. (Ed.). (1995). *The spirit of teaching*. Calgary, AB: Detselig Enterprises Limited.

   This book is a collection of rich essays from a variety of contributors on what it means and what is does *not* mean to be a teacher. Its purpose is to inspire and to uplift and give purpose to teaching and to those who aspire to the profession. This book is all about the pursuit of excellence in teaching; it is also a pursuit of the self in the journey of becoming a teacher.

Classroom Management

Learning Objectives

After reading this chapter, you should understand

1. How to create a well-planned and comprehensive approach to classroom management
2. The explicit rules required for effective classroom management, including appropriate rewards and consequences
3. That the absence of good student behaviour is a performance deficit rather than a skill deficit
4. That the way teachers achieve classroom order is more important than whether order is achieved
5. That the teacher cannot be the only individual responsible for good classroom order
6. How to define, be reasonably flexible with, and firmly implement good classroom order

Schools have changed. No longer can educators focus on academic skills while ignoring the emotional well-being of students. This change in perspective should not, however, be considered a mere moral obligation for you as a teacher, something you may choose to implement or ignore. There is too much compelling evidence that a student's sense of belonging and security forms the educational bases for motivation, learning, and self-discipline. In their comprehensive analyses of behaviour and classroom management in preparation for the second edition of *Understanding and Managing Children's Classroom Behavior: Creating Sustainable, Resilient Classrooms*, Goldstein and Brooks (2007) state that

> . . . schools must now provide social, emotional intervention hand-in-hand with academic education . . . instilling what we have called a *resilient mindset* in students. The basic feature of resilient children is that their self-esteem and sense of competence are intact, [they] possess feelings of hope and optimism, of ownership and personal control . . . nurtured by charismatic educators capable of providing experiences to reinforce their strengths and their feelings of self-worth. When students are actively involved in the learning process, when they feel connected and make contributions, discipline, as E.B. White once wrote, "Will take care of itself." (p. 4)

This chapter introduces the reader to the underlying psychological principles of behaviour and the motivating forces that cause students to act as they do. It also describes how teachers can design and implement an effective model of classroom management. The example included in the Appendix at the end of this book provides a rich narrative description of the types of student and teacher discourses that need to take place if students are to become invested in the management of their own educational environments.

Classroom and Behaviour Management

So you might ask, what exactly is **classroom management**? It is generally defined as the actions teachers undertake to create environments that enhance academic learning and appropriate social skill development. Classroom management is often described as the methods and strategies that teachers use to maintain a classroom environment that is favourable to student learning and achievement. **Behaviour management**, on the other hand, consists of the actions that teachers take to diminish or decrease poor behaviours and to increase desirable behaviours. In this manner, behaviour management is considered an essential subset of classroom management. This means classroom management is not a "bag of tricks" that is suddenly whipped out whenever students act improperly, nor is it a method of "controlling" students so that they obediently respond to teacher demands. You want to think of classroom management as a coherent set of principles and skills that need to be integrated into the everyday activities of teachers and students who are working together. From this perspective, the teacher is not the only person who will have responsibility for classroom order. A broader definition of classroom management can be described as "the ability of teachers and students to agree upon and carry forward a common framework for social and academic interactions, by creating an ethos of effort within a social fabric that is built over time, and ultimately leads to student self-discipline" (Freiburg & Lapointe, 2006). More than anything, though, it is important for you to understand that classroom management is critically important to the social, emotional, and intellectual development of students. It provides the structure, consistency, and reliability that students need to thrive in your classroom.

classroom management
The actions teachers undertake to create environments that enhance academic learning and appropriate social skill development.

behaviour management
The actions that teachers take to diminish or decrease poor behaviours and to increase desirable behaviours. Behaviour management is considered an essential subset of classroom management.

Effective classroom management approaches are in great demand because there is ample evidence that (a) student misbehaviour is one of the most serious problems facing schools (Evertson & Weinstein, 2006a, 2006b), and (b) no other educational factor undermines student learning and achievement as much as poorly managed classrooms and the problematic behaviours that result from students feeling disconnected (Lewis, Newcomer, Trussell, & Richter, 2006). In fact, one in five students exhibit disruptive behaviours, and one in twenty exhibit aggressive behaviours (Myers & Holland, 2000). On average, teachers can spend 30–80% of their time addressing problem behaviours within the classroom (Walsh, 1983).

However, not all students exhibit behaviours that detract from effective teaching practices. Sugai and Horner (2002) found that 80% of students in any classroom behave appropriately, 5% of students display chronic problem behaviours that negatively affect the classroom environment, and the remaining 15% can be swayed either way depending on the effectiveness of classroom management strategies. It is also well documented that classroom management problems are the major cause of teacher burnout and job dissatisfaction; teachers repeatedly rank discipline as the first or second most serious problem they face in schools (Evertson & Weinstein, 2006b).

Impact on Today's Teachers

From your own school years, can you recall a student who frequently exhibited problematic behaviours? How did this student's behaviour affect the overall classroom environment? How did you and your classmates respond to this student? What do you remember about how this student was disciplined? Can you think of ways that this student's behaviour could have been addressed more effectively?

Problem Behaviour

What is interesting about challenging student behaviours is that these are not random acts, as many seem to claim. We know that all behaviours serve some function, but they are mostly attempts to communicate human needs. When we closely examine their base functions, all human behaviours are an effort to get something or avoid something, and all behaviours are maintained, changed, or shaped by positive or negative consequences. B. F. Skinner, the prominent behavioural psychologist who did the earliest work on operant conditioning, provided us with the notion that all behaviours have a purpose (Skinner, 1974). While we agree with this fundamental premise, we also know that some challenging student behaviours are due to a lack of congruence between the task or the social demands being placed on a student and his or her limited skills to respond appropriately. In this regard, behaviour is both an intrapersonal (within-person) and an interpersonal (between-person) phenomenon in that while we have to learn how to properly manage ourselves to meet our own needs, we must do so while simultaneously getting along with others. Therefore, because behaviours mostly emanate from human interaction, this makes behaviour a relational phenomenon. Albert Bandura, the renowned Canadian psychologist who conceptualized social learning theory, established the concept of *reciprocal determinism*. This theory explains how ongoing social interactions between students and teachers reciprocally determine how they interact with each other in the future (Bandura, 1977, 1986). For example, if you have a great first encounter with a student in your class, you are likely to enjoy more of the same despite the student engaging in problematic behaviours. This is more than simply getting off on the right foot; it means that over several positive interactions you will both expect that you will be well treated by the other person.

Levin, Nolan, Kerr, and Elliott (2009) proposed the following to encapsulate how educators should interpret the term *problem behaviour*: It is behaviour that (a) interferes with the teaching act, (b) interferes with the rights of others to learn, (c) is psychologically or physically unsafe, or (d) destroys property. These interpretations dovetail nicely with Demchak and Bossert's (1996) motivations that drive human behaviour:

1. They serve a specific purpose or function for the individual.
2. They have communicative intent.
3. They are directly related to events in the environment that influence and reinforce such behaviours.
4. A single challenging behaviour can serve multiple functions.

The most widely accepted explanation for why students behave badly comes from the seminal works of Dreikurs and Cassel (1972). They developed a pragmatic means of understanding the purposes of bad behaviour and for finding ways to elicit co-operative behaviour. They believed that the root of behaviour could be best understood using four key premises:

1. People are social beings who have a need to belong, to be recognized, and to be accepted.
2. Behaviour is goal oriented and has the purpose of gaining recognition and acceptance.
3. People choose how they behave. Behaviour is not outside of their control; it is often a deliberate act to achieve a desired goal.
4. People try a wide variety of behaviours to see which ones will gain recognition and acceptance. When socially sanctioned behaviours do not produce recognition and acceptance, people will use socially unacceptable behaviours in the mistaken belief that these will produce the recognition they desire (Dreikurs, 1964).

We have paraphrased Dreikurs and Cassel's concepts below and have included examples representative of students' misguided attempts to achieve these concepts:

1. Gain attention (*negative attention is better than being ignored or considered unimportant—nobody pays attention to me when I am good*). A student continually asks for help or assistance despite clear directions, asks for approval, calls out answers, or shows off to the class. The teacher acknowledges the student's attention-seeking behaviour, thereby reinforcing the student because he or she is getting the desired attention. The behaviour continues.
2. Gain power/control (*I only feel good about myself when I have control—I won't try because I don't like taking risks*). The student displays stubbornness or questions the authority of the teacher in an attempt to take control. When the teacher exercises his or her authority, a power struggle ensues. This leads to student tantrums or other more aggressive behaviours.

3. Exact retribution for personal slights (*I protect/enhance my personal well-being by attacking others*). Retribution behaviours, such as stealing; acting sullen; showing defiance; hurting animals, peers, adults, or themselves; and lashing out aggressively, occur because a student feels that he or she lost a power struggle and is seeking revenge for his or her embarrassment.
4. Conceal inadequacy (*I cannot do it—if I demonstrate I cannot do it, I cannot be held responsible*). The student displays a sense of hopelessness and behaves so others think he or she is incapable, gives up easily, participates infrequently, or tries to remain alone and does not accept teacher help.

On the other hand, when it comes to good student behaviour there is no evidence whatsoever that the absence of good classroom behaviour is a skill deficit problem; rather, it is becoming more widely accepted and viewed as a performance deficit problem (Gresham, 2002; Lane, Falk, & Wehby, 2006; Maag, 2004). This means that all students have the basic skills to behave appropriately—they just do not know how to use them or they are not being encouraged to use them properly. Teachers must therefore provide a classroom atmosphere and management structure that models, encourages, and supports the optimal use of desired behaviours.

Goldstein and Brooks's (2007) extensive research determined four classes of behaviour that appear to disturb teachers the most: social immaturity, disobedience, motor and physical activity, and purposefully disruptive behaviour. Among classroom teachers, outright student defiance is consistently rated as the most disturbing problem followed by aggression and poor peer co-operation. Teachers find that a lack of motivation, anxiety, and learning difficulties are the least disturbing student behaviours and the most tolerable.

Ineffective Approaches to Classroom Management

School systems have a long history of relying heavily on rapid-suppression techniques for managing problem behaviours. Students who committed offences were typically punished with in-school suspensions, expulsions, and sometimes corporal punishment. These punitive interventions are after-the-fact reactions by teachers and administrators designed to immediately stop the behaviour and send a warning to not engage in the behaviour again. Unfortunately, rapid-suppression techniques do nothing to promote good behaviours, nor do they provide constructive instruction about preferred pro-social behaviours. Within rapid-suppression systems, there is a strong expectation that students know what to do and what not to do and, if they do not know, they are expected to figure it out by deciphering the implied message behind the punishment. To some degree, this attitude by educators still exists.

Most educational systems, at one time or another, have used punitive discipline as their primary way of responding to challenging behaviours. Advocates of such policies tend to see bad behaviour as unacceptable and they often enact "zero-tolerance" policies as a way of compensating. This results in reactive models of discipline that view poorly behaved students as "the problem" with no regard for why the behaviours occur. When educators encounter students who exhibit problematic behaviours, their speculations about the cause of the problem usually blame the student or his or her family for being a "bad" student. These not-so-subtle inferences place the onus for reform entirely on the student, who has now become the scapegoat for the problem. This mindset conveniently blames students for all disruptions stemming from problem behaviour. On the other hand, it also establishes a student mindset that their behaviour is only wrong if they get caught. Chandler and Dahlquist (2002) documented the negative assumptions that educators often formulate about students who persistently exhibit problematic behaviours:

1. The student misbehaves because he is bad.
2. The student's disability causes bad behaviours.
3. The student's family (poor parenting) causes the child's dysfunction in school.
4. The student's home is dysfunctional.
5. Trauma suffered by the student causes bad behaviours.

Furthermore, teachers often describe students who display problem behaviours as lazy, unmotivated, belligerent, aggressive, angry, or argumentative. Although these characteristics may be accurate classifications of student behaviours, they are primarily used to provide educators with a form of emotional release from their responsibility to properly deal with these students. A common example of this is the teacher who says a problematic student is too belligerent to work with, not because the student is overly obnoxious, but because the teacher will have to spend a lot of time and effort to adequately deal with the student's issues, which can be frustrating. This approach is not conducive to the practices of an effective classroom nor does it contribute to the emotional and behavioural development of students.

Obstacles to Effective Classroom Management

In a comprehensive and widely regarded synthesis of research on classroom management, Brophy (2006a) highlighted two predominant inhibitors to the design and implementation of effective classroom management interventions:

> Although the fundamental importance of classroom management is universally recognized, it has not received proportional attention as a topic of empirical research. Furthermore, the most important time in which to conduct such research is at the beginning of the school year, when many schools or individual teachers do not want researchers visiting their classrooms. (p. 38)

Research conducted in both elementary and secondary schools has identified other prevalent sets of reasons why most existing approaches and interventions do not work well. There is evidence that schools are overreliant on punitive methods of management, educators have unclear or implied-only rules for student behaviour, there is a lack of staff–administrator agreement on behaviour policies, and most interventions do not attend well to student behavioural differences (Mayer, 2001).

According to Edmunds and Edmunds (2010), classroom management interventions are ineffective for four major reasons. First, well-researched behaviour and classroom management principles are not translated into comprehensive/practical interventions. Teachers are left on their own to decipher complex and overlapping findings and to design systematic plans that are only used in single classrooms. Second, some interventions are not designed based on explicit observations of teachers' and students' actions/interactions—they are based on improving things like attendance and achievement. Third, related to the previous point, intervention evaluations are decontextualized whereby investigators examine *indirect* influences on behaviour (e.g., time on task, classroom transition efficacy, academic achievement) rather than measuring classroom-specific behaviours for the expressed purpose of misbehaviour identification, prevention, and reduction/elimination. Finally, and perhaps most importantly, program fidelity—the strict adherence by educators to the fundamental tenets of the program and its implementation—is inconsistently applied or is compromised. A further explanation of program fidelity is found later in the chapter.

There are other logistical issues that contribute to the lack of successful management interventions. Despite strong evidence of the effectiveness of school-wide approaches, most teacher-based interventions are not designed, monitored, and evaluated on a school-wide basis (Burke, Ayres, & Hagan-Burke, 2004). Despite striking evidence that interventions implemented on the opening day of school are more effective, little research has involved the implementation of classroom management systems at the beginning of the school year (Brophy, 2006a). In addition, many interventions are based on misperceptions of behaviour and its management (Lane, Falk, & Wehby, 2006) failing to recognize that *how* a teacher constructs and maintains order is as important as whether order is achieved (Fallona & Richardson, 2006). Another flaw is that many interventions are only implemented over one- to two-day time frames with little or no follow-up and no evaluation of long-term effects. Together or separately, these conditions typically result in no lasting impact for either teachers or students.

The pervasive problem here is that these flaws significantly compromise program fidelity. This means that users do not follow the foundational principles originally designed to govern the intervention so that it will be effective and sustainable. Compromising program fidelity can range from innocently changing the implementation timing (such as the inconvenience of starting at the beginning of the year) to blatantly disregarding one of the key elements (such as teachers not holding students accountable for their behaviours for fear of being portrayed as a mean person). For any classroom management approach to be effective, it needs to be consistent in its application of the exact principles and practices that made it successful in the first place.

The Emotional Needs of Students

Edward Deci's research on motivational factors affecting students (Deci & Chandler, 1986; Deci & Flaste, 1995; Deci, Hodges, Pierson, & Tomassone, 1992) revealed that students are more motivated and will be resilient in the face of adversity if teachers construct environments that satisfy three fundamental needs:

1. To belong and feel connected and to sense that teachers believe in them and will treat them with respect; satisfying this need reduces the likelihood of disruptive, angry student behaviours.
2. To feel autonomous and possess a sense of self-determination, and to feel they are expected and permitted to have ownership, responsibility, and accountability for their actions; satisfying this need increases positive behaviours.
3. To feel competent, successful, and accomplished; satisfying this need appeases our basic motivation to enhance our self-esteem, the primary motivating force for all human activity.

Goldstein and Brooks (2007) extended this research by outlining six strategies teachers can use to nurture the above needs:

1. Provide an orientation period at the beginning of the school year/term to plant the seeds for a positive student mindset of behavioural responsibility and an overall attitude toward building a successful classroom climate.
2. Develop realistic expectations and goals for behaviour and learning and make accommodations when necessary.
3. Reinforce responsibility by providing opportunities to contribute to the welfare of others.
4. Provide opportunities to make choices and decisions and solve problems, which reinforces a sense of ownership.
5. Establish self-discipline by learning to discipline effectively.
6. Assist students to deal more effectively with mistakes and failures.

The premise here is to help students develop a mindset of being active and effective participants in their own environments. Students can emulate teachers' behaviours and will adjust their own behaviours to suit the positive and energizing environments that teachers create. The predominant mindset of successful students is that they believe that they are active participants in their learning environments, not simply passive receivers of it. This belief is driven in part by a strong desire to be involved in the processes that govern their environments. Goldstein and Brooks's (2007, p. 29) synthesis of the characteristics of successful students highlights the following commonalities:

- They believe that whether they learn or not is based in great part on their own motivation, perseverance, and effort. If students view themselves as passive recipients of what is being taught, their interest and enthusiasm for learning will be greatly diminished.
- They recognize that making mistakes and not immediately understanding certain concepts or material are part of the learning process. They appreciate that learning takes time and effort.
- They perceive the teacher as a supportive adult. When confronted with difficulty with academic or nonacademic issues, successful students feel comfortable in taking the initiative to ask their teachers for assistance.
- They understand their learning style, learning strengths, and learning vulnerabilities. The more that students gain an understanding of their learning profile, the more they can develop strategies for learning actively and successfully.
- They treat classmates with respect and avoid teasing or bullying, recognizing that such behaviours work against a positive school climate and adversely affect the learning of all students.

The Case Study below is an account of an incident experienced during practicum by Alan Hillis, a student in the Bachelor of Education program at Western University.

CASE STUDY

I Like You, but Not What You're Doing

Chris can be a difficult student to handle. He gets off-task easily, and when he is not watched closely, Chris creates disruptions. These behaviours are especially noticeable when the teacher is away and a substitute teacher is present or when the teacher steps out of the room and he is left with me (the student teacher).

On one occasion, when the teacher was away and I was working with a substitute teacher, Chris was a problem all day. He was more disobedient than usual, often talking and laughing during instruction, and he kept making noises and actions where he would pretend to be trying to pull-start a lawnmower. Unfortunately, Chris's lawnmower would not start, and he felt the need to pull the cord repeatedly during the day. It was so obvious he wanted attention and he did not care that he was getting negative attention, at least from the teachers, including me.

During the substitute teacher's read-aloud exercise, I had heard enough of Chris. I ordered him out into the hallway for a talk. I asked him "What is the problem today? Why are you being so disruptive? Why are you being like this?" and so forth. His posture was very defensive and his replies were "I'm not doing anything," "It's not me," "You aren't saying anything to anyone else," etc. I decided to try something I had learned in my behaviour management class at the faculty. I said to him, "Chris, you are a great kid and I like you a lot; I just don't like what you're doing."

I could immediately see the look on his face change as the words came out of my mouth. He went from being completely defensive to having this almost bashful look, as if saying, "Yeah, I know I'm being a pain. I'll stop." And that was it. I had no problems with him for the rest of the day and he has responded to me very well ever since.

The part of my course that made the difference in this case was the section about how teachers' perceptions of student behaviour can affect how we deal with them. I knew from class that students often feel *"the teacher doesn't like me"* when a teacher reprimands them. The key for me in this situation was to separate the person from the behaviour and make sure the message was about the behaviour, not about Chris's personality. It worked really well.

Teacher Orientations to Discipline

In 1994, Johnson, Whittington, and Oswald examined the opinions and beliefs of 3,400 teachers regarding the management of classrooms. Teachers responded to open-ended questions such as "How should students behave at school?" "Why should students behave in these ways?" "What strategies are appropriate to ensure students behave in these ways?" "Why do some students not behave in these ways at school?" "Who should decide these matters?" "Who determines how students should behave and who ensures this behaviour?" Using this data, Johnson and his colleagues identified four teacher orientations to discipline: traditional, liberal progressive, socially critical, and laissez-faire. The following descriptions are all derived from the above work.

Traditional: Management Theories

Advocates of this orientation call for strict adherence to class rules, a range of escalating punishments for rule-breakers, and a discipline regime in which the authority of teachers is largely unquestioned. Advocates assertively promote the right of teachers to teach without the distractions of disruptive and disinclined students (Canter & Canter, 1976) in the interests of achieving skills, subject-based knowledge, and values related to conforming to the wider society. Advocates also assert that all children have a propensity to misbehave if not restrained by school officials. Parents are expected to accept and support school authority and discipline policies, and while at home parents should enforce the school rules—such as attendance, homework, and the code of conduct.

Liberal Progressive: Nondirective/Leadership Theories

Advocates of this orientation believe that democratic principles should prevail in all social situations, including in schools. Within this orientation, students should share power and be part of the decision-making process within schools and classrooms; there is more concern with co-operation. Advocates assert that teaching social skills is necessary to prepare students for collaborative in-classroom activities and their participation in a democratic society. In contrast to the traditional values of domination, competition, rewards and punishments, social inequality, pressure from above, sole responsibility, and lack of respect, the preferred values of the liberal progressive orientation include social equality, mutual respect, shared responsibility, co-operation, and self-discipline.

Socially Critical

Advocates of this orientation believe that it is the student's role to challenge inequalities and undemocratic power relationships and that teachers have a responsibility to support power sharing in classrooms. They view students' behaviours as neither good nor bad, but believe that behaviour is influenced by alienation and undemocratic exercises of social power. Disruptions are seen to emanate from a disjunction between the culture and interests of students and the curriculum content and the school organizational ethos. The exertion of group power is justified to oppose and rectify inequities.

Laissez-faire

Advocates of this orientation strive for student self-actualization, inner harmony, and true self-discipline. The teacher's role is to provide a stimulating environment that offers choices consistent with student interests, emphasizing freedom of choice and expression. Teachers are to reject their obvious status of authority and recognize that students have the power to choose to reject the power and authority of others. This orientation was included to make the framework conceptually complete; however, due to the highly structured settings of schools, a strictly laissez-faire approach to discipline is impossible in practice.

As with most typologies, few teachers adhere to only one orientation and typically hold beliefs from several orientations, depending on the situation, even though one perspective will tend to dominate their thinking. Johnson and colleagues (1994) found that the vast majority of the 3,400 teachers surveyed were either traditional or liberal progressive—67% of elementary teachers held liberal progressive views and 30% held traditional. Of all teachers, 3% were socially critical teachers and none were laissez-faire.

Classroom Discipline Models

Effective classroom management requires a broad repertoire of skills that teachers can derive from various theories and models. Because no single model can address all the required aspects, choosing complementary elements from a variety of approaches is necessary to provide the most comprehensive classroom program. There are four predominant theories or models that drive most of the practices used by educators: (a) behaviour modification, (b) assertive discipline, (c) logical consequences, and (d) reality/choice theory. Further, these models differ across four dimensions: (a) beliefs about the root causes of misbehaviour, (b) the required degree of intervention for misbehaviour, (c) the form that interventions should take, and (d) the degree of freedom students should have within classrooms. Before teachers design their approach to discipline, they should identify the level of freedom they feel students should have. Deciding this in advance will allow the other components of your model to facilitate rather than hinder what you want students to experience. For example, behaviour modification and assertive discipline allow students very little autonomy and are mostly dependent on teachers carefully monitoring and controlling student behaviour. On the other hand, logical consequences and reality/choice therapy are more liberal orientations that advocate for considerable freedom for students, as long as they can use it responsibly.

Behaviour Modification

As mentioned earlier, behaviour modification theory resulted largely from the work of B. F. Skinner, who formulated reinforcement strategies to be used by teachers in classrooms. Based solely on work with animals, Skinner believed that all human behaviour could be attributed to environmental stimuli because humans did not have the internal will to guide their own behaviour. Thus, for students to behave appropriately they require teachers who control the environment by reinforcing or punishing displayed behaviours.

Assumptions of Behaviour Modification

1. Human beings respond to external environmental stimuli and thus have no will. They are regulated by influences that satisfy basic needs.
2. Students require guidance from an authoritative figure to behave appropriately.
3. Students are incapable of self-regulating; they require someone to employ reinforcers appropriately.
4. Discipline problems, crime, poverty, war, and other social ills will be the result if student behaviour is not directly controlled by someone with power (Edwards, 2008).

Typical Classroom Practices

1. Reinforcement or punishment always follows behaviour.
2. Reinforcement or punishment should follow the target behaviour as soon as possible.
3. Reinforcement or punishment must fit the target behaviour and have meaning to the individual.
4. Multiple reinforcers or punishers are more effective than single reinforcers or punishers.

Forms of Reinforcers

1. Conditioned reinforcers (e.g., a smile, written comments in a journal, facial expressions)
2. Material reinforcers (e.g., a gold star on a test, stickers on student work around the room)

3. Activity reinforcers (e.g., reading with a friend, free time within the classroom)
4. Edible reinforcers (e.g., candy, gum, cookies, juice boxes)

The primary criticisms of behaviour modification are that (a) there are no guarantees that the effects will generalize across time or settings, (b) inadequately trained teachers become too controlling and merely coerce or bribe students into behaving, and (c) it is unwise to offer extrinsic rewards for tasks students will perform without rewards. Notwithstanding the above, there is much to be lost by refusing to acknowledge the benefits of extrinsic rewards (Kauffman & Landrum, 2009).

Assertive Discipline

Assertive discipline (Canter & Canter, 1976) directs teachers to control the classroom by insisting on appropriate student behaviour and rewarding it, and by responding assertively to inappropriate behaviours with consequences.

Assumptions of Assertive Discipline

1. Students are required to comply with the rules set out by the teacher.
2. Students are incapable of setting out rules and following them.
3. Punishment will result in avoidance of negative behaviours and engagement in positive behaviours.
4. Positive behaviour is encouraged by positive reinforcement.
5. Parents and administrators must be involved with the enforcement of classroom rules and follow through with them (Edwards, 2008).

Typical Classroom Practices

Teachers who use assertive discipline develop classroom rules, rewards, and consequences. Canter and Canter (1976) highlight six steps that teachers should follow when applying assertive discipline:

1. *Create positive student–teacher relationships.* Teachers are encouraged to become better acquainted with their students. They should also be clear about expected behaviours.
2. *Establish rules or expectations.* Whatever the classroom rules are, the most important rule is to follow the direction and expectations of the teacher. Students are not permitted to act outside the rules or a consequence will result.
3. *Track misbehaviour.* Misbehaviour is tracked by writing student names on the board when the student breaks the rules. This also makes the consequence clear. If the behaviour is exhibited again, the consequence gradually increases; for example, a 10-minute timeout for the first infraction and up to 30 minutes for the fourth.
4. *Use consequences to enforce limits.* Agreed upon consequences are used, such as sending the student to the office, writing a letter to the parents, giving a detention, withdrawing a privilege, and so on.
5. *Implement a system of positive consequences.* Rewards for positive behaviour over a predetermined time frame are used, such as special privileges, awards or certificates, personal attention within the classroom, material rewards, and so on.

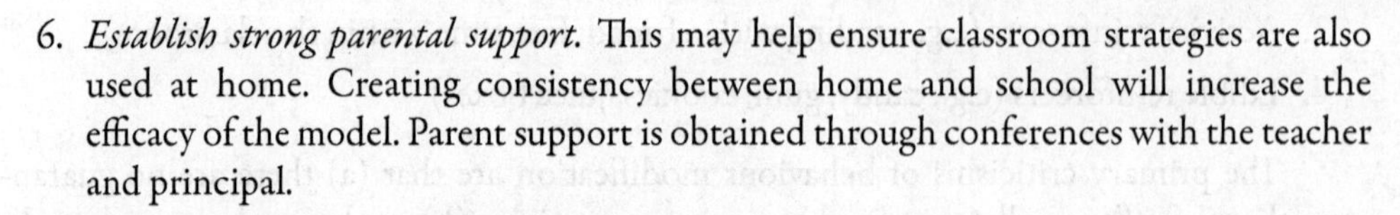

6. *Establish strong parental support.* This may help ensure classroom strategies are also used at home. Creating consistency between home and school will increase the efficacy of the model. Parent support is obtained through conferences with the teacher and principal.

Assertive discipline shares many of the same criticisms that are directed at behaviour modification. In addition, assertive discipline is criticized for being amoral and too narrowly focused on teacher-made (top-down) rules and consequences, especially when the rules and consequences fail to emphasize what it means to be morally good (Fallona & Richardson, 2006).

Logical Consequences

Logical consequences, a discipline model developed by Dreikurs (1964), is more concerned with the inner drives of students and proposes a more directive role for teachers in dealing with behaviours arising from such drives. Dreikurs felt that students are more likely to respond positively to logical consequences of a behaviour because they will not see such consequences as unfair, whereas they may argue when faced with an illogical or unrelated consequence.

Assumptions of Logical Consequences

1. Inappropriate behaviour is a product of a student's drive to gain attention, exercise power, exact revenge, or display inadequacy.
2. Inappropriate behaviours can be avoided by helping students find legitimate ways to satisfy their needs.
3. Teachers can help students learn to understand their own motives and eliminate misbehaviour by helping them explore why they behave as they do.
4. When students suffer logical consequences for their actions, they behave more appropriately.
5. When students are presented with choices among alternative behaviours, it provides them with an opportunity to be responsible and choose appropriate behaviours (Edwards, 2008).

Typical Classroom Practices

Dreikurs was the first to state that discipline is not punishment. Students should be responsible for their actions and must respect themselves and others. Students are free to choose how they behave, but teachers should ensure that each student understands the potential consequences. In order to distinguish between punishment and discipline, Dreikurs, Grundwald, and Pepper (1982) created a list of dos and don'ts, which are outlined in Table 2.1.

Reality/Choice Therapy

Reality or choice therapy was derived from Glasser's (1965) belief that schools, given their organizational structure, competitiveness, and streamlined approach to learning, frequently cause disruptive behaviours. Glasser hypothesized that if teachers created warm, supportive,

TABLE 2.1 The Dos and Don'ts of Logical Consequences

Do	Don't
• Always try first to understand the purpose of a child's misbehaviour. • Give clear-cut directions for actions expected of children. • Focus on children's present, not past, behaviour. • Build on positive aspects and avoid the negative. • Build trust between yourself and children. • Discuss children's behaviour problems only when neither you nor they are emotionally charged. • Use logical consequences instead of punishment. • Treat children with consistency. • Use the whole class to create and enforce rules. • Be kind but firm with children. • Show that you accept children, not their misbehaviour. • Make sure that students understand the limits.	• Do not be preoccupied with your own prestige and authority. • Refrain from nagging and scolding, which may reinforce misbehaving children's quest for attention. • Do not ask children to promise anything. They will use a promise to get out of an uncomfortable situation with no intention of fulfilling it. • Avoid giving rewards for good behaviour. Doing so will only condition children to expect rewards for positive behaviour. • Refrain from finding fault with children. • Do not hold your students and yourself to different standards. • Do not use threats. • Do not be vindictive.

Source: Dreikurs, Grunwald, & Pepper, 1982.

student-centred learning environments, students could examine the underlying causes of their misbehaviours with insight and guidance from teachers.

Assumptions of Reality/Choice Therapy

1. Human beings are capable of managing their own behaviour and are basically self-governing.
2. Children develop the ability to examine the consequences of their behaviour and to make value judgments about their actions.
3. Children learn to accept responsibility for their behaviour rather than making excuses when provided with the opportunity to explore motives.
4. Human behaviour consists of an effort on the part of each individual to satisfy needs for love, power, freedom, and fun.
5. Each person has a unique way of satisfying needs.
6. Children cannot be forced to change what they believe about how to best satisfy their needs (Edwards, 2008).

Typical Classroom Practices

The teacher's role in reality therapy is to help students learn to behave in ways that satisfy their needs. Teachers must help students take responsibility for their actions by acknowledging the reality of their own behaviour and changing it as necessary. Teachers can achieve this by interviewing students in environments that promote understandings of trust and respect between student and teacher. Glasser identified five functions of the interviews:

1. Help students identify their inappropriate behaviour. Do not accept excuses. Do not invite excuses by asking students why they behave as they do.
2. Have students identify various consequences if their inappropriate behaviour continues.
3. Have students make value judgments about their behaviour and its consequences.
4. Help students create plans to eliminate inappropriate behaviour.
5. Help students stick to their plans or suffer the consequences if they fail to do so.

Choice therapy requires teachers to infuse student choice-making opportunities into all instruction. Choice-making interventions provide students with a method of manipulating antecedent events to better suit their preferences, thereby increasing the reinforcing value of the task. This also enhances socioemotional development and quality of life by increasing students' sense of control and influence over their environment.

This approach has been empirically validated as an effective method of increasing academic engagement, improving task accuracy, and reducing behaviour among students with disabilities (Lane et al., 2006). The most common criticisms of both logical consequences and reality/choice therapy are that they lack firmness and direction, the models are difficult to implement, and because the models focus on the individual and not on the social–political contexts of behaviour, the processes do not prepare students for life in a hierarchical society (Johnson et al., 1994).

Teacher Behaviours That Diminish Student Behavioural Problems

It is unmistakable that teachers are the linchpins that hold all models of classroom management together. According to Goldstein and Brooks (2007), persistently disruptive and problematic student behaviours, and especially aggressive and noncompliant behaviours, are consistently diminished, if not eliminated, when teachers consciously engage in the following actions:

1. Provide positive, specific feedback to students.
2. Offer sustained feedback to students.
3. Respond supportively to students in general.
4. Respond even more supportively to low-ability students.
5. Respond supportively to students with behaviour problems.
6. Ask questions that students are able to answer correctly.
7. Present learning tasks for which students have a high probability of success.
8. Use time efficiently.
9. Intervene in misbehaviour at a low rate.
10. Maintain a low ratio of punitive to positive interventions.
11. Be punitive at a low rate.
12. Use criticism at a low rate.

13. Keep the need for disciplinary interventions low through positive classroom interventions.
14. Waste little student time on transitions.
15. Keep off-task time to a minimum. (p. 18)

Wentzel's (2006) comprehensive summary of how and why social motivation plays a vital role in classroom management asks two very important questions:

> If teachers are able to implement specific practices and conditions that result in socially competent students, what is it about these practices that motivates students to participate willingly in classroom activities and even contribute in positive ways to the overall climate of the classroom? Are there ways in which students enable each other to adapt to the demands of the classroom? (p. 635)

Wentzel's responses to these questions are strikingly similar to the descriptions Goldstein and Brooks (2007) provided about successful students. Socially and behaviourally competent students are those who have positive beliefs about themselves, have an effective repertoire of behavioural skills, can solve social interaction problems, and have positive interpersonal relationships. Social competence is fostered when all these personal abilities are exercised within the contexts and boundaries of various social environments. In turn, these experiences influence the further development and refinement of one's personal social skills and resulting behaviours. Like all other abilities such as mental competence, having a moral compass, and being physically able, social competence is a goal-directed behaviour and individuals will naturally strive to strike a balance between achieving their own goals and helping to achieve the goals of their social groups. "Social competence is achieved to the extent that students accomplish social goals that have personal as well as social value in a manner that supports continued psychological and emotional well-being" (Wentzel, 2006, p. 620).

In 1994, Rogers and Freiberg asked students "Why do you love school?" Some of the responses students who "loved" school gave are as follows:

1. They were trusted and respected—school personnel cared about them.
2. They were part of a family.
3. They felt teachers were helpers, encouraging them to succeed and listening to their opinions and ideas.
4. They had opportunities to be responsible, with freedom and choices, but not licence to do whatever they wished.

We can see, then, that the motivational influences of teachers and peers are significant when they create contexts and goals that make individual students feel like they are integral and valued parts of the process. Teachers typically promote pro-social and responsible behaviours such as being courteous and looking out for others. These explicit understandings of what is socially expected have a considerable effect on student self-regulation. Given that teachers and peers are the most influential people students encounter, it follows that their overall influence on each other increases when they agree on common behavioural goals and expectations. This influence is further increased when the collective goals and expectations are made explicit, openly and freely discussed, and mutually agreed to. This enhances all students' sense of self-determination of why it is important to behave in certain ways.

Another perspective that causes problems is a teacher's expectation that students "know" the rules. With this thinking, teachers immediately believe students are intentionally misbehaving when they act out. This is especially the case for students in Grade 3 and higher. Teachers expect that all students have somehow implicitly learned all the rules and have figured out which ones to apply in each specific instance, even though every teacher will have different expectations for good and bad behaviour. After meting out disciplinary action, teachers often ask the following question: "Why should I have to tell them what's right and what's wrong? They're old enough to know better," when in fact no student is old enough or wise enough to have it all figured out. Teachers seem to think that students "get it" by some sort of school-based osmosis, when what students really need (like a lot of adults) is to be told what the precise parameters of acceptable behaviour are. Better still, students should be asked to co-determine those parameters. All students like to achieve successes (individual or group goals) as measured by their own standards and by the positive social reactions they receive from teachers and peers. From this perspective, social competence "is achieved not just by one person's efforts but often as the result of compromise or conflict resolution among two or more individuals" (Wenzel, 2006, p. 621).

Positive Behaviour Intervention Support

applied behaviour analysis
The study of socially relevant human behaviour in naturally occurring applied settings.

Much of the theory and principles that drive what is currently practised in behaviour and classroom management have evolved from **applied behaviour analysis**, the study of socially relevant human behaviour in naturally occurring applied settings. Applied behaviour analysis was designed to allow individuals to understand, prevent, and remedy behaviour problems by using systems that are performance based, analytical, socially and contextually relevant, and which hold individuals accountable for their actions. Positive behaviour intervention support (PBIS), the most predominant theory currently used in schools, is considered an improvement on applied behaviour analysis because it relies much more on positive approaches to changing social environments, it teaches alternative positive behaviours, and it employs meaningful consequences instead of simple punishments. PBIS has at its core a high regard for student quality of life and, therefore, is composed of empirically based interventions that focus on specific behaviours and value nonaversive approaches. The three prominent characteristics of PBIS are as follows:

1. It operates from a person-centred value base and is designed and delivered specific to the needs and preferences of the individual, thus it represents socially valid goals.
2. It recognizes the individuality of each person in the delivery of services and supports and takes into consideration the need for flexibility to accommodate the individual's needs as necessary, given life demands in the delivery of behaviour supports.
3. It works toward meaningful outcomes that enhance the overall quality of life for the individual, including participation in inclusive education and community environments (Anderson & Freeman, 2000).

PBIS was first conceptualized by Sugai and colleagues (Lewis & Sugai, 1999; Sugai et al., 2000) in direct response to the US Surgeon General's call for systems of behaviour to address the contextual factors within schools that contribute to problematic behaviour. It was mandated that such systems should proactively emphasize universal, primary prevention methods while at the same time include a continuum of interventions and supports for students with chronic behavioural concerns.

Using PBIS, educators strive to understand what causes and sustains student misbehaviour rather than always/only using punishment to manage bad behaviour. Instead, students and teachers identify desirable behaviours and develop reward structures for successful actions (Scott, Gagnon, & Nelson, 2008). Based on feasibility, desirability, and effectiveness, student–teacher-mediated rewards and consequences are designed to have a direct impact on students' abilities to act properly. For example, while it is not reasonable to reward students for good behaviour by taking them to Disneyland, it is reasonable that they could negotiate some time for electronics use. PBIS also places considerable emphasis on interventions drawn from historically successful evidence-based practices and systemic, preventative school-wide approaches that enable accurate implementation and sustainability across multiple prevention levels (Sugai et al., 2000). These levels include *primary prevention* of the development and occurrence of problematic behaviours, *secondary prevention* via efficient and rapid response mechanisms, and *tertiary prevention* that reduces the intensity and complexity of escalated behaviours (Lewis et al., 2006).

The most important feature of PBIS approaches and that which separates them from others is its instructional and educational features, whereby behavioural expectations are clearly defined and taught to all students. Students' explicit understandings about behaviour requirements have been shown to virtually eliminate the interpretations students use to deny or abdicate their behavioural responsibilities. The goals of PBIS are to promote supportive environments that emphasize classrooms designed for student success, to teach positive replacement behaviours that enhance learning and security, and to use interventions that try to address the overall quality of life for each student.

The school-wide use of PBIS systems has broadened our appreciation for addressing problematic behaviours before they have a chance to develop. This has meant an emphasis on activities that promote the awareness of good behaviours and the prevention of poor behaviours. Sugai et al. (2000) provided a comprehensive delineation of the different levels of behaviour supports and interventions:

1. *Level 1: Primary Preventions:* These are designed for the 80–90% of students who do not experience serious problem behaviours. These approaches target all students and emphasize the prevention of misbehaviours by teaching and making expectations clear, including students in decision making and ownership of the rules, and providing feedback about positive behaviours.
2. *Level 2: Secondary Preventions:* These are directed toward the 5–15% of students who are at risk for engaging in problematic behaviours. These supports are individualized to meet the needs of students who require more intense interventions. The primary distinction between levels 1 and 2 is that Level 1 focuses on group interventions whereas Level 2 focuses on individualized approaches. Level 2 interventions are likely to be part of a student's IEP.
3. *Level 3: Tertiary Preventions:* These are targeted at the 1–7% of students who have chronic and intense behaviours. These supports are intended for students with the most problematic, persistent, and challenging behaviours whose needs cannot be met by Level 1 or Level 2. These students have impeding behaviours that negatively affect

their quality of life across multiple settings (Sugai et al., 2000). In this way, PBIS has relevance for all students across all educational environments.

What is clear from the work of Sugai and colleagues (2000) is that schools that fail to design and implement effective Level 1 school-wide approaches will increase the number of students who will need Level 2 and Level 3 intensive supports.

The National Center on Education, Disability and Juvenile Justice furthered this line of thinking by outlining three different levels of behaviour prevention that are directly related to the three levels of supports advocated by PBIS. *Primary prevention* focuses on avoiding the initial occurrence of problems using a school-wide plan to help all students meet behavioural expectations. *Secondary prevention* provides additional support with a focus on preventing repeated problem behaviours through more targeted interventions. For example, students with more than one disciplinary referral for fighting would be provided with instruction in conflict resolution or social skills. *Tertiary prevention*, the most intensive level of support, attempts to reduce the impact of a problem on the student's ability to function in the least restrictive setting. For example, the needs of students identified as having an emotional/behavioural disability can be addressed through special education services and behaviour intervention plans. (More information about behaviour intervention plans can be obtained from www.edjj.org/prevention/LevelsPrevention.html.)

Successful, school-wide, positive behavioural support approaches usually define a carefully selected but limited number of expectations. This prevents overwhelming students with too many details and gives them the opportunity to exercise self-control, learn how to improve their social skills, and engage in desirable behaviours more often. These approaches also allow for creative methods of rewarding good behaviours. While good behaviour is always the main focus, there are also clear consequences for undesirable behaviours. All preferred and undesirable behaviours and their commensurate rewards or consequences are jointly and mutually decided upon by students and teachers. As you will see later in this chapter, school-wide PBIS approaches include evaluations by students, teachers, and administrators.

The Effectiveness of PBIS

Within the last 15 years, the use of PBIS across a variety of school settings has resulted in several positive and reliable findings. The consistent features of schools that use PBIS principles include the following:

1. The use of school-wide teams in design and delivery
2. Administrative buy-in and support for school-wide behaviour interventions
3. A school culture that is defined by a limited number of behavioural expectations
4. Behaviour expectations are taught to all students
5. Students are given recognition by a system designed to acknowledge performance
6. Students who engage in disruptive/dangerous behaviours are corrected, not ignored or rewarded
7. Student performance is evaluated in an ongoing manner and is used for decision making. (Horner & Sugai, 2000)

Luiselli, Putnam, and Sunderland's (2002) four-year study of a school-wide PBIS approach found that detentions for disruptive antisocial behaviours, vandalism, and substance abuse decreased while student attendance increased for the same period. Similarly, Scott (2001) found that disciplinary referrals and suspensions were significantly reduced after one year of a Level 1 PBIS school-wide intervention. Lewis and colleagues' (2006) comprehensive review of empirically validated research to date on the efficacy of school-wide PBIS approaches concluded that there was overwhelming evidence that when empirically based preventative measures are integrated into school systems, schools reported "reductions of 40% to 60% in discipline referrals . . . continue[d] declines in behavioral problems . . . drops in daily office referrals, [and] 65% to 75% reductions in out-of-school suspensions and in-school detentions" (p. 845).

In the United States, the importance of PBIS extends beyond ensuring the security and peace of classrooms. The 2004 Reauthorization of IDEA (the Individuals with Disabilities Education Act) mandated legislation that *requires* educators to use positive behavioural support interventions to address challenging behaviours that are impeding student learning or the learning of other students. This process *requires* the use of functional behavioural assessments to deduce the problematic areas accompanied by a behaviour intervention plan specifically designed to implement the changes. All of the above form an integral part of a child's individualized educational program (IEP).

Similarly, but without the legal obligations of the US law, the Ontario Ministry of Education Safe Schools Act (2002) outlines the suspension and expulsion guidelines to be considered when educators are contemplating disciplinary action. The act also requires that teachers and administrators consider mitigating factors when deciding whether a student should be suspended or expelled. This includes whether the student has the ability to control his or her behaviour, can understand the consequences of his or her behaviour, and whether the student's continued presence creates an unacceptable risk to others.

Dynamic Classroom Management: The Application of Positive Behavioural Support Theory

Analytic behavioural application was exemplarily described by Baer, Wolf, and Risely (1968) as the process of applying the sometimes tentative principles of behaviour to the improvement of specific behaviours, and to simultaneously evaluating whether any changes occur. One of the most important understandings to emerge from research on PBIS in recent years is the principle of antecedent management. This means paying strict attention to the environmental conditions and behaviours of others in students' lives that appear to trigger problem behaviours in them. We consider antecedent management as a good first step because it calls attention to what may be causing the behaviour rather than emphasizing after-the-fact consequences. The primary intent here is to try to prevent problem behaviours rather than reactively repair the damage. The main tenets of effective antecedent management, therefore, are teachers' advance instructional cues to inform students about preferred behaviours, the provision of behavioural choice-making opportunities for students, and the positive supports provided to individual students in executing choices and in self-evaluating outcomes.

However, we do not feel this systematic approach goes far enough. The problem remains that antecedent management (like punishment) still relies too heavily on implicit messages and the authority of the teacher to "manage" student behaviours. The underlying, old-school, behavioural thinking here is that if teachers change or manipulate the antecedents, unbeknownst to students, teachers will prevent problematic student behaviours. While antecedent management provides educators with some insights into how to potentially correct some behaviours, it is still primarily an inferential approach that, by design, completely absolves students from being responsible. Nowhere does antecedent management take advantage of students' abilities to think for themselves and to make conscious and deliberate behavioural choices. If students do not have to be responsible, they do not have to think about how they are supposed to interact with their environment—they simply do whatever they want and then rely on someone else to do all the thinking. Not only are students given permission to abdicate responsibility for their actions, they can also expect someone else to do all the hard work of thinking about, choosing, monitoring, and evaluating their behaviours. In this regard, the only person who is fully responsible for all student behaviour is the teacher. We strongly contend that it would be much better to "educate" students about school- and teacher-preferred behaviours, to offer students a reasonable set of behavioural choices, and to make it worth their while to choose appropriate behaviours and evaluate those choices. These expectations should be accompanied by complete descriptions of rewards for good behaviour and consequences for bad behaviours. It makes sense, therefore, that students would be intimately involved in establishing all target behaviours (both good and bad), all rewards, and all consequences. The main idea we want to convey to you is that students are more likely to rise to the level of expectation agreed upon as a group and to be responsible for their actions.

Consistent with the above, an emerging line of research is demonstrating that well-behaved students are not behaving themselves because of the classroom management skills of the teacher; they're behaving themselves because they have the thinking skills to handle challenges in an adaptive fashion (Greene, 2008). Schalock (2000) has reported several times that quality-of-life factors are crucial features of behavioural interventions. *Quality of life* is the degree to which an individual enjoys the important possibilities of his or her life. This concept is consistent with current transitions in educational psychology toward more positive attributes and supports with less emphasis on human deficiencies. Schalock's eight quality-of-life indicators are (a) emotional well-being (having good self-control), (b) interpersonal relations (being connected to others), (c) material well-being (not being destitute), (d) personal development (realizing your own strengths and needs), (e) physical well-being (good health), (f) self-determination (having a modicum of control over your life and its direction), (g) social inclusion (being part of a group or groups), and (h) rights (having rights and freedoms). It stands to reason, then, that schools that use these indicators to promote a goodness of fit between students and their environments will enhance student quality of life. In other words, the more schools advocate for and support the quality-of-life indicators found throughout society, the more likely students will feel like they fit into school, rather than feeling ostracized. The outcomes that can result from such approaches will be students who are happier in school, who have enhanced self-determination, higher degrees of satisfaction with school, greater feelings of safety, and better overall well-being. It is their sense of belonging that will cause them to consider their actions and behaviours. This preventative aspect of schooling cannot be something that is told to students—they have to feel it.

Features of Good Classroom Management Plans

It is well documented that schools with effective behavioural interventions have cultures and climates that explicitly demonstrate that they have the best interests of all students at heart. These schools put the prevention of misbehaviour at the forefront of their approach and intentionally design policies to promote positive and proactive interventions. These effective learning environments have the following common qualities:

1. Behaviour expectations are defined and shared amongst administrators, teachers, students, and families.
2. Expectations are published and visually apparent within all areas of the school.
3. Students are taught all behavioural expectations so they become explicitly aware of and informed about each of them. These skills are modelled by school personnel and are reinforced throughout the school.
4. Appropriate behaviours exhibited by students are frequently acknowledged and celebrated within the school by teachers and administrators (Sugai et al., 2000).

These schools also tend to have far more interactions between adults and students and they tend to use much more positive feedback for both behaviour and achievement than negative comments. Based on our research and the evidence in the literature, there appear to be six prerequisites for building a plan that will provide an effective school-wide approach to discipline:

1. A school-wide needs assessment to determine the focus of the intervention and to act as baseline criteria for the evaluation of change.
2. The establishment of a school-wide behaviour support team led by administrators.
3. Clear evidence of administrator support for all teacher interventions.
4. The commitment and participation of all teachers and administrators in an intervention that has a consistent overall theme but is still adaptable to suit individual classroom or teacher requirements.
5. A system of implementation that is based on proven research and is designed to address the elements brought to light by the needs assessment.
6. A data tracking system that requires regular and timely evaluations of changes in student behaviours and the effectiveness of the intervention.

A school's assessment of its behavioural needs has to be integrated into its overall mission, goals, and objectives. In these instances, all stakeholders have to come together to discuss what the problem is or what it looks like and what they want to do about it. This collaborative process will bring out into the open the beliefs, values, and experiences of all school personnel related to student misbehaviour and the conditions that cause teachers and administrators to be on "different pages" regarding discipline. This results in a shared intention for the chosen intervention, why and how the intervention will be implemented, and what potential short- and long-term goals can be achieved. A written plan for the implementation of the intervention should be constructed and should be periodically reviewed, discussed, and modified as needed, otherwise it will become a perfunctory document instead of a useful one. Included in this process must be a plan to obtain feedback from all educators and students about whether the intervention is working. Without feedback from all stakeholders, the process will not hold up under any type of scrutiny that attempts to hold the process accountable.

A Model for Classroom Management

While many models of classroom management exist, teachers still have the onerous task of interpreting the varied and multifaceted components of different models and incorporating these into a usable plan based on their personal predilections or the characteristics of their classroom or school. Dynamic classroom management (DCM) (Edmunds & Edmunds, 2008, 2010; Johnson & Edmunds, 2006) was one of the first approaches to transform a multitude of research findings into a comprehensive and systematic plan for teachers. It brings together many of the effective components found across several different models and it applies them in a format that is easily adapted by all educators.

DCM was developed in response to Lewis and colleagues' (2006) and Brophy's (2006a) calls for studies to design and validate classroom management interventions within a school-wide process so that broader systemic applications across multiple schools could be entertained. DCM adheres to the tenets of PBIS (Scott, Gagnon, & Nelson, 2008) and was designed to address the obstacles to effective classroom interventions documented above (Edmunds & Edmunds, 2010). DCM was developed using well-known research-based behavioural principles combined with evidence from classroom-based testing. It is consistent with PBIS theory in that it emphasizes communication, social skills, and self-management. Approaches that have used PBIS concepts have proven successful because it is primarily a teaching method (Scott et al., 2008).

Complementing the PBIS structures mentioned above, DCM also adheres to the principles of **process–outcome research**, which states that students learn better and more efficiently in environments that are orderly and psychologically secure. A psychologically secure classroom is one in which students feel comfortable and safe and at ease in their surroundings. This does not mean these classrooms are always devoid of minor/distracting behaviour problems, but it does mean that at no time should they feel out of control or chaotic or be home to recurring and persistent problematic behaviours. In addition, in its implementation phase, DCM uses the principles of **classroom discourse research** (Morine-Dershimer, 2006), which advocates for explanatory and collaborative teacher–student discourses to explicitly establish rules and classroom routines, a process that has proven more effective than implicit rules and punishment-based approaches.

process–outcome research
Research that focuses on creating learning environments that are orderly and psychologically secure so that students can learn better and more efficiently.

classroom discourse research
Research that advocates for explanatory and collaborative teacher–student discourses to explicitly establish rules and classroom routines.

The most important management principle guiding DCM is that it emphasizes clarifying what students are expected to do and helping them learn to do it rather than focusing on misbehaviour and after-the-fact discipline. Moreover, psychologically secure classrooms established via student–teacher discourse demonstrate clear evidence of reduced misbehaviours (Brophy, 2006a), which is particularly so when evidence-based school-wide interventions include the explicit teaching of student behavioural expectations (Sugai et al., 2000). A student's sense of belonging and security positively support all aspects of motivation, learning, and the self-discipline inherent in the good behaviours that schools expect and appreciate (Lewis et al., 2006).

DCM is a new, first-wave PBIS approach to classroom management that incorporates the five global principles of classroom management found in the gold standard text on the subject, *Handbook of Classroom Management: Research, Practice, and Contemporary Issues* (Evertson & Weinstein, 2006a):

1. Develop caring, supportive relationships with and among students.
2. Organize and implement instruction in ways that optimize students' access to learning.
3. Use group management methods that encourage students' engagement in academic tasks.
4. Promote the development of students' social skills and self-regulation.
5. Use appropriate interventions to assist students with behaviour problems. (p. 5)

It is noteworthy that Evertson and Weinstein stated that the impetus for their handbook came from observations consistently reported by numerous researchers and educators:

> Classroom management is a topic of enduring concern for teachers, administrators, and the public. Beginning teachers consistently perceive discipline as their most serious challenge; management problems continue to be a major cause of teacher burn out and job dissatisfaction; and the public repeatedly ranks discipline as the first or second most serious problem facing the schools. (Evertson & Weinstein, 2006b, p. 3)

Along the same lines, Charles (2002) made a very bold but accurate statement when alluding to the most serious educational problem facing teachers:

> That problem is student misbehaviour. If you are now teaching, you have had ample experience with it. If you are preparing to teach, be forewarned: It is the major obstacle to your success and has the potential to destroy your career. (p. 1)

To address all these issues DCM (a) translates the theoretical principles of behaviour and classroom management into a pragmatic and systematic approach, (b) is directed toward and is based upon observations of teacher and student interactions within classrooms, (c) is evaluated based on pre- and post-assessments of school- and classroom-specific problem behaviours, (d) maintains program fidelity via researcher-directed training and participant monitoring, and (e) is implemented at the beginning of the school year (or at the start of a school semester in the case of secondary school).

What makes DCM different from all other interventions is that instead of trying to inferentially change student behaviours (as intended by the stimulus–response mechanism of punishment), DCM focuses on changing how students think about their actions. Within punishment systems, behaviours will recur as soon as the punishment or the threat of punishment is removed. For example, students who frequently misbehave when they have a substitute teacher do so because they do not anticipate that the substitute teacher will enforce the rules as ardently as their actual teacher. This sends a clear message to students that their "problem" is more about getting caught, not that their behaviour is unacceptable. However, when students are explicitly taught about and rewarded for desired behaviours, they change their thinking about which actions they want to engage in and for what reasons (rewards), thereby willingly changing their own behaviours.

DCM is not a "canned program" or a one-size-fits-all approach. As you will see in the next sections, once the principles of DCM are understood, it can be customized by elementary and secondary school educators to suit any school or classroom. Using DCM, teachers provide structures that model, encourage, and support desired behaviours based on PBIS (Lewis & Sugai, 1999; Sugai et al., 2000). To adhere to this principle, DCM applies the two primary instructional tenets of classroom discourse research:

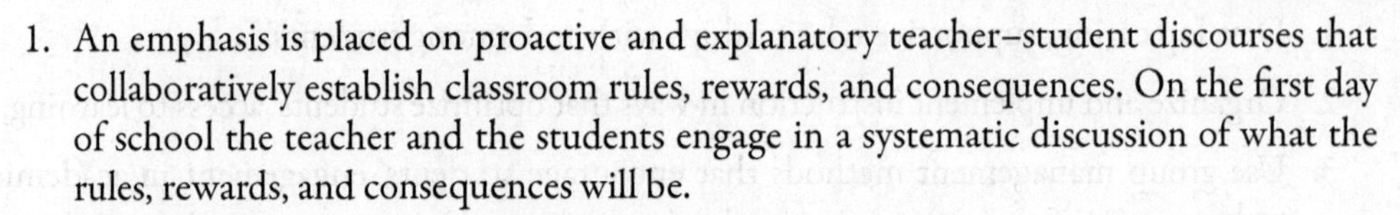

1. An emphasis is placed on proactive and explanatory teacher–student discourses that collaboratively establish classroom rules, rewards, and consequences. On the first day of school the teacher and the students engage in a systematic discussion of what the rules, rewards, and consequences will be.
2. DCM includes overtly explicit rules, rewards, and consequences as well as the development and use of reminder mechanisms so that explicit rules and routines do not fade or become invisible after extended or regular use (Morine-Dershimer, 2006).

Practical Applications

Consider classrooms that you have visited or been assigned to for practicum. What rules did the students have to follow? Were these rules made explicit in any way (e.g., posted on a classroom wall)? How well were these rules understood by students? How could you tell? Were there rewards for good behaviour and consequences for bad behaviour? How consistently were rewards and consequences applied?

In DCM, all rules, rewards, and consequences are clearly spelled out, discussed, and voted on. This is done to eliminate the inference that "this has already been covered by other teachers." This process automatically makes use of the motivational dynamics of self-regulated behaviour: (a) making choices, (b) considering the meaningfulness of choices, (c) executing choices, and (d) reflecting on action outcomes (McCaslin et al., 2006). By proactively engaging students in the design of explicit rules, rewards, and consequences, teachers promote student self-control and investment in how their classroom will operate. This mechanism impedes impulsivity and the potential for students to wilfully abdicate their behavioural responsibilities.

While it is well known that orderly school environments promote student learning and enhance student social growth, current research now emphasizes that how a teacher constructs and maintains order in the classroom is more important than whether or not order is achieved (Nucci, 2006; Fallona & Richardson, 2006). The modern classroom contains far too many interactions and complexities of human behaviour for the teacher to be the lone manager; students of all ages have the capacity and ability to regulate their own behaviour within it, thereby helping the teacher better manage the classroom. The research on creating student self-regulated behaviour has moved beyond simply providing students with choices that transfer behaviour "control" from the teacher to the student. Contemporary conceptions advocate strongly for teachers to go further by providing students with and engaging students in explicit cognitive strategies for (a) making choices, (b) reflecting on the personal meaningfulness of these choices, (c) seeing their choices through to completion, and (d) reflecting on the outcomes of their actions. To maximally enhance the overall behavioural tone of a classroom or school, DCM uses these cognitive strategies collectively. The student discourses that take place while working through all the rules, rewards, and consequences will draw disparate behavioural perceptions and attitudes into the conversation. Through discussion and compromise, DCM promotes more universally accepted student responsibilities for behaviour. In this light, classrooms are best conceived of as co-regulated environments. By proactively engaging all students in the design of explicit rules, rewards, and consequences, teachers promote classroom-wide student self-control. This enables students to award (or suffer) self-determined consequences for behaviours that they have a vested interest in promoting (or diminishing). If teachers make their behavioural expectations clear to students and allow them to match their personal and collective goals to these expectations, this motivates each student to "buy into" the process. And, because each student will want to protect his or her own vested interests (rewards) and maintain his or her own psychological well-being, they will readily, and with just cause, exert positive pressure on students who misbehave. In this regard, DCM is direct and prescriptive about the types of discourses teachers must use to convey their intentions for how exemplary management processes can regulate student behaviour. These include

- An emphasis on explicitly clarifying what students are expected to do; this diminishes student passivity or compliance-only attitudes.
- A collaborative and collective emphasis by teachers and students on before-the-fact problem prevention while only using after-the-fact disciplinary measures as needed; this diminishes punishment-based management and the perception that the only owner and enforcer of the rules is the teacher.
- An emphasis on classroom management as an integral part of instruction rather than as a separate and disconnected part of teacher practice; this increases the coherence and continuity of all that takes place in the classroom.

A comprehensive example of a teacher implementing the entire DCM procedure is found in the Appendix to this text. We suggest that as you read Annette's story you place yourself in her shoes and envision yourself having the same conversation with your students. Draw on your past experiences for rules, rewards, and consequences that will suit your teaching style and will appeal to students. Also, keep in mind that while DCM is designed as a school-wide intervention, there is no reason why you cannot implement it in your own classroom. A brief description of the DCM procedure is provided below to get you thinking.

Implementing DCM

Edmunds and Edmunds (2008) described the key features of DCM that you need to focus on to make your implementation of DCM effective. Before school starts, decide on the non-negotiable rules that you will put in place for the year (you can collaborate with colleagues or the principal on these, but your students will have no input into these rules). Next, discuss your classroom management plan with the principal and other school personnel (e.g., colleagues, educational assistants, resource room teachers) and decide how these individuals can support your approach. Once you have that in place, think about how you will go about setting a positive, engaging, and determined tone on the first day of school. When your students finally show up, welcome them and let them know that your goal is for everyone to have a successful school year, both academically and behaviourally. We urge you to be explicit about how the class will be managed and let them know your goal is to be fair and firm. At this point, you should introduce the non-negotiable rules and by following the DCM model allow your students to develop additional classroom rules that are specific to your and their wishes.

After the rules are established, encourage your students to participate in the design of meaningful rewards for adhering to the rules and meaningful consequences for breaking the rules. This will give them ownership and responsibility. Once this process is completed, post the complete list of rules, rewards, and consequences on the classroom wall and set a time frame for a review of all rules, rewards, and consequences. The message you want to convey is that the rules, rewards, and consequences are not set in stone and that reviewing them from time to time is beneficial. At a minimum, a full review should be conducted every four to five weeks, even if that only means having a brief discussion to make sure everything is working as it should.

The process to design rules, rewards, and consequences is not difficult. One of the authors of this text has experienced that hundreds of students in many classrooms have proven more than reasonable in what they want as rewards and what they think are fair consequences. Once all the rules, rewards, and consequences have been determined, use the following processes to maintain your positive classroom environment:

- Immediately and consistently enforce the rules (while consequence enforcement is the teacher's responsibility, students can call attention to justified rewards).
- Ensure that all stated rewards and consequences are implemented.
- Plan how you will deal with a student who is displaying problematic behaviour. (Suggested dialogue: What is the problem we are having? Which of our rules is being broken? What did we agree the consequence would be if this rule was broken? Let's do what we decided upon. Let's check in later and see how we are doing.)
- Plan how you will deal with a student who is returning to class after being sent to see the principal. (Suggested dialogue: Welcome the student back to the class. Have a private conversation with the student about what has transpired, emphasizing his or her behaviour, not the punishment. Indicate to the student that you have confidence in his or her ability to be better behaved from now on. Tell the student you will be monitoring his or her behaviour, and in one to two days you will review with him or her how things are going.)
- Review the rules with the class periodically and make adjustments where necessary.

As we hope it has become clear, the key to effective classroom management is for you to design and implement a management system that always requires your students to think about how they will behave, rather than simply reacting without thinking. The more invested students are in helping design your management system, the more they will think about their behaviours within it, especially if they anticipate being rewarded for good behaviour.

Principles of Evaluation

To properly evaluate outcomes, teachers and students need to make defined and deliberate judgments about predetermined and targeted objectives at the end of a specified period—it is necessary to evaluate whether the intervention had an immediate effect to determine its credibility and whether it had a long-term effect to determine its sustainability. While an immediate effect is desirable, a sustainable effect is a better indicator because it shows that real changes were maintained over time. To evaluate outcomes such as quality of life, school climate, effects on families, and social relevance, educators and researchers typically use qualitative data-gathering methods such as interviews, questionnaires, rating scales, and document analysis in conjunction with quantitative measures such as frequency charts and behaviour log books. Regardless of the methods chosen, the process should be conducted in a logical, clear, and straightforward fashion that is transparent to all concerned. While school climate is an abstract concept that may seem difficult to measure, it is imperative that educators be given an opportunity to comment on whether it has changed. If educators state that they feel the climate is better than before, this is likely true, since they have no reason to provide a socially desirable answer. It is highly unlikely that educators would not want to acknowledge when an intervention is not working because this would inhibit improvements and render what they are doing a waste of time and energy.

To evaluate something is to determine its value or significance. This is sometimes a judgment that cannot be expressed in numerical terms or by statistical tests of significance. For example, the fact that a lonely and troubled student makes a new and real friend at school is quite significant despite the fact that he still gets sent to the office several times a week. The same can be said for a teacher who says her classroom has a "better climate" because of small changes in student behaviours that are not apparent on a checklist. Formal evaluation needs to be structured, systematic, thorough, and based on explicit behavioural criteria. Relative to classroom behaviour, it is important to make a direct connection between evaluation and what is commonly referred to as **ecological validity**: an explicit judgment of the meaningfulness and usefulness of a behavioural intervention in the context of the routines, experiences, and performance of a classroom or school. For example, it would not be ecologically valid to design an intervention to stop students from throwing things if throwing things is not a prevalent problem. For these reasons and other similar intangibles, DCM evaluations focus on whether teachers and administrators perceive that things are better or worse in terms of specific behaviour problems evidenced in their particular school.

ecological validity
An explicit judgment of the meaningfulness and usefulness of a behavioural intervention in the context of the routines, experiences, and performance of a classroom or school

DCM Program Fidelity

As described previously, numerous behavioural interventions have been compromised by program fidelity problems. The foremost issue in the design of DCM implementations was to develop key functional procedures to eliminate known barriers to program fidelity. What follows is a description of DCM's key procedures, the program fidelity elements required, and the rationale behind both.

The main objective of DCM is for the whole school to function around mutually agreed upon guidelines regarding student behaviour and to fully understand all the procedures involved. While this includes consequences for particularly egregious offences, the primary focus of DCM is to encourage students to choose agreed upon preferred behaviours and to be rewarded for their actions. To this end, one of the program fidelity requirements of DCM is that every student will actively participate in democratically establishing the rules, rewards, and consequences for their classrooms. Under this premise, all student- and teacher-mediated rules, rewards, and consequences are allowable as long as they do not contravene DCM's five non-negotiable rules of the school's code of conduct. While this may initially sound undemocratic, each of these five rules has stood the test of time in many schools, and students, teachers, administrators, or parents have never judged any to be unsuitable or unreasonable. More importantly, the **Big Five**, as they are commonly called, have been consistently been shown to support and complement all school and school board codes of conduct:

Big Five
Five non-negotiable school-wide rules that underlie all classroom-specific rules, rewards, and consequences developed by teachers and students under dynamic classroom management.

1. All our rules will be fair and reasonable and will be democratically decided upon. The rules will be posted on the wall for everyone to see and they will be enforced.
2. No disrespectful behaviour.
3. No touching others and no touching their stuff.

4. Other than when the teacher is teaching, speaking to someone, or giving directions, or when we are writing a test, we are allowed to talk. We understand that this is an earned right and that with it comes responsibility.
5. The principal will be aware of all class rules. He or she will support us for our good behaviour and will deal with our bad behaviour according to the rules of the classroom/school.

Practical Applications

If you were implementing DCM in your classroom, what mandatory rules would you require your students to follow? In other words, what rules do you consider so important that they are not up for discussion in terms of their inclusion on the list of classroom rules?

Another of the program fidelity requirements for DCM is that its implementation takes place at the beginning of the school year or the beginning of the second term in secondary schools. The objective here is to get everyone started on the right foot and not have to suddenly change gears as would be required if the program started after the year had begun. Thus, before the school year starts, all educators and adults must participate in the professional development training provided about DCM. This includes all secretaries, custodians, educational assistants, itinerant professionals and, where possible, all frequently used substitute teachers. In some instances, teacher-candidates who were to do their practica in a school have participated. The rationale here is that everyone needs to be on the same page; teachers need to feel confident that administrators will follow up on students sent to the office, all nonteachers must be given the authority to report student misbehaviour, and most importantly all students must be aware that all adults in the building know the parameters for behaviour and will report it. Next, everyone who plays a significant role in the school must attend a mandatory school-wide assembly on the first day of school. The principal outlines the basic premises for DCM and its implementation. This is the school's first chance to share the Big Five, discuss their relevance and importance, and convey to students that every adult in the school is aware of these behavioural parameters and each has been given the authority to report both good and problematic behaviours.

Immediately after the assembly, all teachers and students, in their respective classes, engage in a collaborative and democratic process to determine the rules, rewards, and consequences of their classroom. This is accomplished by students working in groups of four to come up with one or two rules and the rewards and consequences that apply to each rule. One by one, each of the groups is asked to share one of their rules and its respective reward and consequence. The teacher asks for class discussion and comments about the rule, and the rule is voted on. Once a rule is agreed to, the same democratic process is followed for its reward and consequence. This type of student-to-student and student-to-teacher discourse typically results in minor refinements to all three parts. While the end product of the process is rules, rewards, and consequences, it is the explicit explanations—the thinking and reasoning behind the rules—that will have the most impact. The research on classroom discourse is quite clear—it is the conversation that is key!

At this point, another of DCM's program fidelity requirements kicks in. Once all the rules, rewards, and consequences have been decided, all the administrators of the school (yes, *all* of them) are required to visit the classroom where two students will tell the administrators how and why they chose their rules, rewards, and consequences. The administrators are encouraged to ask the students for explicit details about the process and their resulting rules, rewards, and consequences to draw out the important underlying principles at play. It is also required that when the administrators leave the classroom they take with them an exact copy of all the rules, rewards, and consequences. This happens for all classes.

Now two more DCM program fidelity requirements come into play. First, the administrators are required to keep their copy of each classroom's rules, rewards, and consequences in a special binder in their office, and second, the students (possibly with help from their teacher) are required to create a Wall of Rules. This typically involves having the students create a poster (or something like it) containing all the rules, rewards, and consequences and pinning the poster on the wall in a highly visible place. The Wall of Rules acts as a deterrent and a handy reference when students seem to "forget" what the rules, rewards, and consequences are. It also serves as a public reminder that students can choose their actions and behaviours as long as they operate within the guidelines of the classroom. The administrator's copy (all administrators must have a copy) provides a much-needed consistency of interpretation when students are sent to the office for breaching the rules. This eliminates students' tendency to not always reveal what they actually did, to play the teacher off against the principal, or to complain that they are being unfairly treated. The administrators are also required to keep a behavioural log to document all student referrals to the office and the disciplinary actions taken (the log book is often a requirement by school boards). It is from this data that accurate judgments can be made about whether the DCM program is reducing office referrals.

Another way that DCM program fidelity is maintained is through the requirement that the principal has all teachers' permission to enter any classroom at any time while the democratic rule, reward, and consequence decision-making process is underway. Experiences across several DCM implementations in a variety of schools have revealed that this requirement assures the administrators that all teachers and students in all classrooms are actively participating and benefiting from the process. What has emerged from these experiences is a recognition that student-to-student and student-to-teacher discourses have demonstrable effects in terms of raising student awareness about appropriate conduct and the resulting Wall of Rules.

As part of the DCM procedures, the entire teaching staff is also required to engage in a democratic process to determine the rules, rewards, and consequences for all nonteaching spaces such as the cafeteria, the gym, hallways, the schoolyard, field trips, and during bus duty. Obviously, the school-wide behavioural parameters will apply in all cases, but specific alternatives may have to be designed to properly handle certain behaviours in particular contexts. Another requirement is that DCM has to be a main item on the agenda of every staff meeting. Experience has shown that this ever-greening process keeps the issue fresh and in the forefront of all educators' thinking. It also serves as an opportunity to share ideas and to collectively problem solve to deal with particular issues or to make changes.

Evaluation of DCM

The focus of DCM is to change student behaviour and to create psychologically secure learning environments that benefit both teachers and students. A key feature of DCM that separates it from nearly all other available interventions is that it requires systematic evaluation.

The evaluation of DCM is designed to determine whether changes in the frequency of student behaviours occur and whether, as a result, the overall social atmosphere of the school improves. This means that the educators who use it evaluate its effectiveness (i.e., Was there a decrease in problematic behaviours?) and separately evaluate its utility (i.e., Did the educators find DCM easy to use and useful?). To garner an accurate reflection of whether changes have occurred, the evaluation must focus on overall school and classroom changes, not on individual students. For example, keeping records of classroom discipline incidents and office referrals is more informative than charting the performance of a particular student. The best sources of information about schools undergoing this transformation process are all educators, students, and other individuals who play a role in the school, including custodians, secretaries, parents, or itinerant professionals. Therefore, all these key players need to be involved in any evaluation of behavioural change.

Another important factor of DCM is the degree that all educators clearly understand its philosophy and methodology. The evaluation of potential change and improvement is imperative, so for a school-wide intervention, the process of evaluation must be built in from the start. The objective here is to predetermine the desired changes rather than globally determine whether change has occurred. Behavioural evaluation is not a difficult task if it is intentionally kept simple. Thus, the four basic elements evaluated by DCM are (a) changes in student behaviours, (b) changes in the number of behavioural referrals and disciplinary actions, (c) changes in the overall school climate, and (d) satisfaction with the plan and its implementation. These criteria match the common objectives stated by many schools seeking to improve their behavioural climates; namely, to reduce disciplinary actions and referrals, to reduce in-school suspensions and expulsions, and to increase student, teacher, and administrator satisfaction with the school's climate relative to behaviour (Brophy, 2006a).

Immediately before the professional development training for DCM starts, all educators and attending adults complete a short-response survey. This preintervention baseline data documents (a) all prevalent and persistent problematic student behaviours, (b) the incidence of disciplinary actions, and (c) the predominant behavioural atmosphere of the entire school and each classroom. After five weeks and then five months of nonmonitored implementation, data are gathered comparing changes in students' problematic behaviours, classroom and school atmospheres, required administrative disciplinary actions, and overall intervention effectiveness.

Results

The predominant data-gathering methods of DCM involve the use of various instruments that ask educators to evaluate how things are at a precise moment in time (e.g., five weeks and then five months postintervention) compared to how things were before the intervention started. Therefore, it is possible that this subjective comparison allows for social desirability bias. **Social desirability bias** is a research term used to denote the tendency of respondents to reply in a manner that will be viewed favourably by others, usually by overreporting good behaviours or underreporting bad behaviours (Crowne & Marlowe, 1960). Nonetheless, we feel confident that educators can rely on any evaluative data gathered about the effects of DCM for a variety of reasons. First, persistent problematic student behaviour typically interferes so much with an educator's professional life that it invokes a visceral and often deflating reaction. Thus, educators have no reason to lie about their perceptions of their working environment. In many schools, student misbehaviour causes very real problems for all educators, and it often takes a lot of courage and determination for a school to

social desirability bias
A research term used to denote the tendency of respondents to reply in a manner that will be viewed favourably by others, usually by overreporting good behaviours or underreporting bad behaviour.

admit they need help with these problems. Given these circumstances, we are confident that educators will immediately inform the evaluators if DCM did not work. They collectively have no reason to say that DCM worked when it was not effective. Therefore, there is no risk that any evaluative data would reflect educator social desirability bias.

The processes and procedures of DCM have been implemented in both elementary and secondary schools over several years. This has provided data collected under real-world educational conditions. Collectively, all DCM teacher, administrator, and student data have consistently revealed the following:

1. Demonstrable improvements in student behaviours as measured by teacher ratings of existing baseline (preintervention) behaviours.
2. Demonstrable reductions in referrals to the principal's office as measured by administrator ratings and comparisons with previous years' log book data.
3. Heightened student awareness of the negative impacts of problematic behaviour.
4. Overall enhancements of the tone of classrooms and schools as measured by administrator ratings. (Edmunds, 2010a, 2010b, 2011a)

Tables 2.2 and 2.3 outline teacher perspectives of changes in student behaviour after implementing DCM. Table 2.2 contains data from one elementary school after five weeks and then five months of implementation, and Table 2.3 contains data from one high school at the same time intervals. There are a few things you should note as you interpret this data: First, the evaluation criteria are different for each school. This is because, according to the DCM process, each school individually outlines its primary behavioural areas of concern and seeks to remedy them via its own specific rules. This customizes DCM for each school. Second, not all criteria are reported in both five-week and five-month evaluations. This occurs for several reasons: criteria not outlined preintervention are reported spontaneously, teachers notice good or bad changes they never anticipated, and some criteria cease to be concerns. For example, while attendance was a preintervention issue for the elementary

TABLE 2.2 Elementary Teachers' Perspectives on Student Behaviour Five Weeks and Five Months Postintervention

One school: $N = 42$ teachers

Five Weeks Postintervention	Five Months Postintervention
61% stated students were more respectful	72% stated students were more respectful
63% stated students had better attitudes	74% stated students had better attitudes
74% stated students better understand the rules	78% stated students better understand the rules
68% stated students were better at following the rules	80% stated students were better at following the rules
63% stated students were working harder	70% stated students were working harder
63% stated students were kinder to others	72% stated students were better at helping others
64% stated students were better at paying attention	68% stated students were less disruptive
	72% stated students better resolved conflicts
	68% stated students argued less

Source: Edmunds & Edmunds, 2013.

TABLE 2.3 Secondary Teachers' Perspectives on Student Behaviour Five Weeks and Five Months Postintervention

One school: $N = 67$ teachers

Five Weeks Postintervention	Five Months Postintervention
81% reported less physical violence	83% reported less physical violence
67% reported less outright defiance	65% reported less outright defiance
69% reported less swearing	72% reported less swearing
67% reported less arguing with teachers	70% reported less arguing with teachers
65% reported better adherence to the rules	75% reported better adherence to the rules
60% reported students working harder	72% reported students working harder
62% reported students were kinder to others	76% reported students were kinder to others
69% reported students paid more attention	74% reported students paid more attention
65% reported less lost instructional time	80% reported less lost instructional time
85% reported better attendance	84% reported better attendance
65% reported less referrals to the principal	80% reported less referrals to the principal
72% reported less locker checks	74% reported more completed homework
64% reported less theft	

Source: Edmunds, 2010b, 2011b.

school, it was not an issue at the five-week evaluation, a testament to the effect of the school-wide approach. Also, the school changed the five-week criterion of "being kind to others" into "resolving conflict" for the five-month evaluation. This demonstrates how schools can adjust their behavioural goals as the DCM process moves along.

As you can see from Table 2.3, the secondary school had quite different behavioural concerns than the elementary school did. Its criteria show that this school had a harder edge to its problems. Nonetheless, the staff experienced noticeable changes in the most egregious criteria—for instance, "theft" and "locker checks" were no longer an issue by the five-month evaluation, and more homework was being completed by the five-month report.

The DCM data presented in Tables 2.2 and 2.3 are consistent with multiple evaluations of PBIS Level 1 and Level 2 interventions conducted by other researchers; these interventions typically result in fewer behavioural referrals to the office, a qualifiable (and sometimes quantifiable) change in overall student behaviours, improved school climates, and improved teacher satisfaction (Sugai et al., 2000).

There is indisputable historical and empirical evidence detailing the positive impact of practices, interventions, and system-change strategies employed by approaches using the principles of PBIS. Based on the evidence above, these types of positive effects are largely attributable to DCM's preventative and educative approach rather than a reliance on reactive/punitive and coercive measures that these schools employed before they used DCM. More importantly, DCM supports teachers and administrators with a process that emphasizes positive psychology and the prevention of problematic behaviours (Lewis et al., 2006).

Discipline without education will only temporarily stop problematic behaviours because the causes of these behaviours still exist; once the causes re-emerge, so too will the problematic behaviours. DCM's emphasis on student–teacher discourse is designed to educate students about and engage students in the rule-making process. With DCM, educators do not need to *change* student behaviour. This is a misconception that inherently absolves students from their much-needed responsibility to actively participate. DCM's purposeful student–teacher discussions are designed to evoke students' natural vested interests in the way their classrooms should operate. Through this process educators can change how students think about their behaviour, and they will change their own behaviours.

The story found in the Impact on Today's Teachers box recounts what a Western University teacher-candidate experienced while on practicum. It demonstrates her use of the principles that underpin PBIS and the DCM approach she learned about in a course taught by the first author of this text.

Impact on Today's Teachers

The School Within a College (SWAC) dual-credit program was created to help at-risk students graduate from high school and make successful transitions to college. Students accepted into SWAC represent the most disengaged students—they have already left high school—and they often enter the classroom with additional disadvantages such as addiction, abuse, poverty and mental illness. Other obstacles to learning can include teen pregnancy, sexuality and gender differences and bullying. During my practicum at SWAC I observed and worked with students with one or more of these difficulties on a daily basis. Nevertheless, I did not observe any significant classroom management or behaviour problems due to the structure of the space and the practices of my Associate Teachers.

Consistent with the idea that students cannot learn if their basic needs are not met, SWAC identifies needs that are not being adequately addressed in students' lives. Using Abraham Maslow's hierarchy of needs as a framework to encourage student success, SWAC provides nutritious food in the classroom, access to condoms, and a food and personal hygiene bank. By focusing on these primary concerns, SWAC avoids some of the classroom management issues found in environments where student needs are given little or no attention. Once fundamental inadequacies have been attended to, teachers are able to focus on higher-order needs. To this end, the school board provides a social worker and tutor mentor three days each week. These practitioners meet with each student to focus on emotional well-being and to resolve potential academic problems.

I saw that a fundamental factor in ensuring student success is the creation of a safe space and a compassionate classroom community. Using 'Tribes' strategies such as community circle and four corners, the SWAC teachers actively seek to create a learning community, or SWAC Family, that forestalls some of the negative social interactions that undermine student success. In addition to creating class rules, similar to the process and rules used by Annette Elkins (see the Appendix), SWAC teachers also introduced technology to communicate with students each day regarding barriers to attendance. Some of these barriers include family and financial problems, relationship problems and substance abuse problems. If students exhibit any of these issues during class, or are unnecessarily disruptive, one of the associate teachers invites that student to go for a 'Walk and Talk' to defuse the situation before it escalates.

continued

I arrived at SWAC on my first day of practicum armed with strategies acquired from my behaviour and classroom management course. I was anxious to see if any could be implemented with adult learners and whether I could successfully translate what I had learned in the lectures into a model for classroom management. I was pleased to see that some of these strategies were already a part of the classroom. Class rules that had been agreed upon and signed by the students were prominently displayed, and techniques of effective communication had been developed. While attendance was mandatory only on Tuesdays and Thursdays, many of these students came to class nearly every day. While it might seem counterintuitive to view attendance as a classroom management issue, it nevertheless presented one of the few problematic aspects of the SWAC class.

Due to the self-study nature of SWAC, students can complete their course work entirely online or through hardcopy booklets. Some SWAC students came to class having completed their course work or were unprepared or uninterested in working. The stable space of the classroom sometimes became a site of safety and belonging for them and they sometimes attended in order to socialize and pass the time. This could become distracting for those students who had come to class to work and would occasionally result in the harder-working students going home or to another, quieter location. I developed a strategy of proactively engaging students in a daily goal setting dialogue that incorporated not only educational goals, but also social and personal goals. Like Annette Elkins, I used the concept of positive classroom relationships, in which students are motivated by the knowledge that "their teacher cares about them as well as their academic well-being." In this way I was able to redirect their energy to another task, or to move the conversation out of the classroom space. However, this strategy had to be subtle and my ability to transition smoothly from space to space improved as time passed.

I found the middle ground between authoritarianism and permissiveness a difficult space to occupy as students will attempt to push boundaries. Alternately, a lack of flexibility on the part of teachers and institutions is also counterproductive to student success. I found this especially true for disengaged or disadvantaged students in SWAC. I found the course materials on socioeconomic considerations and poor or dysfunctional homes to be quite relevant and helpful in developing my own teaching practices. After re-reading it and thinking about it for a while, I began to gain confidence in sharing with my students the importance of education in my own life. In this way I was able to deepen my relationships with my students and develop a connection with them based on mutual appreciation. This proved extremely effective in minimizing classroom disruptions, as students did not want to jeopardize the mutual respect that derived from our commonalities.

Conclusion

There is no question that properly managing student behaviour is a vital part of any teacher's approach to teaching. However, as you can see from this chapter, classroom management is something that takes careful thought and planning and requires a comprehensive understanding of the principles that drive the process. Foremost of these principles is the notion that teachers need to talk to students in a systematized manner to co-establish the rules of engagement.

It is more and more evident that teachers engaging in the process of co-establishing rules, rewards, and consequences is more important than the fact that rules, rewards, and consequences are established. The primary purpose is to demonstrate to students that they can choose preferred positive behaviours and be rewarded for them, as opposed to not engaging in negative behaviours simply to avoid punishment. The evidence reported by many teachers and administrators from a wide variety of schools, both elementary and secondary, clearly demonstrates that this process provides numerous and sustainable positive effects.

Discussion Questions

1. Based on your experiences to date, what could the drawbacks be to implementing the DCM approach, and what would you do to address those problems?
2. Discuss with your colleagues how comfortable you would be in providing students with the rights and responsibilities described in DCM. If applicable, what would you put in place to make you more comfortable?
3. Based on the principles provided in this chapter, critically evaluate the classroom management practices you have witnessed.
4. Not all classroom management systems can be instantly converted to an approach like DCM. What elements of DCM would you start with if you wanted to make slow but incremental changes to an existing approach?
5. Establish two teams and debate the following statement: "The DCM approach is reasonable and logical."

Further Resources

1. Cameron, J., & Pierce, W. D. (2002). *Rewards and intrinsic motivation: Resolving the controversy.* Westport, CT: Bergin & Garvey.

   Many social psychologists have been critical of the practice of using incentive systems in education and other applied settings. The concern is that money, high grades, prizes, and praise may be effective in getting students to perform an activity, but performance and interest are maintained only so long as the reward keeps coming. The claim is that rewards destroy people's intrinsic motivation. This widely accepted view has been enormously influential and has led many teachers to question the use of rewards and incentives. Contrary to this view, the research by Cameron and Pierce indicates that rewards can be used effectively to enhance interest and performance.

2. Goldstein, S., & Brooks, R. (2007). *Understanding and managing children's classroom behavior* (2nd ed.). Hoboken, NJ: John Wiley & Sons, Inc.

   This is the classic guide to creating a positive classroom environment. This new edition covers the most recent relevant findings regarding behaviour management. It has been completely updated to reflect the current functional approach to assessing, understanding, and positively managing behaviour in a classroom setting. Unlike other resources, it explains the concept of temperament and its impact on children's behaviour and personality.

3. Johnson, F. L., & Edmunds, A. L. (2006). *From chaos to control: Understanding and responding to the behaviours of students with exceptionalities.* London, ON: The Althouse Press.

This comprehensive book outlines the behaviour and classroom management issues related to students with exceptionalities. It provides clear descriptions of the factors that influence the behaviours of these students and suggests remedies that may be appropriate based on the students' extenuating circumstances. It is an excellent resource for teachers who spend a large portion of their instructional time with students with moderate to high needs.

4. Lane, K., Falk, K., & Wehby, J. (2006). Classroom management in special education classrooms and resource rooms. In C. M. Evertson & C. S. Weinstein (Eds.), *Handbook of classroom management: Research, practice and contemporary issues* (pp. 439–460). Mahwah, NJ: Lawrence Erlbaum Associates.

   This chapter from the *Handbook of Classroom Management* is an excellent complementary resource to the Johnson and Edmunds book described above. It provides a more theoretical description of the issues and cites some of the most important research of our times. Contained within it are many of the principles described in this chapter that are used in the DCM approach.

5. Guardino, C. A., & Fullerton, E. (2010). Changing behaviors by changing the classroom environment. *Teaching Exceptional Children, 42*(6), 8–13.

   This exceptional article asks and answers questions that have important implications for teachers. What impact does the classroom environment have on overall class behaviour and learning? Many teachers face disruptive behaviour in their classrooms; how can they target and change problem areas in the classroom environment? The authors demonstrate that by collecting data on student engagement during instruction, disruptive behaviour, and teacher observations, teachers can identify which physical aspects of their classroom need to be improved. They then show how changing the classroom environment can increase academic engagement and decrease disruptive behaviour.

Curriculum: Designing Meaningful Learning Experiences

Learning Objectives

After reading this chapter, you should understand

1. The varied definitions of curriculum
2. The ideological influences upon curriculum
3. The features of curriculum across Canada
4. The role of outcomes in curriculum planning
5. Curriculum planning for deep understanding

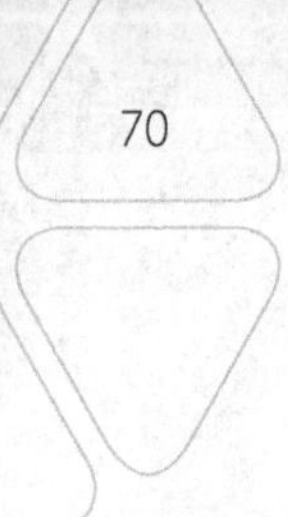

Types of Curriculum

The word *curriculum* finds its roots in the Latin word *currere* which means "the course to be run." Like a race or obstacle course, students must pass through a series of courses of study or learning experiences. The two main questions of curriculum are related to content and process: "What shall we teach?" and "How shall we teach it?" In Canada, the first question is mostly addressed by provincial/territorial curriculum guides, which outline the key content that must be included at each grade level. This is often called the **formal** or **intended curriculum**—that is, what the province/territory mandates. Because the curriculum is a written document, it can be inspected and criticized, and it can be shared and used in various contexts. In Canada, each province/territory generally designs its own curricula with a team of teachers, content experts, and government staff. The curriculum identifies the required topics to be taught, but it often also includes the levels of abilities students should be achieving at each grade.

formal (or intended) curriculum The key content that must be included at each grade level, as mandated by the provincial/territorial government.

informal curriculum Activities that take place during lunch hour or after school, such as clubs and teams. Also called *extracurricular experiences.*

extracurricular experiences Activities that take place during lunch hour or after school, such as clubs and teams. Also called *informal curriculum.*

received curriculum The method by which teachers deliver the formal curriculum and thus the way the curriculum is received by students.

A broader definition of curriculum is "a series of planned events that are intended to have educational consequences for one or more students" (Eisner, 2002, p. 31), or "all learning which is planned and guided by the school, whether it is carried on in groups or individually, inside or outside of the school" (Kerr in Kelly, 2009, p. 12). The formal curriculum includes those activities that have time allocated in the daily schedule, while the **informal curriculum** includes lunch hour and after-school activities such as clubs and teams, often called **extracurricular experiences**.

The **received curriculum** is what unfolds in particular classrooms or schools, and it responds more to the second question, "How shall we teach?" While the formal curriculum includes the topics set out in the provincial documents, teachers have significant flexibility in how they "deliver" those topics and thus in the way the curriculum is received by their students. Earlier, we suggested that these universal curriculum documents could be inspected, criticized, and shared; what happens inside the classroom is less tangible and more varied. Teachers can select diverse ways of achieving the same outcomes. For example, the Alberta Education Program of Studies for Social Studies in Grade 7 (2006) proposes the following knowledge and understanding outcomes:

> *Students will:*
>
> 7.1.3 compare and contrast diverse social and economic structures within the societies of Aboriginal, French and British peoples in pre-Confederation Canada by exploring and reflecting upon the following questions and issues:
>
> - What were the different ways in which Aboriginal societies were structured (i.e., Iroquois Confederacy, Ojibwa, Mi'kmaq)?
> - How did the structures of Aboriginal societies affect decision-making in each society (i.e., role and status of women, consensus building)?

In one school, a teacher can cover these concepts through a series of textbook readings and end-of-chapter questions; in Chapter 6 you will encounter an example of how one teacher had her class imagine themselves as members of one of those societies and, using an iMovie presentation of researched facts and images, had to convince the king of France about the value of their culture. In both cases, the students learned about the social and economic structures of these societies, as mandated by the formal curriculum, but the information was received in very different ways in these two Grade 7 classes. The first class memorized a series of facts, while the second class was challenged to defend an Aboriginal group against historical critiques. Arguably the second group had to think more critically about the facts they learned, resulting in more lasting understanding.

The received curriculum also impacts the **learned curriculum**. Sometimes students do not learn what teachers intend. If teachers only lecture or expect rote memorization, as did the social studies teacher who assigned textbook reading and end-of-chapter questions, students may simply recall terms for a test without truly understanding the content. Later in this chapter, we will examine what is meant by using the curriculum documents to design learning experiences (received curriculum) to promote genuine understanding and deeper student learning.

learned curriculum
What students actually learn; it is not always the same as what teachers intended.

Both the formal and received curricula are relatively explicit—the teachers articulate and plan learning experiences to achieve particular outcomes. However, schools also communicate many implicit messages, often called the **hidden curriculum**. Students learn that in a busy classroom of 25 students, they must share the teacher's attention with their classmates. They learn that compliance is rewarded and that punishment is not necessarily meted out fairly, particularly if one gender or group or individual is targeted or favoured, even if subtly. In one Grade 1 classroom, table groups were rewarded with points if they put their heads down to signal their readiness after a transition, but when asked about this process at least one child seemed not to understand the teacher's goal of achieving order in the classroom.

hidden curriculum
The subtle messages learned in school regarding what is valued, including things like compliance and gender norms.

Boy: When we come in from recess we have to have our heads down.
Researcher: Why?
Boy: Because um, our teacher says.
Researcher: Do you know why she wants you to do that?
Boy: Because we'll get points.
Researcher: There's another reason. Do you know what it is?
Boy: Um—listening.
Researcher: Why does she ask you to listen?
Boy: Because we'll get points . . . maybe.
Researcher: But it's more than that. What would happen if you weren't listening?
Boy: We wouldn't get any points.
Researcher: What else? What would happen in your classroom if nobody listened?
Boy: Not having playground or recess?
Researcher: Wouldn't it get kind of crazy? Kind of loud?
Boy: It would get kinda loud. (Nickel, 2004, p. 210)

Students play the game of trying to read the teachers' minds to discern "what he or she wants" to achieve approval or an A grade. These types of messages, which are often unconscious, are part of the hidden curriculum. Explicit classroom rules described in Chapter 2 help illuminate this hidden curriculum to some degree, but the anecdote described above illustrates that mismatches can occur between what students understand and what teachers intend.

Structural and organizational decisions can also be part of the hidden curriculum. The scheduling of the arts, often on Friday afternoons, suggests "that the arts are forms of play that one can engage in only after the real work of schooling has finished" (Eisner, 2002,

p. 92). School buildings and classroom furniture themselves often send messages about efficiency and individual pursuits, not a comfortable workshop atmosphere. Interestingly, many schools in the past couple of decades have switched from individual desks to table groups where students can more easily collaborate with one another. This sends a message about the kind of learning activities that are expected. Texts also include hidden messages. For example, picture books and textbooks historically portrayed men and women in very stereotypical roles—mothers caring for children in the home and fathers working out of the home. In the last 50 years there has been greater attention paid to eliminating stereotypical sex roles in texts, but it is still difficult for many students to identify with the characters in the stories they read, particularly if their own cultures are not highlighted.

null curriculum
Information, activities, or content that is not included in the curriculum, either formal or informal.

Finally there is the **null curriculum**—what gets left out of the school curriculum. Elliot Eisner questions why "law, economics, anthropology, psychology, dance, the visual arts, and music are frequently not offered or are not required parts of secondary school programs" (2002, p. 193). He is not suggesting that these subjects should replace what is currently in the curriculum; rather, that what exists is in place more as a matter of tradition and not necessarily because of careful analysis of all possible alternatives. What is included and excluded from the explicit curriculum reflects the values of the curriculum writers, and what is included in the received curriculum often reflects the values of the teacher. For example, if the teacher, in selecting the literature for an English course, only includes the works of European writers and omits writers from other cultures, the writers of those other cultures become part of the null curriculum. Religion is often part of the null curriculum in public schools. Rather than risk offending or excluding some religious groups, teachers may avoid the topic entirely or simply give it minimal attention when it is required in social studies. The null curriculum may also include those subjects that are given short shrift because the teacher lacks expertise or resources to teach them adequately. For example, some schools may not have certain sports teams because they lack the resources to include these as extra-curricular options.

educational curriculum
A concept developed by British curriculum scholar A. V. Kelly that provides "a liberating experience focusing on such things as the promotion of freedom and independence of thought, of social and political empowerment, of respect for the freedom of others, of an acceptance of variety of opinion, and of the enrichment of the life of every individual in that society, regardless of class, race or creed" (Kelly, 2009, p. 8).

enacted curriculum
The pedagogy that emerges from the interests and passions of both the teachers and the students.

A. V. Kelly, a British curriculum scholar, argues for what he calls the **educational curriculum**, which should "provide a liberating experience focusing on such things as the promotion of freedom and independence of thought, of social and political empowerment, of respect for the freedom of others, of an acceptance of variety of opinion, and of the enrichment of the life of every individual in that society, regardless of class, race or creed" (2009, p. 8). His definition counters the trend in Britain toward vocational education or curricula that are narrowly focused on technical aims. He argues that a narrow curriculum focused on basic objectives is in fact immoral because it limits the pupil's capacity for criticism and ensures political conformity. This is similar to Catherine Cornbleth's (1990) **enacted curriculum**, which is the pedagogy that emerges from the interests and passions of both the teachers and students; it is shaped by the local context, and the students have significant influence on the shaping of the curriculum.

Curriculum Ideologies and Influences

Curriculum is often caught in the push and pull of shifting ideologies—beliefs about what and how teachers should teach and why. Ideology, like worldview, is a comprehensive vision of the world that influences the decisions people make. In his seminal text *Ideology and Curriculum*, Michael Apple (1990) notes that ideology typically involves legitimation (justification for a group's actions) and a power conflict between those seeking power and those who hold power. Regarding curriculum he writes

> Until we take seriously the extent to which education is caught up in the real world of shifting and unequal power relations, we will be living in a world divorced from reality. . . . The decision to include some group's knowledge as worthwhile to pass on to future generations while other group's culture and history hardly sees the light of day says something extremely important about who has power in society. (pp. viii–ix)

Apple argues that educational institutions seek to maintain the status quo, including the existing economic, political, and cultural arrangements.

The following section discusses some of the more prominent influences drawn from the work of curriculum theorists Elliot Eisner (2002), Valerie Janesick (2003), and Michael Schiro (2008). Each of these ideologies has had some impact on curriculum development both historically and currently. You will inevitably see parallels to these ideologies when you read Chapter 6 on the philosophical roots of education.

Religious Orthodox Ideologies

All religious orthodox ideologies hold their belief in God as central to curriculum development. Canada's first settlers followed the European tradition of developing schools in co-operation with local churches or religious orders, either Catholic or Protestant. Catholic missionaries set up the first schools in Quebec in the seventeenth century. The Anglicans started the first English schools in the 18th century followed by other denominations such as Presbyterian, Baptist, and Methodist (Ontario Ministry of Education, 1994). By the 1840s, there were two school systems in Ontario, one Catholic and one nondenominational, but both were Christian; non-Christian religions were not considered. Schools were charged with the moral education of students, and this moral training was grounded in Christian teaching. Most other provinces and territories followed Ontario's lead in establishing two systems. During the 20th century, increasing diversity led the Protestant system to be gradually replaced by a secular system. Today, some provinces retain a publicly funded "separate" Catholic school board; in other provinces, all religious schools tend to be private though with some public funding. Religious schools teach a religious education course and the religious worldview is pervasive throughout the curriculum.

religious orthodox ideologies
Ideologies that maintain that education should initiate children into the beliefs of the religious group.

For families with conservative religious views, they view childhood as a time to transmit the values of their faith, not a time to necessarily acquire a critical attitude toward faith. When families feel their faith is being undermined by curricular content, they may ask that their children be exempted from classes where the content of the course has explicit religious or sexual content that runs counter to their beliefs. In fact, Bill 44 in Alberta requires teachers to notify parents of such content so that parents have the opportunity to remove their children from these classes. In some cases parents may even choose to remove their children from the school permanently, electing to home school them or pay for a private education that reinforces their worldview. Some argue that home schooling and even private schools effectively silo various groups with differing belief systems and that this isolation may weaken our democracy. The influence of the religious orthodox ideology on curriculum is not as pervasive as it was when all schools had a religious purpose but, nevertheless, it does impact curriculum, particularly for those in religious schools or who are exempted from aspects of the curriculum because of their religion.

CASE STUDY

Religious Teaching in Schools

Case #1

As of 2008, high school students in Quebec are required to take an "Ethics and Religious Culture" (ERC) program that replaced the previously entrenched Catholic and Protestant programs of religious and moral instruction. Two parents asked that their children be exempted from the ERC program, appealing first to the school board; when they were unsuccessful they appealed to the Supreme Court, who upheld the prior decision. The parents claimed

> that the ERC Program is not in fact neutral and that students following the ERC course would be exposed to a form of relativism which would interfere with their ability to pass their faith on to their children. They also maintain that exposing children to various religious facts is confusing for them. (*S.L. v. Commission scolaire des Chênes*, 2012)

The courts argued that exposing children to various religions without forcing them to join any of them does not infringe on freedom of religion and is in fact a reality of contemporary society. "Given the religious diversity of present-day Quebec, the state can no longer promote a vision of society in public schools that is based on historically dominant religions" (p. 11). In the legal statement, the courts cited the Quebec Minister of Education of 1997:

> All schools must teach students to respect different allegiances. However, our schools must not altogether dismiss religious education. They must show that they are open and able to recognize, regardless of specific convictions and from a critical point of view, the contribution made by the different religions in terms of culture, values and humanism. (*S.L. v. Commission scolaire des Chênes*, 2012)

Do you agree with the court's decision in this case? Does the right of the school system to promote religious tolerance trump the rights of the parents to promote their religious views with their own children? How does catechistic teaching of religion conflict with the rights of those who do not share that religion?

Case #2

Morinville, Alberta, is a small community north of Edmonton of approximately 8,500 residents. Morinville was settled mainly by Catholics, and until recently the only public schools in the area were Catholic. Non-Catholic parents lobbied for the right to have their children educated in a secular school system. Initially the Alberta Human Rights Commission would not hear their complaint, but as of September 2012 one school in the area has been reassigned to the public board so that families have the right to choose between Catholic and public schools as they do in most other Alberta communities (*Global News*, 2012).

Why do you think the Alberta Human Rights Commission would not initially hear the parents' complaint? When the majority in the community are religious, do those who are not religious have the right to expect a secular education?

Rational Humanism

Rational humanism is an ideology that values the capacity of human beings to think critically and rationally, particularly in their reading of philosophical and literary classics. (You will recognize many of the ideals of rational humanism in the perennialist philosophy you will encounter in Chapter 6.) Proponents of this curriculum ideology oppose most modern standardized tests because the typical multiple-choice format does not align well with the careful reading and analysis of texts that rational humanism values. Teachers are charged with the task of helping students acquire all the knowledge that has been accumulated by a society, including the content, concepts, and ways of thinking. All students should be exposed to a common curriculum, regardless of social class, so that all are exposed to the best cultural artifacts. Curriculum electives and vocational courses (e.g., cosmetology, auto mechanics, sports medicine) are eschewed because students are considered too immature to choose wisely.

Rational humanism has not been particularly influential outside of elite private schools. It is regarded as too intellectual and lacking in the practical skills that are promoted in more typical curriculum. It gives primacy to disciplinary knowledge over the development of the student. Critics argue that a rational humanist ideology ignores both the concerns and issues of the local context, but perhaps more importantly it ignores the individual student.

rational humanism
An ideology that values the capacity of human beings to think critically and rationally. Proponents of this curriculum ideology believe that all students should be exposed to the same curriculum, regardless of social class, so that they are all exposed to the best cultural artifacts.

Social Efficiency Ideology

Proponents of the social efficiency ideology (also referred to as *traditional ideology*) believe that the curriculum should efficiently provide the skills necessary for students to become functioning members of society. Franklin Bobbitt (1918), a proponent of a social efficiency model of curriculum, wrote

> The central theory [of curriculum] is simple. Human life, however varied, consists in the performance of specific activities. Education that prepares for life is one that prepares definitely and adequately for these specific activities. However numerous and diverse they may be for any social class they can be discovered. This requires only that one go out into the world of affairs and discover the particulars of which their affairs consist. These will show the abilities, attitudes, habits, appreciations and forms of knowledge that men need. These will be the objectives of the curriculum. . . . The curriculum will then be that series of experiences which children and youth must have by way of obtaining those objectives. (p. 42)

social efficiency ideology
An ideology that holds that curriculum should efficiently provide the skills necessary for students to become functioning members of society.

This ideology was particularly influential in the first half of the 20th century when schools were heavily dominated by a business management model of education in which labour tasks were divided into discrete subskills or competencies. To be accountable to society, this ideology also emphasizes the importance of using standardized tests to prove that educators have met the educational task set out for them by society.

The social efficiency ideology relies on behaviouristic principles of psychology: A stimulus (learning activity) will cause a response (learning as evidenced by behavioural change). Teachers employ strategies to help learners acquire the behavioural objectives prescribed by local curriculum makers (behavioural objectives will be discussed more fully later in this chapter). For example, Schiro (2008) describes *Type to Learn,* a computer program used to teach typing skills, as a classic programmed curriculum using behavioural principles. The program provides a stimulus—an auditory and visual presentation of letters, words, or sentences to be typed—and when learners are successful at producing the desired response they are rewarded with the next step in the program, updates on their speed and accuracy, and eventually a game to practise the acquired skills. You might observe parallel structures in math classes, where students are sent back to their desks with corrections and are finally relieved of this task (rewarded) when all the questions are correct.

"Teacher-proof" curricular materials—those that are so highly prescriptive that teachers can apply them exactly as the developers planned—are informed by an efficiency mindset. However, in practice the developers' aims are seldom realized. Schools, teachers, and students are idiosyncratic with varied needs, and the materials seldom meet all those differing needs. As clearly outlined in Chapter 1, professional teachers should engage in reflection to discern how to adapt and develop materials for their classes, for the local context, and for individual students.

The social efficiency ideology was and continues to be criticized for turning teachers into technicians who simply "apply" the curriculum to the students and measure the success of their application. As Smith (2000) argues, teacher judgment is "sidelined":

> In order to measure, things have to be broken down into smaller and smaller units. The result . . . can be long lists of often trivial skills or competencies. This can lead to a focus in this approach to curriculum theory and practice on the parts rather than the whole; on the trivial, rather than the significant. It can lead to an approach to education and assessment which resembles a shopping list. When all the items are ticked, the person has passed the course or has learnt something. The role of overall judgment is somehow sidelined.

One of the major criticisms of social efficiency ideology is the emphasis on curriculum as a product to be delivered rather than curriculum as a process with a focus on the interactions between teachers and learners and knowledge. If we regard curriculum as a process, we rely much more upon the skill of the teacher to develop appropriate curricular concepts and teaching strategies and to interact with students organically by building on their prior experience, contributions, and needs. In Chapter 6 you will read Paulo Freire's critique of a social efficiency ideology of education, which he refers to as a banking model of education in which teachers "deposit" information into passive students, rendering them even more passive (Freire, 2000). Apple (1990) echoes Freire; he is particularly critical of the social efficiency ideology of education because it turns students into consumers who consume what "the holders of real knowledge" (p. xiv) have deemed important. Instead he calls for students to be creators of knowledge, something that a progressive ideology can potentially offer.

Progressivism

progressivism
A learner-centred ideology that focuses on the growth of the individual. A progressive curriculum motivates students to delve into a problem.

Progressivism is a learner-centred approach to education that focuses on the growth of the individual. A progressive curriculum is problem centred or inquiry based; the teacher constructs curriculum that motivates students to delve into a problem. For example, one Grade 8 class engaged in an interdisciplinary project partly in response to the 2012 film *Contagion* to examine how viruses spread and how ideas and trends can be similarly "contagious" (Scott, 2012).

In order to construct a learning environment for a progressive curriculum, the teacher must understand the individual students well enough to know their prior experience and developmental capabilities. Although each of the provinces and territories mandates a framework for curriculum development, progressive teachers hold significant responsibility for curriculum design because they plan its delivery with an awareness of the students and the local context. Progressive teachers often complain that provincial curricula are too prescriptive, particularly when provincial exams are used to enforce the coverage of the curriculum. Provincial curricula organized around broad ideas, however, are more flexible and better lend themselves to progressive approaches to curriculum implementation. Inquiry-based learning as an example of progressive ideology will be discussed more fully later in this chapter.

Critical Theory

critical theory
An ideology that aims to cultivate an awareness of the hidden curriculum—that is, the unspoken values that permeate schools.

Critical theory is an ideology that is more influential in academic circles than among curriculum developers or teachers. Its aim is to cultivate an awareness of the hidden curriculum—the unspoken values that permeate schools. Critical theorists are "concerned with raising the consciousness of unsuspecting parents, students and educators to the insidious and subtle ways through which an unequal and often unjust social order reproduces itself through schools" (Eisner, 2002, p. 73). They lament the hierarchical structure of schools that make students dependent on authority and less likely to formulate their own goals. In his seminal text *Deschooling Society*, Ivan Illich (1971) argued that the selection of content for the curriculum must inevitably involve the imposition of values and a form of social and political control.

According to Eisner, critical theorists have not had a significant impact on curriculum development because they lack a positive agenda: "[I]f their material was less strident, more hopeful, more generous, and more concretely constructive, it would be much more likely to influence practice" (2002, p. 76). However, many teachers informed by critical theory try to involve their students in projects that combat social injustice. The social studies curriculum in many provinces, particularly at the high school level, tries to raise students' awareness of ways in which bias and injustice limit democratic aims. You will see the influence of critical theory on social reconstructionism in Chapter 6.

Reconceptualism

reconceptualism
An ideology that challenges the managerial values in education and focuses on the lived experience of the learner, particularly aesthetic experiences.

Reconceptualism is a curriculum ideology advanced largely by William Pinar, a curriculum theorist at the University of British Columbia. Reconceptualists argue for "a deep respect for personal purpose, lived experience, for the life of the imagination, and for those forms of understanding that resist dissection and measurement" (Eisner, 2002, p. 77). They believe that schools have been influenced by an industrial model, churning out uniform graduates like products on an assembly line, which leads to alienation and indifference. Instead, educators should try to understand the child and his or her experience. This requires sensitive educators who are attuned to the influence of their own prior experience on their teaching practice and their interactions with students.

Several Canadian curriculum theorists have been influential in the reconceptualist movement, most notably Max van Manen and Ted Aoki, both professors emeritus at the University of Alberta. One of van Manen's (1991) best-known contributions to reconceptualism is the concept of a *pedagogical relation*, which highlights the teacher's careful interactions with students. Teachers must act with sensitivity in the learner's best interests and may tactfully "hold back" to permit learner autonomy. Aoki (2005) wrote about the distinction between planned curriculum and *lived curriculum*; the latter must allow space for the stories the students bring to the classroom that bring the curriculum to life. This requires teachers to "listen with care to the voice of the silent other" (p. 213) to draw out the questions and stories that are meaningful to the students. A recent publication compiling the work of Canadian scholars focuses on reconceptualist curriculum themes related to the Canadian context, including the experience of indigenous students and the importance of environmental education for sustainability (Stanley & Young, 2011).

Overall, reconceptualism is less an organized approach to curriculum and more an attitude held by the teacher. To the degree that teachers can be true to this vision, the

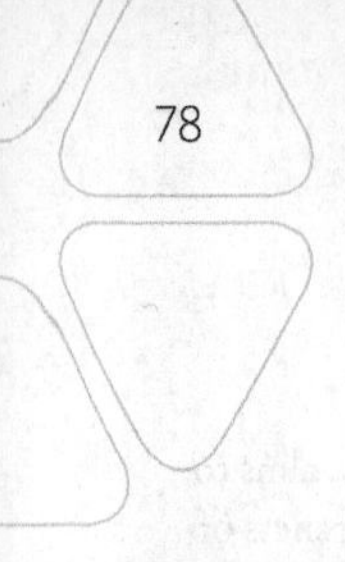

received curriculum in their classrooms may feel much more personalized than the mechanistic classrooms that reconceptualists decry.

Cognitive Pluralism

cognitive pluralism
An ideology that proposes that there are multiple ways to know and express our knowledge.

Proponents of **cognitive pluralism** propose that there are a variety of ways to know and express our knowledge. Humans have the distinctive ability to create and manipulate symbols and in doing so give public expression to inner thoughts that can later be reflected upon. Our ideas can be communicated using various types of symbols and representation—through mathematics, science, poetry, prose, music, and the arts. If there is a plurality of ways to communicate one's understanding, there is also a plurality of intelligences. According to Gardner's (2006) theory of multiple intelligences, humans possess nine different types of intelligence to varying degrees. These are not just aptitudes but are ways of solving problems. The curriculum of the classroom communicates what kinds of intelligence are "valued and practiced":

> If the kind of mind that children can come to own is, in part, influenced by the kinds of opportunities they have to think, and if these opportunities are themselves defined by the kind of curriculum schools provide, then it could be argued that the curriculum itself is . . . a kind of mind-altering device. (Eisner, 2002, p. 81)

Schools have traditionally valued success as demonstrated through linguistic or logical–mathematical intelligence. By inviting various forms of curricular tasks that use different types of intelligence and celebrating accomplishments in areas that have not been traditionally valued, the potential for student success and equity is increased.

Gardner's Multiple Intelligences and Implications for Curriculum Planning

When Howard Gardner (2006) proposed the theory of multiple intelligences, he argued that traditional measures of intelligence privilege linguistic and logical–mathematical intelligence, and in so doing mostly ignore other ways of being intelligent. So too the curricula in schools elevate these two forms of intelligence. The original seven and subsequent two multiple intelligences are shown in Table 3.1.

In translating these intelligences into educational practice, Gardner recommends paying attention to three principles:

1. *Individual-centred education:* Most schools teach children the same things in the same way and assess all children in the same way, which is perceived by educators to be the most fair approach. Gardner argues that this approach privileges those with logical–mathematical and linguistic intelligences but ignores those with other intellectual talents. It is the responsibility of the teacher to learn as much as possible about how children learn best and to provide alternatives where possible to help them learn more effectively. Numerous resources have been developed that help teachers discern assignment alternatives that may better capitalize on the talents of their students. These may include learning experiences such as musical or artistic responses to literature or co-operative learning that may benefit those with interpersonal intelligence. Gardner is not suggesting that some students be excused from core subjects, only that subjects may be taught and assessed in more varied ways.

2. *Priority of educational goals:* Gardner argues that teachers' first priority should be clarity about educational goals. In many cases, multiple intelligence approaches may help teachers to achieve those goals, but they should not be viewed as an end in themselves.
3. *Multiple representations of key concepts:* Mastering disciplinary concepts typically requires multiple exposures to those concepts. Multiple intelligences provide a means for revisiting ideas in ways that may activate different neural networks and appeal to those with different intelligences.

TABLE 3.1 Gardner's Multiple Intelligences

Intelligence	Description
Logical–Mathematical Intelligence	People with strong logical–mathematical intelligence are able to easily problem solve using numbers and make logical deductions. Typical math and science tasks require this type of intelligence.
Linguistic Intelligence	Students who read and write well usually achieve strong grades in school because almost every subject requires reading about ideas and communicating their understanding of these ideas in writing. Those with exceptional linguistic intelligence are often creative and skilled in the communication of their ideas.
Musical Intelligence	Music is a form of communication. Even autistic children who cannot communicate verbally can often play music beautifully. Musical prodigies provide evidence that musical intelligence may be biologically based.
Bodily–Kinesthetic Intelligence	Like musical prodigies, athletic prodigies often show talent at first exposure to a sport. Physical development typically progresses through clear developmental milestones, but children with bodily–kinesthetic intelligence are often significantly advanced. Gardner shows how the steps involved in the effective execution of athletic skills like hitting a tennis ball requires skilful problem solving such as calculating timing and force, coordinating muscles, and thinking strategically about ideal ball placement.
Spatial Intelligence	Those who have strong spatial intelligence can easily visualize what is not concrete. Spatial intelligence is useful for navigation, games like chess, and the artistic use of space in visual arts.
Interpersonal Intelligence	Interpersonal intelligence is manifest in the ability to interpret others' motivations and intentions. It is particularly important for those who lead others; such leaders are often characterized as having charisma, perhaps due to their keen ability to work with the complexities of various personalities.
Intrapersonal Intelligence	Individuals with strong intrapersonal intelligence are especially adept at self-knowledge. They are often characterized as reflective because they can label their own emotions and use this knowledge to guide their behaviour.
Naturalist Intelligence	Those with naturalist intelligence have a strong ability to distinguish between subtle differences in the natural world, which is particularly useful in biology.
Existentialist Intelligence	Individuals who ask "big questions" (Where did we come from? What happens when we die?) are considered to have strong existential intelligence. This type of intelligence is important for philosophers, politicians, and religious leaders.

Practical Applications

REGGIO EMILIA AND CURRICULUM IDEOLOGIES

Several of the above curriculum ideologies are evident in the Reggio Emilia approach to education. Reggio Emilia is a town in Italy that reconceived preschool and primary education in the years following World War II in an effort to provide a child-centred curriculum and to develop a respectful community. Reggio teachers are keen observers of their students' experiences and these observations inform the design of the curriculum. Reggio classrooms are characterized by the following features:

- *Long-term projects*: Teachers' observations help them understand the children and develop appropriate long-term projects for them to participate in together, such as examining light and shadows or the concept of crowds.
- *Multiple symbolic languages*: Children are encouraged to represent their understanding through one of the "hundred languages of children," including sculpture, dramatic play, drawing, and writing.
- *Environment as the third teacher*: The observations help the teachers design environments that will invite the children's curiosity; the environment is considered "the third teacher" in Reggio classrooms and is often flooded with light and with natural materials such as plants and found artifacts from the outdoors.
- *Documentation for assessment*: Teachers document the children's learning through photographs and displays of student work that can later be revisited and discussed to invite reflection.
- *Teacher as researcher*: While functioning as an expert guide, teachers are also researchers who carefully document children's learning and meet with other teachers to discuss their observations. This research helps them discern the best ways to provoke thinking and stimulate learning.

Teachers from Canada and other countries now visit the schools of Reggio Emilia on study tours, and groups like the North American Reggio Emilia Alliance support teachers in achieving the ideals of the Reggio schools. For more information, visit www.reggioalliance.org.

Here are some questions to ponder. These are designed to challenge you to compare and contrast the ideologies that have been presented in this chapter:

1. In what ways would social efficiency ideologues object to a Reggio curriculum?
2. While progressivism and Reggio are both focused on inquiry- or project-based learning, how could the "hundred languages" concept enrich a typical progressive inquiry project?
3. How does a Reggio curriculum align with the reconceptualist concepts of pedagogical relation and lived curriculum?
4. What parallels might there be between cognitive pluralism and the "hundred languages of children"?

Impact on Today's Teachers

Ideology has been the root of many curriculum debates over the decades. For example, in what is often called the "math wars," progressives and traditionalists argue over the best way to teach mathematics. (You may note parallels to the phonics/whole-language debate from Chapter 1.) Progressives suggest that children learn mathematics effectively when solving real-world problems that help them develop number sense, reasoning, and deep, conceptual understanding. Traditionalists argue that computational skills should be memorized and practised before students begin defending multiple answers or ways to solve problems.

WISE Math—Western Initiative for Strengthening Education in Math—is a Canadian group started by mathematics professors at the Universities of Manitoba, Winnipeg, and Regina to improve math education in Canada. They fear that the curricular emphasis on conceptual understanding in math has undermined some aspects of math learning, in particular, algorithms for arithmetic (e.g., carrying and borrowing for addition and subtraction) and automatic recall of mathematics facts. According to WISE Math's website, these skills are missing from the Western and Northern Canadian Protocol, the common math curriculum for the Western provinces and territories. WISE Math's critics agree that algorithms are important, but argue that they don't need to precede problem-solving and conceptual work; such knowledge can be developed during problem-solving tasks. The curriculum may lack the emphasis WISE Math wishes to see, but teachers are the pedagogical decision makers who translate the curriculum into learning experiences; they recognize when their students need more support in basic skills to help them better solve the mathematical problems.

Curriculum in Canada

In Canada, each province and territory is responsible for its own curriculum, usually developed with a team of experts that includes teachers. According to Canada's Constitution Act of 1867, "in and for each province the Legislature may exclusively make Laws in relation to Education" (Section 93). The curriculum documents for each province represent large-scale curriculum planning. **Curriculum guides** are year- or term-long outlines of school subjects that are differentiated by grade. These comprehensive guides specifically outline what students are to be taught and the knowledge, skills, and dispositions they are expected to acquire for each subject at each grade level. Sometimes, but not always, these guides also outline provincial/territorial expectations for student achievement.

curriculum guides
Year- or term-long outlines of school subjects that are differentiated by grade. They are developed by each province and territory by a team of experts that includes teachers. In Alberta, they are referred to as Programs of Study.

Despite varied provincial curricula, the Canadian Ministers of Education (which includes all of the provincial Ministers of Education) have published a series of documents to guide curriculum developers across the country. There has also been some interprovincial curriculum collaboration, such as the Western and Northern Canadian Protocol signed in 1993 by the Ministers of Education for Manitoba, Saskatchewan, Alberta, British Columbia, Yukon, and Northwest Territories (Nunavut joined the group in 2000). Projects in this collaboration included the development of curriculum frameworks with common learning outcomes in mathematics (1995), language arts (1996), and international languages. As noted in Table 3.2, the Atlantic provinces have a common curricula for science.

As you can see from Table 3.2, despite significant overlap there are notable differences in topics as well. For example, every province and territory addresses the topic of plant growth in Grade 3 science except Alberta, where plants are a topic of study in the Grade 4 science curriculum.

Curriculum documents will often specify recommended or required time allotments for each subject. For example, the elementary program in Saskatchewan requires the time allotments shown in Table 3.3, which includes a note about locally determined options. For example, in Regina, public school students are required to take 90–120 minutes per week of core French in Grades 1–8 in addition to the subjects listed in the time allotment chart. Some school boards, particularly those in northern Saskatchewan, may have a Cree language requirement, and Catholic schools require time blocks for religious education. Locally determined options like language and religion require teachers to make time reductions in other areas of the curriculum. In elementary classrooms, where teachers are usually generalists, cross-curricular integration helps teachers meet the time requirements. Often science and social studies involve reading and writing instruction to understand the forms of nonfiction texts; responses to literature may take artistic forms and promote integration

TABLE 3.2 Grade 3 Science Curriculum Topics across Canada

To illustrate the similarities and differences in content across the country, the following topics of study have been drawn from the Grade 3 science curriculum in each province and territory:

	Life Science	Physical Science	Earth Science
British Columbia	Plant growth and change	Materials and structures	Stars and planets
Alberta	Animal life cycle Hearing and sound	Building with a variety of materials Testing materials and designs Hearing and sound	Rocks and minerals
Saskatchewan	Plant growth and changes	Structures and materials Magnetism and static electricity	Exploring soils
Manitoba	Growth and changes in plants	Materials and structures Forces that attract or repel	Soils in the environment
Ontario	Growth and changes in plants	Magnetic and charged materials Forces and movement Stability	Soils in the environment
Quebec	*Curriculum combines some topics for cycle 2 and 3 (Grade 3–4/Grade 5–6), so specific topics are not easily listed*		
Atlantic provinces	Plant growth and changes	Invisible forces Materials and structures	Exploring soils
Yukon	*See British Columbia Program of Studies*		
Northwest Territories	Growth and changes in plants	Magnetic and charged materials Forces and movement Stability	Soils in the environment
Nunavut	Refers to curriculum documents of other provinces: "The following curriculum and resources have been produced in Nunavut or have been adopted from other jurisdictions including Northwest Territories, Alberta, Saskatchewan, and Manitoba. All of these resources form the foundation of educational programs in Nunavut." (Nunavut Department of Education, 2010)		

TABLE 3.3 Curricular Time Allocations in Saskatchewan

Area of Study	Required Minutes per Week
Language Arts	560
Mathematics	210
Science	150
Social Studies	150
Health Education	80
Arts Education	200
Physical Education	150
TOTAL	**1,500 minutes**

*Time for locally determined options may be gained by reducing areas of study by no more than 20% in any area. This creates a maximum of 300 minutes per week for locally determined options.

Source: Saskatchewan Ministry of Education, 2011.

between language arts and fine arts curricula. In inquiry-based units, several subjects may be integrated to develop a well-rounded perspective on the inquiry topic.

Curriculum implementation is also influenced by various groups, particularly those who develop supporting resources. Physical and Health Education Canada provides resources for teachers to promote effective teaching of fundamental movement skills and the promotion of "quality daily physical education." Textbook publishers often use the concepts in provincial curricula to develop new texts. In fact, some texts will note directly that it is the "Ontario edition" to show alignment with the Ontario curriculum, or Western, Northern, or Atlantic provinces editions. Since some teachers adhere closely to textbooks, these texts can have a significant impact on how the curriculum is received by students. Often the provincial ministries will develop supporting resources such as Learn Alberta or the Ontario Curriculum Unit Planner that align with the local curriculum and are accessible only to teachers in that province. For example, the Grade 3 social studies curriculum in Alberta requires students to "demonstrate an understanding and appreciation of how geographic, social, cultural and linguistic factors affect quality of life in communities in India, Tunisia, Ukraine and Peru" (Alberta Education, 2005a, p. 3). Since it can be difficult to find readable texts about these countries for Grade 3 students, the Learn Alberta site provides a helpful series of video clips that follow a Peruvian child on a tour of her country. Organizations like Science World British Columbia or local art galleries also provide teachers with lesson ideas and resources to support the provincial curriculum.

Curriculum Planning

To the layperson, curriculum is simply what is taught in schools. Everyday people are mostly unaware of the knowledge, planning, and analysis of curricula that are the basis for expert teacher practice. Without an understanding of the importance of curriculum design and planning, teaching would remain a mystery, even to educators. Darling-Hammond and colleagues (2005) define *curriculum planning* as the learning experiences and goals that teachers develop for their classes in light of the characteristics of students and the teaching context. According to these researchers, an emphasis on the social contexts and purposes of education within curricular planning is important for three critical reasons: First, the preparation of a citizenry for life in a democracy must be considered as a foundation for decision making about what is taught and how it is taught; second, successful learning is closely tied to the social contexts of learning environments, including the school, the classroom, and the community; and third, teachers need to be aware of policies so they can advocate for parents, children, and conditions that allow their work to be successful (p. 171). Further, Darling-Hammond and colleagues outline the three interrelated elements of the curricular planning process:

1. *Educational purpose* is a conception of what is important to study based on social needs and expectations, learning standards, and research and how these broad goals can be translated into more discrete objectives that can guide particular lessons and units of study.
2. *Learning experiences*, systematically selected and organized into what is often called a "scope and sequence," refers to the kinds of information, demonstrations, models, inquiry opportunities, discussion, and practice students need to acquire the requisite knowledge and skills.
3. *Evaluation* is the collection and analysis of student academic performance data to provide feedback about the effectiveness of teaching and learning relative to the desired curricular objectives.

In commenting on all of the above relative to beginning teachers, Darling-Hammond and colleagues strongly indicated that "this kind of analysis is a good start toward the ability to thoughtfully steer a classroom and to discuss curriculum improvements needed within a school" (p. 200).

Across Canada, teachers often decide what to teach by adhering to the top-down approach depicted in Figure 3.1. This approach includes (a) determining the curriculum for the year and for each term, (b) breaking the curriculum down into units that extend over several weeks, and (c) determining what will be taught on a daily basis.

To conceptualize an entire year's worth or term's worth of instruction, teachers make extensive use of the various curriculum guides produced by their provincial/territorial Ministry of Education. Once educators have these guides in hand, they divide the year or the terms of the year into large units of instruction that are centred on topically related themes

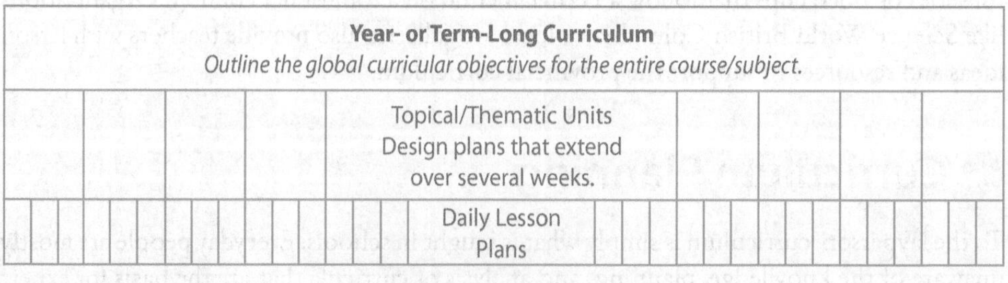

Year- or Term-Long Curriculum
Outline the global curricular objectives for the entire course/subject.

Topical/Thematic Units
Design plans that extend over several weeks.

Daily Lesson Plans

FIGURE 3.1 Curriculum Planning Template

or clusters of educational outcomes or learning objectives. Typically a unit of instruction should encompass at least one week's worth of teaching. On the other hand, some units will extend over several weeks because of a teacher's desire to incorporate more or broader issues related to the topic being taught. It is also a good idea to leave at least a little room in each of these units for unexpected circumstances that arise, like breaking news stories related to the topic or the sudden availability of a guest speaker whose particular expertise will expand upon the information provided in the unit.

The main objective at the beginning of the planning process is to establish and visualize "the big picture" for all of your teaching and to determine the basic sequencing of all topics. This can be accomplished by using the sequences and thematic units suggested in the curriculum guides, by modifying other units to suit your teaching preferences, or by designing completely new and different units based on your knowledge about your students and the community and region you live in. Throughout this process, we suggest you tentatively label your units as they occur to you. Then, when the time comes to narrowing your units down into daily lessons, follow these two rules that have been consistently proven for designing lesson plans:

1. The purpose of each lesson will be clear.
2. The theme or essence of each lesson will be flexible enough to accommodate interruptions or teachable moments.

The Role of Objectives and Outcomes in Curriculum Planning

Many beginning teachers feel that the actual act of teaching is the most important thing they have to accomplish. More experienced teachers, however, come to understand that next to reflective practice (see Chapter 1), the most important element of teaching is planning. Good planning results in excellent teaching, enhanced student learning, and exemplary environments within which effective teaching and learning can take place. In teaching, the opposite of good planning is not poor planning—it is not planning at all. Poor planning may result in occasional mistakes and setbacks, but not doing any planning will certainly result in teaching that is vague and directionless, students who do not learn despite their best efforts, and classrooms that lack predictability, structure, and routine. To this end, good instructional planning involves a careful and simultaneous consideration of the following questions:

1. What educational purposes should schools seek to attain? (objectives)
2. What educational experiences can be provided that are likely to attain these purposes? (design)
3. How can these educational experiences be effectively organized? (scope and sequence)
4. How can we determine whether these purposes are attained? (evaluation) (Tyler, 1949, p. 1)

These questions are quoted from Ralph Tyler, whose book *Basic Principles of Curriculum Instruction* is still widely available and often cited more than 60 years after it was first published in 1949. Tyler is sometimes associated with the social efficiency ideology and with an overly simplistic and technical conception of curriculum. Nevertheless, it is perhaps the simplicity of his principles that makes them continue to be so useful today. Many Canadian curriculum documents draw at least generally on these principles, and the Ontario Curriculum Unit Planner cites Tyler directly. When thoughtfully applied, these principles give teachers a clear sense of direction for curriculum planning. Later in this chapter we will examine a curricular planning approach called "backward design." It draws on Tyler's principles and sensibly applies them in a way that focuses on "big ideas" rather than discrete and narrow behavioural objectives.

For several decades, curriculum developers focused mainly on behavioural objectives. Teacher education programs required lesson plan objectives to be prefaced with the acronym SWBAT ("Students will be able to . . .") because objectives are intended to identify something specific and observable that students are able to do at the end of the lesson or unit. Behavioural objectives, at least traditionally, need to be precise and clear, avoiding vague terms like "understand," "introduce," or "appreciate," and they need to refer to specific content that students are able to identify, describe, analyze, or whatever verb the action might take. Typically a behavioural objective should identify a criterion—at what level of success should the student be able to perform the required action? Must students be able to identify five different triggers for the Renaissance, or is one trigger adequate?

Behavioural objectives became common in the early 1900s at a time when schools were seeking the advice of industry to address perceived deficits in school achievement. A new piece of machinery will usually repeat its performance with little variation, but the problem with behavioural objectives is that schools, students, and teachers include so many variables that are not nearly as predictable as the materials of industry. It is not that one cannot judge aesthetic qualities in a student's artwork, personal voice in writing, or skilful argumentation in a debate, but these qualities must be assessed using various criteria and professional judgment, not the "mechanical application of prespecified standards" (Eisner, 2002, p. 115). Furthermore, not every educational activity has a clear objective; exploration and play can yield unexpected results. Eisner argues that in some cases, what a teacher might aim for is a problem-solving objective: "how deterrents to smoking might be made more effective, or how to design a paper structure that will hold two bricks 16 inches above a table, or how the variety and quality of food served in the school cafeteria could be increased within the existing budget" (p. 116). The problems and criteria are clear, but solutions may vary. Unlike a behavioural objective that typically elicits homogenous responses, a problem-solving objective may yield solutions that surprise the teacher and students:

> The use of problem-solving objectives places a premium on cognitive flexibility, on intellectual exploration, on the higher mental processes. It tends towards the formulation of curriculum activities that are likely to be taken seriously by scholars. . . . It is reasonable to expect that when students have a set of clear criteria and are free to meet those criteria in ways that require ingenuity, they will take a deeper interest in coping with the problem. (Eisner, 2002, p. 118)

While some topics lend themselves well to behavioural objectives, others do not. For example, students "must be able to swim four laps of the pool in order to be able to swim in the deep end" (p. 116) is a perfectly appropriate behavioural objective, but other learning tasks are not so easily quantified. How does one quantify how effectively a student in Grade 5 can "assess peer influence and demonstrate a readiness to prevent and/or avoid potentially dangerous situations involving peer pressure (including lying, substance use, and bullying)" (Saskatchewan Ministry of Education, n.d.)? As you read the curriculum outcomes in your provincial documents, consider how they use behavioural language to add clarity and specificity, but also how they capture problem-solving outcomes that are more open ended and invite varied responses.

Eisner also notes that teachers tend to hold implicit objectives in mind all the time. When helping a frustrated student solve a mathematical problem, a teacher may recognize that the more important issue at the moment is not the mathematics but the frustration that is making the student so agitated. To foster a positive attitude toward learning, the teacher may decide this is the perfect time to send that student on an errand to the office to provide a mental break. The mathematical objective may not be achieved that morning, but some of the less tangible educational outcomes may take priority for the time being.

At any moment in any day, teachers should be able to relate what is happening in their classroom to the broader objectives of the curriculum and to the overall philosophy of education espoused by their school board (or province or territory). Teachers are likely to open a curriculum document and turn directly to the outcomes because this lists the specific content they must be sure to address. However, the front matter of many curriculum documents gives an interesting perspective on how the specific outcomes are related to the broader purposes of the curriculum. It is easy to get bogged down in the minutia of content, but these front pages may help you to look more philosophically at why the subject matters. Figure 3.2 demonstrates the range of objectives from broad to specific.

In this process, society decides on the overall purpose of education (*Philosophical Objectives*) and the government of the day is charged with designing curriculum guides that outline the various topics to be taught/learned in order to properly educate a member of society (*Global Curricular Objectives*). Teachers break curricula down into large manageable units of instruction (*Broad Learning Objectives*) and then into daily lesson plans

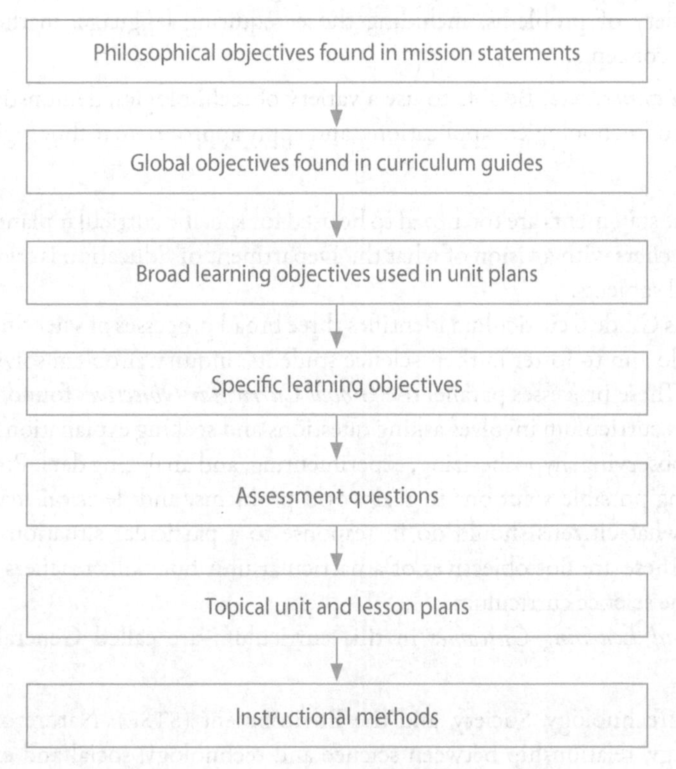

FIGURE 3.2 The Common Thread of Learning Objectives

(*Specific Learning Objectives*) and assessment questions. As you can see, the complexity and broader application of a specific learning objective builds from the bottom upward. The skills, knowledge, and dispositions contained in each level are embedded within successive higher levels. In this way, every one of your daily lessons will be hierarchically connected by a coherent thread of continuity.

Varied Levels of Objectives

To illustrate how this range of objectives is evident in a curriculum document, let's examine the *Atlantic Canada Science Curriculum* (Nova Scotia Department of Education, 2008) for Grade 6 (you may notice that the term *objective,* which is used throughout this textbook, may be replaced with the term *outcome* in your curriculum documents, but the intent is similar). The parallel term to *Philosophical Objective* in this curriculum is the Essential Graduation Learnings expected of all high school graduates:

- *Aesthetic expression*: Respond with critical awareness to various forms of the arts and be able to express themselves through the arts.
- *Citizenship*: Assess social, cultural, economic, and environmental interdependence in a local and global context.
- *Communication*: Use the listening, viewing, speaking, reading, and writing modes of language(s), as well as mathematical and scientific concepts and symbols, to think, learn, and communicate effectively.
- *Personal development*: Be able to continue to learn and to pursue an active, healthy lifestyle.
- *Problem solving*: Be able to use the strategies and processes needed to solve a wide variety of problems, including those requiring language, mathematical, and scientific concepts.
- *Technical competence*: Be able to use a variety of technologies, demonstrate an understanding of technological applications, and apply appropriate technologies for solving problems.

These outcome statements are too broad to be used for specific curricular planning, but they do provide teachers with a vision of what the Department of Education is trying to achieve throughout all subjects.

Next, this Grade 6 curriculum identifies three broad processes of scientific literacy that teachers should aim to foster in their science students: inquiry, problem solving, and decision making. These processes parallel the *Global Curricular Objectives* found in Figure 3.2. Inquiry in this curriculum involves asking questions and seeking explanations and requires skills such as observing, hypothesizing, experimenting, and analyzing data. Problem solving involves testing possible solutions to real-world problems, and decision making involves determining what citizens should do in response to a particular situation (e.g., overuse of landfills). These are not objectives of a particular unit but skills teachers aim to foster throughout the science curriculum.

The *Broad Learning Outcomes* in this curriculum are called General Curriculum Outcomes:

- Science, Technology, Society, and the Environment (STSE): Nature of science and technology, relationship between science and technology, social and environmental contexts of science and technology

- Skills: Initiating and planning, performing and recording, analyzing and interpreting, communication and teamwork
- Knowledge: Life science, physical science, Earth and space science
- Attitudes: Appreciation of science, interest in science, science inquiry, collaboration, stewardship, and safety

Finally, there are the *Specific Learning Objectives* related to each grade level grouped under the first three general outcomes (attitude outcomes are not listed for specific units; rather they are written for the end of Grades 3, 6, 9, and 12 and are meant to help teachers foster positive attitudes to science). The curriculum organizes the content in four columns:

Outcomes	Suggestions for Learning and Teaching	Suggestions	Resources
100s—STSE outcomes 200s—Skill outcomes 300s—Knowledge outcomes		Including formal or informal observation, performance assessment, journals, interviews, presentations, portfolios	

In a microorganisms unit, you will find knowledge and skill outcomes combined in this outcome: "Identify and use correctly appropriate tools to examine and describe some living things that cannot be seen with the naked eye (204-8, 300-19)" and an STSE outcome such as this one: "Describe products and techniques that can be used at home to protect against unwanted microorganism growth (107-1)." STSE outcomes are important for recognizing the relevance of the knowledge and skills to everyday life. To cycle back to the philosophical purpose of education as described earlier in this chapter, the specific learning outcomes of science have to be framed by the larger aims of schooling: Students who prevent unwanted microorganism growth are demonstrating technical competence and citizenship, which are essential outcomes for all graduates.

While the language of the curriculum is supposedly neutral, it is important to note that a government document is never apolitical and inevitably privileges some content and some perspectives over others. Similarly the work of teachers is also political—your own ideological commitments and teaching philosophy will influence what you emphasize, how you present the ideas, and the values you implicitly communicate. A teacher who has only a nominal commitment to environmental issues will design learning experiences much differently than a teacher who is passionate about such issues and energizes her students with her commitment.

Backward Design in Curriculum Planning

In *Understanding by Design*, a seminal book on curriculum planning, Grant Wiggins and Jay McTighe (2005) describe the concept of **backward design**: designing learning experiences by first selecting the aims or outcomes you wish to achieve. All too often, curriculum planning is undermined by the "twin sins" of activity-based planning or coverage-based planning. In activity-based planning, teachers plan activities that seem engaging and interesting

backward design
A curriculum planning strategy where learning experiences are designed first by selecting the aims or outcomes teachers wish to achieve.

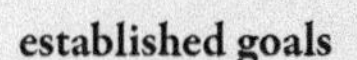

and have the potential to result in learning, but there is no explicit articulation of the understandings that learners will gain or how they will demonstrate this understanding. Teachers who commit the second sin, coverage-based curriculum planning, are so concerned with covering each curriculum objective, particularly when constrained by provincial exams, that they do so with insufficient depth to achieve genuine understanding. The former sin is more typical of elementary teachers and the latter of middle and high school teachers, but both groups could fall into the same pitfalls.

To avoid these pitfalls, Wiggins and McTighe present a three-stage curriculum planning template (see Figure 3.3). Curriculum planning should begin at Stage 1 with the **established goals**, which typically refer to the broad curriculum outcomes, often called general learning outcomes in Canadian curricula. It is important that these big picture priorities guide the planning process so the teacher does not immediately get lost in the minutia of specific objectives or outcomes. Next, they suggest teachers consider the **enduring understandings** and **essential questions**. While these might seem redundant with the previously stated curriculum outcomes, it is important to consider that these "big ideas" connect the facts and questions that require inquiry to be deeply understood:

established goals
In curriculum planning, these are typically the broad curriculum outcomes—the "big picture" priorities that should guide the planning process.

enduring understandings
Ideas that are key for the discipline and have significance beyond the classroom.

essential questions
Broad, timeless questions that bring relevance and depth to curriculum.

> Indeed, the greatest defect in teacher lesson plans and syllabi . . . is that the key intellectual priorities—deep understandings of transferable big ideas, and competence at core performance tasks—are falling through the cracks of lessons, units, and courses devoted to developing thousands of discrete elements of knowledge and skill, unprioritized and unconnected. (p. 58)

For example, the essential questions in a nutrition unit might ask students to consider why so many people eat poorly despite an abundance of healthy food options and information about how to eat well (see Figure 3.4). Enduring understandings include the importance of eating well for one's own physical and mental health and the struggle involved in making good choices—the learning teachers hope will last. These are understandings and questions of genuine inquiry, not those that have a simple correct answer.

Next, Wiggins and McTighe suggest teachers should identify the specific *knowledge* and *skills* students need to acquire; in many cases Canadian curricula also identify *attitudes* or *values*. These are more specific than the established goals. In a nutrition unit, these might include knowledge of key terms such as *protein*, *fat*, and *carbohydrate*, and skills such as the ability to analyze food labels or meal plans for nutritional value.

In Stage 2, the teacher identifies the assessments or performance tasks that will help the students provide evidence that they understand and have achieved the identified knowledge and skills. Unlike the typical curriculum planning model, in which teachers plan learning experiences, teach lessons, and then try to discern what the students have learned from those learning experiences after the fact, backward design asks, "What do I expect students to learn and how can the performance task provide evidence of that learning?" For example, students might create a menu for an outdoor school activity and demonstrate that it meets all the requirements of the Canada Food Guide. A rubric that identifies each of the key understandings that should be evident in the menu helps illustrate how students have succeeded or achieved the understandings. Other evidence of student learning might include journal reflections, observations, quizzes, and other artifacts that indicate understanding.

Finally, in Stage 3 the teacher identifies the learning experiences and conditions that will allow students to achieve the desired results. This includes the smaller learning tasks that prepare students for the performance tasks identified in Stage 2 (see Figure 3.3). An

Stage 1: Desired Results

Established Goals: What relevant goals (e.g., content standards, course or program objectives, learning outcomes) will this design address?

Understandings: Students will understand that . . .

- What are the big ideas?
- What specific understandings about the big ideas are desired?
- What misunderstandings are predictable?

Essential Questions:

- What provocative questions will foster inquiry, understanding, and transfer of learning?

Students will know . . .

Students will be able to . . .

- What key knowledge and skills will students acquire as a result of this unit?
- What should they eventually be able to do as a result of such knowledge and skills?

Stage 2: Assessment Evidence

Performance Tasks

Through what authentic performance tasks will students demonstrate the desired understandings?

By what criteria will performance of understanding be judged?

Other Evidence

Through what other evidence (e.g., quizzes, tests, academic prompts, observations, homework, journals) will students demonstrate achievement of the desired results?

How will students reflect upon and self-assess their learning?

Stage 3: Learning Plan

Learning Activities: What learning experiences and instruction will enable students to achieve the desired results? How will the design accomplish the WHERETO:

W = Help the students know **W**here the unit is going and **W**hat is expected; help the teacher know **W**here the students are coming from (prior knowledge, interests)

H = **H**ook all students and **H**old their interest

E = **E**quip students, help them **E**xperience the key ideas and **E**xplore the issues

R = Provide opportunities to **R**ethink and **R**evise their understandings and work

E = Allow students to **E**valuate their work and its implications

T = Be **T**ailored (personalized) to the different needs, interests, and abilities of learners

O = Be **O**rganized to maximize initial and sustained engagement as well as effective learning

Source: Wiggins & McTighe, 2005.

FIGURE 3.3 Planning Template with Design Questions for Teachers

Stage 1: Identify Desired Results

Established Goals: *Students will make responsible and informed choices to maintain health and to promote safety for self and others. (W–6)*

What enduring understandings are desired?

Students will understand that . . .

- A balanced diet contributes to physical and mental health
- The Canada Food Guide presents relative guidelines for nutrition
- Dietary requirements vary for individuals based on age, activity level, weight, and overall health
- Healthy living requires an individual to act on available information about good nutrition, even if it means breaking comfortable habits

What essential questions will be considered?

- What is healthy eating?
- Are you a healthy eater? How would you know?
- Why are there so many health problems caused by poor nutrition despite all the available information?

What key *knowledge or skills* will students acquire as a result of this unit?

W–6.5 Students will analyze personal eating behaviours—food and fluids—in a variety of settings (e.g., home, school, restaurants).

These may include more specifics, such as those identified by Wiggins and McTighe:

- Key terms: protein, fat, calorie, carbohydrate, cholesterol
- Types of foods in each food group and their nutritional values
- The Canada Food Guide
- Variables influencing nutritional needs
- General health problems caused by poor nutrition

What key *attitudes* will students develop as a result of this unit?

W–6.1 Students will evaluate the need for balance and variety in daily activities that promote health (e.g., physical activity, relaxation, learning, sleep, reflection)

Stage 2: Determine Acceptable Evidence

Healthy Retreat Plan: Students will demonstrate knowledge of nutritious meals and healthy lifestyle factors and how to balance these factors in a planned program that reflects informed, healthy choices. Students design a two-day program. This program can take the form of a weekend retreat, winter or spring break program, outdoor school or in-school fun day. The program should have a theme and address nutritional, physical, social, and cognitive issues, and it should consider the safety of the participants. Students will create a schedule with times and events outlining the activities for participants. The schedules must include the menus for the balanced meals/snacks. Students become "health program consultants" to create a program for an audience of peers, parents, home and school association members, or community groups.

Promoting the Healthy Retreat: Students create promotional materials in a visual format to describe the program they have developed and to "sell" the plan to their peers, parents, teachers, and community. This presentation can be a poster, brochure, flyer, commercial, or HyperStudio or PowerPoint presentation. For this activity, students add "marketing experts" to their role as "health program consultants" to sell their program to an audience of peers, parents, home and school association members, or community groups.

What other evidence needs to be collected in light of the Stage 1 desired results?

- Quiz: The food groups and *Canada's Food Guide*
- Prompt: Describe two health problems that could arise as a result of poor nutrition and explain how these could be avoided.
- Skill Check: Interpret nutritional information on food labels.

FIGURE 3.4 Completed Planning Template for Grade 6 Health Unit

Student self-assessment and reflection

- Self-assess the Healthy Retreat Plan and Promotion brochure
- Reflect on the extent to which you eat healthfully at the end of unit (compared with the beginning)

Stage 3: Plan Learning Experiences

What sequence of teaching and learning experiences will equip students to engage with, develop, and demonstrate the desired understandings? Use the following sheet to list the key teaching and learning activities in sequence. Code each entry with the appropriate initials of the WHERETO elements.

1. Begin with an entry question (Can the foods you eat cause acne?) to hook students into considering the effects of nutrition on their lives. **H**
2. Introduce the essential questions and discuss the culminating unit performance tasks. **W**

Note: Key vocabulary terms are introduced as needed by the various learning activities and performance tasks. Students read and discuss relevant selections from the health textbook to support the learning activities and tasks. As an ongoing activity, students keep a chart of their daily eating and drinking for later review and evaluation. **E**

Introduce the Canada Food Guide and identify foods in each group. Students work in groups to develop a poster of the Food Guide containing cut-out pictures of foods in each group. Display the posters in the classroom or hallway. **E**

Give quiz on the food groups (matching format). **E**

Review and discuss a nutrition brochure. Discussion question: Must everyone follow the same diet to be healthy? **R**

Working in co-operative groups, students analyze a hypothetical family's diet (deliberately unbalanced) and make recommendations for improved nutrition. Teacher observes and coaches students as they work. **E-2, T**

Have groups share their diet analyses and discuss as a class. **E, E-2** (Note: Teacher collects and reviews the diet analyses to look for misunderstandings needing instructional attention.)

Each group designs a meal plan for an outdoor school activity. **E, T**

Students exchange meal plans with other groups for a peer assessment based on a criteria list. Allow students to make revisions based on feedback. **E**

Show and discuss the video "Nutrition and You." Discuss the health problems linked to poor eating. **E**

Students listen to and question a guest speaker (e.g., a nutritionist from the local hospital) about health problems caused by poor nutrition. **E**

Students respond to written prompt: Describe two health problems that could arise as a result of poor nutrition and explain what changes in eating could help to avoid them. (These are collected and graded by the teacher.) **E-2**

Teacher models how to read and interpret food label information on nutritional values. Then have students practise using donated boxes, cans, and bottles (empty!). **E**

At the conclusion of the unit, students review their completed daily eating chart and self-assess the healthfulness of their eating. Have they noticed changes? Improvements? Do they notice changes in how they feel and their appearance? **E-2**

Students develop a personal "eating action plan" for healthy eating. These are saved and presented at upcoming student-involved parent conferences. **E-2, T**

Conclude the unit with student self-evaluation regarding their personal eating habits. Have each student develop a personal action plan for their "healthy eating" goal. **E-2, T**

Source: Adapted from Wiggins and McTighe, 2005; Alberta Assessment Consortium, 2012.

FIGURE 3.4 *continued*

acronym that is used for the design elements to help teachers set students up for success is WHERETO. It includes how teachers ensure students know the expectations, engage the learners and support them in developing the skills needed to fully engage with the projects, build metacognitive self-assessment skills, and differentiate instruction to meet the needs of all learners, including those who cannot engage in the performance tasks without support (see Stage 3 in Figure 3.3). Figure 3.4 provides an example of a completed planning template.

The backward design template encourages teachers and curriculum planners to first "think like an assessor" before designing specific units and lessons, and thus to consider up front how they will determine if students have attained the desired understandings.

Wiggins and McTighe's fictional teacher who is planning this nutrition unit expressed some uneasiness as he reflected on his prior experience teaching nutrition. He described how a typical three- to four-week unit might include a project, one or two quizzes, and an end-of-unit test. However, he wondered if the previous grades really reflected students' understanding of the important ideas or just their efforts at memorization. He also worried that he was using assessments for grading and not really to track and improve learning. The goal of performance assessments is for students to demonstrate deep understanding of the big ideas of the unit; this teacher now feels more confident that the new task of designing a nutritious menu will require students to demonstrate what he really wanted them to learn from the unit, and there will be opportunities for formative assessment during the task completion.

Selecting Curriculum Priorities

In discerning content priorities, Wiggins and McTighe (2005) remind us that there is a range of possibilities (see Figure 3.5). They suggest that the centre, the big ideas framed as understandings and core tasks, should be the most important priorities. While the first two priorities, those ideas that are "worth being familiar with" and those that are "important to know and to do" may be assessed through traditional paper-and-pencil tasks, the big ideas and core tasks typically require a performance task or project to discern deep understanding of these concepts.

Let's consider an example from the British Columbia social studies curriculum for Grade 8, where students are asked to examine the society and cultures of civilizations from 500–1600. Prescribed learning outcomes include the following:

- Identify periods of significant cultural achievement, including the Renaissance
- Describe how societies preserve identity, transmit culture, and adapt to change (British Columbia Ministry of Education, 1997, p. 14)

Given these outcomes, teachers might decide it would be *worthwhile* to be familiar with key figures and their accomplishments during the Renaissance, such as Leonardo da Vinci and Michelangelo. It would be *important* to be able to analyze what social factors came together to create the conditions for the Renaissance. For example, preceding and during the Renaissance, classical Greek texts were reintroduced creating a new excitement for scholarship, a growing group of artisans were able to escape the tyranny of feudalism and make their living independently, and increasing trade meant a broader sharing of ideas. But most importantly, teachers should help students understand *big ideas* such as how societies shift given particular social contexts. To show the relevance of these big ideas in today's society, one group of teachers invited students to respond to the question, "Does our

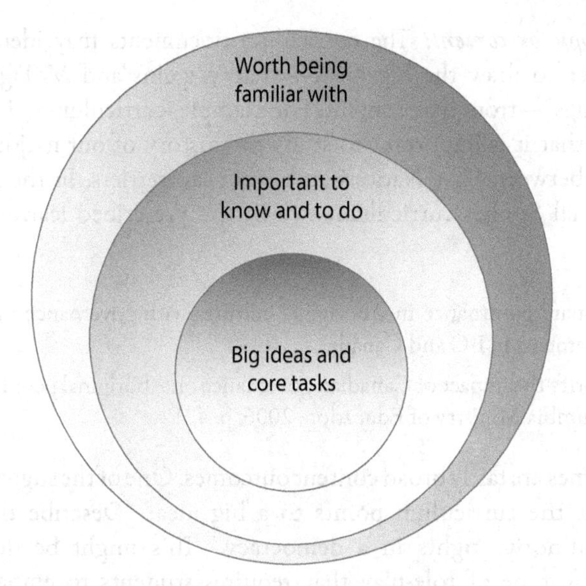

FIGURE 3.5 Content Priorities
Source: Adapted from Wiggins & McTighe, 2005.

city have the necessary conditions to be a Renaissance city?" The students' first core task included doing some research on one aspect of the Renaissance (education, science, arts, and other topics) displayed in iMovie format. Local experts in those fields were invited to view the student presentations and comment on how those particular conditions exist in their city today. Students then used their research and the expert comments to debate the question, "Does our city have the conditions to become a Renaissance city?" (For more information, see Connect! 2011a.) The initial report, something that many Grade 8 classes might complete, focuses on the outer two circles—ideas that are worth knowing and some analytical skills to analyze the impact of social changes. However, to deeply understand the big idea—how societies shift in different social contexts—students needed to see the relevance of the Renaissance concepts in their own modern-day community. This type of performance task surely helped the students achieve a much deeper understanding of the big ideas.

Wiggins and McTighe (2005) suggest that curriculum design may emerge from one of several starting points, but for each you must discern how a backward design process ensures you do not fall into the previously mentioned traps of "coverage" or "activity":

1. *Provincial curriculum:* Clearly this is the most obvious starting point because you are obliged to address these outcomes in your teaching. However, your task is to discern the big ideas that should animate a unit using the prescribed content. As the backward design template illustrates, you must focus on what you want students to learn, not the content you must cover.
2. *A significant test:* In some provinces, students must write an exam based on the provincial curriculum at various grade levels. If the test is well designed, it seeks some type of transferability and deep understanding. Although you need to help students develop familiarity with the test format, the performance tasks you set will ultimately create deeper understanding than will "teaching to the test." The issue of tests constraining curriculum implementation will be addressed later in this chapter.

3. *Important topic or content:* The curriculum documents may identify content, but you may have to draw the big ideas—what Wiggins and McTighe call "enduring understandings"—from that content. For example, curriculum writers across Canada have agreed that it is important to study the history of our nation, particularly the interactions between First Nations and European settlers. In the British Columbia Grade 4 Social Studies curriculum, two of the prescribed learning outcomes read as follows:

   C1 compare governance in Aboriginal cultures with governance in early European settlements in BC and Canada

   C2 identify the impact of Canadian governance on Aboriginal people's rights (British Columbia Ministry of Education, 2006, p. 42)

   These outcomes are fairly broad content outcomes. One of the suggested achievement indicators in the curriculum points to a big idea: "Describe the importance of protecting minority rights in a democracy." This might be deeply understood through some type of role-play that requires students to empathize with other perspectives. The content itself may at first seem to point to simple knowledge and facts, but careful reflection should draw out the larger and more important ideas related to those facts.
4. *A key text or resource:* As an English teacher, you might well argue that Shakespeare's plays are critical texts for inclusion in the high school curriculum and, in fact, you will likely be required to teach Shakespeare. Backward design ensures that you not only "cover" the plays but that you also help students genuinely understand the universal themes and their modern-day relevance (e.g., ambition, corruption, social class), perhaps by retelling the story in some alternative format that illuminates these themes.
5. *A favourite activity or unit:* Perhaps you were excited by the student engagement and learning you witnessed in your practicum when Grade 1 students used puppets to retell their favourite fairy tales. This may be an excellent learning experience, but you must clearly identify the understanding, skills, and big ideas that you hope to observe during the puppet play. Clarity about your goals will help you intervene where necessary to support those who are not showing the level of skill or understanding you hope for (see the Case Study below for discussion).
6. *An important skill or process:* Jardine, Friesen, and Clifford (2006) tell the story of a student teacher who was perusing resources to discern how best to teach Grade 6 math students about percentage until he remembered that he ought to instead consider some "essential questions": "What *is* percentage? How did we come to have such a topic in our world? Why would we want to pass along such a topic to our students? . . . What are the sorts of questions in the lives of students for which percentages might be the answer?" (pp. 207–208). These questions do not tell the end of the story, which was the learning activities that responded to these questions. However, countless student questions and survey possibilities come to mind (e.g., "What percentage of parents, students, and teachers favour school uniforms?"). The skills become relevant when students see them addressing their own questions.

CASE STUDY

A Learning Experience Guided by Specific Learning Objectives

Hannah was exhilarated as she considered her Grade 1 class at play with their puppets. The students had been buzzing with excitement and were genuinely engaged in preparing their plays. As she gathered the students to watch the last group's play, *The Three Little Pigs*, she glanced at her clipboard with the four key learning objectives she wanted to reinforce through this activity:

- Demonstrating Understanding 1.4: Demonstrate an understanding of the information and ideas in oral texts by retelling the story or restating the information, including the main idea.
- Extending Understanding 1.6: Extend understanding of oral texts by connecting the ideas in them to their own knowledge and experience; to other familiar texts, including print and visual texts; and to the world around them.
- Point of View 1.8: Begin to identify, with support and direction, who is speaking in an oral text and the point of view expressed by the speaker.
- Presentation Strategies 1.9: Begin to identify some of the presentation strategies used in oral texts and explain how they influence the audience (Ontario Ministry of Education, 2006, pp. 36–37).

After the last play, the four Grade 1 students stepped from behind the puppet theatre to the sounds of their classmates' applause.

Hannah: Okay, Grade 1s. Two stars and a wish. Tell this group two things you liked and one suggestion to make their puppet play even better.

Sean: I liked the deep voice Justin used for the wolf.

Hannah: I agree. It was really scary with that deep growly sound!

Samira: I thought it was funny when the three little pigs all talked at the same time and said "Not by the hair of our chinny-chin-chins."

Hannah: I wonder if pigs really do have hairy chins. Does anyone know?

Cassidy: Yes, my grandma has pigs at her farm and they look like they have little white fluffs by their chin.

Hannah: Any wishes? Something that would make the puppet play even better?

David: I know the first little pig is supposed to be little, but when his voice is too little and squeaky we can't hear what he's saying.

Hannah: Can you show us how you could make a pig voice that is loud and clear but still sounds like a little pig's character?

David: (in a clear, loud, but high-pitched voice) Not by the hair of my chinny-chin-chin.

Hannah: Could you hear his words clearly Grade 1s?

Class: Yes!

Hannah: Very nice. I agree that the voices were easy to hear even though we couldn't see your mouths. Thank you for using such big strong voices. I also thought you did a very nice job of using voices that matched your characters. Justin, what's the lesson we learn from *The Three Little Pigs*?

Justin: I think it's that you should do things good and not sloppy. The first two pigs didn't build good houses and then the wolf just blew them down.

Hannah: Sometimes when I'm sloppy with my work I can't find things I need later,

continued

like your stories that we want to put in your portfolios for your family to see. Now, I want all of you to think about your group's fable. Do you see any ways in which this story is like the story your group shared with us?

Ashton: They have talking animals. In ours the wolf talks to Grandma and Little Red Riding Hood.

Hannah: Great noticing. Lots of fables have talking animals. Other similarities?

Karim: The wolf is the bad guy.

Hannah: Ah, yes. The wolf in *Little Red Riding Hood* is also trying to eat the characters. Andrew, is there a villain or "bad guy" in your story?

Andrew: Um, I don't really know.

Hannah: You're doing *Goldilocks and the Three Bears*, right? Why did the bears get angry?

Andrew: Because Goldilocks ate their porridge and broke the chair and slept in their beds.

Hannah: What do the rest of you think? Do you think Goldilocks was trying to hurt the bears like the wolf was trying to hurt the pigs?

Navneet: I don't think she meant to hurt the bears. I think she was just being snoopy but when they got mad then she knew she shouldn't have snuck into their house.

Hannah: Navneet, I think you're doing some good thinking. She didn't intend to harm them the way the wolf did, so it's a bit different isn't it?

If each group had simply performed their puppet play with their classmates' applause and little discussion, this experience could possibly have been criticized for being "activity based." Surely the children would have learned something from the activity, but the discussion Hannah led ensured that they actually achieved the outcomes she had in mind. What else might you have said or done to help the students achieve the outcomes listed above?

Deep Understanding and Transfer

The title *Understanding by Design* (Wiggins & McTighe, 2005) suggests two key features of curriculum planning: that teachers are designers of learning experiences and the learning experiences aim to foster deep understanding of important ideas. Having considered how curriculum is designed by teachers, let's now consider the importance of designing for deep understanding.

Cognitive science has taught us much in the past 20 years about how people learn (Bransford, Brown, & Cocking, 2000). First, students come to school with misconceptions, which often persist despite teachers' best efforts to teach those concepts. In a video filmed at a Harvard University commencement, students were asked, "Why do we have seasons?" Despite graduating from one of the most prestigious universities in North America, their explanations revealed that they still held the same misconception—that Earth is closer to the sun in the summer—their grade school teachers surely tried to correct when they studied seasons as part of the elementary science curriculum. They failed to truly understand that seasons result from the tilt of the Earth's axis (away from the sun in the winter and toward the sun in the summer). This reveals why curriculum "coverage" can be so counterproductive if it delivers the content without attention to the students' prior knowledge and misunderstandings. Instead, Wiggins and McTighe suggest curriculum "uncoverage":

- Uncovering students' potential misunderstandings (through focused questions, feedback, diagnostic assessment)

- Uncovering the questions, issues, assumptions, and grey areas lurking underneath the black and white of surface accounts
- Uncovering the core ideas at the heart of understanding a subject, ideas that are not obvious—and perhaps are counterintuitive or baffling—to the novice (2005, p. 46)

In a meta-analysis of over 800 studies relating to student achievement, Hattie (2012) ranked the most powerful influences on student achievement and highlights here the critical importance of understanding students' misunderstandings:

meta-analysis
An overview of existing research on a topic.

> The act of teaching requires that there is cognitive change in the student; thus the key ingredients are being aware of the learning intentions, knowing when a student is successful in attaining those intentions, having sufficient understanding of the student's prior understanding as he or she comes to the task, and knowing enough about the content to provide meaningful and challenging experiences so there is some sort of progressive development. It involves a teacher who knows a range of learning strategies with which to supply the student when they seem not to understand, who can provide direction and redirection in terms of the content being understood and thus maximize the power of feedback, and who has the skill to "get out of the way" when learning is progressing towards the success criteria. (p. 16)

A second critical finding about how people learn suggests that students must develop deep factual knowledge but also be able to understand those facts conceptually to be able to transfer and apply them in different contexts (Bransford et al., 2000, p. 16). Research suggests that transfer is impeded by trying to memorize too many facts too quickly (Bransford et al., 2000, p. 58). Transfer requires application, a higher-level thinking skill than memorization; students cannot just memorize facts but must be able to apply them to a particular situation. It is not enough to memorize the division facts; students must be able to use those facts to fairly divide materials between groups and recognize that division is the mathematical operation required in that context.

A transmission style curriculum that presents facts will not result in lasting learning. A transformational approach to curriculum that invites students to apply their factual understanding in the development of real-world solutions has the potential to result in deep learning—a type of enacted curriculum described at the beginning of this chapter. For example, it is not enough to know the fact that it is important to make sustainable food choices. To truly value this ideal, students need to engage in projects that analyze how consumerism influences the food choices we make, examine the impact of our food choices, and help provide solutions to current food issues, as in the example described in the Practical Applications box.

Practical Applications

AN INTEGRATED CURRICULUM PROJECT

The excerpts below describe how Grade 9 students at one school were challenged to make more sustainable food choices as part of an integrated curriculum project. Guiding questions the students could consider included:

1. What are sustainable food choices?
2. Where does your food come from?
3. What percentage of the garbage we generate in our lunchrooms is made up of food waste?

continued

Students were encouraged to engage in inquiry using activities such as the following:

1. Tracking garbage in the lunchrooms for one week.
2. Trace the origin of the food you eat for one week.
3. Research the environmental impact of fair trade and organic food choices as compared to factory farming.
4. Arrange a videoconference, phone call, or personal interview with an expert in the field you are researching.

Finally, students were asked to create a reflection video identifying their solution to the challenge regarding ways to make more sustainable food choices. The video required the following:

1. *Title:* A restatement of your challenge (X school fights pollution, etc.)
2. *Team members:* A list of first names and the school name.
3. *Solution description:* A concise description of your solution, including the challenge, an overview of key guiding questions and activities, how and where you implemented your solution, your results, and what was learned.
4. *Sources:* A three- to five-item bibliography of sources that support the solution.
5. *Individual reflection videos:* Individual students presenting what they personally learned: "aha" moments, connections with content, how the experience differed, etc.

Curriculum outcomes included some from social studies, health, science (environmental chemistry), math, language arts, and information and communications technology from the Grade 9 Alberta Education Program of Studies. The web link below shows a student exemplar video exploring the issue of food packaging, with extensive research that included both locally collected data and data drawn from outside sources: http://calgaryscienceschool.blogspot.ca/2011/06/making-sustainable-food-choices.html#more.

Try to imagine a contrasting unit that consisted of mundane coverage of this topic with few opportunities for hands-on learning. Perhaps students read a chapter or watched a video and completed some worksheets classifying how food is marketed. To what degree do the criticisms below from prominent psychologist Jerome Bruner describe this mundane unit? To what degree has the inquiry unit described above counter Bruner's worries, creating intellectual excitement, the opportunity to generalize, and an understanding of the structure of ideas related to sustainability?

> Teaching specific topics or skills without making clear their context in the broader fundamental structure of the field of knowledge is uneconomical in several deep senses. . . . Such teaching makes it exceedingly difficult for the student to generalize from what he has learned to what he will encounter later. In the second place, [such] learning . . . has little reward in terms of intellectual excitement. The best way to create interest in a subject is to render it worth knowing, which means to make the knowledge gained usable in one's thinking and beyond the situation in which the learning has occurred. . . . Third, knowledge one has acquired without sufficient structure to tie it together is knowledge that is likely to be forgotten. An unconnected set of facts has a pitiably short half-life in memory. (1966, p. 31)

The notion of transfer is critical to reading comprehension and is articulated as a clear expectation in most curriculum documents. For example, in the Ontario language arts curriculum for Grade 3, Reading Expectation 1.6 is articulated as follows: "Extending Understanding: extend understanding of texts by connecting the ideas in them to their own knowledge and experience, to other familiar texts, and to the world around them" (Ontario Ministry of Education, 2006, p. 67). A common reading comprehension strategy described by Keene and Zimmerman (1997) builds on the idea of transfer by asking students to make connections beyond the story in three ways: text to self, text to text, and text to world. Text-to-self connections help readers make connections to their own lives; for example, after reading Paulette Bourgeois's *Franklin Has a Sleepover,* children might be reminded of their own anxiety when sleeping away from home for the first time and thus better understand the apprehension of Franklin's friend Bear. Text-to-text connections help readers recognize similarities to other books, perhaps in the same genre or the same topic. They might notice that in many fables, there is often magic, events happen in threes, and animals can talk. One young boy made an insightful text-to-text connection between Madeleine L'Engle's *A Wrinkle in Time* and J. K. Rowling's *Harry Potter and the Philosopher's Stone*; he noticed that in the climax of both stories, evil was repelled by the protective power of a family's love. Awareness of these broader themes in literature shows deep understanding. Text-to-text connections might also help students understand text features in nonfiction books such as headings, captions, and tables of contents and to use these features to seek out answers to their own questions. Finally, text-to-world connections are the connections readers make between the ideas in the text and events in the world at large. Students might read about the feudal system and be asked to identify parallels to contemporary economic injustice. A novel about an abusive parent might prompt students to examine local resources to support students in similar circumstances and learn how abusive relationships are a sadly prevalent problem in our society. Strong readers often make these connections spontaneously, but others may need guidance to develop comprehension; curriculum outcomes in reading prompt teachers to promote this deep understanding.

Wiggins and McTighe remind teachers that careful attention to essential questions is an important way to provoke deep understanding. Essential questions should do the following:

1. Prompt inquiry into big ideas and concepts
2. Provoke thought, engaged discussion, and more questions
3. Demand evidence, justification, and consideration of alternative views
4. Require rethinking of assumptions
5. Connect to prior experience
6. Transfer to other situations

They also distinguish between topical questions and overarching questions. Topical questions are smaller in scope but still require deep thinking. For example, an elementary unit on friendship could examine the overarching question, "What is a true friend?" while a topical question might be "Should Frog have lied to Toad?" (Lobel, 1970). The overarching question clearly meets all the criteria of an essential question. Discussions about story characters could help students reconsider their assumptions that a friend is simply a person you spend time with and help them establish and defend a more robust definition of friendship.

Intellectual Engagement and Deep Understanding

Another thing we know about how people learn is the critical role of genuine intellectual engagement. In a Canada-wide study of 93 schools, Willms, Friesen, and Milton (2009) surveyed students in Grades 5–12 to determine their levels of social engagement, academic engagement, and intellectual engagement defined as follows:

- Social engagement: A sense of belonging and participation in school life (feeling accepted by peers, participating in extracurricular activities)
- Academic engagement: Participation in the formal requirements of schooling (mainly attendance)
- Intellectual engagement: A serious emotional and cognitive investment in learning to use higher-order thinking skills (such as analysis and evaluation) to increase understanding, solve complex problems, or construct new knowledge (p. 7)

They found that intellectual engagement declined steadily throughout middle school and remained low throughout high school, and the level of intellectual engagement was more varied than the other two measures. Four of the 93 schools scored as low with 25% of students experiencing intellectual engagement, while just seven schools scored above 60%. This research suggests that there is a high correlation between intellectual engagement and the level of challenge; therefore, students who lack skills or those who are confident in their skills but face low levels of challenge are both likely to experience a lack of intellectual engagement. In their discussion of curriculum implications, Willms and colleagues emphasize the importance of designing learning tasks that help students "learn their way around a discipline" and the importance of knowledge building. They echo Wiggins and McTighe and Bransford and colleagues when they emphasize designing engaging tasks that require deep thinking, disciplinary inquiry, real-world connections, intellectual rigour, and rich conversation. They also cautioned that students require appropriate levels of challenge for full engagement.

CASE STUDY

Intellectual Engagement through an Interdisciplinary Unit

The following case study documents how one Canadian Grade 7 class translated the provincial science and social studies curriculum outcomes into an interdisciplinary unit on the Arctic. For more information, including links to resources and assessment rubrics, go to www.iostudent.com/5254.

Social studies outcomes (in condensed form) included recognizing, appreciating, or assessing

- the positive and negative aspects of immigration and migration,
- the challenges of coexistence among peoples, and

- political decisions and change and their impact on individual and collective identities.

Science outcomes (in condensed form) were drawn from three strands:

1. Planet Earth: Describe methods used in the scientific study of Earth to recognize changes through earthquakes, volcanoes, erosion; interpret examples of changes
2. Interactions and ecosystems: Analyze the link between human impacts on ecosystems and human wants and needs; analyze personal and public decisions involving environmental impact; interpret food webs and effects of changes on that web; illustrate through examples alternative sources of understanding such as Aboriginal knowledge based on long-term observation
3. Heat and temperature: Illustrate and explain how human needs have led to technologies for obtaining and controlling thermal energy and to increased use of energy resources; describe the nature of thermal energy and its effects on different forms of matter, using informal observations, experimental evidence, and models

Although not specified, there were undoubtedly some language arts and math outcomes related to this unit as well. The unit plan describes four preparatory learning activities and two broader performance assessment tasks.

Activity 1: How Do Animals Survive in the Arctic?

a) You have been provided a listening and viewing chart in which you will capture as much information as you can about the documentary *Arctic Tale.* Following this documentary you will be asked to engage in a discussion about the documentary.
   - Which perspective is this documentary being told from? Which voices are not represented?
   - What adaptations do the animals have to survive?
   - What is impacting the animals' ability to survive?

b) On a blank piece of paper, create a basic food web based on the movie. See examples.

Activity 2: Viewing *Adapting to Change*
www.cbc.ca/player/Shows/Shows/The+Nature+of+Things/2008-09/ID/1335284461/
You have been provided a listening and viewing chart in which you will capture as much information as you can about the documentary *Adapting to Change.* Following this documentary you will be asked to create a food web using knowledge you have gained from *Arctic Tale, Adapting to Change,* and the websites you have explored. Once you have completed your food web, you will need to show how human impact might affect that food web.

1. Draw a possible food web that might exist in the Arctic. Make sure there is evidence of producers, consumers, and decomposers.
2. Your food web is being impacted by mining, oil and gas, or climate change. Choose one impact and explain how the impact made its way to your food web. Predict what the outcome will be.
3. Identify how these pollutants enter and move through your food chain and which organisms or species are most impacted.
4. What role does the carbon cycle play in the Arctic?

Task 1
Your first task is to create a mini Arctic survival handbook. The purpose of your Arctic survival guide is to provide knowledge for explorers to prepare for their Arctic journey. You will need to base

continued

your survival tips on Inuit traditions, modern heat technologies, and the adaptations of Arctic wildlife to provide an informative guide for an upcoming expedition to the Arctic.

Your mini Arctic survival handbook needs to explain how your Arctic explorer would meet his or her basic needs to survive (i.e., clothing, shelter, food). You will be referring to all that we have and will explore in science class and the lab to inform what you include in your survival handbook. Please also refer to the book *This Vanishing Land: A Woman's Journey to the Canadian Arctic* by Dianne Whelan to help you in your research.

Task 2: Call for Submissions: "Documentaries"
In order to tell the stories of the Arctic, we would like to sponsor a documentary film festival in the spring. Your task is to explore a story of the Arctic by creating a documentary that could be presented at the festival.

What is a documentary? It is a nonfiction story told through moving images and sound about something you are passionate about. While selecting your topic you must ask yourself, "What's at the heart of this story and how do I show that visually?"

Activity 3: Research Activity: How are fossil fuels formed? How are diamonds formed?
We know that oil and gas come from fossils, but how are they formed? Where do diamonds really come from? How do we mine for diamonds? How do we extract oil, gas, and coal from the earth?

Please use the suggested websites to conduct your own research about these questions. Collect your answers and wonders in your green journal or in a document on your computer. Conducting this research will help you make sense of how these sought-after resources came to be in the Arctic.

Activity 4: Humanities Activity: Organizing Information
Please complete this activity after viewing the documentary *Arctic Rush*.

It is our understanding that you have recently viewed a CBC documentary entitled *Arctic Rush*, which detailed many of the unique perspectives held pertaining to the potential opening up of the Northwest Passage. We recognize that each of you has recorded valuable information into a listening and viewing chart. It will be essential for you to organize this information into categories based on the Google Drive file that was assigned to you. We have therefore designed the following task to aid in your synthesis of research:

- In your table groups, discuss with each other and fill in any gaps in your listening and viewing charts.
- As a large group, your class and your teacher will discuss the following questions: Was there anything that surprised you? Is there anything you want to know more about?
- Each group will then be given a specific term to investigate. Your group must come up with your own definition for the specific term or category and record it in your Google Drive file.
- Each group should then decipher what information recorded from the listening and viewing chart would fit into their category.
- Each group will present their term and categorized information to the class, and your classmates will discuss the results and decide what pertinent information to record in their Google Drive tables.

Discussion
This Arctic unit exemplifies what many curriculum resources provide—a series of learning activities that seem to be related to a set of curriculum outcomes. For you to translate these resources into successful learning experiences for your students, you will need significantly more detail. Let's analyze this unit according to the WHERETO principles of backward design to consider some of the specific supports necessary to promote student success.

W = Help the students know Where the unit is going and What is expected; help the teacher know Where the students are coming from (prior knowledge, interests) **H** = Hook students and Hold their interest	Often an artifact or discussion such as a KWL chart (Know/Want to Know/Learned) can hook the students and help teachers understand their prior knowledge and specific questions. What Arctic issues could serve as hooks to help students understand why scientists and social services staff are worried about those issues (e.g., the impact of global warming, the impact of changing eating patterns on the health of Arctic people)? This would help them see the current relevance of those outcomes. You may also want to get the students excited about the projects to come by talking a bit about creating a documentary, newsletter, and field guide, all of which are projects that allow for significant creativity.
E = Equip students, help them Experience the key ideas and Explore the issues	The teachers have identified some powerful videos to help students experience the ideas. Do you think the learning experiences will help them deeply explore the issues raised in the videos? How will drawing a web help them see the impact of humans on the Arctic ecosystem? How will communicating their understanding through the creation of a documentary help them better understand and communicate the issues?
R = Provide opportunities to Rethink and Revise their understandings and work	Do students receive feedback on their smaller activity tasks (the food web, video viewing chart) to ensure understanding?
E = Allow students to Evaluate their work and its implications	The assessment rubrics give students specific criteria to use when assessing the larger tasks, but are there opportunities for self-assessment throughout the unit?
T = Be Tailored (personalized) to the different needs, interests, and abilities of learners	What supports are in place for those who have specific learning needs (font size, graphic organizers for tracking notes, peer support, breaks for attention span, etc.)? Is there sufficient choice to meet students' interests (flexibility in completion of webs, resource newsletter, topic choice for documentary)?
O = Be Organized to maximize initial and sustained engagement as well as effective learning	

Problem-, Project-, and Inquiry-Based Learning

The Arctic unit in the preceding Case Study is a type of inquiry-based learning project. Problem-, project-, and inquiry-based learning are slightly different teaching methods, but they all are strong approaches for promoting deep understanding and intellectual engagement. While each method can be used separately, many teachers (and university

problem-, project-, and inquiry-based learning (PPIL)
A student-centred, constructivist instructional approach in which students (a) help teachers design comprehensive curricular tasks in response to key questions, (b) collaboratively solve problems with peers, (c) create specific educational products, and (d) reflect on their learning experiences.

instructors) prefer to use them together. Therefore, it is useful to think of **problem-, project-, and inquiry-based learning (PPIL)** as a student-centred, constructivist instructional approach in which students (a) help teachers design comprehensive curricular tasks in response to key questions (inquiry base), (b) collaboratively solve problems with peers (problem base), (c) create specific educational products (project base), and (d) reflect on their learning experiences. Educators of all stripes use PPIL because while it maintains their role as instructional leaders, they are predominantly acting as a learning process facilitator and guide rather than simply a provider of curricular knowledge. The combined PPIL elements are often used together as an interactional entity that closely mirrors real life outside of school; individuals are involved in figuring out which problems to solve, they collaborate to solve them and design an end product, and they collectively reflect on what they have learned and how efficient the learning process was. As a result of this reflection, the students are in a much better position to efficiently solve more complex problems; learning these types of cognitive courses of action is as important as the information acquired or the final product presented.

In the authors' own uses of PPIL, learning is predominantly driven by challenging, open-ended problems that are teacher and student designed and mediated. With instructor guidance, students work in small collaborative groups and take primary responsibility for their group's activities in organizing and directing their learning. During the process, our students discuss problems, define what they know, generate hypotheses, set out learning goals, organize their work to achieve these goals, and reflect on their learning. To round out the entire process, it is required that the results of the activity be presented by each group to the rest of the class. This allows students to develop and demonstrate their presentation skills (a commonly required learning objective) and it provides instructors with an added educational element that can be assessed.

Despite all of its obvious benefits, there is ample evidence that teachers have to model the entire PPIL process with well-constructed examples before students can be expected to take on such comprehensive learning activities. Just as students cannot be expected to develop efficient thinking and learning strategies on their own, many are not initially capable of processing and organizing all the new information included in problems with such wide-ranging applications. It is critical, therefore, that teachers provide lots of support to facilitate the original processes then reduce their support as student autonomy increases and their thinking and problem-solving abilities become more routine (i.e., scaffolding).

A noteworthy feature of PPIL is how its emphasis on information processing simultaneously taps into a broad range of cognitive and social skills. Students have to analyze the overall problem and pick out the important aspects, activate their prior related knowledge, individually and collectively process and construct new understandings, form hypotheses, problem solve, present their findings/solutions, and throughout the entire process carefully monitor and evaluate their progress. The most important aspect of this learning strategy is that it makes both the curricular content and the learning process highly contextual and meaningful, and it requires considerable social interaction for implementation. The authors of this text have also found that these wide-ranging and comprehensive forms of academic assignments improve students' content knowledge and foster the development of communication, problem-solving, and self-directed/self-regulated learning skills. Many of these skills would not develop as well if student assignments had an overly narrow focus or were predominantly completed by individuals.

Disciplinary Thinking

Many advocates of inquiry-based learning emphasize the importance of **disciplinary thinking**. Different disciplines have different cultures or ways of thinking and practising in the discipline. Historians, scientists, musicians, writers—they all create and inquire in different ways. Curriculum should not simply inform students *about* the facts or approaches realized by disciplinary experts, what Perkins (2009) calls *aboutitis*, but should instead help students to be creators and inquirers who learn the culture and ways of thinking practised by those in various disciplines. In science, students should be urged to ask questions about what is puzzling and to look for disconfirming evidence, not just hope that their experiments will work. In English, students should be encouraged to read like writers (pay attention to the writer's craft while reading) and write like readers (pay attention to what will appeal to the audience).

disciplinary thinking The different ways of thinking and practising that different disciplines have. In an educational context, students learn to "think like a scientist" or "think like a historian."

For example, one Canadian resource site for social studies teachers identifies the following as the concepts or ways of thinking engaged in by historians:

- Establish historical significance
- Use primary source evidence
- Identify continuity and change
- Analyze cause and consequence
- Take historical perspectives
- Understand ethical dimensions of history (Centre for the Study of Historical Consciousness, n.d.)

Lesson plans at this site demonstrate ways in which teachers can engage students in thinking like historians with direct links to the curricula of various provinces. For example, one series of lessons examines Aboriginal rights and title in British Columbia, focusing on the concepts of "Continuity and Change" and "Historical Perspectives."

Disciplinary experts are not only consumers of others' knowledge—they are also knowledge builders and producers. Scardamalia and Bereiter (2003), education researchers at the Ontario Institute for Studies in Education in Ontario, discuss three ways schools could try to equip knowledge builders. The first is to teach students the foundational knowledge that exists in the disciplines so they will have the facts necessary to later embark on their own research. A second way is to teach the subskills such as critical thinking, collaboration, and the scientific method that will give students the opportunity to apply these skills to knowledge-building projects. Finally, teachers might engage in problem-based learning that allows students to simulate adult teamwork with real-world content and varied information. The challenge with the first two approaches is that the real work of knowledge building is postponed until a time when the students have developed the knowledge and skills necessary to take on a project. The authors of this text prefer the third option, but we acknowledge that if teachers are not careful this approach can degenerate into "shallow constructivism" whereby students are engaged in activities such as measuring shadows but do not have a clear sense of the purpose of the activities—that is, the knowledge they are trying to build. "Deep constructivism," by contrast, involves students in clear knowledge building: identifying what is not understood, revising goals as new knowledge is learned, gathering ideas, responding to questions, and reporting to others what is learned. According to Scardamalia and Bereiter (2006), knowledge building has the following characteristics:

- Community, not individual achievement: Creating "epistemic artifacts" that help to advance knowledge when they are shared with others
- Idea improvement: moving beyond idea generation to various iterations that improve ideas over time; acknowledges that there is always more to learn
- Knowledge of a subject, not knowledge about a subject: rather than declarative knowledge about a subject, students learn actively to develop procedural knowledge they can use
- Using discourse for problem solving, not argumentation: rather than debate, students work together to help improve ideas
- Constructive use of authoritative information: using various sources to help build knowledge
- Understanding as emergent: developing conceptually rich understandings as students see the interaction between ideas

These characterizations are almost all evident in an inquiry project called "Naming the West," which was undertaken in rural Alberta as a collaboration between two First Nations schools and nine public schools along with support from local museums and the Galileo Educational Network. The Galileo Educational Network, the group that supported these projects, is an organization committed to the promotion of inquiry-based learning with an emphasis on knowledge building. Students in Grades 2, 5, and 9 learned that when they examined the names of places (towns, schools, streets, etc.), the stories of their ancestors and the local heritage were revealed. Students were working as archivists, historians, and toponymists (someone who studies place names), and their work extended beyond the school. They created videos using images of these places to help others learn about their discoveries (Galileo Educational Network, n.d.). Let's examine how the features of this project parallel Scardamalia and Bereiter's (2006) characteristics of knowledge building:

- Community, not individual achievement: The projects were undertaken collaboratively and resulted in artifacts (videos) that were shared widely on the Internet.
- Idea improvement: They developed more detailed and specific understandings by sharing their artifacts with teachers, museum curators, and other staff to improve their ideas. Their research often revealed new information about specific places and the people who influenced their town's development.
- Knowledge of a subject, not knowledge about a subject: They developed procedural knowledge about the kind of work that historians and archivists engage in and the uncertainties they face in their work.
- Using discourse for problem solving, not argumentation: They had the opportunity for peer feedback and revision of their artifacts.
- Constructive use of authoritative information: They were working with various sources to clarify and refine their understanding.
- Understanding as emergent: By comparing similarities and differences in the stories they researched, students developed a conceptual understanding about the ways communities were formed and made decisions about their values.

In a fascinating approach to knowledge building, Kieran Egan (2010), a professor of education at Simon Fraser University, has initiated a program called Learning in Depth. On the first day of school, each student is assigned a topic and continues an inquiry into this topic throughout his or her elementary and secondary school years, building a portfolio to showcase his or her growing knowledge of the topic. A fascinating list of topics with cross-disciplinary possibilities includes worms, clouds, flags, navigation, mountains, and skin. Egan defends the assigning of topics, because what is interesting to a young child is not necessarily a topic that will sustain his or her interest over time. In response to the worry that some of his recommended topics are developmentally inappropriate for children, he quotes Jerome Bruner, who said "any subject can be taught effectively in some intellectually honest form to a child at any stage of development" (1966, p. 33). While Learning in Depth projects are ideally introduced in kindergarten or Grade 1, the projects can be initiated by teachers at any grade level. The level of student engagement is reportedly remarkable, and the projects are now being undertaken across Canada and internationally.

Egan illustrates the effects of this approach by telling the story of Sarah who, in a special ceremony, is assigned the topic of apples on her first day of school. She begins by going with her parents to the supermarket to buy various kinds of apples and compares the similarities and differences, eventually learning that there are over 7,000 kinds of apples! She goes on to consider songs and poems with apples in them and begins a list of sayings about apples, like "An apple a day keeps the doctor away." By the end of her formal education, Sarah will know about the medicinal properties of apples, the role of an apple in beginning the Trojan War, statistics on apple production in various countries, and countless other knowledge about apples. She, like her classmates, will become an expert on one topic, and she will develop skills that transfer across the curriculum.

Strategy and Skill Instruction

Bransford and colleagues (2000) caution that knowledge-centred environments must also be balanced with activities that promote understanding and "automaticity of skills necessary to function effectively without being overwhelmed by attention requirements" (p. 139). According to Nancy Maynes (2011), a professor of education at Nipissing University, teachers often rush through a critical phase she calls "structured consolidation" (see Figure 3.6). When teachers introduce a new concept, they often motivate students with some hook, model the new learning, and check students' prior knowledge, but then they too quickly move on to application—giving students the opportunity to apply the new learning in activities such as co-operative learning, centres, or inquiry projects. Before moving to independent application, Maynes advocates that students need some form of monitored practice where they have the opportunity to receive feedback on their first attempts. For example, the students developing solutions to the sustainable food challenge need to examine the strategies used by professional advocates before applying these to their own documentaries. Wiggins and McTighe (2005) remind teachers that their plans should include "opportunities to Rethink and Revise their understandings and work," but often this aspect of instruction is given short shrift. Maynes's caution is worth noting if teachers are to help students avoid frustration and achieve genuine understanding.

In keeping with the current emphasis on the teaching of thinking skills, educators want to help students develop "routine thinking expertise" whereby students become more

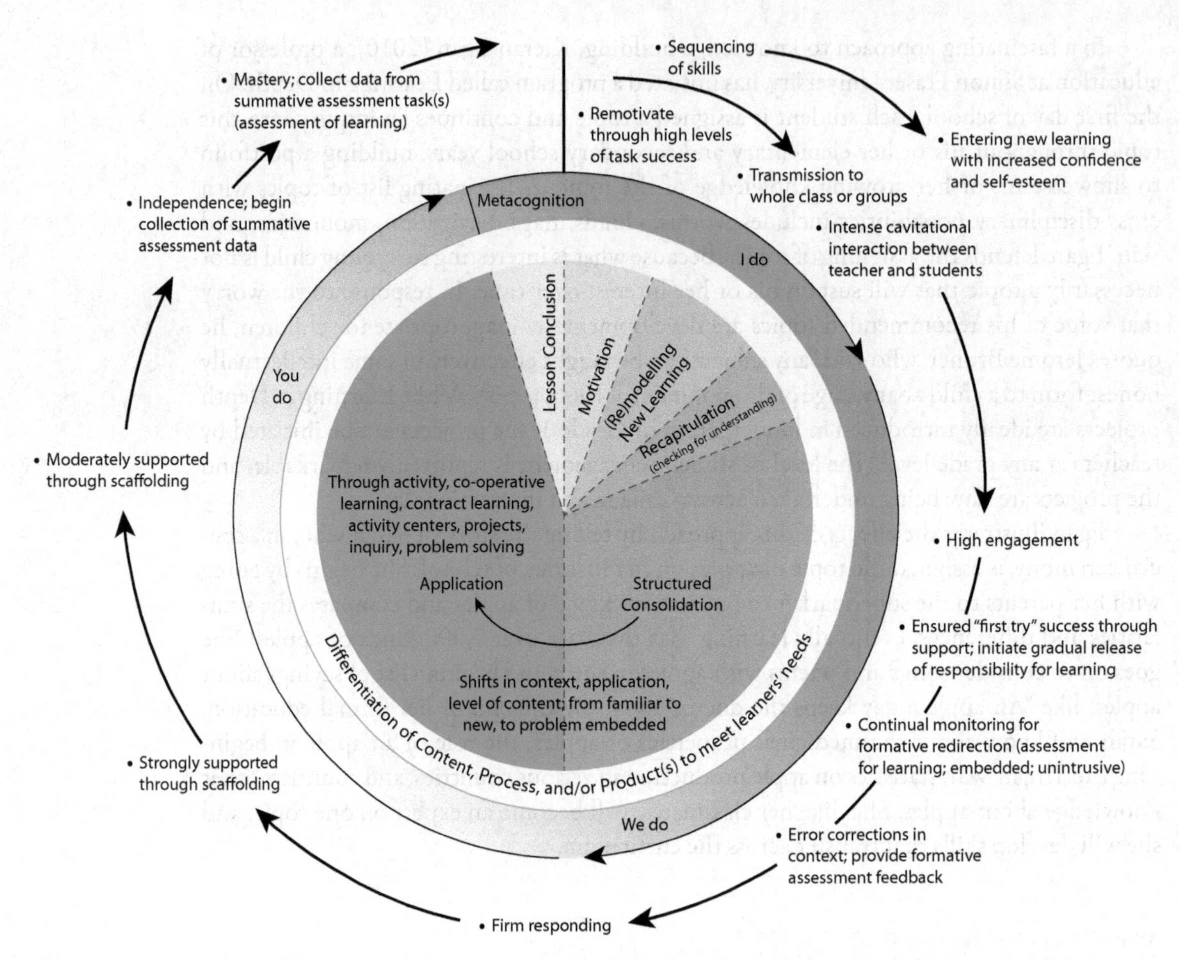

FIGURE 3.6 Direct Instruction: The Launch for Efficient Learning in a Differentiated, Multi-Dimensional Context

Source: From Maynes, Julien-Schultz & Dunn, 2010.

efficient (faster and more accurate) at solving recurring forms of academic problems—problems that, as children progress though the grades, become more sophisticated and complex. Problem solving, then, from your perspective as a teacher, should be focused on trying to turn nonroutine or new problems into routine problems by teaching your students how to develop and apply new thinking strategies and procedures.

The more strategies students have, the better their learning becomes. Children are able to use more strategies as they get older; some they develop on their own as they work through academic tasks while others need to be explicitly taught by you. If we have learned one thing about students' thinking abilities over the years, it is that we should never assume that students of a particular age or grade have developed the use of a particular thinking or learning strategy or that they can use it in the most efficient fashion. Invariably, when we have helped some students who did not use an effective strategy we have found that all students in the class benefited from direct instruction in strategy knowledge and application. On many occasions, several of our competent students have stated that they learned something new when we re-explained a strategy or demonstrated its use again by using a different example.

Although our constructivist propensities make us more inclined to allow students to "discover" thinking strategies for themselves, we know that the research in this area consistently indicates that students do not do this very well on their own and, even if they do, they do not consistently use their newly developed strategies in the most efficient ways. We caution you to remember that a student's self-development of thinking strategies is not a substitute for teacher-taught strategies—students cannot replicate your ability to think of all the variations of strategy use that are possible, nor can they anticipate the probable errors or misuses of particular strategies. Also, you will know best what the efficient use of a strategy looks like; students may not. Pressley and Harris (2006), primarily known for their research on cognitive instruction strategies to improve student learning, summed up this perspective in their analysis of cognitive strategy development and use by students of all ages across curricular domains:

> [W]e have encountered little evidence in any task domain that children certainly discover and consistently use the most effective strategies that can be used to accomplish tasks . . . there is one approach that works better than any other for ensuring that learners actually learn strategies: strategies instruction. (p. 270)

Moreover, students' abilities to consistently and efficiently use domain-specific learning strategies significantly improve under two specific teacher-led instructional conditions: (a) when instruction is meta-cognitively rich (the teacher explains and demonstrates their own use of executive processes), and (b) when instruction relies on student self-regulated use of strategies (students are encouraged to select from or improve upon their own repertoire of proven strategies).

Ultimately, there are only two ways that teachers can know when students have made efficient use of a thinking or learning strategy: (a) When students attempt a task or problem, teachers can infer their strategy ability from the demonstrated outcome; or (b) when students describe their thinking or talk out loud as they complete a task. Because teachers are highly interested in determining their students' learning and problem-solving abilities, most of their teaching processes will require students to explain their thinking. We think it is important to note here that having students explain their thinking is one of the instances in education where a preferred and effective instructional practice is also preferred as a research methodology. According to Pressley and Harris (2006), verbal protocol analysis—the documenting of conscious cognitive processing—has proven to be one of the most illuminating approaches to studying efficient strategy use by students. There is also clear evidence that requiring students to explain their problem-solving strategies (procedural knowledge) improves their understandings of facts (declarative knowledge), enables them to refine their strategies, and improves their ability to transfer their strategies to other types of problems. This happens because when students are asked to explain their thinking about either acquired knowledge or a new problem they have encountered, they consciously activate their working and short-term memory. These efficient cognitive functions allow students to think about and manipulate information and processes stored in long-term memory, and then apply them to their knowledge or to the problem to be solved. In other words, student explanations of their own understandings or problem-solving strategies act as a self-feedback mechanism that allows for reflection or refinement because attention is paid to the logic behind their thinking.

Curriculum Dilemmas

> Provincial restrictive expectations for student preparation for standardized tests is THE most limitative factor in my teaching the way I aspire to teach. Students have no opportunities to inquire and explore topics of their own inspiration. There is no TIME anymore, none. Test scores are the driving force in education in my province, in my board, in my school and, with a guilty conscience, partially in my classroom. (Canadian Education Association, 2012, p. 12)

> I feel that there are far too many curriculum expectations to be met in the Ministry documents and too much overlap of expectations from one grade level to the next. This has taken away opportunities to be flexible and creative in the classroom because there is too much to cover in too little time. (Canadian Education Association, 2012, p. 13)

These two quotes from Canadian teachers capture a common frustration. They would like to teach using authentic performance tasks, but they have too much content to teach and they believe the best way to raise scores on standardized tests is to "cover" all the material and practise the test format. However, Wiggins and McTighe (2005) counter this by saying that "The speaker asks us to believe that the only way to raise test scores is to teach worse" (p. 304). In fact, large research projects suggest that these teachers are wrong:

> Students who received assignments requiring more challenging intellectual work also achieved greater than average gains on the Iowa Tests of Basic Skills in reading and mathematics, and demonstrated higher performance in reading, mathematics, and writing on the Illinois Goals Assessment Program. Contrary to some expectations, we found high-quality assignments in some very disadvantaged classrooms and found that all students in these classes benefitted from exposure to such instruction. We conclude, therefore, that assignments calling for more authentic intellectual work actually improve student scores on conventional tests. (Newmann, Bryk, & Nagaoka in Wiggins & McTighe, 2005, p. 308)

Even with such evidence and a belief that authentic tasks result in more learning, teachers still face the genuine dilemma of how to fit in everything they are required to teach. Fortunately, many curriculum revisions, such as the curriculum redesign in Alberta (Alberta Education, 2010a), are shifting from breadth to depth and a greater focus on competencies, which may ease this anxiety for teachers.

Another curriculum dilemma that teachers face is the balance between big ideas and skill development. The inquiry projects and authentic tasks described in this chapter can be highly engaging, but students are not engaged if they are frustrated because they cannot read well enough to do the research or struggle to organize information meaningfully. Coaching in specific skills must also be part of the curriculum; ideally these skills are also applied to meaningful tasks. As constructivists we may prefer to teach inductively and may argue that a certain degree of ambiguity and even stress may challenge students, but too much of either sends students spiralling into frustration.

Teachers also face dilemmas regarding their assessment workload. Traditional knowledge and skills-based tests are efficient to grade and relatively easy to prepare, but they often lack the contextual richness and deep understanding of performance tasks. Performance tasks are "messy" and involve complex judgments to assess fairly, so it may not be practical or even preferable to assess everything using performance assessments. (Assessment challenges will be discussed more fully in the next chapter.)

As with any true dilemma, there are seldom simple responses to these curriculum issues. A reflective teacher must weigh the issues involved and make thoughtful decisions. Recall the reflective steps from Chapter 1:

Step 1: Identify and analyze the elements of your teaching you think need attention.

Step 2: Gather new information about these elements (or these types of elements).

Step 3: Decide *whether* the new knowledge has implications for your identified elements (it may not).

Step 4: Design and implement your desired changes.

Step 5: Choose a time when you will go through this process again.

These dilemmas will require you to analyze what needs attention in your curricular planning, gather new information about the best way to proceed, decide upon implications, and implement necessary changes. Your action may lead you to conclude that your plans may need to be adjusted yet again, but that is the nature of reflective practice!

Conclusion

The best way for you to develop as a curriculum planner is to simply jump in and begin! Open the provincial curriculum documents and identify the big ideas you want your students to learn for a particular unit, or perhaps to map out tentative plans for an entire year. Next aim for learning experiences that will help your students achieve those outcomes in the most engaging ways possible, complying with as many of the WHERETO principles as possible to equip your students for success. Be mindful of your own ideological presuppositions and how these may influence the curricular decisions you make. Finally, recognize that the curriculum dilemmas described at the end of this chapter may challenge you and test your reflective capacity. The challenging work of curriculum planning is a significant part of what makes you a professional! The concluding Practical Applications box summarizes principles of good teaching that marry explicit instruction with curricular objectives.

Practical Applications

THE GUIDING PRINCIPLES OF GOOD TEACHING: TEN BEST PRACTICES AND 12 GENERIC GUIDELINES

Regardless of what an approach to teaching is called or labelled, there appears to be some common ground in the variety of methods used by good teachers. Brophy's (2006b) analysis and synthesis of the considerable research done on "good teaching" resulted in the following lists of the 10 best teaching practices and the 12 generic guidelines. It is best to think of the 10 best practices as being specific teaching methods that teachers can use in classrooms, and to think of the 12 generic guidelines as broader rules that teachers should always be considering as they construct and deliver their teaching.

continued

Ten Best Practices

These were derived from a distillation of instructional commonalities that have been proven effective across all subject areas.

1. *Goals of teaching for understanding, appreciation, and life application*: Teaching for the understanding of networks of connected knowledge that are structured around big ideas and retained in forms that make them available for life applications
2. *Addressing multiple goals simultaneously*: Attending in a balanced way to multiple mixtures of knowledge, skills, attitudes, values, and dispositional goals (in particular, content and process goals)
3. *Inquiry models*: Frequent use of models that begin by engaging students in problem solving and decision making after sufficient orientation, structuring, and scaffolding
4. *Discourse management*: Teaching students to use related discourse, typically involving the co-construction of understandings through discussion and collaborative problem solving
5. *Authentic activities*: Activities that engage students in doing what disciplinary practitioners do and activities that allow students to apply what they are learning to their lives outside of school
6. *Debriefing*: Teaching students to use post-activity discussions to assess and reflect on what was learned
7. *Working with artifacts*: In association with authentic activities, having students work with the field of study's artifacts
8. *Fostering metacognition and self-regulated learning*: Teaching in ways that help students become metacognitively aware of goals and strategies and better able to self-regulate their learning (also connected to inquiry approaches and discourse management)
9. *Trajectories, misconceptions, and representations*: Being familiar with typical trajectories in the development of understanding or skills, teachers should scaffold students' progress through trajectories and avoid false starts, dead ends, and misconceptions by using well-chosen sets of representations to ensure that students did not construct overly specific or otherwise distorted understandings.
10. *Social aspects of learning*: Learning is most likely to be meaningful and accessible for use when it is socially negotiated through classroom discourse, culminating with whole-class debriefings (pp. 774–775)

Twelve Generic Guidelines

These have been consistently shown to be applicable under ordinary classroom conditions and are associated with progress toward desired student outcomes. Moreover, these guidelines are considered to be mutually supportive components within a coherent model of teaching that can be applied across school subjects.

1. *Supportive classroom climate*: Students learn best within cohesive and caring learning communities.
2. *Opportunity to learn*: Students learn more when most of the available time is allocated to curriculum-related activities and the classroom management system emphasizes maintaining students' engagement in those activities.
3. *Curricular alignment*: All components of the curriculum are aligned to create a cohesive program for accomplishing instructional purposes and goals.

4. *Establishing learning orientations*: Teachers can prepare students for learning by providing initial structuring to clarify intended outcomes and cue desired learning strategies.
5. *Coherent content*: To facilitate meaningful learning and retention, content is explained clearly and developed with emphasis on its structure and connections.
6. *Thoughtful discourse*: Questions are planned to engage students in sustained discourse structured around powerful ideas.
7. *Practice and application activities*: Students need sufficient opportunities to practise and apply what they are learning and to receive improvement-oriented feedback.
8. *Scaffolding students' task engagement*: The teacher provides whatever assistance students need to enable them to engage in learning activities productively.
9. *Strategy teaching*: The teacher models and instructs students in learning and self-regulation strategies.
10. *Co-operative learning*: Students often benefit from working in pairs or small groups to construct understandings or help one another master skills.
11. *Goal-oriented assessment*: The teacher uses a variety of formal and informal assessment methods to monitor progress toward learning goals.
12. *Achievement expectations*: The teacher establishes and follows through on appropriate expectations for learning outcomes. (pp. 775–776)

Discussion Questions

1. As you consider the curriculum ideologies discussed in this chapter, which do you see as most influential in your school or school board and in your own practice? Are these healthy or destructive influences?
2. Consider a lesson you have recently taught or observed. What was the desired outcome? How do you know if all the students achieved the outcome?
3. To practise using the backward design approach to curriculum development, choose a topic from one curriculum guide in your province and sketch out responses to the following questions:
   - What are the enduring understandings and essential questions you hope students will learn about this topic?
   - What performance tasks could lead them to ask these questions and achieve these understandings?
4. What aspects of problem-, project-, and inquiry-based learning are most exciting to you? Most daunting?
5. Discuss an example of when strategy instruction enhanced students' success on a performance task.
6. Which of the curriculum dilemmas presented in this chapter seems most troublesome in your own practice or for teachers you have worked with? What is helping you to manage these complex dilemmas, and what action might you take in the future?

Further Resources

1. Alberta Education. (2004). *Focus on inquiry: A teacher's guide to implementing inquiry-based learning.* Retrieved from http://education.alberta.ca/media/313361/focusoninquiry.pdf.

   This freely accessible document provides a framework for planning an inquiry-based unit with provincial content from any subject area and grade level easily applicable to the rest of Canada. It begins with the *planning* phase when a question emerges that learners are curious about. Teachers often pique curiosity and guide the initial phases of inquiry toward a question that will address curriculum outcomes. In the *retrieving* phase learners begin searching for information related to their topic. This can be overwhelming, so teachers need to provide students with tools like graphic organizers to help them manage the information they are finding or interviews/surveys they are conducting. In the *processing* phase, students may narrow their topic to something more specific that is particularly interesting to them. For example, a student inquiring into electricity might decide to examine electric cars like the one his parents just purchased, while his classmate may be more interested in how much energy her family is using at home. *Creating* and *sharing* gives students the opportunity to put the ideas they are learning into a meaningful format that will be clear and interesting to others—perhaps through an iMovie, a PowerPoint presentation, a dramatic presentation, or a story. Finally, in the *evaluating* phase students engage in self-assessment to reflect on what they have learned.

2. Bransford, J. D., Brown, A. L., & Cocking, R. R. (2000). *How people learn: Brain, mind, experience and school.* Washington, DC: National Academy Press. This book is available for free download at www.nap.edu/openbook.php?isbn=0309070368.

   To effectively plan curricula, teachers must have a clear understanding of how students learn. This oft-cited text provides a strong research base to help discern how the mind works and how to foster deep learning in the design of learning experiences.

3. Jacobs, H. H. (Ed.). (2010). *Curriculum 21: Essential education for a changing world.* Alexandria, VA: ASCD.

   Heidi Hayes Jacobs is a well-known advocate of curriculum mapping: showing clear alignment between curriculum, assessment, and instruction. In this text, Jacobs shows how the curriculum can be enriched with attention to 21st-century learning ideals, including technology integration, globalization, and sustainability.

4. Perkins, D. (2009). *Making learning whole: How seven principles of teaching can transform education.* San Francisco, CA: Jossey-Bass.

   David Perkins argues that schools often suffer from what he calls *elementitis* and *aboutitis*: Teachers teach students the *elements* of writing instead of encouraging them to use these elements in original writing; they teach *about* scientific facts when they ought to help students use those facts to practise science in ways that scientists would practise. He encourages teachers to help students "play the whole game"—or at least a junior version of the game—as soon as possible. Designing a curriculum around tasks that replicate real-world problems seems to be a promising way to play the whole game.

5. Western and Northern Canadian Protocol for Collaboration in Education. (2011). Guiding principles for WNCP curriculum framework projects. Retrieved from www.education.gov.sk.ca/adx/aspx/adxGetMedia.aspx?DocID=7413,1429,107,81,1,Documents&MediaID=15800&Filename=Guiding_Principles_FEB2011.pdf.

This online text, written through a collaboration of provincial representatives, discusses the emerging research from cognitive science concerning how people learn and the implications of this research for curriculum development in Canada. First, they emphasize the importance of developing deep understanding. Next, they remind readers that diversity is critical for a healthy system and thus our curriculum should value diverse ways of knowing. Third, they focus on the importance of developing competencies and how these unite learning experiences. Finally, they emphasize how learning and living well together leads to a sustainable future.

6. Wiggins, G., & McTighe, J. (2012). *The Understanding by design guide to advanced concepts in creating and reviewing units.* Alexandria, VA: ASCD.

This book is a companion to the *Understanding by Design* text discussed extensively in this chapter. It has specific suggestions for selecting evaluative criteria for assessments, "sharpening" essential questions and understandings, and refining and differentiating the learning plan. It is a useful text to assist teachers in curriculum unit and lesson planning.

Classroom Assessment and Student Evaluation

Learning Objectives

After reading this chapter, you should understand

1. The purpose and application of diagnostic, formative, and summative assessment
2. The integral role of the lesson plan learning objective within student assessment
3. The purpose and application of Bloom's taxonomy of cognitive skills within instruction and assessment to establish assessment validity
4. That student assessment must be considered before instruction can be planned or delivered
5. How to construct a Table of Specifications
6. The purpose and application of selected-response and constructed-response questions
7. The use of authentic problems to design authentic assessment
8. How and why teachers need to analyze and review all assessment tools

Impact on Today's Teachers

A COMMON ASSESSMENT CONUNDRUM

As a secondary English teacher was arranging her materials for her class, her students filed in talking about a test in their science class. Many of them felt they failed the test because "who ever heard of answers being "A and B but not C or D, or A and B and C but not D. It was totally confusing." One of them stated firmly, "Well, at least it's better than that stupid 'higher-order thinking test' we did—that was so bad. How could you ever study for that? None of the questions made any sense." They clearly were not happy with their science teacher. "Yeah," said another, "that first test in September was so easy . . . it was all about facts and figures, simple stuff that anyone with half a brain would know. That was too easy, but at least I could do it. I've practically failed every test since. I'm not the sharpest knife in the drawer, but I'm not that stupid. There's no point coming to class or studying because it doesn't make any difference!"

The more they talked, the more it became clear that the science teacher was caught in a common teaching conundrum. Later in a staff room conversation, the English teacher learned what happened. The science teacher began by teaching factual knowledge; he taught the lists of information found in the curriculum guide and had students write down what he was saying verbatim. When it came time for a test, the students who studied got perfect or near-perfect grades. Word got around that this course was easy, so to restore his credibility, the teacher made his next test more demanding by, unfortunately, asking higher-order questions. This compounded the problem because the types of questions he asked did not match what he taught or how he taught it. It was no surprise that the students did poorly. Faced with increased criticism about failing grades and being at a loss as to how to test differently, he resorted to using complicated multiple-choice questions in an attempt to make the simple concepts he was teaching seem more demanding. Unfortunately, his poor answers only made students feel they were being tricked just to keep their grades down. Eventually, this increased the number of failures and exacerbated student and parent frustrations. Ultimately, the teacher was forced back to assessing his students in a way that matched his teaching style; he returned to the easy tests that tested for factual knowledge, and his students' scores improved markedly.

This scenario, or something like it, plays out more often than educators would like. It is a clear example of what happens when a teacher does not understand the fundamental principles of assessment. This chapter has been specifically designed to provide you with the knowledge and skills to make sure this problem never happens to you.

Curricular Planning

It is impossible to describe the fundamental tenets of **classroom assessment** and **student evaluation** without including a detailed discussion of instruction. This is because the design and implementation of instruction and assessment are inextricably intertwined. To treat assessment and instruction as separate entities would be to contradict many if not all of the principles that make both function so well. We will start this chapter with a brief review of curricular planning, as described in Chapter 3, and outline how these planning decisions

classroom assessment
The systematic process of gathering reliable information about student understandings of critical knowledge, skills, attitudes, and behaviours.

student evaluation
The process of making educational judgments based on assessment data.

influence instruction. This is followed by a careful delineation of instructional design and the creation of lesson plans. By doing this you will see how the key features of curricular planning and instructional design play key roles in the design and use of various assessment methods. Assessment is the process of teachers determining what students know and can do. To accomplish this, teachers use a variety of assessment tools and procedures such as assignments, tests, and portfolios, to name a few. Throughout this chapter we variously refer to these assessment tools as tests, measures, indicators, exams, and so on, but they all mean basically the same thing.

Experienced educators know that good planning results in excellent teaching, enhanced student learning, and exemplary environments where effective teaching and learning take place. To accomplish this, the following issues must be considered: (a) what to teach, (b) in what order, (c) which teaching methods and materials will be used, (d) the type of environment the teaching will take place in, and (e) how and when students will be assessed. Educators use the thematic units suggested in curriculum guides to divide the year into large units of instruction. These are then broken down into smaller units and then into daily lessons.

diagnostic assessment
Determining what students already know and what skills they possess for the purpose of guiding future instruction.

At the start of every new year or term, teachers often only have a general idea of what their students were taught previously. Rather than making assumptions about what your students know and can do, your *very first step* in your instructional journey is to assess your students' levels of knowledge and skill. This is known as **diagnostic assessment**—the determination of student knowledge and skills for the purpose of guiding future instruction. Since it is impractical to assess knowledge and skills in all domains, teachers usually assess the language arts skills of younger students since that is the basis of most elementary programs. At the secondary level, teachers typically assess the knowledge and skills of domain-specific courses such as English, algebra, civics, and so on. Regardless of the topics chosen, the point of this activity is to gain a preinstructional indication of the relative strengths and needs of all students. This knowledge will enable you to better prepare your lessons to "meet the students where they are" and to avoid making incorrect assumptions about their abilities. Another benefit to diagnostic results is that they can be compared to other information in each student's file pertaining to their academic abilities. It is important to reassure your students that your diagnostic assessment is simply a measure designed to determine what they need to work on this year or term.

An excellent means of preparing diagnostic assessments is to modify the previous year's end-of-year assessment tools. These can be final tests or other tools such as checklists, rating scales, or group activities. This process may sound onerous, but it is actually an easy and quickly accomplished task. Read the assessment tool over and, with some help from the curriculum guide, reduce it to between 10 and 20 questions; 10–14 questions for younger students and 15–20 questions for Grades 7–12. For each modified assessment tool, more than half the questions should assess global or general objectives while the remaining questions need to assess specific knowledge or skills. After summer breaks, students will remember general concepts better than specific topical details. This consideration is even more important for secondary students, who may go up to 12 months between subjects; they could take Math 10 in the fall of Grade 10 and Math 11 in the winter of Grade 11. Each of these prediagnostic evaluations should only take 45 to 60 minutes. Diagnostic assessments in elementary grades might include conducting a running record (listening to a child read while recording errors) to determine reading level and strategy use. Writing samples will also give some indication of students' ability to express themselves in writing and their use of writing mechanics.

One of the advantages of diagnostic assessment for beginning teachers is that the information can help quell the common worry that he or she lacks the knowledge and expertise required to teach a particular subject. We worry we will teach something that insults students' abilities or is so far above their knowledge base that they tune out. Reading each subject's curriculum guide is extremely helpful because they are designed with developmental appropriateness and topic specificity in mind. As you become more familiar with curriculum guides, what should be taught will become clearer. Based on your faculty of education methods courses and your practicum experiences, you will be able to see where and how you can extend student learning and where you will probably need to go more slowly.

Instructional Planning

The next step in developing your system of assessment is to lay out your overall approach to teaching. Once you know what you will teach, you can design proper assessment tools. For this reason we first present more details about the fundamentals of teaching in this chapter, then we outline assessment. We also want you to connect what we present here about teaching to the related content in Chapter 3.

Aspiring teachers invariably become aware of a variety of instructional methods they can use, but they typically have difficulty articulating them as an overall approach. This takes considerable thinking when starting your career. Therefore, faculties of education often ask teacher-candidates to outline their entire methodology and to rationalize each element. The primary purpose is to feel confident not only in your content knowledge but also in your choice of teaching methods. By taking the time to think things through and provide rationales for your various methods, you give yourself the best opportunity to be an effective teacher. In this chapter we introduce you to the underlying principles of how and why instruction is integral to the assessment of student performance. The rest of the chapter provides examples of how you can develop your overall approach to assessment and explains why you need to justify and make connections between it and your teaching methods.

Determining Exactly What to Teach: Learning Objectives and Lesson Plans

At its core, education is about two predominant teacher functions: teaching and then assessing whether students have learned. The symbiotic interrelationships between teaching, learning, and assessment cannot be overstated, but this critical interplay best occurs when assessment and instruction are planned and designed together.

Both beginning and experienced teachers are often quite good teachers but less skilled at designing good assessment tools. This disconnect typically occurs because most teaching is designed and delivered without a priori consideration of assessment. In fact, many practising teachers do one of two things when it comes to assessment, neither of which is very reliable or effective: They either wait until after they have taught a series of lessons to construct their assessment tools, or they simply re-use the same tests/exams they used last time. While both methods appear to save time and effort, both have the potential for glaring problems. Making up tests or exams after teaching a unit over several weeks usually results in the teacher forgetting to assess something that was taught. Similarly, using the

same tests over and over usually results in assessing something that was not taught. Assessing material that was not covered is the most unpopular aspect of assessment for students. In both instances, teachers lose professional credibility in the eyes of students and parents and they cannot justify their assessment practices to principals and administrators.

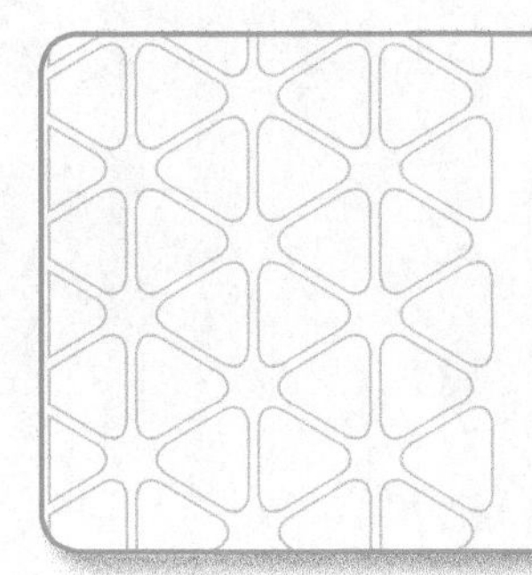

Practical Applications

Consider some assessments of your own school work (e.g., marks on tests, feedback on presentations, feedback on essays and papers). Do you feel these assessments were fair and accurate? Why or why not? How well did the in-class instruction prepare you for the assessment tasks? How could the instruction have been more effective in preparing you for these tasks?

As we mentioned previously, teachers must consciously keep assessment considerations in mind when planning their teaching. This process, called *backward design* (see Chapter 3), is accomplished by asking and answering two key assessment questions *and then* asking two key instructional questions:

1. What do I want my students to learn?
   - ▶ *What I want students to learn is called an instructional goal/learning objective.*
2. How will I determine whether they have learned?
   - ▶ *The educational device that determines whether the learning objective has been learned is called an assessment question.*
3. What will I teach?
   - ▶ *I will teach topics/units/lessons that directly address my instructional goal/learning objective.*
4. How will I teach it?
   - ▶ *I will choose the best way to teach the topic/unit/lesson so that my objective is fully achieved/realized.*

learning objective
An instructional goal that teachers want to achieve. They provide teachers with a systematized method of knowing where they want to take their students, charting a plan to take them there, and confirming that they have arrived in good order.

Backward design is the development of curricular units and lessons derived from the identical instructional goals or **learning objectives** used in creating assessment tools. This process allows teachers to "map backwards" from the desired result of measuring student achievement. It provides teachers with a systematized method of knowing where they want to take their students, charting a plan to take them there, and confirming that they have arrived in good order. Figure 4.1 illustrates how knowing the precise learning objective and how it will be assessed predicates what will be taught and how teaching will take place.

For example, let's say the specific learning objective is "To be able to successfully calculate two-column addition without carrying." To properly determine whether students have learned this, the teacher will assess their abilities using the following questions (or other variations):

$$\begin{array}{r} 23 \\ \underline{+\,15} \end{array} \qquad \begin{array}{r} 11 \\ \underline{+\,55} \end{array} \qquad \begin{array}{r} 71 \\ \underline{+\,18} \end{array}$$

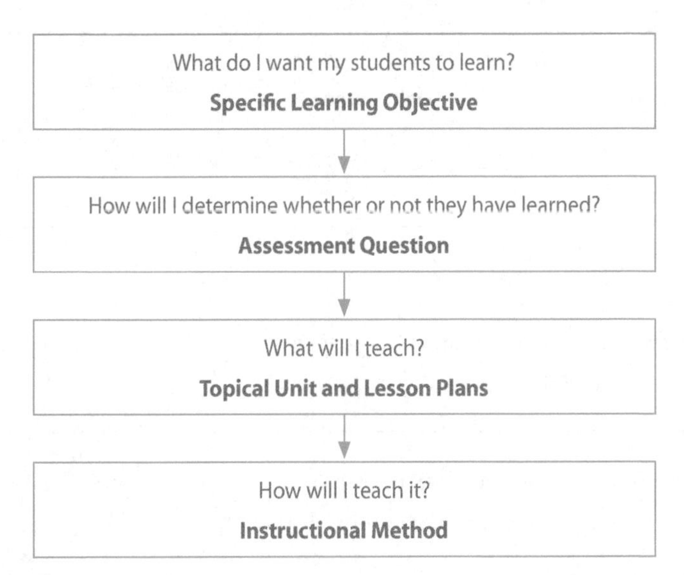

FIGURE 4.1 Learning Objectives: Relationship to Assessment, Lesson Planning, and Instruction

Source: Edmunds & Edmunds, 2010.

Now that the teacher knows precisely what students are supposed to learn and how their understanding or application of this knowledge or skill will be assessed, he or she can properly and confidently design his or her teaching to make sure this happens. Accordingly, the teacher's lesson plan will contain the following learning objective: "As a result of this lesson, my students will be able to calculate two-column addition without carrying." The reason the learning objective must be so clearly stated in the lesson plan is because it is the supreme focal point for all parts of the lesson plan, such as the resources required and how the material will be taught (see Figure 4.2).

The teacher then decides on the best way to teach the material and proceeds to teach the lesson. Students may then engage in various learning activities to help them practise the skill. These will be more engaging if the addition seems relevant for responding to authentic, real-world questions that require addition. Once the teacher is satisfied that students have learned, he or she uses the previously constructed test questions to assess their understandings and skills. *By adhering to the sound assessment and instructional principles involved in this approach, what is expected to be learned, what is taught, how it is taught, and the questions used to assess student learning are all derived from the same learning objective.* This provides the entire process with instructional continuity and integrity. Furthermore, by devising assessment questions during the planning of each daily lesson, teachers will have a comprehensive, ready-made test when they have finished teaching a series of lessons. They do not have to struggle to remember what they did or did not teach. These direct and explicit connections between teaching and assessment generated via a precise learning objective make assessment authentic.

Another important function of the learning objective is that teachers can use it to direct student expectations. For example, the teacher can say (or indicate on an overhead or PowerPoint slide), "Today we are going to learn about fractions. At the end of this lesson, I want you to be able to add and subtract fractions with different denominators." The teacher's statement acts as a cognitive readiness cue and allows students to get into the right

Daily Lesson Plan

Subject ______________________ Date/Time/Period ________________

Topic of Lesson ____

Administration

- ❑ Reminders/due dates for homework, projects, etc.
- ❑ Field trip permission

1. Learning objective statement (be very precise):
   - ❑ As a result of this lesson, my students will be able to …
2. Assessment questions:
   - ❑ Build test items immediately
3. Teaching Method:
   - ❑ Select best teaching approach "for the objective"
   - ❑ Review last day—make explicit connections
   - ❑ Teach, demonstrate, discuss, etc.
   - ❑ Review lesson?
4. Materials required:
   - ❑ Handouts/overheads/videos/music/tools
   - ❑ All parts for demonstrations
5. Anything special about this lesson or this day?

FIGURE 4.2 Lesson Plan Template
Source: Edmunds & Edmunds, 2010.

frame of mind. Teachers can reinforce this by asking students to repeat it and explain their understanding of it. When students are explicitly aware of what they are expected to learn, they can better direct their learning energies and they can better monitor and evaluate their understandings. This sets up an active rather than a passive learning process and creates a dynamic relationship between teachers and learners.

Bloom's Taxonomy

Obviously, learning objectives play an important role in teaching, learning, and in the assessment of learning. But not all learning objectives are created equal; some address fairly simple knowledge and concepts which only require basic cognitive skills to understand and

Level	Cognitive Objective	Description of Thinking
6	Evaluation	Judging the respective worth/value of something
5	Synthesis	Bringing ideas together; generating/creating new ideas from other related ideas
4	Analysis	Breaking concepts into parts; indicating relationships
3	Application	Being able to use information to solve a problem
2	Comprehension	Interpreting/understanding information
1	Knowledge	Remembering or recognizing something factual

FIGURE 4.3 Bloom's Taxonomy

Source: Edmunds & Edmunds, 2010.

apply, while others deal with more complex information and require more sophisticated thinking. For example, knowing and remembering that Canada is composed of 10 provinces and three territories is far less complicated than being able to contrast the primary economic contributors in these 13 jurisdictions. This means that teachers have to use different types of assessment questions to properly address the various concepts covered in lessons. Educational psychologist Benjamin Bloom (Bloom, Englehart, Furst, Hill, & Krathwohl, 1956) established a hierarchical classification of cognitive learning objectives that is commonly referred to as **Bloom's taxonomy** (see Figure 4.3).

Bloom's taxonomy
A hierarchical classification of cognitive learning objectives developed by Benjamin Bloom and colleagues.

This taxonomy explains a hierarchy of intellectual abilities involved in the acquisition and use of knowledge. Educational objectives and the types of thinking required to learn and apply them are sorted into six distinct levels from simple recall to the ability to evaluate learned material: (a) knowledge, (b) comprehension, (c) application, (d) analysis, (e) synthesis, and (f) evaluation. Bloom's six categories are "progressively inclusive," meaning that for students to successfully process information demanded in higher-order categories they must first understand the information contained in lower-order categories. For example, students cannot be expected to understand the respiratory system (Level 3: Application) unless they first understand the parts that make up the system (Levels 1 and 2: Knowledge and Comprehension). Similarly to properly evaluate a position or theory (Level 6: Evaluation), students must first be able to analyze and synthesize the material (Levels 4 and 5). Therefore, the same principle must be applied when assessing student learning: Students cannot be expected to answer a question requiring knowledge or skills that they have not yet acquired.

Bloom's distinction between different types of knowledge allows teachers to easily generate different-but-related learning objectives for a unit of study. By paying close attention to the cognitive verbs used in learning objectives, teachers can be sure that each learning objective is taught at its intended level of understanding. **Cognitive verbs** are used to specifically delineate the way that teachers want students to think as a result of participating in any given lesson (see Figure 4.2). Consider the learning objective stated earlier: "To calculate two-column addition without carrying." This objective, like each and every learning objective in each and every lesson plan, has three required parts:

cognitive verbs
Verbs used in a learning objective that specifically delineate the way that teachers want students to think as a result of participating in any given lesson.

Part 1:
Basic Form *As a result of this lesson, my students will be able to . . .*

Part 2:
Cognitive Verb *calculate . . .*

Part 3:
Topic Description *two-column addition without carrying.*

To be sure that the thinking required for a learning objective is properly assessed, the same cognitive verb is used to build assessment questions. In the example below, the test direction tells students what to do (using the same cognitive verb—*calculate*) and the test includes questions formulated when initially planning the lesson:

Calculate the following:

23	11	71
+ 15	+ 55	+ 18

To make sure that the intended thinking of a learning objective is properly realized, teachers use the cognitive verbs that are associated with the six cognitive levels of Bloom's taxonomy (see Table 4.1).

From Bloom's list, we can see that all forms of thinking can be classified into six basic cognitive processes: remembering, understanding, applying, analyzing, creating, and evaluating. These six processes are brought to bear on four different types of knowledge: factual, conceptual, procedural, and metacognitive. An easy way to determine the proper cognitive verb for a learning objective is to analyze the cognitive processes involved in the learning tasks and focus on the process that is most relevant. For example, the mental processes involved in solving a math word problem are (a) reading for understanding, (b) determining the math calculation form (addition, multiplication, etc.), (c) recalling and properly using memorized math facts, and (d) solving the problem. By the time word problems are introduced

TABLE 4.1 Verbs Used in Cognitive Objectives

Cognitive Objective	Cognitive Verbs That Activate Learning Objectives
Evaluation	compare, critique, evaluate, choose, estimate, judge, defend, criticize, justify
Synthesis	design, hypothesize, support, schematize, write, report, discuss, plan, devise, compare, create, construct, formulate
Analysis	analyze, organize, deduce, choose, contrast, compare, distinguish, differentiate
Application	solve, illustrate, calculate, use, interpret, relate, manipulate, apply, classify, modify, put into practice, compute, determine
Comprehension	summarize, explain, interpret, describe, compare, paraphrase, differentiate, convert, demonstrate, visualize, restate
Knowledge	list, name, identify, show, define, recognize, recall, state

Source: Edmunds & Edmunds, 2010.

in math, math facts (knowledge) and calculation abilities (application) are presumed to be consolidated. Therefore, the learning objectives for word problems will focus on verbs that address the cognitive skills involved in reading, analyzing, and deciphering word problems, such as *analyze, organize,* or *deduce.* This example also illustrates how simple cognitive tasks (remembering and calculating) are often embedded in complex tasks (analyzing). It stands to reason that students who cannot remember math facts or calculate properly will not be able to complete word problems even if they have good deciphering skills.

Stiggins's Achievement Targets

Rick Stiggins (2001) is said to have improved on Bloom's taxonomy by creating a hierarchical structure for achievement targets: a set of specifications for what students should learn or do (see Table 4.2). Two of the primary differences between Bloom's and Stiggins's taxonomies are that Stiggins purposefully targets the development of (a) the combined use of knowledge with specific thinking processes to create products and (b) the preferred attitudes and dispositions that students should bring to bear on their academic endeavours. Stiggins's attitude and disposition target is consistent with mainstream conceptions of educational psychology. These conceptions advocate that students need to be mindful of their learning and be explicitly purposeful in applying their thinking and learning processes rather than allowing themselves to be passive learners.

achievement targets
A set of specifications for what students should learn to do. Developed by Rick Stiggins, they purposefully target the development of (a) the combined use of knowledge with specific thinking processes to create products and (b) the preferred attitudes and dispositions that students should bring to bear on their academic endeavours.

The approaches described above are the building blocks of effective lessons. Once these fundamentals are in place, teachers can be creative and inventive to make lessons that suit their personality, their teaching approach, or the group of students they are working with. Finding innovative ways to make learning fun and engaging students in stimulating and challenging learning experiences makes everyone in the classroom feel excited about school.

TABLE 4.2 Stiggins's Taxonomy of Achievement Targets

Targets	Description
Knowledge	Declarative knowledge: facts, terms, concepts, and generalizations Procedural knowledge: procedures or problem-solving methods
Reasoning	Process of answering questions through analytical problem solving
Skills	Abilities required to put procedural knowledge to use in a fluent fashion and in the appropriate context
Products	Student creations that reflect current skill and ability levels
Attitudes & Dispositions	Interests in certain topics; the desire to learn more about a topic

Source: Edmunds & Edmunds, 2010.

Choosing Effective Instructional Practices

Next to who you are as a person, how you teach will become the primary way you develop your identity as a teacher. It is impossible for you to fully articulate your preferred and proven methods at this point, but in due course the various ways you choose and reject teaching mechanisms will become consolidated. Your ability to completely understand your teaching methods will make day-to-day planning much easier.

The Case Study below provides an example of one teacher's detailed description of her preferred instructional methods. As you read it over, listen for the reasons why she chose or rejected certain methods. By understanding the pros and cons of particular methods, excellent instructional choices are made. These comprehensive understandings then make for exemplary teaching and effective learning.

CASE STUDY

My Preferred Instructional Mechanisms

There are a variety of instructional mechanisms that teachers can choose from, but it is rare that any one teaching method will do everything required. It is also rare that a teacher will use a particular teaching method exactly as it is described or use the entire method. For the most part, teachers pick and choose and modify different parts to develop their own approach. I will first describe the theoretical basis that governs my approach to teaching. Then I will describe why I use certain elements from a variety of established methods. Together, these parts form a cohesive instructional whole that is consistent with (a) my views of teaching, (b) my approach to classroom management, and (c) the ways that I think about and conduct assessment.

My Three Guiding Principles

There are three foundational principles that guide my teaching. The first is the principle of universal instructional design (UID). The roots of UID originate in the architectural concept of "universal design," which advocates for physical spaces and objects that consider the needs of all users, especially those of individuals with disabilities. By extension, UID conceptualizes teaching as an instructional system that, when designed and delivered with the needs of the least independently able students in mind, is more accessible and effective for all (Rose & Meyer, 2006). With inclusiveness and equity at its core, UID creates classroom environments that respect and value diversity. I have incorporated the principles of UID into my approach to teaching; this includes my instructional approach as well as my approach to classroom management. The UID principles I adhere to are as follows:

1. Create a welcoming classroom environment that emphasizes academic and behavioural success.
2. Determine the essential academic components to be taught/learned and the preferred behavioural outcomes.
3. Provide students with clear expectations for learning and feedback about their learning progress and social conduct.
4. Implement a variety of topically suitable instructional methods.
5. Provide a variety of ways for students to demonstrate what they have learned (assessment).
6. Make appropriate use of technology to enhance learning.
7. Encourage and initiate teacher–student and student–student discourses about learning topics/tasks and behavioural expectations.

The second principle that guides my teaching is my realization that the vast majority of teaching is accomplished by either explaining or demonstrating. I use examples, pictures, questions, models, manipulatives, student discourse, student-read passages, and various forms of teacher and student re-explaining to reinforce concepts I am teaching. Therefore, my approach is constructivist in nature even though it includes several teacher-centred applications. It allows students to construct their own knowledge and knowledge-producing structures with my guidance. While my teaching includes student-centred approaches, I also make use of specialized teacher-centred approaches, like direct instruction, to satisfy my responsibility as the instructional leader. All these elements, in conjunction with the meaningful tasks inherent in problem-, project-, and inquiry-based learning, are used collectively to have a direct, positive influence on student achievement and student self-regulated learning. My primary instructional purpose, therefore, is to guide and assist students toward constructing their own understandings and acquiring the skills necessary to responsibly regulate their own learning.

The third principle that guides my teaching is that learning is a highly complex function that involves academic skill acquisition, the development of cognitive understanding, and the formation and enhancement of a variety of cognitive processes used for further learning. All of these abilities are dependent on students making adaptations and adjustments based on their environment and the level and type of cognitive stimulation they encounter. If learning is a function of thinking, then student thinking must be a function of teacher instruction. For me, good teaching is mostly about using these elements to cause students to think. My overall approach to teaching is primarily geared toward generating student thinking, because without thinking neither knowledge construction nor the regulation of learning can happen.

How People Learn (HPL) Framework

To organize what is known about teaching and learning, the National Academy of Sciences Committee (National Research Council, 2000) developed the **How People Learn (HPL) framework**. Bransford, Derry, Berliner, Hammerness, and Beckett (2005, p. 41) outline how the four components of this framework incorporate the various "mini-theories" that educators tend to have about teaching:

How People Learn (HPL) framework
A framework developed by the National Academy of Sciences Committee to organize what is known about teaching and learning.

1. Knowledge-centredness: What should be taught, why is it important, and how should this knowledge be organized?
2. Learner-centredness: Who learns, how, and why?
3. Community-centredness: What kinds of classroom, school, and school–community environments enhance learning?
4. Assessment-centredness: What kinds of evidence for learning can students, teachers, parents, and others use to see if effective learning is really occurring?

Figure 4.4 provides a schematic diagram of the HPL framework.

It is in balancing and integrating all four components of the HPL framework in the following ways that teachers are effective:

1. Knowledge-centredness: Teachers consult their respective national, provincial, and district standards in deciding what to teach and why.
2. Learner-centredness: As well as intensive curricular and instructional planning decisions, teachers need to make moment-by-moment teaching decisions based on ongoing assessments of their learners' current levels of understanding.

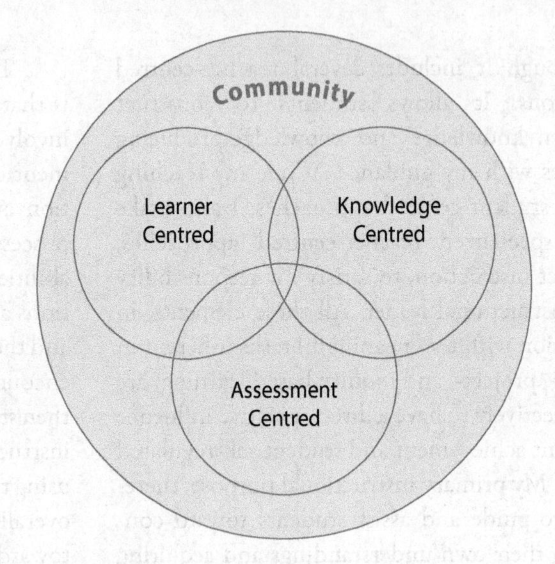

FIGURE 4.4 Diagram of the HPL Framework
Source: Adapted from Bransford, Darling-Hammond, & LePage, 2005.

3. Community-centredness: Teachers need to create climates of shared learning and respect for learning, the sense of community among fellow teachers and other adults in the school, and build upon the goodwill and intellectual resources of the community.
4. Assessment-centredness: Teachers focus on ways that different teaching and learning goals affect what teachers do to assess academic progress (Bransford, Derry, Berliner, Hammerness, & Beckett, 2005).

In conclusion, Bransford, Derry, Berliner, Hammerness, and Beckett (2005, p. 75) illustrated how the HPL framework influences student motivation:

> If students know they are learning content and skills that will be important in life, this is motivating. If courses connect with their interests and strengths, and provide interesting challenges to their preconceptions, this is motivating. If students receive frequent feedback that allows them to see their progress in learning and gives them chances to do even better, this is motivating. And if students feel as if they are a valued part of vibrant, "high-standards" learning communities—at the classroom level, school level, and overall community level—this is motivating as well.

Direct Instruction

direct instruction
A systematic instructional method that prescribes the teaching of small amounts of information and providing lots of student practice to attain mastery of basic facts and skills.

Direct instruction, or *explicit teaching*, as it is sometimes called, is a systematic instructional method that is often portrayed as prescribing the teaching of small amounts of information and providing lots of student practice to attain mastery of basic facts and skills. In our opinion, however, if teachers are not careful this definition and use of the term *direct instruction* can be an overly narrow view of its potential broader application. The following Case Study represents some of the more global and functional benefits garnered by an experienced teacher. She felt that these elements made direct instruction an appealing part of her overall approach:

CASE STUDY

Using Direct Instruction in the Classroom

Direct instruction emphasizes well-developed and carefully planned lessons with clear learning objectives that are purposefully presented to students. Not only do such lessons provide structure and predictability for both me and my students, I feel that the rich structure and clear instruction based on well-planned lessons eliminates misinterpretations that inhibit student learning. While I am a constructivist at heart, I know of far too many instances of student-centred teaching and learning that led students off track and fostered misconceptions of lesson content.

Direct instruction requires teaching via some form of explanation (either lecture, demonstration, or both) and guiding students through complex concepts and problems (either as a group or one on one). In my mind, I must lead my students' learning because no one else knows better the intended learning objective of each of my lessons.

As part of every lesson, direct instruction requires students to complete problems or exercises related to the material or to explain their understandings of the concepts to the class. Once I have explained the key parts of the content, I *always* use two linkage questions: "Can anyone tell me how this is related to what we already know?" and "Why is this information important?" By assigning in-class problems and tasks and by having the students respond to my linkage questions, I activate my students' own constructions of knowledge. I also like how teaching in this manner provides all of us with constant interaction. It is much better than teaching that is primarily me talking and them listening.

Therefore, I strictly adhere to the following aspects of direct instruction for the structure it provides:

1. I review previous related material to activate students' prior knowledge to immediately clear up any lingering misunderstandings.
2. I explicitly describe how new material is related to previous lessons.
3. I allow for both guided and independent practice/homework through the use of in-class problems and tasks and questioning for student understanding.
4. I provide feedback about guided and independent practice.
5. I provide a "common thread" review at the end of related lessons or units of study whereby the common thread links all the concepts. I also do this between all units of instruction to connect everything back to the broader curricular objectives.

I am confident that my constructivist alterations and additions to these elements (such as problem- and project-based learning outlined in the next section) keep my lessons from feeling stiff or rigid. Most importantly, I have found that this modified approach helps my students both prepare for learning and organize how they will approach learning tasks.

A quote from one of the authors' former education students provides a useful summary for the importance of choosing effective instructional practices:

> I think the most interesting thing about my overall teaching methodology is that it is very different from when I began my career. I was always encouraged to have an open mind, and while in the early days I still had to "survive" in my classroom, I found that trying new ideas every now and then kept my approach fresh and expanding. Not all my ideas worked

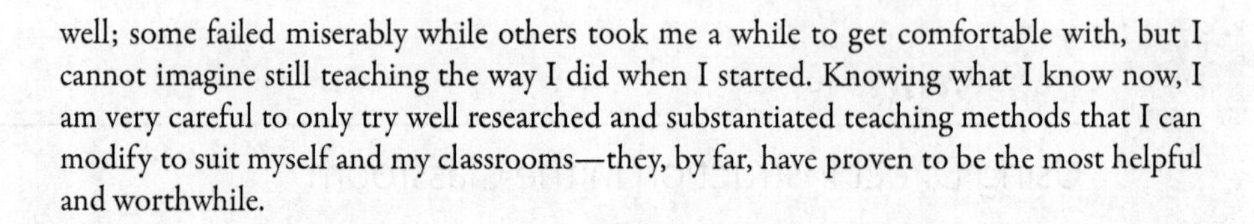

well; some failed miserably while others took me a while to get comfortable with, but I cannot imagine still teaching the way I did when I started. Knowing what I know now, I am very careful to only try well researched and substantiated teaching methods that I can modify to suit myself and my classrooms—they, by far, have proven to be the most helpful and worthwhile.

Assessment

The first sections of this chapter described how instruction and assessment are integrally connected. The remaining sections will focus on classroom assessment. They outline the underlying principles of the assessment of student performance and provide an overview of how teachers can develop an integrated approach to assessment. They also describe how a well planned approach to assessment provides students with optimal opportunities to demonstrate their learning. Detailed approaches to assessment that are directly connected to instruction allow teachers to professionally justify the assessment choices they make and implement them effectively.

Deciding on an Approach to Assessment

If students understand what they have to do to learn effectively and are clear on how their learning will be graded and reported, they are far more likely to positively self-direct their learning and studying energies. As well as providing students with this important sense of control, teachers can also eliminate misperceptions students may have about how grades and marks are assigned. If teachers take the time to heighten student awareness about assessment criteria they will also heighten student responsibility for assessment outcomes.

This clear and simple message conveys to students that they have a responsibility to be active and diligent learners and that their grades will be a reflection of how seriously they have carried out their role. Upon hearing this message, students quickly realize that if they are responsible and do the things they should do, they will do well. If they do not, they will not achieve their potential. Not only does this straightforward message reduce the need for teachers to pressure students to pay attention, work hard, complete assignments, and study for tests and exams, it also virtually eliminates the common excuses that students use to absolve themselves of their responsibilities for their actions and resulting grades. We have all heard excuses like "I didn't know it was due today," "That test was unfair," or "You didn't give us enough time." In cases where assessment methods are appropriate, fair, and clearly understood, these excuses indicate nothing more than poor planning or a lack of effort on the part of the students. This is not to say that students never have legitimate reasons for forgetting to hand in assignments or for failing to plan or study properly. These innocent occurrences will happen, and educators are constantly faced with having to judge these situations on their individual merits and provide remedies as they see fit; for example, due date extensions, test rewrites, and alternate assignments are always a possibility. But by being explicit with students about everything related to assessment, teachers can significantly reduce students' use of excuses for poor scholastic performance.

The following Case Study is an example of how one teacher explained how he would assess his students' progress and performance.

CASE STUDY

Talking to Students about Assessment

One of the most important things I'd like to point out during our first day together is that I want all of you to be successful. So, what does that really mean? Well, in my mind, academic success is all about learning. It's my job to assess how much and how well you have learned so I can determine your progress and assign appropriate grades. Today, I want to share with you how your work will be assessed and what you have to do to get good grades. I know you are all very capable students and I can think of no reason why anyone should not do well. I am going to do my very best to make our lessons exciting and interesting, and I will create assignments, tests, and exams that are demanding but fair. That way your grades will be a true reflection of your learning. I also want you to know that I am always available for extra help during class, before or after school, or during any of our breaks. For the most part, I'm going to leave this up to you, but I know students are sometimes embarrassed to ask for help, so I will check with you from time to time to see how things are going. Here is a chart that explains what you need to do to be successful in my classroom.

How to Be a Successful Learner

Come to school every day—I can only help you learn and achieve if you are here.

Make sure you have everything you need (e.g., pencils, pens, scribblers, calculators, homework, lunch, and indoor shoes)—I cannot help you learn if you are not prepared.

Pay attention during class, take notes, and do the assigned seatwork—I will tell you when seatwork will be marked or not marked.

Complete all assignments—I will not give you very much homework, but what I assign will be important and you will be marked on all of it.

Study for all tests/exams—I will give you lots of notice about each test/exam, and I will also provide a brief review of the material you will be tested on. It is your responsibility to be well prepared by studying a little bit every day.

Ask questions if you do not understand something—If you have a question, it is very likely someone else in the class is wondering about the same thing. If you do not ask questions, I will not know when you need help.

Source: Edmunds & Edmunds, 2010.

continued

Homework is an important part of my overall method for assessing your learning. Here are some important tips about the homework you will be given in this class:

1. Homework will only be used to reinforce difficult concepts, provide extra practice, or introduce new topics. It will not be used to teach new topics.
2. Homework is an opportunity for you to demonstrate what you have learned and for me to gauge how well my instruction is working.
3. All homework will be marked; if you do the work, you should get credit. Homework will not be worth as much as tests or major assignments, but it will certainly make a difference in your overall grade.
4. Homework, often started in class, will consist of small assignments requiring less than one hour to complete, and you will have plenty of time/days for completion.
5. Homework will not be due the same day as a major assignment or the day of a test.
6. Homework will not be assigned on weekends or assigned just for the sake of making you do extra work.
7. Homework will be a preview of what will appear on tests; completing homework is advanced studying for tests.
8. Copying someone else's homework will be problematic in the long run.

Practical Applications

THE USES AND MISUSES OF HOMEWORK

Much has been written about the benefits and misuses of homework. The following is a synthesis of the benefits that can be realized from assigning homework and the factors that make homework a worthwhile educational endeavour for both teachers and students:

- Additional practice or the reinforcement of concepts and skills learned in the classroom
- Higher educational achievement at the secondary level (Cooper & Valentine, 2001)
- The development and enhancement of study, organizational, and time management skills (O'Donnell, D'Amico, Schmid, Reeve, & Smith, 2008)
- The development of elementary students' study strategies and self-regulatory skills even though homework has little if any effect on their academic performance (Cooper & Valentine, 2001)

These benefits are minimized or eliminated unless homework is

- linked to high expectations for student academic success (Newmann, 1991)
- governed by an overall homework policy that focuses on how assignments affect learning and how assignments are related to classroom instruction (O'Donnell et al., 2008)
- composed of smaller, frequent assignments rather than larger, less frequent assignments (Cooper, 1989)
- appropriate, challenging, and meaningful and graded and returned promptly (Berliner & Calfee, 1996)
- differentiated according to whether the teacher wants students to practise or reinforce concepts, be exposed to new material (usually by reading), or extend their learning beyond the classroom, usually involving student interests and preferences (LaConte, 1981).

A teacher's approach to assessment must consist of different methods. It typically will include graded tests and essays but it should also include marks for homework, projects, in-class presentations, and portfolios. Not all students do equally well on all forms of assessment tools. By using a variety of assessments, teachers give every student a fair chance to demonstrate what they have learned. This variety also provides teachers with a more accurate picture of how well their teaching is going. For example, if the grading of a homework assignment reveals that students are having difficulty with a particular topic, the teacher can make instructional adjustments.

Once a teacher establishes his or her assessment system, it is advisable that he or she allow students the option of dropping their lowest assignment or test mark in each subject. Students will be more inclined to work and study more effectively if they know (a) exactly how things are graded, (b) that they can maintain a good average even if they forget an assignment or have one bad test or project, and (c) that one low mark does not mean they are a poor student. In this way, students will feel their grades are the result of hard work and good studying rather than being lucky in choosing what to study.

Students will also learn more and do better if they are provided with short tests and assignments that are completed more frequently. For example, a short test every week or two is better than one long test every month. Teachers will have more chances to provide students with accurate and timely feedback about how they are doing and what they can do to improve, which helps increase student motivation.

Assessment of Student Learning

Except for the social part of school, most of what happens in education revolves around teaching then assessing whether or not students have learned. The foremost goal of instruction is to optimize student learning. The best educational interplay between good teaching, excellent learning, and appropriate assessment occurs when assessment principles are used a priori to guide instruction (see Figure 4.5).

Optimally, teachers first consult curriculum guides to determine what they want students to learn and then decide how to best assess student learning. From there, they establish *what* to teach to achieve that learning and, finally, they come to a conclusion about *how* to best teach the material to achieve all of the above.

What educational devices do teachers use when assessing student progress? As we mentioned earlier, *classroom assessment* refers to the use of a variety of teacher-generated assessment tools. The term **assessment tool** can refer to either a single question or assignment that assesses student knowledge or skills, or to a collection of different types of questions in the form of larger assignments, tests, or exams. Given that teachers teach a variety of concepts and topics while purposefully using a variety of different instructional methods, teachers *must* be open to using a variety of different assessment tools so that they can properly ascertain the full scope of student learning. For example, there is no reason why students cannot write paragraphs to explain math concepts (instead of always completing calculation questions) and, similarly, there is no reason why students cannot draw and use flow charts to demonstrate their understanding of written material (instead of always writing an essay). Regardless of whether it is one question or several, and despite the type of tool used, the primary function of a good assessment tool is to allow students to demonstrate what they have learned; its secondary function is to provide grades to indicate student learning performance.

assessment tool
A mechanism by which teachers assess student learning. It can refer to either a single question or assignment that assesses student knowledge or skills, or to a collection of different types of questions in the form of larger assignments, tests, or exams.

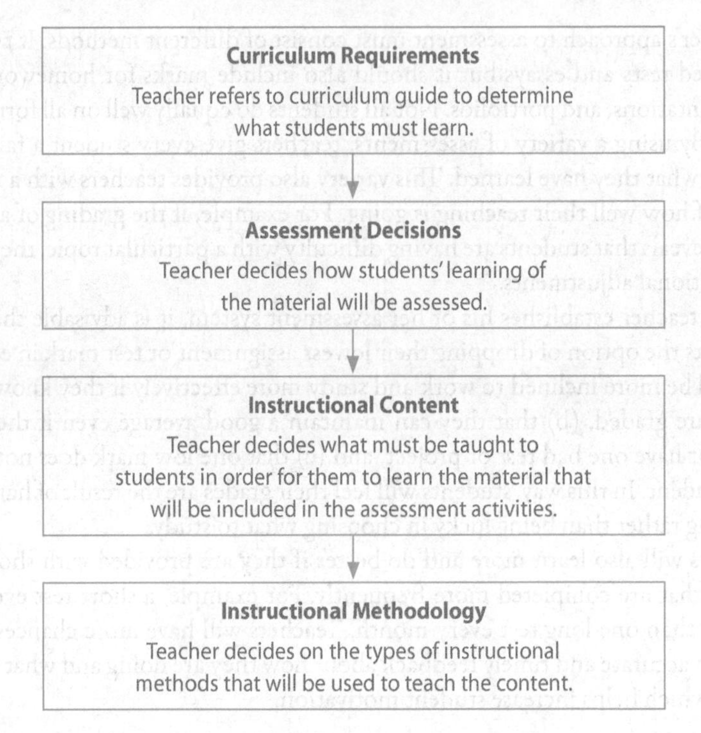

FIGURE 4.5 Interplay between Teaching, Learning, and Assessment

Source: Edmunds & Edmunds, 2010.

But where, exactly, do assessment questions come from? Furthermore, how can teachers be confident that their questions, assignments, and tests/exams are appropriate given what is being taught? The following sections present the systematic process of designing appropriate assessment tools followed by more specific details on the different types of questions available and their appropriate uses. But first it is important to consider the educational reasons for assessment.

The Purposes of Assessment

As already stated, the overarching purpose of academic assessment is to measure and indicate student achievement. Within an assessment system, there are three subsidiary purposes of assessment which exert significant influence at different stages of the teaching process. *Diagnostic assessment* (described earlier in this chapter) is done *before* instruction to determine instructional starting points and to refine or adjust teaching methods. **Formative assessment** takes place *during* instruction, and **summative assessment** takes place *after* instruction.

formative assessment
Assessment that takes place during instruction for the purpose of improving teaching and learning.

summative assessment
The most common type of assessment that is used after instruction to indicate how well students have learned the material and to provide an overall grade for a particular reporting period.

Formative Assessment

There was a time in education and schooling when, for assessment purposes, it was acceptable that teachers would simply construct and administer tests and assignments that matched the learning objectives of the curriculum and then assign grades accordingly. While these elements of assessment are still critically important, research in educational psychology has continually demonstrated that student assessment is far more effective if teachers also use assessment tools to discover what students understand or do not understand. They do this with a view toward improving both student learning and teacher instruction. The process of carrying out assessment for the purpose of improving teaching and learning is known as formative assessment. The seven vital elements that underpin formative assessment (Shepard, Hammerness, Darling-Hammond, Rust, Snowden, Gordon, et al., 2005, pp. 275–288) are as follows:

1. Teachers must have a deep understanding of the formative assessment process and understand its close relationship to instructional scaffolding.
2. Students should be afforded multiple ways to demonstrate their proficiency.
3. Student progress should be judged in relation to performance expectations rather than in comparison to other students.
4. Students must have a clear understanding of the criteria by which their work will be assessed.
5. Teacher feedback from assessment must occur strategically throughout the learning process (not only at the end when teaching on that topic is finished).
6. Feedback is most effective when it occurs on particular qualities of a student's work in relation to established criteria, identifies strengths as well as weaknesses, and provides guidance about what to do to improve.
7. Teachers can dramatically improve the effectiveness of feedback by focusing on three questions: What is the key error? What is the probable reason the student made this error? How can I guide the student to avoid the error in the future? (Elawar & Corno, 1985).

To best discover what students understand and do not understand, teachers should use various types of seatwork, assignments, and test questions that examine students' problem-solving and metacognitive abilities, not merely those that examine knowledge and comprehension. In grading these more sophisticated and complex types of questions, teachers have to be sure that they are looking for the special elements in the students' answers that demonstrate the *quality* of their work and not only grade what is easy to count or quantify.

In the first predominant type of formative assessment, teachers assess or get a sense of student understandings by constantly asking students curricular questions as they teach lessons and by closely monitoring students' performance and understanding as they complete in-class seatwork and group work. Teachers use this steady form of feedback to refine and modify all aspects of their teaching as it unfolds to ensure that their lessons present information that is suitably challenging but attainable. This is one of the main reasons why teacher–student and student–student discourses are important parts of the instructional process. Asking questions and the resulting discourse allow teachers to check for understanding and clear up potential misconceptions.

In the second and most common type of formative assessment, teachers use assigned seatwork, homework, class participation, or short quizzes to provide accumulating grades for student work completed during units of instruction. This data also provides feedback that can be used for monitoring instructional progress, modifying teaching methods, or adapting future assessments. For example, if grades on a short quiz indicate mastery of the material by the vast majority of students, teachers can eliminate further lessons (or parts of lessons) or homework related to that topic. Conversely, if the quiz reveals nonmastery or considerable misunderstandings, teachers should provide a review or assign extra seatwork to make sure that the concepts are consolidated before moving on. This is an important consideration because many topics and concepts are predicated on student understandings of preceding topics and concepts.

Summative Assessment

Summative assessment, by far the most common of the three stages of assessment, takes place *after* instruction, preferably immediately following the completion of an instructional unit. The main purpose of summative assessment is to indicate how well students have learned the material and, when combined with all of the accumulated formative assessment grades mentioned above, to provide an overall grade for a particular reporting period. This collection of data on student performance/progress also forms the basis for teachers' decisions regarding potential reviews of specific curricular material as well as student promotion and graduation.

The Assessment Design Process

Just as research about effective classroom practices for both behaviour management and instruction is founded upon systematized and proven design processes, so too is assessment. Effective assessment design produces tools and measures of student achievement (questions or collections of questions) that consistently and accurately test what students know or can do.

Designing Questions

Where do assessment questions come from? Like good lesson planning, the keystone of assessment design is the teacher's adherence to the fundamental principle of backward design. This principle dictates that assessment questions must be derived from exactly the same learning objectives used to create larger units of instruction as well as daily lesson plans (Wiggins & McTighe, 2005). For example, consider again the lesson plan that contains the following specific learning objective: *To be able to successfully calculate two-column addition without carrying.* When developing this lesson plan, the teacher created the following questions to use when assessing whether or not students have attained this particular skill:

$$\begin{array}{r} 23 \\ +\ 15 \\ \hline \end{array} \qquad \begin{array}{r} 11 \\ +\ 55 \\ \hline \end{array} \qquad \begin{array}{r} 71 \\ +\ 18 \\ \hline \end{array}$$

These questions are conceptually identical to the examples the teacher will use when she teaches the concept, and they are similar in content to the questions her students will do during seatwork or for homework. Because the teacher knows precisely what her students are supposed to learn and exactly how she will assess their knowledge/skills, she designs her teaching of the math content to make sure this happens. This process provides her with ready-made assessment questions for that specific learning objective once the lesson or unit is finished. Moreover, because these questions were based on exactly the same learning objective, the teacher can be quite confident that the questions are appropriate.

It is impractical, however, to formatively assess each and every learning objective as it is taught, so teachers often finish a unit of instruction that has taken several days to present and then design a test or assignment that assesses several related learning objectives together. For example, two-column addition without carrying would likely be assessed at the same time as single-column addition without carrying and single- and two-column subtraction without borrowing, or it might be included with single- and two-column addition with carrying and single- and two-column subtraction with borrowing. Determining when a learning objective is assessed, and which other related objectives are assessed at the same time, depends on its placement within the teacher's sequence of instruction.

Designing Tests/Exams

Given that the overarching purpose of assessment is to indicate student achievement, by extension assessment is also used to hold teachers accountable for student performance. Educators have lived in an era of increasing teacher accountability for several decades, but with a recent growing demand for less reliance on standardized tests and an increased reliance on classroom-based assessment, teacher-made tests must be able to withstand considerable scrutiny. The very best criteria to judge the suitability of a test, including one designed by a teacher, is to determine its reliability and validity. **Reliability** is the extent to which a test produces consistent results, and **validity** is the extent to which a test assesses what it is supposed to assess. **Content validity** is the most important criterion in teacher-generated assessments because it pointedly evaluates whether a test (and the questions contained therein) properly addresses the essence of the content that was taught.

reliability
The extent to which a test produces consistent results.

validity
The extent to which a test assesses what it is supposed to assess.

content validity
The extent to which a test (and the questions contained therein) properly address the essence of the content that was taught; this is the most important criterion in assessing teacher-generated tests.

There is a simple but effective two-step process for making sure a teacher-made test has high validity. The first step establishes the validity of each individual test question while the second establishes the validity of the entire test:

1. If the principles of backward design have been followed, whereby identical learning objectives were used for lesson plan design and for assessment question generation, then the assessment questions will usually have very high validity. We know this because content validity is typically evaluated and confirmed by comparing test questions to the lessons that were taught to see if they are both addressing the same curricular content. In other words, when teachers adhere to the principles of backward design, they not only create both precise lessons and suitable test questions, they also ensure that their test questions have high validity. This important first step provides teacher-made tests with curricular and instructional credibility. On any given day, it allows teachers to confidently explain, should anyone ask, how their teaching is directly related to indicators of student learning.
2. With high validity established for all assessment questions, the second step for teachers is to make sure that their entire test has equally high validity and is well constructed. Building a valid test or exam, however, is not simply a case of using all the assessment questions contained in all the lesson plans in a unit. First, this would likely result in too many questions, but more importantly, it would result in too much emphasis on some concepts and not enough on others, or too much emphasis on lower-order thinking at the expense of higher-order skills or vice versa. In other words, even though each of the individual questions has high content validity, the overall test would be inappropriate because it does not accurately reflect the emphasis of what was taught. Such a test would have poor validity.

In order to be confident that they are constructing tests that are reflective of a teacher's instructional emphasis and have high validity, educators use a **Table of Specifications** (Chase, 1999; Guskey, 2005). This is a table, or chart, that systematically outlines (a) the topics covered by the test, (b) the number of questions to be used to assess each topic, and

Table of Specifications
A table or chart that systematically outlines (a) the topics covered by the test, (b) the number of questions to be used to assess each topic, and (c) the level of thinking required for each category of questions based on Bloom's taxonomy of cognitive skills.

(c) the level of thinking required for each category of questions based on Bloom's taxonomy of cognitive skills (see Table 4.1). For assessment purposes, the six levels of thinking in Bloom's taxonomy are reduced to three levels in a Table of Specifications because (a) the thinking skills within each group are very similar and (b) it is easier to differentiate between the thinking skills across groups. The three levels are

1. Knowledge
2. Comprehension/Application
3. Analysis/Synthesis/Evaluation

Impact on Today's Teachers

TABLE 4.3 Table of Specifications: Educational Statistics 521

Topical Domains	Bloom's Levels of Thinking			Topic Emphasis & Question Totals
	Knowledge	Comprehension/ Application	Analysis/Synthesis/ Evaluation	
Measurement	3	2	0	5 (10%)
Central Tendency	1	2	2	5 (10%)
Norms	3	3	4	10 (20%)
Validity	4	6	5	15 (30%)
Reliability	4	7	4	15 (30%)
Bloom's Level Totals	15 (30%)	20 (40%)	15 (30%)	50 (100%)

Source: Edmunds & Edmunds, 2010.

All the steps in constructing this table of specifications were predicated by the fact that the university assessment policy required instructors to assign an end-of-term test with a maximum time limit of two hours. In most schools, the time frame for teacher-made tests is usually one instructional period (or less) or, in the case of secondary schools, a set amount of time during an exam period, typically one to two hours (or less).

Step 1: The professor filled in the five Topical Domains (Column 1). These are the major units of instruction that she covered in the first half of her Stats course: Measurement, Central Tendency, Norms, Validity, and Reliability.

Step 2: Then, based on the different types of questions contained in her lesson plans, she decided that in two hours students could easily answer a total of 50 questions (bottom right cell) and still have about 15–20 minutes left for review. She confirmed this time frame by completing the test herself (in about 25–30 minutes) and then allowing three to four times that amount of time for her students.

The primary purpose of the Table of Specifications is to ensure that a test contains a fair and representative set of questions that properly reflect the curricular emphasis of the instruction provided. This enhances the validity of the test. Once the purpose and process of creating the Table of Specifications are understood, and if the teacher has used backward design to construct both the lessons and the assessment questions, building a valid test or exam becomes a fairly straightforward fill-in-the-blank exercise. The Impact on Today's Teachers box includes Table 4.3, which illustrates the Table of Specifications a university professor used to construct an end-of-term test in her statistics course followed by an explanation of the step-by-step process the professor used.

Step 3: Next, based on her time spent teaching or the emphasis she placed on each unit or topic within a unit, she decided on the emphasis percentage for each topical domain and, as a percentage of 50 total questions, she determined the number of test questions per unit (Column 5: Topic Emphasis & Question Totals). For example, her instruction on Norms took 20% of the time/emphasis of the course, so she allotted 10 questions to cover Norms (20% of 50).

Step 4: Based on the verbs used in her lesson plan objectives, she determined the proportion of Bloom's levels of thinking within each unit and assigned questions to match. For example, her lessons on Measurement emphasized slightly more Knowledge than Comprehension/Application processing but did not require Analytic, Synthetic, or Evaluative thinking; therefore, she allotted three questions, two questions, and zero questions, respectively. It is obvious from this breakdown that her Measurement unit dealt mainly with the knowledge of basic facts and the understanding and use of measurement applications/calculations. Similarly, it is clear that her units on Norms, Validity, and Reliability dealt with more abstract concepts so, consequently, she used more higher-order thinking questions. (Note: Details on the types of questions to be used for Bloom's different levels of thinking are contained in the next section.)

Step 5: Finally, she summed and filled in the Bloom's Level Totals (bottom row) and cross-checked these numbers with the ones in Column 5 to make sure that (a) each level was proportionally reflective of the thinking emphasis in her lessons/units and (b) the total number of questions was consistent at 50.

The primary benefit of using a Table of Specifications is that *it recycles many of the instructional tasks that teachers have already completed.* Teachers have already divided the entire curriculum/course into smaller instructional units (Column 1), and based on the thinking verbs contained in their learning objectives they have already designed assessment questions for all lessons in each unit (Columns 2, 3, and 4). The Table of Specifications simply reuses these instructional elements in a systematized way to ensure that the number of questions per unit and per type of thinking accurately reflect the instructional emphasis. When assessment questions and instruction are created using the learning objective principles contained in backward design and when tests are constructed by following the Table of Specifications process, tests are said to have excellent content validity.

Testing Issues

The two main issues teachers face regarding assessing student learning is the appropriateness of the test questions used and the frequency of assessment. In terms of appropriateness, test questions must be designed as described above—they must match the information that was taught as well as the teaching methodology used. Students should never be surprised or confused by the type and content of the questions on a test.

Frequency of Testing

Rather than assessing students infrequently by using lengthy tests that cover a large amount of material, it is recommended that testing occur more frequently based on natural separations between or within units of study. Frequent, shorter tests encourage students to be active rather than passive learners because studying is required on a consistent basis and cannot be put off for weeks at a time. In fact, it has been demonstrated that frequent tests serve as powerful memory enhancers; testing actually enhances the long-term recall of material studied for a test, even if the material does not appear on the test (Chan, McDermott, & Roediger, 2006). In addition, over extended periods of instruction the cognitive demand of learning new material can interfere with the recall of material that has already been learned. More frequent studying and testing can, therefore, solidify the continuous process of learning new knowledge and skills rather than confuse or interrupt it. Ideally, testing should occur within one or two days after finishing a unit or a designated section of a unit.

Testing that follows these principles is more effective than testing that is infrequent and typically preceded by curricular reviews by teachers and cramming sessions by students who have put off studying until just before the big test. This is not to say that longer tests covering more material should be avoided. Shorter, more frequent tests usually emphasize basic knowledge and skills, and they prepare students for the longer tests that occur at the middle or end of a term. These longer and more cumulative tests can then be designed to have more of an emphasis on integrating knowledge and thinking processes.

Types of Assessment Questions

There are a variety of assessment questions that teachers can use, but it is important to understand that all questions measure either the retention of knowledge (remembering) or the transfer of knowledge (application) or both. To properly examine the basic knowledge accumulated by rote learning or memorization, teachers usually ask recognition or recall questions, often called **selected-response items**, which are questions that require students to select an answer from the options that are provided. The teaching that occurs before these types of assessment questions are employed indicates to students that "knowing information" is important. However, to properly examine the application of knowledge and to test the transfer skills that are acquired through much more meaningful types of learning experiences, teachers usually ask problem-solving questions, often called **constructed-response items**, which are questions that require students to think about, construct, and write their answers. The type of teaching that occurs before these types of questions are employed indicates to students that "applying knowledge" is important.

selected-response items
Questions that require students to select an answer from the options that are provided. These questions test students' understanding of basic knowledge.

constructed-response items
Questions that require students to think about, construct, and write their answers. These questions test students' ability to apply the basic knowledge they have learned.

The important distinction being made here is that there are certain basic knowledge elements within every curriculum that have to be known or established before teachers can examine whether students can extend or transfer their understandings of that knowledge.

With recent educational emphases on higher-order thinking skills in both teaching and assessment, assessing basic knowledge and skills by using selected-response questions has often been somehow dismissed as a less legitimate form of assessment. In reality, only assessing higher-order understandings can be just as inappropriate as solely measuring basic knowledge and skills. Unless teachers have taken steps to ensure that basic knowledge is consolidated, designing assessment tools that focus exclusively on application or transfer questions doubly, and unfairly, penalizes students who have learned the required basic knowledge and skills but are unable to complete the higher-order, problem-solving questions.

For several decades, educational psychologists and educators held the view that selected-response or objective questions, such as multiple-choice and matching items, were only suitable for determining students' knowledge and skills, while constructed-response questions were best suited for assessing problem-solving abilities, even though the marking of constructed answers involves a great deal of subjectivity on the part of the teacher. (As illustrated later in this section, the design of answer rubrics for marking problem-solving questions has removed much of this subjectivity.) In light of the better connections that teachers can now make between instruction and assessment, this overly negative view of selected-response questions along with the overly positive view of constructed-response questions is no longer valid.

In the previous sections of this chapter we demonstrated how Bloom's taxonomy helps situate and define the thinking processes associated with particular cognitive tasks. Table 4.4 demonstrates how Bloom's taxonomy can also be used to construct assessment questions that could be used to examine students' knowledge about water or test their ability to apply and transfer their understandings about the characteristics of this substance. Depending on the age and grade of the students and on the teacher's curricular emphasis, each of the questions could be legitimately included in a test.

TABLE 4.4 Assessment Questions According to Bloom's Taxonomy

Cognitive Objective	Thinking Involved	Sample Questions
Knowledge	Know/Remember	Which of the following is the chemical symbol for water? What are the two elements that make up water?
Comprehension	Understand	Water is two parts X and one part Y. Explain the ratio of hydrogen to oxygen in a water molecule.
Application	Use knowledge "to do something"	Build/draw a water molecule and explain its composition.
Analysis	Deduce	Why does water extinguish fire?
Synthesis	Create/Organize	How is it that we can walk on ice but not on water or steam?
Evaluation	Judge according to criteria	Present a case for/against why water is considered the basis of life.

Source: Edmunds & Edmunds, 2010.

More recently, there has been a growing emphasis on the importance of assessment that is designed to directly support and complement instruction and learning. Therefore, the current primary guiding principle for selecting the best type of assessment question is to choose the question format that provides the most direct measure of the learning objective. A broad rule of thumb for choosing the question type is to simply duplicate the activity or learning mechanism that was used to teach the concept. If a concept in geography is taught using maps, then the best assessment tool for that concept will involve the interpretation of a map. If an English unit focuses on learning how to write a persuasive essay, then requiring students to write a persuasive essay is the best assessment tool. Similarly, if calculation questions are used to teach math concepts, then calculation questions are the best assessment tool. As outlined previously, when teachers generate specific assessment questions based on the learning objectives from their lesson plans and then use the Table of Specifications to systematically organize questions into suitable tests, their tests will assess their students' use of the same thinking processes that they used to learn the material. However, it should be noted that while assessment questions are primarily learning objective dependent, they are also somewhat student dependent. Students have different learning styles and modes of expressing knowledge, which significantly affects their ability to perform well on different types of test questions. Some students do best on essay-based tests while others do better on tests that are composed of selected-response questions. Therefore, if the main objective of assessment is to allow students to demonstrate what they have learned, teachers must use various yet suitable types of assessment questions. Adopting this mindset provides all students with the best opportunity to show the knowledge and skills they have acquired because it mimics how they learned it and how they practised it.

Selected-Response Questions

A selected-response question typically asks students to choose or select an answer from several options. The most commonly used selected-response type items are true/false (T/F), matching, and multiple-choice (M/C) questions. All three types are generated from the specific learning objectives that guide teachers' lesson plans.

true/false questions
A type of selected-response question where students are asked to identify whether a given statement is true or false. These questions are good for quickly testing students' understanding of basic knowledge.

matching questions
A type of selected-response question that typically requires students to indicate that a concept or term from one list matches or is related to a corresponding concept or term in a second list. These questions are best used to assess students' understanding of associations and linkages between concepts.

True/false questions require students to indicate whether a given statement is true or false. These questions are best written as declarative statements and are best used for examining unambiguous fundamental facts (i.e., Bloom's Knowledge and Comprehension levels) that need to be known to complete higher-order cognitive tasks. They place less demand on reading skills than multiple-choice questions, and a 10- or 15-item T/F test is an accurate and quick way of reviewing material and clearing up misconceptions or misunderstandings. These types of "quick quizzes" are usually used as formative assessment devices within a unit of instruction or as a summative assessment for a section of an instructional unit that involved many small but important details. Then, once the information and concepts on a T/F test have been reviewed and clarified, teachers can confidently use higher-order questions about the same material on a future test. T/F questions are good substitutes for multiple-choice items when it is difficult to generate a suitable number of wrong answers.

Matching questions typically require students to indicate that a concept or term from one list matches or is related to a corresponding concept or term in a second list. Students do this by either drawing a line between the matching concepts or by writing in the number or letter of the selected response. Matching questions usually examine Bloom's levels of Knowledge and Comprehension because students merely have to recognize or recall information. A way to increase cognitive complexity is to provide some concepts in the second list that either match more than one item in the first list or have no match at all. A matching question can also be transformed into a multiple fill-in-the-blank question to increase the

Practical Applications

TRUE/FALSE QUESTIONS

Strengths of True/False Questions

1. Can cover a lot of content in little time (about two questions per minute)
2. Excellent for basic knowledge and facts
3. Less demand on reading ability than multiple-choice questions
4. Scoring is easy and reliable

Limitations of True/False Questions

1. Difficult to write questions beyond the knowledge and comprehension levels that are unambiguous
2. Scores are more subject to guessing than with any other question
3. Requires that the statement is absolutely true or false

Tips for Writing True/False Questions

1. Statements must be definitely true or false.
2. Test only one idea in each question.
3. Use relatively short statements.
4. Use an unequal number of true and false questions.
5. Have students circle T or F rather than write the letter.
6. Avoid absolute terms such as *never* or *always*.
7. Always state questions positively.

question to Bloom's Application level. In this case, students are required to fill in the blanks opposite the first list with the corresponding words or phrases (e.g., naming the capital city of the listed provinces). Matching questions are best used to assess students' understanding of associations and linkages between concepts and can be used in the same formative assessment fashion as T/F questions (i.e., frequent testing to examine whether required knowledge is consolidated before examining higher-order thinking about the same material). To avoid making matching questions unfairly confusing, limit the number of concepts in each list to no more than 10.

multiple-choice questions A type of selected-response question that requires students to read a question or statement (called the stem) and select one correct answer from preferably four but sometimes five options. These are the most common type of selected-response questions. They are ideal for testing basic knowledge, but carefully worded questions can also be used to test student understanding.

Multiple-choice questions, by far the most commonly used selected-response format, require students to read a question or statement (called the *stem*) and select one correct answer from preferably four but sometimes five options (called *distractors*). While M/C questions are mostly used to test for factual knowledge, well-thought-out questions can also be used to measure complex reasoning skills and the application of student understanding. Sometimes M/C questions are purposefully designed to have answers with varying degrees of correctness rather than simply having one correct answer and several incorrect answers. These types of questions are excellent for examining concepts that have subtle but important distinctions between related pieces of information. However, when designing these types of questions, teachers must be careful that the most correct answer is not susceptible to interpretation; they must pay close attention to the learning objectives from which the questions were generated and the content specificity that was highlighted when the material was taught in class. If the teacher cannot be 100% confident that this is exactly how the concepts were differentiated, this approach should not be used.

Practical Applications

MATCHING QUESTIONS

Strengths of Matching Questions

1. Very well suited to measuring associations between concepts/information
2. Easy to construct
3. Short reading and response time allows for more content coverage
4. Reduces and almost eliminates guessing

Limitations of Matching Questions

1. Difficult to measure learning objectives requiring more than basic knowledge

Tips for Writing Matching Questions

1. Provide more Column B options (7–10) than Column A statements/words (5–8).
2. Do not use options for more than one statement.
3. Number Column A statements and use letters for Column B options.
4. Make sure all statements and options address elements of the same concept as it was taught.

Example

Match the inventor's name with each invention and record the letter indicating your choice on the line next to the invention. Each inventor may only be used once.

Inventions	Inventor
____ 1. Airplane	a. John Baird
____ 2. Steamboat	b. Sir Frederick Banting
____ 3. Automobile	c. Henry Ford
____ 4. Radio	d. Benjamin Franklin
____ 5. Iron stove	e. Robert Fulton
____ 6. Television	f. Guglielmo Marconi
	g. Orville Wright
	h. James Watt

Excellent M/C questions have clearly stated, unambiguous questions or statements presented in language that is consistent with the language used to teach or discuss the concept. Students perceive the use of vastly different language as an attempt to trick them. The use of "All of the above" or "None of the above" as possible answers should only be implemented if, and only if, "all" or "none" of the information forms a critical understanding of the concept that was taught. Otherwise, totally inclusive or completely exclusive possible answers merely encourage test-taking strategies that have nothing to do with the knowledge learned. Furthermore, unless "all" or "none" of the information forms a critical understanding of the concept, students will perceive these answers as attempts to make the test harder rather than attempts to assess what they actually know.

To properly measure higher-order thinking skills, M/C questions must require students to analyze material that is similar to the content they originally encountered in their course and to answer a question or several questions based on the new material. The material

Practical Applications

MULTIPLE-CHOICE QUESTIONS

Strengths of Multiple-Choice Questions

1. Can cover a lot of material very efficiently
2. Good for measuring student achievement
3. Scores are less influenced by guessing than true/false questions
4. Scores are more reliable/consistent than essays
5. Scoring is easy

Limitations of Multiple-Choice Questions

1. Constructing good questions is time consuming
2. Without plausible distracters, redesign question as a completion item
3. Scores can be influenced by reading ability
4. Often fails to test higher levels of cognitive thinking

Case-Based Multiple-Choice Questions

The case-based method uses a comprehensive example or case study that is representative of the topics taught. It acts as the stimulus information for the multiple-choice questions that students have to answer. This method allows teachers to test complex thinking, the application of knowledge, and the ability to use and transfer the knowledge and skills taught in the course.

Tips for Writing Good Multiple-Choice Questions

1. Use cases or real-world situations.
2. Use diagrams/maps/charts/tables/figures to tap applied, analytical, or evaluative thinking.
3. Use direct quotes and ask for an interpretation or evaluation.
4. Use straightforward statements/questions and four possible answers.
5. When using the "best answer" format, make sure one choice is obviously better than the rest.
6. Always word stems positively. If needed, negative words should be underlined.
7. Avoid "all of the above" and "none of the above" unless it is vital to the concept.
8. Use plausible distracters; no tricky options.

presented in the question can be in the form of paragraphs, charts, maps, pictures, graphs, or anything that is directly related to the course content. Teachers who want to use these detailed types of M/C questions must keep in mind that such questions place a high demand on students' reading abilities and require more time to complete.

Each of these types of selected-response questions can be scored quickly and easily and can be used to assess a broad array of factual content. However, they are susceptible to students being able to guess the correct answer, with T/F having the highest probability of guessing correctly, M/C having moderate probability, and matching questions presenting the lowest chance (based on 7–10 perfect matches). All three formats are easily and quickly scored and can be used to assess student understandings across a broad array of factual course content.

Today, no curriculum is solely devoted to unambiguous facts and knowledge, so it is inappropriate for teachers to use only selected-response questions and tests to assess student learning. Selected-response questions and tests are appropriate assessment tools when they examine unambiguous knowledge/skills and the type of understandings that were emphasized during instruction. For example, if a series of lessons taught only the names and functions of the individual parts of the human circulatory system, questions that examine individual names and functions are perfectly appropriate. However (and here is where many teachers encounter problems), asking students questions that examine how all body parts work together within an integrated system would be completely inappropriate *unless these explicit connections were taught and demonstrated by the teacher*. Moreover, even if these explicit connections were taught and demonstrated, this does not make selected-response questions the best way to examine such intricate understandings and descriptions of integrated systems. For a proper examination of such detailed understandings, a constructed-response question is best. It is highly recommended, therefore, that selected-response questions and tests be used as part of a broad array of teacher-generated assessment methods wherein the types of questions used are appropriate for the respective content covered and how it was taught.

Constructed-Response Questions

The most commonly used constructed-response type questions are short-answer, restricted-essay, and essay questions. Like selected-response questions, all three types are generated from the learning objectives that guide teachers' lesson plans. However, unlike selected-response questions, all three types require students to provide an answer rather than to merely select one. The requirement to generate an answer eliminates a student's ability to simply recognize a correct answer that may have been forgotten or is only vaguely understood. In other words, the probability of students guessing the correct answer to a constructed-response type question is extremely low.

Another unique feature of constructed-response questions is that teachers must gauge or judge the correctness of the constructed answer. Where possible, it is highly recommended that students be given the benefit of the doubt for answers that are close to the intended answer but not necessarily word perfect, even if only partial credit is awarded. Teachers can easily accomplish this by asking students something like, "Can you please tell me what you meant by this word/term/phrase?" and then judging the correctness of the written answers based on students' explanations. There are two reasons for taking this generous perspective. First, most teachers adhere to constructivist perspectives of education; they believe that students use and interpret language slightly differently when constructing their own knowledge, thus they are likely to have slightly different but still correct understandings of the concepts taught. Therefore, in testing situations, teachers have to expect varied or imprecise words, terms, or phrases that still convey the critical meaning of the required answer. Second, and perhaps most important, if teachers want their students to be consistently active learners instead of passive recipients of information, they must let their students know that their efforts to learn are valued. Nothing will dampen a student's enthusiasm for learning faster than the perceived unfairness of not getting credit for an answer that "means the same thing."

short-answer questions
A type of constructed-response question where students either write a word, phrase, or few sentences to provide a correct answer or where they complete a sentence by filling in the correct word, number, or symbol.

Short-answer questions typically come in two formats. In the first format, students have to answer direct questions by writing a word, phrase, or a few sentences to provide a correct answer. Here are some examples:

1. Question: Who discovered insulin and what country was that person from? Answer: Dr. Frederick Banting discovered insulin and was from Canada.
2. Question: Name the national park that is located on the west coast of Newfoundland and briefly describe the predominant and unique elements of its geography. Answer: The national park on the west coast of Newfoundland is Gros Morne National Park. Its predominant and unique geography is that it has fjords similar to those found in Norway.

These types of questions contain one main point or one primary concept that may have several related parts. Depending on a teacher's overall emphasis for the course, students write their multiple-part answers in either point form or in complete sentences.

The second format of short-answer questions, commonly called **completion** or **fill-in-the-blank questions**, requires students to demonstrate their understanding by completing a sentence with the correct words, numbers, or symbols. The blank can be at the beginning, in the middle, or at the end of the sentence, but it is imperative that the blank require the critical piece of content knowledge while the rest of the sentence provides the context for that answer. This requires the basic recall of information, which is a slightly better indicator of higher-order learning than the simple recognition of information. Fill-in-the-blank questions should only contain one main point and require only one correct response.

completion or fill-in-the-blank questions
A type of short-answer question that requires students to complete a sentence with the correct words, numbers, or symbols. This requires the basic recall of information, which is a slightly better indicator of higher-order learning than the simple recognition of information.

Both formats of short-answer questions are excellent examples of the purposeful connections that teachers can make between instruction and assessment, because these questions can mimic exactly the types of questions teachers constantly ask when teaching. When students then encounter similar questions on a test, the language used in framing the question and the thinking required to answer it are familiar, thereby making it easier for the students to demonstrate what they have learned. Short-answer questions place less demand on reading skills than M/C questions but place a higher demand on understanding

Practical Applications

COMPLETION/FILL-IN-THE-BLANK QUESTIONS

Strengths of Completion/Fill-in-the-Blank Questions

1. Provides a wide sampling of content
2. Efficiently measures knowledge recall
3. Minimizes guessing
4. Takes less time to complete than multiple-choice questions

Limitations of Completion/Fill-in-the-Blank Questions

1. Difficult to phrase so that only one answer is correct
2. More time consuming to score
3. Multiple similar answers have to be considered

Tips for Writing Completion/Fill-in-the-Blank Questions

1. If more than a one-word answer is required, they must constitute a complete answer.
2. Avoid the use of multiple blanks.
3. Omit only key words.

because they eliminate the simple recognition of answers. Like most of the selected-response items described above, short-answer questions typically examine Bloom's Knowledge and Comprehension levels and are best used for examining unambiguous fundamental facts. Therefore, they work well as formative assessment tools if teachers plan to assess higher-order skills later in the unit. Like T/F questions, short-answer questions are excellent substitutes for multiple-choice items when it is difficult to generate a suitable number of credible wrong answers.

While short-answer and fill-in-the-blank questions typically place a low cognitive demand on students' knowledge and thinking, both **restricted-essay** and **essay questions** typically demand higher-order thinking. In providing an answer, students are expected to recall knowledge, organize it, and present it in a logical manner as an indication of their ability to integrate their new knowledge *and* thinking skills. This is accomplished by requiring students to compose extended responses to statements, scenarios, or problems. These types of questions are best if teachers want to get a comprehensive picture of student understanding.

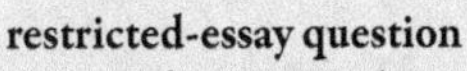

restricted-essay question
A type of constructed-response question that requires students to write an essay in response to a question that is limited in terms of the length and/or the depth of the response required.

essay question
A type of constructed-response question that requires students to recall knowledge, organize it, and present it in a logical manner as an indication of their ability to integrate their new knowledge and thinking skills.

The basic difference between a restricted-essay and an essay question is the scope of the question asked and the length and depth of the response required. Restricted-essay questions are best used when time is a factor; in these cases the unrestricted essay may be an unfair examination of the students' ability to write under pressure. Like all other test questions, essay questions must be designed with clarity in mind. The prompting statements, problems, or scenarios must be unambiguous even though they are usually longer and deal with more complex topics.

Essays can be used to examine all levels of Bloom's taxonomy once basic knowledge is consolidated. They are best used to examine high-level and complex understandings and they are effective for allowing students to demonstrate what they know, particularly when they are asked to defend their position using important concepts taught in the course. While guessing is virtually eliminated, essay questions place a high demand on writing skills. It should be noted as well that there is a curricular trade-off that teachers need to keep in mind when using restricted-essay and essay questions. While these types of questions allow teachers to examine an issue more deeply, they do so at the expense of limiting the content covered on a test. Therefore, teachers should make sure that restricted-essay and essay questions delve primarily into the broader and more critical issues taught in a unit.

Essay questions are obviously inappropriate for early elementary students who are still learning complex language skills. However, once these skills are well consolidated in the later elementary grades, students should be able to respond to fairly simple essay questions. Restricted-essays are good assessment tools to use starting in Grade 4 or 5, but only if students have had experience with essays (e.g., homework and seatwork) and only if they have had experience in writing drafts and revising and editing their work. Prior to Grade 4 or 5, students' emergent writing skills will probably provide inaccurate portrayals of their underlying knowledge and skills. Once students reach middle school and beyond, essays are more appropriate measures of knowledge and abilities. By this time in their cognitive development, students are able to handle the more complex questions that require critical thinking.

One of the best ways that teachers can help students prepare for essay questions is to specifically point out the conceptual differences between various parts of the curricular material. By purposefully demonstrating the difference between "knowing" factual information, like the various names and functions of the different parts of the circulatory system,

Practical Applications

RESTRICTED-ESSAY AND ESSAY QUESTIONS

Strengths of Restricted-Essay and Essay Questions

1. Easily and quickly designed
2. Allow students to express their individuality
3. Require students to organize and express answers in their own words
4. Efficiently measure higher-order cognitive skills

Limitations of Restricted-Essay and Essay Questions

1. Time consuming to mark
2. Complaints about subjectivity increase when no marking rubric is used

Tips for Writing Restricted-Essay and Essay Questions

1. Specify the length of the answer (e.g., number of words or pages).
2. Require all students to answer the same questions.
3. Indicate the mark value of each question.
4. Write an ideal answer; then create your scoring rubric based on those criteria.
5. Read and evaluate all answers to the same question at the same time.

Essay Questions Reflective of Different Levels of Bloom's Taxonomy

Question	Bloom's Level
What are the two predominant types of assessment questions?	Knowledge
What are the primary differences between these two types of questions?	Comprehension
Construct one question of each type pertaining to this chapter.	Application
Explain your rationale for grading homework. Specify the benefits and potential drawbacks.	Analysis
Build a test that uses all types of selected-response and constructed-response questions and explain your rationales for each.	Synthesis
Given what you know about selected-response and constructed-response questions, explain and defend your preferred use of one or the other.	Evaluation

and being able to "apply" their understandings, as in describing how the entire system is integrated and works together, teachers are making it clear to students that they either have to think about and study facts or they have to think about and study the associations between various facts. By making these types of direct and explicit connections between how the content is taught and how the content will be assessed, teachers further enhance the validity of their tests. This explicitness also motivates students to study and learn, because they can predict what the tests will require of them.

marking rubric
An assessment mechanism that outlines all the potential elements of a correct response to a restricted-essay or essay question.

The critical element in using essay questions is to make sure that each essay is marked using the same evaluative criteria. The reliability of the marking scheme (its ability to fairly and accurately grade all essays) is critical to further improving the validity of the essay question. The assessment mechanism that outlines all the potential elements of a correct response to a restricted-essay or essay question is called a **marking rubric**. Just as designing assessment questions precedes deciding what to teach and how to teach it, designing all the critical response elements of a marking rubric *precedes* assigning the question on a test or assignment. When designing assessment questions, teachers ask themselves, "What do I want my students to know?" Similarly, when designing a marking rubric, teachers ask themselves, "What do I want my students to tell me that will indicate that they have learned the material related to this question?" By knowing in advance exactly what the complete answer is, based on specific learning objectives from lesson plans, teachers are more likely to ask more precise and comprehensive questions. Constructed in this manner, essay questions accurately reflect what was taught and are fair, reliable, and valid assessments of student learning.

One of the keys to designing a good marking rubric is to distinguish the important content criteria from the important writing elements. In other words, teachers must separately grade *what was written* from *how it was written*. For example, if there are 10 critical parts to the complete answer for a particular essay question, the teacher must decide whether or not a student's answer must contain all 10 parts to receive a perfect score. Or would it be more appropriate, based on how the material was taught, to award a perfect score for only 8 of the 10 parts? The teacher must also decide whether or not students who are good writers will get better marks than those who do not write as well. Are spelling, grammar, and punctuation important enough to be graded? If conveying or eliciting emotion *is not* a critical aspect of an English essay, how are marks awarded if an answer does this exceptionally well/poorly/not at all? As you can see, determining in advance the various degrees of latitude to be allowed when marking all types of essays is as important as making sure the specific answer criteria are met.

Some elements of an essay response can be easily marked via a checklist wherein an element is either present or absent. Even so, teachers must be prepared to determine whether partial marks will be awarded if a required key concept is implied but not precisely indicated. Other elements of essay answers will have to be graded via a rating scale wherein students get differentiated marks for varying degrees of correct answers. Awarding more or less marks for these types of elements usually depends on the quality and precision of the explanations. Therefore, it is best if the rubric includes the bare minimum answer, the perfect answer, and several points in between. Then the teacher can consistently and confidently award the respective marks for each variation and justify such differences to students, parents, and administrators (if necessary). In all instances, regardless of the number of marks awarded for a particular question or test, the total score determined by the rubric should add up to 100%. Students readily identify with percentage scores rather than a grade of 120 marks, for example.

In summary, using a rubric that includes explicit criteria provides for more consistent and reliable marking and virtually eliminates teachers' judgments based on prior expectations of student performance. When employed in this manner, rubrics are concrete evidence upon which constructive criticism of student learning performances can be based, thus they are supportive of the precise instructional goals teachers are expected to fulfill. It should be noted that rubrics are also designed to evaluate other complex academic performances such as group assignments, comprehensive projects assigned as long-term homework, science fair projects, in-class presentations, and portfolios of student work. The Case Study shows how one teacher described and defended her use of various assessment tools.

CASE STUDY

My Use of Assessment Tools

In order to properly assess the wide range of curricular knowledge/skills covered in my courses and to allow each of my students to have an equal opportunity to demonstrate their learning, I know I must use a variety of assessment tools. This does not mean that I use all the different types of assessment tools available; rather, I choose different assessment tools that precisely match my instructional methods. In this way, my assessment system is consistent with my teaching.

Grade weighting for my assessment tools depends on my teaching and curricular emphases. I do not think it is appropriate to merely assign a series of tests and then calculate each student's average mark. Therefore, I use various types of selected- and constructed-response assessment tools based on their appropriate applications. These forms of assessment comprise about 40–45% of my students' overall grades. The other 55–60% of their grades comes from *authentic assessments*: These are tests or assignments that ask students to use their knowledge and skills to carry out academic tasks that replicate or are similar to those found in real-world activities.

However, as I learned the hard way, not all curricular topics lend themselves to precise real-world applications. In my previous attempts to use more real-world scenarios, I found many were so contrived they appeared disingenuous. Not surprisingly, these did not go over well with my students. Therefore, I use the term *authentic assessment* to indicate that my overall approach to assessment is an *authentic reflection* of my teaching and curricular emphases. For example, based on a series of science lessons, I had a group of students participate in a project that required them to gather and analyze data about a local ecosystem that was showing early signs of abuse and deterioration. The students also had to devise a plan of action to help restore the viability of the ecosystem. Based on my constructive comments about the data and the comments of an expert/mentor, a local biologist I recruited to help with the project, the students finalized their own recommendations on how to enhance the area's biodiversity and water cleanliness.

As an important evaluative feature of this process, one that typically distinguishes authentic assessment from other forms of assessment, the mentor and I provided feedback as part of the project activities. In other words, the students received feedback about their recommendations before finalizing them; the intent was to have them rethink or defend their recommendations as necessary. Then the biologist helped me guide the students as they actually implemented their ideas at the site.

Where possible, I like to allot 55–60% of my students' grades to authentic assessments because this accurately reflects the percentage of time, effort, and emphasis that my students and I dedicate to meaningful learning. By duplicating the problem-solving processes inherent in having to resolve meaningful and real-world problems, I find that students improve their problem-solving skills. They learn to think beyond providing simple answers that require no justification. Based on this premise, I always require students to gather and select relevant information and to either analyze or manipulate it, or both, to find solutions to complex problems. For complex assignments and where appropriate, I will often require that students' final products be revised based on teacher feedback and evaluated according to how well they followed my (or someone else's) advice and comments.

By definition, the best forms of authentic assessment are open-ended student-selected

continued

projects/assignments (chosen from a teacher- or teacher/student-generated list) that are accomplished within an extended time frame, usually two to four weeks. If assigned as a group project, the marking rubric should provide criteria for both group and individual contributions and, where possible, allow for individual creativity and ingenuity. Single but clearly defined and shorter problems can also be used in a test format; the only limitation is that authentic assessment problems or questions, like essay questions, restrict the scope of the curriculum that can be evaluated in one test. Authentic assessments are also preferred because they allow students to demonstrate what they know and what they can do, whereas tests often emphasize what students do not know. I try to make ample use of project- and test-based authentic assessments because there is clear research evidence that these types of assessment tools are excellent for distinguishing between students' abilities to represent problems, explain concepts, logically present solutions, and self-monitor their learning during both instruction and project completion. This approach also leads to far richer discussions with my students about the content of the assessment; there are far fewer conversations about whether an answer is merely right or wrong.

The final piece in my assembly of assessment tools is the *portfolio*: a collection of a student's work that demonstrates his or her abilities, achievements, and growth over time in a particular curricular area, as well as his or her range and diversity within/across specific curricular topics. Because portfolios are growth oriented as well as product oriented, they provide systematic feedback about student development (Hebert, 2001). Portfolios are considered authentic assessments because they are representative of real growth and change. The two basic forms of portfolios are writing and artistic collections. The writing portfolio has the broadest range of applications in education because schooling predominantly requires students to write to indicate their learning. Nearly all topics in all curricular subjects can be the focus of a student's portfolio, such as social studies, math, English, languages, physical education, technology, and vocational education, to name a few.

Under my guidance, all my students are individually responsible for developing their own portfolios and for selecting appropriate contributions. To make their portfolios truly effective, I make sure each one is directed or regulated by a specific learning outcome (or two) that the student and I agree upon. The student writes the learning outcome statement(s) on the outside flap of his or her portfolio folder. I also ask the student to indicate a growth time frame and the different categories for possible entries. Eventually, the portfolio contains student-, teacher-, and student/teacher-selected items and, from time to time, the student is required to reflect on the contents of the portfolio and his or her own growth and progress. I always have my students include examples of their seatwork, homework, draft copies, final copies, or a series of reports. The main criterion for selection into the portfolio is that an item must be a clear indication of student growth relative to the learning outcome(s) or previous entries. Where practical, the portfolio should also contain copies of the stimulus materials that were analyzed or reflected upon, such as newspaper or magazine articles, pictures, printed reports/information from the Internet, and even excerpts from recommended curriculum resources. Ideally, the portfolio will contain a broad array of a student's work and it will reflect all of his or her abilities and achievements. The portfolio should never become just a convenient place to store everything the student completed over a particular period of time.

An added feature and benefit of the portfolio is that my ongoing evaluation of these student productions results in formative as well as summative grades. Based on student growth or performance indicators, formative evaluations help me determine the changes I need to make to my instructional plans and it also helps students better understand the direction and purpose of their portfolios. Perhaps the most important feature of portfolios is the fact that a student's accomplishments are all in one place rather than haphazardly stored or discarded or lost. In my classrooms, students have always taken great pride in their portfolios. They are quite enthusiastic about reflecting upon their learning and growth as they review the work they have collected. I always encourage students to realistically specify where they think growth and improvement have been demonstrated. This is efficiently accomplished because students simply have to compare their work products to the learning outcome(s) that were identified when the portfolio was originally developed. These self-evaluations are particularly effective for students who do not experience a lot of scholastic success because they act as reminders of the student's ability to persevere and make progress toward their learning goals.

The marking and grading of portfolios is typically *criterion based* in that the teacher evaluates whether the portfolio (or each selection within it) has met the established standards (criterion) for good performance. These standards, identified and established when the portfolio is originally developed, are mostly teacher determined but a reasonable proportion can also be student and teacher generated. Depending on what the teacher wants to emphasize, each of the established standards can be scored in two ways:

1. Present/correct = 1, or absent/wrong = 0
2. On a five-point descriptive scale such as Poor = 1; Acceptable = 2; Average = 3; Above Average = 4; and Excellent = 5

Because portfolios are mostly growth oriented, all evaluative criteria should reflect desired changes within the student and should never be reflective of student-to-student comparisons. Figure 4.6 contains examples of the six different evaluative criteria I used for a social studies portfolio scored on the above five-point scale. The portfolio focused on urban versus rural development, a unit of study that spanned four weeks of instruction in a high school classroom. During the four weeks, my students were required to write five reports. The primary learning outcome was for the students to improve their expository report writing, therefore, there was no evaluation of their basic writing skills. These were not the writing attributes that required growth at that time.

Each of the following criteria will be scored on a scale of 1–5:

- demonstrates an understanding of the nature of the problem,
- presents information in a logical fashion (opening, support/argument, conclusion),
- makes appropriate use of urban/rural and city/farm statistics,
- incorporates appropriate media reports (both positive and negative commentary),
- integrates statistics and media reports, and
- provides logical conclusions and recommendations (where possible).

FIGURE 4.6 Social Studies Writing Portfolio—Evaluative Criteria
Source: Edmunds & Edmunds, 2010.

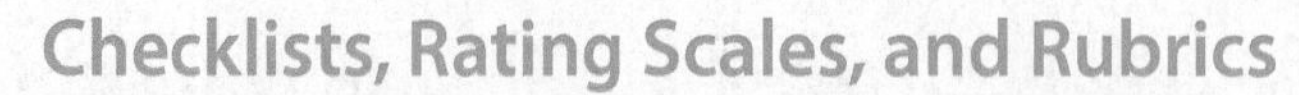

Checklists, Rating Scales, and Rubrics

The assessment principles described in the previous section are applicable for all students in all grades. The aforementioned practices (the construction of questions and tests) can be used with students as young as Grade 4. From junior kindergarten to about Grade 4, however, teachers should make use of the practices illustrated in the following section. The same basic tenets and principles of assessment still apply, but the actual assessment procedures used are quite different. It should also be noted that the practices and procedures we are about to describe can also be used for students up to Grade 12 and beyond.

What is important to keep in mind as you progress through this section is that the learning outcome of the lesson plan(s), described in Chapter 3, is still the primary source for determining the emphasis of the assessment tool that is being created. The three criteria-based instruments detailed in this section are checklists, rating scales, and rubrics. As you will see, they can be used separately to assess simple but specific knowledge and skills, or they can be used in combination to assess more complex knowledge and skills in finer detail.

Checklists

checklist
A list of performance criteria that a teacher uses to indicate whether some or all of the criteria are evident when a student or group of students performs or demonstrates something.

A **checklist** is a list of performance criteria that a teacher uses to indicate whether some or all of the criteria are evident when a student (or group of students) performs or demonstrates something. Checklists can be used for diagnostic, formative, or summative purposes. The criteria that make up the checklist are derived from the learning outcome in the lesson plan(s) and the teacher places a check mark next to those that were evident when the knowledge or skill were demonstrated or performed. On the other hand, IN (incomplete) is used to indicate that the skill was observed but that some sort of improvement is needed before the teacher can state that the skill is consolidated. For example, let's say a kindergarten teacher's lesson was about understanding shapes, drawing shapes, cutting out shapes, and then gluing them onto a piece of Bristol board in an organized fashion. There is an awful lot going on in this lesson, and all of his 19 students will be attempting to follow his example when he instructs them to carry out the classroom activity. A checklist containing all of the important elements of the learning outcome is the easiest and most efficient system for evaluating each student's abilities and progress. The checklist could look something like the following:

Students	Know/Draw	Cut	Organize	Paste
Alan	✓	✓		
Jodi	✓	✓	✓	✓
Ken	✓	✓	✓	✓

The teacher infers that students know/understand shapes when they draw them, so the check mark indicates both criteria. It is obvious from the above that Alan did not demonstrate adequate organizing or pasting skills. The teacher can assess a student's proficiency by comparing it to a predetermined criteria or by comparing a student to how well all other or most kindergarten students do on a particular skill. The completed checklist can be used as the basis for a discussion of student performance/progress with the student, his or her parents, other teachers, or the principal.

If the teacher's lesson was the first of many to address these particular skills, this checklist provides a diagnostic analysis. It can also be used later after the subsequent related lessons in a formative manner to indicate improvement. In both instances, the student can use this type of feedback to work on weaknesses. It is not advisable to use checklists in a summative fashion. The main reason for this is the checklist format restricts the teacher to indicating whether the skill is performed or not performed with no middle ground or method of describing extenuating circumstances.

Rating Scales

This is where rating scales can play a significant role in classroom assessment. A rating scale enables teachers to make qualified judgments about the skills observed, not merely indicate whether the skill was evident or not. This is often referred to as judging performance on a continuum as opposed to implementing simply a yes or no judgment. Depending on the number of descriptive separations for each criteria, teachers are provided with from three to five categories of judgment as opposed to the two categories in a checklist. As you can see in Table 4.5, the rating scale can be numerical or descriptive or both, depending on the level of detail that the teacher requires. We have extended the first two segments of the cutting and pasting checklist from the lesson above to provide examples of how numerical and descriptive scales could be constructed. You will note that we have chosen the four categories of description that are most widely used and most easily understood. Another set of four descriptors that is commonly used to determine the frequency of a skill, such as asking permission before speaking, will contain the descriptors "Always," "Usually," "Seldom," and "Never" on a 4-3-2-1 scale. Scales with more than four descriptors usually contain categories that are not as well defined, thus they are hard for teachers, students, and parents to comprehend.

rating scale
An assessment tool that enables teachers to make qualified judgments about the skills observed, not merely indicate whether the skill was evident or not. A scale usually contains between three to five descriptors that a teacher can use to judge how well a student has demonstrated knowledge or a skill.

It must be noted that even though a teacher may have a clear idea of what kindergarten students should be able to do, Alan's slightly less proficient abilities in Table 4.5 should be compared to that standard, not compared to how well Jodi and Ken did their cutting. If a rating scale is to be used, it must use the same descriptors for all the criteria being evaluated. Different descriptors only lead to confusion and less reliable assessment. There are some in education who would call the above rating scale a rubric. We present the differences in the following paragraphs.

Rubrics

A rubric is a set of specific criteria that describe and qualify various levels of student performance on some sort of educational product. In a way, a rubric is an expanded checklist that also contains elaborated descriptive rating scales that are used to confer summaries of student performance. The descriptive criteria in a rubric often match learning outcome statements closely. In this manner, rubrics help teachers and students focus on what is crucial to each and every lesson and all classroom activities. One of the main differences between rubrics and rating scales is that rubrics are used for more complex and interconnected tasks than rating scales. The criteria of a rubric should be viewed as being subcomponents of the learning outcome statement.

rubric
A set of specific criteria that describe and qualify various levels of student performance on some sort of educational product. In a way, a rubric is an expanded checklist that also contains elaborated descriptive rating scales that are used to confer summaries of student performance.

Here are the important things to consider when building a rubric:

1. Make sure that you build your own rubric—do not use generics from books or the Internet. Only you know intimately your full intentions for the learning outcomes of your lessons.

TABLE 4.5 Numerical and Descriptive Rating Scales

Numerical Scale with Descriptive Indicators

Students	Know/Draw			
	Excellent 4	Very good 3	Good 2	Needs Improvement 1
Alan	✓			
Jodi	✓			
Ken	✓			

This rating scale indicates that all three students knew and were able to draw the shapes required to the highest level expected by the teacher.

Descriptive Scale

Students	Cut			
	Excellent Cuts exactly on the line	Very good Cuts mostly on the line	Good Mostly misses the line	Needs Improvement Hardly follows the lines at all
Alan		✓		
Jodi	✓			
Ken	✓			

This rating scale indicates that Jodi and Ken were able to cut to the standards expected by the teacher while Alan was not quite as proficient.

2. Make sure the assignment (or seatwork) is designed to precisely tap into the specific learning outcomes of the lesson(s).
3. Make sure the rubric criteria or descriptors are an exact breakdown of the learning outcomes for the assignment and contain clear and unambiguous language that accurately reflects what was contained in the lesson(s).
4. Make sure each criteria/descriptor has a number assigned (four is the preferred number of criteria/descriptors) and that each element is qualitatively different.
5. Make sure each element of the criteria differentiates between the cognitive levels of Bloom's taxonomy.
6. Make sure each element of the criteria is observable and measureable.
7. Make sure that the rubric criteria represent a 100% correct answer.
8. Make sure you share the rubric with the students when the assignment/seatwork is assigned.
9. Make sure you have exemplars on hand to show students (if appropriate).

If you follow the advice above regarding making sure that your assignments and their respective rubrics closely adhere to the learning outcomes of your lesson(s), you will further add to the validity of your overall approach to assessment (see the previous discussion of validity earlier in this chapter).

The Ontario Ministry document *Growing Success: Assessment, Evaluation, and Reporting in Ontario Schools* (Ontario Ministry of Education, 2010) contains two excellent examples of rubrics that act as both checklists and rating scales. The elementary example on pages 22 and 23 of the document outlines the classifications and criteria for achievement levels in science and technology for grades one through eight. The secondary example on pages 24 and 25 outlines the classifications and criteria for achievement levels in English for grades nine through twelve. It is worth noting that both of these rubrics are quite broad in scope and apply to the entirety of their respective curriculum guides. Teachers will have to construct their own rubrics to suit smaller units of instruction and the individual assignments and/or tests that are used to determine student learning. You can access *Growing Success: Assessment, Evaluation, and Reporting in Ontario Schools* at http://www.edu.gov.on.ca/eng/policyfunding/growsuccess.pdf.

Practical Applications

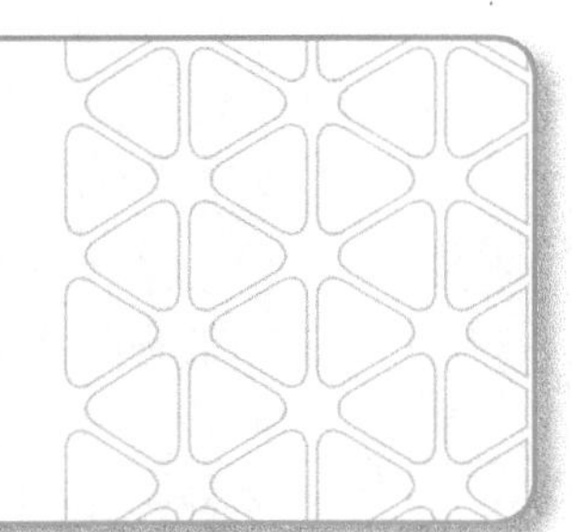

Based on the information presented above, determine whether what you taught while on practicum could be evaluated in this manner or if it would be better evaluated using some of the other assessment methods described in the chapter. Explain the pros and cons of the different methods you have considered.

Authentic Activities, Problems, and Questions

It is becoming increasingly evident that society's transition from a manufacturing-based to a knowledge-based economy necessitates a rethinking and reshaping of teaching and instruction. To better understand whether there is a need for alternative forms of knowledge and alternate forms of instruction to precipitate them, Canadian scholars Carl Bereiter and Marlene Scardamalia (2006) examined the instructional objectives and methods tied to the rising importance of knowledge creation. They concluded that students, as part of their learning process, need to more actively participate in the knowledge creation process rather than only view, learn, and use knowledge as consumers. To accomplish this, the authors recommend that teachers engage students in more **design work**: the ability to work creatively *with knowledge*, as distinct from working creatively on tasks that use knowledge. Working *on* ideas, as opposed to using ideas to do work, typically addresses practical concerns such as the following:

design work
Student work that demonstrates the ability to work creatively with knowledge rather than working creatively on tasks that simply use knowledge; that is, working *on* ideas as opposed to using ideas to do work.

1. What is this idea (concept, design, plan, problem statement, theory, interpretation) good for?
2. What does it do and fail to do?
3. How could it be improved? (p. 701)

Bereiter and Scardamalia identified four constructivist instructional approaches that use authentic but ill-defined problems to prepare students to work creatively with knowledge. While the term *authentic task* applies to each of the activities, problems, and questions used in all approaches, each has a slightly different but important meaning for the term. The four identified approaches and their respective connotations of authenticity are as follows:

1. *Learning by Design* (a trademarked name of Holbrook & Kolodner, 2000): The challenge for students is to design something that can be built and tested; authenticity means designing things that actually work and that appeal to students' interests in toys and games.
2. *Sophisticated versions of project-based learning:* Student-designed inquiry is organized around investigations to answer important questions; authenticity means activities and issues drawn from real-life concerns and controversies.
3. *Problem-based learning:* Students are engaged in solving important problems, but authenticity means that these problems are modelled as closely as possible after problems currently being encountered in their profession.
4. *Knowledge building:* Students build models, conduct experiments, and write reports as a means of producing an innovation or to advance a knowledge frontier; authenticity means the problems and questions used are the ones that students actually wonder about (Bereiter & Scardamalia, 2006, p. 705).

Applying sound assessment principles to evaluate the student learning provided by these four instructional approaches will, necessarily, result in authentic assessment.

Evaluating Teacher-Based Assessments

Every teacher wants their students to do well and know all the correct answers to all test questions. This would indicate that his or her instruction was effective and students learned all that they were supposed to learn; everybody would be satisfied. In reality, this rarely happens. Instead of being disappointed at this regularly occurring phenomenon, teachers can use disparities between what they teach and how well their students learn to improve tests. Based on what and how topics are taught and on how well assessment questions correspond with Bloom's taxonomy of cognitive skills, teachers should build tests based on the expectation that some questions will be answered correctly by all students. These are usually Knowledge and Comprehension questions, and depending on the emphasis of the unit of instruction may include some questions from the Application category. While this sounds like simple and "easy" testing, students will not be able to answer most of these questions if they do not take notes, ask questions, and study. Teachers should also expect that the majority of students will get numerous other questions correct, but again, only if they have worked hard and paid attention in class. These slightly tougher questions will mostly involve Application skills and perhaps some that examine for Analysis skills and understandings. Finally, there are usually a few questions (about 10%) that teachers should expect to be answered correctly by a smaller percentage of students, those who truly understand the content, have studied hard, and can make higher-order connections between concepts (usually 20–25% of students). Teachers do not want most of their students to find these particular questions difficult and there is no doubt they would prefer that all students could answer these questions correctly. Rather, the reality of teaching and learning is such that these types of questions will solicit answers that demonstrate complete understandings of complex concepts and the ability to transfer this thinking to other similarly complex concepts. Students acquire these types of knowledge and skills by attending all classes, paying attention and taking notes as needed, asking and answering questions in class, doing all seatwork and homework assignments to the best of their ability, seeking help to clarify misunderstandings, and diligently preparing and studying for tests and exams. In other words, if students work hard, these educational activities will help them develop skills that will allow them to answer Analysis, Synthesis, and Evaluation types of questions. Unfortunately, as much as teachers encourage students to do so, this level of success does not happen for all students.

It is also clear, however, that poor student responses to particular test questions or assignments cannot be solely attributed to a lack of work or studying. While the primary purpose of assessment is to determine whether students have learned and its secondary purpose is to assign grades, neither of these purposes is properly realized if assessment tools do not ask questions that elicit proper student responses. Therefore, the final process in a teacher's assessment system is a procedure whereby he or she evaluates whether or not the assessment tools (all questions in all tests) have been effective. To complete this process, teachers carefully review all questions and respective responses that are graded, including those assigned as homework. This is typically done after an assignment or test is graded, but of course some evidence of these issues will arise while doing the marking. Teachers should operate from the basic premise that, in theory, all questions should be appropriate and should elicit suitable responses from students because both the questions and the answers were derived from the specific learning objectives used in the daily lessons. However, we know from experience that it is not unusual that critical parts of some lessons get overlooked, the emphasis of a lesson gets a little off the mark, or students interpret material differently than intended. Despite all the careful planning and preparation that teachers do, these things tend to happen occasionally.

There is also the slight possibility that the overall emphasis of the test questions produced by the Table of Specifications did not exactly match what was done or taught during the lessons. By reviewing all questions and answers and eliminating the questions that were not effective, teachers will avoid the following pitfalls that research frequently cites as being common in teacher-based assessments:

1. Poor questions that don't reflect the intended learning outcomes
2. Students being graded unfairly because of poor questions
3. Students feeling that tests are intended to trick them and therefore they are unable to truly demonstrate their learning
4. Valuable feedback on how to improve both teaching and assessment practices is lost because efforts are not made to determine why some questions do not produce the desired results

When examining each assessment question and the various answers the students have provided, teachers need to keep the following guidelines in mind and apply them differentially based on (a) the type and level of question asked, (b) the answer the question was intended to solicit, (c) how the material was taught/emphasized, and (d) the teacher's expectations for correct responses based on knowledge of the students' abilities. Below are some guidelines for determining the effectiveness of assessment questions:

1. A question that does not solicit proper responses from the majority of students is a poor question and must be eliminated from the grading scheme (e.g., answers are all over the map, many responses missed the intent of the question, many students indicated confusion about the question during the test). This is particularly true if the majority of students includes those whose knowledge/skills and work/study habits are exemplary.
2. If a constructed-response question solicits very few or no perfect answers, the mark allocation must be revised so as not to penalize anyone. For example, if a perfect response is worth 5 marks and only one or two students get 5 while the majority of

students get 2, 3, or 4, either the value of the question should be revised down to 4 or 3 or the entire question should be eliminated from the grading scheme.

3. When grading constructed-response answers, give students the benefit of the doubt by awarding partial marks for "near misses that mean the same thing" rather than no marks. This rewards effort and indicates that learning is valued, even if perfection is not achieved.

Once the teacher has identified the poorly worded questions using these guidelines, she or he needs to closely examine the daily lessons and Table of Specifications to decipher why the question did not do what was intended. It is imperative to look for mismatches between the material that was taught, how it was taught, how it was tested, and how the students responded. In the rare instance when this in-depth process does not clear up the ambiguity of a question or two, teachers need to review the question(s) with their students to determine if the intent of the question was understood or why the question elicited a different-than-intended response. In all instances, teachers then need to make appropriate changes to lessons, teaching methods, and assessment tools—or to all three—to make sure there is continuity between instruction, learning, and assessment. By doing this careful review and making necessary revisions, teachers improve the overall validity and reliability of their assessment system. In other words, their assessment questions become better reflections of the material that was taught and how it was taught, and the answers they solicit become true indicators of student learning.

Standardized Achievement Testing

One of the most controversial issues in education is the use of standardized tests to measure student achievement. Governments use standardized tests as accountability measures. The premise is that if schools are funded by the public purse, the government and the public are entitled to know whether students are learning. Prior to 2007, all Canadian 13- and 16-year-olds wrote tests that measured proficiencies in mathematics, reading, writing, science, inquiry, and problem solving. Since 2007, only 13-year-olds are tested and only in math, reading, and science. Nearly all Canadian provinces/territories use various standardized tests for similar purposes. The controversy arises because of perceptions, often by teachers but also by others, that standardized tests (a) are biased toward certain types of knowledge, (b) differentiate between students across race, ethnicity, class, or gender, (c) are stressful and time consuming for students and teachers, (d) do not increase student learning nor their motivation to learn, and (e) assess different learning objectives than those taught in classrooms. Due to space constraints, we cannot provide detailed descriptions of the various opinions on these issues; you can find many good arguments about all of them in various media and on numerous websites. Instead we present a procedure by which a standardized test should be constructed. If this process is followed, the resulting test will be fair, appropriate, and rigorous and it will provide much-needed accountability.

Identical to our detailed discussion of classroom assessment in this chapter, the two fundamental principles this test-construction procedure will adhere to are (a) the test will be reflective of the content teachers are mandated to teach by government curriculum guides, and (b) student knowledge and skills will be compared to criterion-based standards—criteria intended to measure whether or how well a student has learned a specific body of knowledge. This type of test is developed through a rigorous design and pilot-testing process. The following example is excerpted from Edmunds and Edmunds (2010).

The province of Ontario wants to know how well Grade 10 students are doing in English. They ask some secondary English curriculum experts and some experienced, practising secondary teachers to design a test based on the Ontario Grade 10 curriculum guide. Paying strict attention to the learning objectives of the curriculum guide, this group of experts creates a series of multiple-format questions for each and every learning objective. (While standardized tests have historically used selected-response format, more tests now use constructed-response questions that assess reasoning, thinking, and problem solving.) The experts then present all the questions to numerous other practising Grade 10 English teachers across the province. They ask them to consider whether each question accurately represents the curriculum being taught and whether each question is a good question. Based on this feedback revisions are made and the resulting questions are equally divided into three different tests so that each test contains questions that measure performance across all curricular topics.

In a series of pilot tests, the three tests are administered to different sets of classes of Grade 10 English students in a standardized manner (i.e., identical test, same amount of time, same conditions, same time of year). Educators and test developers monitor the test-taking process and make notes about potential test, question, or administration revisions. The results from the three different tests and classification systems to indicate performance are developed. The very best questions comprise the final draft of the test. This test is administered to a larger set of classes of Grade 10 students that is representative of all Grade 10 students in the province (e.g., urban, rural, private/public). Based on the test results, and once scores are adjusted for testing anomalies, scoring criteria are finalized and a test manual is prepared. The final test is administered according to its standardized procedure to all Grade 10 English students. The answers of all students are compared to the established criteria. For example, if the average score on the test for the representative sample is 38 out of 50, the province can report that students who scored above or below 38 are either above or below the provincial standard for Grade 10 English. This is an accurate and fair interpretation of their English performance compared to the rest of the students in the province. Subsequent versions of this test should include its exemplary questions as well as new questions that accurately reflect curricular change. These questions will need to be pilot-tested and new criterion standards will need to be established.

Conclusion

Too often, discussions among educators are too focused on which forms and types of assessment are "better" than others. This type of debate should be encouraged as long as it centres on discussing and evaluating assessment tools in terms of their appropriateness of application. As demonstrated in this chapter, the best application of assessment tools occurs when each is purposefully connected to specific learning objectives. Another contentious issue is the use of teaching assistants to mark school assignments. Most teachers prefer to mark all their own assignments because only they know precisely how the assignment fits into what was taught. Some teachers write very few comments on most students' papers. Their naive justification for providing limited written feedback is typically that most papers are well done and that any errors are minor, usually involving grammar or writing style. In a related manner, many teachers' comments focus on students' weaknesses rather than on what the students did well. In doing this, teachers evidently do not understand the intrinsic value of providing students with written feedback and appear more caught up in assigning a correct numerical grade for each paper. It is clear that not all tests and assignments warrant extensive feedback about learning performance, as that is impractical, but research indicates that students appreciate constructive comments on assignments and they also find it helpful when teachers review some parts of some tests to clear up misunderstandings.

Kadriye Ercikan's (2006) work analyzed and distilled the historical and evolving developments in student assessment and concluded that the true value of assessment lies in the provision of evaluative feedback to students, not simply in the assignment of a grade. Ercikan, in citing Black and Wiliam's (1998) extensive review of more than 250 books and articles on classroom assessment, stated clearly that "ongoing assessment by teachers, combined with appropriate feedback to students, can have high impact on learning" (p. 931). Except for summative assessments or grades for which student feedback is mostly irrelevant (final exams), feedback is essential for students to monitor and regulate their learning. Ercikan summarized four critical aspects of education that are positively affected by ongoing and constructive feedback based on student assessments:

1. *Student self-esteem:* To maintain and promote student self-esteem, feedback should focus on positive qualities of student responses/assignments and include advice on how the responses could be improved.
2. *Student self-assessment:* Training in self-assessment teaches students the purpose of learning, makes clear connections between assessment tasks and learning outcomes, requires realistic views of personal performance, and allows students to govern their learning and studying accordingly.
3. *Interactions in learning environments:* Opportunities for students to express their understandings are necessary if assessment is to support the teaching and learning process. Question-and-answer sessions allow teachers to respond to and orient students' thinking, clarify misunderstandings, and demonstrate the thinking processes used to learn and manipulate information.
4. *Teacher–student dialogue:* This type of dialogue is more thoughtful and reflective and explores understandings more deeply than question-and-answer sessions. It is designed to engage students in thoughtful exploratory dialogue with ample time for thinking and reflecting upon understandings.

In summary, assessment is best when immersed in an interactive teaching and learning environment, it should foster student self-esteem and self-assessment, and it should be the catalyst for thoughtful and meaningful curricular conversations between teachers and students.

Discussion Questions

1. What are the instructional and assessment purposes and applications of Bloom's taxonomy of cognitive skills?
2. How can you develop an overall approach to instruction based on guiding principles and specific instructional methods?
3. How can a discussion of assessment motivate students to learn and study?
4. What are the purposes and applications of selected-response and constructed-response questions?
5. How can teachers analyze and review their assessment tools?

Further Resources

1. Airasian, P. W., Engemann, J. F., & Gallagher, T. L. (2012). *Classroom assessment: Concepts and applications* (2nd Canadian ed.). Toronto, ON: McGraw-Hill Ryerson.

   This text is designed to provide support for learning about assessment and evaluation within a Canadian context. It covers the broad range of assessments that confront teachers both in the classroom and beyond. It contains an overview of the critical concepts, terms, practices, and issues associated with assessment and evaluation, including numerous Canadian examples, illustrations, and strategies for application.

2. Joint Advisory Committee. (1993). *Principles for fair student assessment practices for education in Canada.* Retrieved from www2.education.ualberta.ca/educ/psych/crame/files/eng_prin.pdf.

   This resource is a concise but accurate description of the principles for proper assessment and evaluation in Canada. It contains the guidelines generally accepted by professional organizations as indicative of fair assessment practice within the Canadian context. It outlines how and why assessment is based on sound professional judgment and describes the issues to be considered in exercising this professional judgment. The result is the fair and equitable assessment of all students.

3. Popham, W. J. (2003). *Test better, teach better: The instructional role of assessment.* Alexandria, VA: ASCD.

   This text by a renowned educator explains how to create and use tests to guide everyday teaching. It describes how and why tests can tell you what to teach, how to teach it, what to put on a test, and the rules for choosing and writing good test items. It also outlines the measurement concepts every teacher must know to design accountable tests, including sample test questions and steps to guide you in interpreting assessment data and making sound judgments about whether instructional practices are achieving the desired results.

4. Popham, W. J. (2010). *Classroom assessment: Principles and practice for effective standards-based instruction.* New York, NY: Pearson Education.

   This text provides teachers with a concise, nontechnical, and practical guide to conducting a full range of high-quality classroom assessments. Assessment methods are integrated with instruction and presented according to when teachers evaluate students (before, during, and after an instructional unit), the learning targets that are measured, and standards of testing. There is considerable emphasis on the nature of learning outcomes and which assessments are most appropriate. Suggestions for effective practice are presented with examples, case studies, and teacher interviews as well as additional emphasis on formative assessment for student learning.

5. Popham, W. J. (2013). *Classroom assessment: What teachers need to know.* New York, NY: Pearson Education.

   This text provides practical ways in which teachers can develop and use well-written assessment tools to improve their effectiveness. It pays considerable attention to the instructional implications of educational assessment so that teachers can understand the fundamental concepts and processes of educational assessment. The text recognizes and highlights the exponential increase in the importance of educational assessment in an era of common core standards. This approach helps teachers feel part of an exciting and evolving profession.

5

The History of Education

Learning Objectives

After reading this chapter, you should understand

1. The basic elements of how several ancient societies approached education
2. Educational changes through the medieval and early modern periods
3. Educational developments in the 19th century, especially the widespread move toward common schools
4. Educational changes in Canada from before Confederation until the 21st century
5. Contemporary currents and recent changes in education

Approaches to the History of Western Education

In this chapter we want to help you understand the broad outlines of the history of formal education. We recognize that throughout history all societies have depended on the kind of informal education that happens in homes, in communities, and in such activities as hunting, fishing, harvesting, and cooking. But this textbook focuses on organized schools, so we focus this history on formal education.

Much of the history of Western educational practice has been the product of ongoing interaction between the classic traditions of Greek and Roman education and the religious traditions and thought of the ancient Jews and Christians. One could almost view these four traditions as the two sets of grandparents of Western education. More recently, many other ideas and strains have entered the gene line, but until the advent of the modern period these four influences dominated educational thought and practice.

None of these traditions is monolithic. Even cursory study of any of the four elements we just named would show great variety of thinking and practice within each of the traditions. As we will show in this chapter, Greek education varied from city to city and evolved over time. Likewise, Roman education changed forms as Rome's power increased. Within the Hebrew–Christian tradition, one finds advocates for a dramatically wide range of responses to such questions as whether subjects such as astronomy and music belong in the curriculum at all and, if they do, whether they do because they have inherent value or only because they enhance one's understanding of faith and the divine. To push the grandparents' image slightly, then, these grandparents were not the kind who just sat around—they were constantly on the move.

Historians of education do not agree on how to structure a chapter like this one. Some say that the best chapter is one that surveys chronologically how societies have historically answered the enduring questions in education, a few of which appear in the Practical Applications box. Some claim that the history of education should include a survey of educational thinkers at different points in history, examining what each of them has claimed should be done to educate succeeding generations. Others say the history of education should survey actual educational practices in different societies throughout history. This approach has some appeal because actual educational practices sometimes vary dramatically from the desires of respective societies; exploring the contradictions can perhaps teach the watchful student of education important lessons about our contemporary situation. Still others argue that the history of education should abandon any portrayals of educational neutrality and should recognize that societies establish education systems to perpetuate the status quo social and economic arrangements. Viewed from such a perspective, educational history is not just one thing after another, happening haphazardly, but begins to look more like a systematic process put in place by a succession of societies for specific purposes, many of them doubtless beneficial but some nefarious (as a large body of historical documents clearly demonstrates). In short, only the naive writer of history thinks it possible simply to tell what happened. The self-aware writer (and reader) of educational history knows that things always end up cast in either this light or that light; every decision about what to include and what to exclude colours the story.

Practical Applications

ENDURING QUESTIONS ABOUT EDUCATION

Below are some enduring questions about education that have been asked and answered in many different ways by different societies throughout time.

- Should all children have equal access to education? Or should a society's finite educational resources be distributed unevenly, giving more resources to those children most able to take advantage of what is offered or to those children whose parents can most easily afford education?
- Should societies divide finite educational resources in favour of those who prove most capable of learning?
- Should schools focus on producing critical thinkers, patriotic citizens, moral persons, or workers prepared to take their place in the economic life of the community?
- Should societies direct educational resources only to their own citizens? Or should all persons that reside in a geographic area have equal access to education?
- Should religious organizations have the right to tax-supported schools?
- How much direction from teachers do learners need?
- Should schools offer military training to their students?

In view of these issues, should a chapter such as this one always keep its eyes on contemporary Canadian educational thought and practice? Written that way, the history of education implicitly takes on a judgmental function, assessing education throughout history against contemporary sensibilities, as if educational developments constitute a natural and inevitable progression toward what we see now and as if no further changes will occur. In this chapter, we will blend several approaches to the history of education. We do want to explore the visions and ideals suggested throughout history by various individuals who have thought deeply about education. We also want to examine what transpired at different times in classrooms (and other learning settings) populated by actual teachers and students. We do not want to miss the substance and nuances of educational history as it unfolded in a variety of contexts historically, but we do want to tie it to the questions and practices of our own time in our own context. We believe this approach will add relevance and interest to what might otherwise seem like a meaningless assemblage of historical information.

Further to the caution about inevitable progression toward contemporary forms, when we examine the practices of other societies, whether in our time or in the ancient world, we may fall into the trap of considering our own patterns the right patterns, not just our patterns. When we think about how the Romans or the Greeks educated, for example, several differences from contemporary Canadian society may strike us as odd—the subordination of women, for example, or the emphasis on physical strength and military preparedness. As readers of history, we must set our own standards aside temporarily (to whatever degree we are able) and recognize that historical arrangements were as they were, as offensive as some of those might be to our contemporary sensibilities.

Also, when we speak about contemporary French education, German education, and American education we must remember that these are not monolithic. The kind of education delivered in these places has changed over time and continues to evolve. And education looks different in different parts of Germany even though Germany, unlike Canada, has a national curriculum. When we speak of Canadian education we recognize that there are great differences in curriculum from one province to the next, that there are differences between kinds of schools in Canada, that some children are home schooled, and that Aboriginal Canadians educated for centuries without schools at all. Such variety has characterized education at most times and in most places. So we recognize a certain looseness in how we use language when we employ phrases such as *American education* or *Canadian education*.

Throughout this chapter we focus mainly on educational traditions in Europe because those traditions most powerfully shaped Canadian education, not because of a lack of awareness of the systems of education developed by other societies. Also, this chapter focuses on formal schooling, because most of the intended readers are seeking certification as teachers who will work in formal schools. As should Canadian school teachers, this textbook recognizes that children today, as they have done historically, learn a great deal outside of school. That includes learning at home, through travel, through informal and organized sports, through music and other community involvements, through religious organizations, and on their own through reading and engaging with other media. We recognize all of the educational venues and agencies that contribute significantly to the formation of children, but our task here remains to focus on formal education.

Ancient Education

Among the many places and periods we might start our exploration of the history of education, we have chosen to examine education in Sparta, Athens, Rome, and China. We treat ancient education in some detail, both because the ancient period is a legitimate subject of study in itself, but also because ancient educators set many patterns of learning and teaching that persist to our own time. We will find that the ancient curricular disagreements largely remain unresolved in the 21st century. We will find discussions about effective pedagogy, and we will find complaints about students that will be repeated this week in staff lounges throughout Canada. So we study ancient education for two good reasons, not just one. We begin our study in Sparta, Greece.

Spartan Education

Today, the word *Spartan* carries connotations of material scarcity and rough living conditions, and for good reason. Spartan education included extensive military training as an expression of patriotism to the city-state. Boys participated in military training, in one harsh form or another, from the age of seven onward. But Spartan values became evident long before that. This passage from the chapter about Lycurgus in Plutarch's *Lives*, section I, part 105, gives some insight into Spartan society:

> Nor was it in the power of the father to dispose of the child as he thought fit; he was obliged to carry it before certain triers at a place called Lesche; these were some of the elders of the tribe to which the child belonged; their business it was to carefully view the infant, and, if they found it stout and well made, they gave order for its rearing . . . but if they found it puny and ill-shaped, ordered it to be taken to what was called the Apothetae, a sort of chasm under Taygetus; as thinking it neither for the good of the child itself, nor for the public

> interest, that it should be brought up, if it did not, from the very outset, appear to be healthy and vigorous. (Plutarch, 1888)

Once the male child was identified as worthy of keeping alive and therefore of education and citizenship, he required training. Plutarch gives insight into that process as well:

> [N]or was it lawful, indeed, for the father himself to breed up the children after his own fancy; but as soon as they were seven years old they were to be enrolled in certain companies and classes, where they all lived under the same order and discipline, doing their exercises and taking their play together. Of these, he who showed the most conduct and courage was made captain.

The military spirit and training Plutarch described continued for Spartan boys and young men through to about age 30. As foreign as this may seem to 21st-century readers, it was nevertheless the case that Sparta spared literally no effort—and apparently recognized few limits—in fulfilling an educational ideal that had at its foundation the views that children belonged not to parents but to the state and that the primary function of the state was to prepare for and engage in war.

Spartan education focused not only on military discipline and preparation. The Spartans also held speaking ability in high regard. For example, in *The Iliad*, Homer has Phoenix, a teacher, say to Achilles, the student, that Achilles's parents had asked him to help Achilles develop into both a warrior and a rhetor, a typical ideal of Spartan parents. According to Plutarch, Spartan boys were to "comprehend much matter of thought in few words. For Lycurgus, who ordered, as we saw, that a great piece of money should be but of an inconsiderable value, on the contrary would allow no discourse to be current which did not contain in few words a great deal of useful and curious sense" (Plutarch, 1888).

We will encounter the rhetors again in Athens and Rome. Today, the word *rhetoric* has somewhat different connotations from those it carried in ancient Greece (and in Rome). Now, as then, the purpose of rhetoric is to persuade. But like other parents in ancient Greece, Achilles's parents wanted their son to learn to persuade so that he could get what he wanted in society; Spartans considered it a basic necessity for males. Interestingly, Spartans viewed rhetoric as a skill to be used without regard for whether one's goals were ethical or not. Set in this moral framework (or lack thereof), rhetors became known for their sophistry, for winding their listeners up with sophisticated arguments to which those listening could offer no good counterarguments. To some degree, one might compare rhetors to some contemporary salespeople who persuade people to take actions against their own best interests.

We might ask, legitimately, why Spartan parents would focus on military and rhetorical skill when they hired tutors for their sons. To the extent that Sparta had an education system—albeit with no Ministry of Education or local school board—why would this society choose these two values over all the other possible curricular emphases or purposes that one might list? This question is worth asking and its answer is simple: These were the things Spartans held dear. In the Spartan vision of the good life, or what we might call the Spartan worldview, these were important values. Throughout this chapter we will see that every society creates an education system, formal or informal, to perpetuate its values. And while today we may find Spartan values harsh, unusual, or packaged in strange combinations, we can generalize and remember that, as far as the general purposes of education, Spartan society was like all others inasmuch as it wanted to survive as a society and therefore found ways to transmit its own story and its chief values to its young.

Athenian Education

As is the case in every society, how the Athenians understood education changed over time, notably around the fifth century BCE. Prior to that time, Athenian education had aimed at the ideal of the mind (reason), the will (morals), and the physique (body) all being trained to a level of excellence. Insofar as Athenian education saw value in training one's body, it overlapped with the Spartan system that we just reviewed. But dramatic differences appear as well, especially regarding the relationship of reason and virtue, a great concern of the three most famous Greek philosophers, Socrates, Plato, and Aristotle.

As do all societies today, Athens had to answer this question: Should all citizens be educated? If virtue can be taught and society wants virtuous citizens, then perhaps Athens should have answered yes to that question. However, according to both Homer and Plato, virtue could not be taught and therefore not all should be educated. For Plato especially, one must be born into the aristocracy to be the kind of person who would benefit from education. With that view, Plato might support increasing university tuition fees in contemporary Canada, or he might advocate looking at students' scores on a standardized test as the basis of admissions, regardless of financial status.

Aside from whether luck in birth qualified one to receive an education, gender also played a decisive role in Athens (as it did in Sparta). Recall, for example, that Penelope, wife of Ulysses, stayed at home—the expected place for her in Athenian culture. We know that the story of Ulysses and Penelope's role in it are simply elements of Homer's poetry, but that story and therefore Penelope's minor part in it figured in the Greek curriculum for centuries. Homer's assignment of a minor role to Penelope obviously reflected Greek society, but it influenced Greek society as well and, because his poetry was so central to the curriculum, it did so for several centuries. Considered alongside the nearly complete silence about women's education in the literature we have about Athenian society, or even the beliefs of some, such as Aristotle, that women were men's property, we can safely conclude that Athenian women received either no education or else informal, at-home training in the skills necessary to function as Athenian women.

The high regard for rhetoric characteristic of Sparta also characterized Athens. Like Spartan parents, Athenian parents would hire tutors to teach their sons rhetoric and argumentation (see Figure 5.1). As happened in Rome much later, more successful tutors would gather several students to teach together, either in rented space or in the plaza. Plato portrays Socrates as one such teacher.

Writing existed for centuries before the rise of Athens, but that city held writing in particularly high regard. Plato has left us some significant reflections on the place of writing. This passage, about the inherent value of writing, appears in Plato's *Protagoras,* a conversation recounted by Socrates:

> But you should not assume, Hippocrates, that the instruction of Protagoras is of this nature: may you not learn of him in the same way that you learned the arts of the grammarian, or musician, or trainer, not with the view of making any of them a profession, but only as a part of education, and because a private gentleman and freeman ought to know them? (Plato, 2008)

Notice that Plato does not argue some instrumental value for writing. It is simply part of one's education, something one ought to know.

Plato also left us a strong warning about writing, or perhaps about all technologies. In the *Phaedrus,* he recounts a story Socrates told about the discovery of writing. In this

FIGURE 5.1 A Typical Educational Setting in Ancient Greece

story, the lesser god, Thoth, discovers writing and runs with the news of his discovery to the king of the gods, Thamous. Thamous warns Thoth that, with writing available, people will no longer need to remember. This argument is not too dissimilar from arguments we hear today at the introduction of nearly each new technology related to communication, reading, or writing. We note this story from the *Phaedrus* because it tells us something important about the qualities of Athenian education. We know that Greek boys recited Homer from memory, learning it from the tutors who themselves knew it from memory. We also know that Greek pupils used what we now call workbooks or scribblers (we know because some grammar workbooks have survived to the present day). But the story from the *Phaedrus* indicates self-awareness about writing. In fact, if you substituted in a few words here and there, Socrates's warning about the possible death of memory would sound like any number of warnings about the death of the printed book at the hands of ebooks, or how texting will lead to the demise of good writing. In other words, Athenian education enjoyed the luxury of deep reflection, not only about such enduring questions of beauty, justice, and the relationship of the individual to the state, but on the meaning and character of language itself. The fact that we still read the works of Socrates (none written by himself, all of them recorded by Plato), Plato, Aristotle, and other Greek rhetors, grammarians, mathematicians, and philosophers attests to the quality of Athenian education.

Roman Education

Our study of Greek education has revealed that the phrase *Greek education* glosses over some of the differences between, for example, Athens and Sparta. When we turn to Roman education, we must exercise similar care in our use of labels. On the one hand, we should likely refrain from distinguishing Greek and Roman education too strongly because Rome, although it conquered Greece politically and militarily between 197 and 146 BCE, adopted many aspects of Greek thought, especially some of its forms of education. On the other hand, Roman education evolved over time, just as Greek education did. It also took varied forms; one child might receive a formal education leading to a life in law, politics, or public speaking while another child went into apprenticeship before the age of 10 to learn a trade.

As in most societies, the initial stage of education for the Roman child was informal. Both boys and girls learned at home, usually from the parent of the same sex. Romans considered educating one's own child to be honourable and important work. The underlying purposes were moral: to build character and to teach the child to value loyalty, hard work, Roman citizenship, and patriotism. More visibly and practically, this first informal stage of education entailed apprenticeship into the family business, whatever that was. Many Roman parents, while holding home education as an ideal, often turned the actual tasks of teaching over to their slave, who would have been living in their home anyway, or to a hired tutor (see Figure 5.2). Slaves were not necessarily uneducated; many were educated foreigners brought to Rome in the context of military expansion.

With the growth of Roman wealth and power—especially among the wealthy and nobles—boys would advance to more formal education, which, by the time the empire formed (in the first century BCE), took place at three distinct levels.

The first teacher a young student would encounter was called a *magister* or *litterator*. At what we now consider middle school age, about 10 or 11, boys from some families went to study with a *grammaticus*, a teacher who focused on writing, poetry, and the study of Greek, but who also taught his students music, astronomy, science, and philosophy. These disciplines were ancillary and were meant mainly to aid the student's understanding of the literature he was studying at the time.

© PRISMA ARCHIVO / Alamy

FIGURE 5.2 A Roman Tutor and His Students

This scene from a Roman tombstone shows a tutor working with a landowner's two sons. The younger brother, holding his writing tablets, waits behind for his turn to recite.

By age 14 or 15, the Roman boy's parents might send him to study with a rhetor. This teacher would train the boy in speech but would also teach him music, mythology, and literature as well as philosophy, astronomy, geography, and geometry—a wider range of subjects than the earlier Greek rhetors had concerned themselves with. Again, these latter subjects were considered secondary in Roman education; the first three were more important, and rhetoric occupied the pinnacle of the curriculum hierarchy. The rhetor's job was to prepare the future politician, someone capable of persuading others in public settings by speech alone. Given this goal, the rhetor's students studied in painstaking detail the component parts of persuasive speech, even analyzing how rhythm, sentence length, and paragraphing contributed to or undermined effectiveness. Interestingly for teachers today who use stories or case studies in their teaching, Roman rhetors frequently used case studies as a prompt for students to develop a debate or speech. Even in Rome case study teaching had its critics, some of whom were concerned that students were spending their time debating fictional cases based on far-fetched scenarios involving poisonings and insanity rather than the more normal events that would demand the focus of a real-world politician. Other critics lamented the loquacious style that some rhetors taught their students, a speech style that focused on just that—style—rather than on the content of the arguments in question.

These various teachers taught in homes and in public places such as town squares. If they were successful enough to afford the rent, they would teach in a rented space. With no system of teacher certification in place, teachers attracted students on the combined basis of their reputation and the level of tuition fees they charged. Because of the scarcity of reading materials, few teachers or students in Rome could afford to purchase written works. The teacher typically recited curricular material from memory and expected students to memorize it in turn. Because Roman education aimed openly at producing citizens who followed a certain moral code, much of the Roman curriculum was unapologetically moral in its tone. The Roman school day typically ran from daybreak until noon, with some teachers continuing after lunch.

Oratory

In our discussion of Athens, we noted the role of rhetoric in Athenian education. Roman education assigned rhetoric or *oratory* an important place as well. In our own time, educational jurisdictions everywhere face budget constraints. In response, they ask what the curriculum absolutely must include and what can be omitted. Discussions of the value of the liberal arts inevitably arise in these circumstances. We are not the first generation to have such discussions. The Romans also asked how broadly one needed to be educated. In his book *On Oratory*, Cicero argues that students should have a thorough grounding in the liberal arts:

> My own private opinion is, that no one can be a real orator in the full sense of the word unless he first acquire a knowledge of all the great subjects of human study; for a wide knowledge is needed to give a luxuriance and richness to language which, unless the speaker has thoroughly mastered his subject, suffers from what I may perhaps call a puerile vapidity of expression. (Cicero, 1942, Book I 7–10, Book II 48–49)

Although Cicero lived in ancient Rome, his words could easily appear on the editorial page of a contemporary Canadian newspaper. Then, as now, societies debated how best to prepare the next generation to become effective and contributing members of society. In ancient Rome, an orator needed three qualities: He had to be of good moral character, he

Practical Applications

OLD QUESTIONS ARE NEW AGAIN

Question: Are teachers paid enough?

Historical answer: They weren't in Rome, according to the Roman author Juvenal:

> But it is seldom that the fee can be recovered without a judgment of the Court. And yet be sure, ye parents, to impose the strictest laws upon the teacher: he must never be at fault in his grammar; he must know all history, and have all the authorities at his finger-tips. If asked a chance question on his way to the baths, or to the establishment of Phoebus, he must at once tell you who was the nurse of Anchises, what was the name and birth-place of Anchemolus' step-mother, to what age Acestes lived, how many flagons of Sicilian wine he presented to the Trojans. Require of him that he shall mould the young minds as a man moulds a face out of wax with his thumb; insist that he shall be a father to the whole brood, so that they shall play no nasty game, and do no nasty trick—no easy matter to watch the hands and sparkling eyes of so many youngsters! (Juvenal, 1918, 7.215–243)

Even when we grant that Juvenal used hyperbole to achieve his comic effect, we must admit that he paints a grim picture of the teacher's salary.

Question: Should teachers adopt behaviourist techniques?

Teachers today sometimes debate to what extent they should implement behaviourist reinforcement practices or competition in their classrooms. We are not the first to deal with that question. The Roman author Seutonius writes in his *Book about Schoolteachers* (section 17) about one Marcus Verrius Flaccus, who gave an old book as a reward for the student who won the in-class essay contest.

Question: What about study abroad?

Historical answer: Go. A semester or year's study in another country is not a new idea. Many Roman young men would spend a year elsewhere, usually in Greece, once they had completed their studies with their rhetor.

had to know his audience, and he had to be good at speaking. Regarding the third quality, one needed a good memory. Quintilian (who lived during the first century) argued that one could develop or train one's memory by learning a foreign language first. He anticipated his critics' objections by arguing that one would learn one's native tongue anyway:

> For there are other subjects of education which must be studied simultaneously with literature. These being independent studies are capable of completion without a knowledge of oratory, while on the other hand they cannot by themselves produce an orator. The question has consequently been raised as to whether they are necessary for this purpose. What, say some, has the knowledge of the way to describe an equilateral triangle on a given straight line got to do with pleading in the law-courts or speaking in the senate? Will an acquaintance with the names and intervals of the notes of the lyre help an orator to defend a criminal or direct the policy of his country? They will perhaps produce a long list of orators who are most effective in the courts but have never sat under a geometrician and whose understanding of music is confined to the pleasure which their ears, like those of other men, derive from it. To such critics I reply, and Cicero frequently makes the same remark in his Orator, that

> I am not describing any orator who actually exists or has existed, but have in mind an ideal orator, perfect down to the smallest detail. (Quintilian, 1920, Book I, Chapter 10)

Without stretching Quintilian's complaint too far, readers will find similarities to some criticisms of contemporary students and teachers. By 75 CE Tacitus was already complaining that the broad education Quintilian called for was not valued by the rhetoricians:

> Who does not know that eloquence and all other arts have declined from their original glory, not from dearth of men, but from the indolence of the young, the carelessness of parents, the ignorance of teachers, and neglect of the old discipline. (Tacitus, 1893, p. 179)

Tacitus provides the reader today with a litany of complaints that are typically raised against contemporary education, such as declining standards and a watered-down curriculum. How should educators today respond knowing that others have voiced their complaints since at least the time of the Roman Empire? Pessimists might conclude that educators are collectively on a fool's errand—that we will never complete our work. Optimists might conclude that things may not be in as serious decline as the latest doomsayer alleges if writers in Rome were lodging the same complaints.

Oriental Education

In its origins, Oriental education was heavily influenced by the teachings of Confucius, who lived about 551–479 BCE. The purposes of classical education in both China and Japan were to produce moral citizens, with morality understood more as duty to family and society than as individual moral integrity or individual authenticity (a modern concept). In this framework, morality is understood as living nobly, and nobility implies understanding and accepting one's station in life and its attendant duties. Whether one is a subject, a parent, a wife or husband, a child, a friend, or a neighbour, one has duties. The noble realization of each of those roles implies understanding and following principles. Thus, education is largely moral education.

Confucius himself (see Figure 5.3a) was more of an itinerant teacher, walking from place to place and teaching whomever wished to accompany and engage him. Those who came after him, as much as they loved his writing, formalized his teaching into a curriculum that required direct instruction, specifically recitation. The teacher would read one line and the students would repeat it until they had learned it. Eventually, they would memorize entire lessons. As we would also expect in classrooms today, such a method would engender its own resistance and classroom management problems. In these circumstances, punishment became part of Chinese education.

Confucian teaching was especially important in the Mandarin class, the class that carried out the work of the civil service. The Mandarin class consisted of males who communicated between their local communities and the emperor, a role consistent with the thinking of Confucius, who taught that a stable society depended on good leaders who served as moral exemplars to their subjects. To join this class of privileged civil servants, a boy had to pass literacy and literary examinations. These examinations reinforced the conformity that already characterized Chinese education.

We should note that not all Chinese philosophers agreed with Confucius. Lao Tzu (see Figure 5.3b), who probably lived before Confucius, argued that citizens should have no restraints placed upon them by governments and that the ultimate purpose of life was to

FIGURE 5.3 Statues of Confucius (a) and Lao Tzu (b) in Contemporary China

achieve harmony with the universe itself. Mencius, who lived after Confucius, argued that rulers could rule only by the consent of their citizens, an idea we recognize in the contract theory of government that gives shape to the political structures of contemporary democracies. Mencius's teaching about the importance of gaining the consent of those one rules also applies to classroom teachers today who, although perhaps armed with expertise, a degree, a certificate, and a contract, must also have the support of their students if they are to implement and carry out their classroom program effectively.

The political and social vision of Confucius dominated throughout Chinese history, resulting in the creation of a national examination system for civil servants that appears to be somewhat like that proposed by Plato in *The Republic* inasmuch as it prepares an elite cadre of rulers. The curriculum meant to prepare administrators for these exams consisted of studying the works of Confucius. Instruction consisted of memorization under the tutelage of a single instructor.

We have treated ancient Chinese education briefly by comparison to the attention we gave to Greece and Rome. Nevertheless, we see in ancient China a model of curriculum and instruction that worked in that place and at that time. Interestingly, Chinese educational leaders today are working to wean teachers and students off instructional models that are not too different from what we have described here. And they are moving away from standardized testing. Because critical thinking does not develop when the teacher serves as the sole source for information and the student's job is to copy down what the teacher says, some Chinese educators worry that Chinese students will not be able to compete in the global economy against students from the West. This worry seems ironic in light of Western worries that Chinese students outpace Western students in international comparisons of scholastic ability.

Medieval and Renaissance Education

Church Control of Education

As we might expect, historians disagree on the state of education in the years between the end of the classical period and the start of the Renaissance. They do generally agree that learning declined as the classical period ended, and they agree that it underwent revival at about 1000 CE. Those agreements are sufficient for our purposes here. In its revived forms, medieval education proceeded largely—almost completely—under the control of the Christian church. The church wanted religious leaders who could read the Scriptures in their original languages as well as read commentaries on those Scriptures written during the last centuries of the classical period. And it needed administrators who could manage church and civic affairs. With pragmatic motivations such as these, and the structures in place to deliver education across the European continent, the church emerged as the major provider of education throughout medieval Europe. This widespread provision may have had its roots in the 700s, when the bishops of the churches required that local churches offer education. The first purpose was to prepare clergy for the church itself; the secondary purpose was to educate others. Thus, the parish school or local, church-run school had its origins centuries before Europeans discovered the Americas by sailing west to find a route to the east.

Monasteries also founded schools (see Figure 5.4). Primarily, these were meant to educate the monks so that they might better attend to their religious duties and carry out the requisite recordkeeping related to the business and administrative activities of the monasteries themselves. These included such activities as agriculture, wine making, cheese production, and honey production, which were all meant to provide a measure of economic self-sufficiency for the respective monasteries.

FIGURE 5.4 A Medieval Classroom Setting, from a Monastery School

Because of the rigid class structure in the medieval world, with education mostly reflective of the feudal system, only the aristocracy had the prospect of extensive education. For the aristocracy, part of education was to learn the manners and obligations of nobility—*noblesse oblige*. Ordinary people would receive no education unless they associated themselves with the church.

Medieval guilds, while we might not recognize them as educational organizations, also served a clearly educational purpose inasmuch as they established apprenticeship programs whereby a young person, usually a boy, could attach him- or herself to a master to learn a trade. Given that apprenticeships and the guild examinations were noted for their rigour, one might be inclined to consider whether or not we should classify the guilds as educational organizations rather than simply as trade organizations. They offered, in effect, highly specialized vocational training within formalized structures, and they required that the apprentice pass rigorous examinations, leading us to classify them as educational organizations.

In many towns, the bishop would appoint an officer to oversee the development of schools, a development not quite warranting the phrase *school system* but coming close to it. For various reasons, in the 1300s some towns began to set up their own schools that were separate from church control. For some, establishing municipal schools was an act of resistance against the church's hegemony in so many dimensions of life. For others, it was a matter of expedience: The cathedral schools and monastery schools could not produce a sufficiently plentiful supply of clerks and scribes to meet the growth of trade. Related to the matter of supply, for some it was a matter of finding people who were able to write in the local or vernacular language instead of in Latin. This development had numerous effects, the most notable of which was that the church now faced competition in its provision of education and citizens of medieval towns and cities now had a measure of educational choice.

High Medieval Education and the Scholastics

The 12th and 13th centuries saw the rise of European universities. These were not the first universities. Recall that the Romans, when they sacked Alexandria, Egypt, destroyed a library with at least 700,000 scrolls, a library that scholars had for generations travelled long distances to study in. Some have argued that Athens, in essence, had a university. Those questions notwithstanding, the story of the founding of the universities is an important part of the larger story of medieval education in Europe. Through the late 1100s and early 1200s, universities began in Italy, France, Germany, and England, all of which still operate to this day. The early stories about these institutions have their share of rumours and intrigues, such as the claim by some that Cambridge University was founded by teachers and students who had been banned from the city of Oxford because of their repeated late-night excesses involving drink and noise. The story of the rise of universities has been told repeatedly elsewhere and we will give no more detail here.

Western Europe had largely lost or forgotten the body of Greek and Roman philosophy and literature, but the Arab world had kept the classical legacy alive. A fortunate side effect of the crusades—an unfortunate chapter in history—was the reappearance in Europe of the classics. Returning crusaders brought back to Europe otherwise unknown Greek and Roman works of philosophy and literature (we will note in a later section of this chapter that these documents, long preserved and read by Arabs, helped bring about the Renaissance). Earlier, we noted the church's practical motivations for education. Those who began to read classical works in the 11th and 12th centuries had no such practical goals in view; they wanted to study these works simply for intellectual purposes. In the case of classical fiction, some medieval readers read simply for the pleasure of reading. The side-by-side presence in the medieval period of two distinct motivations for education, one practical and one purely intellectual, anticipates by a thousand years a question about the aims of contemporary education: Should schools prepare students with skills for the practical necessities of life, or should they provide children the opportunity to engage with the rich traditions of liberal learning? We do not propose to solve that question here, only to note that 21st-century educators are not the first to ask it. It is interesting to look at the charter for the University of Avignon in France from 1303, which addresses some of these issues:

> The city of Avignon for many reasons is eminently suited and fitted to become the seat of a university. Believing that it would be for the public good if those who cultivate wisdom were introduced into the city, and that it would in time bear rich fruit, by this document we grant that a university may be established there, in which masters may teach, and scholars freely

> study and hear lectures, in all faculties. And when those who study in the university attain a high degree of knowledge, and ask for the permission to teach others, we granted that they may be examined in the canon and civil law, and in medicine, and in the liberal arts, and that they may be decorated with the title of Master in those faculties. All who are to be promoted to this honor shall be presented to the bishop of Avignon.
>
> . . . Those who are examined and approved in Avignon and receive the license to teach, shall thereafter have the full and free right to read and teach everywhere, in that faculty in which they have approved, without further examination or approval by anyone else. (Thatcher & McNeal, 1905, pp. 334–335)

The recovery of classical knowledge in medieval Europe forced the church to deal with the problem of synthesizing sacred and secular knowledge. In short, how could the Christian Scriptures and the Greek and Roman classics both tell the truth and hold the insights necessary for living the good life if they were, at some points, incompatible? Medieval theologians and philosophers—often called the **Scholastics**—gave much effort to resolving this apparent conflict, with some focusing their discussion on Saint Anselm's (1033–1109) claim that one believes in order to understand, as opposed to understanding so that one may believe. Pierre Abelard (1079–1142) suggested that linguistic analysis could help clear up apparent tensions between classic and Christian works; if through careful analysis one came to understand what the authors of works really meant, then one would find no real conflict. In more recent decades, literary theorists and scholars in hermeneutics have debated to what extent readers can know what authors mean by their written words, or whether texts can even be said to have meanings. In the 12th century, Hugh of Saint Victor (1096–1141) proposed that while authors of works of literature may have intended a particular meaning, those works also contained an inner meaning, which he called God's meaning. Albeit unwittingly, Hugh may have anticipated some current controversies in literary theory.

Scholastics
Medieval theologians and philosophers who studied Greek and Roman classics and debated issues such as how to synthesize sacred and secular knowledge and whether education should have a practical purpose or simply provide the opportunity to engage in liberal learning.

Besides the project of synthesis, some medieval scholars undertook a project of organizing knowledge. Medieval scholars had differentiated the academic divisions or disciplines, as we now know them, beginning with philosophy and logic, theology, medicine, grammar and rhetoric, literature, and law. But how did these disciplines relate and connect to each other? Were they equally important, or should we view them as a hierarchy? Various philosophers and theologians proposed overarching, integrating frameworks, some based on Christian theology and others based on classical philosophy. These medieval attempts at organization were somewhat like today's scholarly discussions of the meta-narratives offered by Darwin, Freud, and Marx, or the search in contemporary physics for what in *A Brief History of Time* (1988) Stephen Hawking has called a theory of everything.

The Medieval Curriculum

The scholastic effort to make sense of and integrate all the subjects of the curriculum in a theological framework brings us to the matter of the medieval curriculum. Knowing that the bishops first asked the churches to form schools in the 700s and that theologians were attempting to synthesize all knowledge by the 1200s helps us understand that the medieval curriculum evolved over time.

By the end of the medieval period, most teachers believed that every subject of study belonged in the syllabus because they all helped the student understand the Bible correctly. Zoology, minerals, mathematics, astronomy, and music all fit together harmoniously and beautifully. As well, they all aided students in understanding both their place in the universe and the mysteries of God's ways. Saint Augustine of Hippo (354–430) left Africa and moved to Milan as a young man. By his own accounts, he taught rhetoric by day and partied by night. He came to the Christian faith through the teaching of Bishop Ambrose, and over the next several decades he wrote numerous volumes of Bible commentary, philosophy, and theology. We note his life here rather than in the classical section of the chapter because the medieval church considered his work to be as important as that of the Apostle Paul, the Biblical writer, and of Aristotle, the Greek philosopher. In Augustine's framework rhetoric was important because, having understood the world and its mysteries, one's duty was to teach others, a practice that required rhetorical ability. The medieval period may have ended long ago, but 21st-century readers still read Ausgustine's works on language, theology, and the liberal arts.

Another strong influence on the medieval curriculum was the book *Divine and Secular Learning* by Cassiodorus (485–585). This book was divided into two large sections: Biblical studies and liberal studies. Cassiodorus viewed the two as a unity, and like Augustine he believed that both liberal and scientific study would deepen one's understanding of matters of Scripture and faith. However, the history of the publication of Cassiodorus's book tells a story quite different from what he intended. It seems that most preferred to treat the subjects as separate and unrelated, even publishing the two parts of the book separately.

This book and its vision of the curriculum anticipate two questions that continue to dog those who develop curriculum today: Around what overall central principles do we organize curriculum? And what purpose do schools serve? We have already noted in this chapter that different societies believed that schools and curriculum should produce rhetors, loyal citizens, or good soldiers. Today, the school and the curriculum continue to be contested spaces, with some saying that students must learn to compete in the marketplace while others say that democratic citizenship requires critical thinking skills, to name just two contrasting conceptions of the purposes of schools. And educators today offer a variety of different organizing principles by which the whole curriculum might achieve coherence.

Aristotle's logic, much recovered in the 12th century, came with a worldview attached—that every dimension could be organized, simplified, and systemized so that it could more readily be understood. Statements and arguments could be reduced to a number of basic forms. Some have argued that part of the appeal of Aristotle's logic to medieval scholars was its orderliness in a world in which there was much disorder and much that defied understanding.

The Eclipse of the Medieval Worldview

Historians generally agree that the Renaissance began in the late 1300s, but they do not agree so readily about when it ended. At the root of this disagreement is that different scholars point to different events to mark the end of the Renaissance. In this section we will first discuss the great flowering of mathematics, philosophy, art, and theology that followed the reintroduction to Europe of classical Greek and Roman texts; we say *reintroduction* because these works had been largely lost to Europe for centuries, although Arab scholars had continued to study the classics and had thereby protected the classical heritage. As we noted already, the crusades, one of the sadder chapters of European history, had at least one good result: When they arrived in the Middle East, the crusaders discovered Greek and Roman writing and brought it back to Europe. This factor alone did not end the medieval period but it served to raise the standards of European scholarship.

At least three other events and processes ended the dominance of the medieval worldview. First, the age of exploration challenged the essentially bounded Eurocentric view of the world that dominated European society. Maps dated through the 1600s would continue to label the massive white blotches on Africa, Asia, and the Americas with such uninviting words as "Wild Beasts Dwell Here." Such cartographic threats notwithstanding, explorers insisted on exploring and the bounded worldview that had been in place for a thousand years became unbounded.

Second, the Protestant Reformation broke the Roman Catholic hegemony in religion and its near hegemony in civil society. In our own century, we of course believe that we can construct any worldview we want—we can choose. This was not the case on October 31, 1517, when Martin Luther (1483–1546; see Figure 5.5) posted 95 theses—debate topics, really—on the church door in Wittenberg, Saxony (now Germany). Luther did not pick this location by accident; the church owned a vast collection of religious relics. From studying the Bible, Luther had concluded that such relics had no value to the Christian. Additionally, a church officer named Tetzel was aggressively selling indulgences to raise funds for the church. In effect, according to Tetzel, one could pay money so that one could sin more. Luther found Tetzel's practices and promises infuriating. Many of his 95 theses related to the abuse of indulgences. None of Luther's theses states that he wanted to start a new church, but the unplanned happened. So as the age of exploration had ended the Eurocentrism characteristic of people at that time, the Reformation broke the church's control over society. In fact, the age of exploration and the Reformation are remarkably close together chronologically—Christopher Columbus had sailed to America only 25 years before Luther lodged his complaints.

Third, from the 1400s through the 1500s, scientific and philosophical knowledge dramatically expanded. We could cite many philosophical and scientific works here, but two important ones will suffice to make our point. A 1620 book by Francis Bacon (1561–1626; see Figure 5.6) illustrates the growth—and perhaps the ambitions—of science in the early 1600s. Bacon published *Novum Organum Scientiarum*, probably best translated as *New Scientific Instrument*, in which he proposed what we now call the *scientific method* or *empirical method*. Until that point in time, scientists had relied more on reason and deduction than on observation and induction. Given this historical and social context, Bacon's immodest proposal was revolutionary. Following 1620 and the publication of this book, Europe increasingly viewed empirical knowledge as superior to the knowledge claims based on revelation, authority, or intuition that had passed the epistemological tests of European society for the previous thousand years.

FIGURE 5.5 Martin Luther

Bacon appears in this chapter because his explanation and justification of empirical scientific work had a profound effect on all education, not just on how scientists conducted their work. Some consider him one of the founders of the modern era because of his approach to scientific discovery (at about the same time that René Descartes, 1596–1650, was searching for a path to certainty through rational thought alone). To this day, he remains a key figure in the shift in authority that characterizes modernity. After Bacon, church authority, deductive reasoning, and scholastic debate would henceforth be less important than evidence gained through experimentation and observation. Millions of schoolchildren who today learn the steps of the scientific method in some sense have Bacon to thank.

FIGURE 5.6 Francis Bacon

Overlapping with Bacon chronologically, in 1640 and 1641, René Descartes published his *Meditations on First Philosophy*. In the *Meditations* he presented his famous epistemological argument *cogito ergo sum* (I think, therefore I am). For Descartes, the one thing a person can be certain of is that he or she is thinking. From this single certainty, Descartes argued upwards all the way to God's existence. A very brief background might help contemporary readers who wonder why Descartes would bother wondering if he existed. For a century following the Protestant Reformation, Europe had put a lot of energy into religious war. If your sovereign worshipped with Catholics, the nation would need to be Catholic; if the sovereign aligned with the Protestants, the nation would become Protestant. These were serious wars in which people died and property was destroyed wholesale. Understandably, Descartes, along with thousands of others, pondered what one could be certain about. In response to his own ponderings—his *Meditations*, so to speak—and based on a purely philosophical argument, he built a framework with a rock-solid philosophical claim at its base. We noted that Bacon launched (or certainly boosted) the empirical tradition in science; with the *Meditations*, Descartes launched (or certainly boosted) a rationalist tradition in philosophy.

These three events—the age of exploration, the Reformation, and the scientific revolution—put an end to the medieval worldview. People in the West would never think the same way again.

Education in the Modern Period

Up to this point, we have presented events and processes roughly chronologically and by looking at one geographic area and then another. We will switch modes in this section and proceed biographically. We do so for good reason. The modern period of educational history in Europe is marked by noticeable similarities. First, several important educational thinkers and writers, whether they lived and worked in Germany, Switzerland, England, or America, tended to have international influence. Second, a movement for the creation of common schools gathered steam throughout the late 1700s and, more markedly and fruitfully, in the 1800s. With educators travelling to other countries to observe schools, this movement recognized no borders. We will discuss the common schools movement later in this chapter, but in this section we will focus on some of these educational thinkers, writers, and leaders. Out of this series of vignettes, which viewed one at a time may seem like a random collection, one will see a new understanding of education emerging that is quite different from what had been in place for the six or seven centuries before it.

Richard Mulcaster

Richard Mulcaster (1531–1611), from England, warrants mention because he believed that instruction should be individualized for each child so that education helps every child reach a state of perfection. His vision of a classroom included both boys and girls studying music, drawing, reading, and writing in their native language. Mulcaster believed that the nature of the child trumped the content of the curriculum in importance, perhaps anticipating the somewhat ill-conceived debate heard today about whether teachers teach students or teach subjects.

Wolfgang Ratke

Wolfgang Ratke (1571–1635), from Germany, remains noteworthy in educational history because of his defence of mastery learning and the inquiry method. He believed that children should be taught all subjects, even foreign languages, in their native tongue. In his view, children should completely master one topic before moving on to the next, and inquiry was more important than memorization as a means of learning. On reflection, for someone to have promoted the inquiry method or mastery learning four centuries ago may strike contemporary educators as radical. Indeed, Ratke was ahead of his time. His name for his approach—the *new method*—may indicate his own awareness of that fact.

His view that children should learn in their native language bears on contemporary debates about pedagogy for second-language learners. Should the children of immigrants to English or French Canada be forced to study in the primary language of the region to which they have come? Or should they be allowed to continue, for a time, to study in the language of their previous national home? Those arguing for mastery of subject-area content say that children should continue in their first language for up to three years in their new setting. Those favouring immersion approaches to learning argue that new Canadians should take their subject-area instruction in French or English upon arrival here. That Ratke waded into this debate nearly 500 years ago may help us realize that a clear and compelling answer to the question will not likely appear on our own horizon easily or soon.

© GL Archive / Alamy

FIGURE 5.7 Jean-Jacques Rousseau

Jean-Jacques Rousseau

In reaction to both rationalism and the Industrial Revolution, Jean-Jacques Rousseau (1712–1778; see Figure 5.7) from France, like the romantic poets, elevated feelings, or what we now call the *affective dimension*. He advocated naturalistic education. The boy after whom *Émile* (published in 1762) is named was to learn morality through noticing the consequences of his own actions rather than through instruction, so for Rousseau morality was thus not adherence to divinely mandated laws and rules. *Émile* became a bestseller that scandalized both the Protestant and Catholic church leaders of Rousseau's day and has influenced educators ever since.

With *Émile*, Rousseau in fact launched a revolution in education and in how we think about children and their learning. Though others had previously suggested that children are not simply miniature adults, Rousseau argued the point persuasively. His conception of children's capacity for choosing well began a long tradition in education—which some call the **romantic tradition**—which includes such names as Johann Pestalozzi, Maria Montessori, John Dewey, and more recently Mr. Keating, the fictional character played by Robin Williams in Peter Weir's 1989 film *The Dead Poets Society*. In that film, Mr. Keating inspired his students to accompany him on an adventure filled with mystery and an increased love of learning. He expressed his deep belief in the capacity of the boys at Welton Academy to direct their own learning by asking such questions as, "Gentlemen, what will your verse be?" *The Dead Poets Society* appeared more than two centuries after Rousseau's *Émile*, but it captures Rousseau's philosophy very well.

romantic tradition
An educational tradition started by Jean-Jacques Rousseau that views children as naturally good and as having the capacity to choose well.

Johann Heinrich Pestalozzi

As a young person, Johann Heinrich Pestalozzi (1746–1827; see Figure 5.8a), from Switzerland, had found Rousseau's *Émile* particularly persuasive and it was to have a lifelong influence on his thinking about children and how they should be educated. Pestalozzi did not agree with Rousseau on every point. For example, where *Émile* portrays the benefits of unlimited freedom for the pupil, Pestalozzi believed in combining freedom with discipline and obedience; in Pestalozzi's work, genuine learning required genuine effort on the part of the pupils. Pestalozzi's reservations with Rousseau notwithstanding, as a student he became involved in a society that thought Swiss civil life could be restored on the basis of the image of traditional rural life. This rural romanticism would run as a theme through his educational philosophy and it would influence students for generations to come.

At the age of 29, Pestalozzi started a small charity school in his home in Neuhof, near Frankfurt, Germany. He took in 50 poor children from the area and involved them in agricultural activities in summer and indoor craft activities in winter, teaching mathematics, language, reading, and religion through songs and recitation. This farm school failed in 1779, but Pestalozzi believed his educational approach was sound (the failure being a result of his being a poor businessman). Partly as a result of the failure of the Neuhof school, he shifted his interest to developing teachers, and starting in 1804 he spent 20 years in Yverdon, Switzerland, where he continued to focus on his philosophy, methods, and teacher training.

Pestalozzi modelled a best-selling novel, *Leonard and Gertrude* (1781), after Rousseau's *Émile*. The Gertrude in Pestalozzi's title raised her children by the principles of natural education, such as treating children kindly in a home where the children experience emotional security. Although the village where Pestalozzi set this fictional family had Hummel, a corrupt and manipulative policeman, its schoolteacher, Leonard, was morally upright and Pestalozzian in his educational philosophy and practices (meaning that he believed in the innate capacity for goodness in children). The local church minister and the local nobleman also had the best interests of the community at heart. In these positive circumstances, Gertrude's children matured into responsible and independent adults, a story illustrating Pestalozzi's view that people are not inherently bad but that society has the capacity to corrupt individuals. Education has the power to help those individuals develop in another positive direction, a theme to which Pestalozzi returned in his *How Gertrude Teaches Her Children* and a debate that continues to this day. His three sequels did not sell as well as his first book, but *Leonard and Gertrude* nevertheless gave Pestalozzi great public exposure and attracted a wide following to his ideas.

Pestalozzi accepted Rousseau's romantic ideal of the child in a natural state as the correct starting point to understanding and conducting education. He wanted to shape instruction to the circumstances, capacities, dispositions, and interests of the developing child. According to Pestalozzi, children will sense the truth of what they are learning if it accords with their experience and observations. The central concept in Pestalozzi's understanding of instruction was *Anschauung*, the gradual development of the child according to natural processes. With these ideas, one might classify Pestalozzi as an early developmentalist as well as the romantic we have already noted. He had a strong interest in the child's sense impressions, observations, and perceptions, and he believed that children possessed innate intellectual, physical, and moral powers. Because he believed that children were naturally active, he argued that schools should engage children by using activities that led to their development in all aspects of life: moral, physical, aesthetic, vocational, and intellectual. Because children learn best through sensory experience, it is essential that teachers have actual objects and artifacts in the room as curriculum materials. Where necessary, graphics may be used as a substitute for the real, but for Pestalozzi verbal descriptions were the poorest substitute for the real and should be the last resort of teachers.

For Pestalozzi, education represented a natural, symmetrical, and harmonious development of all the faculties of the child, a development that should be in harmony with nature. Ideally, learning should happen in homes. Given that this ideal cannot always be achieved, school structures should imitate the home. Because natural laws governed society, Pestalozzi believed that education conducted according to his principles had the power to transform society into a natural society that ran according to natural laws.

Here is a list of several of Pestalozzi's methods:

- Arithmetic instruction based on activities and children's interactions with objects
- Drawing based on observations of actual objects rather than theory and imitation of great works
- The schoolyard as a resource in nature study and geography
- The gymnasium for moral and affective development
- Music instruction for moral and affective development
- Deduction and teaching from theory are less effective than building instruction upward from the children's own sense experiences

He offered more than this list, of course, but it gives us a sense of his holistic and romantic view of the child and of instruction.

Pestalozzi attracted followers and achieved several significant results. Many educators came to accept that children's sense experience should serve as a source of curriculum and instructional activity (echoing Rousseau's ideas and anticipating John Dewey's philosophy). Pestalozzi's view that instruction must be matched to the child's capacities and interests gained widespread acceptance. Dramatic changes came about in teacher training because of the view that teachers must be taught to work with the child and draw out of the child instead of simply reciting to the child what the child must memorize.

The school in Yverdon became a destination for educators from several nations. These educators wanted to observe Pestalozzi's natural method first-hand, and many went home with glowing reports about is effectiveness. In response to a visit by some of its officials, the Prussian government, for example, sent many teachers there so that Prussia could implement Pestalozzian education throughout its school system.

© Classic Image / Alamy

© bilwissedition Ltd. & Co. KG / Alamy

FIGURE 5.8 Johann Heinrich Pestalozzi (a) and Johann Friedrich Herbart (b), Major Forces in the Romantic Educational Tradition

To this day, Pestalozzi's educational ideals continue to motivate many educators. His motto "Learning by head, hand, and heart" is still a key principle in many successful 21st-century schools. With or without the motto, and in many cases without even knowing his name, many educators today continue in the Pestalozzian tradition.

Johann Friedrich Herbart

Among the many visitors to Pestalozzi's school in Yverdon was Johann Friedrich Herbart (1776–1841), who served for some decades as a philosophy professor at the University of Königsberg. Herbart became fascinated with the details of teaching. Regarding teachers, he stressed the importance of the teacher's moral character; regarding instruction, he insisted that children could assimilate new learning best when they encountered it in patterns. For Herbart, the lesson plan that attended to his concern for assimilation and patterns had five steps: preparation, presentation, association, generalization, and application. Although he lived 200 years ago, Herbart was describing what educators today call *scaffolding*.

Some credit Herbart with founding the study of education as an academic discipline. His interest in teaching was sparked initially when he worked for three years as a tutor, during which he met Pestalozzi, the Swiss school reformer we just discussed. Many years later he founded a teachers' college where he lectured until his death. At the core of Herbart's view of education was an idea we have already encountered in this chapter: that the purpose of education is to help children become productive citizens. The best kind of education to produce such citizens was formal and rigorous, and classrooms shaped on those concerns were the ideal place to produce moral and intellectual adults. A debate that most teachers encounter in their first psychology class as undergraduates is whether human tendencies are inherent or learned. Herbart believed that most tendencies were learned, thus placing more importance on the educational process.

On Herbart's account, effective pedagogy involved five steps: preparation by the teacher of the curriculum materials; instruction of the prepared contents; inductive questioning of the students by the teacher so that the students associate their new learning with what they already know; reflection on and summary of the curriculum contents, which Herbart called generalization; and finding and establishing connections to the good life, also known as application.

Friedrich Froebel

Pestalozzi's school in Yverdon, Switzerland, attracted visiting educators from many nations, but especially from Britain, Germany, and the United States. Friedrich Froebel (1782–1852), from Germany, came to Yverdon in 1808 and then founded a school in 1816 at Griesheim, Germany, and another at Keilhau, also in Germany, in 1818. In these schools he implemented his adapted version of Pestalozzi's principles. Central to his conception of education was his view that the child is an essential part of the universe, which is itself a divinely created community. Children were inherently good, implying that the teacher's task was to provide an environment where they could flourish.

Today, Froebel is best known for founding kindergarten, not for starting the Griesheim and Keilhau schools. He began the first kindergarten in 1837 in Blankenburg, Germany. Froebel studied with Pestalozzi at Yverdon for some time and was heavily influenced by him. Many credit Pestalozzi with inventing kindergarten, but Froebel coined the word *kindergarten* sometime between 1837 and 1840. In his view, kindergarten should be based on two central curriculum concepts: *gifts* and *occupations*. Gifts included symmetrical forms such as cones, rods, and blocks. He believed that such shapes as these pointed to the harmony and perfection of the universe itself. Occupations included physical materials such as clay and paper that pupils could touch and use. Educators today recognize that Froebel was recommending what are now called *manipulatives*.

Educators quickly accepted kindergarten as a good idea, and Froebel's followers started kindergartens in Germany, England, and the United States within a few years. Notice both the romantic and quite openly religious threads running through his philosophy of education:

- Humans are in a fundamental unity with nature and education must be organized to recognize and foster this unity.
- All that exists is to reveal God, and children will find God in nature.
- Education is a part of life, not preparation for life.
- The importance of play to children's proper development is paramount.
- We must discipline children to be mild.
- Music is important in children's education.

With views such as these, we should not be surprised that the fundamental purpose of kindergarten for Froebel was to aid in the individual development of the child. That development entailed movement, music, self-directed activity, and social settings that demanded co-operation. Froebel also believed that children should learn using fantasy and fairy tales, a matter on which Maria Montessori would later register her disagreement. She believed that children should not learn anything that they would later have to unlearn. According to her, the natural world provided sufficient curriculum materials for all the learning that children would ever need to do.

Froebel had enormous influence on the development of North American education, especially in the United States. Conservative reaction to the 1848 revolutions in Europe led to the Prussian government's suppression of kindergartens, although that suppression ended in 1861. Margarethe Schurz, who was impressed with Froebel's work but exiled herself from Prussia after the reactions to the 1848 revolutions, founded the first kindergarten in the United States in 1855 in Watertown, Wisconsin. That kindergarten operated in the German language, but five years later Elizabeth Peabody founded the first English-language kindergarten in the United States. After visiting Froebel-inspired schools in Europe and Schurz's Watertown kindergarten and converting to Froebel's ideas about children and instruction, she founded her kindergarten in Boston. In 1873, St. Louis, Missouri, became the first city to implement kindergartens throughout its public school system when schools superintendent William Torrey Harris became convinced that kindergarten provided children with an essential foundation for elementary education. By this time, state-sponsored elementary schools, known as **common schools**, were required by law in every state, and as we shall see in most Canadian jurisdictions (see Table 5.1). Pestalozzi's romantic educational ideals and his conception of the child influenced Herbart, Froebel, and others. That influence peaked in the very decades when the push for common schools and national education systems was at its strongest. This confluence guaranteed the further spread of the ideas of these three educators, and it also gave significant shape to the schools founded in North America.

common schools
Nineteenth-century state-run elementary schools that were required by law in every state in the United States and in most jurisdictions in Canada.

Maria Montessori

For several reasons, we view Maria Montessori (1870–1952; see Figure 5.9), from Italy, as an educator who fits in the same tradition as Rousseau, Pestalozzi, and Froebel. She believed that children learned through self-directed activity, but she did not come to this view without reflection and much experience. While studying medicine in Rome, Montessori became interested in children in poverty, especially in how to reach them educationally. In 1909 she

TABLE 5.1 Common Schools: When Schools Became Compulsory and Available

Nation	Date	Required Attendance Age
Spain	1857	6–15
Mexico	1857	6–14
Massachusetts (US)	1861	6–16
Georgia (US)	1868	6–16
Japan	1871	6–15
Illinois (US)	1871	6–17
California (US)	1874	6–18
France	1881	6–16
England and Wales	1891	6–16

FIGURE 5.9 Maria Montessori

Italy's most famous educator, Montessori was featured on an Italian bank note prior to Italy's adoption of the euro.

published *The Montessori Method* in which she explained her views of how humans develop optimally when they learn to interact with their environment. Foundational to her view of development was her conviction that humans had several inherent, constructive tendencies that, when allowed to flourish, would result in focused, significant learning. These tendencies included exploration, exactness, abstraction, repetition, and purposeful activity. She constructed a complete philosophy of education on this model of development, and she provided detailed descriptions consistent with this philosophy of how she believed classrooms and schools should be organized for the maximum educational benefit of children. In the century since that publication, Montessori schools have been established around the world, many of them independent but some within publicly funded school boards.

Montessori classrooms characteristically include children of different ages. Visitors to Montessori classrooms sometimes gain an impression of disorganization, but Montessori was very clear that given large blocks of time and appropriate learning challenges and materials, children could become initiators of their own learning within the clear parameters of the environment the teacher prepares and establishes. Using materials especially developed for Montessori classrooms, these children become independent learners. Although no educators used the word *constructivist* when Montessori wrote more than a century ago, she described a constructivist model of learning. Her learning model shapes not only those schools that carry her name; many teachers in non-Montessori schools have implemented some of Montessori's recommended practices.

John Dewey

As you recall from Chapter 1, John Dewey (1859–1952) remains the best-known American educator and possibly the most important educational thinker of the 20th century. He is widely quoted and misquoted, and in fact he takes the blame for many of the ills in contemporary education, often unjustly. Along with many books on psychology, philosophy, politics, and religion, Dewey wrote several educational titles ranging across several decades from *My Pedagogic Creed* in 1897 to *Experience and Education* in 1938. Several themes run through these educational writings, prominent among them that instruction should begin with the child's experience rather than with the curricular objectives or contents. Dewey argued this viewpoint most forcefully in *The Child and the Curriculum*, first published in 1902. In his view, seeing the curriculum simply as content to be transmitted by the teacher to the students through direct instruction left the students as inactive recipients rather than as engaged learners. This criticism may sound like a sideways swipe at Johann Herbart and his five steps but it was not—it was a direct attack. In *How We Think* (published in 1910) Dewey presented his own five steps to teaching, but they were five steps of *thinking* and his intention was to help teachers understand how to set up problems that students would solve. He believed that schools should help students become citizens who could properly frame and consequently think through complex problems. Today we are quite familiar with discussions of the benefits of inquiry learning or with debates about active learning versus passive learning, but when Dewey proposed his ideas over a century ago many considered them to be new and radical. To use today's educational language, Dewey was calling for *scaffolding* and *engagement* to ensure that students have a sufficient knowledge base to engage in new instructional materials.

Dewey's critics, to the present day, have viewed this experiential approach in sinister terms as a complete rejection of the curriculum and a complete adoption of child-centred education. As his popularity grew, Dewey himself expressed concern that some had taken his views too far by starting and ending with the child and abandoning the curriculum altogether. For Dewey, teachers were to provide the connection points between the child and the curriculum, not to abandon their leadership of classrooms altogether.

Developments in German Schooling

We have reviewed the ideas and work of several educational thinkers, most of them European. We end this section of the chapter by noting briefly developments in two settings, Germany and the United States. We start with Germany.

Johann Gottlieb Fichte (1762–1814) was well known in his own time in Germany as a philosopher. Our interest in him stems from his important role in spreading Pestalozzi's ideas. Fichte gave a series of lectures in 1807–1808 known as the *Addresses to the German Nation*. In those lectures he promoted Pestalozzian understandings of curriculum and instruction. He was appointed first chancellor of the newly chartered University of Berlin in 1809, a year after the German government had created a new Bureau of Education within the Ministry of the Interior with Wilhelm von Humboldt as director. Humboldt created a new national system of secondary education—the Gymnasium schools—which followed a national curriculum that combined study of the classics with science and modern languages. In 1810, Humboldt introduced a national system of teacher certification.

In 1817, Germany folded the Bureau of Education into a Ministry of Religion, Education, and Public Health. Under this umbrella, the clergy had greater influence over education, resulting in the requirements that teachers be of upstanding moral character and that they teach their students to obey legitimate institutions. By 1834, success on the national exams that signified the end of one's secondary education were accepted nationally as the equivalent of an entrance exam to the university, further legitimizing the Gymnasium schools.

Jumping several decades ahead, in 1890 Kaiser Wilhelm II convened a national education conference to address the need for schools to prepare students more adequately in science and in the practical skills needed in the workplace. The conference also addressed the questions of how schools could attend more carefully to German language and history in the interests of promoting national identity.

This very brief review includes only a few details but these details are sufficient for the 21st-century reader to see that some of our contemporary educational policy debates did not begin in the last few decades. In fact, educators and policy-makers in many nations have dealt with these same questions at many other points in history.

Developments in American Schooling

As does the British North America Act for Canada, the US Constitution deprives the federal government of a role in education. It leaves individual states to decide what to do about the instruction of children. Several states do address education in their own state constitutions. For example, the Pennsylvania Constitution of 1776 prescribes that schools be "established in every county by the legislature for the convenient instruction of youth, with such salaries to masters, paid by the public, as may enable them to instruct the youth at low prices, and all useful learning shall be duly encouraged and promoted in one or more universities" (Noble, 1938, p. 117). The Constitution of the Commonwealth of Massachusetts also requires that schools be maintained by the state; the reason for their establishment warrants repetition here: "Wisdom and knowledge, as well as virtue diffused generally among the body of the people being necessary for the preservation of [the citizens'] rights and liberties" (Noble, 1938, p. 117). Other state constitutions are less specific about education, but all state governments have taken on the responsibility for both K–12 schooling and, to varying degrees, higher education.

In three bills submitted between 1776 and 1779, Thomas Jefferson outlined his proposals for education in what is now the US state of Virginia. He wanted control over schools to be local, with a ward of about 30 square miles controlling its own elementary school. Counties were to assist those wards lacking the resources to operate their own school. Jefferson's reasons for proposing universal elementary education are, by now, familiar: to keep the population out of ignorance and to have "the whole people respectably enlightened" (Arrowood, 1930, p. 71). Interestingly, he believed that three years of primary school would meet that concern. Unlike Egerton Ryerson, who would profoundly influence Canadian education 75 years later and who envisioned a curriculum with over a dozen subjects, Jefferson saw the need only for reading, writing, and arithmetic.

In outline, Jefferson's plan sounds democratic, but his reason for limiting universal primary education to three years had its foundation in a view of human learning that is quite at odds with what we now take for granted: He believed that since only a few people had the capacity to learn beyond three years, further study would be of no benefit. (Recall Plato's similar concern that education be offered only to the most capable who would be most likely to benefit from study.) School superintendents, appointed by local judges, were to select those boys most suited to study in a state-supported secondary school or a grammar school beyond the three years on offer in each local elementary school. Boys thus selected on the basis of capability were not to be charged fees for their secondary education. Jefferson's suggestion that secondary education should be made available to any boy who showed suitability, regardless of economic status, may make him sound a bit more generous or democratic, but some numbers may help: He envisioned that only one boy would be selected from every 20 primary schools.

In 1783, when Britain ceded lands not included in the 13 original colonies to the United States, the 1785 ordinance that circumscribed the governance of those territories repeated the sentiments of the Massachusetts Constitution regarding the purposes of education. The ordinance specified that "religion, morality, and knowledge were necessary to good government and happiness of mankind [and that] schools and the means of education [were to] be forever encouraged" (Noble, 1938, p. 117).

In the late 1700s, various American educators discussed the creation of a national university. One organization even offered a prize for the best plan for such an institution or system. However, these plans never came to fruition. Meanwhile, many groups of people, especially church denominations, created private colleges, with 17 such institutions chartered by the year 1800, an increase from 10 at the time of independence in 1776. The 19th century saw the creation of literally thousands of colleges in the United States, most of them founded by churches and many of them still in operation today.

The Morrill Act, passed by the US government in 1862, granted to each state 30,000 acres of public land for every senator or representative from that state. The proceeds from the sale of this land were to be used to found universities and colleges whose primary purpose was practical and agricultural education, along with other studies. Many of these so-called land-grant colleges exist to this day, some having become state universities. A second Morrill Act in 1890 mandated further federal funds for these colleges and new funds for the creation of colleges for Black students.

At the same time that an increased number of land-grant colleges and universities were offering practical and general education, research-oriented universities based on the model of the University of Berlin were growing. These universities saw the expansion of knowledge through research as their mission, not the propagation of knowledge through teaching. Some colleges already in existence, such as Harvard (1636), changed directions to become research universities that focused on graduate study. Other universities, such as Johns Hopkins (1876), were founded for the purpose of conducting research and offering advanced study.

Returning to K–12 education, in 1847 John Philbrick of Quincy, Massachusetts, built the first school with separate rooms for different classes. Edward Shelton returned to Oswego, New York, from visiting Pestalozzian schools in Europe and introduced the object lesson to instruction in the United States, and he founded a teacher training college to spread the idea. After observing the success of Philbrick's school in Quincy, Francis Wayland Parker worked to implement what educators would now call integrated learning or literacy across the curriculum. He wanted spelling taught in context in other classes, and he wanted scientific subjects introduced in language classes. Manners, ethics, history, and geography were also to be integrated into other subjects.

The first American secondary school, in a form that is recognizable today, opened in Boston in 1821 as the Boston English Classical School. Note the date in relation to Germany's founding of the Gymnasium schools in 1809. A 21st-century educator or student would recognize a majority of its curriculum, although courses such as navigation and moral philosophy might now be considered curricular misfits. Applicants had to take an entrance examination and were expected to attend for three years. Five years after the Boston English Classical School began operations, a similar school opened for girls, although it ceased operations after only two years. By 1840, there were over two dozen high schools in Massachusetts similar to the Boston English Classical School.

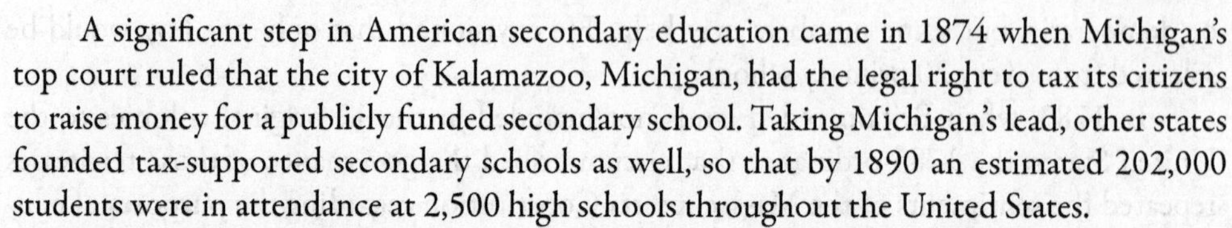

A significant step in American secondary education came in 1874 when Michigan's top court ruled that the city of Kalamazoo, Michigan, had the legal right to tax its citizens to raise money for a publicly funded secondary school. Taking Michigan's lead, other states founded tax-supported secondary schools as well, so that by 1890 an estimated 202,000 students were in attendance at 2,500 high schools throughout the United States.

With a patchwork of new schools of so many kinds spread across such a large country, standardization of quality in secondary education inevitably became an issue. The University of Michigan instituted what educators today would consider a system of accreditation by inviting high schools from across Michigan to submit to an inspection by the university. Graduates of those schools that met the University of Michigan's standards could enter the university without further testing. By 1885, the first regional accreditation board for colleges had formed in New England, and soon regional boards formed across the country. The system of K–12 education and higher education in place in the United States today had largely taken shape by 1885.

Native American Education

The story of Native American education is less happy than the story of American education in general. While we do not tell it here, we do note the parallels to the Canadian experience and we point our readers to a couple of excellent references. Native American education has sad similarities to Canadian and Australian education. We recognize that people groups have moved en masse throughout history. Europeans came to North America and, to various degrees, subjugated those already resident here. In both Canada and the United States, residential schools featured as a key component in an official policy of forced cultural assimilation. Some say, in fact, that American residential schools had one main purpose: to assimilate Native Americans into White American life (Adams, 1995). Note this citation from a 1902 circular from Indian Commissioner William Jones regarding the tendency of boys returning from residential school to the reservation to grow their hair long upon return: "The returned male student far too frequently goes back to the reservation and falls into the old custom of letting his hair grow long. He also paints profusely and adopts all the old habits and customs which his education in our industrial schools has tried to eradicate" (in Adams, 1995, p. 292). The passage of a century since Jones wrote those lines does little to soften the language of cultural eradication.

Another researcher has called the residential schools a "generally horrendous system" whose sole purpose was the subjugation of Native American culture (Fletcher, 2008, p. 3). Ironically, treaties often included provisions for the US government to oversee Native education, implying that for good reasons or bad, Native Americans became complicit in their own subjugation. Treaty provisions hide some deep problems inherent in residential school education, one of which is the inevitable collision of worldviews when American educators functioning in the modern paradigm set out to educate students with a fundamentally different epistemology. Recall from earlier in this chapter that the modern period characteristically privileges empirical and rational claims to knowledge over all other claims. This tradition, which we have inherited from Bacon and Descartes among others, is suspicious at its foundations of claims to knowledge based on intuition, tradition, the authority of elders, or spiritual encounters in nature. Hair length may be an obvious or presenting point of tension when we think about residential schools, but we realize on closer inspection that hair length is also a metaphor for the deep cultural conflict in which residential schools placed Native American students. In his book *White Civility*, Daniel Coleman (2006), from McMaster University, has traced aspects of the Canadian story, which we look at in Chapter 8.

We conclude this brief survey of the history of American education by returning to the American Constitution's assignment of responsibility for education to the individual states. As this book goes to press, a new national initiative known as the Common Core State Standards is underway in the United States. Forty-five states have so far agreed to give up some measure of their state sovereignty over education in favour of the benefits of what some critics call a national curriculum. Once these standards are adopted, all participating states will aim at the same educational ideals and will use similar curriculum to achieve those ideals. We note this as neither a good thing nor a bad thing, simply as part of an ongoing process. In this case, a nation is moving its education system toward the very kind of national model that the nation's founders considered undesirable.

Canadian Education

Some historians of Canadian education have argued that the three great forming influences on formal Canadian education are the French and English educational traditions and the example of how education evolved in the newly formed United States just across the border (Wilson, Stamp, & Audet, 1970). Whether Canada wanted these conversation partners or not when it created its various systems of schooling, these are the partners it found itself with. In this section of the chapter we tell only part of the story of the evolution of Canadian education. The history of Acadian education (in Nova Scotia) is as bumpy as Acadian history itself, we give only brief detail about the growth of education in Newfoundland, and we do not deal at length with the three Western provinces. We do provide some detail about Quebec and Ontario, and we give some detail about what became known as the Manitoba Schools Question, one of Canada's first crises in federal–provincial relations. In Chapter 8, which focuses on law, policy, and funding of Canadian schools, we briefly discuss a crisis in New Brunswick that is similar in important ways to the Manitoba crisis. In short, we cannot tell the whole story in detail, but we will tell representative parts of the story.

Newfoundland

The development of education in Newfoundland proves interesting for at least two reasons. First, no recorded evidence remains of any school in Newfoundland before 1722. However, by the end of the 1700s, schools began operating in many settlements as well in the major centres. The second noteworthy feature of Newfoundland education is that until relatively recently its schools were operated largely by churches with funding from the provincial Department of Education. In 1967, 13 churches folded their school systems into one system, known as the Integrated Education Council (IEC). That union yielded four main systems of schools: the IEC schools, the Roman Catholic schools, the Seventh Day Adventist schools, and the Pentecostal schools. These four systems were folded into a single public system in 1998 despite the objections of many of the churches.

Upper Canada

The history of education in what is now Ontario provides a parallel to the story of education in Quebec. Education in New France mirrored education in France. Education in Ontario echoed that in England. At the time of settlement, England had a variety of schools, including apprenticeships (practised since the middle ages), parish schools run by local churches, various schools for the poor, some common schools, and Sunday schools established to enable children who worked in factories to gain some social mobility by learning—on their one day off work—to read and write. Notably, in England, the wealthy ensured that their own children attended fine schools or had tutelage at home. The same pattern emerged in Upper Canada, the name of the colony from 1791 to 1841.

The first lieutenant-governor of Upper Canada, Lord Simcoe, illustrates this repetition of the English patterns in Upper Canada. He called for educational institutions that would foster the development of a loyal and learned clergy; that is, education's aim was to supply the church with its needed ministers. Educational leaders, promoters, and visionaries in Upper Canada spoke repeatedly of starting schools that, apart from training church ministers, would also teach children religion, virtues, and good morals.

Egerton Ryerson

The best-known figure in Canadian educational history is, without doubt, Egerton Ryerson (1803–1882; see Figure 5.10). His fame rests on his having founded a system of public schools in Upper Canada. Ryerson made official visits to the United States, Britain, Germany, and other European countries to examine their school systems. After his extensive first-hand study he made several recommendations, such as the founding of teacher-training institutes, the development of a system of teacher certification, that all schools have libraries, and that teachers be encouraged to attend to their professional development by attending conventions. Ryerson wrote a great deal about education, but the kernel of his philosophy and program can be found in the report he wrote following his inspection tour to Europe, *Report on a System of Public Elementary Instruction for Upper Canada* (Ryerson, 1847). The word *report* in Ryerson's title is an understatement. He wrote his report with the desire, in his own words, to "elevate the character of both the teachers and schools and to encourage every plan and effort to educate and improve the youthful mind of the country" (Ryerson, 1847, p. 6). He offered simply what he believed to be "required by the circumstances of the country" (p. 8). Inevitably, the authors of such reports end up articulating their own conceptions of education, and Ryerson does so in fine detail. In the early pages, he offers these simple but powerful propositions:

- Education should be universal.
- Education should be practical.
- Education should be founded on religion and morality.
- Education should attend to both intellectual and physical dimensions (a section in which he offers several pointed observations about American education).
- Education should be based on a specific curriculum (which, for Ryerson, includes 15 subjects ranging from religion to agriculture to vocal music).

From contemporary perspectives, not all of Ryerson's proposals were particularly helpful. In an 1847 report he submitted to the Assistant Superintendent General of Indian Affairs, he recommended the development of residential schools, a recommendation that was eventually implemented.

Starting in 1844, Ryerson served as superintendent of education in Upper Canada, and in the years following he worked tirelessly to develop a public school system. As one might expect, Ryerson's interpreters do not all agree on his motives for starting public schools. Some say that he simply wanted to see more widespread availability of schools, as was happening at the same time in the United States and some European nations. Others say that he had a clear secularizing agenda: to keep educational power out of the hands of the Church of England, who he suspected of wanting to become an established church, as was the Anglican Church in England.

In 1855, the Government of Upper Canada (now Ontario) published *Copies of Correspondence between the Chief Superintendent of Schools for Upper Canada, and Other Persons, on the Question of Separate Schools* (Government of Upper Canada, 1855). This correspondence, much of it mundane but some of which is quite contentious, reveals many of the day-to-day details of organizing and funding two tax-supported school systems in Upper Canada, mainly in Toronto. Many of the funding principles and practices that evolved under Ryerson's direction when he served as Superintendent of Schools in Toronto ended up being reflected in the British North America Act of 1867 and then in the Constitution Act of 1982, both of which we deal with in greater detail in Chapter 8.

In summary, Ryerson believed that the wealth, morals, and general happiness of the world's nations were in direct proportion to the spread of free, public education. And he worked tirelessly in Ontario to develop an education system that would bring about those conditions.

FIGURE 5.10 Egerton Ryerson, Canada's Most Famous Educator

New France, Lower Canada, and Quebec

New France

From 1608 to 1760, when Quebec was known as New France, the Roman Catholic Church had almost complete responsibility for education. Initially, in fact, no other party even expressed interest in education. In 1635 the Jesuits founded the first college (likely more akin to a secondary school in today's terms) in the new world in Quebec City (Magnuson, 1969). Most educational histories place Harvard (in Massachusetts), founded in 1636, as the first such college. However, the Jesuit order was founded some decades earlier as a teaching order. To this day, they have colleges on some Canadian university campuses, such as Campion College at the University of Regina. Those who organized the first schools in New France actually represented several Catholic orders besides the Jesuits and the Ursulines. The Récollets and Sulpicians were especially active in New France. By today's standards, there is no doubt that New France suffered from a shortage of schools, even relative to its sparse population. But today's standards are inappropriate for measuring education 350 years ago. And we should recall that in the 1600s Europe itself, including France, did not enjoy widespread schooling. That said, records attest to the existence of at least 32 schools in New France by 1700, most of them in Montreal, Trois-Rivières, and Quebec City. Several of these were girls' schools operated by the Ursulines, a teaching order of nuns from France, and by the Sisters of the Congregation, an indigenous Canadian order of nuns based in Montreal.

One early argument for schooling in New France was based on the premise that schools were needed to keep boys with guns out of trouble. Governor General of New France Jacques-René de Denonville, who served from 1685–1689, complained about uncontrollable boys who spent all day in the woods under the pretense that they were hunting. Unsupervised, they got into all manner of mischief (Parkman, 1908). We note this rationale for schools because it echoes complaints about the young from the Greeks about 25 centuries ago, and it could easily appear as a contemporary blog entry on a Canadian educational website. Presumably, boys such as these might prefer a less-than-classical curriculum. In fact, Canada's first vocational school began operations in the town of Quebec in 1668, teaching rug making, carpentry, masonry, shoe making, and other practical subjects.

We noted at the beginning of this section of the chapter that one of the obvious themes in the history of Canadian education is the early place of religion in education. The schools of New France, being operated almost exclusively by churches, were unapologetically religious in their character. Even when students took secular courses such as mathematics or Latin, they never forgot where they were or what the ultimate purpose of their education was. Such was church-sponsored education in New France.

Lower Canada

Britain defeated France in 1760, and the 1763 Treaty of Paris formalized the transfer of all French land in Canada to Britain. Despite the 1774 Quebec Act's recognition of French institutions and traditions, the British victory ultimately undermined Quebec education. Royal education subsidies stopped coming from Paris, the British government forcibly closed some institutions, and many teachers returned (or moved) to France. On some accounts, the literacy rate dropped from close to 80% in the early 1700s to about 20% by 1784.

When the British finally did begin to address Quebec's educational questions, their proposals were met with suspicion. A 1787 commission chaired by William Smith recommended free common schools and a nonsectarian university. An 1801 law, the Act for the Establishment of Free Schools and the Advancement of Learning in This Province, also suggested a system of free public schools. The French in Quebec viewed both the 1787 proposal and the 1801 law as attempts at English subjugation. In their view, removing school control from the church would lead not only to secularization but to Anglicization. After two decades of negotiation by French Catholic representatives, the provincial assembly finally passed the Fabrique Act in 1824, which recognized the parish as the foundation of educational provision. Five years later, the School Act established that school boards would be established in parishes. It also created a provincial funding structure so that educational grants could be directed to those boards for the support of all students' learning. By all accounts this act succeeded, inasmuch as hundreds of funded schools came into being or entered the formal system between 1829 and the Act of Union (with Upper Canada) in 1840.

From Confederation onward, the Quebec government had a fully functional Department of Education, but it assigned to the Catholic Church most of the responsibility for the actual operation of schools.

Quebec

In Quebec today, the Roman Catholic Church does not control education. But the end of direct church provision of education came relatively recently. The first stirrings of the movement to wrest control out of the church's hands actually began in 1844 when a group known as the Institut Canadien formed with the chief goal of separating church and state in matters of education, health, and social services. In a distinct show of power, the church excommunicated all members of the Institut in 1868, effectively ending that group's agitation.

A similar group was formed in 1902, the Ligue de l'enseignement, whose stated goal was also the secularization of Quebec education. Like its predecessor, this group enjoyed little success, a failure interesting in part because, as we have seen, during these same decades many jurisdictions witnessed the widespread creation of common schools that were not controlled by churches. In 1966, the Royal Commission chaired by Alphonse-Marie Parent submitted its report about all aspects of Quebec education. That report asserted that the state, not the church, should control education. Sparked by this report, arguments for secularization of schools began anew.

This enduring pressure to construct a public school system akin to that in other Canadian provinces resulted in the National Assembly of Quebec unanimously voting in 1997 to request a constitutional amendment allowing Quebec to be exempted from the British North America Act, Section 93 (which was retained in the Constitution Act of 1982). This section protected the rights of religious minorities in Ontario and Quebec to have funded denominational schools. The federal government granted this request, and Quebec then established a single, funded public school system.

At the time of this writing, Quebec education's posture toward religion in education continues along a bumpy path. After trying a series of models in succession from 1997 to 2008, and after invoking the notwithstanding clause of the 1982 Constitution (which meant that the law was temporarily not open to judicial review for any perceived Charter violations), the Department of Education now requires that all schools (including private schools) teach an "Ethics and Religious Culture" course (as we noted in Chapter 3). This course, which involves education about religions in Quebec but is definitely not religious education, has as its two founding principles the recognition of others (respect) and the pursuit of the common good. Opponents of this requirement have taken the course to court, noting that religious parents in Quebec now have fewer educational rights than those in several other provinces, an irony given that the church essentially controlled education in Quebec for three centuries.

In the 1960s, Quebec education underwent massive changes, reflecting the larger transformation now referred to as the Quiet Revolution. Specifically, Quebec raised the age at which students are allowed to leave school to 15 and eliminated the family costs of secondary education (making it free). It began providing greater support to private education and higher education, consolidating school units into larger boards, and streamlining provincial funding structures. It also addressed perceived weaknesses in teacher training. Regarding pedagogy specifically, the province addressed the reliance on rote learning and the dearth of varied teaching methods. Regarding curriculum, Quebec de-emphasized language and literature and pushed for more attention to scientific and technical subjects while also calling for more child-centred elementary schools. From our perspective today, these changes perhaps make complete sense—they may even seem inevitable. But at the time they seemed nothing short of revolutionary. In 10 years, the province began to overturn more than three centuries of educational tradition, affecting funding, governance, curriculum, instruction, and almost every other aspect of the work and operations of Quebec's schools.

The Manitoba Schools Question

Shortly after Manitoba entered Confederation, it passed a law that initiated deep discussions about the constitutional division of educational powers. In brief, Manitoba joined Canada in 1870, three years after the British North America Act guaranteed school funding to religious minorities in Ontario and Quebec. Recognizing the sizable Métis and French Catholic minorities in Manitoba, the 1870 Manitoba Act, which brought that province into Confederation, guaranteed in Section 22(1) the same school-funding rights and provisions to Manitoba's Roman Catholics. However, in 1890 the Manitoba provincial government declared that it would have only one public school system; in this act, it overturned the guarantees to the denominations. Historians now refer to this action and its repercussions as the Manitoba Schools Question or the Manitoba Schools Crisis.

The path to Manitoba's 1890 action is relatively straightforward. Upon joining Confederation, about 55% of Manitoba's population was Catholic. Settlement patterns shifted after 1870, however, and by the 1880s Manitoba's Catholics were clearly a minority. The second Métis rebellion in 1885 fuelled anti-Catholic sentiment in Manitoba. Scandals erupted involving the provincial government and its land and financial dealings with the Canadian Pacific Railway, increasing the need for the government to help its citizens focus on something else. Anti-French and anti-Catholic sentiments had spawned new organizations in Ontario and Quebec, and the Orange Order agitated across Canada against Catholic rights. As we describe in detail in Chapter 8, New Brunswick in the 1860s had become embroiled in a good deal of controversy over the funding of denominational schools and had emerged with funds going toward a single, public system. Combine some of these contextual factors, and the next step the Manitoba government took becomes somewhat more understandable. Without much consultation, the then-Premier and the Minister of Public Works declared in 1890 an end to the dual education system that had been in place since 1870. Protestant and Catholic denominational schools alike could continue to exist but would receive no government funds; Manitoba would have a single, public school system.

Not surprisingly, many Manitoba Catholics and a few Protestants (mainly Anglicans) protested that while they would now have to pay for their own schools, their taxes would support other schools, contrary to the provisions of the Manitoba Act itself. To this day, independent school parents refer to this as *double taxation*. Even in the face of these appeals the Manitoba government refused to budge, so the opponents of the action looked to Ottawa. The Supreme Court responded with five separate opinions, three of them in favour of the Manitoba government. Obviously dissatisfied with the court's findings, the minority appealed to the federal government itself. Finally, in March 1895, the Judicial Committee of the federal government found that the Manitoba government had acted out of order and demanded that it restore funding to denominational schools.

As removed from these events as we are, we may not catch the degree of tension generated by the Manitoba Question. Nevertheless, the Manitoba Schools Question remains an important chapter both in Canadian constitutional history and Canadian educational history.

Conclusion

Newfoundland, Ontario, Quebec, and Manitoba present four quite distinct pictures of how education developed in Canada. They illustrate both pre-Confederation and post-Confederation patterns of development. They also illustrate that nothing is typical about the history of education in Canada. One area, called New France at the time, developed church-operated schools like those in France. Newfoundland, a largely English-speaking colony and then province, also gave control of education over to churches. In Ontario, however, with the purpose of ensuring that no single church had control over education, Ryerson built a public school system that looked like the common schools being founded at the same time in the United States. And Manitoba led Canada into a constitutional crisis because it attempted to override the linguistic and religious guarantees given to French-speaking Roman Catholics in the Manitoba Act. These four stories illustrate the ongoing and sometimes problematic place of both religion and language in Canadian education.

Contemporary Movements in Educational History

A century from now, teacher-candidates reading about the history of education will read about changes that took place in the first decades of the 21st century. Of course we cannot be certain what they will read, but having looked at 25 centuries of educational history, and especially at the last century or two, we can likely predict some of what future educators will identify as important in our own time. In this final section of the chapter, we offer a handful of current trends—changes in which we as educators right now find ourselves. Some or all of these may turn out to be less significant than we suggest and will not warrant the word *historic*. But they will all be historical, and we suggest them as a way to close this chapter.

Tightened Educational Funding

Throughout the world, Canada included, both K–12 and higher educational funding have come under increasing pressure. We can identify several sources. First, society has added to the tasks they expect educators to do. For example, many schools provide food to students at lunch time. And many schools assign full- or part-time educational assistants to classrooms with children identified with special needs. As you are aware from other courses, the range of those special needs is wide, running from behaviour issues through to delayed development and a variety of learning difficulties. And of course the educational assistants who help these children receive salaries. These two examples raise some good questions: Is it reasonable that society expects such levels of service? Does the respective School Act in a given jurisdiction require that schools provide such services? Do schools go looking for more work? These questions must be answered elsewhere. Our point is that providing the services—expected or not—drives up the cost of education.

A second source of the pressure on educational funding is the broader pressure on governments to provide more services in all sectors of society. The Ministry of Education must compete with other ministries, all of which are aware of other needs in society. In jurisdictions collecting fewer tax revenues than they once collected (because of demographic shifts or a shrinking economy), responding to the many perceived needs becomes more and more difficult. In fact, citizens in some American states have gathered petitions with the required number of names (usually 5% of the electorate) to force state-wide votes meant to reduce educational funding. Canadian citizens have not engaged in such actions. Nevertheless, the pressure on schools to deliver more while facing budget constraints is historic, at least with reference to the period of educational history that began following World War II.

A third source of pressure on educators is declining government revenue. In some jurisdictions, one often hears that cutting taxes will solve all manner of economic problems, including some problems that, in every historical case, have gotten worse when tax revenues shrank. Nevertheless, decreased tax revenues have become a part of the real political environment in which contemporary educators do their work.

Assessment

Since the 1990s, both K–12 and higher educators have faced increased demands that they document student learning. As we noted in some detail in Chapter 4, this increased emphasis on assessment has a variety of roots: Some people accuse educators of doing what they like outside of any accountability structures; rising costs of education have pushed some to ask what society gets for its money; periodic horror stories of high school graduates who cannot read appear in the media. Such stories may catch the public's attention only briefly, but they leave a residue of diminished confidence. If we keep these varied roots in mind, we should not be surprised that the focus on assessment has become so dominant in educational discussion.

This change in focus has several aspects. Decades ago, the word *assessment* denoted something along these lines: a teacher graded a test or other assignment and the individual student's grade or the whole class's average grade indicated the degree of the student's or students' understanding and mastery of the material. Two changes have taken place since then, both deserving of mention in a chapter on educational history. First, under pressure from parents, employers, legislators, and several other stakeholder groups, officials in Ministries of Education have required students to participate in a larger number of standardized tests than ever before in history. Canadian educators have seen this shift, but to a smaller degree than, for example, the United States or Britain. Not incidentally, higher education has begun to face similar accountability pressures because students, parents, governments, and accrediting associations all want to know if universities and colleges are delivering on their promises.

Critics of the move toward widespread standardized testing raise two quite distinct objections. First, and most obvious, such standardized tests take up instructional time; when a class writes a standardized test required by a jurisdiction, that class is not receiving instruction or participating in whatever learning activities the teacher might otherwise have planned. Second, do standardized tests (or any tests) measure what they claim to measure? We cannot develop this criticism at length in this chapter, but we will note that classroom teachers, academics, some students, and many others object to standardized testing because some learning perhaps cannot be measured, because the particular test may not reliably or validly measure what it claims to, and because in some cases so much rides on students' performance on a single day (which is why we often hear the phrase *high stakes* used to describe standardized testing).

Second, contemporary educators have come to understand assessment rather differently from how educators in earlier decades understood it. A classroom teacher still believes that an individual grade or a class average indicates something important about student learning. But in our new understanding of assessment, we believe that such grades also indicate something about our teaching. If the whole class demonstrates that they do not understand a process or concept, and the assessment mechanism is valid, then something might have been wrong with how the teacher taught the material. Before the teacher uses that material again, he or she will make adjustments to the curriculum materials or the instructional strategies. Thus, assessment leads to continuous recalibration. This new understanding has already brought about improvements in both K–12 and higher education. Formative assessment as a means of providing students with ongoing feedback about their performance to foster greater student ownership is also a prevalent trend in assessment (Wiliam, 2011).

Higher Professional Standards for Teachers

We are currently witnessing what we might call a historic rise in the professional development of teachers. This has two aspects. First, the number of years of education required to teach has risen and continues to rise. Second, more and more jurisdictions are requiring that their teachers participate in ongoing, formal professional development. We will address this matter again in Chapter 8, but it is worth noting here that, historically, some teachers entered the profession with as few as one or two years of higher education as late as the mid-1960s. By 1970, this standard moved to four years. As this book goes to press, the standard is moving toward five years of higher education in most jurisdictions and six years in some.

The Digital Revolution

Without writing at length, we do wish to register the digital revolution as having produced major shifts in education. We do not know how this particular revolution will turn out, but we have already witnessed the changes it has brought to many aspects of curriculum and instruction. We note, for example, that computers make it possible for tens of thousands of students to take the same course; this was literally unthinkable through the entire history of education prior to the digital revolution. We note also the chorus of people who claim that the Internet has rendered schools redundant. Mark Zuckerberg and Bill Gates regularly remind educators that they dropped out of Harvard and are doing fine and that everything anyone really needs to know is available on the Internet. Finally, we note what some call the *flipped curriculum*. In this model, students get access to the teacher's course materials from their teacher's blog or a course wiki. Class time is not given over to information transfer; instead, with the material in hand, students and teachers can spend class time working, clarifying, and solving problems.

We have given just three examples of the impact that the digital revolution has had on education: massive online courses, Internet believers who criticize formal schooling, and the flipped curriculum. These three examples are different in kind from each other, and they help prevent anyone from predicting too confidently how the digital revolution will eventually change education. All we know for sure is this: It will.

All contemporary educators have found themselves participants in the changes outlined in this concluding section of the chapter. We do not know where these changes will lead, when the change process will end, or if it will end. But they help us remember that we are part of educational history, and decades from now teacher-candidates will read about our responses to the changes in which we now find ourselves.

Conclusion

Large volumes have been written about every topic in this chapter; here, we have written only briefly about educational history. At that, we have selected only a handful of topics and people from the thousands of options at our disposal. Nevertheless, we have provided enough material for a reader to catch a sense that almost all societies establish formal education systems, that those systems have both similarities and important differences, and that the range of ideals societies have articulated for their schools have varied dramatically over the years, from soldiering to self-discovery. We ended the chapter with a brief look at current trends to remind ourselves that this process has not stopped. Schools have not reached a point of stasis; they will continue to evolve as our own and future societies articulate different ideals that they want education to meet, in whatever forms that education takes.

In the early pages of this chapter, we listed some enduring educational questions: questions of access, funding, the purposes of schools, the mix of teacher- and student-directed learning, and the curriculum that schools should follow. We have seen how various societies throughout history have answered these questions. On every question, it seems, societies have had good reasons for choosing as they did. In some cases, those choices might be reversed later in the same society. In other cases, other societies may have been deciding differently at the same time with the same information available to them. If anything, this history shows both the recurrence and endurance of certain themes and practices at the same time that it reveals the range of creativity and variety humans bring when they answer the question of how best to pass on cultural riches to succeeding generations.

Discussion Questions

1. Identify several elements in ancient education to which contemporary Canadian educators would likely take exception. On what grounds would they likely object to these elements? Suggest some elements or trends in contemporary Canadian education that future educators might identify as mistaken or destructive.
2. What are some of the key differences between ancient education and medieval education? Suggest what social changes might have resulted in the medieval world as a result of these changes in educational provision.
3. Identify one or two of the major educational thinkers we treated in this chapter with whom you find your own approach to education most in alignment. In two or three sentences, summarize his or her approach to education and explain the sources of the alignment with your own understanding of education.
4. The shift from church sponsorship of education to tax-supported common schools occurred in many jurisdictions during the 19th century. What, in your view, are the strongest arguments for developing systems of common schools?
5. In the last section of the chapter, we suggested several current trends that we consider to be of historical importance. What trends or changes would you add to those we listed herein?

Further Resources

1. Coleman, D. (2006). *White civility: The literary project of English Canada*. Toronto, ON: University of Toronto Press.

   While interacting with original works or literature and journalism, this volume traces how the British idea of civility helped shape Canadian identity during the 19th and 20th centuries. Coleman reveals the racism that undergirded much of the curriculum and made possible the residential schools program.

2. Glenn, C. L. (1988). *The myth of the common school*. Amherst, MA: University of Massachusetts Press.

Faced with the need to assimilate immigrants, Massachusetts and other states formed common schools with the overt purpose of socializing students into American values. This volume compares American, French, and Dutch approaches to public schooling, asking throughout about the balance of state and parental rights to shape children's thinking.

3. Gutek, G. L. (2011). *Historical and philosophical foundations of education* (5th ed.). New York, NY: Pearson.

   Gutek surveys major figures and trends throughout the history of Western education with his comprehensive reading and thorough grasp of historical and philosophical detail evident on every page. Although intended as a graduate-level textbook, this book serves equally well as a readable reference.

4. Magnusson, R. (1969). *Education in the province of Quebec.* Washington, DC: U.S. Department of Education.

   This history of education in Quebec traces education from Quebec's colonial beginnings to the time of publication. Magnusson writes with a factual tone, appearing not to take sides on any historical or ideological issues.

5. Wilson, J. D., Stamp, R. M., and Audet, L. P. (1970). *Canadian education: A history.* Toronto, ON: Prentice-Hall.

   This clear and comprehensive volume traces the development of Canadian education through to the date of the book's publication. The book remains a standard volume even after almost five decades in part because the authors deal honestly and, at points, critically with Canadian education.

6

The Philosophical Roots of Education

Learning Objectives

After reading this chapter, you should understand

1. How metaphysics, epistemology, and axiology raise questions relevant to philosophy of education
2. How the philosophies of idealism, realism, pragmatism, and existentialism have influenced philosophies of education
3. How the philosophies of education (perennialism, essentialism, progressivism, and social reconstructionism) reflect particular values about education
4. The importance of articulating your own beliefs about education to guide your practice

Practical Applications

EXAMINING YOUR PHILOSOPHICAL ASSUMPTIONS

Let's begin this chapter with an exercise that should help you articulate the assumptions you make about teaching and learning and how these align with the philosophies of education we will explore in this chapter. For each statement, select the number that most closely fits your beliefs.

0—Strongly disagree 1—Disagree
2—Agree 3—Strongly agree

Question	0	1	2	3
1. The purpose of education is to prepare students for work.				
2. The purpose of education is to cultivate the intellect, fostering students' use of critical thinking and careful reasoning.				
3. Teachers create learning environments and then guide students to reflect on their learning experiences.				
4. Schools should promote social change more than the preservation of traditional values.				
5. Schools should prepare students for the workforce, providing them with essential skills they will need.				
6. Everyone should read the great classics in literature.				
7. Learning experiences should not be set before determining students' interests.				
8. Schools play a role in criticizing and transforming society.				
9. Society should share the same value system, so teachers need to inculcate these traditional values at school.				
10. Despite changing trends, there are certain ideas that persist and students should learn these important ideas.				
11. Teachers should facilitate interdisciplinary projects.				
12. "Traditional values" often mask racist and sexist beliefs.				
13. Teachers should be efficient in transferring knowledge to students and should stick to tried and true teaching methods.				
14. Education should be the same for all, not varied by the social setting or the teacher.				
15. Classrooms should be democratic so students learn how to participate in a democratic society.				
16. Schools should level the playing field by providing equal opportunities for all children.				

continued

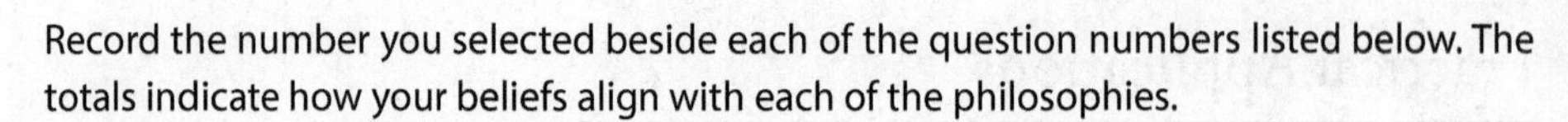

Record the number you selected beside each of the question numbers listed below. The totals indicate how your beliefs align with each of the philosophies.

1) ______ 5) ______ 9) ______ 13) ______ = total for Essentialism

2) ______ 6) ______ 10) ______ 14) ______ = total for Perennialism

3) ______ 7) ______ 11) ______ 15) ______ = total for Progressivism

4) ______ 8) ______ 12) ______ 16) ______ = total for Social Reconstructionism

It is important to note that your scores are only a provisional indication of your philosophical alignment. These scores could differ depending on the grade level or subject discipline you were considering when you answered or the particular wording of the question. As you read about the philosophies that follow, consider your scores on this survey and whether you still consider your highest score to be a good indication of your philosophical assumptions about education.

Although teachers may not consciously concern themselves with issues of philosophy when planning a lesson or marking an exam, much of what we do as teachers is impacted by philosophy. Education is often caught in the push and pull of ever-changing philosophies or belief systems. This chapter will first describe three branches of philosophy: metaphysics, epistemology, and axiology and how they address questions relevant to the philosophy of education. Next, we consider some of the major philosophical systems and assess their impact on education including idealism, realism, pragmatism, and existentialism. We will then turn our attention to some of the philosophies of education that emerged and continue to emerge from debates in philosophy itself, including perennialism, essentialism, progressivism, and social reconstructionism.

Current philosopher of education Robin Barrow (2010) reminds us that these "isms" are but one way to study philosophy of education and these are not homogenous belief systems. Other approaches to philosophy of education may focus on influential thinkers or questions that emerge from philosophical study, such as "What does it mean to be educated?" and "What is the role of schools in moral education?" We shall try to introduce some of these influential thinkers and some of the questions that are important to particular philosophies in the context of the philosophical systems. It is important to note that the philosophies discussed in this chapter are based primarily in the foundations of Western civilization because these traditions have had the most influence on Canadian schools. As our schools become increasingly multicultural, it is altogether possible that other philosophies will influence our schools.

Besides introducing these various "isms," this chapter will address two interrelated questions: (a) Why is it important for me as a teacher to reflect upon the philosophical issues related to education? and (2) What impact should these philosophical positions have on me as a classroom teacher? As a teacher, it is important that you begin to formulate a philosophical position in response to some historical and contemporary anxieties in the philosophy of education. This formulation will help you reflect on the underlying principles guiding your pedagogical choices and will also help you understand those whose assumptions and actions may differ from your own.

The way you interact with students and structure learning experiences reflects many of your beliefs. For example, what do you believe about human nature? Are children by nature basically good (beneficent, charitable, co-operative), bad (egocentric, self-seeking), or neutral (dependent upon experience to form character)? What do you believe about knowledge and how we come to know? Is knowledge justified true belief, the sum total of all the beliefs in a society, or is knowledge something that is constructed through experience? Understanding your own personal philosophy will help you move from executing the many practical details of teaching to a reflective examination of the reasons for your decisions and the reasons your colleagues and superiors may provide for the decisions they make (see Chapters 1 and 2). Finally, philosophy of education can also help you understand the significance of education and educational issues for our society at large.

 Branches of Philosophy

Metaphysics

metaphysics
The branch of philosophy that seeks to understand what is real.

Metaphysics is the branch of philosophy that seeks to understand what is real. Metaphysics asks questions about abstract concepts: What is time? Do numbers exist? Does beauty exist? How we categorize knowledge is also part of the metaphysical project. Metaphysicians believe that when we think carefully, we divide the world into meaningful categories. For example, the science curriculum is often divided into physical sciences, life sciences, and Earth sciences; scientists and most metaphysicians would argue that this language represents the way the world really exists.

Recently, scientists and metaphysicians have pondered the question, "Do planets exist?" especially when the International Astronomical Union demoted Pluto from a planet to a dwarf planet. For decades, science students have been taught that there are nine planets, but there is now a new category for bodies that don't meet all the conditions to be labelled as *planets*. Our language categorizes the world in ways that suit our needs, and in doing so we shape reality, or so the argument goes.

Metaphysics is important to education because the disciplines, experiences, and skills in the curriculum reflect what our society has determined to be real. Teachers and curriculum developers are trying to help students understand particular features of reality in each of the subjects. As you read about each of the education philosophies, consider how proponents of each would define what is real and what is "out there." As you will see, the traditional Greek philosophies care very much about what is real, while the more contemporary philosophies are somewhat indifferent to claims about ultimate or basic realities and opt instead for a more subjective "local truth"—facts we can agree on based on common observations.

Sometimes teachers have presuppositions that have metaphysical relevance. For example, philosophers have long been interested in the issue of causation—a paradigmatically metaphysical concept. They have wondered to what extent human choice is free (caused by oneself) or determined (caused by something external to the self). Teachers may presuppose that students from less-privileged backgrounds are less likely to be successful in school, or they may believe that their role as teachers is to foster the exercise of free will and ultimately student responsibility regardless of the students' personal circumstances. It

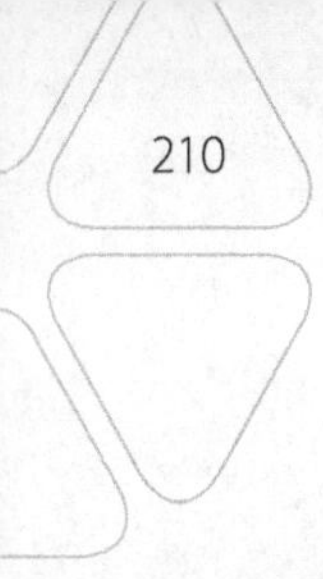

is important to clarify such presuppositions about causal determination because they can influence teachers' expectations and create self-fulfilling prophecies.

Epistemology

epistemology
The branch of philosophy that addresses what knowledge is and how we acquire it.

Epistemology is the branch of philosophy that addresses questions like, "What is knowledge and how do we acquire it?" According to the Platonic tradition, knowledge is justified true belief. However, some philosophers have dismissed this conception of knowledge, taking a more sociological view that knowledge is simply what people believe, disregarding concerns over justification and truth. This recent trend raises some unsettling questions. Did people in the Middle Ages *know* the Earth was flat and was the centre of the universe? It would be more accurate to say they *believed* claims we now know to be mistaken. For Plato, the idea of false knowledge is a contradiction; for any belief to rise to the status of knowledge it must be justified and true. Epistemologists are divided on how both justification and truth are to be discerned. This division has implications for what should be included in the curriculum. Must teachers confine education to those things we know to be true, or can we wade into topics where the truth is less clear? Social studies is certainly one subject where truth is elusive. For example, which is true: that Louis Riel was a terrorist or a hero? Education aspires to give students the tools for discerning the justification for their beliefs. Some philosophies are more flexible than others about what counts as true.

Philosophers disagree about the second central question of epistemology: how knowledge is acquired. If knowledge is viewed as the justified true beliefs accumulated by a society, schools then transmit that accumulated knowledge through lectures and demonstrations so that students may acquire it. If knowledge is viewed as what people believe and understand, then educators help learners engage in exercises that will help them clarify beliefs and construct understanding. For example, the Alberta Education Program of Study for Grade 8 Social Studies requires students to "examine, critically, the factors that shaped the worldview evolving in western Europe during the Renaissance." Teachers typically require students to read and respond to texts that help them acquire the knowledge of these factors. However, one group of Calgary teachers invited students to respond to the question, "Does Calgary have the necessary conditions to be a Renaissance city?" Students completed research on some aspect of the Renaissance (education, science, arts, and other topics), and then local experts in those fields were invited to watch a student-generated presentation and comment on how that particular condition exists in their city today. Students then used their research and the expert comments to debate the question, "Does Calgary have the conditions to become a Renaissance city?" (For more information, see Connect! The Professional Learning Journal of the Connect Charter School, 2011a). While the teachers clearly wanted students to acquire the knowledge required by the provincial curriculum, it would seem they were also epistemologically committed to helping students understand and clarify their own beliefs—beliefs that are debatable and not necessarily objective. In the philosophies that follow, you will see varied perspectives on how knowledge is best acquired and understood.

Axiology

axiology
The branch of philosophy concerned with aesthetics and ethics; that is, how we define what is beautiful and what is morally good and valuable.

Axiology is the branch of philosophy concerned with aesthetics and ethics; it addresses the questions: What is beautiful and what is morally good and valuable? It would be easy to assume that aesthetics is best studied within art class, but aesthetics is also a way of looking at the world:

> There is something of interest and value in every event, but we systematically neglect or pass over the quality of most events. As one poet put it, we casually measure the world. Development of efficient ways of doing things, smoothly functioning habits, sometimes produces in us a kind of functional blindness, deafness, or insensitivity to the quality of the world in which we live. The poet, however, cultivates sensitivity to sights, sounds, and feelings; and he or she has developed techniques for breaking up our habits, or putting them in a context which helps us see, feel, and experience the quality of our world, and presenting familiar objects in fresh fashion—the footworn stone or wayside flower. (Hahn, 1984, pp. 73–74)

An aesthetically conscious teacher helps students to appreciate beauty in various aspects of the curriculum and everyday life, whether in poetry and the natural world (as philosopher Lewis Hahn suggests in the above quote) or in the fine arts. Advocates for the arts often fear that teachers feeling the pressure of provincial exam preparation in the academic core subjects may give the arts short shrift and opt instead for efficient coverage of academic material while ignoring a sensitivity to sights, sounds, and feelings. The philosophies in this chapter vary regarding the value they place on aesthetics in the curriculum.

As for **ethics**, modern ethical theories are typically divided between **consequentialism** and **deontology**. Consequentialism seeks the greatest good for the greatest number; since happiness is the greatest good, we should do what will produce as much happiness as possible. A consequentialist considers lying to be morally wrong because it generally produces bad consequences, but there may be cases in which lying is permissible, such as to protect another's feelings. By contrast, deontology obliges us to do what duty requires regardless of the consequences. The most famous deontologist was philosopher Immanuel Kant (1724–1804), who argued that we are never justified in lying, even to a murderer when we know where his potential victim is hiding. A much older ethical theory, **virtue ethics**, is associated primarily with Aristotle and Plato. It suggests that ethical behaviour originates from the character of individuals rather than consequences or any rules. A virtue ethicist is more interested in what the lying or truth telling says about the individual's character.

ethics
Principles and norms that govern human conduct.

consequentialism
Also called utilitarianism, consequentialism seeks the most useful consequence; the greatest good for the greatest number of people.

deontology
An ethical theory that claims humans have an obligation to do what duty requires, regardless of the consequences.

virtue ethics
An ethical theory that suggests that ethical behaviour originates from the character of individuals rather than consequences or any rules.

Arguably all three of these ethical systems may influence teachers and some may be more influential depending on the teacher's philosophy. Teachers often create classroom rules that require students to respect school property, show consideration to others, and to give their best effort to their school work. They might argue that students have a duty to obey and also that obeying such rules will have good consequences for the student and the class. Many contemporary character education programs find their foundation in virtue ethics, often focusing on a virtue of the week that is promoted and recognized (patience, perseverance, truthfulness, and others). Virtue ethicists claim that students may be habituated into good behaviour and in the process develop a moral character. Critics argue that such programs are more interested in compliance than character.

In her famous book *Caring: A Feminine Approach to Ethics and Moral Education* (2003), philosopher and educator Nel Noddings argues that the basis for moral action is not in the application of some rigid rule but in our care for others. She suggests that schools should not only celebrate reason and academics but also sensitive response to moral concerns. While Noddings is not without her critics, her argument has been influential among teachers who find intuitive appeal in promoting empathy and care for others.

Some of the philosophies that follow take a very directive role in the ethical training of young people. Other approaches use the same pragmatic problem-solving approach for academics and moral problem solving, judging the best course of action based on the possible outcomes of each course of action. Still others encourage students to question the status

quo and take action to correct injustice, sometimes even acting against given rules. As you read the philosophies covered in this chapter, consider how each might regard metaphysics, epistemology, and axiology.

Major Philosophical Systems

Each of the philosophical systems discussed over the next few pages takes particular perspectives on great human questions. We will focus primarily on the questions most relevant to education and then show how these philosophies were foundational to philosophies of education.

Idealism

idealism
A philosophical system often traced to Plato, who believed that there is an ideal world of perfect ideas; that is, ideas that express truths are universal.

Idealism is most often traced to the ancient Greek philosopher Plato who believed that in addition to the sensible world we experience, there existed an ideal world of perfect ideas—the Form of the Good, containing all truth, goodness, justice and beauty. Beauty is an idea that exists independent of any flower, and justice exists independent of any courtroom. The real world is too variable and unpredictable to represent truth, but ideas that express truths are universal. For example, provided one is working in a base 10 number system, 5 + 5 will always equal 10; this truth is not influenced by the environment or by any sort of psychological attitude a person might have.

In the famous allegory of the cave (Plato, 1997), Plato illustrates that humans are like prisoners in a dark cave who can only see shadows reflected on the wall but cannot see the actual objects. He asserts that our senses only provide us with distorted images of reality and we must "leave the cave" so that we can use reason to understand ideas as they truly are. To the extent that we persist in the shadow world of sense perception (i.e., subjective experience), we continue to live in the dark. For example, adolescents may accept the political views of their parents as real without reasoning, but this is not true knowledge because they are relying on unreasoned assumptions. The cave illustrates the sensory world, with its reliance on sense perception and assumptions, while universal truth can be found through careful reasoning.

While some other philosophies see truth as culturally relative or constructed by individuals, idealists typically believe students need to be freed from such relativistic beliefs and discover enduring truths. These truths are often brought to awareness through teaching strategies such as the Socratic dialectical method that uses questions to stimulate the learner's ability to reason. The teacher then becomes a midwife, not *giving* knowledge to students but helping to *draw out* or *birth* knowledge while fostering students' ability to reason. The Socratic method is practised in many contemporary classrooms, but today's teachers are probably more interested in fostering students' ability to reason and think critically than in arriving at enduring truths or knowledge of the forms.

Idealists argue that the classics in literature, art, and music are transhistorical sources of universal truths and should form the core of the curriculum. Mathematics, especially pure math, is also highly prized by many idealists—the perfection of mathematics is considered a thing of beauty. A teacher might draw a triangle on the blackboard, but it is a feeble substitute for the true form—a perfect triangle conforming to the Pythagorean theorem: in any right triangle, the square of the hypotenuse is the sum of the squares of the legs. Plato wants humans to ascend beyond the merely sensible realities to truly know the forms; therefore, theoretical science such as astrophysics is more highly valued than science that is based upon empiricism and experimentation.

The forms are also important in idealist elementary school curricula where children learn basic literacy and numeracy to prepare for later study of the classics. Friedrich Froebel (1782–1852) is a famous idealist who designed a series of "gifts," including balls, blocks, and rods, for children to use in their play. He believed playing with these materials would help children develop conscious awareness of the concept or ideal form of the sphere or cube and ultimately the interrelationships of forms in the world. Using each gift, the children would identify similar shapes in the environment and manipulate the gift to represent mathematical and geometric concepts and aesthetic ones as well. Froebel is famously credited with inventing the concept and the term *kindergarten*, a "garden" where children could blossom and become who they were destined to be. Although few contemporary kindergarten teachers would identify themselves as idealists, most would agree that block play seems to set the foundation for mathematical and scientific understanding of concepts such as angles, size, balance, volume, and dimension.

With respect to ethics, idealists believe that the great works in theology, philosophy, literature, and art are storehouses for the culture's values and provide models for ethical action. They emphasize perspective—that students learn what is ethical and beautiful over time by repeated exposure to literature, art, and music. Students should also be exposed to exemplars whose ethical models they can emulate.

Realism

realism
A philosophical system often traced to Aristotle, who believed that reality could be perceived with one's senses, and one could abstract concepts from those experiences.

Realism can be traced to Aristotle, Plato's most famous student; however, it is also associated with the scientific revolution of the 17th and 18th centuries. While most idealists believe in an unchanging reality that can be understood through philosophical reasoning, Aristotle and the early modern scientists and philosophers believed that reality could be perceived with one's senses, and one could abstract concepts from those experiences. To know the world we use sensation and abstraction—sensation to learn data about the world and abstraction to extract the necessary qualities to form a concept about an object. For example, repeated walks in the forest help children understand the necessary qualities of trees (leaves, branches, bark) and perhaps to make distinctions between trees and shrubs or deciduous and coniferous trees. Aristotle investigated many scientific concepts to learn verifiable information about how the world works. In fact, he helped develop distinctions between genus and species and the understanding of categorization that is so central to science today. As previously noted, categorization can be regarded as one aspect of the metaphysical project of defining what is real.

For realists, education helps learners develop abstract concepts. The ability to build concepts from our observations begins in the early years. The classic *Sesame Street* song "One of These Things (Is Not Like the Others)" helps young children develop concepts and the ability to make distinctions between things like shoes and boots or numbers and letters. In later years, students develop the ability to understand more complex concepts such as themes in literature or scientific concepts like force and energy. In fact, the disciplines of history, mathematics, language, biology, chemistry, and physics include groups of related

© Stuart Robertson / Alamy

FIGURE 6.1 *School of Athens,* **Raphael**

The distinction between Plato's idealism and Aristotle's realism is illustrated through Raphael's famous *School of Athens* painting, where Plato points to the sky and Aristotle to the earth. Aristotle believed humans should seek understanding in the empirical world, while Plato believed understanding could be found in the universal forms beyond the sensible world.

concepts that help learners to develop vocabulary and conceptual understandings related to those disciplines.

A key principle of realist ethical education is virtue ethics: to foster habituation in the virtues for young children until they are able to use reason to help them act virtuously. For example, young students are encouraged to take turns even when they are too egocentric to recognize the important principles of fairness and justice underpinning that expectation. Human beings have an end, a goal, a *telos*: *eudaimonia*. **Eudaimonia** is most frequently translated as "happiness," but "fulfillment" may better capture its essence. For Aristotle, *eudaimonia* is impossible without rationality to moderate our actions and emotions. Until such time as children can behave rationally, teachers must require obedience to foster moral habits and develop character.

Theistic realism (or *Thomism*), developed by Thomas Aquinas (1225–1274), is a fusion of Aristotle's ideals and Christian theology and is influential in many Christian schools today. While Aquinas agreed with Aristotle that humans' goal in life was to achieve *eudaimonia*, he also believed that to experience the presence of God was a higher goal. Moral education habituates the students to behave in virtuous or Christlike ways. Like other realists, Thomist educators aim to cultivate reason and favour an educational approach that transmits subject area knowledge to students. However, this aim to cultivate reason sits alongside the complementary aim to cultivate spirituality.

Realist schools are typically charged with transmitting bodies of knowledge and scientific inquiry skills to students. Judgments about scientific concepts are best made by experts, so prospective teachers should study with these subject area experts to master these ideas and then transmit them to their students. Realist teachers should not be distracted from their central purpose by social issues that are better left to social service agencies. The elementary school curriculum should provide the basic skills of reading, writing, mathematics, and basic research skills necessary for later advanced subject matter study in high school. The curriculum is important for realists because it has the potential to "get the world right"—to transmit truth—while the philosophies that follow, existentialism and pragmatism, deny that the world can ever be captured accurately.

eudaimonia
A Greek word translated as happiness but better defined as human fulfillment or flourishing.

theistic realism
A fusion of Aristotle's realism with Christian theology, marrying the educational goals of cultivating reason and spirituality. Also known as *Thomism* after its developer, Thomas Aquinas.

Existentialism

Existentialism is a relative newcomer to the philosophical landscape, emerging in the mid-1800s in the writings of Søren Kierkegaard (1813–1855) and rising to prominence around World War II. Existentialism differs from the traditional philosophies of idealism and realism by ignoring metaphysical questions about reality; such questions are regarded as a distraction from human beings' responsibility to make choices about real-life issues. Noddings (2007) suggests that it should not be called a "philosophy" because it has so many varied interpretations, and existentialists generally reject systematic philosophy. Idealists and realists claim that the good life is prescribed and we have the responsibility to live up to that ideal. By contrast, Jean-Paul Sartre's famous existentialist statement asserts that "existence precedes essence." We first exist and then determine our essence by the choices we make. In the absence of absolute authority or reality, the existentialist teacher aims to foster students' responsibility and autonomy—for students to take ownership of their choices to become authentic human beings. The aim is to be true to oneself despite external pressures.

existentialism
A philosophical system that emphasizes personal responsibility for one's choices and living an authentic life.

Existentialist educators sometimes critique schools for mirroring the efficiency values of the Industrial Revolution. They want to address the depersonalization of education by encouraging a more authentic student–teacher relationship and the students' right to find personal meaning in their learning. Teachers must be careful that students' individuality is not sacrificed to the group. While realists believe there is some reality that can be transmitted, existentialists rely on the learners to determine what is meaningful to them as individuals. Ambiguity and openness are important ideals for existentialists. They reject the idea of order; by whose standards would one judge order, especially if all students have the personal responsibility to live authentically? Not surprisingly, then, ethics and morality are largely defined by the students with minimal teacher intervention.

An existentialist curriculum prizes the arts and humanities because these subjects invite personal meaning making. Literature often illustrates characters' choices in complex human issues. Learning activities such as autobiographical writing help students reflect on their own self-identity. Existentialists invite aesthetic education to prompt creative expression, not to emulate the styles of classical artists. Science is regarded as a necessary body of knowledge that can inform students about their context, but it does not help them make themselves. Existentialists are typically opposed to standardized tests that set specific skills and content as necessary; these high-stakes tests mean that priority is given to the content to be tested at the expense of fine arts and other opportunities that are more likely to foster students' creative expression.

The story *The Wizard of Oz* is sometimes used to illustrate existentialism. Over the rainbow is a wizard who will give the characters what they need: courage, a brain, and a heart. When the wizard turns out to be a hoax, Lion, Scarecrow, and Tin Man learn that these "gifts" they were seeking could be found within; they made themselves on the journey. (See the Practical Applications box on page 216 for another example from a movie of an existential classroom.) For existentialists, education should be an important part of one's journey, helping students determine who they are. Chapter 1 of this text also reflects teachers' existentialist journeys toward being reflective professionals who define themselves through the choices they make.

Pragmatism

While realism and idealism find their roots in ancient Greece, **pragmatism** is a uniquely American philosophy developed in the 19th and 20th centuries. Like the realists, pragmatists take a scientific orientation to understanding the world, but they are not limited by the metaphysical or epistemological commitments of the realists; reality is what is observed

pragmatism
A philosophical system that believes that knowledge is constructed by individuals and groups to solve problems they encounter. Pragmatists believe that reality is what is observed or experienced and truth is what works.

or experienced and truth is what works. Pragmatism shares with existentialism a rejection of truth as traditionally understood; however, while existentialists romanticize the human predicament and the loss of meaning, pragmatists quickly get to work in searching for practical solutions to human problems. For pragmatists, truth is justification: In as much as any belief is justified, it is knowledge.

Practical Applications

AN EXISTENTIALIST CLASSROOM

In the film *Dangerous Minds* (1995), there is a confrontational classroom scene in which the teacher invites the students to leave if they are so unhappy. One student sneers that people in her neighbourhood don't have choices. The teacher counters that, in fact, they do: While some of their neighbours have choose to sell drugs and even kill people, these students have chosen to come to school. She refers the class to the lyrics of a Bob Dylan song they had been discussing when the confrontation erupted and asks them again what they think it means.

> *I will not go down under the ground because someone tells me that death's comin' round.*
>
> *I will not carry myself down to die, when I go to my grave my head will be high.* (Dylan, 1962)

Students begin to analyze the text, noting that the writer is not going to wait for death but rather is choosing to die with pride. The words of the famous lyricist urge the students to recognize the choice that is before them: When faced with death, what would it mean to die with pride? In a neighbourhood where their futures seem predetermined, the teacher challenges the students to choose—to make their own lives.

Existentialists prize the potential of literature for exploring life's meaning and the choices confronted by characters. Existentialism as a philosophy leads to social reconstructionism, an educational philosophy concerned with social justice that will be explored in future pages. As individuals take ownership for their own lives, they often see the way their social context has constrained them and others around them. They may seek to address these constraints so that others may live more authentically.

Consider a piece of literature for children or young adults that invites discussion of existentialist themes. What questions would you pose to students to draw out these themes? What parallels do you see between existentialism and the psychological concept of locus of control?

Teachers with a pragmatist orientation oppose the idealist and realist view that there exists a body of knowledge to be transmitted to students. Rather, knowledge is constructed by individuals and groups to solve problems they encounter; the curriculum is open ended, growing out of the students' needs and interests. Imagine curriculum as Lego blocks. Realists want to provide the blocks with the models included, for example, models to construct the Star Wars X-Wing Starfighter, while pragmatists are content to provide the blocks out of which children construct their own creations. For pragmatists, the end in view is not to build the models as instructed but to employ the building blocks to problem solve in order to meet human needs and preferences.

Pragmatists aren't opposed to transmitting knowledge as long as that knowledge can be extended through the students' inquiry. The Renaissance study described in the epistemology section of this chapter is compatible with pragmatic philosophy, because the students learned knowledge about the Renaissance but then extended it through their own inquiry to show its relevance for contemporary issues. Basic skills are regarded as building blocks but not ends in themselves. In a pragmatist classroom, skills instruction is typically integrated with a practical task. Phonics is not taught in isolation but instead is taught to help decode words in the context of a story. Multiplication facts may be memorized but then used to calculate the classroom area. Subjects are tentative understandings about topics like history and biology, but these understandings can be refined. Even moral development proceeds from group problem solving, considering the possible outcomes of each proposed course of action. In that sense, pragmatists would generally take a consequentialist view of ethical questions.

Of all the pragmatist philosophers, John Dewey (1859–1952) has been most influential to education in the United States and Canada. Dewey established a Laboratory School that involved children in co-operative activities such as play, construction, and nature study, all designed to help the learners construct their own understanding through experiences. In fact, Dewey preferred the term *naturalism* to *pragmatism* because he found explanations in natural phenomena. Pragmatists rely on the scientific method (used in other subjects besides science) in which learners recognize and define problems, suggest possible solutions, consider the possible consequences of those solutions, and then experiment to find the most workable solution. For this reason, pragmatists are also sometimes referred to as experimentalists:

> The change of attitude from conservative reliance on the past, upon routine and custom, to faith in progress through intelligent regulation, of existing conditions, is of course, the reflex of the scientific method of experimentation. The empirical method inevitably magnifies the influences of the past; the experimental method throws into relief the possibilities of the future. The empirical method says, "Wait till there is a sufficient number of cases;" the experimental method says, "Produce the cases." (Dewey, 1933, p. 154)

The scientific method involves holding all truth up for careful interrogation, an ideal that runs counter to the traditional view that the Western canon contains eternal truths. Dewey asks us not to rely upon truths laid out by others in the past but to create solutions to the everyday problems we encounter. This interrogation of truth requires careful reflection on one's own beliefs and the use of evidence and arguments to make decisions.

As noted in Chapter 1, the type of problem solving required by the scientific method is a critical aspect of teachers' reflections as they search for the best ways to help children learn. The influence of pragmatism on education is especially evident in the educational philosophy of progressivism, which is discussed later in this chapter.

 Normative Philosophies of Education

The preceding philosophies are broad philosophical systems that comment on a variety of problems and questions. These philosophies have led to some historical and contemporary anxieties about education that are addressed by the following philosophies of education. They address philosophical issues related specifically to education and are normative in the sense that each prescribes how education *ought* to proceed.

CASE STUDY

Preservice Teachers' Beliefs and Assumptions about Teaching and Learning

As part of an introductory Foundations of Education course, preservice teachers visited several innovative schools including a charter school where all students were provided with a laptop and learned much of the curriculum through inquiry-based learning projects. One project required Grade 7 students to engage in the following exercise:

LEARNING ACTIVITY: Some Europeans believe you are a "strange and savage people without faith, without laws, without religions, without any civilities, but living like unreasoned beasts" (André Thévet, 1651). Like Donnacona and his sons, you have been taken back to Europe and have been asked to give an account of your people. This is your opportunity to convince the Europeans of the value of the way of life back in your First Nations community. You must create a speech in support of your First Nations community. Your speech must contain the following:

- Information on the different elements of your First Nations community (social structure, art, spirituality, values, etc.)
- Arguments why you are not "strange and savage" people in need of civilizing
- Specific historical details about your First Nations community
- Some piece of advice or lesson that the Europeans (or people today) could learn from your First Nations way of life

(Learning Activity excerpted from Connect! The Professional Learning Journal of the Connect Charter School, 2011b. Used with permission.)

Miriam was skeptical of this project: "I know the students are expected to research one of the tribes and use that information in their speech, but I'm sure they'll miss a lot of key ideas. The task is too wide open and unstructured for them to learn all the content the Grade 7 social studies curriculum includes."

"So would you rather see the teacher just give them notes on each of the tribes?" asked Khaled. "Boring! They might cover more content but would they remember it? I like this approach because students can be actively involved in using the ideas they research to create the speech. They get to choose the tribe and the ideas they include and how to present it—posters or iMovie or whatever they want. It makes it more authentic to imagine themselves as one of those people."

Jennifer nodded, "I think he's right, Miriam. When students can interpret the content and use the parts that are most meaningful to them, that's learning that lasts. They might even recognize aspects of their own culture that they'd want to celebrate."

"I like the application to life today," said Thomas. "Drawing a lesson for today from a tribal group living centuries ago gets the students to think outside their own ethnocentric worldviews. Hopefully they'd see how the racism of that time is still evident in our own community today."

Brow furrowed, Miriam remained uncertain. "I see what you mean, but I still worry that the classroom would be a free-for-all and the projects wouldn't be very thorough. These kids have provincial exams to write; how would that teacher explain to the parents why their child bombed on the social studies exam because they were writing fictional speeches and playing with iMovie instead of learning the content? It's too easy to miss things if the teacher lets the kids just teach themselves."

These preservice teachers' reactions to this learning experience reflect their values and their beliefs about how schools should proceed with the work of education. Whose values are most closely aligned with your own? Do you recognize others whose beliefs would be more like one of the other teachers in this scenario? As you read the philosophies that follow, consider which ones are most likely held by Miriam, Khaled, Jennifer, and Thomas.

Perennialism

perennialism
A philosophy of education that believes great truths are universal and unchanging, so education should foster rational powers and transmit these truths, often through classic texts.

Perennialism is a philosophy of education often drawn from idealism and especially realism. You may recall that idealists typically believe knowledge is acquired by using reason to understand the archetypal forms while realists believe one abstracts concepts from observing the empirical world. While idealists and realists differed in these epistemological commitments, both were committed to transmitting a core curriculum, and thus both were influential in the development of perennialism, one of the earliest philosophies to specifically address educational questions.

Like a perennial plant that returns each spring, ideas are perennial, universal, and unchanging. For perennialists, education should foster rational powers and transmit these truths. Since human nature is basically unchanging, the great ideas of the past are useful in addressing contemporary problems. They caution that if we mistake progress for wisdom, we may overlook the wisdom of the past, often found in the "Great Books." The Great Books include texts such as Homer's *Iliad* and *Odyssey*, the writings of the early philosophers and theologians, Shakespeare, and Einstein. *Ad fontes* is a Latin expression that means "to the sources" or "to the fountains"; it represents Renaissance educational reforms designed to return to the sources of great ideas—the Greek and Latin classics. The fine arts also teach us about great human ideals. Because human nature is unchanging, education should be the same for everyone; it should not differ according to the history, intellectual capacity, socioeconomic background, or culture of the learners because such variations may be undemocratic. Contemporary realists are particularly wary of relativism in education because they believe it undermines intellectual rigour and moral judgment. Like their idealist and realist

Practical Applications

SOME CRITICISMS OF PERENNIALISM

Critics of perennialism argue that it is elitist and does not help teachers motivate students, particularly the students who lack the educational background of their more privileged peers. Do you agree that education should be the same for everyone, or should it differ for some individuals or communities?

Perennialism is also criticized by educators focused on culturally relevant pedagogy because of its heavy reliance on the Western canon. Do you think all students should study the Western canon, or should there be more time for texts from other cultures, particularly those that reflect the cultural background of the students in the class?

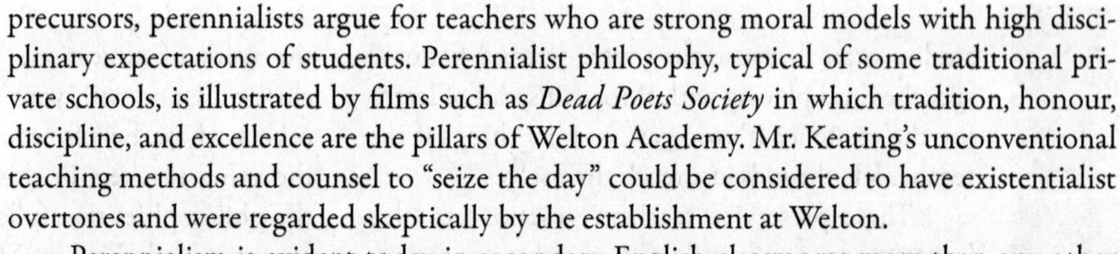

precursors, perennialists argue for teachers who are strong moral models with high disciplinary expectations of students. Perennialist philosophy, typical of some traditional private schools, is illustrated by films such as *Dead Poets Society* in which tradition, honour, discipline, and excellence are the pillars of Welton Academy. Mr. Keating's unconventional teaching methods and counsel to "seize the day" could be considered to have existentialist overtones and were regarded skeptically by the establishment at Welton.

Perennialism is evident today in secondary English classrooms more than any other discipline because this is where students are most likely to read the great classics in literature. At its best, perennialism can lead students to look carefully at themes like justice and human rights in the context of current social issues.

Essentialism

essentialism
A philosophy of education that emphasizes basic skills and subjects, mastery of the content checked by standards, and preparing students to be productive citizens through classrooms that are orderly, disciplined, and efficient.

If perennialism represents education that goes back "to the sources," **essentialism** is education that goes "back to the basics." It emphasizes basic skills and subjects, mastery of the content checked by standards, and preparing students to be productive citizens through classrooms that are orderly, disciplined, and efficient. It shares with ancient realism and idealism an epistemological optimism that the world is knowable and teachers have an obligation to represent those objective realities about the world accurately to their students. Essentialists believe that what is essential to education is the transmission of basic knowledge that is critical for human civilization. Philosophies of education that depart from this cultural transmission place society in peril. This core knowledge includes all the liberal arts and sciences developed from the time of the ancient Greeks and Romans to the present. To learn all of this material in a limited amount of time, teachers must be deliberate and efficient (one can see the relationship to the social efficiency ideology described in Chapter 3). Rather than experimenting with new methods, essentialist teachers rely on tried and true instructional methods like note taking, worksheets, and comprehension questions. They may employ scope and sequence charts to cover the curriculum in the most logical and efficient way.

While essentialists and perennialists may both value a relatively teacher-led classroom, the underlying values are quite different. Essentialism is sometimes associated with an industrial model of education in which schools are compared to a standardized and efficient assembly line, producing obedient students who can be used in the economic system to create wealth. By contrast, perennialists see education as a type of cultural womb, a way to replicate the culture and produce thoughtful citizens to sustain it.

Assertive discipline (Canter & Canter, 1976), which was discussed in detail in Chapter 2, is an approach to classroom management that aligns closely with essentialism. Teachers have a responsibility to enforce rules and students are placed in clearly subordinate roles. Teachers establish a few clear rules and assertively apply consequences for compliant and noncompliant behaviour. This squares with Aristotle's admonition that children must be habituated in virtues. However, assertive discipline may be overly pessimistic about children's ability to act rationally, something Aristotle urged adults to cultivate. In her famous book *Democratic Education* (1999), philosopher Amy Gutmann argues that education ought to develop in children the capacity to deliberate: "To the extent that a democracy is not deliberative, it treats people as objects of legislation, as passive subjects to be ruled, rather than as citizens who take part in governance" (p. xii). For Gutmann, schools must foster citizenship, and this is best achieved in a classroom that permits students a reasonable amount of voice. Most essentialists place a lower value on student voice than some other philosophies. Essentialists may also subscribe to character education programs.

Essentialism arose as a response to progressivism, a pragmatist philosophy of education that will be discussed in future pages. Essentialists believe these liberal approaches to education undermine academic rigour and lead to lax moral standards. Arguably, essentialist philosophy influences many contemporary teachers. Teachers who are desperate to gain control of unruly classrooms may resort to authoritarian management techniques. To some degree, the pressure of provincial exam preparation leads teachers to be efficient in their curriculum coverage, even when they may feel uncomfortable with the level of engagement observed in their students or the depth of understanding they are able to promote in their limited time. Essentialists are generally more supportive of standardized tests than other philosophies because demonstrating one's mastery of essential skills is a critical component of essentialist education. In the previous Case Study, Miriam likely held essentialist ideas; she seemed to believe that toying with technological presentations and a fictional role would not help students "cover" the required facts.

Impact on Today's Teachers

TRADITIONAL LEARNING CENTRES AND ESSENTIALIST VALUES

While essentialism may seem out of vogue, it continues to be apparent in some schools and programs such as Traditional Learning Centres (TLC), a program of choice for students in the Calgary Board of Education. TLCs advocate

- High expectations for academic excellence and character development, which are clearly defined
- Direct whole-group instruction that is sequential and enriched, building on a foundation of knowledge, virtues, critical thinking, and inquiry
- Structured, orderly, safe, and nurturing environments that maximize student learning
- Staff that are committed to continuous learning within a community of learners (Calgary Board of Education, 2011)

Essentialist themes are evident in this program's emphasis on academic excellence, character education, sequential direct instruction, and structure to maximize student learning. Some parents may feel more comfortable with this type of education, particularly parents who grew up in school systems with more traditional educational approaches.

Review the mission statement of various types of schools and see if you can identify essentialist themes in their statements. Schools do not operate in a vacuum, so it is inevitable that schools will be influenced by the dominant ideologies.

Conservatism

Conservatism, which is more of a political ideology than an educational philosophy, is a subset of essentialism that is having a significant impact on education. The root word, *conserve*, means to preserve or keep in a safe state. It is born out of many of the preceding philosophies

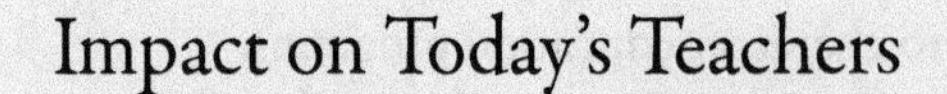

Impact on Today's Teachers

CONSERVATIVES AND CREATION SCIENCE

The teaching of evolution in science has been an ongoing debate between Christian conservatives and their opponents. Conservatives argue for a curriculum that includes "intelligent design," a repackaging of creation science asserting that the irreducible complexity of life on Earth must have been initiated by an intelligent higher power. Philosophers of education are interested in this issue because it raises many metaphysical, epistemological, and axiological questions.

1. What is *real*? Christians claim God is real and created the world, while scientists claim as real what is scientifically verifiable.
2. What is *knowledge*? Christian conservatives believe knowledge is the revealed truth in the Bible and schools must present the Bible's creation account alongside the scientific accounts of evolution; scientists believe knowledge includes the accumulated discoveries of science over the centuries, including the theory of evolution.
3. What is *ethical*? Christians claim that it is unethical to impose secular scientific theories on their children, thus undermining their faith in God; scientists believe that students should be taught the scientific facts and be allowed to make their own decisions about faith and science.

Courtesy of Owen Egan

Brian Alters, a professor of science education at McGill University, established the Evolution Education Research Centre (EERC) to address the scientific illiteracy he perceives in Canadian science education. Research suggests that one third of teachers report pressure from parents to teach creationism or intelligent design (Alters, Asghar, & Wiles, 2005). Teachers often avoid the topic of evolution completely or tiptoe around it, explaining that some faiths believe in a creation story. Alters warns that when science can't offer an explanation for some natural phenomenon, divine intervention is credited and this undermines the inquiry that is critical to science. He argues, "You can't teach biology without teaching the one thing that unifies the whole discipline" (Laidlaw, 2007). Alters's current research examines the place of evolution in provincial science curricula across Canada. Preliminary analysis suggests that the term *evolution* is avoided (often replaced with "change over time") seemingly in an effort to avoid controversy (Alters et al., 2005).

What do you think? What is *real* with respect to the origins of Earth? How do we *know*? Is it *ethical* to teach material that runs counter to your students' faith? Is it ethical to withhold ideas from students?

who together claim, "We have found something worth conserving." Conservatism resists rapid change; in education, it endorses basic skills instruction and rigorous academic standards to transmit cultural heritage. In keeping with its essentialist cousins, it also endorses strict disciplinary standards.

conservatism
A subset of the educational philosophy known as essentialism that resists rapid change in education. It endorses basic skills instruction, rigorous academic standards, and strict disciplinary standards.

Christian fundamentalists in Canada and more so in the United States are associated with conservative ideology. They argue for the restoration of "family values" and are especially resistant to teaching about abortion, premarital sex, and homosexuality. In April 2010, the Institute for Canadian Values spoke out and threatened demonstrations in response to changes to the Ontario sex education curriculum. "It is unconscionable to teach eight-year-old children same-sex marriage, sexual orientation and gender identity," said Charles McVety, head of the Canada Christian College (*CBC News*, 2010). Ontario Premier Dalton McGuinty agreed to reconsider some of the language and content in the curriculum; currently the *Health and Physical Education Curriculum, Grades 1–8* from the Ontario Ministry of Education is labelled "Interim Edition."

Conservatives who align with perennialists argue that schools should transmit the cultural heritage of Western civilization, while conservatives who align with essentialists emphasize developing skills that are critical to the economic growth of a nation. To prepare graduates to function in the economy, they recommend strict enforcement of standards including the retention (grade repetition) of children who do not master the content of their grade level. This practice is usually discouraged in Canadian school boards because research suggests retained students are less likely to be successful than similar peers who are promoted, and that retained students are more likely to drop out (Jimerson, 2001). While conservatives generally oppose change and nonacademic additions to schools, technology is now considered a new basic requirement that is necessary for economic prosperity.

Progressivism

Progressivism finds its early origins in the work of Jean-Jacques Rousseau (1712–1778), especially his famous book *Émile* (1762/1998). For Rousseau, children's natural goodness was corrupted by adults and institutions like schools. Émile, the pupil who is the focus of his book, was encouraged to follow his own instincts in exploring the environment. Rousseau was criticized for having an overly sentimental conception of children during a time when children were to be "seen but not heard." However, his views ultimately contributed to a shift in society's views of children, including the abolition of child labour (Friquegnon, 1997).

progressivism
A child-centred philosophy emphasizing problem solving while capitalizing on students' curiosity and creative self-expression.

The Progressive Education Association organized in 1919 brought together educators who were committed to common principles including encouraging students' initiative and creative expression, with teachers who serve as facilitators of research activities that promote students' development (Gutek, 2009, p. 343). Progressives want to promote the development of the whole child—physically, cognitively, socially, and emotionally. Topics should arise from the children's interests, not the teachers' goals. They also believe that learning should be active, collaborative, and build reflective skills. Formative assessment and scaffolding to support learners is critical to building this reflective capacity. Inquiry-based and problem-based learning typical of many contemporary schools are approaches to learning that align with progressivism, at least in many respects.

Although existentialism has been perhaps most influential to social reconstructionists (which are discussed below), to some degree its themes resonate in progressive ideals, particularly the importance of student choice. However, for existentialists the emphasis is on the development of the *individual* and the personal meaning he or she finds in learning those chosen ideas. Students in progressive classrooms make choices about the content and presentation of ideas, but they are more likely to collaborate with others who have similar interests. Progressives are interested in fostering citizenship in addition to personal development so students tend to work together to solve problems.

Early progressives drew heavily on the philosophy of pragmatists like John Dewey. They were particularly influenced by Dewey's Laboratory School, where educators experimented with various educational methods. Dewey shared progressives' disdain for what he referred to as "traditional education" because students were "rendered callous to ideas, . . . associated the learning process with ennui and boredom [and] dull drudgery" (1938, p. 27). Furthermore, traditional education taught content in isolation, disconnected from the real world, so there was little transfer; the ideas were "not available under the actual conditions of life" (p. 48). Progressive schools initially had intuitive appeal because they were more humane. They lacked the harshness and autocratic feel of traditional schools and, unlike traditional schools, took seriously "the importance of personal impulse and desire as moving springs" (p. 71).

However, despite being called "the father of progressivism," Dewey actually took issue with many progressive ideals, particularly their naive optimism about children and an overemphasis on a child-centred curriculum. They seemed to cater to children's whims, engaging them in activity for activity's sake but with little intellectual value:

> But this is no reason why progressive education should identify impulse and desire with purpose and thereby pass lightly over the need for careful observation, for wide range of information, and for judgment if students are to share in the formation of purposes which activate them. . . . I have heard of cases in which children are surrounded with objects and materials and then left entirely to themselves, the teacher being loath to suggest even what might be done with the materials lest freedom be infringed upon. . . . It is impossible to understand why a suggestion from one who has a larger experience and a wider horizon should be at least as valid as a suggestion arising from some more or less accidental source. (Dewey, 1938, p. 71)

Dewey argued that it was the teacher's role to select ideas from within the students' experience that have the potential to present a meaningful problem "such that it arouses in the learner an active quest for information and for production of new ideas" (Dewey, 1938, p. 79). He cautioned, "failure to give constant attention to development of the intellectual content of experiences and to obtain ever-increasing organization of facts and ideas may in the end merely strengthen the tendency toward a reactionary return to intellectual and moral authoritarianism" (p. 86). Notice the attention to "development of intellectual content" and "production of new ideas"; problem-, project-, and inquiry-based learning described in Chapter 3 seem to be approaches to teaching and learning that would very likely conform to Dewey's ideals—a type of progressivism done well.

William Heard Kilpatrick, one of Dewey's students, developed the *project method* to integrate the ideals of progressivism with Dewey's scientific method of problem solving, an approach to education that continues in contemporary classrooms. He argued that the best learning happens when children, in response to their own curiosity, seek answers to problems in their environment. Students, individually or in groups, define a problem or project. Progressive teachers in a project-based classroom may seem to play a secondary role, but in fact they play a critical role in establishing an environment with rich opportunities for learning and guiding their students through meaningful projects and problems. They must know their students well, including their background experience, interests, and needs.

Current initiatives in the project approach have been led by Sylvia Chard, a scholar at the University of Alberta. Although the project approach has been most influential in prekindergarten to Grade 3 settings, Chard's website (Chard, n.d.) provides examples of projects in all age groups, including high school. Projects include examination of trees, creation of a healthy snack bar, robotics, and sustainable housing. One project involved preschoolers in Baton Rouge, Louisiana, a city that hosted thousands of evacuees after Hurricane Katrina. Children visited a demonstration centre where they learned about sustainable housing with steel beams and long nails. They used fans to examine the impact of wind on objects of varying weights and had the opportunity to construct their own "homes" with pretend steel (silver pipe cleaners). This project aligns with progressive ideals because the topic arose from a current local issue, the children were actively involved in exploring the topic in hands-on ways, and it stemmed from their own experience.

Inquiry-based learning, which is somewhat similar to the project approach, is a current iteration of progressivism practised in many Canadian schools. The Galileo Educational Network is an organization that supports teachers in inquiry-based learning. Their website argues that *inquiry* can be distinguished from *projects* in that projects often supplement the curriculum and use broad-based assessments while inquiry is part of the regular curriculum and there is a deliberate effort to build inquiry questions around essential questions arising from the curriculum. (Advocates of the project approach would likely disagree with this distinction and find much that is similar in their approaches.) Inquiry-based learning has been defined as follows:

> Inquiry is a study into a worthy question, issue, problem or idea. It is the authentic, real work that someone in the community might tackle. It is the type of work that those working in the disciplines actually undertake to create or build knowledge. Therefore, inquiry involves serious engagement and investigation and the active creation and testing of new knowledge. (Galileo Educational Network, 2011a)

Inquiry projects rest on the following pillars:

- *Authenticity:* The inquiry study emanates from a question, problem, issue, or exploration that is significant to the disciplines, has meaning to the students, and has significant influence in determining the scope of the study. It addresses real-world problems and students have the opportunity to create or produce knowledge.
- *Academic rigour:* Students use methods of inquiry that professionals in the field would use to respond to the problem or question. They are encouraged to develop habits of mind that help them to question evidence, viewpoint, causes, and significance.
- *Assessment:* Students have a clear sense of assessment criteria and use those criteria to critique their own work and establish learning goals. They receive ongoing feedback from multiple sources—teachers, peers, and those outside the classroom.
- *Beyond the school:* The inquiry explores a question that is relevant to curriculum outcomes and some topic beyond the school. Students develop skills relevant to the workplace such as organization, communication, teamwork, and problem solving.
- *Use of digital technologies:* Students select technology to research, share information, solve problems, and communicate with various audiences beyond the classroom throughout the study. They employ sophisticated software for multimedia, videoconferencing, simulation, and databases.

- *Active exploration:* Students are actively involved in fieldwork, labs, interviews, and construction. They communicate what they are learning through presentations and exhibitions.
- *Connecting with experts:* Students interact with adults who have expertise relevant to their study. The teacher collaborates directly or indirectly with experts to design the inquiry task.
- *Elaborated communication:* Students regularly support, challenge, and respond to others' ideas as they develop an understanding of the concepts. They express their ideas in various forms such as by using PowerPoint or iMovie or through mime, artwork, dance, and other forms and share their learning with various audiences. (Galileo Educational Network, 2011b)

The Renaissance project described previously achieved many if not all of these outcomes. The study emanated from an *authentic* question, "Does Calgary have the conditions to be a Renaissance city?" which built on the social studies curriculum and local ideas. *Academic rigour* was achieved through researching historical and current data as well as debate. Students received ongoing *assessment* feedback from their teachers, peers, and the local experts. Applying a historical question to an analysis of their own city provided relevance *beyond the school* and fostered many of the organization and communication skills suggested by this pillar. Students were involved in *active exploration* through interviewing and presenting their learning and had direct *connection with experts* who commented on their work and provided ideas for the debate. Students developed *elaborated communication* through videos, audio files, wikispaces, interviews, and debate.

Modern progressives argue that given the explosion of information in contemporary society, mastering the traditional subject matter may well be less critical than developing the skills of problem solving and the ability to collect and analyze information (Gilbert, 2011). This focus on fostering complex problem solving is an important rationale for the 21st-century education movement. Influential journalist Thomas Friedman (2007) writes, "The first and most important ability you can develop in a flat world is the ability to 'learn how to learn'—to constantly absorb, and teach yourself, new ways of doing old things or new ways of doing new things" (p. 309). Friedman also argues that collaboration, passion, curiosity, and creativity are far more valuable in education than mastery of content; these less tangible assets are critical for solving the problems in contemporary society. Although he is not an educator, Friedman has clearly thought deeply about education and seems to be critical of essentialist ideals like "mastery of content"; he would undoubtedly favour the pillars of inquiry-based learning.

Alberta Education (2010), in consultation with a wide variety of stakeholders (teachers, businesspeople, academics, and others), produced a document called *Inspiring Education: A Dialogue with Albertans* in which they articulate a renewed vision for education in the province. They question the adequacy of an industrial model of education and, like Friedman, advocate for an education system that better prepares students for a knowledge-based society. Rather than mastering the specific content in the curriculum, this document argues instead that high school graduates should be able to

- know how to learn—to gain knowledge, understanding or skills through experience, study, and interaction with others.
- think critically—conceptualize, apply, analyze, synthesize, and evaluate to construct knowledge.

- identify and solve complex problems.
- manage information—access, interpret, evaluate, and use information effectively, efficiently, and ethically.
- innovate—create and generate new ideas or concepts.
- create opportunities—through play, imagination, reflection, negotiation, and competition—with an entrepreneurial spirit.
- apply multiple literacies—reading, writing, mathematics, technology, languages, media, and personal finance.
- demonstrate good communication skills and the ability to work cooperatively with others.
- demonstrate global and cultural understanding.
- identify and apply career and life skills. (p. 26)

The writers admit that a "focus on competencies will shift education away from a process of disseminating information to a process of inquiry and discovery" (p. 26). Dissemination implies a perennialist and essentialist philosophy of education in which students are "given" the facts of the culture and learn the basic skills required by society. Many would argue that the existing provincial exams incline teachers to pedagogies of dissemination rather than inquiry. One of the goals of the report is to revise assessment to align with a competency-based system (p. 39). The Alberta curriculum is currently being redesigned to comply with these recommendations, particularly with a focus on competencies. Perhaps progressive teachers may find it easier to be faithful to their beliefs about teaching and learning with an assessment system that measures the competencies they value.

Think back to the Case Study featuring Miriam, Khaled, Thomas, and Jennifer's discussion about the First Nations learning activity. Khaled and Jennifer had progressive ideals. What advice would you give to ensure that this project is an effective learning opportunity that addresses Miriam's objections?

Impact on Today's Teachers

PROGRESSIVISM AND SKILLS INSTRUCTION

In Chapter 1 you read about the dispute over whether phonics or whole language constitutes the best approach to reading instruction. As you may have surmised, phonics represents an essentialist philosophy while whole language represents a more progressive philosophy of language learning. We demonstrated that current reading instruction does not recommend a simple combination of these approaches; rather, reflective teachers must examine the outcomes of their practices to determine which approaches are most effective.

Victoria Purcell-Gates (2001) details her first teaching experience with junior high students who lacked basic skills in reading and writing. In keeping with the established program, students did daily phonics workbooks, read short reading selections, and responded to basic comprehension questions. Inspired by a course in whole-language reading strategies and discouraged by the students' boredom and lack of progress,

continued

Purcell-Gates engaged the students in self-directed reading and responses to authentic texts with tremendous success. However, she points out that the effectiveness of these progressive strategies depended on what she calls "side-of-the-pool" instruction:

> Side-of-the-pool activities are those that isolate parts of the reading process for concentrated teaching or practice. They are so named because they are akin to hanging onto the side of the swimming pool in order to practice kicking for a while before going back to actual swimming.... After working through these skill-based activities, the reader returns to the "pool," returns to functional reading activity, practicing the worked upon skill. I and others have termed this instruction whole-part-whole. (pp. 124–125)

This example illustrates how reflection upon her own beliefs about teaching and the outcome of her practices led one teacher to find ways to incorporate the best aspects of essentialism (explicit skills instruction) with a student-centred progressive philosophy that aligned with her own beliefs about reading instruction.

Social Reconstructionism

social reconstructionism
A philosophy of education that maintains that teachers and schools ought to be change agents in creating a new and more equitable social order.

Social reconstructionism is a philosophy of education that maintains that teachers and schools ought to be change agents in creating a new and more equitable social order. The term was first coined by George Counts (1889–1974) who wrote the book *Dare the School Build a New Social Order?* (1932). After World War II social reconstructionism was further developed by educator and philosopher Theodore Brameld (1904–1987) who viewed society and education through anthropological lenses. Every society practises some form of education, where education is defined as a type of enculturation. However, when a society experiences a cultural shift that prompts significant social change, education helps society to rebalance by integrating the new ideas with the old. In response to the feminist movement, schools have been deliberate about removing sexist ideas from the curriculum and have contributed to a significant shift in society's views of women. According to social reconstructionists, the curriculum often reflects the status quo—the existing society with all its injustices and unresolved issues. For Brameld, the curriculum should include the examination of that status quo and of controversial issues in politics, economics, morality, science, religion, and society. Not surprisingly, moral education for social reconstructionists involves activating the social conscience of students.

Brameld rejected the traditional definitions of philosophy, defining it "not as metaphysics, epistemology, and axiology but rather said it is 'the persistent effort of both ordinary and sophisticated people to make life as intelligible and meaningful as possible'" (Gutek, 2009, p. 372). Like their existentialist precursors, social reconstructionists hold the concept of truth lightly. Truth has been defined by the powerful but does not necessarily reflect the realities of less-privileged groups. Realists accuse reconstructionists of being motivated more by radical ideology than philosophy and leading schools into cultural relativism. Even progressives and pragmatists who support reconstructionists' social reform ideals worry that the social reconstructionists' political agenda might indoctrinate and undermine students' abilities to think independently.

Another key figure in social reconstructionism is Paulo Freire (2000), a Brazilian Christian Marxist scholar devoted to advancing the plight of the illiterate peasants of his homeland. The relationship between social reconstructionism and existentialism is evident in the following statement concerning the "banking model of education," which draws on a similar metaphor developed by famous existentialist Jean-Paul Sartre:

> The teacher's task is to organize a process which already occurs spontaneously, to "fill" the students by making deposits of information which he or she considers to constitute true knowledge. And since people "receive" the world as passive entities, education should make them more passive still. (Freire, 2000, p. 57)

Instead, Freire recommends "problem-posing" education: "Students, as they are increasingly posed with problems relating to themselves in the world and with the world will feel increasingly challenged and obliged to respond to that challenge" (p. 62). Not surprisingly, conservatives are suspicious of this "obligation" and regard reconstructionists' consciousness raising as a form of indoctrination.

Wayne Urban, an educational policy analyst, considers social reconstructionism helpful in countering contemporary attacks on public schools, including "standardized testing that threatens to rob the pedagogical process of any flexibility" and "fundamentalist religious groups who advocate home schooling as an alternative to what they perceive to be public schools' secular values" (quoted in Gutek, 2009, p. 361). It may be a philosophy that has greater value in helping teachers think critically about educational issues than in actually guiding their pedagogical decision making. Nevertheless, the inquiry approaches of progressive educators often activate the social conscience of students and can look much like a social reconstructionist classroom. In the Case Study earlier in this chapter, Thomas represented a social reconstructionist philosophy because he recognized how defending First Nations' values would challenge students' ethnocentrism and help them see discrimination in their own community.

As noted at the beginning of this chapter, Western philosophies have been most influential in the Canadian education system. Social reconstructionists and other critics remind us that there are other philosophies that can and should inform schooling in Canada. For example, feminist philosopher of education Nel Noddings (2007) laments that the curriculum, while celebrating the work achieved in the public sphere, devalues the work of mothers and neighbourhoods in shaping society. Noddings also argues that a traditional epistemology that extols rational autonomy may exclude other ways of knowing.

The call to take seriously diverse epistemologies is echoed by Battiste (2002), an Aboriginal scholar. She shows how the identities of Aboriginal peoples are largely shaped by a deep sense of interconnectedness, particularly a connection to the natural environment. Aboriginal knowing seldom sees information as separate parts but looks for connections to other ideas. Experiential education is central as learners observe, listen, and participate, often through ceremonies and stories; introspection, meditation, and other forms of self-directed learning are valued.

Buddhism has similarly challenged education, reminding educators to value reflection, co-operation, and self-sacrifice more than the instrumental and pragmatic goals that often dominate our school systems. Influenced by Buddhist and Daoist teachings, Heesoon Bai (2012), a philosophy of education professor at Simon Fraser University, suggests that an instrumental view of education has diminished the value of the arts, has contributed to an exploitive relationship with the Earth and its resources, and that the pursuit of ego-driven success has suppressed human emotion, leading to psychological alienation. Mindfulness practices emerging from Buddhist teachings have become more widely employed in schools to address such concerns.

Practical Applications

PROJECT IMPACT INSPIRES STUDENTS TO MAKE A DIFFERENCE

© franckreporter/iStockphoto

One Canadian teacher challenged her Grade 10 and 11 social studies students to make an impact in their lifetimes. More than 100 students took part in Project IMPACT, a semester-long project involving research, exploration, reflection, and self-assessment based

Although feminism, Buddhism, and Aboriginal philosophy do not necessarily fall under the mantle of social reconstructionism, all of these philosophies remind us to question the status quo and educational approaches that value academic achievement at the expense of human flourishing. While it is beyond the scope of this chapter to explore the philosophies of education emerging from various cultures, suffice it to say that immigration and globalization are bound to challenge the Western philosophies that have so dominated the Canadian education system for the last century.

Comparing Philosophies of Education

In the introductory chapter of this text it was suggested that good teaching may be measured by indicators of student achievement or more humanistic measures like fostering students' inter- and intrapersonal growth. Depending on your philosophy, you may value one of these measures more highly than the other. In some cases, you may have ideals that align with a particular philosophy, but in practice you rely on teaching approaches that contradict those ideals. For example, many new teachers may claim to be progressive teachers who value hands-on student problem solving, but in practice they rely on methods they experienced on a social justice topic related to their social studies curriculum. Students picked their own topic, examined it deeply, and considered it in light of our current world. As part of the assignment each student had to take a personal and public action that challenged their own and society's assumptions about the chosen topic.

Students studied global warming, aids, mass media and consumption, arms dealing, discrimination, bullying, homelessness, family violence, homosexual rights, and genocide. They demonstrated their commitment by volunteering for community organizations, presenting at local junior high schools, meeting with experts, and writing letters to major corporations and government officials on the issues they were exploring.

Students kept journals of their successes and difficulties and explored new and more complex questions related to their topics. In their final reflections, students were asked to describe the impact that the project had on them. One student said her project on global warming changed her perspective and helped her to encourage others to make changes in their lives to address this problem. Another described her commitment to standing up against discrimination. One group created a social justice club in their school as a result of their project.

At the end of January, students held a special event to celebrate and present the work that they had done throughout the semester (Calgary Board of Education, 2007).

Critics of social reconstructionism claim that teachers indoctrinate students to their own viewpoints. How do you think this teacher raised the social conscience of her students without indoctrinating them? If you were the teacher, how would you ensure that students were epistemologically sound—that is, able to defend their positions with clear evidence and argument?

when they were students: teacher-directed instruction to deliver information. The reflective process described in Chapter 1 can help you address these inconsistencies so that your teaching practice matches your values.

Chapter 1 asserts that teaching elements are viewed as testable possibilities to adopt or discard depending on their value in advancing student learning. Teachers are urged not to trust an authority but to trust their own minds, to trust their own judgments about what is best practice. You should not be surprised if this language seems to connote Dewey's pragmatic ideals. There is little question that pragmatism and the educational philosophies born from it are tremendously influential in contemporary education.

Have we been toying with you, suggesting there is a smorgasbord when really we expect you to find pragmatism and progressivism to be the most compelling philosophies? We argue that the philosophies in this chapter are less an inventory of ideas from which you may choose and more of a history showing the trajectory of educational ideas over time. As we have shown, some of the traditional ideas of essentialism and perennialism still influence education, but some of those ideas are certainly outmoded and no longer represent strong pedagogy. The teacher in Chapter 1 with the carefully prepared overheads seemed to regard himself as the source of knowledge helping students to "get the information."

We would argue that this teacher was operating from an essentialist perspective, and this perspective did not lead to good teaching. Educators now recognize that learning is significantly increased when students are motivated and interested and that transmission methods typical of perennialist and essentialist philosophies often run counter to good teaching. Existentialist and social reconstructionist philosophies, with their attention to students' personal development and social justice, often have some intuitive appeal and may find their way into progressive projects, but not every topic in the curriculum will have personal appeal or significance to every individual learner and not every topic lends itself to social change. To respond to the question that opened this paragraph, yes, a thoughtful version of progressivism is likely the set of ideals you will most often hear espoused in your education courses. You will need to discern the degree to which you agree with these ideals and can enact them in practice.

Teachers might argue that their own beliefs about education incline them to a progressive approach but the mandated curricula stands as a body of knowledge that they must "transfer" to their students; they may struggle to reconcile their own beliefs with the daunting amount of material they are responsible for teaching. You read quotes from some of these teachers in Chapter 3 with respect to curriculum dilemmas. Sometimes stakeholders such as parents and employers expect greater attention to the classics or to basic skills and see inquiry projects as diversions from the real work of schools. Teachers must find ways to respond to these pressures without abandoning their own beliefs about the best way to educate students.

This chapter has given you some philosophical lenses through which to examine your teaching decisions in the hopes that you may be more philosophically reflective. Good teachers espouse philosophies that represent good teaching—philosophies that invite rich pedagogy, student engagement, cultivation of critical thinking, skill development, and genuine learning. Good teachers should reject philosophies that invite outmoded pedagogies that run counter to what is regarded as best practice. Good teachers should also be mindful of the philosophical objections to their methods. Each of the philosophies may influence you in some ways, and this may vary depending on your subject area expertise and the grade level you teach. Be mindful of the following ideals and possible objections to your philosophical position:

- *Perennialism:* We can value the perennialists' esteem for the classics; Shakespeare and other texts of the Western canon contain some powerful insights about history and human nature and contain much of our cultural heritage—they have become classics for very good reasons! However, we must be aware of the criticisms of perennialism. Perennialist teachers may fail to show students the contemporary relevance of ancient texts, may give insufficient attention to current events, and may fail to interrogate the stereotypical ideas about race and gender included in texts composed in bygone eras. If you are a lover of the classics, you will need to find those that will appeal to the interests and abilities of your students and show the timelessness of the ideas for contemporary society. You may also invite students to look critically at the texts in light of the current context.
- *Essentialism:* One can hardly argue with essentialists' interest in basic skill instruction; the public depends on schools to produce students who can read, write, and do mathematics effectively as well as understand the key curricular concepts of science, social studies, the arts, and other subjects. However, skills divorced from a meaningful

context can quickly sap the curiosity of learners. Furthermore, an essentialist philosophy may lead to authoritarian discipline that can undermine the development of genuine student responsibility and citizenship. If critics argue that your approach is too structured and divorced from the real lives of your students, you must show how it is possible to be relevant and genuinely engage students while establishing the skills you believe are critical to success. If critics argue that your strict classroom privileges compliance over moral development, you must be able to show that you are indeed fostering students' ability to deliberate and act morally.

- *Social reconstructionism:* Students in a social reconstructionist classroom can be very empowered by activism projects and certainly learn about their own social context. However, parents may criticize teachers who relegate math and explicit language instruction to the back burner while pursuing projects. Reconstructionist teachers, passionate about their own beliefs on issues like homophobia, the environment, and poverty, can be accused of indoctrinating and cutting off the critical dialogue about such issues that should characterize thoughtful education. If social reconstructionist ideals appeal to you, remember your ethical responsibility to the students and foster open-minded discussion and debate.
- *Progressivism:* A progressive philosophy of education is arguably most influential in Canadian schools today and there is much in progressivism that aligns with principles of strong pedagogy, including ideals like student choice, collaboration, and problem solving. So how will you avoid the unfortunate label of "permissive progressive" that even John Dewey launched at his progressive colleagues? You must be able to carve out a teacher role that provides sufficient direction to genuinely challenge your students and provide necessary skills and content. In Chapter 1 you read about the phonics versus whole-language debate, the latter informed by progressive ideals. Mem Fox (2001) writes about the mistaken application of whole language:

> But alongside the liberating advances there occurred a distressing loss of expectation. Whole language (or at least I, as an advocate of whole language) never intended to convey the message that correctness didn't matter, but somehow invented spelling held sway in the end over the need for flawless final drafts. Teachers forgot to tell children that writing is essentially a message from inside one's head to inside other heads, and that when that message is ill-spelled, ill-organized, and expressed in an ill manner, so to speak, the message gets badly mangled. (p. 107)

As Chapter 1 explained, there is now a consensus around effective reading instruction that includes explicit skills instruction in the context of authentic reading and writing opportunities. Progressive teachers must be careful that in their enthusiasm to engage children in authentic projects they also provide the skills instruction children will need to tackle those projects successfully.

You may recall that pragmatism and progressivism have rather modest epistemological expectations. While inviting students' construction of understanding, some might question by what standards you might judge students' conclusions? You will need to promote the type of academic rigour espoused by inquiry learning that will invite students to provide evidence for their claims and careful consideration of bias and viewpoint.

Each of the philosophies has its potentials and pitfalls, perhaps some more than others. It is critical that you draw upon the best in each while considering the criticisms.

Philosophy of education is not merely explanatory and descriptive; rather it is normative. Sociology of education describes what teachers often do and educational psychology describes how people learn, but philosophy of education requires teachers to ask themselves questions like the following:

- What *should* my goals for my students be?
- What *should* the aims of education be? (academic or social and moral aims)
- Why *should* I teach this way? What teaching approaches *should* I use? What makes these goals or approaches *valuable* or good in the first place?
- How *should* I contribute to students' moral development?

Your answers to these questions have normative import; they remind you what you should do. The world philosophies and philosophies of education that we have surveyed provide some material that can help you respond reflectively to these questions.

Table 6.1 summarizes the philosophies we have discussed in this chapter.

TABLE 6.1 Philosophy of Education Continuum Chart

Modernity <————————> Postmodernity
Traditional and Conservative <————————> Contemporary and Liberal
Authoritarian (Convergent) <————————> (Divergent) Nonauthoritarian

General or World Philosophies	**Idealism**	**Realism**	**Pragmatism**	**Existentialism**
	Ideas are the only true reality, the only thing worth knowing. Focus: *Mind*	Reality exists independent of the human mind. World of physical objects is the ultimate reality. Focus: *Body*	Universe is dynamic and evolving. Purpose of thought is action. Truth is relative. Focus: *Experience*	Reality is subjective and found within the individual. Individual rather than external standards are key. Focus: *Freedom*
Originator(s)	Plato, Socrates	Aristotle	Pierce, Dewey	Sartre, Kierkegaard
Curricular Emphasis	Subject matter of mind: literature, history, philosophy, religion	Subject matter of physical world: science, math	Subject matter of social experience; creation of new social order	Subject matter of personal choice
Teaching Method	Teach for handling ideas: lecture, discussion	Teach for mastery of facts and basic skills: demonstration, recitation	Problem solving: project method	Individual as entity within a social context
Character Development	Imitating examples, heroes	Training in rules of conduct	Making group decisions in light of consequences	Individual responsibility for decisions and preferences

TABLE 6.1 *continued*

Related Educational Philosophies	**Perennialism** Focus: Teach ideas that are everlasting. Seek enduring truths that are constant, not changing, through great literature, art, philosophy, and religion.	**Essentialism** Focus: Teach the common core, "the basics" of information and skills (cultural heritage) needed for citizenship. (Curriculum can change slowly.)	**Progressivism** Focus: Ideas should be tested by active experimentation. Learning is rooted in the questions of learners in interaction with others. Centred on experience and the student.	**Reconstructionism/ Critical Theory** Focus: Critical pedagogy: analysis of world events, controversial issues, and diversity to provide vision for a better world and social change.
Key Proponents	Robert Hutchins, Jacques Maritain, Mortimer Adler, Allan Bloom	William Bagley, Arthur Bestor, E. D. Hirsch, Chester Finn, Diane Ravitch, Theodore Sizer	John Dewey, William Kilpatrick	George Counts, Jürgen Habermas, Ivan Illich, Henry Giroux, Paulo Freire
Related Theories of Learning (Psychological Orientations)	**Information Processing** The mind makes meaning through symbol-processing structures of a fixed body of knowledge. Describes how information is received, processed, stored, and retrieved from the mind.	**Behaviourism** Behaviour is shaped by design and determined by forces in the environment. Learning occurs as a result of reinforcing responses to stimuli. **Social Learning** Learning is achieved by observing and imitating others.	**Cognitivism/ Constructivism** The learner actively constructs his or her own understandings of reality through interaction with the environment and reflection on actions. Student-centred learning focuses on conflicts to present knowing structures.	**Humanism** Personal freedom, choice, and responsibility are key. Achievement is the motivation toward the highest levels. Control of own destiny is emphasized. It is child-centred and focuses on interaction with others.
Key proponents	Robert Gagné, Robert Sternberg, John R. Anderson	Ivan Pavlov, John Watson, B. F. Skinner, Edward Thorndike, Albert Bandura	Jean Piaget, Urie Bronfenbrenner, Jerome Bruner, Lev Vygotsky	Jean-Jacques Rousseau, Abraham Maslow, Carl Rogers, Arthur Combs

Source: Cohen, 1999.

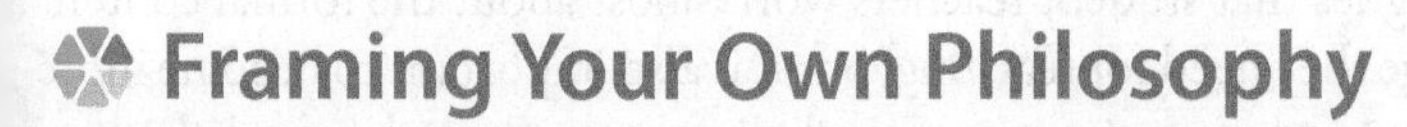

Framing Your Own Philosophy

Return to the exercise in the Practical Applications box entitled "Examining Your Philosophical Assumptions" at the beginning of this chapter. Now that you have learned about the key features of each of the philosophies, do you still agree with your responses to those initial questions? In writing your own philosophy of education statement, you should articulate your beliefs about the aims of education, the curriculum and methods you will include, and your role in moral education. Consider each of the prompt questions below and the way each of the philosophies might respond to these prompts. Note that these are truncated points; you may return to preceding pages for more detail on each philosophy.

1. What do you believe are the primary *aims* of education?
   a) Perennialism: Train the intellect
   b) Essentialism: Acquisition of basic skills
   c) Progressivism: Develop problem-solving skills
   d) Social reconstructionism: Develop a more just society
2. What do you believe are the most appropriate *curriculum and methods*?
   a) Perennialism: Discussion of classics
   b) Essentialism: Structured practice of essential skills
   c) Progressivism: Co-operative inquiry-based learning projects
   d) Social reconstructionism: Student projects on social issues
3. What do you believe is your role in *moral education* and *classroom management*?
   a) Perennialism: High expectations; helping students learn from the moral examples in classic literature
   b) Essentialism: Requiring compliance with appropriate rules
   c) Progressivism: Helping the group make decisions based on consequences
   d) Social reconstructionism: Fostering individual responsibility for one's actions

A clear philosophy prevents you from being pulled in multiple directions by fads and reactionary thinking. As a new teacher in a Grade 1 classroom, one of the authors of this text used a writer's workshop approach, and her students eagerly filled reams of booklets with stories using invented spelling. In keeping with her progressive ideals, she believed that their motivation to write was at least as important as the discrete skills of writing. However, from time to time she found herself doubting their skill development and pulled out phonics worksheets; they responded with groans and there was little transfer of these skills to their actual writing. She tried to find ways to more effectively integrate skills instruction into the writer's workshop as Victoria Purcell-Gates did with her side-of-the-pool instruction (see the Impact on Today's Teachers box entitled "Progressivism and Skills Interaction"). She similarly vacillated about her role in classroom management when behavioural issues arose; sometimes in frustration she simply demanded compliance rather than fostering students' reflection and problem solving. While these reactions are not uncommon for new teachers, a clearly articulated philosophy can help you to remain true to your vision.

Korthagen (2004) argues that student teachers worry most about the formal content and pedagogical knowledge they need for teaching, but it is also important to become more conscious of their philosophical commitments—the beliefs and values that lead them to make the choices they do. The model shown in Figure 6.2 shows how teachers may react to events in the environment and how the environment in turn influences their behaviours. These behaviours are also informed by layers below—the teacher's competencies, beliefs, identity, and at the core their sense of mission, "what is deep inside us that moves us to do what we do" (Korthagen, 2004, p. 85). These inner three layers are closely aligned with a teacher's philosophy of education and often receive less attention in teacher education than the outer layers (teachers' behaviours and competencies) despite the fact that beliefs affect behaviours. "For example, if a teacher believes that attention to pupils' feelings is just 'soft' and unnecessary, he or she will probably not develop the competency to show empathic understanding" (pp. 80–81).

In the example just outlined of the experience of one of the authors of this text with her Grade 1 class writer's workshop, when she pulled out the phonics worksheets her behaviour was a knee-jerk response revealing her fear that the students were not developing the skills they needed. She needed to return to her philosophy—her beliefs about how children learn to write (meaningful writing supported by "side-of-the-pool" instruction), her identity ("I am not an essentialist, so why am I teaching like one?"), and her mission ("I became a teacher to empower joyful independent learners"). Only with careful reflection could she practise in ways that matched her philosophy.

In the introduction to this chapter we asked a couple of questions: (a) Why is it important for me as a teacher to reflect on the philosophical issues related to education? and (b) What impact should these philosophical positions have on me as a classroom teacher? We hope that you now realize that these philosophical issues can have a significant impact on the way a classroom operates and ultimately on students. Your philosophy of education defines what is worth knowing and the best ways to help students acquire that knowledge. It

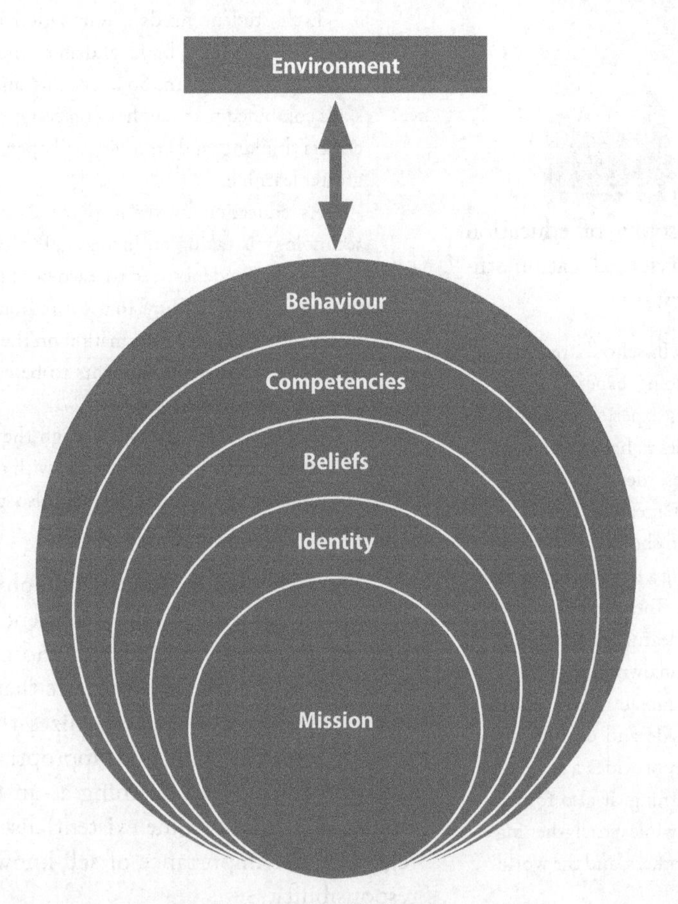

FIGURE 6.2 The Onion Model: Levels of Change
Source: Korthagen, 2004.

defines your approaches to moral education and the place of aesthetics. However you ultimately define your aims, teaching approaches, and beliefs about moral education, your philosophical position should lead you to create optimal learning opportunities for your students and avoid the potential criticisms of your position. The Case Studies below include two examples of teachers' reflections on their philosophy (for other examples of relevant prompt questions and sample philosophies written by preservice teachers, see Cohen, 1999).

CASE STUDY

A Preservice Teacher's Philosophy Statement

Courtesy of Jon Wynder

Jon Wynder wrote his philosophy of education statement as a first-year preservice education student at Mount Royal University.

> Learning is a lifelong activity. In schools, teachers act as guides, designing learning experiences to engage students. These learning experiences should include a wide range of activities to help the learner better understand themselves, develop a sense of community, and construct meaning from the world around them. Education should be inquiry-based, active learning providing a balance between student, teacher, and subject. These relationships are essential for creating a safe learning community and a sense of responsibility and ownership.
>
> There are opportunities for authentic learning and engagement both inside and outside the classroom. Outdoor education provides a sense of exploration and hands-on learning. It also fosters self-discovery and curiosity while strengthening the connections with oneself, others, and the world in which we live.
>
> Teachers should be engaged in designing structured learning experiences rather than just delivering content. Teachers can make a difference. Good teaching is both an art and a science, and good teachers are constantly learning and working to improve. Teachers need to be flexible and adapt to different students and situations to be most effective.
>
> Each student needs a foundation of knowledge upon which to build, and an essential skill is knowing how to learn. Solid reading and writing skills combined with emphasis on communication, critical thinking, and creativity will open doors for greater learning.
>
> As education moves into the 21st century, technology is taking an increasingly vital role in our schools. Students need to learn not just how to use it effectively, but how to use it responsibly and discern the quality of information on the Internet. Technology can enable students to be creators of content and not just consumers.
>
> As I grow and develop through the activities of learning and teaching combined with reflection, my philosophy of education will also grow and develop along the way.

You likely see more than one philosophical orientation influencing Jon's statement. While his focus on inquiry-based learning and adapting to the needs of the students suggests that he is primarily a progressive, he recognizes the importance of essential skills and appropriate teacher direction for effective learning as an essentialist would. He also has some existentialist intuitions regarding the importance of self-knowledge and responsibility.

CASE STUDY

An Experienced Teacher's Philosophy

Courtesy of Neil Stephenson

Neil Stephenson is the District Principal of Innovation and Inquiry for the Delta School District in Delta, British Columbia. In this role, Neil helps support teachers in designing meaningful, inquiry-based learning. Previously, Neil was a Grade 6 and 7 humanities teacher at the Connect Charter School where he was awarded both the Prime Minister's Award for Teaching Excellence and the Governor General's Award for Excellence in Teaching. Neil shares his thoughts on his blog www.thinkinginmind.com.

Like most, when I think back over my public school experience the memories that remain are the times there were opportunities to create or produce something. I remember doing early stop-motion animation movies in Grade 5 and building physical models of Aztec pyramids in Grade 6. I remember music performances and writing projects that had relevance to my own interests and passions. As a child who loved to draw, I have clear memories of the projects that allowed me to express myself or solve problems in visual ways. Looking back now I can see that my philosophical attraction to progressive or constructivist approaches to teaching and learning comes from these positive experiences I had in my own schooling.

After graduating with my education degree I was elated to be offered a job at a school with a deep focus on inquiry-based learning. This school was designed to engage students in authentic learning projects, and it had a number of supports in place to help teachers create these tasks. The school had a culture of risk taking and innovation; it encouraged teachers to continually try new things and push their teaching practice forward. During my first few years of teaching I definitely took advantage of the culture of risk taking. I had my Grade 6 and 7 students engaged in all sorts of different learning tasks and projects; my classroom was often buzzing with students engaged in different experiential, hands-on activities.

As my experience with designing inquiry-based learning has grown, my understanding of what constitutes strong student work has changed. When I look back now I can see that some of my early experiments into inquiry-based learning were full of energy and activity, but not always directed at learning something important about a topic. Through my own professional development, including a sustained mentoring relationship with the Galileo Educational Network, I have come to a place where I believe that strong inquiry-based teaching is a delicate balance built on a teacher-structured process, directed at students developing deep understanding of an important and engaging topic while providing opportunities for students to participate, imagine, engage, and create.

Recently I've become quite interested in the idea of play as a framework for approaching inquiry-based learning. My understanding of play is that it's a unique experience that lives in the space between structure and freedom, between what is known and what is unknown. As is familiar to all, what makes play possible are the rules or boundaries that govern a particular game. If we think of young children engaged in imaginative play, their ability to stay in character and take subtle clues from other children allow the game to continue. Or think of any sport we might play. As soon as one of players decides to ignore the rules, the game falls apart and the

continued

experience of play is gone. However, while the structure is important, we know that play is not a completely planned activity. What makes play enjoyable is the possibilities that emerge; even within a set of clearly defined set of boundaries, the outcome is not yet known. Not everything is decided up front.

I find this notion of play to be a powerful way to understand how teachers might approach inquiry-based learning. I believe there is a misconception around inquiry-based teaching that it's completely student centred; that it's just about what the students want to learn. While my teaching philosophy has elements of constructivist theories (I think students learn best when creating new knowledge, applying information, solving problems, etc.), my development has led me to strive for a balance between student passion and interest, and them coming to know something important about the world. My starting point for learning is always the topic—I start by asking questions such as "What is worthy about this topic?" or "Where does this topic actually live in the world?" What makes teaching incredibly enjoyable and stimulating for me is the challenge of designing tasks that are creative and engaging yet are intentionally chosen so that students learn to think or act in meaningful ways.

As an example, a few years ago I had my Grade 7 students work through a year-long Canadian history experience called the Cigar Box Project. Inspired by an online exhibit at the Canadian Museum of Civilization called "Canada in a Box," students were challenged to create five different labels for a historical cigar box that they would physically build. Over the course of the year, students worked through different eras in Canadian history and for each one they collected and then digitally "remixed" primary source historical artifacts into their own new creations. The purpose of the project was for students to take on different aspects of authentic historical thinking by creating their own unique visual representation of different issues and challenges from throughout Canadian history. Throughout the year, the students were mentored by professors of Canadian history and graphic designers as well as a curator from the national museum. At the end of the year, the student-created artifacts were assembled in their own online gallery, which was linked to the Canadian Museum of Civilization. For me, the project became an example of learning situated in the space between the structure and knowledge of the study of history and the creative possibilities for students afforded by digital technologies.

Courtesy of Neil Stephenson

Neil refers to himself as a progressive educator and has been heavily influenced by the Galileo Educational Network and the ideals of inquiry-based learning. He describes an evolution in his practice from "energy and activity, but not always directed at learning something important about a topic" to "balance built on a teacher-structured process, directed at students developing deep understanding of an important and engaging topic while providing opportunities for students to participate, imagine, engage, and create." Unlike some iterations of progressivism that are overly focused on student interests, Neil's vision aligns with Dewey's recommendations, including attention to "the intellectual content of experiences" and those that "arouse in the learner an active quest for information" (Dewey, 1938, p. 79).

Do you see evidence of other philosophies influencing Neil? Are their indications of social reconstructionist ideals? How does he pass on the cultural heritage in ways that perennialists would value? Do you think the "teacher-structured process" he describes incorporates the skills instruction that essentialists require?

Discussion Questions

1. What are the three branches of philosophy and what questions do they raise about philosophy of education?
2. How have the traditional philosophies influenced education?
3. What are some of the competing values articulated by the various philosophies of education?
4. How do beliefs and values about teaching and learning reflect one's philosophy of education?

Further Resources

1. Bailey, R., Barrow, R., Carr, D., & McCarthy, C. (Eds.). (2010). *The Sage handbook of philosophy of education.* London, UK: Sage.

   This text is divided into three major sections with various authors contributing separate chapters. The first section looks broadly at educational philosophy and theory, as this chapter has done. The second examines some key historical figures in philosophy of education such as Plato, Rousseau, Dewey, and others. The final section examines the impact of philosophy of education on educational practice; it explores broad topics like knowledge, truth, morality, and motivation as well as issues like diversity, religion, skills, and assessment.

2. Cohen, L. M. *Philosophical perspectives in education.* Retrieved from http://oregonstate.edu/instruct/ed416/module1.html.

   This website provides the instructional materials for an educational foundations course at Oregon State University. In addition to a discussion of many of the philosophies of education, you will find a guide for writing your own philosophy of education.

3. Gutek, G. L. (2009). *New perspectives on philosophy and education.* Columbus, OH: Pearson.

   For readers who would like more detail about the philosophies included in this chapter, this text discusses each of the philosophies in significant detail. In addition, it expounds additional ideologies and philosophical perspectives on Marxism, postmodernism, globalization, critical theory, and others.

7

Diversity and the Sociocultural Influences on Teaching

Learning Objectives

After reading this chapter, you should understand

1. The interplay between schools and social class, including how schools contribute to social reproduction
2. How changing immigration patterns have affected the composition of Canadian schools
3. Ways in which cultural patterns can contribute to misunderstandings and discrimination in schools
4. How to interrogate your cultural blind spots to become a more reflective teacher
5. Approaches to multicultural and antiracist education

The Canadian classroom of today is quite unlike the one-room schoolhouse of the early 20th century. Teachers at that time were primarily middle-class young, White women teaching children whose background was much like their own. While a large percentage of today's teachers are still middle-class young women, the classrooms in which they teach include children with varied backgrounds. Schools are microcosms of Canadian society and are thus filled with children from diverse cultural backgrounds and varied social classes. The fundamental question this chapter will address is "How can schools and those who teach within them educate children from diverse social and cultural backgrounds?" To answer this question, attention will first be devoted to discussing the sociocultural changes that Canada has undergone and the related Canadian policies. Besides addressing the political and demographic trends that have created the Canadian mosaic, specific attention will be paid to the student diversity in today's schools, including cultural patterns of communication. Next the chapter will discuss ways teachers might challenge their own blind spots to better understand their students. Finally, models of multicultural education and practical advice on how to teach within diverse classrooms will be offered with the end goal being to equip teachers with the knowledge and skills required to create respectful, equitable, and inclusive learning environments.

It is important to begin by unpacking this chapter's title, particularly the word *socio-cultural*, which literally means to consider both social and cultural factors. We will begin with a discussion of social class, though the interconnections between social and cultural factors will become apparent.

Social Class

Social class describes the social stratification of groups in society. It is typically analyzed using indicators like income, occupation, and parental education and is divided into three groups: upper class, middle class, and lower class (Weber, 1964). MacIonis and Gerber (2014) divide these groups into further subcategories as follows:

social class
The social stratification of groups in society based on indicators like income, occupation, and levels of education.

- Less than 5% of Canadians are considered upper class, and of these less than 1% are considered upper-uppers. For this most elite group, their wealth is often inherited, which is why they are often labelled "old money." They tend to live in exclusive neighbourhoods and their children attend private schools and universities, often studying liberal arts and sciences in the pattern of European aristocrats rather than vocational subjects. Lower-uppers (2–4% of the Canadian population) may have similar prosperity and lifestyles, but their wealth comes primarily from earned income rather than inheritance. Sometimes labelled *nouveaux riche*, they may be excluded from the elite social circles of the upper-uppers with privileged heritage.
- About 40–50% of Canadians are considered middle class; the top half of this group makes $80,000 to $175,000 per year, often through managerial and professional jobs. This allows them to live comfortable lifestyles and often accumulate significant wealth. Most of these upper-middles have a university education. By comparison, the average middles work in highly skilled blue-collar jobs or less prestigious white-collar occupations. They usually have a high school education and perhaps some postsecondary.
- Working-class Canadians make up about one third of the Canadian population. Sometimes called lower middle class, they tend to work in blue-collar jobs. Often

these jobs require little imagination and provide limited autonomy. Many working-class Canadians own their own homes in economical neighbourhoods. Typically they do not have university education.

- About 20% of Canadians are lower class, sometimes called the underclass, with income levels that fall below the poverty line. Some survive on social assistance while others have one or more jobs that do not provide enough money to pay for necessities. Often they live in segregated neighbourhoods that are ethnically or racially diverse.

social mobility
The process of changing social class. If this is accomplished within one's own lifetime it is called *intragenerational mobility*; if the change is relative to one's parents, it is called *intergenerational mobility.*

Social mobility is the process of changing social class. *Intragenerational mobility* is moving up or down the social ladder within one's lifetime, while *intergenerational mobility* is a change in one's income or social status relative to one's parents. Education is generally considered the strongest engine of social mobility—people with more education tend to have higher incomes and social status. Overall, most groups in Canada have benefited from the growth in universities in the 1960s and 1970s; the majority of Canadians have more education than their parents.

Wilkinson and Pickett (2010) argue that the potential to advance in terms of social mobility is highest in countries that are most equitable—that is, countries that have the smallest gap between the rich and the poor: "Public expenditure on education (elementary/primary and high/secondary schools) is strongly linked to the degree of income equality" (p. 161). They are particularly critical of the United States, the least equal of the countries they assessed, where only 68.2% of spending on education is public money; that clearly impacts the quality and equity of education. Among the countries they assessed, Canada is approximately mid-range in terms of income equality but is actually one of the highest countries in terms of social mobility. Wilkinson and Pickett's research is worth referencing in high school social studies, history, and civics courses to help students understand social equity.

Similar results were found by the Programme for International Student Assessment (PISA), a test that compares academic performance in many countries around the world (Knighton, Brochu, & Gluszynski, 2010). Countries strive to achieve strong results but also to reduce the disparities between high- and low-performing students, which is an indicator of equity. "Canada is widely recognized as one of a few PISA countries that has both high performance and high equity" (Knighton et al., p. 18). Despite this promising finding, "socioeconomic status, whether determined by parental background or school composition, continues to be one of the strongest determinants of student performance in all Canadian provinces and participating nations" (Wotherspoon, 2009, p. 259). Social class also frequently influences students' aspirations; whether because of their parents' expectations or their own self-concepts as learners, students from lower classes either do not attend postsecondary institutions or choose programs that provide little social mobility. It is also worth noting that standardized tests are often criticized for class and cultural biases that favour dominant groups (Johnson, 2005, 2007).

consensus perspective
A theoretical perspective that sees society as a system with relative stability, order, and cohesion. This perspective takes a neutral view of schooling and thus assumes no responsibility for the educational failure of disadvantaged students.

Inequity in some countries may be a result of systemic factors that limit working-class children's access to a challenging education. For example, in Germany secondary students were traditionally divided into grammar schools and vocational schools; this system helped maintain social reproduction because the middle- and upper-class students typically attended grammar schools and the working-class students typically attended vocational schools. Now most German students attend a comprehensive school, *Gesamtschule*, intended to provide all students with access to a broad curriculum regardless of financial status or educational achievement.

Theoretical Perspectives on Social Class

Consensus perspectives on social class see society as a system with relative stability, order, and cohesion. Schools are viewed as institutions to provide skills, knowledge, and basic social values: "Society is seen as a meritocracy and schools as level playing fields where all students have equal chance to succeed regardless of their background or gender" (Egbo, 2009, p. 12). Standardized tests are intended to assure that all students receive the same treatment. The consensus perspective takes a neutral view of schooling and thus assumes no responsibility for the educational failure of disadvantaged students. This perspective parallels conservative ideology and the essentialist philosophy of education (see Chapter 6).

By contrast, **interrogative perspectives**, including **conflict theory** and critical theory, recognize schools as politically charged organizations that mirror the power struggles in society; this context warrants educational provision to support those who are disadvantaged. Conflict theorists argue that schools contribute to social reproduction. The seminal work of Bowles and Gintis (1976) showed how schools maintain inequity by socializing children differently depending on their social class. Middle- and upper-class children are educated with the assumption that they will assume leadership positions, while disadvantaged children (working class and minorities) are educated in ways that train them for subordinate positions. The Case Study below describes a seminal study by Jean Anyon (1981) that demonstrates how this socialization process happens in practice.

interrogative perspective
A theoretical perspective that recognizes schools as politically charged organizations that mirror the power struggles in society. Conflict theory and critical theory are two interrogative perspectives.

conflict theory
A theoretical perspective that sees schools as contributing to the reproduction of unequal social relations.

CASE STUDY

Reproduction of Social Class

Jean Anyon's (1981) fascinating study of working-class, middle-class, affluent professional, and elite executive schools showed how social reproduction works in practice. Note that this study, conducted in New Jersey, focuses on social class rather than racial diversity. In the first two schools, 85% of the students were White. In the affluent professional school 90% were White, and in the executive elite school all of the children were White. Students were in Grade 2 and Grade 5.

The working-class children were educated in the basics using behaviourist strategies. Teachers often claimed students were lazy and needed basic skills. Instruction focused on rote learning with little expectation to use higher-order thinking skills or to discuss the relevance of the topic. Social studies texts included few controversial topics. When the interviewer asked 10 Grade 5 children what knowledge is, they talked about facts, skills, and the ability to do worksheets. When asked if they would go to college, all but three said no. They claimed they weren't smart enough: "If it's hard I couldn't do it" (p. 10). Resistance was a dominant theme as students sought to undermine the teachers' efforts to impose curriculum upon them.

In the middle-class schools, teachers claimed they taught what students would need for college. While there was more emphasis on comprehension and also more flexibility in their approaches than in the working-class schools, there was a heavy reliance on texts and an assumption that knowledge is made by experts. Social studies was more conceptual with less focus on facts and skills. When asked what knowledge was, the children said, "It's smartness," "It means you're intelligent," "You go to a museum." They claimed knowledge came from

continued

scientists, museums, books, television, and "everywhere." When asked if they could create knowledge, nine said no and eleven said yes. Possibility was a dominant theme in the middle-class school as children imagined future potential.

In the affluent professional school, teachers said they wanted children to learn from experience and think for themselves. When students asked questions, teachers often replied "You decide" or "What do you think?" Regarding the social studies texts, Anyon writes "Unlike the series in the working-class and middle-class schools, it discusses at length such topics as social class, the power of dominant ideas, and 'competing world views'" (p. 19). Narcissism or extreme individualism was a dominant theme in this school as children were encouraged to think for themselves and express themselves creatively.

Finally, in the elite professional school one might expect even greater student autonomy. However, in this school, where students were often the children of business elites, teachers emphasized logical reasoning and problem solving to equip students to take on the high-level positions held by their parents. The demands of the curriculum left little time for exploring with materials like math manipulatives. They used the same social studies text as the affluent upper-class school, but the class discussions were more "sophisticated, complex and analytical" (p. 26) than the other schools. Excellence was the dominant theme in this school; the children knew they were being prepared to be top-quality performers.

Anyon analyzed how these schools reproduce the existing social order. Children in the working-class school are offered no critical understanding of the American working class or their place in the world. There is an emphasis on mechanical behaviours with little opportunity to develop cultural capital: "knowledge and skills at manipulating ideas and symbols in their own interest" (p. 32). Although they did struggle against teacher control, this struggle was destructive to themselves. Genuine citizenship education would help them to change the system for their own interests.

For the middle-class students, the assumption that knowledge resides with experts may lead to a type of social passivity. Knowledge was commodified and may be exchanged for "objects" like college entrance or a professional job:

> Commodification of knowledge in the middle-class school is reproductive in part because it helps to legitimate and reproduce the ideology of production for consumption, for example, production of knowledge and other cultural products for the market rather than for personal use or for social transformation. (p. 34)

However, such striving may not result in the expected results and may lead to cynicism and a critical view of the system.

In the affluent professional school, children have learned to see knowledge as capital because it provides them access to professional jobs where they can be creative and seek independent development, but this individualism may undermine collectivist values. Anyon grants that independent thought may also foster social critique and transformation; in fact, many revolutionaries in the early Soviet Union and China have come from the professional ranks:

> It is, then, important to provide the children of the affluent professional class with school knowledge that is not just conceptual, analytical, and expressive, but that is also critical and collective. Such knowledge would foster responsiveness not only to the needs of individual "meaning making" and development, but to the development of a wider social collectivity that, not coincidentally, would affirm the needs of the working and middle classes as well. (p. 37)

Finally, in the executive elite school, children learn that wealthy aristocrats have ruled for centuries and this is a natural and rational state of affairs. They learn that struggle may be necessary to maintain one's position in society in a capitalist system where others are competing against you. This may require exploiting others, like the pool of workers who do not have access to power or resources.

In conclusion, Anyon reminds us that class conflict is not dormant nor is there certainty about ideological hegemony:

> Those who would struggle against ideological hegemony must not confuse working-class powerlessness with apathy, middle-class ideology with its inevitability, or ruling-class power and cultural capital with superior strength or intelligence. (p. 38)

She exhorts educators to continue to struggle for social transformation and greater equality regardless of the social class of the students.

This study was published in 1981. Do you see similar evidence of differential treatment of students based on social class in today's schools? Why does Anyon think it is so critical to expose students to social class differences and struggle? How might this look in practice in a Canadian school?

Bourdieu (1977) criticizes the apparent neutrality of schools that claim to offer equal opportunities. Schools favour those who have cultural capital—knowledge, language, experience, even ways of dressing—that promote social mobility. Privileged children who have had the advantage of rich early childhood experiences, museum excursions, and perhaps even vacations abroad are at a distinct advantage over their peers who have not had such opportunities.

Bernstein (1977) argues that middle- and upper-class families also use complex language codes that are compatible with those used in schools. For example, teachers often use something called the IRE sequence: **I**nitiate a question, student **r**esponds, and the teacher **e**valuates the response. For example:

Teacher: What do we need to do in this question?
Student: Subtract.
Teacher: Right. We need to subtract because the question says, "how many more . . . ?"

This IRE pattern begins when parents talk with their preschoolers and say things like, "Look! What's that?" and the child responds by identifying whatever the adult has pointed to. Clearly the adult knows the correct answer but uses this IRE sequence to "test" the child. This discourse pattern is common in schools and is familiar to many middle-class students but may be confusing to working-class students whose families do not pose questions for which they already know the answer.

While conflict theory critiques the role of schools in replicating the existing social order, **critical theory** offers a vision for changing schools. "Critical theorists believe that if schools subordinate some groups in society, they therefore hold the key for change through just and inclusive practices that affirm diversity" (Egbo, 2009, p. 16). Like the social reconstructionist philosophy discussed in Chapter 6, critical theorists believe education can raise consciousness about unequal power structures in society and help students become agents of change.

critical theory
A theoretical perspective that offers a vision of change for society. Critical theorists believe education can raise consciousness about unequal power structures in society and help students become agents of change.

Cultural Diversity

The most basic definition of diversity is difference. The natural world is full of biodiversity—a variety of species within a region. In a group of politicians there may be a diversity of opinions about the best policies to govern the nation. In this chapter we are primarily

cultural diversity
The differences in social values, beliefs, and worldviews that give order and meaning to people's lives.

concerned with **cultural diversity**: "Culture refers to a dynamic system of social values, cognitive codes, behavioral standards, worldviews, and beliefs used to give order and meaning to our lives as well as the lives of others" (Gay, 2010, pp. 8–9).

Canadian society is composed of various cultural groups, and this cultural diversity can create conflict as groups struggle to understand one another.

Each of us typically identifies with one or more cultural groups, and these identities may be influenced by *biological factors* or by *social* and *cultural factors* (Egbo, 2009). Biological or inherited factors include ethnicity, skin colour, personality, and cognitive ability, though the latter two are also influenced by biology and environmental factors such as family and school experiences. Social and cultural factors include language, religion, social class, nationality, citizenship, and education.

You probably belong to the macro-culture we call Canadian culture. You also belong to some subcultures based on your gender, social class, religion, profession, and ethnicity. The personal identity you create is influenced by your worldview and your participation in those subgroups that you identify with. A student who was born in Canada to Chinese parents may feel less affiliation with Chinese culture than his classmate who emigrated from China recently, but both are likely influenced to some degree by the values of their family's culture. Membership in particular groups can help us understand the behaviour of others, but we would be **stereotyping** if we assumed all people from that culture shared the same values and behaved in the same ways. Stereotypes are "an exaggerated and usually biased view of a group" (Vang, 2010, p. 38).

stereotyping
Assuming that all people from a particular culture share the same values and behave in the same ways.

"Race" and Racism

Biologists tell us that *race* is an erroneous term because human beings are biologically all from the same race—*Homo sapiens*. However, society still sees race in physiological features such as skin colour and facial features. Often those with lighter skin colour are provided superior status. For example, European colonizers of Rwanda accorded higher social status to the minority Tutsis because they had lighter skin than the majority Hutus; these status differences contributed to ethnic tensions and ultimately the 1994 Rwandan genocide when approximately 500,000 people were killed. Slavery was also based on assumed superiority of those with lighter skin.

racism
When racial differences are the basis for social discrimination. Racism can occur on an individual level or an institutional/systemic level.

Racism results when racial differences are the basis for social discrimination. "Race matters not because people are inherently different or unequal but because perceived differences may be manipulated as a basis for sorting out privilege and power" (Fleras & Elliott, cited in Egbo, 2009, p. 6). Racism can occur at the individual level when a landlord refuses to rent an apartment to a prospective tenant because of his race (the landlord is assuming that his stereotypes of that race are true of that person). Racism can also occur at the institutional or systemic level when "policies, rules, and regulations of an organization systematically reflect and produce differential treatment of various groups within that organization" (James, cited in Egbo, 2009, p. 6). For example in school systems children who are English language learners (ELL) are sometimes grouped with children who have cognitive delays even though their learning needs are quite different; this can result in a program that does not appropriately challenge the ELL students. Iannacci (1998) shares his autobiographical account of being streamed into special education because he spoke limited English when he began kindergarten. Sadly such experiences still occur when teachers misinterpret the source of the child's learning challenges or lack supports for their ELL students.

While stereotypes involve generalizations about the typical characteristics of a group, prejudice is one's attitude toward members of a group. Prejudices can be positive or negative, but the term tends to be used more frequently to describe negative attitudes. You might have a prejudice that boys like sports and girls like art until you interact with students who are exceptions to this prejudice. Discrimination results when you take action based on your prejudice or stereotypes, such as having lower expectations for students from an ethnic group that you believe has lower cognitive ability. Xenophobia, from the Greek words *xenos* (foreigner/stranger) and *phobos* (fear), is a fearfulness of those who are different. Xenophobia has become particularly worrisome since 9/11, with some North Americans fearing all Muslims are terrorists.

A visible minority in Canada is a category that exists in labour policy to promote equity in hiring and includes all persons (other than Aboriginal people) who are non-White. Visible minorities are certainly not a homogenous group—the category includes many ethnic backgrounds and social classes. In some parts of the country, visible minorities are now the majority, making the term somewhat of a misnomer. The term is important to the concept of *hegemony*, which is the "'invisible' process of maintaining power and social control by dominant groups through state and social institutions" (Egbo, 2009, p. 8). Many diversity scholars argue that oppression of minority groups exists because oppressed groups accept their subordinate position in society as normal, so there is little resistance or opposition. In schools there are minority students who seem to resist educational success, thus reinforcing stereotypes others have of them (Ogbu, 2003). Social reconstructionists, discussed in Chapter 6, seek to raise the consciousness of these students so they might resist disempowerment by the majority.

The advent of the IQ test in the early 20th century corresponded to biologically based deficit theory—a theory suggesting that differences in achievement reflected innate differences. There was an assumption that White people were intellectually superior to racial and cultural minority groups. Deficit theories have been touted even in the last 20 years by a Canadian researcher (Rushton, 1997). In the 1960s, these assumptions began to be challenged by cultural deficit theory. According to this theory, economic circumstances, poor parenting, and students' low motivation contributed to their lack of success. This prompted the initiation of programs that sought to minimize these negative impacts, including early intervention programs like Head Start in the United States that targeted low-income and often minority families. It is particularly important for aspiring teachers to be aware of the pernicious nature of both types of deficit theories because they essentially blame the children, looking to explain achievement differences by something within the child's genetic makeup or family background. As aspiring teachers, you should know that regardless of your students' cognitive ability, you have control over the school factors that can enhance or diminish a student's learning.

prejudice
One's attitude toward members of a particular group. They are usually, although not always, negative.

discrimination
Taking action based on prejudices or stereotypes.

xenophobia
The fear of those who are different. Comes from the Greek word *xenos* (foreigner/stranger) and *phobos* (fear).

visible minority
A category that exists in labour policy to promote equity in hiring and includes all persons (other than Aboriginal people) who are non-White.

deficit theory
A theory suggesting that differences in achievement reflect innate differences among different cultural groups.

cultural deficit theory
A theory that emphasizes economic circumstances, poor parenting, and students' low motivation when looking at differences in achievement among different cultural groups, rather than on innate differences among the groups.

Canadian Diversity Policies

Canadian Immigration Trends

Canada has an international reputation as an immigrant nation. However, the groups who are granted admission to Canada have varied over the decades. The first wave of immigrants was primarily from France, but after the English conquered New France there was an influx of British immigrants. In the late 1800s more immigrants came from Eastern Europe and Asia. Chinese immigrants came to work on the Canadian Pacific Railway, although the Chinese Head Tax (1885) and the Chinese Immigration Act (1923) were clearly immigration policies that were systematically racist. Immigration acts passed in 1910, 1919, and 1923 were intended to limit the number of immigrants from countries other than Britain and those who were considered unsuitable because of poor health, education, or "radical" political views. After World War II, the government recognized a greater need for immigration to support economic development, so large numbers of immigrants were accepted from diverse countries. With the 1967 Immigration Act, race and national origin were explicitly removed from policies and replaced with a point system that acknowledged factors like age, credentials, language proficiency, and demand for the job skills of the applicant. Before 1961, 90% of immigrants came from Europe. This number dropped to 69% during the 1960s, 36% during the 1970s, 25% in the 1980s, and less than 20% in the 1990s. In the same period, the numbers of immigrants from various other parts of the world increased with the largest increase from Asian countries, which comprised 58% of all immigrants to Canada by the 1990s. Figure 7.1 shows that the percentage of visible minorities in Canada has increased from less than 4% in 1981 to nearly 16% in 2006. Figure 7.2 shows the most common visible minority groups in 2001 and projected in 2017. Currently Canada has an annual immigration target of around 300,000, approximately 1% of our overall population.

The point system recognizing education means that immigrants are often well educated compared with the Canadian-born population. One in six Canadian-born participants in one study (25–54 years old) had university degrees, but over half of the landed immigrants in that age group had university degrees (Wotherspoon, 2009). However, these educated immigrants often have difficulty finding work in their field, especially in recent years. In the past these struggles typically diminished as the newcomers gained greater language proficiency and made Canadian contacts. Census data reveals that in 1980, immigrants' salaries were 85% of the salaries of Canadian-born workers, but by 2005 the ratio

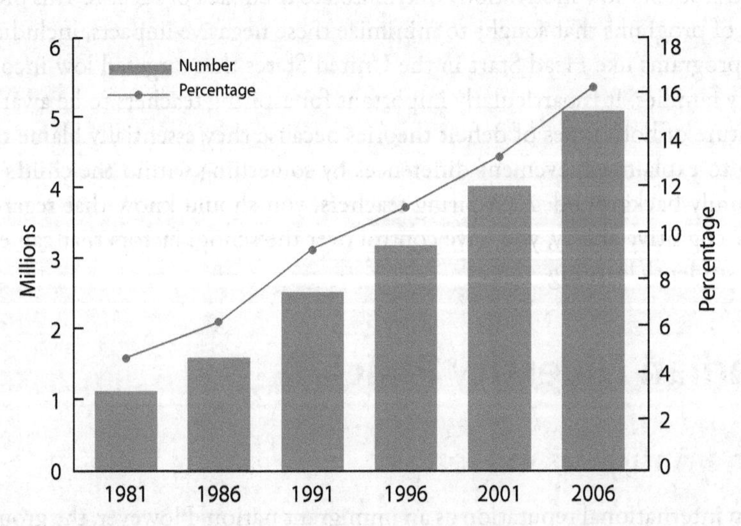

FIGURE 7.1 Number and Share of Visible Minority Persons in Canada, 1981–2006

Source: Statistics Canada, 2006a.

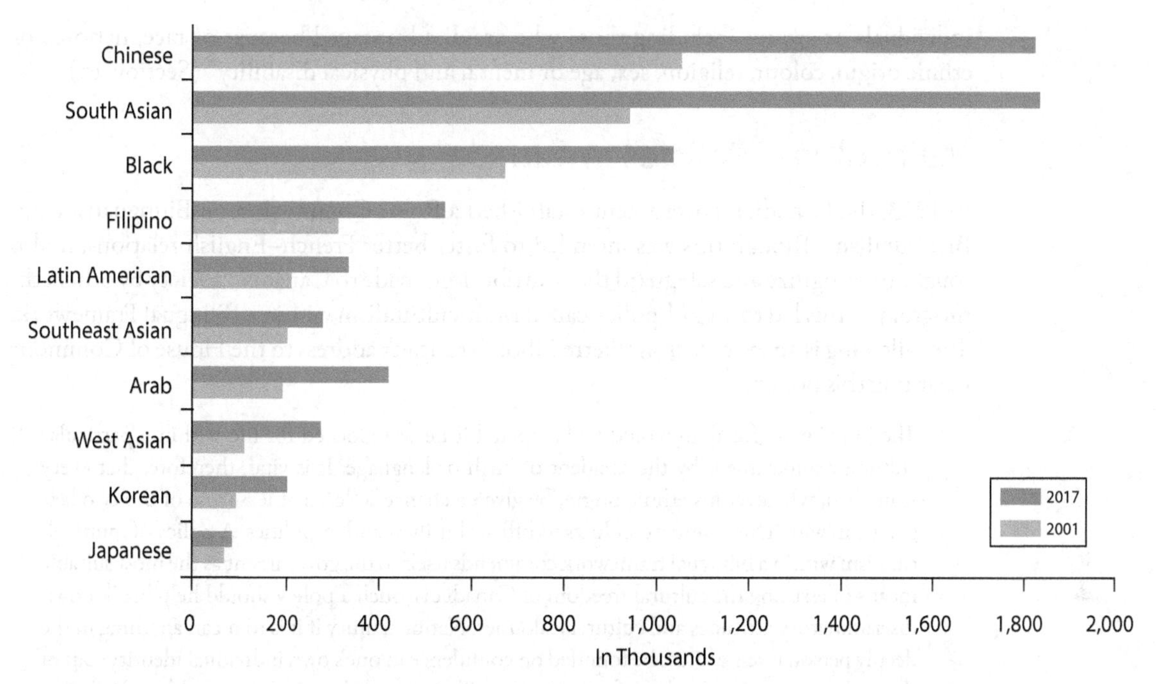

FIGURE 7.2 Visible Minority Groups in Canada, 2001–2017
Source: Statistics Canada, 2007.

had widened to 63% for immigrant men and 56% for immigrant women (Statistics Canada, 2008). This may result because employers fail to recognize foreign credentials and experience. Furthermore, cultural barriers and discrimination may create communication challenges that hinder immigrants from achieving appropriate employment.

A relatively small percentage of immigrants to Canada are refugees, those who flee their home countries for fear of persecution. They may be sponsored by an individual, an organization, or by the government. The Canadian government may provide support through the Resettlement Assistance Program or the Immigration Loans Program. Refugee children in schools require special attention. Often they come from traumatic situations where they may have experienced war, famine, or oppression. They may have witnessed extreme violence and suffer serious emotional damage, including posttraumatic stress disorder (PTSD). Such trauma can result in challenging behaviours; these children require sensitive and thoughtful teachers whose response to such behaviours is not punitive but rather formative and patient.

Canadian Charter of Rights and Freedoms

The Canadian Charter of Rights and Freedoms, which replaced the Canadian Bill of Rights in 1982, is another policy that has influenced diversity and education in Canada. It assures Canadians "freedom of conscience and religion . . . of thought, belief, opinion and expression" (Section 2) and various other democratic rights. The Charter is often invoked to defend the importance of culturally responsive education as a means to achieve equality of rights—not only protecting student rights but also providing the kind of education that will help them to succeed. It calls for "amelioration of the conditions of disadvantaged individuals or groups including those who are disadvantaged because of race, national or ethnic origin, colour, religion, sex, age or mental and physical disability" (Section 15).

Multicultural Policies in Canada

In 1963, the Canadian government established a Royal Commission on Bilingualism and Biculturalism. Though this was intended to foster better French–English relations, it also sought to recognize and safeguard the contributions made to Canadian society by other ethnic groups. This led to a 1971 policy called Multiculturalism within a Bilingual Framework. The following is an excerpt from Pierre Elliott Trudeau's address to the House of Commons regarding this policy:

> The individual's freedom would be hampered if he were locked for life within a particular cultural compartment by the accident of birth or language. It is vital, therefore, that every Canadian, whatever his ethnic origin, be given a chance to learn at least one of the two languages in which his country conducts its official business and its politics. A policy of multiculturalism within a bilingual framework commends itself to the government as the most suitable means of assuring the cultural freedom of Canadians. Such a policy should help break down discriminatory attitudes and cultural jealousies. National unity if it is to mean anything in the deeply personal sense, must be founded on confidence in one's own individual identity; out of this can grow respect for that of others and a willingness to share ideas, attitudes and assumptions. A vigorous policy of multiculturalism will help create this initial confidence. It can form the base of a society which is based on fair play for all. (House of Commons, 1971)

This policy signalled a departure from assimilationist ideals to greater pluralism. The government committed to supporting immigrant groups and providing the necessary assistance to acquire English or French language skills.

Critics of the policy suggest it highlights difference and undermines the development of a Canadian culture; furthermore, minorities may not enjoy equal access to that Canadian culture if they are not assimilated. Others note that the policy may be relevant in urban areas where large numbers of immigrants typically settle but is not meaningful to those in rural areas. The strongest critique suggests that the policy is rhetorical and masks continued inequity. Politicians can appear to support multicultural ideals, but immigrants often do not have access to the jobs and privileges afforded to Canadian-born citizens. They continue to be overrepresented in low-paying service jobs and underrepresented in leadership positions.

Critical Theory Perspectives of Multiculturalism

Critiques of Canadian multicultural policies often come from critical theorist perspectives like those of Joe Kinchloe and Shirley Steinberg (1997), well known in the Canadian post-secondary education system for their work on multiculturalism. They introduce five categorizations of multiculturalism: conservative multiculturalism, liberal multiculturalism, pluralist multiculturalism, left-essentialist multiculturalism, and critical multiculturalism.

- Conservative multiculturalism is a belief in the superiority of Western culture and the deficiency of other cultures. According to conservative multiculturalists, celebrating difference is divisive so they seek consensus, but in doing so they tend to silence the marginalized.
- Liberal multiculturalism claims that people from diverse racial, class, and gender groups "share a natural equality and common humanity [and] compete equally for resources in a capitalist economy" (p. 10). In celebrating individualism and citizenship, they become blind to the structural dynamics that make equality elusive for some groups.

- Pluralist multiculturalism has become the mainstream view of multiculturalism; it is similar to liberal multiculturalism in many respects but does more to celebrate difference and diversity, often through a type of cultural tourism. However, liberal and pluralist multiculturalism both fail to problematize Eurocentrism and imply that "anyone can 'make it' by working hard" (p. 16). This is likely the perspective most evident in Trudeau's quote above.
- Left-essentialist multiculturalism sees minority groups forming an essential group identity that results in a type of "dominant-culture-is-bad marginalized-culture-is-good inverse dualism" (p. 21).

The preferred categorization of multiculturalism for Kinchloe and Steinberg is critical multiculturalism, which seeks to make all people aware of the way power relations are present in schools, workplaces, and daily life: "An individual who has gained such a consciousness understands how and why his or her political opinions, socio-economic class, role, religious beliefs, gender role and racial self-image are shaped by dominant perspectives" (p. 23). Like social reconstructionists, critical multiculturalism aims to promote equity by exposing injustice.

Multiculturalism Policy Indexes

Liberal philosophers argue that multicultural policies are necessary to remedy injustices experienced by some groups in society. In his famous treatise on moral and political philosophy, *A Theory of Justice*, John Rawls (1999) describes the critical importance of equality of opportunity and ensuring equality for those who are least advantaged in society. When these principles are applied to education, all students have an equal right to learn and equity demands that they have a right to the resources they need to succeed.

Will Kymlicka (2012), a Canadian philosopher renowned for his work in multiculturalism, argues that "multiculturalism is first and foremost about developing new models of democratic citizenship, grounded in human rights ideals, to replace earlier uncivil and undemocratic relations of hierarchy and exclusion" (p. 8). Historically, when cultures coexisted there was often a range of undemocratic and hierarchical relationships, but in response to the atrocities of World War II there was a genuine shift toward equality of all peoples and principles of democratic citizenship. Multiculturalism arose in the post–World War II era as part of a human rights revolution and to address continuing inequalities. Kymlicka proposes a Multiculturalism Policy Index (MCP) that includes the most common features of multiculturalism policies:

- Constitutional, legislative, or parliamentary affirmation of multiculturalism at the central and/or regional and municipal levels
- The adoption of multiculturalism in school curricula
- The inclusion of ethnic representation/sensitivity in the mandate of public media or media licensing
- Exemptions from dress codes, either by statute or by court cases
- Allowing of dual citizenship
- The funding of ethnic group organizations to support cultural activities
- The funding of bilingual education or mother-tongue instruction
- Affirmative action for disadvantaged immigrant groups (p. 7)

This index can be used to measure the efforts of nations to implement effective multicultural policies.

Before defending multiculturalism, Kymlicka first outlines the major critiques. Many argue that multiculturalism has failed and has only focused on the trivial, celebratory aspects of cultures ("saris, samosas, and steeldrums," p. 4) and is thus open to several critiques. First, such an approach to multiculturalism ignores continued economic and political inequalities such as poor educational outcomes, poor language skills, and high unemployment. Second, a supposed focus on "authentic" features of a culture needs to attend to the cultural practices that are not worthy of celebration, like forced marriage. Third, focusing on the celebratory aspects of cultures sees them as static, which can reinforce stereotypes and polarization. It assumes that cultures have distinct customs but ignores the fact that as cultures mix they adapt and share commonalities. Finally, this approach can reinforce power inequalities within minority groups; people (often women) within those cultures are then locked into cultural scripts in which they have little autonomy.

Kymlicka acknowledges that the celebratory model of multiculturalism reflects the human tendency to simplify ethnic differences, but he argues that Canadian multicultural policies actually have much loftier goals. He shows how MCPs have ultimately contributed to the advancement of human rights. Critics ignore the fact that MCPs actually include affirmative action policies, processes for political consultation, funding for ethnic groups to self-organize, and support in accessing citizenship. To the degree that these policies are effective, they advance human rights.

Second, critics who claim that multicultural policies ignore the importance of universal human rights fail to see that multiculturalism *is* a human rights movement. It has been the role of multiculturalism to attack those deeply rooted "White" traditions that have marginalized minorities on the grounds that these traditions violate human rights. Dominant groups have been "required to renounce fantasies of racial superiority, to relinquish claims to exclusive ownership of the state, and to abandon attempts to fashion public institutions solely in its own (typically White/Christian) image" (p. 9). Now those who wish to lobby against unjust practices such as cliterodectomy or forced marriage can do so using the language of human rights. "Subordinated groups can appeal to MCPs to challenge their illiberal exclusion, but those very policies also impose the duty on them to be inclusive" (p. 10).

Having considered the aspirations of Canadian MCPs, have we actually succeeded in contesting ethnic hierarchies and creating a more just society? Kymlicka concedes that this is an open question but points to some promising research that suggests we have. He cites the work of Irene Bloemraad, who has studied Vietnamese immigrants to Toronto and Boston. Both groups arrived under similar circumstances—similar time frame, levels of education, wealth, and language proficiency—but the immigrants to Toronto have integrated more successfully: "Canada's proactive MCPs have sent a clear message that Vietnamese political participation is welcome, and have also provided material and logistical support for the self-organization and political representation of the community" (p. 10). Her research shows a similar result among Portuguese immigrants to the same cities. Kymlicka cites other research showing that, compared to other Western nations, immigrants to Canada are more likely to become citizens and to vote and run for office. In addition, their children achieve better educational outcomes, and although they still suffer from an "ethnic penalty" in translating this education into employment, the penalty is lower in Canada. For Canadians, "multiculturalism serves as a source of shared national identity and pride for native-born citizens and immigrants alike. Studies show that in the absence of multiculturalism, national identity is more likely to lead to intolerance and xenophobia" (pp. 11–12).

Kymlicka includes an appendix where he compares the MCP scores of various Western nations in 1980, 2000, and 2010—that is, their incorporation of the relevant policies identified in the Multiculturalism Policy Index. Canada had the highest score of all the countries at each point in time.

Admittedly, certain issues still threaten multiculturalism. States are less likely to treat minorities fairly when they feel insecure, as is the case in post-9/11 United States where there is a fearfulness of Muslims. Some perceive an unwillingness among immigrants to accept liberal democratic norms. Illegal immigration also threatens MCPs; such immigrants are regarded as queue jumpers who are flouting the law and denying fairness to other legal immigrants. It is important that immigration policies continue to welcome immigrants from a variety of nations so that one group does not develop such a strong presence that they fail to integrate with other Canadians:

> Without proactive policies to promote mutual understanding and respect, and to make immigrants feel comfortable within mainstream institutions, these factors could quickly create a racialized underclass, standing in permanent opposition to the larger society. (p. 24)

Kymlicka maintains that these policies are still doing their work and have not achieved all their ideals, but policy-makers should continue to consider MCPs as an appropriate response to the challenges of racism in society.

Diversity within the Classroom

Teacher Diversity in Canada

One yawning gap in the Canadian education system is the shortage of teachers who mirror the diversity in the classrooms. Ryan, Pollock, and Antonelli (2009) contracted Statistics Canada for a specific analysis regarding the number of visible minorities who are teachers in Canada. Table 7.1 shows that while the number of visible minority teachers has increased, their proportion in the teacher workforce has decreased relative to the proportion of visible minority citizens in the Canadian population. Statistics Canada does not include Aboriginal in the "visible minority" category, but the researchers were able to discern that 2.7% of teachers are Aboriginal, while Aboriginal students make up 5.2% of the student population and 3.7% of the Canadian population.

A pipeline metaphor is used to describe children who progress through the school system into postsecondary education and finally into careers such as teaching. Unfortunately, there are leaks in this pipeline, and some groups are clearly not being served as well as others by the K–12 and postsecondary school systems, in part because students do not see teachers who look like themselves. Ryan, Pollock, and Antonelli conclude that the shortage of minority teachers "can be traced to two institutional shortcomings: inequitable schooling practices that limit the number of students willing and able to enter the teaching force, and discriminatory licensing and hiring practices that exclude those who have already completed their teacher education programs" (2009, p. 609).

TABLE 7.1 Visible Minority Teacher Population Compared to the Canadian Population, 2001 and 2006

	Total Teacher Labour Force	Visible Minority Teacher Population	Percentage of Visible Minority Teachers	Percentage of Total Visible Minority Population	Percentage Difference
Canada					
2001	412,955	22,415	5.4	13.4	8.0
2006	429,380	30,715	6.9	16.2	9.3
Quebec (province)					
2001	98,190	2,690	2.7	6.9	4.2
2006	101,365	3,985	3.9	8.8	5.9
Montreal					
2001	42,905	2,305	5.3	13.5	8.2
2006	47,755	3,985	7.2	16.4	9.2
Ontario					
2001	162,240	12,055	7.4	19.0	11.6
2006	179,390	17,085	9.5	22.8	13.3
Toronto					
2001	62,950	9,260	14.7	36.8	22.1
2006	71,165	13,300	18.6	42.4	23.8
BC					
2001	52,055	4,645	8.9	21.6	12.7
2006	51,960	5,985	11.5	24.8	13.3
Vancouver					
2001	23,730	3,935	15.5	36.8	21.3
2006	24,945	5,060	20.2	49.0	28.8

Source: Ryan, J., Pollock, K., & Antonelli, F. (2009). Teacher diversity in canada: Leaky pipelines, bottlenecks, and glass ceilings. Canadian Journal of Education, 32(3), 591–617. Reproduced with permission from the Canadian Journal of Education.

Prospective teachers may also be found in the ranks of internationally educated teachers who immigrate to Canada and secure teaching certification in Canada. These teachers find it tremendously difficult to find employment; they are six times more likely to be unemployed than local graduates. Despite their experience as teachers in other countries, employers often doubt the quality of their credentials and question their ability to "fit" in the Canadian school system.

Some of these internationally educated teachers have enrolled in an eight-month program for francophone teachers at the University of Ottawa. They describe the challenges they faced when their prior conceptions of education did not match their experience in Canadian schools (Duschene & Stitou, 2013). One immigrant teacher learned that calling students Miss and Mr. created discomfort and emotional distance from her students.

Another was surprised by how freely students expressed themselves; he had to question his own ideals regarding respect for authority and the traditional role of the teacher. The authors argue that for these teacher-candidates to be successful in their practicum and in teaching in Canada, they must have support in confronting varied conceptions of education and reconciling the differences between schools in their country of origin and the Canadian school system.

Student Diversity in Canada

So far this chapter has described social class, key terms related to culture and diversity, immigration patterns in Canada, and policies that have shaped the sociocultural landscape in Canada. But who are the students in Canadian classrooms? The following section delineates some key statistics related to Aboriginal students, linguistically diverse students, religious diversity in schools, gender, and socioeconomic status of Canadian children. All of these statistics will be discussed with a view to how they affect classroom teachers.

Aboriginal Canadians

Aboriginal peoples in Canada are sometimes referred to with the acronym FNMI to represent the three major groups: First Nations (formerly called Indians), Métis, and Inuit. It should be noted that the First Nations peoples who inhabited Canada prior to colonization were not a monolithic group (though they were often seen that way by the Europeans). In actuality, they represented diverse cultures with different languages and systems of governance. Colonizers set out to assimilate and "civilize the savages." First Nations children were torn from their parents and sent to residential schools where they were forbidden to speak their own language and were often subjected to harsh abuse. Parents and other adults mirror to children what is expected within their culture—what social scientists refer to as "the looking-glass self" (Garcia, 2011); for Aboriginal children who were separated from their parents, many never developed this strong cultural identity and never learned how to be parents, creating serious dysfunction in the First Nations community and virtual cultural genocide. Residential schools are now regarded as a disastrous social policy. Canadian Prime Minster Stephen Harper offered a formal apology in 2008 on behalf of the government, saying "There is no place in Canada for the attitudes that inspired the Indian residential schools system to ever prevail again" (Woods, 2013). A Truth and Reconciliation Commission has been listening to and cataloguing the stories of those who were harmed in residential schools; the Indian Residential Schools Settlement Agreement seeks to compensate former students.

Aboriginal peoples have sought the right to greater self-governance, including the right to educate their children in Aboriginal ways of knowing. They are critical of multiculturalism policies because they do not recognize First Nations special status as one of the partners in Confederation. These rights have been supported in the *United Nations Declaration on the Rights of Indigenous People* (United Nations, 2008).

In 2006, 50% of First Nations people aged 25 to 64 living on reserve had not completed high school, compared to 30% of off-reserve First Nations people. Among Aboriginal Canadians aged 15 and over, 43.7% do not hold any certificate, diploma, or degree, compared to 23.1% of other Canadians (Sharpe & Arsenault, 2010). Given the devastating history of residential schools and the lack of opportunities for Aboriginal people to represent themselves in educational decisions, it is not surprising that they feel disenfranchised from formal schooling. However, limited education means these Aboriginal Canadians have less access to the workforce. The population of Aboriginal schoolchildren is increasing, particularly in the territories and in cities like Saskatoon, Regina, Winnipeg, Thunder Bay, and Sudbury (Statistics Canada, 2006b). School systems and provincial curricular bodies will need to be intentional about co-operating to meet the needs of this growing population. While challenges persist within the Aboriginal community, recent initiatives to support Aboriginal curriculum content have led to what Colin Power calls, "a veritable renaissance among indigenous peoples in their cultures, languages, histories and traditional ways of learning" (cited in Egbo, 2009, p. 58).

Band schools on reserves, which are federally operated, have the greatest fidelity to Aboriginal ways of knowing. With the shift to band control in the 1970s came more FNMI content, cultural training initiatives, and special teacher education programs to increase the number of Aboriginal teachers, such as the Northern Teacher Education Program (NORTEP) in northern Saskatchewan. Provincial Ministries of Education have policy and curriculum documents to help teachers integrate Aboriginal perspectives. Saskatchewan has also implemented something called the School Plus model, which seeks to integrate a variety of community-based supports and human services agencies to meet the needs of diverse learners, including Aboriginal learners. In Alberta, where provincial policy supports charter schools and is more amenable to alternative programs, children may enroll in Aboriginal charter schools like Mother Earth's Children's Charter School in rural Alberta or alternative programs within the regular public system, such as Piitoayis Family School in Calgary.

Impact on Today's Teachers

FNMI EDUCATION

Several provincial Ministries of Education offer policy statements and resources regarding FNMI education. Learn Alberta's (2012) *Walking Together: First Nations, Metis and Inuit Perspectives in Curriculum* is an especially rich resource on the Alberta Education website. This multimedia resource provides videos of classroom activities, interviews with FNMI leaders, and interactive scenarios to help teachers understand cultural perspectives of the FNMI community.

For example, one interactivity describes a classroom teacher who wants an elder to help his students understand FNMI traditional knowledge about the wetlands, the current unit in his classroom. Viewers are asked to select the best course of action—call an Aboriginal storyteller, place an advertisement in the paper, call a local Native Friendship Centre, or call the FNMI consultant for the school board. By following the various scenarios, it becomes apparent that the teacher needs the support of the FNMI community to find the appropriate person and broker that first meeting, including an appropriate gift to offer the elder. The teacher also needs to meet with the elder to build a relationship before asking the elder to come to the classroom. This beautifully designed resource does not simply *tell* teachers about FNMI culture, rather it *shows* the culture and brings it to life.

Linguistic Diversity

Controversy over linguistic diversity came to the forefront in Canadian policy during the Quiet Revolution that took place in Quebec during the 1960s. This revolution set the foundation for the Official Languages Act of 1969 and the Multiculturalism within a Bilingual Framework policy two years later. These policies seek to address the needs of francophone minorities such as the Acadians in New Brunswick who have the right to a French education for their children. Although the act gave equal status to English and French as the official languages, it also acknowledges the enrichment linguistic diversity brings to Canadian culture.

We have already identified some of the immigration patterns in Canada, which gives some indication of the diversity of students in Canadian schools. Now that many immigrants come from non–English-speaking countries, schools are filled with children who speak many different languages. Figure 7.3 summarizes Canadian census data (Statistics Canada, 2012) and shows a tremendous increase in the percentage of people who speak one

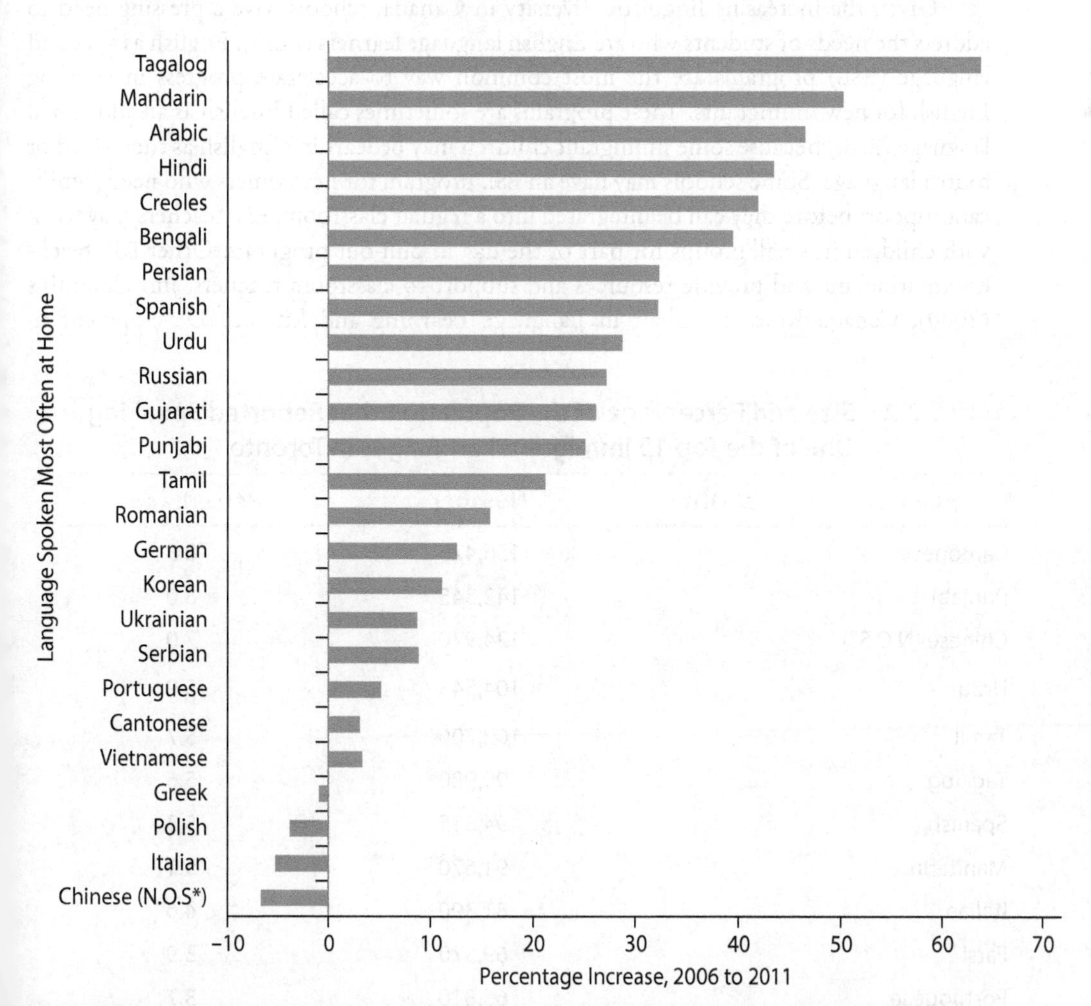

FIGURE 7.3 Population Growth (in percent) of Persons Who Speak One of the Top 25 Immigrant Languages Most Often at Home, 2006–2011

* N.O.S. = not otherwise specified

Source: Statistics Canada, 2012.

of the top immigrant languages at home. For example, respondents who reported speaking Tagalog, a language spoken in the Philippines, increased the most (+61%) between 2006 and 2011. In 2006, 170,000 people spoke Tagalog at home, but this number increased to almost 279,000 people in 2011.

The census reports also show the number and percentage of the population speaking one of the top 12 immigrant languages at home for each of the six urban areas where 80% of immigrants settle. Table 7.2 shows the data for Toronto, where nearly 9% of the population speaks Cantonese and 8% speaks Punjabi. The most common immigrant language in Montreal is Arabic (17.2% of the population), in Vancouver and Calgary is Punjabi (17.7% and 12.1%, respectively), in Edmonton is Tagalog (11.8%), and in Ottawa is Arabic (20.8%). If you wish to see the complete data for each of these cities read the full report, *Linguistic Characteristics of Canadians* (Statistics Canada, 2012; see References list for a URL leading to the report).

Given the increasing linguistic diversity in Canada, schools have a pressing need to address the needs of students who are English language learners (ELLs). English as a second language (ESL) programs are the most common way to accelerate progress in learning English for new immigrants. These programs are sometimes called English as an additional language (EAL) because some immigrant children may be learning English as their third or fourth language. Some schools may have an ESL program for newcomers who need significant support before they can be integrated into a regular classroom. ESL teachers may work with children in small groups for part of the day in pull-out programs. Other ESL teachers are itinerant and provide resources and support to classroom teachers. Jim Cummins (2000), Canada Research Chair in Language Learning and Literacy Development in

TABLE 7.2 Size and Percentage of the Population that Reported Speaking One of the Top 12 Immigrant Languages in Toronto

Language Spoken Most Often	Number	Percentage
Cantonese	156,425	8.8
Punjabi	142,345	8.0
Chinese (N.O.S*)	124,970	7.0
Urdu	104,545	5.9
Tamil	102,700	5.7
Tagalog	99,980	5.6
Spanish	94,315	5.3
Mandarin	91,670	5.1
Italian	81,390	4.6
Farsi	69,570	3.9
Portuguese	65,810	3.7
Russian	64,700	3.6
Other immigrant languages	587,590	32.9

* N.O.S. = not otherwise specified

Source: Statistics Canada, 2012.

Multilingual Contexts, suggests that newcomers need five to seven years of intensive language support but most receive far less. Once students achieve some fluency and basic interpersonal communication skills, teachers may mistakenly think they are able to manage the regular classroom curriculum. However, to read and write about complex academic concepts, students require cognitive academic language proficiency, and this takes several years of targeted instruction. The number of students whose families do not speak English at home is increasing dramatically, but funding for ESL programs is not keeping pace.

Cummins (2000) has been a strong advocate for **additive bilingualism**. His research suggests that it is critical to maintain one's first language while learning a second language and that this does not diminish capacity in the new language. This may be achieved through literacy instruction in both languages, particularly for newcomers. A classroom environment that supports ELLs can make use of their native language even when the teacher does not speak that language. Student-generated books and group-constructed texts are simple ways to build on the students' first language. While all students benefit from guided reading with pre-, during-, and post-reading discussion, this is particularly important to build comprehension skills in ELLs. It is also important to invite artistic (visual, dramatic, musical) learning tasks; written tasks may be particularly challenging for ELLs and may not appropriately showcase their understanding.

additive bilingualism
An approach to bilingualism that ensures one's first language is maintained while learning a second language.

Benchmarks are a tool to help teachers identify students' language proficiency by attending closely to their reading, writing, speaking, and listening skills. Citizenship and Immigration Canada and the Centre for Canadian Language Benchmarks have published documents that provide outcomes for ESL students in Canada (Johansson, Angst, Beer, Martin, Rebeck, & Sibilleau, 2001). Learn Alberta (n.d.) provides similar benchmarks and a website that includes videos, tracking sheets, and support documents to help teachers understand and effectively use the benchmarks to provide explicit targeted instruction. For example, in the domain of speaking alone, teachers assess the following:

- Linguistic Vocabulary: knowledge of words and their meaning
- Linguistic Syntax: knowledge of word order and sentence structure
- Strategic Questioning: knowledge of ways to seek information
- Strategic Clarification: knowledge of ways to confirm understanding
- Discourse: knowledge of how ideas are organized and connected
- Sociolinguistic: awareness of social and cultural factors influencing the way language is used
- Auditory Discrimination: ability to hear differences in sounds of letters and letter combinations

The benchmarks contain a similar list with some variations for reading, writing, and listening. Teachers assess students' benchmark level on each of these components to better identify and support students' specific language learning needs.

Many school districts have the option to choose the second language instruction they offer to their students; while French and English are the most common language offerings, school boards may select other options. For example, in the Calgary Board of Education, students have the opportunity to participate in bilingual education programs in Spanish, Mandarin, or German during the regular school day. The Western and Northern Canadian Protocol (an organization introduced in Chapter 3) provides a curriculum for second language instruction in Aboriginal languages. Unfortunately, the number of people who speak

Aboriginal languages is in decline, and many of the languages are threatened with extinction. The Aboriginal Languages Initiative is a federal program that provides grants to programs that help to preserve Aboriginal languages.

subtractive bilingualism
When a second language learner loses his or her first language because of lack of use.

For some immigrants, the result of ESL programs is actually **subtractive bilingualism**—the loss of one's first language due to lack of use (Cummins, 2000). Because language and culture are integrally linked, some families may want to ensure their children retain the family's language; this may be particularly challenging for second-generation Canadians who have never lived in the family's country of origin. One approach is to send students to special language classes outside of school. For example, the Toronto District School Board organizes after-school and weekend international language courses that cover approximately 60 different languages.

It is easy to become discouraged when the limited English proficiency of students seems to hamper their academic progress. However, there are significant benefits to bilingualism that may not be apparent. People who are bilingual are more cognitively flexible, analytical, think more creatively, and have greater metalinguistic awareness (Baker, 2006). Therefore, it behooves teachers to support students in maintaining their first language.

Religious Diversity

The Canadian Charter of Rights and Freedoms protects the rights of all Canadians to practise their religion. But what should be the role of schools in the religion of their students? As described in Chapter 3, Canadian school systems were initially founded with one of two publicly funded options: public (formerly Protestant) and Catholic. In Newfoundland, Ontario, Quebec, Saskatchewan, Alberta, Northwest Territories, and Yukon, Catholic schools continue to be funded in the same way as public schools. However, this practice has been tested by legal cases such as *Waldman v. Canada*. In this case, the United Nations Human Rights Committee (2000) ruled that

> The Covenant does not oblige States parties to fund schools which are established on a religious basis. However, if a State party chooses to provide public funding to religious schools, it should make this funding available without discrimination. This means that providing funding for the schools of one religious group and not for another must be based on reasonable and objective criteria. (pp. 97–98)

The committee considered it discriminatory to fund Catholic schools at the same level as public schools while not providing the same funding for other religious schools. Despite this ruling, Ontario continues to fully fund Catholic schools.

Several provinces, namely British Columbia, Alberta, Saskatchewan, Manitoba, Ontario, and Quebec, provide some public funding for independent religious schools provided they comply with provincial curriculum. However, unlike the Catholic schools that are fully funded, these parents must still pay out-of-pocket tuition fees to cover the balance of the costs. Critics argue that any amount of public funding of private schools siphons dollars from the public system and weakens it. They argue that it "ghettoizes" students and undermines the development of religious tolerance and understanding that can be developed in a public system. These issues remain contentious in the Canadian education system.

As for students of diverse religions attending public schools, they continue to face challenges. For example, there have been legal cases concerning the rights of students to wear religious symbols like kirpans, a ceremonial dagger carried by Sikhs. Schools argued that these were a safety concern, but the courts upheld the students' right to wear kirpans provided they were small enough to be worn under clothing. In 2013, Quebec raised public ire when it sought to pass a Charter of Values that would require all public employees, including teachers, to refrain from wearing any religious symbols in the workplace.

Public schools welcome children of all religions and must ensure that no religion is devalued. Teachers must be aware of the impact of religious beliefs on the children in their classroom. Children may miss school because of religious holidays or wear religious dress to school. Some parents may not want their children to participate in activities that have a religious tone or even celebrations like birthdays. You must consider how you will accommodate these children when others bring birthday treats to share with the class. Your role as a teacher is to consistently communicate that tolerance and respect are expected.

Gender

Gender is another aspect of diversity that influences the school culture. While the terms *sex* and *gender* are often used interchangeably, sex refers to one's biological makeup while gender refers to learned behaviours that are considered masculine or feminine, which children begin learning from birth. Adults give them names and toys and clothing that reflect their gender. Parents of boys are known to roughhouse and encourage boys to be tough while parents of girls subtly encourage caution and relational tenderness. Such socialization persists into the school years and can lead to gender stereotyping.

Historically, the curriculum and classroom discourse privileged boys and men. Texts showed males in dominant roles, and advanced education for girls was considered unnecessary since they were expected to become wives and mothers. In her seminal book on girls and education, Dale Spender (1982) found that boys consistently dominated the classroom discourse and received more teacher attention, both positive and negative, than girls. Feminist advocacy beginning in the 1960s led to curriculum changes and teaching practices that supported girls. Girls are performing as well as and in many cases much better than boys. On the Programme for International Student Assessment (PISA), girls outperformed boys in reading in every single country, and the gender gap widened between 2000 and 2009 (Organisation for Economic Co-operation and Development, 2010). Boys' math scores were slightly higher in Canada, but in some countries girls outperform boys in math. Unfortunately, boys responding to the PISA survey questions report that they are less interested in reading than girls. Researchers believe some boys may consider school success, and reading in particular, as more appropriate for girls (Blair & Sanford, 2004). PISA analysts believe the best way to improve the reading results of boys is to get more boys engaged in reading by paying attention to their reading preferences. However, they acknowledge that this will require concerted efforts on the part of families, teachers, and society to break the stereotypes about what is acceptable for boys and girls.

Some researchers worry that these test results mask other persistent social issues. Research suggests that boys still get the majority of teacher attention (Beaman, Wheldall, & Kemp, 2006), especially boys who are White and middle class (Grant & Sleeter, 2011); Black male students are reprimanded more often. Socialized to be compliant, girls who are struggling academically may become invisible in the classroom and fail to get the support they need. Violence in schools is an issue for boys and girls, but the sexual nature of this violence is particularly troublesome for girls. The public has been shocked by high-profile stories of girls' sexual exploitation through social media. Girls are also more likely to be involved in self-harm. Boys are often constrained by hypermasculine expectations to be athletic, tough and, put simply, not academic.

Gender stereotypes can also be complicated by cultural expectations. Traditional cultural beliefs downplaying the importance of girls' education still influence some girls' aspirations. Children may struggle when their interests do not fit with parental expectations of acceptable pursuits for their gender. In addition, cultural or religious beliefs may make it difficult for families to accept their homosexual children. Thirty-one percent of gay youth report a suicide attempt compared to 13% of heterosexual youth (Grant & Sleeter, 2011). All of these factors can impact the culture norms of schools.

Are there actual biological cognitive differences between boys and girls, or do these apparent differences reflect differential socialization? Diane Halpern (2012), a psychologist who has studied cognitive differences in males and females, shows that there are in fact some slight differences as measured by cognitive tests. Girls tend to have stronger reading comprehension and writing, fine motor, and perceptual skills and greater general knowledge of language and literature. Boys have an edge in visual working memory such as mental rotations, fluid reasoning, and general math and science knowledge. However, Halpern cautions that the differences among all boys and the differences among all girls are much greater than the differences between the genders. Claims about the different learning needs of boys and girls are often trumped up to justify single-sex schools or other gender-specific interventions.

Both boys and girls need hands-on, relevant tasks that invite their curiosity and engagement. If brains are most malleable when children are young, as neuroscientists like Lise Eliot (2009) suggest, it is important that teachers consistently communicate high expectations for both genders and downplay stereotypical expectations: "Kids rise and fall according to what we believe about them, and the more we dwell on the differences between boys and girls, the likelier such stereotypes are to crystallize into children's self-perceptions and self-fulfilling prophecies" (p. 15). We have provided here only a brief discussion of very complex issues regarding gender and how it might intersect with school culture.

Socioeconomic Status and Schools

Despite the previously cited PISA finding that Canada scores well in terms of equity, social class still has a significant impact on student achievement. Poverty is associated with high absence and dropout rates, high-risk behaviour, and more health problems. Children who grow up in poverty are often underrepresented in challenging programs and have low self-esteem and low educational aspirations (Levin, 2004). According to Campaign 2000 (2011), child poverty rates in Canada have continued to remain at about 15–18% for the last 25 years since their campaign to reduce child poverty was initiated. Schools in low-income neighbourhoods often do not have access to the same services or infrastructure as those in more privileged areas. While schools in Canada are funded on a per student basis that ought to enhance equity, active parent fundraising associations in privileged areas ensure those privileged students have enrichment funds for things like school trips and computers. Table 7.3 shows that a large percentage of the Canadian children living in poverty are new immigrants and Aboriginal children.

The Canadian Teachers' Federation (2009) prepared a report on child poverty in Canadian schools. They quoted children in North Bay, Ontario, who described poverty as

- "feeling ashamed when my dad can't get a job"
- "pretending that you forgot your lunch"
- "being afraid to tell your Mom you need gym shoes"

TABLE 7.3 Prevalence of Low Income among Children in Canada by Social Group

All children (2007)	**9.5%**
Children (<15 years) in recent immigrant families (2005)	39.3%
First Nations children (<15 years) (2005)	33.7%

Source: Parliament of Canada, 2009.

- "not buying books at the book fair"
- "not getting to go on school trips" (p. 2)

This report also interviewed teachers, who discussed their worries about student transiency for families who could not pay rent, lack of participation in extracurricular activities, and students' low self-esteem and hopelessness about their own futures. The Federation recommends that schools advocate for "more effective recruitment, selection, preparation, and placement of teachers for schools affected by poverty," (p. 3) small class sizes (which is especially important for vulnerable children), creating a strong sense of community within schools, and building strong relationships with parents. They also recommend teacher education programs that help teachers see themselves as social advocates to lobby for economic policies to support the poor, such as subsidized housing, healthcare interventions, and fair wages and working conditions.

Cross-Cultural Communication

On one hand it is important for educators to be aware of the cultural values and communication patterns of their students to appropriately interpret and respond to those students. On the other hand, it is difficult to identify these differences without stereotyping. Cultures are not monolithic, but rather comprise individuals with complex and diverse personal influences. We tend to have values similar to those of others in our own culture, but our individual values depend on our experiences. In this section we will consider some of the most common cultural patterns and how these might be evident in a classroom. These include direct and indirect communication styles, individual and collective orientations, high and low power distance, and nonverbal communication.

Communication Styles

Malcolm Gladwell (2008) recounts a fascinating case of miscommunication that had devastating consequences. Korean Air was developing a dismal safety record despite the fact that their safety inspections were sound. A careful analysis of the black box recording in one particular crash helped investigators discern how communication challenges may have contributed to the tragedy:

> When the first officer says, "Don't you think it rains more? In this area, here?" we know what he means by that: Captain you have committed us to a visual approach, with no backup plan, and the weather outside is terrible. You think that we will break out of the

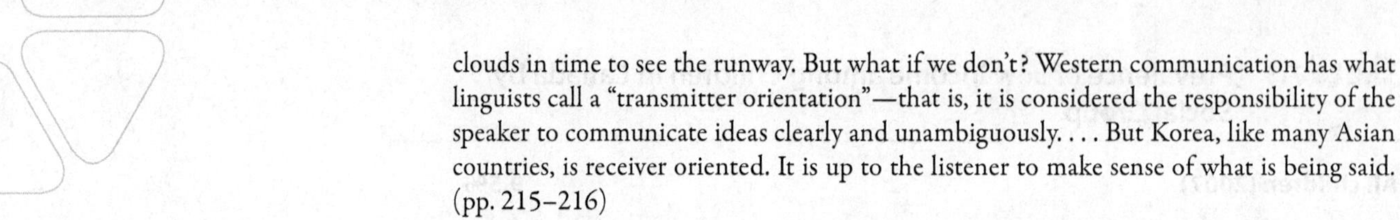

> clouds in time to see the runway. But what if we don't? Western communication has what linguists call a "transmitter orientation"—that is, it is considered the responsibility of the speaker to communicate ideas clearly and unambiguously. . . . But Korea, like many Asian countries, is receiver oriented. It is up to the listener to make sense of what is being said. (pp. 215–216)

The first officer recognized that there was a potential issue. However, it seems he felt it was inappropriate for him to direct the pilot because the pilot had greater authority than he did. Instead, he raised his concerns as questions. Investigators believe that more direct communication would have helped to prevent this crash. Training for pilots now helps them see how critical direct communication is in the time-sensitive realm of the airplane cockpit.

High-context cultures like Korea provide enough context in their speech so that their meaning is self-evident; the onus is on the listener to understand the speaker's message. They also assume the individual they are speaking with is knowledgeable about a subject so they provide very little background knowledge. They prefer to avoid conflict or deal with it subtly, as the first officer did in this scenario. Their emotional reactions are subdued, and they tend to be reserved. Students from these cultures may expect teachers to provide the information they need and may therefore be reluctant to ask questions.

By contrast, low-context cultures assume the other person knows very little, so they are explicit and precise; they also confront conflict openly and are more emotionally demonstrative. In the classroom, those from low-context cultures are likely to provide lengthy responses to teacher questions or in written responses. Those from high-context cultures may provide little background knowledge in their responses, leading teachers to assume they have less knowledge. Because Canadians tend to use a lower-context communication style, you will need to be attentive to your students' nonverbal cues—they may be confused but reluctant to ask for help because of their cultural patterns. Chinese, Japanese, and Arab cultures and to a lesser degree Greek, Spanish, and Mexican are other high-context cultures. German and Scandinavian cultures are the lowest-context cultures with Canadian culture appearing in the middle of the continuum (Alberta Education, 2010b).

Individual versus Collective Orientations

Cultures may have **individual** or **collective orientations**. Canadians mainly have an individual orientation. This means we value freedom, autonomy, and privacy. Canadians present themselves by sharing personal details and value the time and energy they put into achieving individual goals because these are central to their identities. By contrast, students who come from collective cultures identify themselves by their group membership and place priority on loyalty to that group. For this reason, their introductions may identify the group they belong to rather than personal details. When involved in a task, they assume collective responsibility. They place high priority on the time and energy invested in building relationships. Students from collective cultures may be frustrated by the apparent lack of consultation and rapport building when working with classmates from individualistic cultures (Alberta Education, 2010b).

Power Distance

The terms **high** and **low power distance cultures** describe attitudes toward authority. In low power distance cultures, interactions with authorities like teachers are informal; students are usually not afraid to critique the ideas of those in authority positions. They will ask

individual orientation
A cultural orientation that values freedom, autonomy, and privacy. Members of this orientation value the time and energy they put into achieving individual goals.

collective orientation
A cultural orientation that values group membership and places high value on loyalty to that group. Members of this orientation assume collective responsibility for tasks and place priority on building relationships.

high power distance cultures
Members of high power distance cultures are very formal with superiors and they won't contradict them. They expect detailed directions and will seek permission before taking initiative.

low power distance cultures
Members of low power distance cultures are informal with superiors and they are not afraid to critique or contradict the ideas of those in authority positions. They will ask for clarification of questions and will take initiative.

for clarification of questions but expect some autonomy in assignments. They take initiative and expect recognition and support for that initiative taking. High power distance cultures are much more formal with superiors; they won't contradict them and they trust the teacher as the authority. They expect detailed directions and will seek permission before they take initiative. This means they may be frustrated when tasks are ambiguous. The immigrant teachers described earlier in this chapter who participated in the teacher education program at the University of Ottawa expressed their confusion when students were so informal with teachers.

Power distance is measured by a numerical scale ranging from 11 (low power distance, like Austria) to 104 (high power distance, like Slovakia); Canada's score is 39. High scores are also found in Russia, China, Arab countries, the Philippines, and some South American countries, while low scores are found in many countries in Western Europe, Canada, the United States, and New Zealand (Alberta Education, 2010b). However, there are some interesting divergences that should curb our preconceptions; for example, India and Pakistan score 77 and 55, respectively, despite the fact that they are neighbouring countries and might be expected to have similar cultural patterns with respect to authority.

Nonverbal Communication

Nonverbal communication includes things like eye contact, gestures, and personal space. In Western culture, eye contact signals interest and honesty. Those who avoid eye contact may be judged as "shifty" or lacking confidence. Aboriginal people as well as Asian, Middle Eastern, and African people often make only brief eye contact to communicate respect. In those cultures, a speaker who makes continued eye contact might be viewed as haughty. It is easy to see how such nonverbal signals could be interpreted in a classroom. A teacher who confronts two students about a playground scuffle may see the child who avoids eye contact as dishonest and assume that child is at fault. Gestures can also be misinterpreted. An "OK" symbol to Canadians may be regarded as threatening in Arab cultures and disparaging (suggesting "you're a zero") in some European countries. Canadians tend to like having a large amount of personal space and feel crowded and uncomfortable with those who are "close talkers," while some cultures have small personal spaces and don't mind being physically close to the people around them.

Aboriginal Culture

An Alberta-based teaching resource identifies communication styles among Aboriginal students that may influence teacher–student relationships (Alberta Education, 2005b). First, FNMI students may nod or say "yes" to acknowledge the speaker, but this does not necessarily signal their agreement. Some cultures see conflict as a productive way to work out differences, but conflict in Aboriginal culture is embarrassing; parents are more likely to tell a story to teach a lesson than address the issue directly. Aboriginal children and their parents don't like to be the focus of attention and are likely to avoid situations where they are the focus; parent–teacher conferences might be awkward encounters for Aboriginal families. It is prudent for teachers to avoid overly public praise and certainly to avoid public criticism of Aboriginal students. They also like to make decisions with the input of others, so it is important for teachers to build relationships with parents and recognize the time it may take for parents and students to receive others' input to make decisions. Some people build relationships while participating in tasks together, but many Aboriginal people feel it is important to establish relationships first. Thus children who seem to be avoiding tasks may be simply developing relationships with group members before they tackle the academic task they have been assigned. This may also reflect different concepts of time among Aboriginal learners, which may be frustrating for non-Aboriginal teachers. Learning in Aboriginal culture is contextual and meaningful, so if the relevance of a task is unclear a teacher is less likely to get student co-operation. Cultures value different ways of knowing; Euro-Canadian culture tends to value objective book knowledge while Aboriginal culture places higher values on one's inner knowledge and using imagery to communicate that knowledge. Finally, all of us have different boundaries regarding our personal information and emotional transparency. Developing a relationship of trust and showing respect will help foster greater openness with your Aboriginal students and their families.

It is important to remember with all of these cultural patterns that they are generalizations. These patterns may not necessarily be characteristic of all children who come from one of these cultures. This discussion is intended to help you better understand some possible ways students from various cultures may respond so that you can avoid unfair judgments. The following Impact on Today's Teachers boxes provide examples of cross-cultural communication in the classroom.

Impact on Today's Teachers

(MIS)UNDERSTANDING DIFFERENT COMMUNICATION STYLES

Two teachers in the staff room are discussing a new student they both teach.

Geri: Don't get me wrong. I like Mujahid. He's very polite.

Nicole: Always does his work?

Geri: You bet. And it's very neat.

Nicole: Sounds good to me.

Geri: That's just it. It's too neat. Too correct. Never a mistake.

Nicole: Not even a smudge. Yep, that's Mujahid, a perfectionist.

Geri: That's not normal—not for a fourth-grade boy.

Nicole: For a boy! Some of the girls are just as messy. What are you getting at?

Geri: Well, I'm not sure . . . that is, I'm not sure he's doing his own homework.

Nicole: Funny. Who would do it for him?

Geri: I'm not sure, but, well . . . okay, I'll say it, but it won't sound right. I think he's sneaky.

Nicole: Sneaky? Like in he doesn't do his own homework? What makes you say that?

Geri: Haven't you noticed? He sits in the back of the room. When I call on him, he drops his eyes. One time I called him to my desk. He walked up very slow, looking at his shoes all the time. When I tried to talk to him, he just shuffled his feet and answered only yes or no. He didn't really try to talk to me.

Nicole: Of course, silly. He's very respectful. That's what I like about him. He's so polite. His dimples show when he smiles. (pp. 72–73)

How might high- and low-context cultural differences and high and low power distances contribute to Geri's interpretation of Mujahid's behaviour?

Source: Used with permission. From Teaching for Diversity: A Guide to Greater Understanding (3rd ed.) by Ricardo L. García. Copyright 2011 by Solution Tree Press, 555 North Morton Street, Bloomington, IN 47404, 800.733.6786, solution-tree.com.

Impact on Today's Teachers

CULTURAL DIFFERENCES IN COMMUNICATION

The University of the Pacific (LaBrack, n.d.) has prepared a fascinating resource on cultural differences to support their students who study abroad. The difference between their experience and yours as a teacher in Canada is that they are going into other cultures where they must adjust their behaviour to the cultural norms of that country. In your case, your students are coming into your classroom that may have cultural norms that differ from their own. You may not even be aware of the many times each day when they feel confused or offended in the classroom. Doing the exercises in this online resource may help you to better understand the cultural values and communication patterns among your students that make it challenging for them to feel comfortable in your classroom. Often behaviours that seem strange to you are consistent with values that they hold dear.

One of the exercises is adapted below.

In the exercise below, match the behaviour in the column on the left to a value or belief in the column on the right.

Behaviour	Value/Belief
1. Use of understatement	a. Directness
2. Asking people to call you by your first name	b. Centrality of family
3. Taking off from school to attend the funeral of an aunt	c. External control
4. Not helping the person next to you on an exam	d. Saving face
5. Disagreeing openly with someone in a discussion	e. Respect for age
6. Not laying off an older worker whose performance is weak	f. Informality
7. Agreeing with a suggestion you think is wrong	g. Deference to authority
8. Inviting the teaboy to eat lunch with you in your office	h. Indirectness
9. Asking the principal's opinion of something you're the expert on	i. Self-reliance
10. Accepting, without question, that something cannot be changed	j. Egalitarianism

Suggested Responses

Behaviour	Value	Sample Countries/Areas
1. Use of understatement	h. Indirectness	China/Thailand
2. Asking people to call you by your first name	f. Informality	Australia/UnitedStates
3. Taking off from school to attend the funeral of an aunt	b. Centrality of family	Venezuela/Korea
4. Not helping the person next to you on an exam	i. Self-reliance	Switzerland/Canada

continued

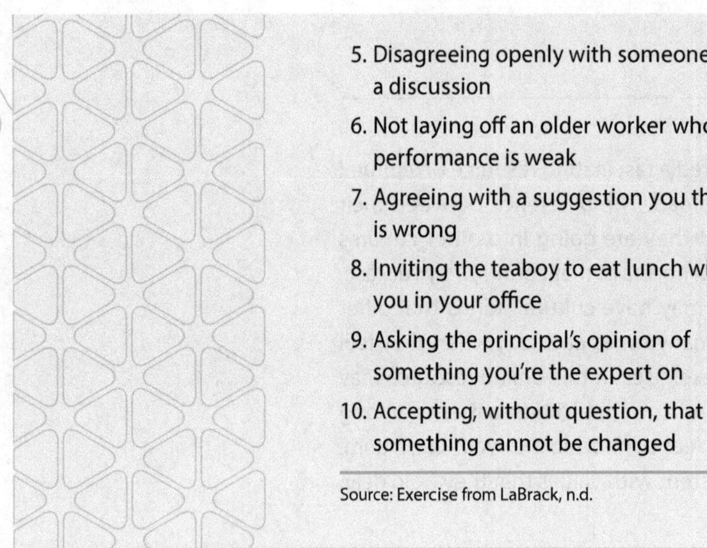

5. Disagreeing openly with someone in a discussion	a. Directness	Germany/England
6. Not laying off an older worker whose performance is weak	e. Respect for age	Japan/Pakistan
7. Agreeing with a suggestion you think is wrong	d. Saving face	Asia generally
8. Inviting the teaboy to eat lunch with you in your office	j. Egalitarianism	Cambodia/Vietnam
9. Asking the principal's opinion of something you're the expert on	g. Deference to authority	India/Brazil
10. Accepting, without question, that something cannot be changed	c. External control	Saudi Arabia/Turkey

Source: Exercise from LaBrack, n.d.

Impact on Today's Teachers

COMMUNICATION PATTERNS

A study of interethnic dialogue in northern Canada revealed fascinating distinctions between the language patterns of the Athabaskan Aboriginal people and the English-speaking Canadians (Bainbridge & Heydon, 2013). Athabaskan speakers were reluctant to participate in conversation when others' points of view were still unknown, while the English speakers used conversation as a way to learn those points of view. English speakers viewed the Athabaskans as aloof, and the Athabaskans viewed the English as overly talkative; they seemed to assume their own dominance over the Athabaskans.

In raising children, Athabaskan adults provide models for children to emulate, but the English-speaking teachers encouraged Athabaskan children to display their abilities to their teachers at school. Such cultural differences could clearly lead to misunderstandings in a school setting. Ball and Lewis (2005), who showed similar findings, were particularly concerned about how this affected the assessment of First Nations children in schools. It is unlikely that they demonstrate their knowledge fully if they are unaccustomed to being questioned by adults. Sensitive teachers must not interpret silence or reluctance to display one's talents as a lack of knowledge or skill.

Diversity Issues and Teachers' Blind Spots

> Teachers who believe that society is fair and just believe that their students are participating on a level playing field and simply have to learn to be better competitors than other students. They also believe in a kind of social Darwinism that supports survival of the fittest. . . . Teachers who [are] culturally relevant assume that an asymmetrical (even antagonistic) relationship exists between poor students of color and society. Thus, their vision of their work is one of preparing students to combat inequity by being highly competent and critically conscious. (Ladson-Billings, cited in Egbo, 2009)

Many well-intentioned teachers claim to be colour-blind because they aim to treat all children in the same way. However, this attitude obfuscates the fact that "the same way" is in fact based on one's own values, typically Eurocentric values. When we treat everyone in the same way, we assume that the cultural norms of the majority benefit everyone equally. For this reason it is important to distinguish between *equality* and *equity*. Equality means treating everyone in the same way; equity means treating people in ways that might even the playing field.

Like Gloria Ladson-Billings, who is quoted above, Gay (2010) presents contrasting views of teaching. On one hand, teaching may be viewed as an apolitical activity in which teachers are technicians charged with imparting knowledge to students. On the other hand, teaching may be viewed as a critical activity in which teachers interrogate practices that privilege some knowledge over other kinds of knowledge.

> How we teach, what we teach, how we relate to children and each other, what our goals are—these are rooted in the norms of our culture. Our society's predominant worldview and cultural norms are so deeply ingrained in how we educate children that we very seldom think about the possibility that there may be other different but equally legitimate and effective approaches to teaching and learning. In a society with (so) much sociocultural and racial diversity . . . the lack of this wonderment about alternative ways often results in unequal education and social injustice. (Gay, 2010, p. 24)

When teachers embrace social justice, they see how some of their students may be disempowered by the school system.

Immigrant families often immigrate to Canada to create a better life for their children. However, these families often face circumstances that complicate their lives in other ways. While their schooling experience in their home country may have been disrupted by political unrest, their schooling experience in Canada is often disrupted by frequent residence changes. Their relocation often involves the loss of extended family and support networks. The stress and vulnerability associated with adjusting to a new language, culture, lifestyle, and school system can negatively affect school achievement (Gay, 2010). Immigrants also face "stereotype threat" when stereotypes about one ethnic group's intellectual ability "[divert] attention onto task-irrelevant worries, creating self-consciousness and undue caution, and (cause) them to disengage from academic efforts. . . . It is most salient for those students who care most about performing well" (Gay, 2010, pp. 18–19).

John Ogbu (2003) was a Nigerian-American anthropologist renowned for his research on the interplay between race, ethnicity, economic status, and educational achievement. In his view, minorities feel marginalized by the education system, which impacts motivation, achievement, and even IQ scores. He also concluded that some minority students did poorly because peers would perceive effort and high achievement as "acting White." Unfortunately, such behaviour reinforces stereotypes others may hold about their academic abilities and contributes to self-fulfilling prophecies. McLaren (2007) observed similar "resistance" among West Indian children at a Canadian school who felt that school success meant denying their blackness.

Gonzalez, Moll, and Amanti (2005) remind teachers how important it is to attend to the students' funds of knowledge—the life experiences outside of school that have shaped them. The more the teacher is different from the students, the more difficult it will be to recognize these funds of knowledge. Teachers need to be deliberate about acquainting themselves with the community where their students live. What assets and expertise are in this community? What barriers do they face? How do students spend their spare time?

It is difficult to see how teachers can be learner-centred if they do not make such efforts to get to know their students and consider how their home lives intersect with their learning.

> Putting learners first is at the heart of learner-centered teaching. The focus is shifted from "what teachers teach" to "what students learn." Learner-centered teachers understand that they must find ways to know their individual students and provide a safe and nurturing context before the job of teaching can begin. Learner-centered teachers also understand that not only is learning a natural lifelong process, but motivation to learn also comes naturally when the learning context is supportive. (McCombs, cited in Grant & Sleeter, 2011, p. 39)

To illustrate this point, Grant and Sleeter (2011) describe a student teacher named Glenda who, as part of the field experience requirement in her course, participated in an after-school tutoring program. The Grade 6 boys, all from diverse cultural groups, were two years below grade level in reading and math. After struggling to engage the boys, Glenda proposed asking one another questions to get better acquainted. The boys took this "assignment" very seriously and asked insightful questions about Glenda's family, her hometown, and her choice to go to university. When they responded to her questions she learned about their responsibilities at home, their families' work, and their interests in sports. After a lengthy and engaging discussion, Glenda asked how she and their teacher could help them be more successful. The students all said they wished that they could have similar kinds of discussions at school. Effective teachers regard prior experience, community, culture, and student and teacher ethnicities as important ecological factors in the classroom (Bronfenbrenner, 1979). How can they claim to know their students if they don't make some effort to know about their cultures and how these may influence the child in front of them?

A subtle way teachers may unintentionally limit some students is through their expectations. "Teacher expectations about students are affected by factors that have no basis in fact and may persist even in the face of contrary evidence. . . . Assumptions about connections among the intellectual capability, ethnicity, gender, and classroom adjustment of students attest to the tenacity of teacher expectations" (Gay, 2010, pp. 64–65). These expectations are particularly pernicious if the assumptions lead to negative expectations. Some teachers expect males and students of colour to be more disruptive and for there to be a correlation between achievement and good behaviour. As they communicate these high expectations to "good" students and communicate low expectations and frustration to others, the sense of hopelessness grows exponentially for the latter group. In two different studies, teachers expected students who spoke African-American and working-class dialects to have lower achievement and they assessed them accordingly (Gay, 2010, p. 65). To overcome such biased expectations, Hattie (2012) cautions:

> Teachers need to stop overemphasizing ability, and start to emphasize increased progress (steep learning curves are the right of all students regardless of where they start); they need to stop seeking evidence to confirm their prior expectations, but rather seek evidence to surprise them and find ways in which to raise the achievement of all. School leaders need to stop creating schools that attempt to lock in prior achievement and experiences (such as by using tracking), and instead be evidence-informed about the talents and growth of all students by welcoming diversity and being accountable for all (regardless of the teachers' and schools' expectations). (Hattie, 2012, p. 82)

Teachers' self-efficacy is also related to their expectations. Insecure teachers attribute students' failure to the students' lack of ability or their impoverished home life rather than to their own teaching quality. More confident teachers continually examine their own practices for ways they can adjust to meet the needs of struggling students.

Angela Valenzuela (cited in Grant & Sleeter, 2011) distinguishes between *aesthetic* and *authentic care* as observed in a school that served mainly Mexican-American students. Aesthetic care was "awarded" to those students who were engaged in school, but authentic care was evident when the teacher and students developed a genuine relationship. Students rejected school when they did not feel cared for. An exercise to probe one's attitudes toward students asks teachers to briefly describe the kids who are easy to like and those who are hard to like, kids who you are sorry for and those you feel threatened by, kids you identify with and those you feel inadequate around, and finally those kids you don't even notice. Students sense your feelings and will react accordingly. The children who are least like you are also least likely to feel that authentic care unless you are deliberate about examining your attitudes and adjusting your actions accordingly.

Grant and Sleeter (2011) present the exercise displayed in Table 7.4. Teachers regularly pass judgments on students' potential to learn based on their effort, behaviour, and the quality of their classwork. But as this exercise shows, there may different reasons for similar behaviour. What does this exercise reveal to you about your expectations and possible misinterpretations of students' behaviour?

Parker Palmer's famous book *The Courage to Teach* (1998) reminds teachers how central our identity is to teaching. He urges us to ask ourselves "How does the quality of my selfhood form—or deform—the way I relate to my students, my subject, my colleagues, my world?" (p. 4). Sometimes we are not even aware of how our identities "deform" our relationship to our students. How do we overcome those blind spots?

Cultural therapy is a process for raising consciousness about one's own assumptions that was developed by American anthropologist and professor of education George

TABLE 7.4 Interpreting Classroom Behaviour

Picture a student who . . .	Describe classroom behaviours of such students	How much effort do students invest in this case?	What should a teacher do?
Is bored, unchallenged, considers the work too easy			
Is in the process of learning English and is not yet fluent			
Sees little point in what is being taught even though he or she is capable of doing the work			
Is frustrated because the work is too difficult, requiring skills or background the student lacks			

Source: Grant & Sleeter, 2011, p. 36.

Spindler (1999): "It helps teachers to 'see' more clearly the imprints of culture in their own and their students' behaviour" (Gay, 2010 p. 71). Spindler describes three forms of cultural knowledge that need to be brought to conscious awareness. The first, *mundane knowledge*, is everyday knowledge such as how to answer a telephone, how to put on clothing, or how to recognize a barn. He describes an exercise where teachers are shown various images including a German *bauernhaus* (a two-storey house that houses humans on the second floor and livestock on the first). North Americans don't notice the manure pile in the yard because there is no category in their culture for a manure pile in front of a house. In discussions with teachers, he helps them to see how such perceptual errors can cause them to miss things in their students because they lack a cultural category for things that may be evident to their students.

Second, *self–other knowledge* is knowledge of how we are perceived by others. Spindler describes a Grade 5 teacher he observed over a period of several months as part of an ethnographic study:

> He prided himself on being open to his students, helpful to those with problems, accessible, and friendly. In reality he was—to those students like himself (White, Protestant, middle to upper middle class, and mainstream). It was not that he was hostile or mean to those who were not. He simply ignored them. He did not know how to relate to them. He did not understand why his classes were not meaningful to them. He was ignorant of the negative perceptions of a sizable number of his students. (p. 468)

When he heard the observations, the teacher was initially angry and defensive but soon resumed the consultation and began to better understand himself. Until teachers see themselves as students see them and honestly confront such unpleasant perceptions, they work in blind and often self-protective ways that fail to meet the needs of all students.

Finally, *submerged knowledge* can best be described as tacit knowledge or hidden assumptions. Spindler describes an exercise where German and American teachers watched a video of one another's classrooms and compared their observations using an exercise he calls a *cross-cultural interview*. For example, they observed that German teachers worked with struggling students to bring them up to the level of the group while American teachers sought to maximize the individual's potential. In another example regarding authority and control, American teachers tried to provoke guilt for disturbances that occurred in their absence while German teachers tended to dismiss the issues that occurred in their absence. These submerged cultural attitudes only became apparent when they could observe, discuss, and analyze their teaching practices.

While not all teachers will have the opportunity to participate in such rich cultural therapy discussions, a series of questions like those in Table 7.5, when tackled bravely, critically, and honestly, can prompt the kind of personal and professional self-awareness necessary for effective teaching. Exercises like these are designed to enhance intercultural and transcultural understanding—the ability to communicate outside one's own culture and recognize how all of our interpretations are constrained by our cultural lenses (Takkula, Kangaslahti, & Banks, 2008).

In the same way that teachers can engage in careful introspection to identify their own blind spots, students can be led through learning experiences that help them consider perspectives they might not have considered and how they misunderstand others. The United Nations Association in Canada (Abboud, Chong, Gray, Kaderdina, Masongsong, & Rahman, 2002) has created the following exercise to stimulate critical thinking about antiracism; readers may recognize some of these prompts, which are similar to Peggy McIntosh's

TABLE 7.5 Checklist for Conducting Critical Self-Reflection and Analysis

Area of Self-Reflection	Sample Questions
Personal History	• In what ways do my personal history and worldviews affect my teaching practice? • What are the privileges or oppressions that come with my identity? • In what ways does my background facilitate or hinder my success in Canadian society? • What are my personal beliefs about diversity and equity issues?
Pedagogical Beliefs and Approaches	• What is my basic approach to teaching? • Does this approach best serve the interests of my diverse students? • In what ways could I be reinforcing stereotypes through my teaching practices? • In what ways do I create space for promoting democratic values in my classroom? • How often do I reflect upon my classroom practices? • What kinds of resources do I use in my everyday practice?
Knowledge of Diversity Issues	• What are the key debates about diversity in Canadian society? • How current am I with research on diversity? • What does the research say? • How can I become culturally literate? • What cross-cultural competencies do I have? • What do I know about the following groups in Canadian society: First Nations peoples, visible minorities, women in Canadian history, people with disabilities?
Knowledge of Students	• How well do I know my students? • To what extent do I interact with members of diverse communities? • What are the various first languages of the minority students in my class? • In what ways do I support first language maintenance among my students?
Assumptions about Learning	• What are my basic assumptions about learning? • What are my beliefs about learning styles? • To what extent is learning style socially and culturally influenced? • Am I meeting the instructional needs of my students? • What are my expectations for my students? • To what extent am I contributing to the success of all my students? • How relevant are my expectations to the life experiences of all my students?
Assumptions about Knowledge	• What are my basic beliefs about schooled knowledge? • What should Canadians learn in school? • Who controls this knowledge? • Whose knowledge do students currently learn? • To what extent is this knowledge inclusive? • To what extent do I question and engage in curricular materials?
Beliefs about Society	• What are my beliefs about how society functions? • Who controls power in society and how do I feel about this? • To what extent do I share in that power dynamic? • Do I believe that equity and social justice for all are marginal or important issues in Canadian society? • Who determines educational priorities, and how do I feel about this? • What are my beliefs about the link between education and society?

Source: Egbo, 2009.

seminal article on White privilege (1990). Students are invited to ask themselves, "Which of the following applies to you because of your skin colour?"

1. I can turn on the television or open the front page of the paper and see people of my race widely represented.
2. I can, if I wish, arrange to be in the company of people of my own race most of the time.
3. I can say something positive about my own race without feeling that I'm saying something racist.
4. When I am told about our Canadian heritage or "civilization," I am shown that people of my colour made it what it is.
5. I can go into an art gallery and find the work of artists of my race hanging on the walls.
6. I can go into a university/high school and find professors of my race in all the departments.
7. I can go into a hairdresser's shop and find someone who knows how to cut my hair.
8. I can be at any cultural gathering or event and feel completely comfortable.
9. I can swear or not answer letters without having people attribute these choices to the bad morals or the illiteracy of my race.
10. I can do well in a challenging situation without being called a credit to my race.
11. I can criticize our government and talk about how much I disagree with its policies without being told to go back to where I came from if I don't like it here.
12. I can be pretty sure that if I ask to talk to the person in charge, I will be facing a person of my skin colour.
13. If a traffic cop pulls me over, I can be sure I haven't been singled out because of my race.
14. I can talk about my ancestors without feeling guilty about what people of my race may have done in the past.
15. I can take a job with an equal opportunity employer without having my co-workers on the job suspect that I got it because of my race.
16. If my day or week or year is going badly I wonder if each negative situation has racial overtones.
17. I can walk onto a bus or train or into a cafeteria or school room and find it easy to sit next to someone of my race.
18. I can choose blemish cover (cover-up) or bandages in "flesh" colour and have them more or less match my skin.

Such an exercise can open students' and teachers' eyes to the experiences of their classmates and colleagues who are visible minorities.

Multiculturalism and Antiracist Education

Given the diversity of Canadian schools, educators have been striving to ensure not only the equality of all students but equity for all students—to even the playing field for those who may have been disadvantaged by their background. Multicultural education has been defined as

> an idea, an educational reform movement, and a process whose major goal is to change the structure of educational institutions so that male and female students, exceptional students, and students who are members of diverse racial, ethnic, language and cultural groups will have an equal chance to achieve academically in school. (Banks & Banks, cited in Egbo, 2009, p. 53)

multicultural education Education that seeks to be inclusive of many cultural ideas and values by appreciating diversity or preserving cultural heritage.

James Banks (2004), one of the leading researchers in multicultural education, outlines the five dimensions of **multicultural education**. First, *content integration* is the way in which teachers integrate examples and information from diverse cultures to illustrate key concepts in a subject area. For example, there have been various curricula developed and supports offered for integrating Aboriginal perspectives in the Canadian curriculum. Unfortunately this leads teachers of math and science to dismiss multicultural education as important for the humanities but irrelevant to their disciplines. Second, *knowledge construction* aims to illustrate how knowledge is developed by people and how the diverse backgrounds of those creators influences the knowledge that is developed. In Canada, our curriculum tends to reflect a Eurocentric worldview. Third, *prejudice reduction* involves specific strategies to reduce the prejudicial attitudes that students have and aims to help them develop a greater sense of democratic citizenship. Fourth, *equity pedagogy* involves teachers adjusting their teaching approaches to support the academic achievement of students from diverse groups by examining their preconceptions and adjusting their practice. Finally, an *empowering school culture* includes restructuring the organization of the school by reconsidering grouping practices, labelling practices, the social climate of the school, and expectations of all staff.

Egbo (2009) analyzes several models of multicultural education, each with its own particular pitfall:

1. *For common values:* This model of multicultural education seeks to highlight the similarities among all cultures. While society has some broad values that everyone can agree upon, which can create a strong sense of unity, this emphasis may obfuscate the fact that some values are culturally specific and render these cultural values insignificant.
2. *As education of the culturally different:* This model of multicultural education presupposes that culturally different students are at a deficit, and a curriculum catered to those students that builds on their cultural background will help to address this deficit. Not only does this assume the superiority of the mainstream culture, it also fails to engage those mainstream students in developing broader perspectives. They also can benefit from learning about the cultural background of others.
3. *As education for cultural understanding:* Developing an understanding and appreciation of differences and similarities in cultures to build greater social unity is the aim of this model. While this is a laudable approach and preferable to the preceding models, it fails short in its capacity to empower minority students.
4. *As education for cultural accommodation:* The aim of this model is to foster awareness of the dignity of one's ethnic group so as to become a special interest group negotiating for fair resources. This may be regarded as paternalistic since the dominant group charitably concedes for the benefit of the minority.
5. *Bicultural education:* Like the approach advocated by Lisa Delpit in the Case Study below, bicultural education values retaining one's own culture while developing competencies in another to create broader opportunities.
6. *As education for cultural preservation:* This segregationist model places the group's interest above the broader society, such as allowing families to educate their children in separate schools. It is considered pernicious because it violates the autonomy of young people who are precluded from learning about other cultures by the decisions their parents have made on their behalf.

7. *As education for multicultural adaptation:* Like bicultural education, this model encourages all students to develop a deep understanding of another culture, perhaps through immersion experiences or second language learning. In Canada this is clearly more feasible for immigrants who are thrust into Canadian culture, but it is more difficult for Canadian students unless they travel abroad, join some organized cultural immersion experiences, or become well acquainted with a friend's culture through socialization.

The rationale for each of these models as well as the critiques should be evident from the descriptions above.

CASE STUDY

Accessing the Culture of Power

Lisa Delpit (1988, 2006) is a well-known Black educator who explores how issues of power are enacted in classrooms. She describes how there are codes or rules for participating in the culture of power. These include ways of speaking, dressing, writing, and interacting. When people are explicitly told about these codes it makes it easier for them to access power. Those who have power are least aware of these codes and believe that making these codes explicit will impose upon the autonomy of others. She suggests we are most explicit about power in settings where the power dynamics are clear. Parents have no difficulty directing their teens to "Turn that music down!" but in a job interview people tend to subtly and indirectly coach the interviewee about appropriate responses, and these cues can be easily misunderstood, especially when there are cultural differences.

> Many liberal educators hold that the primary goal for education is for children to become autonomous, to develop fully who they are in the classroom without having arbitrary outside standards forced upon them. This is a very reasonable goal for people whose children are already participants in the culture of power. But parents who don't function within that culture . . . want to ensure that the school provides their children with discourse patterns, interactional styles, and spoken and written language codes that will allow them success in the larger society. (Delpit, 1988, p. 285)

This concern was at the root of parents' apprehensions when well-intentioned educators introduced dialect readers. One parent complained, "My kids know how to be Black—you all teach them how to be successful in the White man's world!" (p. 285). A Black teacher had similar criticisms of a new writing program that focused on fluency:

> Our kids are fluent. What they need are the skills that will get them into college. I've got a kid right now—brilliant. But he can't get a score on the SAT that will even get him considered by any halfway decent college. He needs skills, not fluency. This is just another one of those racist ploys to keep our kids out. White kids learn how to write a decent sentence. Even if they don't teach them in school, their parents make sure they get what they need. But what about our kids? They don't get it at home and they spend all their time in school learning to be fluent. I'm sick of this liberal nonsense. (Delpit, 2006, p. 16)

Delpit (1988) describes the seminal work of Shirley Brice Heath (1983) who analyzed the interaction patterns of neighbouring towns. The White middle-class teachers she observed said things like "Is that where the scissors belong?" or "You want to do your best work today." By contrast, many Black teachers are more likely to say "Put those scissors on that shelf" or "Put your name on the papers and make sure to get the right answer for each question" (Heath cited in Delpit, 1988, p. 288). White teachers used indirect speech that is considered less authoritarian. This put Black students at a disadvantage when they entered school because they often misinterpreted teachers' "directives" as suggestions and then were viewed as defiant when they did not comply.

Delpit provides a poignant description of one Native American teacher's masterful efforts to give her students access to the codes of power. She covered one side of the bulletin board with phrases from the students' writing and labelled this side "our Heritage English." The other side of the bulletin board showed corresponding statements with the heading "Formal English":

> They think everybody needs to talk like them. Unlike us, they have a hard time hearing what people say if they don't talk just like them. Their way of talking and writing is called "Formal English." We have to feel a little sorry for them because they have only one way to talk. We're going to learn two ways to say things. (p. 293)

The teacher made the distinction between a picnic where people may eat with their hands and a formal dinner party where the cutlery is placed in specific places and the rules of etiquette are adhered to more closely. The class then dressed up and participated in a formal dinner party where only "formal English" was allowed and a picnic where only "heritage English" was allowed. Delpit argues that such explicit instruction helps students understand that language standards are arbitrary but also politically charged and such bilingualism provides access to power.

Delpit believes that minority students need cultural capital, sometimes called *high-status knowledge*. What cultural capital would make it easier for your students to access status and how could you make this knowledge explicit as the Native American teacher did?

In the last 20 years, many theorists have argued that multicultural education is doomed to fail until it explicitly addresses the problem of racism and structural inequality. Instead they argue for **antiracist education**. Antiracist education does not simply appreciate diversity or preserve cultural heritage but rather raises awareness of social inequity. Multicultural education assumes that racism results from ignorance and the racist attitudes of individuals, but advocates of antiracist education argue that racism is embedded in unequal power structures in society, including the society of schools. Antiracist education is embedded in the interrogative perspectives of conflict theory and critical theory discussed earlier. In the Practical Applications box below we will consider some examples of how these approaches to multicultural and antiracist education might unfold in practice.

antiracist education
Education that raises awareness of social inequity based on racism.

Practical Applications

British Columbia has developed an antiracism resource called *Make a Case against Racism: A Guide for Teachers of Grades 4–7*. One of the learning activities is excerpted below.

Note: In a prior lesson, students are expected to define in their own words the following vocabulary. Suggested discussion points below:

- *Prejudice:* Explain to students that the underlying meaning of the word *prejudice* is *pre judge*; discuss how they think prejudging (prejudice) and making broad generalizations about groups and/or individuals (stereotyping) lead to poor treatment of people.
- *Discrimination:* Point out the fundamental unfairness and the limitations involved in treating people with disrespect on the basis of difference.

continued

- *Racism:* Point out the ways in which racism can adversely affect an entire community (e.g., limiting access to opportunity, limiting development of society's full potential, undermining members' sense of belonging).

The suggested instructional approach is to provide students with each of the scenarios and ask them to respond individually to the questions before discussing them as a class.

Scenario 1

In September at the start of each school year, the students in Mr.__________'s class go away on a two-day camp, so the students can get to know each other and Mr. __________, and so the class can establish some shared experiences that will allow all members to better work together throughout the year. The last day of the camp is a Friday and the tradition is to hold a final camp jamboree and camp circle after dinner. This event is something the students look forward to, but on this particular year the Friday evening of the camp coincides with Yom Kippur, which begins at sundown on the last day of camp. There are several students in the class who observe Yom Kippur. There is now the question, "To respect this holiest of days in the Jewish religion, should the camp end before sundown or should it be rescheduled to another date?"

- What do you think should be done? Why?

Scenario 2

Mydori brought her school lunch into the multipurpose room. Her lunch consisted of sushi (which everyone liked) and also kimchi (a Korean dish that is similar to pickled coleslaw and has a very strong vinegary odour). The kimchi was something Mydori's classmates were not used to. As students entered the multipurpose room, they could smell the strong vinegary kimchi. Some students made faces as they entered the room, some students laughed while looking in Mydori's direction. No one sat down at the table where Mydori was eating her lunch.

- What do you think Mydori is feeling or thinking as she tries to eat her lunch?
- Are the behaviours of the students who are making faces, laughing, and not sitting at Mydori's table a form of discrimination?
- What are the reasons for your answer?

Scenario 3

Omar seems to get into trouble a lot. Then he says it's not his fault. Sometimes he cries. None of the other students seem to want to be his friend, although Omar wants very much to fit in and have friends. Joanne, Steve, Miki, and Samira and other students in their class know that Omar is easily upset. They often tease him, hiding his jacket or taking things out of his lunch and saying nasty things about him and to him. One day last week they wrote mean things about him on the sidewalk in front of the school. This made Omar very angry on that day. After school he looked for Miki and, in front of his friends, challenged him to a fight. Miki just laughed and said, "Can't take it Omar? We just wrote what's true." Omar lost his temper and hit Miki in the face, causing it to bleed profusely. One of the students watching the fight ran to the office for help. When Omar met with the principal, he was told he would be transferred to another school, not only for hitting Miki but to give him an opportunity for a fresh start in a new school.

- Why do you think some of the Grade 6 students bullied Omar?

Student Performance Assessment

When conducting assessment (e.g., formative assessment) in relation to students' group work and contributions to the class discussion, consider and give feedback on the extent to which students are able to

- identify (and empathize with) feelings that someone might experience if being bullied (e.g., fear, sadness, hurt, anger, anxiety)
- recognize the range of hurtful ("bullying") behaviours in the scenarios (e.g., punching, name-calling, excluding, spreading false and "belittling" rumours)
- identify possible motivations for bullying behaviour (e.g., having been ill-treated themselves, allowing someone to feel more important or powerful, attempting to impress someone else)

Does this learning activity represent any of the models of multicultural or antiracist education we have discussed in this section of the chapter? If multiculturalism education assumes that racism results from racist attitudes of individuals and antiracist education highlights unequal power structures, do these scenarios invite sufficient critique of those structures? Or do they focus on changing the attitudes of individuals?

Source: British Columbia, 2008.

If you are engaging in antiracist learning activities such as the one from British Columbia included in the Practical Applications box, it is important to set ground rules, because the sensitive topics may prompt disagreement or misunderstanding. Behaviours and slurs that are simply unacceptable must be banned. You might generate a list as part of a classroom discussion or invite students to submit written ideas anonymously.

The antiracism curriculum from British Columbia may be a helpful resource for what Banks (2004) refers to as prejudice reduction, but in a crowded schedule learning experiences that are not directly linked to required curriculum content are often crowded out. It is also important to consider multicultural integration in the regular curriculum. As you learned in Chapter 3, curriculum planning is more than a series of learning activities. It requires careful attention to essential questions the topic raises. Christine Sleeter (2005) models infusing regular curriculum planning with a multicultural focus by building on the principles of backward design (Wiggins & McTighe, 2005). As teachers identify the big ideas for their curriculum planning, she encourages them to consider from whose perspective that big idea is usually presented in school and if there is a particular ideology reflected. Often the curriculum pits Western against non-Western perspectives, highlighting the accomplishments of Western civilization from the Greeks and Romans to modern-day governments and ideals while other cultures are often given a peripheral role. Similarly, Judeo-Christian ideas are highlighted with a nod to other religions. She encourages teachers to select a sociocultural group whose perspectives relate to the big idea but are not highlighted in the curriculum and research how members of that social group address the big idea.

Illustrating the continuum from shallow to deep curriculum design, Sleeter along with her colleague Carl Grant (2011) present four typologies of multicultural curriculum design by using the concept of wellness in the health curriculum. The first, "contributions, add-and-stir, or human relations" involves teachers adding famous historical figures or celebrations to regular curriculum topics. In a wellness unit, a teacher might introduce nutritious foods from diverse cultures. This is the simplest but also the most shallow design because students don't genuinely learn about the values that shape cultures. The second, single group studies, involves studying the knowledge and worldviews of a nondominant group. The initiatives around Black History Month fall into this typology. A wellness unit might bring in a women's studies perspective to highlight the media's role in selling unrealistic body images and promoting eating disorders. Wellness studies could also examine the health issues in a particular country and their access to healthcare. Third, a transformative multicultural approach to curriculum examines unique perspectives on the curriculum topic from the perspective of another group with the aim to challenge key assumptions of the mainstream canon. Wellness studies could compare Western medicine with acupuncture and other cultural perspectives on health. Finally, a social action or antiracist typology for multicultural education aims to not only learn about injustice but actually do something to change the unjust situation. The authors suggest examining the distribution of healthcare services and propose fair policies for marginalized groups. Project IMPACT described in Chapter 6 is a good example of social action because students volunteered for community organizations, presented at schools, met with experts, and wrote letters to stakeholders on the issues they were exploring.

Multicultural curriculum design also includes culturally relevant assessments described as "alternative paths that permit elbow room for varied cultural and participatory styles as well as more mediums and strategies for representing knowledge" (Mahari, cited in Sleeter, 2005, p. 72). You may recall from the discussion of cultural patterns of Aboriginal peoples that they value using imagery to communicate knowledge. Many students, including Aboriginal students, could benefit from the opportunity to showcase their understanding artistically. This does not mean that such alternative assessments should replace all traditional assessments, but it reminds teachers that options like these may provide keen insights into a child's thinking process in ways that a written assignment might not. Sleeter (2005) cautions that teachers should be attentive to the students' background knowledge and how this might influence what the assessments tell us about their learning. Teachers should avoid concepts that are not central to what is being assessed. For example, math problems with agricultural terminology may be unnecessarily confusing for an urban child.

For those who aspire to teach elementary school, interrogating ideological perspectives may seem out of reach for your young students. However, antiracist activities can begin even with the youngest students, particularly with the help of multicultural literature. Beverly Slapin and Doris Seale (in Grant & Sleeter, 2011) describe a teacher who asked her students to draw a picture of a Native American and then listen to a rich piece of children's literature written by a Native American author. The children were asked to identify how their drawings presented a limited conception of that culture. She introduced the term *stereotype* and asked the children to examine library books for examples of stereotypes.

Multicultural literature can often be a useful vehicle for rich curricular integration. For example, one Grade 5 teacher coordinated with the school librarian to create a scavenger hunt for books that included various cultural perspectives on the solar system (Sleeter, 2005). In language arts the children analyzed similarities and differences in these stories.

For science, they had to create their own fictitious creation account using facts they had learned about a planet but emulating literary devices from folktales. Cross-curricular integration helped the teacher design a curriculum using big ideas while also integrating diverse cultural perspectives. This approach might not lend itself to social action, but it does reflect Grant and Sleeter's (2011) third approach, a transformative approach to multicultural education, because it considers diverse perspectives on the curriculum topic.

Conclusion

In this chapter we have delved into the complexity of the sociocultural dimensions of teaching. You may have found yourself digging into some uncomfortable realities about your own prejudices and expectations of students.

Now it is time to revisit the five steps of reflection introduced in Chapter 1, beginning with identifying an element of your teaching that needs attention. Perhaps as you were reading this chapter you were thinking about a student you have struggled to reach. We hope that this chapter has helped you consider factors such as differences in socioeconomic status, gender, and culture between you and the student that may be contributing to the disconnect. This should propel you into the second step in reflection—gathering further information that will help you better understand this student and your own reaction to him or her. You may want to learn more about the child's culture and family context; remember that you will have to be diligent about monitoring your own preconceptions and expectations. Revisit Table 7.5: Checklist for Conducting Critical Self-Reflection and Analysis to be sure you have fully questioned your own attitudes. After gathering this information, you need to consider the implications for your practice. Does your reflection suggest you have been subtly communicating your low expectations to this student? Did you recognize that you have been ignoring the student because you don't know how to relate to him or her? If the answer to these questions is yes, you need to decide on a plan of action that will show authentic care and help promote the student's engagement with learning. This may involve greater sensitivity to cultural miscommunication, getting to know the student's community, building on the student's interests, and focusing on ways to build successful experiences. You may want to invoke some antiracist teaching strategies to help classmates confront their preconceptions. Finally, you need to revisit this reflective process. It may be that you slip back into unhealthy patterns and find yourself unfairly judging the student. Hopefully you find that reflective practice has helped you to finally connect with the student and promote more engaged learning. If you truly believe that education is the great equalizer, providing the possibility for social mobility and for human dignity, you must be prepared to teach in ways that make this possible for *all* students.

Discussion Questions

1. How do schools reproduce social inequality? How might your practice challenge this trend?
2. How have your cultural blind spots been challenged through the reading and exercises in this chapter? How do you think this will make you a more culturally responsive teacher?

3. Describe one recent curricular unit you have taught or observed that could be revamped using the recommendations for multicultural curriculum development or antiracist pedagogy.

Further Resources

1. Abboud, R., Chong, J., Gray, D., Kaderdina, R., Masongsong, M., & Rahman, K. M. (2002). *The kit: A manual by youth to combat racism through education*. Ottawa, ON: United Nations Association in Canada.

   This document is intended for youth facilitators to use in racism workshops, but many of the learning activities could effectively be used in a classroom. The document also provides some interesting preliminary background on Canadian policies and issues.

2. Caduto, M. J., & Bruchac, J. (1997). *Keepers of the Earth: Native American stories and environmental activities for children*. Golden, CO: Fulcrum Publishing.

   This book is an excellent resource that helps children understand stewardship of the environment from an Aboriginal perspective.

3. *Stop racism* website (2013) at www.stopracism.ca

   Lest we think racism is a problem of the past, this website includes news stories that highlight current controversies with respect to racism including Aboriginal land claims, dress code restrictions for athletes, hate crimes, and media issues.

4. *Understanding race* website (2011) at www.understandingrace.org/lived/index.html.

   This website provides some fascinating activities, quizzes, videos, and interactivities on race that may help dispel myths and stereotypes among your students.

The Legal, Economic, and Political Aspects of Education

Learning Objectives

After reading this chapter, you should understand

1. How the Canadian Constitution assigns responsibility to the provinces
2. How provinces and territories oversee education in their respective jurisdictions
3. The role of local school boards in school governance
4. The role of school councils in school governance
5. The role of teachers and students in shaping Canadian education
6. How schools and teachers are evaluated

The Core Cycle of Teaching Activities

Students and teachers do not automatically appear in school buildings each morning for 185 to 200 days per year. Towns, cities, and groups of parents do not build schools on a whim. People build school buildings and other people learn and teach inside those buildings within a long-standing and complex legal, policy, and financial framework. In this chapter we look at the details of that framework, aiming to understand especially the impacts it has on the day-to-day work of teachers.

During most of their days in school buildings, teachers focus on curriculum, instruction, and assessment; they also complete administrative tasks, such as taking attendance and attending staff meetings; they meet parents; and they supervise lunchrooms, field trips, and student clubs. But they come to school for one main reason: to engage in the core activities of instruction. Think of this core cycle of activities as a three-strand braided rope where one strand is curriculum, the second is instruction, and the third is assessment (see Figure 8.1), what one educator calls the **CIA rope** (curriculum, instruction, assessment; Tucker, 2013). Without all three strands the rope will not have the required strength. In this metaphor, the sheath is the classroom ethos, the social space in which students and teachers do their work together. The sheath keeps the strands from unravelling and it protects them from damage.

CIA rope
A metaphor used to describe the core cycle of activities that teachers engage in. The rope is envisioned as a three-stranded braid where one strand is curriculum, the second is instruction, and the third is assessment. Without all three strands the rope will not have the required strength.

Other courses in your degree will focus on the component parts of this cycle. The curriculum—what we expect children to learn—is prescribed by school jurisdictions, as articulated in Chapter 3. Jurisdictions may be as small as one independent school or as large as a whole nation, as is the case in Great Britain, which sets a national curriculum. In Canada, provinces establish the curriculum but local school boards and individual schools add to and adapt what the provinces prescribe. School authorities at all levels expect teachers to teach what the curriculum guidelines specify.

Working within the broad parameters outlined by provincial Ministries of Education, teachers plan and carry out their instruction. In fact, those who supervise teachers regularly ask about planning. Rightly, they want to know if teachers have their overall plans ready for the whole academic year or semester. And they want to know if teachers have plans for each unit that show what learning activities the students will be engaged in for each day of the respective units. Some school principals may even want to see the teacher's plans for each portion of each instructional block in a school day—in other words, how the teacher and students will spend every minute of each respective unit. A few American school districts have taken such planning out of teachers' hands altogether, prescribing and providing the exact curriculum materials and detailed instructional plans for every lesson being taught by every teacher in the school district. So far, no Canadian school district has gone that far, preferring to respect the professional judgment of the teachers.

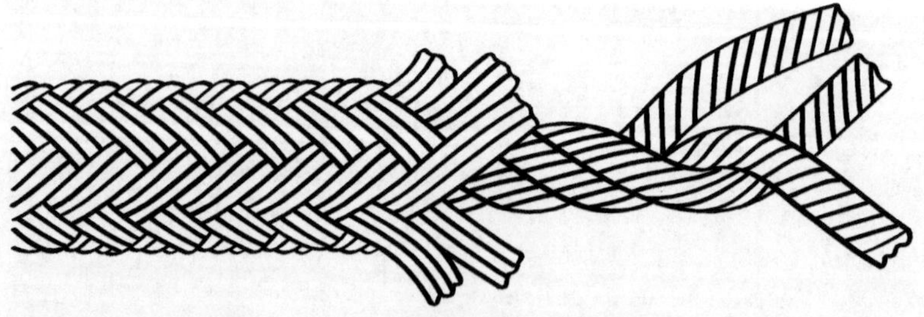

FIGURE 8.1 The CIA Rope

Educators understand assessment of instruction dramatically differently now compared to even two decades ago. From the beginnings of mass education in the 19th century, assessment meant assessment of student work to find out whether or not, or to what degree, students understand the work. In short, did they pass? In the last few decades, phrases such as *assessment for learning* and *assessment as learning* have appeared in educational language. Before these phrases and the mindset they reflect became normal in educational thought, a diagram of the connections between curriculum, instruction, and assessment could have appeared as a straight-line progression without much protest from any corner: The jurisdiction set the curriculum, teachers planned and carried out instruction, and they assessed students' grasp of what they had taught. Students' grades, such as an individual student's grade of 91% or a class average of 68% on a given test, indicated student learning.

Educators now view this process as a cycle (i.e., a circle) because of the recognition that assessment also contains rich information about the instruction itself, not just about what students have or have not learned. A 68% class average on a unit test, for example, may indicate something about the teacher's instruction if no one in the class could answer question #6 correctly or if the students in a same-grade classroom down the hall, with a different teacher, earned a class average of 81% on the same test. Presenting curriculum, instruction, and assessment as a cycle reminds educators that assessment is not the end of the work. Professional educators approach assessment self-critically because they want to recalibrate their instructional approaches before teaching that same material again. They also recognize that assessment gives them information about the needs of individual students so they may differentiate instruction for those students.

The diagram in Figure 8.1 illustrates the core cycle of teachers' work quite well, but it ignores the context in which teachers do their work. As the authors of an educational foundations textbook, we concern ourselves with curriculum, instruction, and assessment as well as the kind of learning and teaching space—the immediate classroom context—that teachers create over time. But we also ask about the wider contexts in which teachers carry out the activities of teaching. What are the philosophical currents that shape various societies' educational ideals? What political forces act on schools? Throughout history, what have various societies expected of schools, and how have those societies tried to meet those expectations? We have treated these and other related questions throughout this book because the answers societies give to these foundational questions shape what members of those societies expect teachers to do each day. In fact, teacher-candidates and teachers new to the profession often discover that society, or at least local (and vocal) representatives of it, hold expectations for teachers that are not written in any policy manual or set of regulations. In fact, sometimes those expectations are the exact opposite of what the regulations prescribe.

Teachers might wish that they could simply get up in the morning and do their work—this is a rather widespread and, on occasion, justifiable sentiment, especially when teachers conclude that they face more new initiatives than they can possibly implement, leading to what one author has called *initiative fatigue* (Reeves, 2010). One difficulty with the desire simply to go to a classroom and do one's work is that so many other people define teachers' work. In this chapter we set that work in its policy context by looking behind the scenes, so to speak, to identify those other people. We ask how the Canadian Constitution, provincial governments, school boards, school councils, and administrators help define the work that teachers must do. In doing so, we show that for teachers to do their work, many other people have to do their work as well. We will begin that examination of the legal, funding, and policy contexts of Canadian teachers' work by noting the broad legal parameters set for education in Canada by the Constitution.

This chapter focuses specifically on the policy, governance, and financial aspects of Canadian education. Teachers everywhere, including Canadian teachers, carry out their core instructional activities in specific policy contexts—someone governs their school. Before any teacher even receives a job offer for a specific post or classroom, someone has determined that all the schools in a jurisdiction or at least that specific school will be financed in this way rather than that way. A group of people have come to some kind of agreement about the ideals that this specific school or all the schools in the jurisdiction will aim at. Someone has decided who will control the curriculum, who will write or approve textbooks, who will hire teachers, and how those teachers will be paid. Someone has made these decisions plus a thousand more.

Like every other nation, Canada has established the legal parameters by which such policies are made. In our case, the provincial governments have control over educational policies. As we noted with reference to Great Britain, some nations have a national educational structure with a national curriculum (Germany, France, and Kenya are three other examples of the dozens that are possible). For reasons we will make clear, Canada's founders passed educational power on to the provinces. The original four provinces (New Brunswick, Nova Scotia, Ontario, and Quebec) and every province that has joined Confederation since all have specific policies governing matters of education.

Governing Canadian Education

The Canadian Constitution likely never comes to most Canadian teachers' or students' minds during a typical school day (other than in a social studies class, of course). Although largely out of sight, the Constitution nevertheless gives broad shape to teachers' work. We begin this governance section by examining the Constitution and its provisions for education in Canada, noting especially the division of responsibilities for education between the federal and provincial governments.

The Constitutional Provisions for Education

British North America (BNA) Act
The legislation passed in 1867 by the British Parliament to create the legal entity known as the Dominion of Canada. The act included specific provisions for education, specifying which level of government has control over and responsibility for maintaining schools, and the relative protections for and rights of linguistic minorities regarding education.

The British Parliament created the legal entity known as the Dominion of Canada when it passed the **British North America (BNA) Act** in 1867. The BNA Act included specific provisions for education that were largely carried forward into the Constitution Act of 1982. In both cases, those provisions focus on two matters: specifying which level of government has control over and responsibility for maintaining schools, and the relative protections for and rights of religious and linguistic minorities regarding education.

Under the BNA Act, Ontario and Quebec (known as Upper and Lower Canada for some years before 1867) joined New Brunswick and Nova Scotia to form the initial Canadian Confederation. Section 93 of the BNA Act guaranteed provincial control over education. Obviously, this assignment of responsibility to the provinces implies in the most general terms that the federal government has no responsibility for education. It also implies that no province must provide for or oversee education in the same way as any other province. Regarding the first implication, the federal government, while having no constitutional responsibility for education, obviously has an interest in education. For example, on behalf of all Canadians, it has an interest in ensuring that Canada have a well-educated workforce to enable it to compete in a global economy. However, Section 91 of the BNA Act assigned to the federal government complete control over all matters related to First Nations, including education, a matter we will return to later in the chapter.

Section 93 of the BNA Act also guaranteed the Protestant, English-speaking minority in Quebec and the Roman Catholic, French-speaking minority in Ontario the right to operate their own tax-supported schools. In effect, parents had the constitutional right to provide denominational education for their children, a provision requiring much more nuancing now than it did in the 19th century, given the social changes that have taken place between the historical context of the BNA Act and today. Despite the restriction of the wording of Section 93 to *denominational education*, Section 93 implicitly pertained to both religion and language. The Roman Catholic minority in Ontario was largely French speaking and the Protestant minority in Quebec was largely English speaking, so Section 93 dealt with the rights of both linguistic and religious minorities in a single paragraph.

Even Section 93 has its own history. The Ontario government did not extend funding for Grades 11–13 in Roman Catholic schools until the 1980s, after various court challenges. Nova Scotia and New Brunswick, the two other provinces that joined Canada originally, interpreted Section 93 to be restricted to the two provinces named in the section. As other provinces joined Confederation, some developed separate schools in light of Section 93 (Alberta, Saskatchewan, and Newfoundland) while others did not, believing the application of the section to be restricted to Ontario and Quebec. In the case of Manitoba, which joined Canada in 1870, the funding of Protestant and Catholic school systems was guaranteed in the Manitoba Act. But the Manitoba provincial government created a single public school system in 1890, overturning the guarantees to the denominations. This action, now known as the Manitoba Schools Question, led to a constitutional crisis that was eventually

THE CANADIAN PRESS/Stf-Ron Poling

FIGURE 8.2 In 1982, Queen Elizabeth, the British sovereign, signed the Proclamation of Canada's Constitution Act.

settled by the Privy Council in London in favour of funded denominational schools. We already provided some detail related to the Manitoba story in Chapter 5.

The educational provisions in the 1867 BNA Act have been carried forward into Canada's 1982 Constitution Act and Charter of Rights and Freedoms. Section 15 of the Constitution Act of 1982 largely reflects the provisions of Section 93 of the BNA Act. Section 23 of the Charter guarantees the right of parents who speak the minority language in a particular province to have their children educated in the minority language in publicly funded schools. In practice, this guarantee means that there are publicly funded English schools in Quebec and publicly funded French schools in the other provinces and the territories.

The Canadian educational landscape continues to change. Secularization, for example, has meant that what were or may have been called *Protestant school boards* in Ontario have become *public* school boards. Religious practices and religious instruction disappeared in Ontario public schools after landmark court cases in the 1980s and 1990s. Through a constitutional amendment in 1999, Quebec replaced its denominational school system with linguistically based school boards, thereby ending nearly four centuries of full or partial church control over education. Newfoundland, which had a denominational school system since 1843 but only joined Canada in 1949, abolished its denominational system in 1998 over the protests of Roman Catholic and Pentecostal churches and educators.

Section 29 of the Charter of Rights and Freedoms recognizes the right of all Canadians to provide for their children the kind of education they desire, including religious education. Various courts have made clear since 1982 that the Charter does not give parents the right not to educate their children; children must be educated. In 1995, the Supreme Court of Canada (*Bal v. Ontario*) declined to rule on an Ontario Court of Appeals finding that Section 15 of the 1982 Constitution Act did not imply that the Ontario government was required to fund religious schools other than member schools of funded Catholic boards. That is, the Charter right to choice in education does not imply the right to funding of that education (see Chapter 7 for further discussion of this issue).

Uniquely Canadian Patterns in Educational Provision

Like lawmakers everywhere, the authors of the 1867 BNA Act and the 1982 Constitution Act and Charter of Rights and Freedoms meant to write unambiguously. But as the Manitoba Schools Question made clear, laws are open to interpretation, and in these cases courts need to render judgments. Since 1982, various parties have asked the courts to clarify the clauses of Canada's current Constitution. In recognizing and funding denominational education, Canada is not unique—many nations fund schools operated by religious organizations, but by doing so it is numbered among a minority of nations. These provisions also produce some interesting anomalies. For example, both Penetanguishene (Ontario) and St. Albert (Alberta) have predominantly Roman Catholic populations. The *public* schools in both these cities are Roman Catholic and the *separate* schools are Protestant, or secular.

The BNA Act assigned responsibility for all matters related to First Nations Canadians to the federal government. Sections 92 and 93 of the BNA Act, which assign responsibility for education to the provinces, do not apply to First Nations education.

School Acts and Education Acts

With responsibility for education assigned to them by the Constitution, the provinces and territories all have passed and now maintain their own Education Act or School Act. In these acts, the provincial and territorial departments specify such matters as who must or may attend school, who may teach in school, who will oversee the school, how schools will be funded, how long the school year will last, and myriad other matters. Throughout this section, we will examine in detail the clauses typically included in School Acts, keeping in mind what they imply for teachers and their work. We will begin by looking at one province's School Act, both its history and its contemporary form. New Brunswick provides an interesting case study because, while parts of its story are typical of other Canadian provinces, it also went through a legal crisis that put some provisions of the BNA Act to the test. Below we have provided some detail of New Brunswick's educational and legal history, but we have omitted a great deal of the story, which at points reads like a detective novel.

The Schools Act of New Brunswick

For the nine years before 1867, when New Brunswick became one of the founding provinces of Canada, its schools operated under the Parish Schools Act of 1858. This act gave a provincial board of education ultimate authority for schools, but it did not require it to establish schools. Some constituencies still operate this way today—for example Kenya, where women's self-help co-operatives, towns and cities, churches and mosques, and various other agencies have organized and operate schools. In the case of New Brunswick, the Roman Catholic and Anglican churches organized most schools and they received some government support for doing so. But without any requirement for teacher certification and lacking a provincial curriculum or inspection system, many of these schools suffered in quality. By 1871, the new provincial government, having grown increasingly concerned about attendance rates and the quality of education on offer, followed the lead of Ontario, which had formed a public school system under the leadership of Egerton Ryerson in 1844, and of Nova Scotia, which had created its public school system in 1864, three years before Confederation.

The bill proposing a nonreligious, public school system in New Brunswick first came before the legislature in 1870 and, after some bumps, became law as the Common Schools Act in 1871, taking effect on the first day of 1872. It allowed teachers to open and close the school day with a Bible reading and the Lord's Prayer, but it made clear that no other religious instruction was to take place in New Brunswick's schools. Significantly, it placed control of all New Brunswick schools in the hands of a provincial board of education.

Reaction to the new Common Schools Act was swift and fierce. Opponents argued that the act placed the duty to educate their children—which belonged to parents—in the hands of the state. Further, it trampled on the rights of religious educators who had operated schools under the 1858 Parish Schools Act. Opponents appealed to the federal cabinet under the *disallowance clause* in the BNA Act (a clause that allowed the federal Privy Council to disallow laws passed in the provinces). When that effort failed, two Members of Parliament from New Brunswick made a motion in the House of Commons to overturn the Common Schools Act, again without success. In response to the Canadian government having sought advice, the British crown gave its opinion that schools in existence before January 1, 1872, had no rights or legitimate claims. In 1873, the New Brunswick Supreme Court gave the same opinion, leaving no recourse for religious educators in New Brunswick.

This New Brunswick story has significance for all Canadian provinces because it functioned, in effect, as a test of the BNA Act clauses regarding the educational rights of religious minorities. The BNA Act specified that the French Catholic minority in Ontario and the English Protestant minority in Quebec had the right to provincially funded schools. It also specifically stated that other provinces joining Confederation could, if they wished, extend the same funding (as Alberta and Saskatchewan ultimately did). But the New Brunswick case illustrates that provinces choosing not to extend funding to such schools had parliamentary and jurisprudential support on their side.

The story of the New Brunswick Common Schools Act did not end with the parliamentary and legal actions we have described. The citizens of one Acadian and predominantly Catholic town, Caraquet, disapproved strongly of the provisions of the Common Schools Act and, in essence, decided not to implement it. The protests and responses to the protests ultimately led to two deaths in Caraquet. This escalated response to the act helped the provincial government realize the level of commitment to religious education among provincial inhabitants and prompted meetings between the province and those arguing for church-based education. The province amended a number of important clauses in the act related to church-owned property, religious instruction, curriculum, and teacher certification.

The New Brunswick Education Act Today

As do the governments in nearly all jurisdictions, the Government of New Brunswick posts all New Brunswick laws online. The Education Act and its regulations are presented in five sections:

- School Administration
- School Districts and Subdistricts
- Governance Structure
- Pupil Transportation
- Teacher Certification

Compared to other provinces, these five headings are simultaneously both typical and atypical. They are typical inasmuch as all the provinces' Education Acts or School Acts need to specify, in great detail and with great care, who takes responsibility for what, how they are to carry out their respective responsibilities, and what happens if they don't. Given that these acts must specify the parameters for educational provision in entire provinces, with all the variety of contexts and needs that implies, one might expect to find a lot of detail. The New Brunswick Education Act is atypical inasmuch as another province's act might, for example, omit "Pupil Transportation" as a heading, but might include "Curriculum" (which in New Brunswick's case appears under "School Administration").

Looking beyond New Brunswick's initial five headings proves interesting. Under the first heading, "School Administration," the act includes regulations regarding such matters as these:

- School attendance
- Administration
- Pupils
- Teacher certification appeals

To give a taste of the level of detail that school regulations include, note the following details related to school attendance, the first subsection of this section of the Education Act.

Courtesy of Dr. Wilson/Wiki Commons

FIGURE 8.3 Caraquet, New Brunswick, was the scene of an early and important test of Canada's constitutional provisions for the education of religious minorities.

School hours

3(1) School hours shall include all the time between the opening and the closing of school for the day.

3(2) The Minister shall provide a minimum number of hours of instruction per day, or the equivalent in a school year, exclusive of the noon recess, as follows

(a) for kindergarten and grades one, two, four hours

(b) for grades three to eight inclusive, five hours; and

(c) for grades nine to twelve inclusive, five and one-half hours.

Closure of schools on holidays

4 No school shall operate on a holiday.

School vacations

5 There shall be in all schools

(a) a summer vacation beginning on the first day of July and ending on the Saturday immediately preceding Labour Day, unless otherwise varied by the Minister for any school district for any school year,

(b) a winter vacation of two weeks, beginning on the Saturday immediately preceding Christmas Day, unless otherwise varied by the Minister for any school district for any school year, and

(c) a spring vacation of one week, beginning on the Saturday immediately preceding the first Monday in the month of March. (Attorney General of New Brunswick, 1997)

We have cited here roughly 60% of one page in a 20-page document containing the regulations under one of the five sections of regulations in New Brunswick's Education Act. This citation from the act illustrates two typical characteristics of all such School Acts, and, for that matter, all laws. First, note the degree of specificity; the Education Act is comprehensive and deals with all aspects of operating a school system in a province. While the Department of Education needs to speak generally because its act must apply in a great variety of circumstances, not all of which can be predicted, it also needs to balance generality with specificity. The Department of Education defines the school day for each grade, it makes clear the length of the school year, and it forbids schools from opening on a holiday.

Second, note the degree of clarity in this sample of regulatory language. Staff at the Department of Education and lawyers in the Department of Justice or at the provincial attorney general's office do not want to spend their time interpreting ambiguous regulations for school board members and staff, school principals, parents, students, and classroom teachers. This combination of specificity and clarity—typical of the School Act or Education Act in every jurisdiction—usually enables education officials in the Department of Education in any provincial capital to set appropriate and legal policies and to give clear answers to questions that students, parents, teachers, and principals might ask. Likewise, it supports school board officials in central offices, principals in schools, and teachers in individual classrooms in their efforts to understand what they must do, what they may do, and what they may not do.

Provincial and Territorial Departments of Education

Provincial and territorial Departments of Education fulfill their constitutional responsibility for education by passing a School Act or Education Act. Someone must organize and carry out the work specified or implied in those acts, and provincial Departments of Education end up with a great variety of work. In this section we provide a sample of some of the branches of the various Ministries.

British Columbia

British Columbia has seven main branches in its Ministry of Education, of which Business, Technology and Online Services is one. In its turn, it has five sub-branches, which we list here to underline how complex the work of fulfilling a province's constitutional responsibility has become: Student Certification Branch, Business Integration, Provincial Learning Network, Information Technology Management Branch, and Open School BC (modelled after Britain's Open University). British Columbia's other six branches within the Ministry of Education (with summaries of their responsibilities) are as follows:

- Liaison: connections among education stakeholders in British Columbia
- Safe Schools: bullying, critical incident and emergency response preparedness, gangs, student physical and mental health
- Governance, Legislation, and Regulation: all matters of governance
- Learning: Aboriginal education, curriculum, assessment, diversity, French instruction, e-learning

- Open Government and Community Partnerships: enhances collaboration with and participation of the public in developing educational policy
- Resource Management: operational and capital funding, financial compliance by school boards (British Columbia Ministry of Education, 2013)

Saskatchewan

The branches in Saskatchewan's Ministry of Education reveal some different priorities from those of British Columbia, but also some overlapping concerns. They are as follows:

- Communications: supports the Minister of Education's communication needs and oversees media relations, advertising, and opinion research
- Corporate Services: financial oversight and budget development within the Ministry of Education (excluding funding for schools)
- Early Years: leadership to early years (0–8) educators, including community-based programs, monitoring and supporting early learning and child care, as well pre-kindergarten and kindergarten programs
- Education Funding: financial support to school districts
- Human Resource Services: advises on teacher classification and oversees staffing within the Ministry
- Information Management and Support: all technology (except student instruction in technology)
- Infrastructure: supports school divisions' building programs
- Provincial Library: legislative and policy framework for the operations of the Saskatchewan public library system
- Literacy Office: public awareness of literacy
- Stakeholder Relations: connections among education stakeholders as well as all ministerial correspondence
- Strategic Policy: helps set and implement government educational policy, as well as oversees privacy and access regulations
- Student Achievement and Supports: curriculum, instruction, assessment
- Teachers' Superannuation Commission: teacher pensions, disability, dental plan and insurance (Saskatchewan Ministry of Education, 2012)

We suggest that Saskatchewan's 12 branches invite critical examination. We want especially to know how many branches directly support the work of students and teachers and how many mainly support other branches of the department. Perhaps British Columbia's seven branches could do the same work done by Saskatchewan's 12 branches. If so, should Saskatchewan have fewer branches? Recognizably, British Columbia may have layers of bureaucracy buried in its sub-branches, but on the surface they seem to have constructed a simpler organization.

Nova Scotia

We jump to Nova Scotia for a third example of the organization of a provincial Department of Education. Nova Scotia places responsibility for K–12 education in one branch of

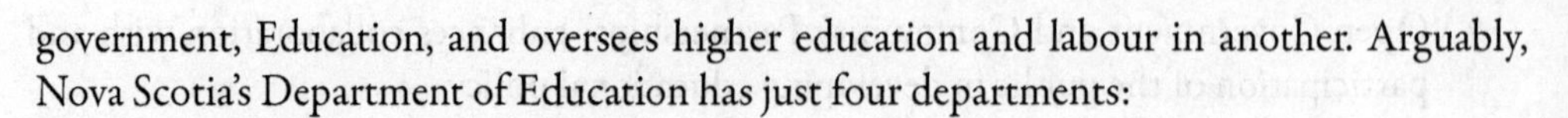

government, Education, and oversees higher education and labour in another. Arguably, Nova Scotia's Department of Education has just four departments:

- Acadian and French Language Services
- Public Schools
- Corporate Policy
- Corporate Services

On first glance, these four branches appear to offer a much simpler model than either British Columbia or Saskatchewan. But on inspection we find it to be at least as complex as the two examples above, with 11 sub-branches under public schools, four under corporate policy, and five more under corporate services:

- Acadian and French Language Services
- Public Schools (with 11 branches)
    - African Canadian Services
    - Education Quality Services
    - English Program Services
    - Equity and Special Projects
    - Evaluation Services
    - French Second Language Services
    - Learning Resources and Technology Services
    - Mi'kmaq Liaison Office
    - Regional Education Service
    - School Board Labour Relations
    - Student Services
- Corporate policy (with four branches)
    - Agencies, Boards, and Commissions
    - Departmental Library
    - Freedom of Information and Protection of Privacy
    - Publishing
- Corporate Services (with five branches)
    - Facilities Management
    - Finance
    - Information Technology
    - Statistics and Data Management
    - Teacher Certification

We will not decide here whether Nova Scotia's Department of Education has four branches or 21. We do want to underline that the work of Departments of Education is complex. In contemporary settings, offering education in a whole province demands that a province provide a great variety of services and programs to a variety of stakeholder groups.

All of us, and most certainly government officials, need to remind ourselves that students and teachers are the main stakeholder groups for whom all these branches and departments should be working. When those main groups fall out of focus, observers of the work of provincial Departments of Education may legitimately want to ask pointed questions about the growth of bureaucracy.

Local School Boards

Historically and very typically, as the population of a district or community grew, parents would express their desire to see a school established. Under the BNA Act, the province had responsibility to provide such a school; in practice, however, the provinces could not operate such schools from the capital. Nor did they want to. Intuitively, it makes sense to give responsibility for a local school to those closest to and most affected by that school. Thus, provinces gave responsibility to locally elected school boards who hired professional staff to oversee the schools in a district. In the mid-1800s this might include only one superintendent whose job was to hire principals and inspect schools. The second person hired might well be a truant officer, someone meant to enforce the compulsory attendance regulations. With urbanization and a growing list of what services the public expected schools to provide, staff numbers grew. A contemporary board might have curriculum experts, literacy consultants, second-language program officers, even psychologists who work with students from several schools in the district. Ironically—especially from a historical perspective—one person absent from such a contemporary board might be the truant officer.

school boards
Locally elected officials given responsibility by each province to run the local school district. School board members are elected (usually every two to three years) and hire professional staff to oversee the schools in a district.

Consolidation of Boards

For decades, waves of school board consolidation have resulted in each province having fewer school boards (see Table 8.1). Declining rural populations and the efficiencies of centralized services drove some of this consolidation. To illustrate efficiencies, a larger school district can hire a literacy or science curriculum specialist to assist teachers in reaching the school district's goals. Smaller school units usually cannot afford such specialization.

Responsibilities of School Boards

Through each respective School Act or Education Act, provincial governments delegate much authority for education to local school boards. School boards end up charged with a variety of tasks, including such typical responsibilities as these:

- Planning for the jurisdiction, setting priorities for the system in light of community wishes, available resources, and sound educational practice
- Setting goals for the jurisdiction, ensuring education stays in step with today's world
- Evaluating the school board superintendent
- Adopting an annual budget for the school system
- Making policy to guide the administration and employees toward district goals

Courtesy of Michelle Welsh

FIGURE 8.4 Typical advertising related to school board elections in Canada. Canadian school board elections typically happen every two or three years, usually in late fall.

- Communicating with the community and staff on behalf of the jurisdiction
- Educating others, with a goal of ensuring education is given a high priority by the public and to make the community aware of the jurisdiction's achievements
- Gathering information to make sound decisions
- Adjudicating in policy disputes

The above list is adapted from the Alberta School Boards Association, but it overlaps significantly with similar lists from across Canada.

An important distinction to keep in mind regarding school boards is that between the elected members of the board and the staff they employ in the central office. Every two years (in some cases every three or four years), the voters within the boundaries of a school district elect a slate of officers to the local school board. In Ontario, Saskatchewan, and Alberta they may vote for members of only one board, the separate school board or the public school board. That elected board then carries the responsibilities given to it under the School Act or Education Act of the province or territory in question. Legally, they become the stewards of that district's schools for the duration of their term. By law, members of this board are members of the public, a reflection of the period when free, mass education began and the government expected a (very) local group of citizens to give oversight to their local school. In most jurisdictions, school board staff are prohibited from running; most jurisdictions also have term limits on school board service. The respective School Act spells out other such regulations.

A trained educator not working in a school in the district may run for school board office, but for the most part members of the board are not experts in education—they are interested citizens. We grant that sometimes they are interested citizens with a single grievance or agenda who believe that the school board is the best venue in which to address their concern. School board legislation thus creates a situation where those charged with

TABLE 8.1 School Districts in Canada

Jurisdiction	School Boards
Newfoundland	5
Prince Edward Island	1
Nova Scotia	8 (7 English, 1 French)
New Brunswick	7 (4 English, 3 French)
Quebec	69 (60 French, 9 English)
Ontario	70
Manitoba	38 public (Catholic schools do not have separate boards; they participate in the Manitoba Federation of Independent Schools)
Saskatchewan	26
Alberta	66
British Columbia	59

oversight of an education system may not know how schools optimally operate day to day. So school boards hire professional educators to carry on the daily contact with schools. Ideally, the elected board works in partnership with its central office staff—it asks for guidance in setting policies for the district. But the people immediately responsible to carry out those policies work in the central office and they, in turn, work with the individual schools in the school district. We note this distinction because people often do not clarify the phrase *school board* when they use it, sometimes meaning the elected board and sometimes meaning the central office staff.

School Councils

In the history of school councils, the observer of how Canadian education is governed confronts a deep irony: Overlapping in time with the nationwide movement to consolidate school boards, the movement to authorize **school councils** gathered steam. The consolidation movement centralized school authority in fewer board offices within any given province. Some of these central offices oversee schools in a geographic area larger than some sovereign states; for example, the Chinook School Division in southwestern Saskatchewan, which covers 42,750 square kilometres, is larger than Switzerland, which is only 41,285 square kilometres. Inevitably, parents and guardians of children in local schools, for example, in Consul, Saskatchewan, will have less influence on the governance and management of their local school when the Chinook School Division office is in Swift Current, which is 215 kilometres away. In short, consolidation reduced local control—critics of consolidation say it removed local control altogether.

school council
An elected group that oversees and directs the work of one school. School councils share responsibility with their respective school boards. School council membership always includes parents, often teachers, and sometimes administrators.

Beginning in the 1980s, provinces have attempted to restore a measure of local control by creating school councils. Across Canada, school councils' responsibilities range from advising schools on matters of shared concern to hiring teachers.

School Council Responsibilities

The list below is a composite, drawn from across Canada. Not all jurisdictions grant school councils all these responsibilities, but in general school councils advise and consult on matters such as these:

- Overseeing school design, planning, renovations, improvement of the physical plant
- Developing school education plans, curriculum, and related policies; achieving school and district learning and achievement goals, and provincial or district policies related to religious education and education about religion
- Developing a positive learning climate in the school
- Understanding student and community needs and communicating with parents and the wider community formally and informally
- Encouraging school building use by the wider community
- Hiring teachers
- Maintaining and overseeing the enforcement of student conduct codes
- Participating in or advising on hiring the school principal; participating in performance reviews of the school principal or the school
- Participating in planning the school budget and spending
- Participating in student transportation decisions

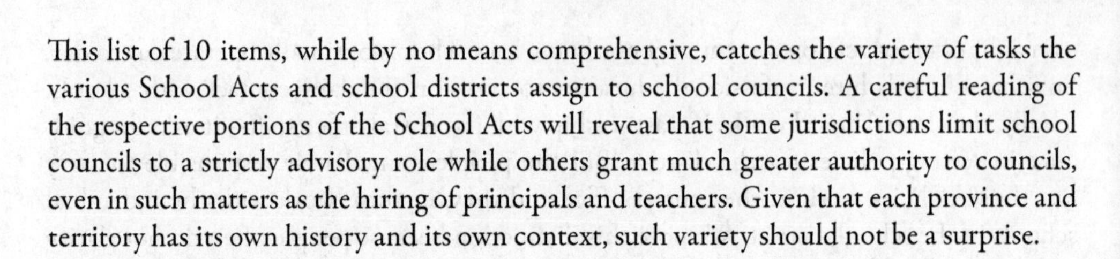

This list of 10 items, while by no means comprehensive, catches the variety of tasks the various School Acts and school districts assign to school councils. A careful reading of the respective portions of the School Acts will reveal that some jurisdictions limit school councils to a strictly advisory role while others grant much greater authority to councils, even in such matters as the hiring of principals and teachers. Given that each province and territory has its own history and its own context, such variety should not be a surprise.

School Council Eligibility, Composition, and Term Limits

With 13 different School Acts in place, the regulations governing the composition of Canada's school councils vary widely. We provide details from a few examples to illustrate this variety.

- In British Columbia, a council consists of the school principal, one teacher, three parents, and one student.
- Under New Brunswick's regulations, council membership can vary from six to twelve members, the majority of which must be parents or guardians of children in attendance at the school or their designated representatives. The council also includes a teacher elected by his or her colleagues, a student elected by the students, a representative of the Home and School Association where one exists, and up to two community members (appointed by the parent members). New Brunswick does not allow the principal to serve on the council, although he or she attends its meetings.
- Nova Scotia elementary school councils consist of six members, including the principal, two parents or guardians, one support staff member, one teacher, and one community representative. Secondary school councils in Nova Scotia have all of the above as well as one more parent or guardian, one more teacher, and two students.
- School councils in Saskatchewan have between five and nine elected parents or community members, the principal, one teacher, up to three students (in Grades 10–12), and one First Nations representative.

These figures underline again the important point that Canadian education is characterized by variety.

Term limits vary across Canada, from one year (council members who are not parents of a child at the respective school in British Columbia) to two years (Yukon) to not more than three years (Nova Scotia). Some people are prohibited from serving on a school council. For example, school board officials may not serve on school councils in British Columbia and Nova Scotia, and a teacher in a school may not serve on the school council as a parent or community member in Nova Scotia or New Brunswick or as parent committee members.

Provinces have prohibited school councils from certain kinds of activities and discussions as well. Here are some examples drawn from the regulations of several provinces:

- Discussion or action related to any individual student
- Action related to any individual teacher
- Paying council members for serving on the council

Who Inspects the School? Evaluation and Accountability

With so many different bodies and agencies overseeing the work of educators, who actually inspects the school? Who inspects the individual classroom? These are important questions that teachers and principals ask and even students ask. The public wants answers to these questions as well.

At its simplest, provincial governments work with school districts, and districts work with schools and school councils. Such a system has built into it an implicit and somewhat hierarchical structure for accountability and evaluation. Given that provincial governments, school board members, and school council members all take office because of voters' actions, we assume that they must account for themselves not only to someone higher up in the hierarchy but also to the voting public. Ideally, accountability in education works in both directions.

Typically, the school superintendent inspects the school. A century or more ago, in fact, many school districts had an officer known as a *school inspector*. A quick web search using the string "Britain school inspection" will reveal that Britain has a national agency whose job is to evaluate schools (see www.schoolinspectionservice.co.uk). Regardless of name, someone remains in charge of evaluating schools' performance, and it is usually the superintendent of the school district who does this job. A district may seek help from a provincial Department of Education in its attempt to deal with a school that consistently fails. In cases of failing schools, a district typically allocates additional funds to build up the instructional program and thereby improve the school climate or support student learning.

Formally, district offices also evaluate principals. As we noted in the section on school councils, some councils also play a role here. A school district ordinarily deals with an administrator it concludes to be incapable of running his or her school; in all but a few cases, districts do not seek provincial help in such cases.

Teacher evaluation is another matter. Many school districts leave it to the principal to evaluate or oversee the evaluation of teachers. In some cases, teachers undergo evaluation only during their probationary period. Ideally, teacher evaluation is part of an ongoing and much wider process and is embedded in a thoughtful program of annual professional growth plans and ongoing professional education that leads to additional qualifications or degrees. Such evaluation should combine thoughtful reflection by the teacher her- or himself, as well as evaluation by colleagues and administrators. Jurisdictions around the world are increasingly requiring teachers to engage in ongoing professional education, an elevation of teacher standards that cannot help but further professionalize teaching and enhance student learning.

We noted above that principals evaluate teachers or oversee that evaluation. In addition, some principals assign a teacher to a mentor who may have an informal role in evaluation. Some teachers participate in professional learning communities with staff colleagues (by choice or because their principal compelled them to do so). Those colleagues also often have a part in informal evaluation, especially of teaching plans, instruction, and assessment, and perhaps in other aspects of the professional growth of the teacher being evaluated. Experience has shown that wise administrators do not ask mentors or colleagues to participate in formal evaluations of teachers because it places the mentor in a conflict of interest. Later in this chapter we will return to the work of teachers and how their work is assessed. For now, this brief introduction to professional evaluation gives one a sense of the accountability mechanisms in place in Canadian schools.

First Nations Education

From the beginning of their history on this continent until well after the arrival of Europeans, First Nations peoples educated their children informally and always in the context of daily life in the community. Their educational purposes were to enable the next generations to survive and thrive in their environment. Under the banner of cultural assimilation, the federal government, under the Indian Act, organized a system of residential schools, requiring First Nations children to attend. In 1969, the federal government shifted its policy away from residential schools, most of which had been operated by churches. Following the 1969 shift in policy, schools began to close, but some operated into the 1990s.

CASE STUDY

Residential Schools in Cinema

The 1997 American film *The Education of Little Tree* (directed by Richard Friedenberg) and the 2002 Australian film *Rabbit-Proof Fence* (directed by Phillip Noyce) tell the stories of children placed in residential schools. Both portray events from the viewpoints of the respective children, in the one case an American Indian boy and in the other case two Aboriginal sisters. Both films contain powerful scenes of the brutality of assimilationist policies. Those who originally articulated and supported the racist, assimilationist purposes of residential schools did so in a historical and ideological context in which their understandings of race, culture, and education made sense, at least to those in charge. Generations of people have inherited the cultural damage inflicted by such schools in the name of assimilation. As most who attended them knew at the time and as all Canadians recognize in retrospect, residential schools did not make sense.

As we noted earlier in this chapter, through the Constitution the federal government retained jurisdiction over First Nations education, despite having assigned authority for education generally to the provinces. Through Aboriginal Affairs and Northern Development Canada, the federal government retains final responsibility for and continues to fund First Nations education (at a per-student level that is below provincial per-student levels). Beginning in the 1970s, the federal government began to shift control over education to the First Nations themselves (see Table 8.2).

TABLE 8.2 Where Do First Nations Students Attend School?

Type of School	Approximate Percentage of First Nations Students
On-reserve, band-operated schools	60
Provincially and territorially funded schools (i.e., public schools)	40

In 1948, a Joint Parliamentary Committee on Indian Affairs first recommended that the federal government move away from its residential school model in favour of on-reserve schools and provincially funded public and separate schools—a move from segregation to integration. A 1969 federal government White Paper recommended complete integration of First Nations students, a recommendation opposed by First Nations groups from across Canada. An illuminating retrospective comment appeared in a more recent Senate committee report: "Not only was integration seen as having failed to improve the social and economic conditions of First Nations, it was also not considered an appropriate foundation for educating First Nations children" (St. Germain & Dyck, 2011, p. 8).

The National Indian Brotherhood (the organizational precursor to the Assembly of First Nations) responded to the 1969 White Paper with its own paper on local control of schools. It published a 1972 paper on Indian Control of Indian Education, in which it outlined an educational philosophy centred on parental responsibility and First Nations local control of education. Then–Minister of Indian Affairs Jean Chrétien accepted the proposal as a basis for federal education policy and, since 1973, Canadian federal policy regarding First Nations education has—at least in principle—followed the goals and principles of that 1972 paper.

Who Really Runs Canadian Schools?

Sociologists of education, among others, often ask if schools actually operate the way that governments, school boards, school councils, and principals say they do. In this chapter so far, we have examined many aspects of how Canadian schools are governed. Throughout this section we have raised only a few questions about alignment between what is claimed about schools and what is actually experienced by those who work and learn in them. And we will not raise further questions here. But we do want to note that many people—journalists, academics, disenchanted students, teachers, custodial staff, parents, even principals—raise serious questions about this desired alignment. Recall from Chapter 5 that such criticisms are not new—schools have had critics for as long as there have been schools.

This question of alignment connects to a standard distinction that sociologists make between formal and informal power. Officially, the authority structure for education runs from the Minister of Education down to the kindergarten student. But many Canadian classrooms have a photo of the reigning monarch of England or perhaps the Canadian prime minister on the wall, leading some to infer that even the Minister of Education is not finally in charge. Sociologists answering the question of alignment would ask who really exercises power. Perhaps a particularly vocal or wealthy parent holds sway in the school council. Perhaps a particularly cranky teacher, administrator, or central office official runs roughshod over people and policy because no one wants to get pulled into a conflict. Or perhaps a very popular and charismatic teacher seems to get his or her way with students, colleagues, parents, and administrators. In some cases, a small group of students may intimidate staff and administrators as well as other students and informally end up "ruling the school," as they might put it. We will not explore all the possibilities connected to this question of alignment, which is more properly the focus of educational sociology or political studies in education, but we do want our readers to note that though we focus in this chapter on one view of governance, we recognize that, for the most part, we have presented the official picture, not the picture that a critic might paint.

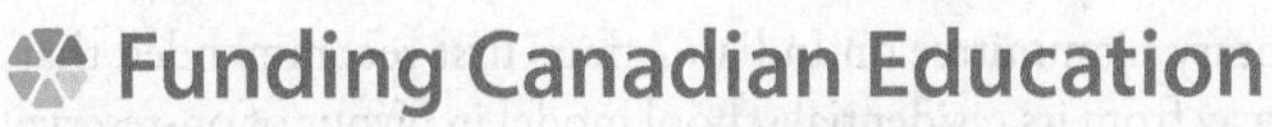

Funding Canadian Education

Funding Public and Separate Schools

Canadians in most provinces are required by law to support a school system with a portion of their property taxes. A portion of their income taxes also goes to schools, inasmuch as the provincial or territorial budget, whose income derives in part from income taxes, includes and funds a Department of Education. Most jurisdictions base school grants on the September 30 registration at each school (or on a combination of the registration on September 30 and on some other date later in the school year). In two of the three provinces with separate school systems (Ontario and Saskatchewan), property owners direct their taxes specifically toward either the separate or the public school system. The exception, Alberta, handles all school funding from the provincial level. At its simplest, this is how public and separate schools in Canada are funded. Independent schools use a variety of other models, some of which we discuss later in this section.

Many nations follow the Canadian pattern of funding schools at the provincial or state level rather than with local funds alone. Speaking in economic terms, in such a model the poorest school in a district gets the same instructional grant as the wealthiest school in that district. And teachers are paid the same regardless of where they teach in a district. In fact, in provinces with a province-wide collective agreement, teachers will receive the same salary for teaching in any school in the province. Compare this funding model to a jurisdiction where school funds derive largely from the school district itself. Over the last decades of the 20th century, such funding schemes have left many urban boards—where the city around them faced postindustrial decline—with little money to operate inner-city schools or attract highly qualified teachers to those schools. The tax money to support schools and many strong teachers fled to the suburbs. In the 21st century, we are witnessing the revitalization and gentrification of urban areas and a corollary suburbanization of poverty. As this process picks up speed, jurisdictions with funding schemes where local taxes are the primary source of school funds will possibly underfund suburban schools while increasing the funding for and attractiveness of their urban schools. They do so simply because the jurisdiction in question has that particular tax and education funding in place. We make this observation as a way to point out that Canada's provinces have adopted funding models that increase equity in education and, in so doing, ultimately increase the cultural and intellectual capital available in our nation. Rather than encouraging the destructive circle where poverty begets poor schools that perpetuate poverty, Canadian funding models generally encourage equality and help break the cycle of poverty.

Funding Formulas in Canadian Provinces

In the above section we noted the similarity of funding models used across Canada—that most provinces combine provincial and local revenue to fund education. That truth notwithstanding, the provinces take different approaches to funding schools. In all cases, the province contributes an annual instructional grant to each respective school district based on the number of students registered. Some provinces expect local boards to levy a local tax and thereby raise a portion of the costs of education. Cities, towns, counties, and municipalities usually raise this tax revenue as part of the taxes charged annually to owners of real property. As we noted, one province provides 100% of educational funding, removing from local school boards the necessity of raising their operating revenue within their community (and also removing from them a measure of control).

The description above, while accurate, misses some of the complexities of providing for and funding education. Calculating the costs of education involves a host of additional and quite specific factors, some of which directly affect teachers, whether in terms of salaries, funds available for teaching materials, or any number of other items that, to be blunt, require money. Here are some examples of the various costs of education:

- The number of staff needed in a school building to allow time for teacher preparation
- Administrative, counselling, maintenance, and custodial staff who are not directly involved in instruction
- Central office staff in such departments as human resources, finance
- Central office staff who provide professional development and direct support to teachers in such areas as subject-area curriculum and instruction
- The cost differences for different grades, different courses and types of programs, and different students
- The cost differences for vulnerable schools, remote schools, and specialized schools
- The costs for educational assistants who work with designated special needs students
- The costs of overseeing home-schooled students registered with schools in the district
- School busing costs

The factors we have listed above do not remain static. For example, for decades educators accepted as commonplace that secondary education cost more to provide than primary education. Secondary schools need laboratory equipment and more specialized teachers (who are typically at a higher step on the salary scale). They will have some smaller classes, like Grade 12 physics, which still require a teacher's full attention. However, in recent years, educators have come to understand the importance of early learning to later school success, especially in literacy and mathematics. The priorities of school budgets have shifted to reflect this awareness. Lowering teacher–student ratios in kindergarten to Grade 3, for example, costs money but pays dividends throughout students' education.

Demographic changes in cities also influence educational costs. With gentrification of a downtown neighbourhood, an inner-city school may need fewer additional resources than it did previously. The reverse may be true as well. As we noted, the suburbanization of poverty will place new financial demands on schools that, perhaps for decades, school boards may have considered stable and relatively without needs besides the basic instructional grant based on student registration levels.

The new focus on the primary grades and the revitalization of downtown areas are just two examples that reveal that school boards and provincial governments must deal with another layer of complexity besides the nine bulleted areas of expenditure we just listed. Determining how to distribute educational funds clearly requires conversation among many partners. And, given that school funds are finite but the needs of students, schools, and school districts inevitably expand beyond the available funds, those conversations take on continued importance.

An Alternative Model: Site-Based Management

A story circulates among educators in Edmonton, Alberta, that a new management and budget model now used in the Edmonton Public School Board arose out of one of those historical situations that a comedian could not make up. A school principal in Edmonton wanted to create a school library. Library services assured him he could obtain funds to buy books, but building services reported that the budget from which the bookshelves would need to come was already spent for that year. A few days after receiving this disappointing news, building services showed up at his school with new doors—it was time for the scheduled replacement of doors. He decided that something was wrong with the budget model and sent the doors back.

In what we might call the standard model of school budgeting, school boards break school budgets down according to a number of quite-sensible categories, such as supplies, services, administrative staff, instructional staff, building and maintenance, and special projects. In this model, the central office of the school district controls the annual budget for each of these budget lines. Managing the district's finances in this way, of course, allows the district to give oversight to the finances of the whole school district. In a small school division, the whole picture might include 10 or 20 schools. In a large urban school board the central office might serve 200 or more schools.

site-based management
A funding model that puts authority over and responsibility for spending decisions in the hands of the principal at a particular school.

Some school divisions have tried another model, usually called **site-based management** or site-based decision making. In the 1970s, Edmonton Public School Board became the first school board in Canada to implement this model, which some school districts in Florida and California had already begun to use. The Edmonton School Board began a trial in seven schools, all of which had volunteered for the experiment. This trial ran from 1976 to 1979. By 1980, the model was in place in all Edmonton public schools. The foundational principle of this model is simple: The principal should function as the superintendent in his or her own school and the central office should offer whatever services principals and schools need to do their work. This model is recognizably different from a model where the central office of a school district sets out a vision for the whole district and the principals of the respective schools, while responsible for their operation, are given little flexibility in how they are to carry out their responsibility.

As one might expect, implementing such a model brought Edmonton public schools some challenges. First, some officials in the central office itself, seeing how some of their authority would shift to schools, resisted the change. The board had to find new management and budget models to support the functioning of the new model. It also needed new models to calculate what level of funding each school should receive. The board needed to provide consulting services and professional development for principals, who now had to allocate a single pool of funds in effective ways so that they could carry out all the needed direct and indirect work to support student learning in their school buildings. Before site-based management, Edmonton public school principals typically received just 2% of their annual budget as discretionary money, a percentage that obviously would change dramatically under the new model. Teachers also needed professional development, because in this model they had new responsibilities to participate in the budget process.

From jurisdictions all over the world, education officials now make their way to Edmonton to learn first-hand how site-based management works. Three decades into its "experiment," Edmonton has continued to work with this model that moves much authority and responsibility out of the central office and into individual schools.

Funding Independent Schools

Government funding of **independent schools** varies from province to province, ranging from zero funding in some provinces (New Brunswick, Nova Scotia, and Ontario) to partial operational support in others (Alberta, British Columbia, and Saskatchewan), depending on levels of teacher certification and adherence to provincial curriculum. Some independent schools have become alternative schools within public boards (notably in Alberta and Saskatchewan), thereby receiving full support for operations and salaries, but not for capital projects.

independent schools Schools that operate independently of the local public or Catholic school board, almost always governed by a parent council or school council.

We should note some areas of tension related to independent schools. First, should elite private academies receive public funding? Listen in on this debate and you will likely hear that parents of children in these schools pay for education twice: first in tuition fees and again in their taxes. Undeniably, they do pay twice. But keep listening and you will hear that if they can afford such an education, then they can afford to pay twice. In fact, they knew that paying taxes for education was not optional and they had the option to make whatever choice they want about the public school or (in three provinces) the separate school that they already would pay for. We will not settle this debate in this book, but it does raise important ethical and philosophical questions for a democratic and pluralist society such as Canada.

Second, should avowedly religious schools be entitled to public funding? We will not settle this question here either, but the question proves interesting partly because it involves a thicket of subquestions. Perhaps those with extreme religious perspectives should be denied funding for their schools while those religious believers with the good of the whole community in mind and who teach responsibly should receive funding. But who is positioned to decide that some groups have extreme views and others not?

Third, what about certification of teachers? If a province does not contribute to the costs of independent schools, what say should it have about teacher certification, curriculum, or the length of the school year? Tied to this question, philosophers have argued for over two millennia about the question "to whom do children belong?" In the latest century we have witnessed several failed experiments where nations—all of them dictatorships—declared that children belong to the state. Most people around the world argue the opposite: that children belong to parents. A few independent school parents argue that children belong to God. How does a Department of Education propose workable independent schools legislation or a funding model with these dramatically opposed perspectives at the table?

CASE STUDY

Funding Independent Schools in British Columbia

The provinces of Canada follow no typical pattern in the funding of separate schools (as defined in the Constitution for Ontario and Quebec) or of independent schools more generally. But the path British Columbia has followed illustrates some of the complexities involved in funding schools that function outside of public school boards.

In 1977, British Columbia began to give partial funding to independent schools that hired certified teachers and followed the provincial curriculum.

continued

Marko Poplasen/Shutterstock

A Montessori school classroom

British Columbia recognizes a variety of independent schools and makes available two different levels of funding for qualified schools: 35% or 50% of the operating grant normally given to public school boards. Even schools that do not qualify to receive funding must register with the Ministry of Education, meaning that under BC law all schools are registered, even those who consider themselves fiercely independent. The level of provincial support for an independent school depends on a number of factors, such as the number of grades offered by the school and how long the school has operated.

To qualify for provincial funding under the 1996 British Columbia Independent School Act, independent schools must meet stringent requirements, summarized below in nonlegal language:

Legal and policy conditions

- Independent schools must be operated by an authority, either a society, a corporation, or a person, when they apply to operate. Schools operated for profit will not receive provincial funding.
- The school must enroll at least 10 students.
- The school must report twice per year the amount of student fees it has collected.
- The school must not promote racial or ethnic superiority or persecution, religious intolerance or persecution, social change through violent action, or sedition.
- The school must have adequate physical facilities that meet all building bylaws and codes.
- The principal and all teachers must be certified to teach in British Columbia.
- All employees of the school must have criminal record checks.

Instructional accountability

- The school must meet the instructional time requirements specified by the BC Ministry of Education.
- The school must have a satisfactory program to evaluate student progress and must participate in such provincial assessments as the Foundation Skills Assessments and Graduation Program Examinations.
- The school must supply the independent schools inspector with reports of student progress, cumulative files, and safety reports.
- The school must undergo an inspection or evaluation at least every two years.

Although this is only a summary it does give a flavour of the difficulties of finding an approach to funding independent schools. At the time of writing, no other province follows the policies that British Columbia follows, although both Alberta and Saskatchewan have seen historically independent schools join publicly funded school boards as alternative schools.

Teachers and Their Work

We began this chapter by noting that for most of the day and for most days of the school year, teachers give their energy and time to the core cycle activities of understanding curriculum, instruction, and assessing students' learning—what we called the CIA rope. We stressed that teachers' work happens in a context, not in a vacuum; the rope has a sheath, which we called the classroom ethos.

Parker Palmer, who has written extensively about the vocation of teaching and the work of teachers, has noted that for teachers, teaching has deeply personal dimensions and we must teach *who we are* (Palmer, 1998). As we learn in educational psychology courses or in workshops about multiple intelligences, learning styles, differentiation, or the developmental stages, we also must teach *who they are*—that is, you must respect the variety of students in your classroom. But we also teach in a historical context, a political and legal context, and in a funding context—so we must also teach *where we are*.

So far in this chapter we have treated the constitutional provisions for education in Canada and the forms those provisions take at the levels of provinces and territories, of local boards, and of school councils. We focus now on some elements of that context that likely come to teachers' minds more often than, say, Section 93 of the British North America Act. Indeed, some of these elements are likely on your own mind as you participate in this foundations course.

In this section we will look at teacher education and certification, the changing landscape of teaching, and teachers' induction into the profession. Teacher evaluation and contracts also warrant our attention. Teachers sometimes have amazing days—days when they exclaim at 3:30 p.m. that they would work for free! However, for the most part teachers prefer to work for compensation; thus, collective bargaining and salaries are of interest. Most Canadian teachers join professional organizations, federations, or unions, and such bodies have codes of ethics, likely overlapped with the codes that boards and individual schools have in place. In what follows we will examine all of these issues, each of which has great importance to teachers.

Teacher Education in Canada

We have described some of the ways in which the provincial and territorial governments ultimately control and supervise the work of most Canadian teachers. Governments do not train teachers in Canada, but all governments certify teachers except one, Ontario, which has a separate certifying body, the Ontario College of Teachers. Government interest in whom they certify and in whom schools hire inevitably will reach back into the teacher education process. With that interest, every Ministry of Education has a branch that focuses on teacher education and certification. But they do not exercise direct control over teacher education—universities and colleges do that. Furthermore, in all provinces, teachers have organized themselves into professional federations and associations. These do function as labour unions, but they also deal with the professional lives of teachers and have specific interests in teacher certification and the ongoing professional development of their members. Thus, at least three partners must carry on the conversation about teacher education and how it leads to certification. In Ontario, with its College of Teachers operating at arm's length from both government and the teachers' federations, the conversation involves a fourth partner. Some provinces have formalized mechanisms for the school board associations or provincial parent councils to join the conversation as well.

From the teacher-candidate's perspective, finishing a university degree or two leads to certification in the province in which you complete that degree (whether at the undergraduate or graduate level)—this is a simple process. But behind that apparently simple process lie ongoing negotiations between the many stakeholders we have listed: the universities and colleges, the teachers' federations, and the certification branch of the respective Ministry of Education.

Canadian teacher education has followed a pattern similar to that in most developed nations. The recent shift among school boards to hire a majority of new teachers who have an undergraduate degree plus a teaching degree represents only the latest movement in a long succession of such changes.

Practical Applications

A CHOICE OF WORDS: TEACHER EDUCATION OR TEACHER TRAINING?

When the provincial and territorial governments argued in 2009 for interprovincial mobility of teaching certification in the Agreement on Internal Trade, they waded into an old discussion within the foundations of education: Do we train teachers or do we educate them?

Like many professions, teaching involves skills. Teachers need a repertoire of instructional strategies, for example, and they need to know how to build a classroom ethos that reflects their educational ideals. Inasmuch as teaching involves this *knowing how* component, we could argue that teachers require training. But teaching involves mastery of both disciplinary and pedagogical knowledge as well, what some have called *knowing that*, a truth about teaching that leads some to argue that teachers require education, not training (or at least not only training). Critics of this position might respond that the construction trades also require a knowledge base and not just skills. For example, electricians must know that the electrical code requires a ground-fault detector in any electrical outlet installed in a bathroom. On this account, training implies a knowledge component, not just skills, and teachers should be trained. Defenders of teacher education might then reply that teaching also involves *knowing to*; that is, the teacher has nurtured certain dispositions (e.g., patience) and has made normative commitments to specific courses of action. Teachers carry out their work within a moral framework. That is, at its core, teaching has more similarities to medicine, law, and social work than it does to electrical work or auto mechanics. If these dispositions and values are not incidental to teaching or simply beneficial add-ons if they are present, but in fact lie at the core of teaching, then *teacher education* should likely be our choice of phrasing, even though we recognize that teachers need to be trained in specific skills if they are to succeed in classrooms.

This discussion is not just about fine points in linguistics. It bears on the day-to-day question of what teachers really need to know if they are to succeed in their classrooms: They do need to know *what* (content expertise), they need to know *how* (teaching/learning strategies), and they need to *know to* (the deeply moral character of teaching). This discussion also bears on the question of qualifications for teaching. Some non-Canadian jurisdictions now require little or no teacher education for teachers in the industrial arts. If this trend spreads to Canada, the question of teacher training or teacher education will certainly become much more than an innocent choice of words.

The generation of Canadian teachers who began teaching in the 1960s include the last teachers hired after completing only a year of normal school or teachers' college. Most of those who began teaching in the 1970s started with a minimum of four years of university. Of course these are generalizations, but they reflect a major step in the professionalization of teaching. Nuancing generalizations may produce a more accurate picture of the story of teacher education and certification in Canada. As early as the 1840s, Upper Canada had passed regulations that tied school funding to the hiring of certified teachers. These regulations did not guarantee that every classroom had in it a certified teacher, but the early date indicates that the concern for certification is almost as old as the concern for common schools.

Teacher Certification and Mobility

Across Canada, a graduate from a recognized education program will receive a provisional or interim certificate from the Ministry of Education in the province where the education program is located. (Yukon, Northwest Territories, and Nunavut have no teacher education programs, although some universities offer education courses by extension at various northern locations.) When certification is described in this way it sounds almost automatic. But as most teacher-candidates know, certification requires that you receive a passing grade in your placement(s), that you pass all of your courses, and in many provinces that you have somewhere on your transcript evidence that you have taken a minimum number of credits in such subjects as Canadian studies or one of Canada's two official languages. We return to these requirements below, but for now we want to underline what perhaps you already know: Certification is not automatic.

Perhaps without many teacher-candidates' awareness, teacher education programs do their own work to ensure that a degree leads to certification. Programs regularly adapt their degree requirements as conversations about optimal teacher preparation reveal an emerging need or as a provincial government identifies a new priority. Education faculty regularly conduct extensive assessments of their own programs in preparation for site visits by accreditation teams. These teams often comprise representatives from the various stakeholder groups: the Ministry of Education, the teachers' federation, and other academic institutions (often the dean of education from another program). Thus, education programs constantly engage in program evaluations—self-assessment—to maintain and improve quality as well as to retain the right to grant degrees that lead to certification. Given that you are currently studying in precisely the kind of program we are describing, we will not go into further detail about the connections between teacher education and provincial certification.

Teacher mobility between Canadian jurisdictions has largely been addressed through a series of agreements made between the various certification branches (and the Ontario College of Teachers, OCT). In summary, these agreements state that those holding a certificate in one province may apply for a similar certificate in another province without any legal barriers. Transferring can be a bit more difficult, as we will see, because some provinces require their teachers to have taken certain courses that may not be required in other provinces. In many cases, teachers provide supporting documentation for their licensure in the province in which they earned their teaching degree and initial licence, they pay a fee, and they receive a certificate that allows them to teach in a new jurisdiction.

In 2009, the 13 territorial and provincial governments committed themselves to the "Labour Mobility" section of the Agreement on Internal Trade. Overall, those formulating the agreement intended to ease movement within Canada for all trades and professions that recognize or require certification. But some have raised objections to such a plan. First, in the case of education (and specifically teacher education), such a national agreement may undermine provincial jurisdiction over education and the differences in teacher education across Canada that reflect the different character of the various provinces. Second, such a plan may reduce teaching to a set of competencies and thereby reduce teacher education to teacher training, as if it were only a case of mastering certain skills. Third, and related to the interprovincial protocols we have just described, the teaching profession already had mechanisms in place to ease such mobility. Thus, the labour mobility initiative, while well intentioned, did little to make it easier for teachers to move between Canadian jurisdictions.

Entering the Profession: New Teacher Induction

Researchers who study attrition among teachers in their first five years offer varying percentage rates, all of which are sobering for governments, universities, school boards, teachers themselves, and even teacher-candidates. Why should individuals and society as a whole expend so many resources preparing someone to teach if he or she stands a 30–40% chance of leaving the profession before the start of the sixth year of teaching?

With these sobering statistics in hand and in mind, educational leaders have begun to take new teacher induction far more seriously than was the case before the turn of the current century.

In what follows, we omit the myriad details about each jurisdiction's specific initiatives and policies. But we can summarize in two bullets what is generally found in the field today:

- Handbooks and manuals are available for new teachers that contain many details ranging from copier codes to how dental plans work to benefiting from mentoring to typical employment expectations beyond the minimum legal requirements of the School Act.
- New teacher induction programs that focus on professional development and improving practice, working with administrators, and understanding how teaching is assessed are mandatory for beginning teachers during the first year, but they seem focused on new teachers earning satisfactory ratings on administrator assessments. Some provinces have begun province-wide programs (British Columbia, New Brunswick) while others leave new teacher induction to boards and schools (Nova Scotia).

For teachers themselves, the research on new teacher induction makes two important points. First, the new teacher should not count on anyone else to arrange for his or her induction into the profession. One's first post might be in a setting with a formal structure established to help new teachers make their way, but it might not be. The second conclusion of the research on induction is sobering, especially in light of the patchwork way that Canadian provinces and boards have addressed induction so far: The teacher without a formal induction setting (e.g., one involving a mentor or a professional learning community) stands a higher chance of leaving the profession. It is not our place in this textbook to tell you what to do when you take up your first teaching post, but our reading of the literature in this area leads us to the undeniable conclusion that new teachers who discover the absence of a formal program should quickly create their own structure to ensure their longevity in the profession.

Practical Applications

FIVE TIPS TO ENSURE A SUCCESSFUL INDUCTION INTO TEACHING

We know your first year of teaching will be busy. You will likely feel swamped a good deal of the time, as was Erin Gruwell, the teacher portrayed by Hilary Swank in the movie *Freedom Writers*. But we believe that new teachers need to and can take partial charge of their own induction into the profession. Based on the latest research into teacher induction, here are five key components of self-directed, successful induction into the teaching profession:

1. Be humble. All teachers can learn to teach more effectively. Ask for advice from your colleagues about lesson planning and curriculum, especially if there is more than one teacher in your department or grade. Ask to sit in on other teachers' classrooms to observe their teaching methods and style (even if they teach a different grade or subject). Do not criticize another teacher's teaching style to anyone even remotely involved with your school community. You need to be and be seen as a professional colleague and teammate.
2. Focus on building professional relationships within your school community during your induction phase. Do not spend all your time preparing, teaching, and grading, even though you will probably feel like you need to. Eat lunch with other colleagues to learn the school culture and foster friendships.
3. Find a mentor. Find a mentor. Find a mentor. If your school did not assign you a mentor, or the one assigned avoids you, personally seek out another mentor. Find a retired teacher living in your community, look for a respected teacher in your school, or even seek out another teacher in your content area at another school. Teaching is not an individual profession and you need support, especially during your inductive years.
4. Be a role model. If you are doing your job right, you will be a positive role model in your school community. Be conscientious in preserving your reputation. Be careful with how you talk and act in public—people are listening and watching. Dress professionally (or, given the variety of school settings, dress appropriately). You are not your students' friend, you are their teacher. Be the person that parents want as an influence on their children. Be a person to emulate in your community.
5. Join or form a professional learning community. If your principal or department head does not assign you to meet with other grade-level or subject-area colleagues, form your own group. Some speak of professional learning communities (PLCs) as if they are the flavour of the month, but they offer real benefits to both new and veteran teachers.

Source: Hollabaugh, 2012; Mitchell, Ortiz, & Mitchell, 1987; Smethem, 2007.

Collective Agreements and Teachers' Rights

The respective School and Education Acts of the provinces and territories each specify how individual school boards or whole provinces are to negotiate salaries and working conditions with teachers (in public schools). In some settings, all the teachers in a province work under one agreement and on one salary scale but local boards negotiate other working conditions like the amount of preparation time. In other settings, both salaries and other conditions are negotiated in separate collective agreements in each district.

Toward the end of their teacher education, teacher-candidates begin to search for teaching jobs. Many aspire to teach in a particular district, often for simple reasons such as friends or family or access to favourite recreation. Many candidates prefer urban boards. One surprise often awaits teacher-candidates and new teachers: Salaries are similar regardless of location. As often as not, that similarity derives from the simple fact that one collective agreement covers teachers from a whole province. Collective agreements in Canada tend to run from one to as many as five years. Boards and teachers' federations sometimes settle after the contract year has started, with both parties launching the school year in hopes of reaching a settlement soon. In rare cases, teachers teach a whole year without a contract.

As this book goes to press, one provincial legislature (Ontario) has moved toward prohibiting teachers from striking. Ontario Bill 115, the Putting Students First Act, would obviously have implications for unionized workers throughout Ontario should it become law. Successful passage of such a bill in one province might also induce other provinces to consider such legislation. We note this move in Ontario not to take sides but to underline that teachers work in a changing labour environment. The Elementary Teachers' Federation of Ontario (ETFO) has told its members that Bill 115 might imply at least these six things about their employment:

- They would not be able to negotiate their own salaries.
- They could lose insurance and other already-negotiated benefits.
- Existent provisions for sick leave could be rolled back.
- The requirements for how teachers spend their work days could change.
- The system for allocating jobs in a district could change.
- Teachers could lose their protections from arbitrary discipline and dismissal without just cause. (Elementary Teachers' Federation of Ontario, 2014)

As you might expect, others interpret Bill 115 in less sinister terms, arguing that such restrictions and reductions are necessary to improve Ontario education. But we summarize the ETFO's position to demonstrate the anxiety that some teachers feel when they think about their changing legal status as workers, especially given that some jurisdictions have already attempted to crush teacher unions altogether.

Impact on Today's Teachers

ONTARIO AND THE RIGHT TO STRIKE

During the early and middle decades of the 20th century, teachers across Canada formed federations to protect members of the teacher profession from various kinds of arbitrary and abusive practices that some teachers had experienced historically at the hands of school boards. Educators, as did many Canadian workers generally, began to assume that the right to negotiate a collective agreement was a basic right in a democratic and free society such as Canada. The Canadian Charter of Rights and Freedoms guarantees the freedom of association (Section 2d), which many interpret as the right to organize into a labour union or professional federation. Into this context, the Ontario government introduced Bill 115 in the second decade of the 21st century. All six teacher unions in Ontario did not respond in the same way to Bill 115, but teachers in general perceived that Bill 115, besides rolling back teacher salaries, would to some degree deny them the right to collective bargaining.

Our task in this text is not to line up for or against Bill 115. Viewed one way, Bill 115 may simply be a provincial government's attempt to spread the necessary sacrifice fairly in a time when it must balance a budget. Viewed another way, it may signal the beginnings of a historic shift in the value a whole society places on educators or even education. Of course, one could take dozens of other views on Bill 115 as well.

Teacher Contracts and Salaries

Regardless of the nature of the particular collective agreement in place in a school district, individual teachers work under several kinds of contracts. The main distinction to bear in mind regarding contracts is that between **permanent** and **temporary contracts**. Many beginning teachers work under a series of probationary one-year contracts for several years. When an oversupply of qualified teachers seeks employment, school boards can become more selective in hiring, finding those they deem most qualified among a strong pool of applicants. To some extent, aspirational boards—those boards in which teachers aspire to eventually teach—enjoy this luxury regardless of the supply of teachers. In almost all school jurisdictions, the School Act or the collective agreement regulates the length of probationary contracts, thus barring school boards from shortening or lengthening a new teacher's probation period based on its assessment of the supply of teachers.

In times when qualified teachers are in short supply (and where the collective agreement permits), boards may reduce the probationary period, moving new teachers toward permanent contracts after one year or, in rare cases, immediately. Governments and school districts may also offer reduced probation or other incentives—including cash—to teachers willing to teach in remote locations or in schools that historically have encountered problems attracting or retaining staff. Nunavut, for example, offers a variety of housing, storage, food, and relocation-in and relocation-out allowances to teachers who work in the territory; several pages of its collective agreement attend to these matters.

permanent contracts
Teacher contracts that are continuous from year to year, which helps stabilize the staff for a particular board but also gives the teacher protection against unwarranted dismissal.

temporary contracts
Teacher contracts that are only valid for a specific period of time. Some examples of the many situations that would require a temporary contract are when the funding for a specific program came from a one-time funding source, or covering a permanent teacher's maternity leave.

Temporary Contracts

School boards use temporary contracts for a number of reasons:

- The funding for a specific program came from a one-time funding source.
- A program or initiative operates with a specific closing or end date.
- The funding for a specific program or position came from a funding pool whose allocations are based on competitive applications.
- A teacher with a permanent contract has taken a planned sabbatical year, or taken a leave for one or two years for the purpose of exchange or service teaching in another province or country.
- A school or school district is phasing out a program.
- A school or school district is offering a new program, but on a trial basis.

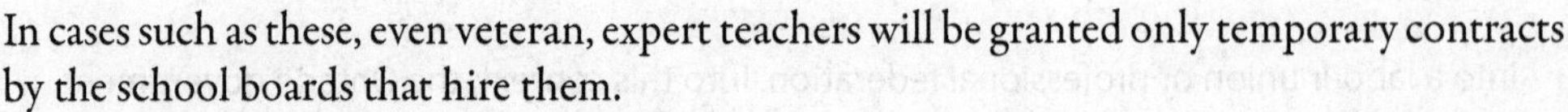

In cases such as these, even veteran, expert teachers will be granted only temporary contracts by the school boards that hire them.

School boards also hire teachers for positions with a term limit of less than a year for a variety of reasons:

- Coverage of a maternity leave
- Coverage of a medical leave or other leave that extends beyond the maximum period that the respective school board can employ a substitute teacher, which is usually specified in the collective agreement
- Coverage of a position that became open because of the death or dismissal of a teacher. In such cases, the school board may move quickly to fill the position for the remainder of the school year while it seeks a permanent replacement. A school board may also seek a permanent replacement immediately, covering the position with supply teachers for the time it needs to fill the position.

Both the above lists could be extended, but the points listed include the major categories under which temporary contracts are used. They also illustrate the variety and range of reasons that school boards might advertise or fill a specific position with a temporary contract.

Salary Scales

We have noted that collective agreements typically recognize six or seven years of education and 10–12 years of experience. The scale shown in Table 8.3, from the collective agreement between the teachers in Elk Island Public Schools (Alberta) and their board, has six steps (for levels of education) and 11 increments for experience.

TABLE 8.3 Salary Scale for Teachers in Elk Island Public Schools

Years of Experience	4 Years of University	5 Years of University	6 Years of University
0	$55,424	$58,678	$62,348
1	$58,657	$61,910	$65,581
2	$61,877	$65,152	$68,817
3	$65,128	$68,368	$72,049
4	$68,351	$71,613	$75,295
5	$71,595	$74,849	$78,519
6	$74,830	$78,082	$81,752
7	$78,064	$81,307	$84,969
8/9	$81,287	$84,550	$88,221
10	$84,485	$87,747	$91,408
11	$88,166	$91,408	$95,091

Source: Alberta Teachers' Association, 2008.

The same school district calculates a principal's or vice-principal's allowance according to the number of students attending the school. The amounts in the middle column of Table 8.4 reflect an allowance in addition to the principal's salary as per the teacher salary grid. The amounts for assistant principals are calculated as 60% of the rate paid to principals.

TABLE 8.4 Principal and Vice-Principal Allowances in Elk Island Public Schools

School Enrolment	Principal Allowance	Vice-Principal Allowance
0–499	$26,001	$15,601
500–649	$27,343	$16,406
650–899	$30,027	$18,016
900–999	$32,712	$19,627
1,000–1,199	$34,053	$20,432
1,200+	$35,395	$21,237

Source: Alberta Teachers' Association, 2008.

The Elk Island Public Schools collective agreement contains much more than these grids. It specifies pay rates for such persons and responsibilities as the following:

- In-school, grade-level instructional coordinators
- Teaching in more than one school building
- Substitute teachers
- Teachers employed at an hourly rate in the board's continuing education program

This particular collective agreement contains nothing unusual when it notes these specific responsibilities or work conditions beyond or outside the normal grid. Every school jurisdiction has unique programs, staffing needs, and situations.

Collective agreements also typically include details on such matters as these:

- How to evaluate industrial trade experience in such fields as construction or cooking
- Support for professional development, for example, tuition support for further education, conference and workshop fees
- Annual professional growth plans and evaluation of those plans
- Paid and unpaid personal leave days, sick days, and long-term disability
- Pension funds contributed by the employing school district or province
- Medical, dental, and life insurance

Teacher-candidates moving into the teaching force can sometimes feel overwhelmed by the volume of paperwork involved in getting an updated criminal record check, selecting insurance plans and options, and even registering for building and room keys. Fortunately, administrative staff from the central office and the school office are there to help and, for most teachers who look back on their first years, the administrative work entailed in taking up a new post will turn out to be a small series of minor tasks compared to the challenges of teaching.

Teacher Salaries and Contracts across Canada

Table 8.5 outlines the salary scales and some interesting notes about contracts in each of the 10 provinces and three territories in Canada. The word *steps* refers to years of education or certification, and the word *increments* refers to teaching experiences recognized for salary purposes.

As one might expect, the three territorial Departments of Education offer financial incentives to encourage teachers to come and stay in remote settlements. We list here a few of the incentives that the Northwest Territories might offer a given teacher who agreed to teach in a remote location:

- Relocation allowance
- Travel and accommodation expenses
- Rapid incremental progression of salary
- Remote locality entitlements (air fares to the outside, remote incentive allowance, remote retention payment, family travel allowance, remote satellite and installation)
- Tax incentives

The above bullets make clear that some school boards must recruit more aggressively and offer more benefits than other boards to attract teachers and retain them in their school districts.

Teachers' Standards and Ethics

Teachers see regular reminders that society holds them to high ethical standards. Sobering stories sometimes appear in the news of teachers who fail professionally in areas related to money or improper relationships with students. Other teachers may run afoul of a provincial or district policy because they have neglected their duties. School districts, teacher associations and federations, and even individual schools publish codes of ethics for teachers, in some cases asking teachers to sign them annually to indicate their willingness to adhere to such codes.

More broadly, as professionals teachers must direct their efforts toward certain professional standards. Obviously, teachers have their own individual ideals—for most teachers that is why they go to work in the morning. But teachers' groups and the officials to whom teachers report have also addressed the matter of educational ideals or standards, producing charter-like documents that describe how optimal teachers carry out their work. We have included in the Case Study on page 320 the full text of two such sets of standards, one from British Columbia and one from Ontario. Read these with a comparative eye, noticing what both sets of standards highlight and noticing which standards appear to be unique to just one province's standards. Also read them with your own employment in mind. Could you work in an ethos shaped by these standards? How do these standards overlap with the ideals that you hope characterize the learning and teaching space in which you and your students will do your work? We suspect you will discover much in common between British Columbia and Ontario, and between these standards and your own.

TABLE 8.5 Salary Scales across Canada

Province/Territory	Salary Scales (*levels* = education *increments* = experience)	Notes about Contracts
Newfoundland and Labrador	7 levels and 11 increments 5 hours of service counted as a day, with total years of service calculated by days of service divided by number of school days in a year	Teachers are responsible to inform their school board when they reach a new level of certification or pay. Collective agreements run for four years.
Prince Edward Island	4 levels and 12 increments	
Nova Scotia	8 levels and 11 increments	
New Brunswick	7 levels and 11 increments	The amount of experience is determined by the Minister's Advisory Committee on Teacher Certification.
Quebec	2 levels and 17 increments	Advanced qualifications are reflected as increments.
Ontario	4 levels and 11 increments (Ontario Secondary School Teachers' Federation). The first level is not four years of study, it is one.	Teachers are responsible for informing their school board when they reach a new level or increment.
Manitoba	7 levels and 9 increments	
Saskatchewan	7 levels and 11 increments	Classification is done initially by the secretary-treasurer of the board of education or at the time of employment or request for reclassification.
Alberta	Scale negotiated by individual boards; typically 6 levels and 10 or 11 increments	
British Columbia	4–5 levels and 9–11 increments, with each board negotiating separately	
Nunavut	7 levels and 11 increments plus a northern allowance	
Northwest Territories	6 levels and 11 increments plus a northern allowance	
Yukon	7 levels and 10 increments plus a northern allowance	

CASE STUDY

Codes of Conduct from British Columbia and Ontario

Case #1: Standards for the Education, Competence and Professional Conduct of Educators in British Columbia

Established by the British Columbia Teachers' Council for individuals who hold a certificate of qualification.

1. *Educators value and care for all students and act in their best interests.* Educators are responsible for fostering the emotional, aesthetic, intellectual, physical, social and vocational development of students. They are responsible for the emotional and physical safety of students. Educators treat students with respect and dignity. Educators respect the diversity in their classrooms, schools and communities. Educators have a privileged position of power and trust. They respect confidentiality unless disclosure is required by law. Educators do not abuse or exploit students or minors for personal, sexual, ideological, material or other advantage.
2. *Educators are role models who act ethically and honestly.* Educators act with integrity, maintaining the dignity and credibility of the profession. They understand that their individual conduct contributes to the perception of the profession as a whole. Educators are accountable for their conduct while on duty, as well as off duty, where that conduct has an effect on the education system. Educators have an understanding of the education system in BC and the law as it relates to their duties.
3. *Educators understand and apply knowledge of student growth and development.* Educators are knowledgeable about how children develop as learners and as social beings, and demonstrate an understanding of individual learning differences and special needs. This knowledge is used to assist educators in making decisions about curriculum, instruction, assessment and classroom management.
4. *Educators value the involvement and support of parents, guardians, families and communities in schools.* Educators understand, respect and support the role of parents and the community in the education of students. Educators communicate effectively and in a timely manner with parents and consider their advice on matters pertaining to their children.
5. *Educators implement effective practices in areas of planning, instruction, assessment, evaluation and reporting.* Educators have the knowledge and skills to facilitate learning for all students and know when to seek additional support for their practice. Educators thoughtfully consider all aspects of teaching, from planning through reporting, and understand the relationships among them. Educators employ a variety of instructional and assessment strategies.
6. *Educators have a broad knowledge base and understand the subject areas they teach.* Educators understand the curricular, conceptual and methodological foundations of education and of the subject areas they teach. Educators must be able to communicate effectively in English or French. Educators teach students to understand relevant curricula in a Canadian, Aboriginal and global context. Educators convey the values, beliefs and knowledge of our democratic society.
7. *Educators engage in career-long learning.* Educators engage in professional development and reflective practice, understanding that a hallmark of professionalism is the concept of professional growth over time. Educators develop and refine personal philosophies of education, teaching and learning that are informed by theory and practice. Educators identify their professional needs and work to meet those needs individually and collaboratively.

8. *Educators contribute to the profession.* Educators support, mentor or encourage other educators and those preparing to enter the profession. Educators contribute their expertise to activities offered by their schools, districts, professional organizations, post-secondary institutions or contribute in other ways. (British Columbia Ministry of Education, 2014. www.bcteacherregulation.ca/Standards/StandardsDevelopment.aspx)

Case #2: Ontario College of Teachers Standards of Practice

Alone among Canadian provinces, Ontario has a College of Teachers. It publishes the Standards of Practice below.

Commitment to Students and Student Learning

Members are dedicated in their care and commitment to students. They treat students equitably and with respect and are sensitive to factors that influence individual student learning. Members facilitate the development of students as contributing citizens of Canadian society.

Professional Knowledge

Members strive to be current in their professional knowledge and recognize its relationship to practice. They understand and reflect on student development, learning theory, pedagogy, curriculum, ethics, educational research and related policies and legislation to inform professional judgment in practice.

Professional Practice

Members apply professional knowledge and experience to promote student learning. They use appropriate pedagogy, assessment and evaluation, resources and technology in planning for and responding to the needs of individual students and learning communities. Members refine their professional practice through ongoing inquiry, dialogue and reflection.

Leadership in Learning Communities

Members promote and participate in the creation of collaborative, safe and supportive learning communities. They recognize their shared responsibilities and their leadership roles in order to facilitate student success. Members maintain and uphold the principles of the ethical standards in these learning communities.

Ongoing Professional Learning

Members recognize that a commitment to ongoing professional learning is integral to effective practice and to student learning. Professional practice and self-directed learning are informed by experience, research, collaboration and knowledge. (Ontario College of Teachers, 2014. Used with permission.)

Language similar to that used in these two sets of standards appears in documents from jurisdictions and from teacher education programs throughout the world. In cases where the language differs, one would probably find similar or overlapping educational ideals expressed. Obviously the OCT's standards have legal bearing only for Ontario teachers; teachers in other Canadian provinces will teach in view of other professional standards of practice, likely overlapping at several points with those listed above.

The Canadian Education Association (CEA) has published a set of professional teaching standards with a somewhat similar purpose to the OCT's but with a slightly different focus. Following a two-page history of curriculum and instruction, the CEA document presents five core characteristics of effective teachers:

1. Teachers are designers of learning.
2. Work students are asked to undertake is worth their time and attention.

3. Assessment practices improve student learning and guide teaching.
4. Teachers foster a variety of interdependent relationships.
5. Teachers improve their practice in the company of their peers. (Friesen, 2009)

Notice the similarities between the CEA standards and the OCT or BC standards—for example, the focus on collaboration in CEA principle #5. Without looking further afield than these three documents, we see clear statements of an important value among contemporary educators. Notably, similar lists of professional standards from a century ago would likely have omitted collaboration. As we should expect, the BC, OCT, and CEA documents all focus on dimensions of student learning and the teacher's role in enhancing and enriching that learning, implying in all cases that teachers themselves have adopted habits of lifelong learning. We point out these similarities to underline the point that when thoughtful, professional educators reflect on education with the purpose of publishing a conception of professional teaching practice (whether it has legal status or not), they will draw similar conclusions. One could examine the regulations governing teachers' work in any number of jurisdictions, even worldwide, and one would find similar emphases and language to what we have shown here.

Tying Certification to Teacher Standards in Alberta: An Example

Certification in Alberta depends on a teacher having met several conditions, which is typical for other jurisdictions as well. Below we summarize Alberta's Certification of Teachers Regulation:

- Alberta teachers must have completed at least four years of postsecondary education, including 48 semester hours in teacher education (which in turn includes at least 10 weeks of internship).
- Alberta elementary teachers' postsecondary education must include at least three semester hours in Canadian studies, mathematics, and science and at least six semester hours in English or French language or literature. Prospective secondary teachers must have a teachable major area of at least 24 semester hours and at least six semester hours in English or French language or literature.
- Prospective Alberta teachers with credentials from or experience in another jurisdiction must show evidence of the relevant credentials or experience.
- Valid certification from the jurisdiction where the teacher completed his or her initial teacher preparation program and from where the teacher is currently teaching or last taught is also required.
- Prospective Alberta teachers must have the right to work in Canada.
- Prospective Alberta teachers must be proficient in English or French. (Alberta Queen's Printer, 1999)

The Certification of Teachers Regulation is part of the Alberta School Act. As is true in all jurisdictions, this act and the regulations under it are updated as needed. Staff in the Ministries of Education in each respective jurisdiction recommend changes as needs arise. Lawyers (usually including members of the respective Ministry of Justice or the provincial attorney general's office) work with the Ministry of Education to develop the policy, which then goes to the government for passage. Once a bill passes (to become law), responsibility for enforcing it falls to the specific branch of government, in this case the teacher certification branch in the respective jurisdiction.

The prospective Alberta teacher must provide the documents and evidence named above to the Professional Standards Branch of Alberta Education, who will issue a teaching certificate if the candidate has met all the requirements. Any hiring board or school must ensure that the teacher possesses a teaching certificate, since Alberta requires such certification to teach in any school recognized by the province. After Alberta Education has issued a teaching certificate that authorizes a teacher to teach in Alberta, the Teacher Qualifications Service (TQS) appraises that teacher's credentials to determine his or her place on the salary scale (based on years of postsecondary education and years of teaching experience). Interestingly, the TQS is a branch of the Alberta Teachers' Association, not a branch of Alberta Education.

So far, the Alberta policies and structures that we have described represent the arrangements that are typically in place across Canada. But here is an important difference between Alberta and other jurisdictions: In 1985 the Alberta government established the Council on Alberta Teacher Standards (COATS), which advises the Professional Standards Branch of Alberta Education on all matters pertaining to teacher education and certification. We note this because of the composition of the council. COATS includes four Alberta teachers appointed by the Minister of Education for three-year terms (teacher members' terms overlap). COATS includes single representatives of the following constituencies:

- Alberta Deans of Education
- College of Alberta School Superintendents
- Alberta Teachers' Association
- Alberta School Boards Association
- Association of Independent Schools and Colleges in Alberta
- Alberta Education

Finally, COATS includes one representative from the public. Note that while COATS advises Alberta Education, it does not tell Alberta Education what to do. But composed as it is with representatives of so many constituencies, COATS functions as a unique forum for discussing Alberta education and for conceiving and formulating policies related to teacher training and certification.

One example of the fruitfulness of the conversation between Alberta Education and COATS is the initiation of a regulation known in Alberta as the Teaching Quality Standard. Like the five professional standards published by the Ontario College of Teachers, this regulation offers a set of ideals that all professional Alberta teachers are expected to aim at. Because we already included details of the standards from British Columbia, the Ontario College of Teachers, and the Canadian Education Association, we will not deal at length with the Alberta Teaching Quality Standard. We provide it as an example of the quality of work that a council can produce when representatives of many constituencies agree to talk and work together. It also serves as a kind of demonstration site to illustrate how certification can be tied to ongoing professional development. We believe that the COATS standards and the other sets of standards we have listed here—along with the conception of professional teaching they collectively present—are worth the attention of teacher-candidates and in-service teachers everywhere.

How Teachers Are Evaluated

Different jurisdictions evaluate teachers in a variety of ways using a range of instruments and rubrics. We begin by noting who evaluates teachers and then discuss how and for how long.

In most cases, the principal oversees the evaluation of his or her teaching staff. In some larger schools, this task may fall to an associate principal who has been assigned the oversight of instruction and staff development. In a few cases, an official from the school board or school district office may be involved in teacher evaluation. When Canadian schools were predominantly rural, this was more often the case because so many teachers taught in one-room schools. With multiroom schools overseen by principals, such central office involvement is not necessary.

Teachers are evaluated according to how well they carry out the specific duties assigned to them. Type the search string "teacher evaluation checklist" into a search engine and you will find literally hundreds of such checklist forms. If you browse through some of the sites the search engine returns, you will quickly get a sense that, regardless of geographic location, school jurisdictions look for the same kinds of knowledge, skills, and attitudes in their teachers. Many of the forms will have unique items, but in general they will reflect the kinds of professional values and work that we noted in the previous section of this chapter about teaching standards.

Obviously, teachers will be evaluated on how well they carry out their professional duties, focusing on planning, instruction, and assessment of students and the knowledge, skills, and attitudes dealt with in the various sets of professional teaching standards. In recent decades, many schools have adopted a model in which teachers reflect on their practice and provide their administrator with an annual professional growth plan. This plan might include such items as these:

- New teaching strategies the teacher plans to incorporate
- New curriculum content or teaching materials the teacher plans to incorporate
- Professional reading, study, workshops, and courses the teacher plans to complete
- Plans for mentoring younger teachers
- Plans to participate in a professional learning community
- Plans for professional involvement and leadership in the school, school district, or provincial subject-area council

Having articulated such goals and plans in writing, the teacher engages professionally through the year and evaluates his or her progress with the building administrator, rather than simply having the administrator assess the teacher's professional work and progress.

Teacher evaluation models that involve teachers writing their own growth plans and aiming at the goals they have articulated are more robust and professional than simple checklist evaluations completed by a principal or vice-principal. The teaching profession has become more professional as the educational requirements for entry to the profession have risen. It likewise becomes more professional as more schools adopt models where teachers become involved in and take ownership of their own ongoing professional evaluation.

Curriculum and Students

So far, this chapter has focused on the laws and policies that govern how Canadian schools and the people who operate them do their work. We began the chapter by noting the core cycle of teaching activities that most teachers spend most of their days on. But so far we have focused more on the legal, financial, and regulatory structures within which teachers do their work, thereby addressing somewhat indirectly the fundamental purpose for which all these regulations and the schools themselves are established: student learning. We turn now to matters of curriculum and school attendance, matters that affect students' lives directly.

Determining Curriculum: A Shared Responsibility

According to each province's School Act, the province retains ultimate responsibility for setting the K–12 curriculum. In practice, the provincial Ministries of Education work closely with boards and subject-area councils to assess curriculum and devise new curriculum plans.

As an example, Quebec has a mathematics subject-area council. In any given year, this council will have on it members who teach mathematics full time in Quebec but who miss several days of instruction per year to attend council meetings. Such council meetings may also include teachers who are seconded (borrowed) from one to three years at a time from school districts throughout Quebec. Especially during a major curriculum revision or launch, provinces will include the budget for such secondments in the budget for development and implementation of a new curriculum. Council meetings may also include full-time staff from the curriculum branch, which might include mathematics specialists or staff whose work focuses on First Nations concerns, on articulating the respective project between the English and French school boards, or on working with prospective publishers of the new materials. If you imagine the group gathered at a table for such a meeting, you would see both full-time Ministry of Education staff and teachers who might have been working in their classrooms yesterday. In this kind of partnership, curriculum is conceived and developed.

A council deciding to produce and implement a new mathematics curriculum, for example, has a lot of work to do. It must listen to the advice of teachers from across the province as well as from curriculum specialists in school boards. It must seek bids from publishers to produce the textbooks it wants. It must find teachers willing to pilot-teach the new curriculum material in their classrooms and then report their students' and their own experiences of the material. It must plan the professional development sessions teachers will need to familiarize themselves with the goals and contents of the new curriculum. It must schedule the phase-in period if upper grades require concepts taught only in the new curriculum of the lower grades. These and many more questions need to be resolved to implement a new curriculum. Listing these questions does help one understand some of the intricacies of devising and implementing a new curriculum, yet the process is actually much more complicated than we have made it sound here.

Returning to the question of subject-area councils, in most provinces vacancies on subject-area councils are advertised in teachers' federation newspapers and newsletters and on federation websites. Teachers who get involved at this level with their subject area almost universally report that it enhances their professional growth, inevitably enhancing their own students' learning directly while also providing a channel of service to the educational community at large.

For our hypothetical example here, we have written about Quebec and a new mathematics curriculum. As you might expect, the provinces have subject councils in many school subject areas besides mathematics. Ontario, for example, has councils in arts education, computer studies, drama and dance education, outdoor education, special education, history, and science—and that is only a handful of the councils and associations that give oversight to the many subjects taught in Ontario. Alberta has 21 such councils; other provinces have a similar number.

Taking Attendance

Between 1830 and 1850, Germany, England, the United States, and Canada began creating free public schools. Legislation requiring that children attend these schools either accompanied or followed the laws that created these school systems within a few years. Viewed from today's perspective, one might wonder how there could ever have been a time when schooling was not compulsory. At our point in history, the knowledge and skills that school aims to provide are absolutely essential, even for minimal participation in society and the world of work, let alone for success. Nevertheless, laws compelling children to attend school are less than two centuries old, and some of the first such laws only required children to attend school until age 11 or 12.

Combined with school-leaving laws, jurisdictions also passed laws pertaining to the age at which children must begin attending school. To this day, school-starting ages vary around the world and even within Canada. In Canada, the various School Acts specify the date range within which a child may begin attending school and must begin attending school. Regarding when they may start, many Canadian provinces specify that children may begin in the fall of the year in which they turn five if their birthday falls on or before December 31 of that school year. Child-development experts, parents, educators, policymakers, and economists debate the relative merits of starting school before the child's fifth birthday. Malcolm Gladwell, the author of the bestseller *Outliers* (2008), has even weighed in on the question, arguing that the older children entering any program eventually succeed at higher rates than their younger peers. Twinned with regulations about when children may start school are the specified dates by which they *must* start. Some provinces require that children attend school beginning in the school year following their fifth birthday (New Brunswick), but most provinces require children to attend school starting at age six (Manitoba, Nova Scotia, Ontario, Quebec), while some require attendance by age seven (Prince Edward Island, Saskatchewan).

Legal school-leaving ages in Canada have inched steadily upward since governments first enacted compulsory education in the mid-1800s. At the time of writing, all but three provinces require that students stay in school until age 16. New Brunswick led the way to a higher school-leaving age, requiring students since 2000 to stay in school until their eighteenth birthday (unless they finish Grade 12 first); Ontario followed suit in 2006 and Manitoba in 2011. Doubtless, 18 will become the new standard across Canada during the careers of those now preparing to work as K–12 teachers.

Controversy inevitably erupts when a province discusses raising the school-leaving age to 18. Some object to what they see as further state intrusion into the sphere of parents and the family; what right does the state have to declare that a 16- or 17-year-old must attend school? That is a good philosophical and political question that we will not resolve here. On the other side, educators, sociologists, economists, and many others point to private

Practical Applications

EARLY DISMISSAL

Some provinces make provisions for a student to leave school before age 16, but only after undergoing a thorough process. Nova Scotia's Education Act, for example, contains these regulations:

> A school board that receives a request from the parent of a student who has not attained sixteen years of age for a certificate issued pursuant to Section 114 of the Act exempting the student from attendance at school may issue such a certificate if
>
> (a) the student has attained the age of fifteen years;
>
> (b) the staff of the school board have
>
> (i) conducted an evaluation of the circumstances related to the request,
>
> (ii) examined alternatives to exemption from attendance, and
>
> (iii) discussed such alternatives in detail with the student and his or her parent; and
>
> (c) the school board is satisfied, after considering the results of the actions described in clause (b), that requiring the student to continue school attendance would not be beneficial to the student. (Nova Scotia Department of Education, 1997)

Given all of the inarguable economic and social benefits of graduating from high school, one might wonder why any jurisdiction would allow a student to leave school at age 15. In some cases, of course, mitigating circumstances might point to the wisdom of such a policy. We cannot weigh the merits of the case here, but like all democratic jurisdictions Nova Scotia's government must weigh competing rights.

benefits, such as increased lifetime income, and public benefits, such as decreased crime rates and a workforce that is more able to compete globally.

One Canadian economist, Philip Oreopoulos, has dedicated much of his professional effort to the argument that staying in school until graduation yields measurable private and social dividends over the student's lifetime. Oreopoulos has researched 17 American states that have raised the school-leaving age to 18, including the five states that have held that standard for decades (Ohio, Oklahoma, Oregon, Utah, and Washington) (Oreopoulos, 2005). And he has studied New Brunswick's first half-decade with a school-leaving age of 18 (Oreopoulos, 2006). With these data in hand, Oreopoulos concluded that raising the age from 16 to 18 usually has less effect than school officials and legislators hope. Specifically, he has observed these positive but small effects:

- The average student stays in school between 0.12 and 0.16 years longer.
- The dropout rate decreases between 1.2% and 2.1%.
- The percentage of young adults with some college or university education increases in the range of 1.5 to 2.1%.

These modest numbers do not deter Oreopoulos from arguing that staying in secondary school longer benefits both students and society. But he is saying that a raised school-leaving age will not serve as a single path to success for all students. His research on American jurisdictions reveals another pattern: Some states have experimented with lowering the school-leaving age (e.g., Mississippi, Wyoming). That state Departments of Education and legislators would enact such policies in the face of overwhelming evidence of the benefits of staying in school may indicate the difficulties encountered by some students in school, the importance of individual rights (versus state rights) in some people's world-views, or several other factors. Certainly, such actions point to the complexity of requiring a single schedule for all students.

Enforcement of compulsory school attendance has remained an issue from the mid-19th century when compulsory school laws first took effect until now. Many researchers, including Oreopoulos, have flagged enforcement as a weak spot in compulsory attendance. One can get a clearer sense of some of the difficulties in implementing and enforcing attendance policies from a set of recommendations the School Leaving Age Task Force made to the New Brunswick government in 1999, just before it raised the school-leaving age. The task force recommended the government do the following:

- Create an information campaign aimed at students aged 15–18, educators, parents and guardians, employers in New Brunswick, and employees of all agencies that serve New Brunswick youth so that they are aware of how their legal responsibilities will change if and when the school-leaving age rises to 18.
- Develop means to identify and support at-risk students, including Aboriginal at-risk students. Designate special funds for this support; ensure that at-risk students have access to (and know they have access to) counselling and other support programs, including transition-to-work programs.
- Develop supports for returning dropouts.
- Address the professional development needs of teachers regarding at-risk students.
- Specifically address at-risk student populations in school improvement plans.

We have not included all of the recommendations that the New Brunswick task force made, but the list clearly shows how complex the process of raising the school-leaving age is. A legislature cannot simply raise the age and tell the respective Department of Education to develop the appropriate regulations. Clearly, implementation and support for those most affected become prominent issues in the process.

We know that Canadian adolescents contemplating dropping out of school will not turn to Oreopoulos's technical arguments, but legislators and educational policy-makers will. This means that the school-leaving age will inevitably rise to 18 across Canada, as it already has done in a handful of countries with national education systems (such as Germany, Taiwan, Poland, Belgium, and the Netherlands) and will do in other developed nations.

The School Year in Canada

Across Canada, different jurisdictions define the school year differently. Some School Acts or Education Acts state the number of instructional days possible; others prescribe a minimum number. Both Yukon and the Northwest Territories allow individual schools to set the length of their school year. In Yukon the year ranges from 173 to 184 days, and in the

Northwest Territories it ranges from 180 to 188 days. In Nunavut, the local district education authority sets the school year's length, typically at 195 days. In Saskatchewan and Quebec school boards set the school year, typically for 197 days in Saskatchewan and 190 days in Quebec.

Several provinces specify how many days must be given to instruction and how many may be given over to administration, professional development, or teachers' conventions. British Columbia requires between 186 and 193 instructional days while allowing six non-instructional days and one administrative day. Manitoba pegs the school year at 196 days, of which 10 may be used for noninstructional purposes; the exact number of noninstructional days is set by each school division and varies across the province. Newfoundland and Labrador start with 190 days, a different number from Manitoba, and allow up to 10 professional days. New Brunswick also grants teachers 10 professional days but starts with 185 days for the school year. Nova Scotia and Prince Edward Island both start with 195 days, with Nova Scotia allowing eight days for professional purposes. Prince Edward Island includes in their formula an orientation day for teachers and up to three days at the end of the year for teachers to attend to year-end activities. Interestingly, PEI recognizes professional development days but does not specify how many teachers may take in a given year. Unique to Canada, Alberta does not specify a number of school days but requires a set number of hours of instruction: 950 for elementary and junior high students and 1,000 for secondary students. School districts can construct the school year any way they like, but they may not require teachers to teach more than 200 days in a school year.

Clearly, the Canadian school year varies from province to province, as one might expect given that the different provinces each have responsibility for their own education systems. Buried not very deeply in the obvious variety, however, is a typical Canadian school year of about 185 to 190 days of instruction. Compared to other countries, this is longer than in some jurisdictions and shorter than in others.

Conclusion

In this chapter we have explored how Canadian schools are governed, operated, and funded. The broadest parameters for education in Canada are set by clauses in the 1867 British North America Act and, in turn, the 1982 Canadian Constitution Act. The provinces have control over and responsibility for funding education, which they exercise in various ways using different but often surprisingly similar structures. The provincial or territorial Department or Ministry of Education oversees the whole system for each respective province or territory and provides some or all of the funding for schools. Local school boards (some of them representing a large land area) operate schools, and many raise some of their funding through property taxes. The administrators of schools work with school or parent councils to operate the schools on a day-to-day basis. Independent schools answer to the provincial Department of Education but are, in most cases, operated by their own council.

Much more could be written about the organization and funding of Canadian education; in this chapter, we have provided only an introduction. It is our hope that in doing so we have simplified the complex nature of the legal, economic, and political aspects of education in Canada.

Discussion Questions

1. Some nations have adopted national education systems (e.g., Great Britain) while others have assigned responsibility for education to states and provinces (e.g., the United States and Canada). From three different perspectives—the K–12 student in the classroom, the K–12 classroom teacher, and the curriculum branch of the Department of Education—consider some strengths of a national education system and curriculum. Note a couple of strengths of a system where provinces and states have the responsibility for educational provision.
2. Using a three-column PMI chart (plus, minus, and interesting), suggest possible advantages and disadvantages to having school councils and local school boards sharing oversight and governance of schools. In the third column, list features of dual governance that you consider neither positive nor negative but simply interesting.
3. We suggested in this chapter that you type "teacher evaluation checklist" into a search engine. Using that search string, "teacher evaluation tools," or "assessment of teachers," explore at least five websites and note some of the expectations of teachers that different jurisdictions have. List these expectations using three columns labelled "knowledge," "skills," and "attitudes." Recognize that many jurisdictions use the word *dispositions* as a synonym for attitudes.
4. Some have argued that universities hold a monopoly on teacher preparation in Canada. Suggest reasons why teacher preparation is best done in the university context. Suggest grounds for one or two alternative models for teacher preparation (such as school board–directed teacher preparation and apprenticeship models).
5. At present, many parties contribute to the curriculum conversation: publishers, teachers, principals, students, school councils, school boards, provincial Departments of Education, and universities. In your view, who should determine the actual curriculum that students engage with in their classes? What is the best mix and why?

Further Resources

1. Friesen, S. (2009). *What did you do in school today? Teaching effectiveness: A framework and rubric.* Toronto, ON: Canadian Education Association. Retrieved from http://www.cea-ace.ca/sites/cea-ace.ca/files/cea-2009-wdydist-teaching.pdf.

   Beginning and veteran teachers alike will benefit from this short booklet that outlines some of the knowledge, skills, attitudes, and practices of the professional teacher.

2. Kutsyuruba, B. (2012). Teacher induction and mentorship policies: The pan-Canadian overview. *International Journal of Mentoring and Coaching in Education, 1*(3), 235–256.

   Every new teacher should read this research article, although Kutsyuruba's conclusions are directed to educational policy-makers and school boards. This research shows that mentoring is the key to successful entry to the teaching profession.

3. Oreopoulos, P. (2006). The compelling effects of compulsory schools: Evidence from Canada. *Canadian Journal of Economics 39*(1), 22–52.

   Oreopoulos brings a lifetime of research in a variety of nations and an economist's eye and thinking to the questions of school leaving and of extending the compulsory attendance age to 18. He concludes that when jurisdictions require students to remain in school longer, their lifetime incomes do increase—that typical claim is not just a fiction.

4. Palmer, P. J. (1998). *The courage to teach: Exploring the inner landscape of a teacher's life.* San Francisco, CA: Jossey-Bass.

   An outstanding teacher and storyteller explores the emotional dimensions of teaching, noting some of the mental habits typical of effective teachers who remain in the profession. Palmer is clear that teaching is a moral activity, and his book is essential reading for new teachers.

5. Smethem, L. (2007). Retention and intention in teaching careers: Will the new generation stay? *Teachers and Teaching: Theory and Practice*, 13(5), 465–480.

   Smethem interviewed 18 first-year teachers in England about their reasons for entering teaching and their plans to stay or leave. Her participants agreed with Parker Palmer—that teaching is a moral task—but they struggled to reconcile that view with what they perceived as an obsession with performance and results.

Appendix

DYNAMIC CLASSROOM MANAGEMENT CASE STUDY

The First Day of School

"Hello everyone," Annette says, "My name is Ms. Elkins and I am very happy to be here as your new teacher. Let's talk a little bit about how we are going to do things in our classroom this year. In order for everyone to enjoy school and have a good chance of doing their best, we are going to have to be very careful about how we behave toward each other. So let's take some time to decide together what our rules and routines will be. I'm sure we all want this classroom to be a safe and pleasant place."

Tara immediately pipes up, "Miss, before . . ., uh, Mr. Dawe just told us all the rules and we had to obey them . . . when we did something wrong, he would yell at us, make us clean the classroom, or make us write lines . . . and some of his rules weren't even fair." Her voice softens, "Are you going to do that, too?"

"What wasn't fair?" Annette asks. She can sense that other students feel the same as Tara.

"Well," Tara looks to her classmates for support, "some of us didn't like having to put up our hand every time we wanted to get out of our seat, and if we forgot to put up our hand, we had to stay in during recess. Mr. Dawe didn't trust us. He thought we would make too much noise if we got up and walked around. He just never gave us a chance . . . it was so not fair."

"Yeah," chimes in Katherine, a Grade 10 student, "I always got in trouble for that and I had to spend recess with the little ones. They had a blast and I was soooo bored. I was supposed to do school work as my punishment but I never got anything done because of all the racket, then I'd have to take it home to do as homework," Katherine continues, "on top of all my other homework . . . all for *getting out of my seat without permission*." Her impression of a male teacher's "very serious" voice draws giggles of approval.

"I'm not going to say that we won't have consequences for misbehaviour," Annette says, "but I'm sure we can make the rules fair for everyone and only use consequences that are suitable and that you agree to."

Very slowly, a skeptical Katherine asks, "What do you mean consequences we agree to? I don't want to be punished for anything."

"I don't mean that you will always like the consequence, but if it is necessary it will be a consequence that you have agreed to beforehand, one that is appropriate. As a class, we can decide together what is acceptable and unacceptable behaviour in our school and decide, also in advance, what rewards people can get for doing things right and what consequences people will have to accept for doing things wrong."

Not yet convinced, Katherine says, "Like, what kind of rewards? What do I have to do to get them—sit still and not say or do anything except school work for the whole day? That's just boring."

The quiet stillness of the other students lets Annette know she is on a roll. "No, nothing that drastic. Actually, it's quite easy. Let's say we agree that one of our rules will be that no one is allowed to talk while someone is speaking to the class, like me or another teacher. If no one breaks the rule during all the morning classes, every student can have 10 minutes of free time just before lunch. How would you feel about that?"

"Can we use the computers? Simon asks, "I'd rather do that than anything."

Before Annette can answer, Katherine asks another question that reveals her skeptical nature: "What if we break the rule about not interrupting? Then what happens?" Her tone clearly indicates a here-it-comes expectation.

"Well," Annette explains, "when we decide on a rule and its reward, we will also decide on what the consequence will be if someone breaks the rule. Let's say that the consequence for breaking the interrupting rule is that there will be no free time or computer time before lunch, but it can be anything we want, like a detention or a visit to the principal's office. We just have to agree to what the consequence will be . . . then, when the rule is broken, everyone knows what will happen."

"So if one person breaks the rule, we all get punished? That doesn't sound fair," exclaims Katherine, becoming more agitated. "What if only one person breaks the rule and spoils it for everyone? That sounds just like the rules we had before. What's the point of being good if someone else can ruin it for the whole class?"

"Well, maybe there shouldn't be a rule where the consequence applies to everyone. As a group we can decide ahead of time if the consequence will only apply to the individual who breaks the rule or to the class as a whole." Annette can see they like the idea of "fair" rules. "If we decide it only applies to the individual, that person loses their free time privilege while everyone else gets free time. You see, rules can be fair." Annette continues, looking directly at Katherine, "but, what makes rules, rewards, and consequences fair is when everyone has a chance to understand them, talk about them, and select them by a majority vote. Except for a few mandatory rules that the principal and I have decided are best for the entire school, everybody here can help me decide what our other rules will be and what happens when our rules are either broken or followed."

Silence descends on the classroom. Annette can sense that the students are thinking hard about what she has said. Undoubtedly, they are struggling because they haven't experienced this process before. "So, rather than talk about rules that don't exist, why don't we figure out a few rules? Once we have examples, things will be a lot clearer," she promises. "Before we begin, I'd like to tell you the five mandatory rules that we will use as our starting point; I call them the Big Five. Like I said before, these are rules that the principal and I decided are best for everyone's welfare. They are fair and necessary but they are not negotiable. Once everyone understands these five basic rules, we can set up whatever other rules we want as long as the new ones do not go against the Big Five." She turns and starts writing on the large white board at the front of the room. "Okay, our first rule is . . ."

Rule #1: All our rules will be fair and reasonable, and they will be democratically decided upon. They will be posted on the wall for everyone to see and they will be enforced.

"This is a pretty straightforward rule but does anyone not understand what it means?" Annette is not surprised at no response because the rule doesn't really state anything the students have not heard from her already. Eventually, a hand goes up. "Yes, Anna?"

Anna is a quiet but bright girl. "This seems pretty obvious to me," she says quite matter of factly, "Why do we need such a rule?"

"Thank you, Anna, that's a great question. There are several good reasons for this rule, but the main reason is because in many classrooms the teacher is the only one who knows all the rules and students have to guess at what they can and cannot do. This especially happens in higher grades because many teachers expect students to already know how to act. Some teachers mistakenly think all students have implicitly learned over time what is good and bad classroom behaviour when, in fact, every student needs to be explicitly told exactly what the rules will be. I don't want you to guess or interpret my thoughts and actions, I want you to know precisely what the boundaries for your behaviours are. By talking about the rules and selecting them in a democratic fashion, we can all be on the same page. Nobody can later claim that they did not know a certain rule existed, or get into trouble because they broke an 'invisible' rule."

"Yeah, that's what happened to me last year," Jackson states with authority, "I got the stapler out of the teacher's desk to staple my assignment and hand it in and I got in b-i-i-i-g trouble." Lots of laughter erupts. "How was I supposed to know we weren't allowed in his desk? He never said anything."

"My point exactly," Annette remarks. "Don't forget that an important part of Rule #1 is that all the rules will be posted on the walls of the classroom where everyone can see them, every day. Another reason we need Rule #1 is because it refers to the democratic process, which is so important. We all want our rules to be fair and reasonable. Our group discussions will allow everyone to get a better understanding of each rule, and everyone will develop ownership for them, and not just see the rules as coming from me or the principal. Clearly stating that the rules will be enforced also reminds everyone of what they are supposed to do or not do and it reminds me, as your teacher, that I am ultimately responsible for everything that goes on in this room. I don't like having to punish students but I will enforce consequences if I have to because we have already agreed that they will make our classroom function best. There's no sense setting up a bunch of rules if they will not be enforced."

"Uh, Miss . . . ," the ever-skeptical Katherine raises her hand. "So it will be your job to give us rewards too?"

"Katherine, you took the words right out of my mouth." Annette says cheerfully. "In fact, I'd rather give out rewards for good behaviour every day than enforce consequences. That would mean that we are all getting along and we have the best opportunity to learn.

"Can time in the gym be a reward?" asks Brandon. "Free time would be better if we didn't have to stay in the classroom."

"Yes, that's possible. Anything that is fair and reasonable is possible." Annette can tell that they are starting to get the basic idea, so she goes back to writing on the white board. "Let's have a look at our next rule."

Rule #2: We will not tolerate any disrespectful behaviour.

As she reads it out loud, she can tell she has their undivided attention. "This means *anything* that is disrespectful, like rude or improper gestures or saying mean things, and it also includes saying mean things in a teasing manner because what is said is still hurtful. I am not including this rule because I'm worried that you will be disrespectful to me; I don't think you will be. The vast majority of disrespectful acts in classrooms are usually directed at other students. Nothing makes a person feel more psychologically insecure than being called names, or being teased, or threatened, or bullied, or put down. All disrespectful behaviour ever does is make people feel bad, and it can encourage more disrespectful behaviour. I cannot think of anything positive that can come from allowing disrespectful behaviour in our classroom. Can any of you?" She pauses and waits.

"Does that mean they can't tease me because I suck at school?" Jackson asks pleadingly. This is obviously troubling him.

"Yes, that's right Jackson, your classmates will no longer get away with teasing you about your grades," says Annette. "However, I don't think it will even be a problem because since no one here can come up with a good reason to allow disrespectful behaviour, I think we can safely assume that you won't be treated that way anymore. However, what do you think the consequence should be if someone does tease you or if they do anything else we consider disrespectful?" The bell rings before anyone can answer. *"Perfect timing!"* Annette says to herself. "Why don't you all think about that question during recess and we'll talk about it when you come back."

Once the students return from their break, there is considerable conversation. The class decides that there will be an escalating list of consequences for being disrespectful and Annette will mete these out according to what she thinks is appropriate based on the offence. As a bare minimum, the offending student will have to publicly acknowledge that they have been disrespectful and sincerely apologize to the victim. Tara thoughtfully interjects, "If everybody knows the rules and the punishments for breaking them, then everybody will know when someone has crossed the line and what will happen next! That will definitely make people stop and think before they do something. Besides, who wants to be embarrassed by having to stand up in class and make an apology? Not me!"

The group also agrees that if the disrespectful behaviour requires a stronger punishment, the following additional consequences are to be levied:

1. No computer privileges (variable duration)
2. No free time (variable duration)
3. After-school detention (variable duration)
4. A note to parents
5. A visit to the principal's office

"Now, what behaviours do you think you should be rewarded for?" asks Annette, only somewhat rhetorically. "Or do you think it's fair and reasonable to expect people to treat each other with respect without being rewarded?"

"Yes," says Katherine, "um . . . oh, I don't know, it's just that you said you wanted us to be good and there would be rewards. . . ." Her voice trails off.

"I know what you mean," says Annette with a smile, "So, I propose this. Rather than rewarding people for being overtly respectful, which can become fake and meaningless, let's decide on a reward for being polite *and* not being disrespectful; that there is more good behaviour and less bad behaviours. You have to remember, we are talking about *your* judgments about respectful and disrespectful behaviours, not only mine or the principal's."

After more discussion, they agree that the reward for not being disrespectful for a whole day will be 10 minutes of free time the following day. Those who break the rule will lose the privilege and suffer one of the previously agreed upon consequences. But Annette feels it is important for the students to see themselves as having the potential to exceed the behavioural expectations inferred in the rule, so she gets them to agree that after a one-week trial period, they will need two good days to earn the same free time. They also agree to re-evaluate everything two weeks after that.

Annette can tell the process of collectively deciding the rules is making the students far more aware of the intent of each rule. *"This never would have happened if I simply told them these things,"* she thinks ruefully. *"Because they all know that everyone knows the rules and has agreed to them, they all will be much more vigilant about adhering to them. More importantly,"* she concludes, *"they now have a behaviour to consciously and meaningfully work on instead of simply obeying vague rules to avoid punishment. This level of student awareness and responsibility makes a lot of sense."*

Annette picks up right where she left off. "I need your attention please. Our next mandatory rule is just as important as the previous one. In fact, you might think of this rule as simply addressing another form of disrespect." She reads what she has written on the whiteboard.

Rule #3: Students are not to touch other students or their things without permission.

Unknowingly but perceptibly, all student heads nod in approval. This tells Annette this rule has struck an appreciative chord. "The reason for this rule is that unwanted touching causes bad feelings, arguments, and fights and it rarely achieves anything positive. We are all very protective of ourselves and our belongings. Like the disrespect rule, this rule is necessary because most unwanted touching happens to students, not to teachers or other adults in the school. Can you think of any time when this rule might not apply?"

"What about when we are helping other students and passing out things that belong to others, like books and scribblers and papers?" asks Sophie, who likes helping out. "That isn't the same, right?"

"That's right Sophie, that's not what this rule is for. Everyone here will still be able to do all of those things. What the rule is for is to keep people from touching or hitting others, because even if it is done in a friendly or teasing manner it can be very irritating and often leads to bigger problems. Touching someone or their possessions when they don't want you to is very disrespectful. The rule will also keep people from going into someone else's backpack, desk, or lunch box. These types of acts create nothing but problems and hard feelings. So, to start with, we will all assume that no one has given anyone permission to touch them or their things. That way everyone is on the same page. Now, let's discuss possible rewards for following the rule and consequences that will be used if it is broken."

Their previous concerted effort with the disrespect rule now pays off handsomely and the class quickly comes to a consensus in less than half the time. They decide that since the "no touching" rule is an extension of the disrespectful behaviour rule, the rewards and punishments will be the same. But Katherine becomes worried that the reward element is now too good to be true.

"Miss, so, does this mean we can get 20 minutes of free time each day if we obey both rules? That could be a lot of free time in one week. Shouldn't we be spending that time on school work?" There are audible groans from the other students.

"You have a good point, Katherine," Annette acknowledges, "but I see it as time well spent because of the positive behaviours that earned the free time. When disruptive behaviours happen, teachers have to interrupt their lesson to correct the student, or they use up even more time when they stop everything to deal with the student directly. Without clear and explicit rules, these extended interruptions happen over and over again and waste a lot of time. Also, these interruptions often involve heated arguments and high emotions by teachers and students. Not only does this make everyone in the room uncomfortable, but everybody worries about the next eruption. If that is my option, I am more than happy give you free time because you were behaving. Yes, teaching time is lost either way, but you have to admit that free time puts it to far better use." She closes on that important point and she goes back to the whiteboard. "Now, the next rule is a little bit longer than the others, but it's one you will definitely like."

Rule #4: Students will be allowed to do lots of talking. Other than when Ms. Elkins is teaching or giving directions, when someone is speaking, or when students are writing a test, students can talk amongst themselves at an appropriate volume.

As she turns back to the group, she is faced with several ear-to-ear smiles. She knows this rule will go a long way toward maintaining harmony. "Look, I know you all want to talk to each other and I think that's a good thing as long as it does not interfere with what I need to do and as long as it doesn't get too loud. Let's do an activity to set a suitable volume. At the same time, I'd like all of you to say out loud your name, birthday, and telephone number . . . and repeat it over and over until I tell you to stop. While you are talking, I will raise or lower my hand to tell you to either raise or lower your voices. When my hand is level with my waist," she demonstrates that position, "that will be the acceptable volume for talking."

After the acceptable volume is established, Annette moves on. "Another time that students like to talk is after they have completed their seatwork, but talking at that time can also be distracting to those who are still working. What I'd like us to agree on is that no one will talk until everyone is finished their work. Once everyone is finished, and if there is time, you can all talk until we move on to the next part of the lesson."

"Ms. Elkins, do we have to just sit here while the others are finishing up?" asks Tara.

"No, that would be a waste of your time," Annette replies, "so I have a better solution. What I want each of you to do is write out a list of five things you want to do whenever you are finished your seatwork, such as reading a book or magazine, working on an assignment, drawing, or just sitting quietly. This can also include moving around the room or using the computer as long you are very quiet. Let's call these things *After Seatwork Options*."

"Can we listen to music on our iPods?" asks Brandon.

"Yes, but you can only use one earplug. It will be difficult for me to get your attention if you have both earplugs in and your music on," Annette explains. "Besides, you are already allowed to listen to your music before school, during recess and lunchtime, and after school while waiting for the bus, so I think this is a fair compromise." Brandon is pleased.

"In addition to your list, I will also make a list of five things I would like each of you to do once your work is done, such as working on a project, revising a draft, reading for the next lesson, getting extra help from me, or helping me get ready for a class activity. I'll meet with each of you individually and we will review both lists to make sure we aren't duplicating anything. You can put both lists in your desk or your planner and I'll have copies of everyone's lists in my planner. Then, when you are finished your seatwork, you can choose something from *your* list on Mondays, Wednesdays, and Fridays, and something from *my* list on Tuesdays and Thursdays. We can change both lists every month, especially if you finish something on either list. That way you will always have something to do while waiting for others to finish. How does that sound?"

"Aw, that sounds like everyone will be bugging me to hurry up because I'm always last and they will want to talk and I'll never get to talk because I'm so slow," says Jackson, not happy at all at that prospect.

"No, Jackson, the others will not pester you to hurry up because that would be disrespectful," says Annette quite pointedly. She can tell this seemingly innocuous behaviour was not something they had previously thought of as disrespectful, but their nods indicate they agree with her logic. "So, I'll tell you what; on days when there will be at least five minutes left after everyone else is finished, you can stop as well and take the rest of your work home as part of your homework. That way, nobody will bother you and you will get to talk like everyone else, or you can do something from your *After Seatwork Options*. It will be your choice, but you will have to be responsible for doing the work at home or I cannot let you have that privilege. How do you feel about that?"

"That's okay, I guess, but it means I will always have more homework than everybody else." Jackson is not convinced the deal is worth it.

"Here's another way to look at it," says Annette. "The seatwork I give you is very important, so it needs to be done. You have to decide whether you want to do it here or finish it at home. It's completely your choice."

"But . . . if I don't do it at home . . . I won't be allowed to take it home anymore." Jackson's statement is almost a question.

Rather than let him dwell on all the possible ways that this could go wrong or end badly, Annette intervenes: "I understand. Let's put our plan in place for the first couple of weeks and see how it goes, then we can decide if we want to continue." Jackson shrugs his shoulders and grins; he seems willing to give it a try.

Jackson's issues aside, the essence of the talking rule seems understood and appreciated by the students, but Annette knows from experience that the bane of many teachers' existence is getting students to stop talking and pay attention as needed. She informs her class that along with their earned right to talk comes a responsibility to stop talking and pay full attention to her when she asks them to. From experience, Annette knows that yelling "Can I have your attention, please?" or "Please stop talking!" does not work because in the past she used these attention-getters without attaching student responsibility for a proper response. In fact, the more she raised her voice, the less effect it seemed to have and the louder the students talked. Annette informs her new students that when she wants their attention, she will briefly turn the lights off, then back on, and when this happens, all students are to stop whatever they are doing, stop talking, and face her. She attaches student responsibility to this action by having them decide on a consequence for not following this rule and a reward for appropriate behaviour. After some concerted discussion, the students agree that a failure to adhere to this aspect of the talking rule constitutes a breach of the overall rule and, thus, the same consequences should follow. However, and this takes a lot of explaining on Annette's part, they eventually agree that being quiet and paying attention to the teacher is a respectful, necessary, and vital component of the teaching and learning process. They also agree, ruefully, that it does not warrant a reward.

Annette starts writing the final rule on the whiteboard. "Here is the last rule in the Big Five."

Rule #5: The principal will be aware of all class rules and she will support us in our good behaviour as well as address our bad behaviour.

From their startled looks, Annette can tell this is new. "There are several reasons why this rule is necessary. First, while I am responsible for what goes on in our classroom, Mrs. Nugent is responsible for what goes on in the entire school. It makes sense, therefore, that she knows exactly what our rules, rewards, and consequences are. She also needs to know about the democratic process we went through to develop our rules. If I have to send you to see Mrs. Nugent for some reason, she can then fairly deal with you according to our rules." Annette knows that because the students will be aware that the principal knows the rules and the process used to devise them, students will not be able to plead ignorance if they break one of them. Knowing that the principal knows will eliminate students' attempts to pit the teacher against the principal (or their parents). It also increases student accountability beyond the confines of the classroom.

To complete the rule-setting process, Annette tapes two large pieces of chart paper on the wall and divides the students into two groups. She directs each group to a piece of chart paper. "I want each group to come up with three to five rules to implement in our classroom. Remember to choose rules that address important issues but which are not contrary to the Big Five. Once you have listed your rules on the chart paper, decide on reasonable rewards and consequences for each. Write them underneath the rule, rewards first followed by consequences." After the students complete the task, Annette says, "Please switch chart papers and discuss the rules, rewards, and consequences developed by the other group. When you are finished, we will discuss everything as a class and everyone can provide feedback."

When they finish, Annette asks Sophie and Simon to combine all rules, rewards, and consequences on the whiteboard. She purposefully asks each group to explain why their rule, reward, or consequence is fair and reasonable. She then asks for class feedback and discussion, followed by a vote. A majority vote is required to add a rule to the list started by the Big Five. Annette is prepared to veto a rule if it is approved but negatively affects a particular student or group. In the end, three rules are added to the overall list:

Rule #6: No cellphones allowed in the classroom.

Students who do not bring their cellphones into the classroom may use them during the entire lunch break.

If a student brings a cellphone into the classroom, the teacher will keep the cellphone until class is dismissed for the day. If this occurs more than twice, the student's parents will have to see the principal to get the phone back.

Rule #7: Students must be on time for class.

If there are less than eight instances of students being late in a two-week period, the class earns the privilege of watching a movie during class time.

A student who is late must stay in the classroom during the morning break. Three lates in two weeks and he or she cannot watch the movie.

Rule #8: Students must be prepared for class (have all the materials they need, including their completed homework).

Students who are prepared for the entire week will have no homework assigned for the weekend.

A student who is not prepared must write a list of what they need for the next school day and have it signed by the teacher and a parent.

Before the rule-making process started, Annette had formulated a series of other rules she thought would be helpful based on past teaching experiences. She keeps careful track of her students' deliberations to make sure that nothing important is overlooked. In the end, Annette is extremely pleased with their overall rules. "Congratulations, you have been a great help in establishing our rules. We have one final step in this procedure but I need a few minutes to set it up. In the meantime, I'd like all of you to list your five *After Seatwork Options* and, obviously, you can talk while you are doing it. This will be our very first test of working and talking at the same time." Annette waits until they are started and slips out of her busy room, assured the students' attention to the activity and their "permission" to talk will keep them on task for the time she needs. Her heart leaps as she returns to a chatty but busy classroom and she is encouraged at her first success. Not only is the noise level acceptable, but each student is finished their list and they appear happy. She briefly turns the lights off, and then back on. Annette is not sure if the immediate silence and inactivity is due to the unexpected darkness or because the students are remembering her attention-getting rule, but she gives them the benefit of the doubt.

"Well," she says with a genuine smile, "Thank you for stopping what you were doing and paying attention. And thank you for working on your lists and for keeping the volume down while I was out of the room."

"You were gone?" Katherine asks.

"Yes, Katherine, I was gone for about two minutes, but it didn't seem to matter because all of you carried on as if I was still here. You should be impressed."

"Really?" says Tara, "I mean, all we did was talk and do our lists. It was kind of normal. We didn't do anything special."

"Tara, that's exactly the point. This should be a normal thing for our class all the time . . . the whole class adhering to basic and fair rules. Doing your lists and talking quietly and paying attention when I flicked the lights are the obvious things, but a lot more happened during that time. There was no disrespectful behaviour, nobody touched anyone else or their things, and nobody was acting out or using their cellphone or iPod when I came back. Yes, this was our first experiment and it was for a short time, but I think it went exceptionally well and I don't see any reason why we cannot do this all the time. It's almost time for lunch so you can head to the lunchroom. Job well done!"

After lunch, Mrs. Nugent arrives as Annette had arranged earlier when she left the classroom. Annette invites her in. "Students, as you will remember, one of our rules states that Mrs. Nugent will be aware of all our rules and the rewards and consequences that go with them. I'd like Sophie and Simon to tell Mrs. Nugent about each of the rules we established. When the group leaders are finished and all of Mrs. Nugent's questions have been answered, I will make a final copy of all the rules, rewards, and consequences to put up on our wall. I will also give a copy to Mrs. Nugent so she can keep it in her office."

The discussion with Mrs. Nugent takes quite a while and finishes with about 15 minutes left in the day. Annette has no difficulty convincing the students to use one of their *After Seatwork Options* for the duration of that time. When the dismissal bell finally rings, Annette congratulates the students again for a successful first day. As they leave for home, she gets busy making copies of the rules. She is tired but happy to have achieved so much. She is hopeful that the tone for the school year has been set and the focus can now turn to learning.

Glossary

achievement targets: A set of specifications for what students should learn to do. Developed by Rick Stiggins, they purposefully target the development of (a) the combined use of knowledge with specific thinking processes to create products and (b) the preferred attitudes and dispositions that students should bring to bear on their academic endeavours.

adaptive expert: A teacher who has the habit of mind to inquire continually into their practice; a lifelong learner who balances instructional efficiency with instructional innovation.

additive bilingualism: An approach to bilingualism that ensures one's first language is maintained while learning a second language.

antiracist education: Education that raises awareness of social inequity based on racism.

applied behaviour analysis: The study of socially relevant human behaviour in naturally occurring applied settings.

assessment tool: A mechanism by which teachers assess student learning. It can refer to either a single question or assignment that assesses student knowledge or skills, or to a collection of different types of questions in the form of larger assignments, tests, or exams.

axiology: The branch of philosophy concerned with aesthetics and ethics; that is, how we define what is beautiful and what is morally good and valuable.

backward design: A curriculum planning strategy where learning experiences are designed first by selecting the aims or outcomes teachers wish to achieve.

behaviour management: The actions that teachers take to diminish or decrease poor behaviours and to increase desirable behaviours. Behaviour management is considered an essential subset of classroom management.

Big Five: Five non-negotiable school-wide rules that underlie all classroom-specific rules, rewards, and consequences developed by teachers and students under dynamic classroom management.

Bloom's taxonomy: A hierarchical classification of cognitive learning objectives developed by Benjamin Bloom and colleagues.

British North America (BNA) Act: The legislation passed in 1867 by the British Parliament to create the legal entity known as the Dominion of Canada. The act included specific provisions for education, specifying which level of government has control over and responsibility for maintaining schools, and the relative protections for and rights of linguistic minorities regarding education.

checklist: A list of performance criteria that a teacher uses to indicate whether some or all of the criteria are evident when a student or group of students performs or demonstrates something.

CIA rope: A metaphor used to describe the core cycle of activities that teachers engage in. The rope is envisioned as a three-stranded braid where one strand is curriculum, the second is instruction, and the third is assessment. Without all three strands the rope will not have the required strength.

classroom assessment: The systematic process of gathering reliable information about student understandings of critical knowledge, skills, attitudes, and behaviours.

classroom discourse research: Research that advocates for explanatory and collaborative teacher–student discourses to explicitly establish rules and classroom routines.

classroom management: The actions teachers undertake to create environments that enhance academic learning and appropriate social skill development.

codification: The assembly, arrangement into order, and systematization of principles that govern a professional body.

cognitive pluralism: An ideology that proposes that there are multiple ways to know and express our knowledge.

cognitive verbs: Verbs used in a learning objective that specifically delineate the way that teachers want students to think as a result of participating in any given lesson.

collective orientation: A cultural orientation that values group membership and places high value on loyalty to that group. Members of this orientation assume collective responsibility for tasks and place priority on building relationships.

common schools: Nineteenth-century state-run elementary schools that were required by law in every state in the United States and in most jurisdictions in Canada.

completion or fill-in-the-blank questions: A type of short-answer question that requires students to complete a sentence with the correct words, numbers, or symbols. This requires the basic recall of information, which is a slightly better indicator of higher-order learning than the simple recognition of information.

conflict theory: A theoretical perspective that sees schools as contributing to the reproduction of unequal social relations.

consensus perspective: A theoretical perspective that sees society as a system with relative stability, order, and cohesion. This perspective takes a neutral view of schooling and thus assumes no responsibility for the educational failure of disadvantaged students.

consequentialism: Also called utilitarianism, consequentialism seeks the most useful consequence; the greatest good for the greatest number of people.

conservatism: A subset of the educational philosophy known as essentialism that resists rapid change in education. It endorses basic skills instruction, rigorous academic standards, and strict disciplinary standards.

constructed-response items: Questions that require students to think about, construct, and write their answers. These questions test students' ability to apply the basic knowledge they have learned.

content validity: The extent to which a test (and the questions contained therein) properly address the essence of the content that was taught; this is the most important criterion in assessing teacher-generated tests.

critical theory: A theoretical perspective that offers a vision of change for society. Critical theorists believe education can raise consciousness about unequal power structures in society and help students become agents of change.

critical theory: An ideology that aims to cultivate an awareness of the hidden curriculum—that is, the unspoken values that permeate schools.

cultural deficit theory: A theory that emphasizes economic circumstances, poor parenting, and students' low motivation when looking at differences in achievement among different cultural groups, rather than on innate differences among the groups.

cultural diversity: The differences in social values, beliefs, and worldviews that give order and meaning to people's lives.

curriculum guides: Year- or term-long outlines of school subjects that are differentiated by grade. They are developed by each province and territory by a team of experts that includes teachers. In Alberta, they are referred to as Programs of Study.

deficit theory: A theory suggesting that differences in achievement reflect innate differences among different cultural groups.

deontology: An ethical theory that claims humans have an obligation to do what duty requires, regardless of the consequences.

design work: Student work that demonstrates the ability to work creatively with knowledge rather than working creatively on tasks that use knowledge; that is, working on ideas as opposed to using ideas to do work.

diagnostic assessment: Determining what students already know and what skills they possess for the purpose of guiding future instruction.

direct instruction: A systematic instructional method that prescribes the teaching of small amounts of information and providing lots of student practice to attain mastery of basic facts and skills.

disciplinary thinking: The different ways of thinking and practising that different disciplines have. In an educational context, students learn to "think like a scientist" or "think like a historian."

discrimination: Taking action based on prejudices or stereotypes.

ecological validity: An explicit judgment of the meaningfulness and usefulness of a behavioural intervention in the context of the routines, experiences, and performance of a classroom or school

educational curriculum: A concept developed by British curriculum scholar A. V. Kelly that provides "a liberating experience focusing on such things as the promotion of freedom and independence of thought, of social and political empowerment, of respect for the freedom of others, of an acceptance of variety of opinion, and of the enrichment of the life of every individual in that society, regardless of class, race or creed" (Kelly, 2009, p. 8).

enacted curriculum: The pedagogy that emerges from the interests and passions of both the teachers and the students.

enduring understandings: Ideas that are key for the discipline and have significance beyond the classroom.

epistemology: The branch of philosophy concerned with the nature and scope of knowledge addressed by questions like, "What is knowledge?" "How is knowledge constructed?" "How do we know what we know?" It is usually accompanied by a healthy skepticism about different knowledge claims.

epistemology: The branch of philosophy that addresses what knowledge is and how we acquire it.

essay question: A type of constructed-response question that requires students to recall knowledge, organize it, and present it in a logical manner as an indication of their ability to integrate their new knowledge and thinking skills.

essential questions: Broad, timeless questions that bring relevance and depth to curriculum.

essentialism: A philosophy of education that emphasizes basic skills and subjects, mastery of the content checked by standards, and preparing students to be productive citizens through classrooms that are orderly, disciplined, and efficient.

established goals: In curriculum planning, these are typically the broad curriculum outcomes—the "big picture" priorities that should guide the planning process.

ethics: Principles and norms that govern human conduct.

eudaimonia: A Greek word translated as happiness but better defined as human fulfillment or flourishing.

evidence-based practice: Teacher practices that are based on established and consistent research findings.

existentialism: A philosophical system that emphasizes personal responsibility for one's choices and living an authentic life.

extracurricular experiences: Activities that take place during lunch hour or after school, such as clubs and teams. Also called *informal curriculum.*

formal or intended curriculum: The key content that must be included at each grade level, as mandated by the provincial/territorial government.

formative assessment: Assessment that takes place during instruction for the purpose of improving teaching and learning.

hidden curriculum: The subtle messages learned in school regarding what is valued, including things like compliance and gender norms.

high power distance cultures: Members of high power distance cultures are very formal with superiors and they won't contradict them. They expect detailed directions and will seek permission before taking initiative.

How People Learn (HPL) framework: A framework developed by the National Academy of Sciences Committee to organize what is known about teaching and learning.

idealism: A philosophical system often traced to Plato, who believed that there is an ideal world of perfect ideas; that is, ideas that express truths are universal.

independent schools: Schools that operate independently of the local public or Catholic school board, almost always governed by a parent council or school council.

individual orientation: A cultural orientation that values freedom, autonomy, and privacy. Members of this orientation value the time and energy they put into achieving individual goals.

informal curriculum: Activities that take place during lunch hour or after school, such as clubs and teams. Also called *extracurricular experiences.*

interrogative perspective: A theoretical perspective that recognizes schools as politically charged organizations that mirror the power struggles in society. Conflict theory and critical theory are two interrogative perspectives.

learned curriculum: What students actually learn; it is not always the same as what teachers intended.

learning objective: An instructional goal that teachers want to achieve. They provide teachers with a systematized method of knowing where they want to take their students, charting a plan to take them there, and confirming that they have arrived in good order.

low power distance cultures: Members of low power distance cultures are informal with superiors and they are not afraid to critique or contradict the ideas of those in authority positions. They will ask for clarification of questions and will take initiative.

marking rubric: An assessment mechanism that outlines all the potential elements of a correct response to a restricted-essay or essay question.

matching questions: A type of selected-response question that typically requires students to indicate that a concept or term from one list matches or is related to a corresponding concept or term in a second list. These questions are best used to assess students' understanding of associations and linkages between concepts.

meta-analysis: An overview of existing research on a topic.

metacognition: Higher-order thinking skills such as planning, monitoring, and evaluating that oversee and control the cognitive processes used in learning.

metaphysics: The branch of philosophy that seeks to understand what is real.

multicultural education: Education that seeks to be inclusive of many cultural ideas and values by appreciating diversity or preserving cultural heritage.

multiple-choice questions: A type of selected-response question that requires students to read a question or statement (called the stem) and select one correct answer from preferably four but sometimes five options. These are the most common type of selected-response questions. They are ideal for testing basic knowledge, but carefully worded questions can also be used to test student understanding.

null curriculum: Information, activities, or content that is not included in the curriculum, either formal or informal.

pedagogy: The principles, methods, and activities of instruction that compose the profession of a teacher; sometimes referred to as "how one teaches."

perennialism: A philosophy of education that believes great truths are universal and unchanging, so education should foster rational powers and transmit these truths, often through classic texts.

permanent contracts: Teacher contracts that are continuous from year to year, which helps stabilize the staff for a particular board but also gives the teacher protection against unwarranted dismissal.

pragmatism: A philosophical system that believes that knowledge is constructed by individuals and groups to solve problems they encounter. Pragmatists believe that reality is what is observed or experienced and truth is what works.

praxis: The process of engaging, applying, exercising, or practising a theory, lesson, or skill such that practice and theory become intertwined.

prejudice: One's attitude toward members of a particular group. They are usually, although not always, negative.

problem-, project-, and inquiry-based learning (PPIL): A student-centred, constructivist instructional approach in which students (a) help teachers design comprehensive curricular tasks in response to key questions, (b) collaboratively solve problems with peers, (c) create specific educational products, and (d) reflect on their learning experiences.

process–outcome research: Research that focuses on creating learning environments that are orderly and psychologically secure so that students can learn better and more efficiently.

professionalism: Teacher professionalism comprises high levels of competence, performance, and conduct in regard to educating students, engaging in professional development, and being an exemplar of the discipline.

progressivism: A child-centred philosophy emphasizing problem solving while capitalizing on students' curiosity and creative self-expression.

progressivism: A learner-centred ideology that focuses on the growth of the individual. A progressive curriculum motivates students to delve into a problem.

racism: When racial differences are the basis for social discrimination. Racism can occur on an individual level or an institutional/systemic level.

rating scale: An assessment tool that enables teachers to make qualified judgments about the skills observed, not merely indicate whether the skill was evident or not. A scale usually contains between three to five descriptors that a teacher can use to judge how well a student has demonstrated knowledge or a skill.

rational humanism: An ideology that values the capacity of human beings to think critically and rationally. Proponents of this curriculum ideology believe that all students should be exposed to the same curriculum, regardless of social class, so that they are all exposed to the best cultural artifacts.

realism: A philosophical system often traced to Aristotle, who believed that reality could be perceived with one's senses, and one could abstract concepts from those experiences.

received curriculum: The method by which teachers deliver the formal curriculum and thus the way the curriculum is received by students.

reconceptualism: An ideology that challenges the managerial values in education and focuses on the lived experience of the learner, particularly aesthetic experiences.

reflective practice: The process of purposefully thinking about one's teaching practice and actively considering whether it can be changed.

reliability: The extent to which a test produces consistent results.

religious orthodox ideologies: Ideologies that maintain that education should initiate children into the beliefs of the religious group.

restricted-essay question: A type of constructed-response question that requires students to write an essay in response to a question that is limited in terms of the length and/or the depth of the response required.

romantic tradition: An educational tradition started by Jean-Jacques Rousseau that views children as naturally good and as having the capacity to choose well.

rubric: A set of specific criteria that describe and qualify various levels of student performance on some sort of educational product. In a way, a rubric is an expanded checklist that also contains elaborated descriptive rating scales that are used to confer summaries of student performance.

Scholastics: Medieval theologians and philosophers who studied Greek and Roman classics and debated issues such as how to synthesize sacred and secular knowledge and whether education should have a practical purpose or simply provide the opportunity to engage in liberal learning.

school boards: Locally elected officials given responsibility by each province to run the local school district. School board members are elected (usually every two to three years) and hire professional staff to oversee the schools in a district.

school council: An elected group that oversees and directs the work of one school. School councils share responsibility with their respective school boards. School council membership always includes parents, often teachers, and sometimes administrators.

selected-response items: Questions that require students to select an answer from the options that are provided. These questions test students' understanding of basic knowledge.

short-answer questions: A type of constructed-response question where students either write a word, phrase, or few sentences to provide a correct answer or where they complete a sentence by filling in the correct word, number, or symbol.

sine qua non: A necessary, indispensable, and essential principle, action, or condition of an entity without which there is nothing.

site-based management: A funding model that puts authority over and responsibility for spending decisions in the hands of the principal at a particular school.

social class: The social stratification of groups in society based on indicators like income, occupation, and levels of education.

social desirability bias: A research term used to denote the tendency of respondents to reply in a manner that will be viewed favourably by others, usually by overreporting good behaviours or underreporting bad behaviour.

social efficiency ideology: An ideology that holds that curriculum should efficiently provide the skills necessary for students to become functioning members of society.

social mobility: The process of changing social class. If this is accomplished within one's own lifetime it is called *intragenerational mobility*; if the change is relative to one's parents, it is called *intergenerational mobility*.

social reconstructionism: A philosophy of education that maintains that teachers and schools ought to be change agents in creating a new and more equitable social order.

Socratic method: A dialogue-based instructional approach where teachers ask students open-ended questions that require generative and rationalized answers. These usually prompt further questions, deeper analysis, and better understandings.

stereotyping: Assuming that all people from a particular culture share the same values and behave in the same ways.

student evaluation: The process of making educational judgments based on assessment data.

subtractive bilingualism: When a second language learner loses his or her first language because of lack of use.

summative assessment: The most common type of assessment that is used after instruction to indicate how well students have learned the material and to provide an overall grade for a particular reporting period.

Table of Specifications: A table or chart that systematically outlines (a) the topics covered by the test, (b) the number of questions to be used to assess each topic, and (c) the level of thinking required for each category of questions based on Bloom's taxonomy of cognitive skills.

temporary contracts: Teacher contracts that are only valid for a specific period of time. Some examples of the many situations that would require a temporary contract are when the funding for a specific program came from a one-time funding source, or covering a permanent teacher's maternity leave.

theistic realism: A fusion of Aristotle's realism with Christian theology, marrying the educational goals of cultivating reason and spirituality. Also known as Thomism after its developer, Thomas Aquinas.

triangulation: The combined analysis of related pieces of information to establish the validity of a research conclusion.

true/false questions: A type of selected-response question where students are asked to identify whether a given statement is true or false. These questions are good for quickly testing students' understanding of basic knowledge.

validity: The extent to which a test assesses what it is supposed to assess.

virtue ethics axiology: An ethical theory that suggests that ethical behaviour originates from the character of individuals rather than consequences or any rules.

visible minority: A category that exists in labour policy to promote equity in hiring and includes all persons (other than Aboriginal people) who are non-White.

xenophobia: The fear of those who are different. Comes from the Greek word *xenos* (foreigner/stranger) and *phobos* (fear).

References

Abboud, R., Chong, J., Gray, D., Kaderdina, R., Masongsong, M., & Rahman, K. M. (2002). *The kit: A manual by youth to combat racism through education*. Ottawa, ON: United Nations Association in Canada.

Adams, D. W. (1995). *Education for extinction: American Indians and the boarding school experience, 1875–1928*. Lawrence, KS: University Press of Kansas.

Alberta Assessment Consortium. (2012). *Healthy retreat*. Retrieved from http://www.aac.ab.ca/wp-content/uploads/2013/10/EMHL6healthyretreat.pdf.

Alberta Education. (2005). *Social studies: Kindergarten to Grade 3*. Retrieved from http://education.alberta.ca/media/456082/sockto3.pdf.

Alberta Education. (2005b). *Our words, our ways: Teaching First Nations, Métis, and Inuit learners*. Edmonton, AB: Author.

Alberta Education. (2006). *Social studies Kindergarten to Grade 12*. Retrieved from http://education.alberta.ca/media/457625/ss7.pdf.

Alberta Education. (2010a). *Inspiring education: A dialogue with Albertans*. Edmonton, AB: Author.

Alberta Education. (2010b). *Handbook for international education administrators*. Edmonton, AB: Author.

Alberta Queen's Printer. (1999). *School Act: Certification of Teachers Regulation*. Edmonton, AB: Author. Retrieved from http://www.qp.alberta.ca/1266.cfm?page=1999_003.cfm&leg_type=Regs&isbncln=9780779733316.

Alberta Teachers' Association. (2008). Elk Island Public Schools Regions Division 14 (2007–2012). Retrieved from http://www.teachers.ab.ca/For%20Members/Salary%20Benefits%20and%20Pension/CollectiveAgreements/Pages/Elk%20Island%20Public%20Schools%20RD%20No%2014%20%282007%20-%202012%29.aspx.

Alters, B., Asghar, A., & Wiles, J. R. (2005). Evolution Education Research Centre. *Humanist Perspectives, 154*. Retrieved from http://www.humanistperspectives.org/issue154/EERC.html.

Anderson, C. M., & Freeman, K. A. (2000). Positive behavior support: Expanding the application of applied behavior analysis. *The Behavior Analyst, 23*, 85–94.

Anyon, J. (1981). Social class and school knowledge. *Curriculum Inquiry, 11*(1), 3–42.

Aoki, T. T. (2005). *Curriculum in a new key: The collected works of Ted T. Aoki*. W. F. Pinar & R. L. Irwin (Eds.). Mahwah, NJ: Lawrence Erlbaum Associates.

Apple, M. (1990). *Ideology and curriculum* (2nd ed.). New York, NY: Routledge

Arrowood, C. A. (Ed.). (1930). *Thomas Jefferson and the education the republic*. New York, NY: McGraw-Hill.

Attorney General of New Brunswick. (1997). *Education Act*. Retrieved from http://laws.gnb.ca/en/ShowTdm/cs/E-1.12//.

Baer, D. M., Wolf, M. M., & Risely, T. R. (1968). Some current dimensions of applied behaviour analysis. *Journal of Applied Behaviour Analysis, 1*, 91–97.

Bai, H. (2012). Reclaiming our moral agency through healing: A call to moral, social, environmental activists. *Journal of Moral Education, 41*(3), 311–327.

Bainbridge, J., & Heydon, R. (2013). *Constructing meaning: Teaching the elementary language arts* (5th ed.). Toronto, ON: Thomson Nelson.

Baker, C. (2006). *Foundations of bilingual education and bilingualism* (4th ed.). Clevedon, UK: Multilingual Matters.

Ball, J., & Lewis, M. (2005). Talking points: What can speech-language partners contribute to Aboriginal early childhood development? In J. Whitehead (Ed.), *Research connections Canada: Supporting children and families: Vol. 1* (pp. 21–40). Ottawa, ON: Canadian Child Care Federation.

Bandura, A. (1977). Self-efficacy: Toward a unifying theory of behavioral change. *Psychological Review, 84*(2), 191–215.

Bandura, A. (1986). *Social foundations of thought and action: A social cognitive theory*. Englewood Cliffs, NJ: Prentice-Hall.

Banks, J. A. (2004). Multicultural education: Historical development, dimensions, and practice. In J. A. Banks & C. A. McGee Banks (Eds.), *Handbook of research on multicultural education* (pp. 3–49). San Francisco, CA: Jossey-Bass.

Barrow, R. (2010). Schools of thought in philosophy of education. In R. Bailey, R. Barrow, D. Carr, & C. McCarthy (Eds.), *The Sage handbook of philosophy of education* (pp. 21–35). London, UK: Sage.

Battiste, M. (2002). *Indigenous knowledge and pedagogy in First Nations education: A literature review with recommendations*. Prepared for the National Working Group on Education and the Minister of Indian Affairs, Indian and Northern Affairs Canada. Retrieved from http://www.usask.ca/education/people/battistem/ikp_e.pdf.

Beaman, R., Wheldall, K., & Kemp, C. (2006). Differential teacher attention to boys and girls in the classroom. *Educational Review, 58*, 339–366.

Bereiter, C., & Scardamalia, M. (2006). Education for the knowledge age: Design centered models of teaching and instruction. In P. A. Alexander & P. H. Winne (Eds.), *Handbook of educational psychology* (2nd ed., pp. 695–713). Mahwah, NJ: Lawrence Erlbaum.

Berliner, D. C., & Calfee, R. C. (Eds.). (1996). *Handbook of educational psychology*. New York, NY: Macmillan.

Bernstein, R. (1978). *The restructuring of social and political theory*. Philadelphia, PA: University of Pennsylvania Press.

Black, P., & Wiliam, D. (1998). Inside the black box: Raising standards through classroom assessment. *Phi Delta Kappan, 80*, 139–148.

Blair, H., & Sanford, K. (2004). Morphing literacy: Boys reshaping their literacy practices. *Language Arts, 81*(3), 452–460.

Bloom, B. S., Englehart, M. B., Furst, E. J., Hill, W. H., & Krathwohl, O. R. (1956). *Taxonomy of educational objectives: The classification of educational goals. Handbook 1: The cognitive domain*. New York, NY: Longman.

Bobbitt, F. (1918). *The curriculum*. Cambridge, MA: Riverside Press.

Bourdieu, P. (1977). Cultural reproduction and social reproduction. In J. Karabel & A. Halsey (Eds.), *Power and ideology in education* (487–511). New York, NY: Oxford University Press.

Bowles, S., & Gintis, H. (1976). *Schooling in capitalist America: Educational reform and the contradictions of economic life*. London, UK: Routledge and Kegan Paul Ltd.

Bransford, J. D., Brown, A. L., & Cocking, R. R. (Eds.). (2000). *How people learn: Brain, mind, experience, and school* (expanded ed.). Washington, DC: National Academy Press.

Bransford, J., Darling-Hammond, L., & LePage, P. (2005). Introduction. In L. Darling-Hammond & J. Bransford (Eds.), *Preparing teachers for a changing world: What teachers should learn and be able to do* (pp. 1–39). San Francisco, CA: Jossey-Bass.

Bransford, J., Derry, S., Berliner, D., Hammerness, K., & Beckett, K. L. (2005). Theories of learning and their roles in teaching. In L. Darling-Hammond & J. Bransford (Eds.), *Preparing teachers for a changing world: What teachers should learn and be able to do* (pp. 40–87). San Francisco, CA: Jossey-Bass.

Brice Heath, S. (1983). *Ways with words: Language, life, and work in communities and classrooms.* Cambridge, UK: Cambridge University Press.

British Columbia. (2008). *Make a case against racism: A guide for teachers of Grades 4–7.* Retrieved from http://www.embracebc.ca/local/embracebc/pdf/make_a_case_teachers_guide.pdf.

British Columbia Ministry of Education. (1997). *Social studies 8 to 10: Integrated resource package.* Retrieved from http://www.bced.gov.bc.ca/irp/pdfs/social_studies/1997ss810.pdf.

British Columbia Ministry of Education. (2006). *Social studies grade 4: Integrated resource package.* Retrieved from http://www.bced.gov.bc.ca/irp/pdfs/social_studies/2006ssk7_4.pdf.

British Columbia Ministry of Education. (2013). Who makes up the Ministry of Education. Retrieved from http://www.bced.gov.bc.ca/departments/.

British Columbia Ministry of Education. (2014). *Standards for the education, competence and professional conduct of educators in BC.* Retrieved from http://www.bcteacherregulation.ca/standards/StandardsDevelopment.aspx.

Brodie, D. (1997). *Writing changes everything: The 627 best things anyone ever said about writing.* New York, NY: St. Martin.

Bronfenbrenner, U. (1979). *The ecology of human development: Experiments by nature and design.* Cambridge, MA: Harvard University Press.

Brookfield, S. D. (1995). *Becoming a critically reflective teacher.* San Francisco, CA: Jossey-Bass.

Brophy, J. (2006a). History of research on classroom management. In C. M. Evertson & C. S. Weinstein (Eds.), *Handbook of classroom management: Research, practice, and contemporary issues* (pp. 17–46). Mahwah, NJ: Lawrence Erlbaum Associates.

Brophy, J. (2006). Observational research on generic aspects of classroom teaching. In P. A. Alexander & P. H. Winne (Eds.), *Handbook of educational psychology* (2nd ed., pp. 755–780). Mahwah, NJ: Lawrence Erlbaum.

Bruner, J. S. (1966). *Toward a theory of instruction.* Cambridge, MA: Belknap Press.

Burke, M. D., Ayres, K., & Hagan-Burke, S. (2004). Preventing school-based antisocial behaviors with school-wide positive behavioral support. *Journal of Early and Intensive Behavior Intervention, 1*(1), 66–74.

Buzan, T. (1993) *The mind map book.* London, UK: BBC Books.

Calgary Board of Education. (2007, January 19). *Project impact inspires Lester B. Pearson students to make a difference.* Retrieved from http://www.cbe.ab.ca/new/impact.asp.

Calgary Board of Education. (2011). *Traditional learning centres.* Retrieved from http://www.cbe.ab.ca/Programs/Choices/prog-tlc.asp.

Campaign 2000. (2011). *Revisiting family security in insecure times: 2011 report card on child and family poverty in Canada.* Toronto, ON: Family Service Toronto.

Canadian Education Association. (2012). *Teaching the way we aspire to teach: Now and in the future.* Retrieved from http://www.cea-ace.ca/sites/cea-ace.ca/files/cea-2012-aspirations.pdf.

Canadian Teachers' Federation. (2009). *Supporting education . . . Building Canada: Child poverty and schools.* Ottawa, ON: Author.

Canter, L., & Canter, M. (1976). *Assertive discipline: A take-charge approach for today's educator.* Seal Beach, CA: Canter & Associates.

Carter, P. (2003). *A review of highly effective teachers in Hamilton County: Analysis of current trends and implications for improvement.* Chattanooga, TN: Public Education Foundation.

CBC News. (2010, April 23). Sex ed opponents claim victory in Ontario. Retrieved from http://www.cbc.ca/canada/toronto/story/2010/04/23/ontario-education.html.

Centre for the Study of Historical Consciousness. (n.d.). *The historical thinking project: Promoting critical historical literacy for the 21st century.* Retrieved from http://historicalthinking.ca/.

Chan, J. C. K., McDermott, K. B., & Roediger, H. L. (2006). Retrieval-induced facilitation: Initially non-tested material can benefit from prior testing of related material. *Journal of Experimental Psychology: General, 135*(4), 553–571.

Chandler, L. K., & Dahlquist, C. M. (2002). *Functional assessment: Strategies to prevent and remediate challenging behaviors in school settings.* Upper Saddle River, NJ: Merrill/Prentice-Hall.

Chard, S. (n.d.) *The project approach.* Retrieved from http://www.projectapproach.org.

Charles, C. M. (2002). *Essential elements of effective discipline.* Boston, MA: Allyn & Bacon.

Chase, C. I. (1999). *Contemporary assessment for educators.* New York, NY: Longman.

Cicero. (1942). *De Oratore.* E. W. Sutton (Trans.). London, UK: William Heinemann Ltd. Retrieved from https://archive.org/details/cicerodeoratore01ciceuoft.

Cochran-Smith, M., Feiman-Nemser, S., McIntyre, D. J., & Demers, K. E. (Eds.) (2008). *Handbook of research on teacher education: Enduring questions in changing contexts* (3rd ed.). New York, NY: Routledge, Taylor & Francis Group, and the Association of Teacher Educators

Cohen, L. M. (1999). *Philosophical perspectives in education.* Retrieved from http://oregonstate.edu/instruct/ed416/module1.html.

Cole, A. L. & Knowles, J. G. (2000). *Researching teaching: Exploring teacher development through reflexive inquiry.* Toronto, ON: Allyn & Bacon.

Coleman, D. (2006). *White civility: The literary project of English Canada.* Toronto, ON: University of Toronto Press.

Connect! The Professional Learning Journal of the Connect Charter School. (2011a). *Renaissance debates.* Retrieved from http://calgaryscienceschool.blogspot.com/2010/03/grade-8-renaissance-debates.html.

Connect! The Professional Learning Journal of the Connect Charter School. (2011b). *First nations defense assignment.* Retrieved from http://calgaryscienceschool.blogspot.

com/2009/09/css-podcasts-first-nations-defense.html.

Cooper, H. M. (1989). Synthesis of research on homework. *Educational Leadership, 47*(3), 85–91.

Cooper, H. M., & Valentine, J. C. (2001). Using research to answer practical questions about homework. *Educational Psychologist, 36*, 143–153.

Cornbleth, C. (1990). *Curriculum in context.* London, UK: The Falmer Press.

Counts, G. S. (1932). *Dare the school build a new social order?* New York, NY: John Day Company.

Crowne, D. P., & Marlowe, D. (1960). A new scale of social desirability independent of psychopathology. *Journal of Consulting Psychology, 24*, 349–354

Cummins, J. (2000). *Language, power and pedagogy: Bilingual children in the crossfire.* Clevedon, UK: Multilingual Matters.

Darling-Hammond, L., Banks, J., Zumwalt, K., Gomez, L., Gamoran Sherin, M., Griesdorn, J., & Finn, L. (2005). Educational goals and purposes: Developing a curricular vision for teaching. In L. Darling-Hammond & J. Bransford (Eds.), *Preparing teachers for a changing world: What teachers should learn and be able to do* (pp. 169–200). San Francisco, CA: Jossey-Bass.

Darling-Hammond, L. & Bransford, J. (Eds.). (2005). *Preparing teachers for a changing world: What teachers should learn and be able to do.* San Francisco, CA: Jossey-Bass.

Deci, E. L., & Chandler, C. L. (1986). The importance of motivation for the future of the LD field. *Journal of Learning Disabilities, 19*(10), 587–594.

Deci, E. L., & Flaste, R. (1995). *Why we do what we do: Understanding self-motivation.* New York, NY: G. P. Putnam's Sons.

Deci, E. L., Hodges, R., Pierson, L., & Tomassone J. (1992). Autonomy and competence as motivational factors in students with learning disabilities and emotional handicaps. *Journal of Learning Disabilities, 25*(7), 457–471.

Delpit, L. D. (1988). The silenced dialogue: Power and pedagogy in educating other people's children. *Harvard Educational Review, 53*(3), 280–298.

Delpit, L. D. (2006). *Other people's children: Cultural conflict in the classroom* (2nd ed.). New York, NY: New Press.

Demchak, M., & Bossert, K.W. (1996). Assessing problem behaviors. *Innovations, 4.* Washington, DC: American Association on Mental Retardation.

Dewey, J. (1933). *How we think.* Lexington, MA: D.C. Heath.

Dewey, J. (1938). *Experience and education.* New York, NY: Collier Books, MacMillan.

Dewey, J. (1988). The public and its problems. In J. A. Boydston (Ed.), *John Dewey, the later works 1952–1953: Vol. 2. Essays, reviews, miscellany, and the public and its problems* (pp. 235–372). Carbondale, IL: Southern Illinois University Press.

Dreikurs, R. (1964). *Children the challenge.* New York, NY: Hawthorne.

Dreikurs, R., & Cassel, P. (1972). *Discipline without tears: What to do with children who misbehave.* New York, NY: Hawthorn Books.

Dreikurs, R., Grunwald, B. B., & Pepper, F.C. (1982). *Maintaining sanity in the classroom: Classroom management techniques* (2nd ed.). New York: Harper & Row.

Duschene, C., & Stitou, M. (2013). Conceptions of learning: The challenge for immigrant student teachers. *Canada Education, 53*(5).

Edmunds, A. L. (2010a). The effectiveness of a school-wide approach to classroom management. Paper presented at the AERA Annual Meeting, Denver, CO.

Edmunds, A. L. (2010b). Managing school-wide behavior from the principal's office. In A. L. Edmunds & R. B. Macmillan (Eds.), *Leadership for inclusion: A practical guide* (pp. 19–31). Rotterdam, Netherlands: Sense Publishers.

Edmunds, A. L. (2011a). Teacher success via effective classroom management. Paper presented at the 34th Annual Conference of the Teacher Education Division of the Council for Exceptional Children, Austin, TX.

Edmunds, A. L. (2011b). Effective classroom management: A "bad" school's success story. Paper presented at the Canadian Society for the Study of Education Annual Conference. Fredericton, NB.

Edmunds, A. L., & Edmunds, G. A. (2008). *Special education in Canada.* Toronto, ON: McGraw-Hill Ryerson.

Edmunds, A. L., & Edmunds, G. A. (2010). *Educational psychology: Applications in Canadian classrooms.* Toronto, ON: Oxford University Press.

Edmunds, A. L., & Edmunds, G. A. (2013). The behavior management network. Paper presented at KNAER Networking Information Exchange, Ontario Ministry of Education Research and Evaluation Strategy Branch, Toronto, ON.

Edwards, C. H. (2008). Classroom discipline and management (5th ed.). Toronto, ON: Wiley.

Egan, K. (2010). *Learning in depth: A simple innovation that can transform schooling.* Chicago, IL: University of Chicago Press.

Egbo, B. (2009). *Teaching for diversity in Canadian schools.* Toronto, ON: Pearson Canada.

Eisner, E. W. (2002). *The educational imagination: On the design and evaluation of school programs* (3rd ed.). Upper Saddle River, NJ: Pearson Education Inc.

Elawar, M. C., & Corno, L. (1985). A factorial experiment in teachers' written feedback on student homework: Changing teacher behavior a little rather than a lot. *Journal of Educational Psychology, 77*(2), 162–173.

Elementary Teachers' Federation of Ontario. (2014). Bargaining and agreements. Retrieved from http://www.etfo.ca/bargainingandagreements/pages/default.aspx.

Eliot, L. (2012). *Pink brain, blue brain: How small differences grow into troublesome gaps and what we can do about it.* Oxford, UK: One World.

Ercikan, K. (2006). Developments in assessment of student learning. In P. A. Alexander & P. H. Winne (Eds.), *Handbook of educational psychology* (2nd ed., pp. 929–952). Mahwah, NJ: Lawrence Erlbaum.

Evertson, C. M., & Weinstein, C. S. (2006a). *Handbook of classroom management: Research, practice, and contemporary issues.* Mahwah, NJ: Lawrence Erlbaum Associates.

Evertson, C. M., & Weinstein, C. S. (2006b). Classroom management as a field of inquiry. In C. M. Evertson & C. S. Weinstein (Eds.), *Handbook of classroom management: Research, practice, and contemporary issues* (pp. 3–15). Mahwah, NJ: Lawrence Erlbaum Associates.

Fallona, C., & Richardson, V. (2006). Classroom management as a moral activity. In C. M. Evertson & C. S. Weinstein (Eds.), *Handbook of classroom management: Research, practice, and contemporary issues* (pp. 1041–1062). Mahwah, NJ: Lawrence Erlbaum Associates.

Featherstone, D., Munby, H., & Russell (Eds.) (1997). *Finding a voice while learning to teach.* Washington, DC: Falmer Press.

Fletcher, M. L. M. (2008). *American Indian education: Counternarratives in racism, struggle, and the law.* New York, NY: Routledge, 2008.

Fox, M. (2001). Have we lost our way? *Language Arts, 79*(2), 105–113.

Freiberg, H. J., & Lapointe, J. M. (2006). Research-based programs for preventing and solving discipline problems. In C. Evertson & C. S. Weinstein (Eds.), *Handbook of classroom management: Research, practice, and contemporary issues* (pp. 735–786). Mahwah, NJ: Lawrence Erlbaum Associates

Friedman, T. (2007). *The world is flat: A brief history of the twenty-first century.* New York, NY: Picador.

Friere, P. (2000). *Pedagogy of the oppressed.* New York, NY: Continuum.

Friesen, S. (2009). What did you do in school today? Teaching effectiveness: A framework and rubric. Toronto, ON: Canadian Education Association. Retrieved from http://www.cea-ace.ca/sites/cea-ace.ca/files/cea-2009-wdydist-teaching.pdf.

Friquegnon, M. L. (1997). What is a child? *Thinking, 13*(1), 12–16.

Galileo Educational Network. (n.d.). *Naming the west.* Retrieved from http://www.galileo.org/initiatives/ntw/index.html.

Galileo Educational Network. (2011a). *What is inquiry?* Retrieved from http://www.galileo.org/inquiry-what.html.

Galileo Educational Network. (2011b). *Inquiry rubric.* Retrieved from http://www.galileo.org/research/publications/rubric.pdf.

Garcia, R. L. (2011). *Teaching for diversity: A guide to greater understanding* (3rd ed.). Bloomington, IN: Solution Tree Press.

Gardner, H. (2006). *Multiple intelligences: New horizons in theory and practice.* New York, NY: Basic Books.

Gay, G. (2010). *Culturally responsive teaching: Theory, research, and practice* (2nd ed.). New York, NY: Teachers College Press.

Gilbert, I. (2011). *Why do I need a teacher when I've got Google? The essential guide to the big issues for every twenty-first century teacher.* London, UK: Routledge.

Gladwell, M. (2008). *Outliers: The story of success.* New York, NY: Little, Brown and Company.

Glasser, W. (1965). *Reality therapy: A new approach to psychiatry.* New York, NY: Harper & Row Publishers.

Global News. (2012, June 1). Morinville area students will have public school this fall. Edmonton, AB: *Global News.*

Goldstein, S., & Brooks, R. (2007). *Understanding and managing children's classroom behaviour: Creating sustainable, resilient classrooms* (2nd ed.). Hoboken, NJ: John Wiley & Sons, Inc.

Gonzalez, N., Moll, L., & Amanti, C. (2005). *Funds of knowledge.* Mahwah, NJ: Lawrence Erlbaum.

Government of Upper Canada. (1855). *Copies of correspondence between the chief superintendent of schools for Upper Canada, and other persons, on the question of separate schools.* Toronto, ON: Lovell & Gibson.

Graham, S. (2006). Writing. In P. A. Alexander & P. H. Winne (Eds.), *Handbook of educational psychology* (2nd ed.) (pp. 457–478). Mahwah, NJ: Lawrence Erlbaum Associates.

Grant, C. A., & Sleeter, C. E. (2011). *Doing multicultural education for achievement and equity* (2nd ed.). New York, NY: Routledge.

Greene, R. (2008). *Lost at school: Why our kids with behavioral challenges are falling through the cracks and how we can help them.* New York, NY: Simon & Schuster, Inc.

Gresham, F. M. (2002). Teaching social skills to high-risk children and youth: Preventive and remedial strategies. In M. R. Shinn, H. M. Walker, & G. Stoner (Eds.), *Interventions for academic and behavior problems II: Preventive and remedial approaches* (pp. 403–432). Washington, DC: National Association of School Psychologists.

Guskey, T. (2005). Mapping the road to proficiency. *Educational Leadership, 63*(3), 32–38.

Gutek, G. L. (2009). *New perspectives on philosophy and education.* Columbus, OH: Pearson.

Gutmann, A. (1999). *Democratic education.* Princeton, NJ: Princeton.

Hahn, L. E. (1984). Aesthetics and education. *CUHK Education Journal, 12*(2), 71–76.

Halpern, D. F. (2012). *Sex differences in cognitive abilities* (4th ed.). New York, NY: Psychology Press.

Hammerness, K., Darling-Hammond, L., & Bransford, J. (2005). How teachers learn and develop. In L. Darling-Hammond & J. Bransford (Eds.), *Preparing teachers for a changing world: What teachers should learn and be able to do* (pp. 358–389). San Francisco, CA: Jossey-Bass.

Hansen, D. T. (2008). Values and purpose in teacher education. In M. Cochran-Smith, S. Feiman-Nemser, D. J. McIntyre, & K. E. Demers, (Eds.), *Handbook of research on teacher education: Enduring questions in changing contexts* (3rd ed.) (pp. 10–26). New York, NY: Routledge, Taylor & Francis Group and the Association of Teacher Educators.

Hattie, J. (2012). *Visible learning for teachers: Maximizing impact on learning.* London, UK: Routledge.

Hebert, E. A. (2001). *The power of portfolios: What children can teach us about learning and assessment.* San Francisco, CA: Jossey-Bass.

Holbrook, J., & Kolodner, J. L. (2000). Scaffolding the development of an inquiry-based (science) classroom. In B. Fishman & S. O'Connor-Devilbiss (Eds.), *Fourth international conference of the learning sciences* (pp. 221–227). Mahwah, NJ: Lawrence Erlbaum.

Hollabaugh, J. (2012). *Exploring the perceptions and experiences of inductive teachers in secondary education: How do inductive teachers find their place in the profession and what motivates them to remain in the field?* Unpublished doctoral dissertation. George Fox University, OR.

Horner, R. H. & Sugai, G. (2000). School-wide behavior support: Am emerging initiative. *Journal of Positive Behavior Interventions, 2,* 231–232.

House of Commons. (1971). *Report of the Royal Commission on Bilingualism and Biculturalism.* Retrieved from http://www.canadahistory.com/sections/documents/Primeministers/trudeau/docs-onmulticulturalism.htm.

Iannacci, L. (1998). *An autobiographical account of first language and culture replacement.* Unpublished master's thesis. University of Western Ontario, London, ON.

Illich, I. (1971). *Deschooling society.* London, UK: Marion Boyers Publishers.

James, W. (1899/1983). Talks to teachers. In G. E. Myers (Ed.), *William James: Writings 1878--1899.* New York: Library of America. (Original work published 1899)

Janesick, V. J. (2003). *Curriculum trends: A reference handbook.* Santa Barbara, CA: ABC Clio.

Jardine, D. W., Friesen, S., & Clifford, P. (2006). "If you want to": Inquiry and the arrival of new information and communications technologies into the world of the classroom. In D. W. Jardine, S. Friesen, & P. Clifford (Eds.), *Curriculum in abundance* (pp. 203–209). Mahwah, NJ: Lawrence Erlbaum Associates.

Jimerson, S. R. (2001). Meta-analysis of grade retention research: Implications for practice in the 21st century. *School Psychology Review, 30*, 420–437.

Johansson, L., Angst, K., Beer, B., Martin, S., Rebeck, W., & Sibilleau, N. (2001). *Canadian language benchmarks 2000: ESL for literacy learners*. Ottawa, ON: Centre for Canadian Language Benchmarks.

Johnson, B., Whittington, V., & Oswald, M. (1994). Teachers' view on schools discipline: A theoretical framework. *Cambridge Journal of Education, 24*, 261–276.

Johnson, D. (2005). *Signposts of success: Interpreting Ontario's elementary school test scores*. Toronto, ON: C.D. Howe Institute.

Johnson, D. (2007). Ontario's best public schools: An update to signposts of success. Toronto, ON: The David Johnson/C.D. Howe Institute. Retrieved from http://www.cdhowe.org/pdf/ebrief_39.pdf.

Johnson, F. L., & Edmunds, A. L. (2006). *From chaos to control: Understanding and responding to the behaviours of students with exceptionalities*. London, ON: The Althouse Press.

Jones, D. C. (1995). *The spirit of teaching*. Calgary, AB: Detselig Enterprises Limited.

Juvenal. (1918). *Satires*. G. G. Ramsey (Trans.). Retrieved from http://www.tertullian.org/fathers/juvenal_satires_07.htm.

Kauffman, J. M., & Landrum, T. J. (2009) *Characteristics of emotional and behavioral disorders of children and youth* (9th ed.). Upper Saddle River, NJ: Prentice Hall.

Keene, E., & Zimmerman, S. (1997). *Mosaic of thought*. Portsmouth, NH: Heinemann.

Kelly, A. V. (2009). *The curriculum: Theory and practice* (6th ed.). London, UK: Sage.

Kerka, S. (1996). *Journal writing and adult learning* (Report No. EDO-CE96-174). Washington, DC: Office of Educational Research and Improvement. (ERIC Document Reproduction Service No. ED399413). Retrieved from http://www.ericdigests.org/1997-2/journal.htm.

Kinchloe, J. L. & Steinberg, S. R. (1998). *Changing multiculturalism*. New York, NY: Open University Press.

Klein, P. D. (1997). Multiplying the problems of intelligence by eight: A critique of Gardner's theory. *Canadian Journal of Education, 22*(4), 377–394.

Knighton, T., Brochu, P., & Gluszynski, T. (2010). *Measuring up: Canadian results of the oecd pisa study the performance of Canada's youth in reading, mathematics and science: 2009 first results for Canadians aged 15*. Ottawa, ON: Human Resources and Skills Development Canada, Council of Ministers of Education, and Statistics Canada. Retrieved from http://www.cmec.ca/Publications/Lists/Publications/Attachments/254/PISA2009-can-report.pdf.

Korthagen, F. A. J. (2004). In search of the essence of a good teacher: Towards a more holistic approach in teacher education. *Teaching & Teacher Education, 20*(1), 77. doi:10.1016/j.tate.2003.10.002.

Kymlicka, W. (2012). *Multiculturalism: Success, failure, and the future*. Washington, DC: Migration Policy Institute.

LaBrack, B. (n.d.). *On-line cultural training resource for study abroad*. Retrieved from http://www2.pacific.edu/sis/culture/index.htm.

LaConte, R. T. (1981). *Homework as a learning experience. What research says to the teacher*. Washington, DC: National Education Association.

Laidlaw, S. (2007, April 2). Creationism debate continues to evolve. *The Star*. Retrieved from http://www.thestar.com/Life/article/198318.

Lane, K., Falk, K., & Wehby, J. (2006). Classroom management in special education classrooms and resource rooms. In C. M. Evertson & C. S. Weinstein (Eds.), *Handbook of classroom management: Research, practice and contemporary issues* (pp. 439–460). Mahwah, NJ: Lawrence Erlbaum Associates.

Learn Alberta. (2012). *Walking together: First Nations, Métis, and Inuit perspectives in curriculum*. Retrieved from http://www.learnalberta.ca/content/aswt/

Learn Alberta. (n.d.). *Benchmarks, strategies and resources for teachers of English language learners*. Retrieved from http://www.learnalberta.ca/content/eslapb/index.html.

Levin, B. (2004). A recommitment to equity in education. *Education Canada, 44*(2), 16–18.

Levin, J., Nolan, J. F., Kerr, J. W., & Elliot, A. E. (2009). *Principles of classroom management: A professional decision-making model* (2nd Canadian ed.). Toronto, ON: Pearson.

Lewis, T. J., & Sugai, G. (1999). Effective behavior support: A systems approach to proactive schoolwide management. *Focus on Exceptional Children, 31*(6), 1–24.

Lewis, T. J., Newcomer, L. L., Trussell, R., & Richter, M. (2006). Schoolwide positive behavior support: Building systems to develop and maintain appropriate social behavior. In C. M. Evertson & C. S. Weinstein (Eds.), *Handbook of classroom management: Research, practice and contemporary issues* (pp. 833–854). Mahwah, NJ: Lawrence Erlbaum Associates.

Lobel, A. (1970). *Frog and toad are friends*. New York, NY: Harper Collins.

Luiselli, J. K., Putnam, R. F., & Sunderland, M. (2002). Longitudinal evaluation of behavior support intervention in a public middle school. *Journal of Positive Behavior Interventions, 4(3)*, 182–188.

Maag, J. W. (2004). *Behavior management: From theoretical implications to practical applications* (2nd ed.). Belmont, CA: Wadsworth.

MacIonis, J. J., & Gerber, L. M. (2014). Sociology (8th Canadian ed.). Toronto, ON: Pearson Education Canada.

Magnuson, R. (1969). *Education in the province of Quebec*. Washington, DC: US Department of Education.

Mayer, G. R. (2001). Preventing antisocial behavior in the schools. *Journal of Applied Behavior Analysis, 28*(4), 467–478.

Maynes, N. (2011). *Focus on learning: The art and science of planning, delivering, and assessing effective lessons*. Toronto, ON: Pearson.

McCaslin, M., Bozak, A. R., Naploeon, L., Thomas, A., Vasquez, V., Wayman, V., & Zhang, J. (2006). Self-regulated learning and classroom management: Theory, research and considerations for classroom practice. In C. M. Evertson & C. S. Weinstein (Eds.), *Handbook of classroom management: Research, practice and contemporary issues* (pp. 223–252). Mahwah, NJ: Lawrence Erlbaum Associates.

McIntosh, P. (1988). White privilege: Unpacking the invisible knapsack. *Independent School, 49*(2), 31–36.

McLaren, P. (2007). *Life in schools: An introduction to critical pedagogy in the foundations of education* (5th ed.). New York, NY: Addison-Wesley Longman.

Mitchell, D. E., Ortiz, F. I., & Mitchell, T. K. (1987). *Work orientation and job performance: The cultural basis of teaching rewards and incentives.* New York, NY: State University of New York Press.

Morine-Dershimer, G. (2006). Classroom management and classroom discourse. In C. M. Evertson & C. S. Weinstein (Eds.), *Handbook of classroom management: Research, practice and contemporary issues* (pp. 127–156). Mahwah, NJ: Lawrence Erlbaum Associates.

Myers, C. L., & Holland, K. L. (2000). Classroom behavioral interventions: Do teachers consider the function of the behavior? *Psychology in the Schools, 37*(3), 271–280.

National Research Council (2000). *How People Learn: Brain, mind, experience, and school* (Expanded ed.). Washington, DC: National Academies Press.

Newmann, F. M. (1991). Promoting higher order thinking in social studies: Overview of a study of 16 high-school departments. *Theory and Research in Social Education, 19*(4), 324–340.

Nickel, J. (2004). *Personal and moral autonomy in primary classrooms.* Unpublished doctoral dissertation. University of Western Ontario.

Noble, S. (1938). *A history of American education.* New York, NY: Farrar & Rinehart.

Noddings, N. (2003). *Caring: A feminine approach to ethics and moral education* (2nd ed.). Berkeley, CA: University of California Press.

Noddings, N. (2007). *Philosophy of education* (2nd ed.). Boulder, CO: Westview Press.

Nova Scotia Department of Education. (1997). *Governor in Council Education Act Regulations.* Retrieved from http://www.novascotia.ca/just/regulations/regs/edgic.htm.

Nova Scotia Department of Education. (2008). *Atlantic Canada science curriculum: Grade 6.* Retrieved from http://www.ednet.ns.ca/files/curriculum/Science6_Web.pdf.

Nucci, L. (2006). Classroom management for moral and social development. In C. M. Evertson & C. S. Weinstein (Eds.), *Handbook of classroom management: Research, practice, and contemporary issues* (pp. 711–734). Mahwah, NJ: Lawrence Erlbaum Associates.

Nunavut Department of Education. (2010). Nunavut approved curriculum and teaching resources. Retrieved from http://www.edu.gov.nu.ca/apps/UPLOADS/fck/file/K-12/NU%20CUR%20GUIDE%20SEPT%20201.pdf.

O'Donnell, A. M., D'Amico, M., Schmid, R. F., Reeve, J., & Smith, J. K. (2008). *Educational psychology: Reflection for action.* Toronto, ON: John Wiley & Sons Canada.

Oberg, A. (1988). Professional development through self-evaluation. In P. Holborn, M. Wideen, & I. Andrews (Eds.), *Becoming a teacher.* Toronto, ON: Kagan & Woo Limited.

Organisation for Economic Co-operation and Development. (2010). *PISA 2009 results: What students know and can do—Student performance in reading, mathematics and science: Vol. I.* Retrieved from http://www.oecd.org/pisa/pisaproducts/48852548.pdf.

Ogbu, J. U. (2003). *Black American students in an affluent suburb: A study of academic disengagement.* Mahwah, NJ: Lawrence Erlbaum Associates.

Ontario College of Teachers. (2014). *Standards of practice.* Retrieved from http://www.oct.ca/public/professional-standards/standards-of-practice.

Ontario Ministry of Education. (1994). *Education about religion in Ontario public elementary schools.* Toronto, ON: Queen's Printer for Ontario.

Ontario Ministry of Education. (2006). *The Ontario Curriculum: Grades 1–8: Language.* Retrieved from http://www.edu.gov.on.ca/eng/curriculum/elementary/language18currb.pdf.

Ontario Ministry of Education. (2010). *Growing success: Assessment, evaluation, and reporting in Ontario schools: First edition Covering Grades 1 to 12.* Retrieved from http://www.edu.gov.on.ca/eng/policyfunding/growsuccess.pdf.

Oreopoulos, P. (2005). Stay in school: New lessons on the benefits of raising the legal school-leaving age. C. D. Howe Institute Commentary #223. Retrieved from http://www.cdhowe.org/pdf/commentary_223.pdf.

Oreopoulos, P. (2006). The compelling effects of compulsory schools: Evidence from Canada. *Canadian Journal of Economics, 39*(1), 22–52.

Palmer, P. J. (1998). *The courage to teach: Exploring the inner landscape of a teacher's life.* San Francisco, CA: Jossey-Bass.

Parkman, F. (1908). *The old regime in Canada (Part IV).* Boston, MA: Little, Brown.

Parliament of Canada. (2009). *Statistical profile of poverty in Canada.* Retrieved from http://www.parl.gc.ca/content/lop/researchpublications/prb0917-e.htm.

Perkins, D. (2009). *Making learning whole: How seven principles of teaching can transform education.* San Francisco, CA: Jossey-Bass.

Plato. (1997). *Republic.* In J. M. Cooper (Ed.), *Plato: Complete works* (pp. 971–1223). Indianapolis, IN: Hackett Publishing Company.

Plato. (2008). *Protagoras.* B. Jowett (Trans.). Retrieved from http://www.gutenberg.org/files/1591/1591-h/1591-h.htm.

Plutarch. (1888). *Lives.* A. H. Clough (Ed.). Boston, MA: Little, Brown. Retrieved from http://www.gutenberg.org/ebooks/674?msg=welcome_stranger.

Pressley, M., & Harris, K. R. (2006). Cognitive strategies instruction: From basic research to classroom instruction. In P. A. Alexander & P. H. Winne (Eds.), *Handbook of educational psychology* (2nd ed., pp. 265–286). Mahwah, NJ: Lawrence Erlbaum.

Purcell-Gates, V. (2001). What we know about readers who struggle. In R. F. Flippo (Ed.), *Reading researchers in search of common ground* (pp. 118–128). Newark, DE: Routledge.

Quintilian. (1920). *Institutio Oratoria.* H. E. Butler (Trans.). Retrieved from http://penelope.uchicago.edu/Thayer/E/Roman/Texts/Quintilian/Institutio_Oratoria/1C*.html.

Rawls, J. (1999). *A theory of justice* (rev. ed.). Cambridge, MA: Harvard University Press.

Reeves, D. (2010). *Transforming professional development into student results.* Alexandria, VA: ASCD.

Rogers, C., & Freiberg, H. J. (1994). *Freedom to learn* (3rd ed.). New York, NY: Macmillan/Merrill.

Rose, D. H., & Meyer, A. (2002). *Teaching every student in the digital age: Universal design for learning.* Alexandria, VA: ASCD.

Rousseau, J.-J. (1762/1998). *Émile.* London, UK: Everyman.

Rushton, J. P. (1997). *Race, evolution, and behaviour: A life history perspective.* New Brunswick, NJ: Transaction Publishers.

Russell, T. (1995). Returning to the physics classroom to re-think how one learns to teach physics: Reflections on teacher education. In T. Russell & F. Korthagen (Eds.), *Teachers who teach teachers: Reflections on teacher education.* Washington, DC: Falmer Press.

Ryan, J., Pollock, K., & Antonelli, F. (2009). Teacher diversity in Canada: Leaky pipelines, bottlenecks, and glass ceilings. *Canadian Journal of Education, 32*(3), 591–617.

Ryerson, E. (1847). *Report on a system of public elementary instruction for Upper Canada.* Toronto, ON: Lovell & Gibson. Retrieved from http://archive.org/stream/reportonsystemof00ryeruoft#page/n9/mode/2up.

Saskatchewan Ministry of Education. (n.d). Health education 5 outcomes. Retrieved from http://www.curriculum.gov.sk.ca/index.jsp?view=outcomes&lang=en&subj=health_education&level=5#.

Saskatchewan Ministry of Education. (2011). Core curriculum: Principles, time allocations, and credit policy. Retrieved from http://www.education.gov.sk.ca/core-principles-time-credit.

Saskatchewan Ministry of Education. (2012). Ministry overview. Retrieved from http://www.education.gov.sk.ca/ministry-overview/.

Scardamalia, M., & Bereiter, C. (2003). Knowledge building. In *Encyclopedia of Education* (2nd ed., pp. 1370–1373). New York, NY: Macmillan Reference.

Scardamalia, M., & Bereiter, C. (2006). Knowledge building: Theory, pedagogy, and technology. In K. Sawyer (Ed.), *Cambridge Handbook of the Learning Sciences* (pp. 97–118). Cambridge, UK: Cambridge University Press.

Schalock, R. L. (2000). Three decades of quality of life. *Focus on Autism and Other Developmental Disabilities, 15*(2), 116–128.

Schiro, M. S. (2008). *Curriculum theory: Conflicting visions and enduring concerns.* Los Angeles, CA: Sage.

Schön, D. (1983). *The reflective practitioner: How professionals think in action.* New York, NY: Basic Books.

Scott, D. (2012). Thoughts and viruses interdisciplinary inquiry unit [Weblog post]. *Connect! The Professional Learning Journal of the Connect Charter School.* Retrieved from http://calgaryscienceschool.blogspot.ca/2012/04/by-dave-scott-grade-8-humanities-this.html#more.

Scott, T. M. (2001). A school-wide example of positive behavioral support. *Journal of Positive Behavior Interventions, 3*(2), 88–94.

Scott, T. M., Gagnon, J. C., & Nelson, C. M. (2008). School-wide systems of positive behavior support: A framework for reducing school crime and violence. *Journal of Behavior Analysis of Offender and Victim: Treatment and Prevention, 1*(3), 259–272.

Sharpe, A., & Arsenault, J. (2010). *Investing in Aboriginal education in Canada: An economic perspective.* CSLS Research Report 2010-03. Ottawa, ON: Centre for the Study of Living Standards.

Shepard, L., Hammerness, K., Darling-Hammond, L., & Rust, F. (with Snowden, J. B., Gordon, E., Gutierrez, C., & Pacheo, A.). (2005). Assessment. In L. Darling-Hammond & J. Bransford (Eds.), *Preparing teachers for a changing world: What teachers should learn and be able to do* (pp. 275–322). San Francisco, CA: Jossey-Bass.

Skinner, B. F. (1974). *About behaviorism.* New York, NY: Knopf.

Skau, K. G. (1995). The journey of the teacher. In D. C. Jones (Ed.), *The spirit of teaching.* Calgary, AB: Detselig Enterprises Limited.

S.L. v. Commission scolaire des Chênes, 2012 SCC 7. Retrieved from http://scc-csc.lexum.com/scc-csc/scc-csc/en/item/7992/index.do.

Sleeter, C. E. (2005). *Un-standardizing curriculum: Multicultural teaching in the standards-based classroom.* New York, NY: Teachers College Press.

Smethem, L. (2007). Retention and intention in teaching careers: Will the new generation stay? *Teachers and Teaching: Theory and Practice, 13*(5), 465–480.

Smith, M. K. (2000). Curriculum theory and practice. *Encyclopaedia of Informal Education.* Retrieved from http://www.infed.org/biblio/b-curric.htm.

Sockett, H. (2008). The moral and epistemic purposes of teacher education. In M. Cochran-Smith, S. Feiman-Nemser, D. J. McIntyre, & K. E. Demers, (Eds.), *Handbook of research on teacher education: Enduring questions in changing contexts* (3rd ed.) (pp. 45–66). New York, NY: Routledge, Taylor & Francis Group and the Association of Teacher Educators.

Spender, D. (1982). *Invisible women: The schooling scandal.* London, UK: Women's Press.

Spindler, G. (1999). Three categories of cultural knowledge useful in doing cultural therapy. *Anthropology & Education Quarterly, 30*(4), 466–472.

Stanley, D., & Young, K. (2011). *Contemporary studies in Canadian curriculum: Principles, portraits, and practice.* Edmonton, AB: Brush Education Inc.

Statistics Canada. (2006a). *Canada's ethnocultural mosaic, 2006 Census: National picture.* Figure 1: Number and share of visible minority persons in Canada, 1981 to 2006. Retrieved from http://www12.statcan.gc.ca/census-recensement/2006/as-sa/97-562/p5-eng.cfm.

Statistics Canada. (2006b). *Aboriginal children's survey* (No. 81-582). Retrieved from http://www23.statcan.gc.ca/imdb/p2SV.pl?Function=getSurvey&SDDS=5108

Statistics Canada. (2007). *Some facts about the demographic and ethnocultural composition of the population.* Figure 29: Visible minority groups in Canada, 2001 to 2017. Catalogue no. 91-003-XWE. Retrieved from http://www.statcan.gc.ca/pub/91-003-x/2007001/4129904-eng.htm.

Statistics Canada. (2008). Earnings and incomes of Canadians over the past quarter century, 2006 Census Findings. Catalogue no. 97-563-XIE2006001. Retrieved from http://www12.statcan.ca/census-recensement/2006/as-sa/97-563/index-eng.cfm?CFID=361281&CFTOKEN=83796207.

Statistics Canada. (2012). *Linguistic characteristics of Canadians.* Catalogue no. 98-314-X2011001. Retrieved from http://www12.statcan.gc.ca/census-recensement/2011/as-sa/98-314-x/98-314-x2011001-eng.cfm.

St. Germain, G., & Dyck, L. A. (2011). *Reforming First Nations education: From crisis to hope.* Report of the Standing Senate Committee on Aboriginal Peoples. Retrieved from http://www.parl.gc.ca/content/sen/committee/411/appa/rep/rep03dec11-e.pdf.

Stiggins, R. J. (2001). *Student-centered classroom assessment* (3rd ed.). Upper Saddle River, NJ: Merrill/Prentice Hall.

Sugai, G., & Horner, R. H. (2002). The evolution of discipline practices: School-wide positive behavior supports. *Child and Family Behavior Therapy, 24*, 23–50.

Sugai, G., Horner, R. H., Dunlap, G., Hieneman, M., Lewis, T. J., Nelson, C. M., et al. (2000). *Applying positive behavioral support and functional behavioral assessment in schools. Journal of Positive Behavior Interventions, 2*, 131–143.

Tacitus. (1893). *The Agricola and Germany of Tacitus*. J. A. Church & W. J. Brodribb. New York, NY: Macmillan.

Takkula, H., Kangaslahti, J., & Banks, J. (2008) Teaching transcultural competence: From language learning to experiential education. *Policy & Practice: A Development Education Review 7*, 88–95

Thatcher, O. J., and McNeal, E. H. (Eds.). *A source book for medieval history*. New York, NY: Scribner.

Tucker, M. (2013, October 3). Concerning standards, curriculum, and assessment. *Education Week*. Retrieved from http://blogs.edweek.org/edweek/top_performers/2013/10/concerning_standards_curriculum_and_assessment.html.

Tyler, R. W. (1949). *Basic principles of curriculum and instruction*. Chicago, IL: University of Chicago Press.

United Nations. (2008). *United Nations declaration on the rights of indigenous peoples*. New York, NY: United Nations.

United Nations Human Rights Committee. (2000). *Report of the Human Rights Committee: Vol. II*. No. 40 (A/55/40). New York, NY: United Nations.

Vang, C. T. (2010). *An educational psychology of methods in multicultural education*. New York, NY: Peter Lang.

van Manen, M. (1991). *The tact of teaching: The meaning of pedagogical thoughtfulness*. London, ON: Althouse Press.

Walsh, D. (1983). Our schools come to order. *American Teacher, 68*, 1.

Weber, M. (1964). *The theory of social and economic organization*. New York, NY: The Free Press.

Wentzel, K. R. (2006). A social motivation perspective for classroom management. In C. M. Evertson & C. S. Weinstein (Eds.), *Handbook of classroom management: Research, practice, and contemporary issues* (pp. 619–644). Mahwah, NJ: Lawrence Erlbaum Associates.

Wiggins, G. P., & McTighe, J. (2005). *Understanding by design* (expanded 2nd ed.). Alexandria, VA: ASCD.

Wiliam, D. (2011). *Embedded formative assessment*. Bloomington, IN: Solution Tree Press.

Wilkinson, R., & Pickett, K. (2010). *The spirit level: Why equality is better for everyone*. London, UK: Penguin.

Willms, J. D., Friesen, S., & Milton, P. (2009). *What did you do in school today? Transforming classrooms through social, academic and intellectual engagement*. Toronto, ON: Canadian Education Association.

Wilson, J. D., Stamp, R. M., and Audet, L. P. (1970). *Canadian education: A history*. Toronto, ON: Prentice-Hall.

Woods, M. (2013). Five years after residential schools apology, Aboriginal groups say they're still waiting for progress. *Postmedia News*. Retrieved from http://o.canada.com/news/national/five-years-after-residential-schools-apology-aboriginal-groups-say-theyre-still-waiting-for-progress.

Woolfolk Hoy, A., Davis, H., & Pape, S. J. (2006). Teacher knowledge and beliefs. In P. A. Alexander & P. H. Winne (Eds.), *Handbook of educational psychology* (2nd ed.) (pp. 715–738). Mahwah, NJ: Lawrence Erlbaum Associates.

Wotherspoon, T. (2009). *The sociology of education in Canada* (3rd ed.). Toronto, ON: Oxford University Press.

Index